W9-CEV-476

Edward Bliss, Jr.

NOW THE NEWS

The Story of Broadcast Journalism

BISHOP MUELLER LIBRARY
Briar Cliff College
SIOUX CITY, IA 51104

COLUMBIA UNIVERSITY PRESS   NEW YORK

COLUMBIA UNIVERSITY PRESS
New York   Oxford

Copyright © 1991 Columbia University Press

All rights reserved

Casebound editions of Columbia University Press
books are Smyth-sewn and printed on permanent and
durable acid-free paper

♾

Printed in the United States of America

c 10 9 8 7 6 5 4 3 2

PN
4784
.B75
B54
1991

Library of Congress Cataloging-in-Publication Data

Bliss, Edward
  Now the news : the story of broadcast journalism / Edward Bliss, Jr.
    p.   cm.
  Includes bibliographical references and index.
  ISBN 0-231-04402-X
  1. Broadcast journalism—United States—History.   2. Broadcasting—
United States—History.   3. Radio broadcasting—United States.
  4. Television broadcasting—United States.   5. Cable television—
United States.   6. Electronic news gathering—United States.
  I. Title.
PN4784.B75B54   1991
070.1′9′0973—dc20   90-22546
                                                          CIP

22731482

TO
ANNE,
LISA, ALISON, AND ANDREW
AND IN
LOVING MEMORY
OF
LOIS BLISS ABSHIRE

Contents

Photos follow p. 304.

Preface

This is the story of what Eric Sevareid has called "inescapably the most personal form of journalism ever." The story begins in the distant, already murky region of early radio and ends with communications satellites feeding news to home receivers from thousands of miles above Earth. It is a story of men and women who, combining electronic wizardry with journalistic skills, worked and on occasion risked death—indeed, did die—reporting the news.

It was a brand-new medium to which these people came, doing something every day, it seemed, that never had been done before. Everyone in the business was trying something new. In research, it was trying to make signals clearer and travel farther. In news, it was, as today, competition to get the report on the air as quickly and accurately as possible. The difference is that what was being covered back then—the air disaster, the trial, the war, the political convention—was being covered electronically for the first time.

The first radio reporters appeared in the 1920s. The networks established their news organizations in the 1930s and in the 1940s covered global war. During the 1950s, television overtook radio. The 1960s saw profound technological change. Videotape arrived. Viewers began seeing their news in color. The first communications satellite was spun off into space. Cable television emerged. An Asian war was televised. Electronic newsgathering (ENG) made television nimbler in the 1970s. More news was reported live. In the 1980s, cable thrived. Viewers by the millions bought, rented, and borrowed videocassettes. With the erosion of their audience, the old networks lost their dominance. It was a new day.

Repeatedly, in writing this story, I wanted to use the word *revolution* — it was all, from the beginning, so revolutionary. And not only in technology and the journalism that technology made possible. Also, at the heart of it, there has been a social revolution, the acceptance, not yet complete, of competence regardless of skin color or sex.

I set out to write this revolutionary story because every source to which I turned when teaching broadcast journalism treated the subject piecemeal. Useful books have been published about the business of broadcasting, its programs and its politics. Fascinating profiles have been written about the major figures. Authorities have expounded on their chosen topic: production, reporting, writing, regulation. Scholars like Erik Barnouw have produced comprehensive histories of broadcasting, which include entertainment programing and promotion as well as corporate management. I have tried to focus on the journalism of broadcasting, from the first reporting of a presidential election by Lee de Forest in 1916, through Vietnam and the Fairness Doctrine to Watergate and television's transformation of the political process.

This is a review of almost a century of broadcast news. I wish I could tell more of the story, but as the managing editor of the newspaper on which I once worked said, "There comes a time, my friend, to stop making over and put the paper to bed."

Acknowledgments

In the preparation of this history, I owe much to many. I am especially indebted to Erik Barnouw, who encouraged me to undertake the task, and to his three-volume history of broadcasting in the United States (*A Tower in Babel, The Golden Web,* and *The Image Empire*), which remains the preeminent source. Three other histories I found invaluable were *Stay Tuned: A Concise History of American Broadcasting* by Christopher H. Sterling and John M. Kittross, *American Broadcasting: A Source Book on the History of Radio and Television* by Lawrence W. Lichty and Malachi C. Topping, and *The First 50 Years of Broadcasting* by the editors of *Broadcasting* magazine.

Early works to which I turned include Paul W. White's *News on the Air,* A. A. Schechter's *I Live on Air,* Mitchell Charnley's *News by Radio,* William L. Shirer's *Berlin Diary,* Eric Sevareid's *Not So Wild a Dream,* Edward Gibbons' *Floyd Gibbons: Knight of the Air,* Graham McNamee's *You're On the Air,* and César Saerchinger's *Hello, America!* Each one of these books is a classic. I also perused, and recommend to anyone who wants to know more of the story, *Due to Circumstances Beyond Our Control* by Fred W. Friendly, *Documentary in American Television* by A. William Bluem, *Those Radio Commentators!* by Irving Fang, *At the White House* by Robert Pierpoint, *Air Time* by Gary Paul Gates, *The Evening Stars* by Barbara Matusow, *Newswatch* by Av Westin, *Empire* by Lewis J. Paper, and *To Kill a Messenger* by William Small.

ACKNOWLEDGMENTS

I needed and was privileged to have recourse to the three fine biographies of Edward R. Murrow: *Prime Time* by Alexander Kendrick, *Murrow: His Life and Times* by A. M. Sperber, and *Edward R. Murrow* by Joseph Persico. I studied with fascination, and some pain, the spate of books concerning the latter-day turmoil at CBS.

In my research, eight magazines proved indispensable. They were *Broadcasting*, the *RTNDA Communicator*, the *Columbia Journalism Review*, *Journalism Quarterly*, *The Quill*, *Televison Quarterly*, the *Washington Journalism Review*, and *Variety*.

And I am beholden to many people. Several teachers of broadcast journalism have written to me, volunteering information. Of these, I am particularly indebted to Jack Shelley, professor emeritus, Iowa State University; David Dary, director of the School of Journalism and Mass Communications at the University of Oklahoma; Robert O. Blanchard, chairman, Department of Communication, Trinity University; and Mervin Block, lecturer at the Columbia University Graduate School of Journalism and the New School, whose mailings of scrupulously dated, immensely useful clippings have filled two file drawers to overflowing.

ABC, CBS, CNN, and NBC could not have been more helpful in providing photographs.

I am grateful to librarians who have helped me. At the ABC general library they were Kitty Lynch and Michele Creary. Others at ABC who answered my questions were Alan Raymond and Julie Hoover. At the CBS Reference Library I received the generous assistance of May Dowell, Shirley Abrams, Roberta Hadley, Marcia Goldstein Ratcliff, Laura Kapnick, and Carol Parnes. (The mere listing demonstrates that on my home grounds I was a real pest.) My library source at NBC was Vera Mayer, but I also was helped by archivist Cynthia Gagen, Jack Van Buskirk, Betty Reed, and Ron Najman. Two other librarians, Catharine Heinz of the Broadcast Pioneers Library and Susan Hill of the National Association of Broadcasters library, helped immensely, whether I came by in person or called desperately by telephone. Like all librarians, these are grand people.

Other people helped me through interviews, telephone conversations, and correspondence. Among them are Martin Agronsky, C. Edmund Allen, Curtis Beckmann, Burton Benjamin, Julian Bentley, Monroe Benton, Elliott Bernstein, Lee Bland, Frank Bourgholtzer, Ed Bradley, Bill Brannigan, Mary Marvin Breckinridge (Mrs. Jefferson Patterson), David Brinkley, George Burnett, Raymond L. Carroll, John Chancellor, Robert Chandler, Mitchell Charnley, Margaret Church, Donald Coe, Tristram Coffin, Charles Collingwood, Walter Cronkite, John Daly, Joseph Derby, Elisabeth Dinsmore, William Dunn, Douglas Edwards, Osborn Elliott, John Faber, Mary Fifield, Ed Fouhy, Reuven Frank, Fred Friendly.

Jean Garnett, Gary Paul Gates, Hinda Glasser, Donna Glenn, Paul Greenberg, J. G. "Jap" Gude, George Herman, Don Hewitt, John J. Hanrahan, John Hart, Larry Hatteberg, Bill Headline, David Hosley, Richard C. Hottelet, Quincy Howe, Paul Hume, Lynda Irvin, Jackie Judd, Dan Karasik, Joseph Keefer, Josephine Kendall, Donald Keyes, Theodore F.

Koop, Charles Kuralt, G. Bennett Larson, Jack Laurence, Bill Leonard, Larry LeSueur, Henry Lippold, Elmer Lower, John MacVane, Tom Mackin, Jay McMullen, Gordon Manning, Anne Mascolino, Don Meaney, Dean Mell, Odessa Memory, Mary Jo Melone, Janet Murrow, Gary Nurenberg, John O'Regan, Barney Oldfield, Lee Otis, Richard Pack, Deborah Potter, Larry Racies, James L. Reine, Ralph Renick, Frank Reynolds, Hewson A. Ryan.

Gene Rider, Bill Ridenour, Tom Roberts, Leo Rosenberg, Elliott Sanger, Diane Sawyer, Ernie Schultz, William Sheehan, Michael Shepley, Bob Schieffer, James M. Seward, Tom Shales, William L. Shirer, Gary Shivers, Lewis Shollenberger, Norman Silverstein, Helen Sioussat, Robert Skedgell, James L. Snyder, Sandy Socolow, Glen Stadler, Frank Stanton, Marcia Stein, Emerson Stone, Vernon A. Stone, Steve Strassberg, Howard Stringer, John Cameron Swayze, Sol Taishoff, Joel Tall, Ruth Ashton Taylor, Craig Tenney, Joe Tiernan, Dallas Townsend, Robert Trout, Joe Vaughan, Thomas Velotta, Henry Wefing, Joseph Wershba, Sylvia Westerman, Av Westin, Palmer Williams, Perry Wolff, Gayle Yamada.

I also am indebted to Lawrence Laurent, Larry Scharff, Mervin Block, Eric Sevareid, Bob Edwards, and Richard S. Salant, who read manuscript. Any mistakes that appear are my own.

I was blessed at the Columbia University Press in receiving wise counsel from Joan McQuary, managing editor, and Jennifer Crewe, senior executive editor. For their patience and guidance, I am profoundly grateful. Also, I must thank William F. Bernhardt, another fine editor, who encouraged me as the writing was getting under way.

Finally, acknowledgment to my dearest colleague, Lois Arnette Bliss, for her steadfast support, and to all former students in the School of Communication, American University, who instructed me and enriched my life.

NOW
THE
NEWS

1

The Natal Circumstances

Where did it begin? One of the hardest things to do is pinpoint a beginning. It has been said that broadcasting began when Stentor, the herald, rallied the Greeks before the gates of Troy.[1] According to Homer, Stentor had a good announcer's voice and "broadcast" to the besieging forces through a great horn.

There was Thales, the Greek philosopher who made a study of frictional electricity and magnetism in the sixth century B.C. William Gilbert, physician to the court of Elizabeth I, also experimented in magnetism. Gilbert is said to have been the first person to use the word *electric,* after the Greek word *elektron,* meaning amber, the fossil resin on which an electric charge can be produced by friction.

In 1752, Benjamin Franklin, who is sometimes called the grandfather of American journalism, flew his kite in a thunderstorm and founded the study of atmospheric electricity. Samuel F. B. Morse harnessed the electromagnetic medium for communication—a momentous breakthrough—by inventing the telegraph. With his invention of the telephone in 1876, Alexander Graham Bell introduced, as he stated in his patent application, "a method of, and apparatus for, transmitting vocal and other sounds telegraphically." Voice had been added. In Budapest, Theodore Puskas linked up 700 telephones to form what he called a telephonic newspaper —a forerunner, surely, of Ted Turner's cable news in the 1980s.

Thomas Edison noticed that sparks leaping between two electrodes tended to spread in all directions. The phenomenon was due, he believed, to a mysterious "etheric force." In Germany, Heinrich Hertz found that the force consisted of electromagnetic waves possessing various frequencies.[2] Although Hertz failed to see the communications potential of these radio waves, other people did, and research toward their practical application was conducted all over Europe. In London, Sir William Brookes, writing in the *Fortnightly Review,* saw "a new and astonishing world" emerging. "Rays of light will not pierce through a wall, nor, as we know only too well, through a London fog. But the electrical vibrations of a yard or more in wave length . . . will easily pierce such mediums, which to them will be transparent." He said, "Here, then, is revealed the bewildering possibility of telegraph without wires."[3]

James Clerk Maxwell, the Scottish physicist, had theorized about the existence of radio waves. Hertz proved they did exist. It remained for Guglielmo Marconi, a young Italian fired up by Hertz's findings, to put the mysterious invisible waves to use. "I could scarcely conceive," he said years later, "that it was possible that their application to useful purposes could have escaped the notice of eminent scientists."[4] But it had, and Marconi went to work. Employing homemade apparatus and a telegraph key, he succeeded in sending Morse code a few meters; then, using an antenna, to the far side of a hill behind his father's country house near Bologna. He had achieved "telegraph without wires"—wireless—but when he went to the Italian government with his discovery, he was rebuffed. So he went to London, and it was in England in 1897 that Marconi received his patent and, with British backers, formed the Wireless Telegraph Signal Company, Ltd.[5]

The Birth of Broadcast Journalism

Now came a small and momentous event. In 1898, through facilities provided by Marconi's newly founded wireless company, the *Dublin Daily Express* received minute-by-minute coverage of the Kingstown Regatta. This was wireless telegraphy—no sportscaster's voice was heard—and the audience was minuscule. But it was news, and it was heard over the air. And the name for news heard over the air is broadcast journalism. Because of this success, the *New York Herald* the next year commissioned Marconi to provide wireless coverage of the America's Cup races.[6] With these two yachting events at the close of the nineteenth century, news and radio were joined. Broadcast journalism, in dots and dashes, was born.

A Legend Questioned

For the next twenty years, radio[7] was confined principally to military and maritime use. Wireless telegraphy was employed extensively by Allied and Central powers in World War I and throughout the period by ships at sea.

In 1912, the "unsinkable" *Titanic* struck an iceberg and sank in the North Atlantic. David Sarnoff, the future chairman of RCA, was then a 21-year-old wireless operator working for Marconi's company in New York City. The legend promoted by Sarnoff himself was that he picked up a message from the S.S. *Olympic* saying the *Titanic* was sinking and then for two days and two nights, while the *Olympic* radioed information and newspapers put out extra editions, took down the names of those who survived and those who were missing. Only after getting the last name, the story went, did Sarnoff take off his earphones and go to bed. Years later, he said, "I passed the information on to a sorrowing world, and when messages ceased to come in, fell down like a log at my place and slept the clock around."[8] It now appears that Sarnoff's role was exaggerated. He may have picked up the *Olympic's* signal and relayed some information, but major New York papers like the *Times* and *Tribune,* reporting the sea disaster in detail, made no mention of whatever Sarnoff did at the time.

Although the origin of the first voice broadcast is debatable, certain facts are known. Reginald Fessenden, working in his Pittsburgh laboratory, succeeded in transmitting his voice by radio in 1901. Logic led him to use a continuous, smooth-flowing electromagnetic wave, instead of trying to use the interrupted or staccato-type wave adopted for the transmission of code. This was a radical departure, a heresy so important to the future of broadcasting that Erik Barnouw calls it "the foundation of radio."[9] Fessenden pursued his research and, thanks to an alternating current generator developed for him by Ernst F. W. Alexanderson, voice transmission became stronger and more distinct.

One of the most intriguing stories in early radio is the story of Fessenden's achievement on Christmas Eve, 1906. On that night, out in the Atlantic, the wireless operator of the S.S. *Kroonland* was amazed to hear in his earphones the sound of a woman singing. This was followed by a recording of Handel's "Largo," then a poetry reading and more music played from phonograph records. To the wireless operator, accustomed to hearing only dots and dashes on his receiver, it seemed a miracle. The impromptu program came from Fessenden's new transmitter at Brant Rock, Massachusetts, near Plymouth. Fessenden himself gave a "live" performance of Gounod's "O, Holy Night" on his violin. Robert St. John calls it "the first real broadcast of history."[10]

A curious story is that of Nathan Stubblefield, who, using ground conduction, transmitted voice signals for short distances as early as 1892. He received a patent for his "wireless telephone" in 1908 but got caught up in ruinous litigation with his business associates. Although Stubblefield is identified on his gravestone in Murray, Kentucky, as the father of radio broadcasting, he never was able to cash in on his invention.

In 1909, Charles "Doc" Harrold was broadcasting regularly scheduled news reports, as well as music, from what he called "the wireless telephone on the Garden City Bank Building in San Jose, California." His first broadcasts were scheduled for brief periods, but by 1915 the experimental station—known later as KQW, San Jose, and today as KCBS, San Francisco—was on the air up to eight hours a day.

On a winter night in 1908, from a radio antenna atop the Eiffel Tower in Paris, came a totally American voice saying, "I will attempt to play into the air the William Tell Overture." It was Lee De Forest, the energetic, Yale-educated son of a minister, introducing a program of recorded music. Two years earlier, he had invented the audion tube which, with its three electrodes, increased the energy of the wireless signals it received and made long-distance voice transmission possible. In the introduction to his autobiography, *Father of Radio*—a not self-deprecating title—he relives the sweet moment of success;

> I hurried to my laboratory carrying in my pocket the world's only supply of three-electrode vacuum tubes. They were just two in number, and I was eager to test them to determine whether my latest invention, a tiny bent wire in the form of a grid inserted between the carbon filament and the platinum plate . . . could bring in wireless signals over substantially greater distances than other receiving devices then in use. . . . To my excited delight I found that it did; the faint impulses which my short antenna brought to that new grid electrode sounded many times louder in the headphones than any wireless signal ever heard before. I was happy indeed.[11]

It would be difficult to overstate the importance of this amplification of sound. The "tiny bent wire" opened up a whole new world of applications, ranging from long-distance telephone service to television. On February 20, 1909, the *Jersey City Journal* called De Forest's predictions for radio "bolder than the dreams of fiction." It said, "He foresees the time when news and even advertising will be sent out to the public over wireless phones."

Briefly, De Forest himself became a broadcast journalist. It was election night, 1916. From his experimental transmitter at High Bridge, on the east bank of the Harlem River in New York City, De Forest read returns in the close race between Woodrow Wilson and Charles Evans Hughes. He got the returns from Hearst's *New York American* and, in the fashion of election night reporters ever since, kept up a running account. On closing down at 11 P.M., he gave his projection of the winner, sans polling sample, sans precinct profile, sans computer. Antedating H. V. Kaltenborn by 32 years,[12] he predicted that the next President of the United States would be Hughes and went to bed.

The next morning, November 8, the *New York Times,* in noting De Forest's "election night innovation," reported that "amateur operators within a radius of 200 miles had been forewarned of the new information service, and it was estimated that several thousand of them received the news, many through using the newly manufactured wireless telephones."

It was a two-paragraph story. And, perhaps because everyone had been fooled, not a word about De Forest's having been wrong about the outcome of the election.

In his autobiography, De Forest claims, "This was the first use of radiotelephone for broadcasting news of general interest, and," he adds, lest the fact be overlooked, "it took place four years before the much publicized broadcast of the Harding–Cox election returns by Westinghouse Station KDKA."[13]

More about KDKA later.

De Forest was a better inventor than businessman. For many years, his companies struggled to compete with the more successful communications endeavors of Marconi and American Telephone and Telegraph and with manufacturing firms like Westinghouse, General Electric, and Western Electric, which in 1919 pooled their radio patents and formed the Radio Corporation of America. But although De Forest acquired and lost several fortunes, his scientific contributions—he is credited with more than three hundred inventions—made him a giant in the communications field.

The Radio Music Box

On September 30, 1915, the vice president of American Marconi, Edward J. Nally, received a memorandum that has become perhaps the most renowned piece of paper in the history of broadcasting. It is the famous "Radio Music Box" memorandum written by young David Sarnoff, whose judgments in the three years since the *Titanic* disaster had come to be respected in the company.

Until this time, the proper function of radio was thought to be the transmission of messages, but Sarnoff foresaw—he was a great foreseer— a whole new profitable field, the broadcasting of information and entertainment for millions of people owning home receivers. This revolutionary concept of a mass radio audience is best described by Sarnoff himself:

> I have in mind a plan of development which would make radio a "household utility" in the same sense as the piano or phonograph. The idea is to bring music into the home by wireless. . . . The "Radio Music Box" can be supplied with amplifying tubes and a loudspeaking telephone, all of which can be neatly mounted in one box. The box can be placed on a table in the parlor or living room, the switch set accordingly and the music received. . . . The same principle can be extended to numerous other fields as, for example, receiving lectures at home which can be made perfectly audible; also, events of national importance can be simultaneously announced and received.[14]

Sarnoff, looking into the future, had recognized that the "box" could deliver news—live—as well as lectures and concerts. He anticipated "handsome profits." He pointed out that there were about 15 million families in the United States and said, "If only one million or seven percent of the total families thought well of the idea, it would, at the figure mentioned, mean a gross business of about $75,000,000, which should yield considerable revenue."[15]

But this was 1915. Sarnoff, ahead of his time, was unable to sell Nally, a cautious man, on the idea. Five years later, after joining RCA, Sarnoff resubmitted his proposal. Even then it was approved grudgingly. Sarnoff, who was thinking in grandiose terms, was allowed no more than $2,000 to design the prototype of his Radio Music Box. His final triumph, however, was complete. In 1922, the first Radiola,[16] manufactured by RCA, went on the market.

The Invisible Trumpet

It could be argued convincingly that broadcast journalism really began in 1920. On August 31 of that year, in Detroit, 8MK covered a primary election. On November 2, in East Pittsburgh, KDKA, as well as 8MK, broadcast the returns in the presidential election in which Warren G. Harding defeated James M. Cox.

These were determined news efforts. Because 8MK was the "baby" of William E. Scripps, publisher of the *Detroit News,* the station—later to be licensed as WWJ[17]—soon became journalistically oriented. It is an all-news station as this is written. KDKA was less news oriented, although it always has made news an important part of its programming. Within the year after Harding was elected, KDKA, besides broadcasting news bulletins, pioneered in what today is regarded as public affairs programming. Even as President Harding delivered his inaugural address in Washington, an announcer at KDKA read a transcript of the speech over the air. At about this same time, the station carried a talk delivered in Pittsburgh by the new secretary of commerce, Herbert Hoover.[18]

Besides such talks and music, KDKA aired market reports, public service announcements, church services, sporting events, and plays— everything, it seems, except commercials. As Sydney W. Head observes in his survey of broadcasting, "Westinghouse [operator of KDKA] had no plan to dilute the favorable publicity the station brought the firm by sharing it with others."[19]

In Detroit, 8MK came into being because Scripps thought it appropriate for a newspaper to get involved in the magical new way of communicating. He bought a de Forest-designed OT-10 transmitter, installed it on the second floor of the *Detroit News* building, tested it, and then, on August 20, 1920, put 8MK on the air with a program of phonograph music and news, making the *Detroit News* the first newspaper in the country to enter the broadcast field.[20]

It was 11 days later, on Tuesday night, August 31, that 8MK, with a voice reaching only 20 or 30 miles, ventured onto the air with returns from the Michigan primary election. In his early work, *News by Radio,* Mitchell

V. Charnley describes the studio, if it can be called that, from which the broadcast was made:

> Up among the bound files in the *News* library, on a table crowded into a corner, rested a de Forest radiophone. It consisted of a rectangular panel about 14 by 16 inches in size, with several control switches and dials, a pair of voltmeters and, at its top center, what looked like a telephone mouthpiece, its primitive microphone. . . . Into the mouthpiece a young man was talking, broadcasting election returns as they came to him from the newsroom, a floor below.[21]

The next day, the *News* reported that "a gigantic step" had been taken "in the history of man's conquest of the elements."[22]

It is doubtful that more than a few hundred people heard the broadcast. 8MK may have reached more listeners when it reported the presidential returns two months later. The *News* had promoted its "radiophone station," sometimes with front-page stories, and more and more amateurs were assembling home receivers. Still, the audience was small. Outside its building, the *News* projected returns by lantern slide. Now and then, a bulletin was delivered by megaphone. Barnouw notes, "The megaphone on that day may have reached more people than the radiophone—but for the last time.[23] Charnley says flat out, "Regular broadcasting of news was born that night."[24]

"Please Send a Postcard . . ."

KDKA's roots go back to 1916. Dr. Frank Conrad, assistant chief engineer for Westinghouse, set up 8XK, a small experimental transmitter in the two-story garage behind his house in Wilkinsburg, Pennsylvania, a Pittsburgh suburb. Unlike most operators, Conrad was allowed to broadcast throughout World War I because of work he was doing on wireless equipment for the Navy. This gave him a headstart when the war ended, and as early as 1919 he was playing phonograph records over the air.

In those days, radio operators were supposed to communicate with each other—just to broadcast was against the law—so Conrad, acting as disk jockey, would announce what he was going to put on the Victrola and add, "Please let me know if you like it." Just a postcard would do. In his book, *The Crowd-Catchers,* Robert Lewis Shayon says, "Dr. Conrad's broadcasts got to be quite a thing in the East Pittsburgh area. His two sons, Crawford and Francis, became radio's first masters of ceremony. They brought in neighborhood talent, vocal and instrumental."[25] The response was so enthusiastic that Conrad began scheduling two hours of music every Wednesday and Sunday night. He also began reporting baseball scores.

These programs on 8XK became so popular that the local Joseph Horne Department Store in Pittsburgh advertised that it had wireless receivers for sale for as little as ten dollars. When H. P. Davis, vice president of Westinghouse, saw the ad, it gave him the idea of founding a company station, one that would promote the Westinghouse name and at the same time create a market for receiving sets the company would manufacture and sell. The result—a deep disappointment to Sarnoff—was that Westinghouse's first civilian receiver, the Aeriola, Jr., went on sale a year before the first Radiola manufactured by RCA.[26]

To whet the appetite of these first listeners, Westinghouse asked Conrad to assemble a more powerful transmitter at its plant in East Pittsburgh. A 100-watt transmitter was set up on the roof of K Building, one of Westinghouse's taller structures, and a special license to inaugurate a regular broadcasting service was applied for. On October 27, six days before the presidential election, it received the now famous call letters, KDKA.

During this time, arrangements were being made for covering the election. A special telephone line was installed, linking the newsroom of the *Pittsburgh Post* with the radio shack on the roof of Building K. Duties were assigned. William Thomas would operate the transmitter. Leo H. Rosenberg of the publicity department would read the returns. Apparently it did not occur to anyone that returns in a presidential election could fill the hours of a whole evening, so a hand-cranked phonograph and music records were brought up to the rooftop station to help fill time. Here is how Rosenberg describes what happened:

> As the returns came in to the *Post*, they were telephoned to the station and recorded by R. S. McClelland and handed to me for reading into the microphone. The private telephone line was constantly monitored by John Frazier, manager of the telephone department of Westinghouse. . . . Periodically, I would say, 'If you are hearing this radio broadcast, please send a postcard to L. H. Rosenberg, Publicity Department, Westinghouse Electric and Manufacturing Company, East Pittsburgh, Pennsylvania.' Hundreds of cards were received from all over the United States and some foreign countries, even New Zealand. This was remarkable for a 100-watt station. It was due, we were told, to the bouncing effect of the atmospheric waves.[27]

Thus, Leo Rosenberg, age 24, became the first person to report presidential returns on a station authorized to provide the general public with a regular service. And the service on this night was journalism. Listeners, telephoning the station, demanded less music and more returns. The station could play the Victrola anytime. So Rosenberg read the results past midnight, though by 10 o'clock it was apparent that Harding, with his plea for "normalcy," had been elected.

Dawn of a New Era

The broadcast heralded a new era in communication. Whereas the *Detroit News,* as Barnouw has pointed out, directed its election reports primarily at radio hams, Westinghouse "presented the activity as something for everyone, a social delight for home and country club."[28]

Soon after the election, KDKA raised its "voice" to 500 watts and committed itself to a nightly two-hour program of music and news. For the first three months, Rosenberg served as announcer for these programs after working from 8:30 A.M. to 5:00 P.M. as manager of the station. Later, he went as manager to WBZ, the Westinghouse station in Boston.[29] In 1940, when Roosevelt defeated Wendell Willkie for a third term, the broadcast pioneer took part with Lowell Thomas in the first televising of election returns at WJZ in New York. He was truly present at the creation.

Looking back on that first election broadcast on KDKA, Rosenberg, at age 80, said, "Most writers have treated this as an isolated broadcast, but it proved to be a much greater 'first' with tremendous impact on journalism." By that, he said, he meant that the time lapse between an event and the reporting of that event had almost disappeared. He cited how, within minutes, the whole world knew the Japanese had attacked Pearl Harbor.[30]

But which of today's broadcasting stations is the oldest station? Which was on the air first? The question interests broadcast journalists because that station, of all existing stations, probably was the first to broadcast news. One has to say "probably" because records of what was broadcast, and when, are incomplete. Broadcasting's pioneers were too busy experimenting with the *means* of wireless transmission to keep accurate, detailed logs of what went on the air. It is impossible to say which station broadcasting today was the first to do news. Even the question of which is oldest is debated.

Impressive research on the subject of "oldest station" was done by Joseph E. Baudino and John M. Kittross and published in the *Journal of Broadcasting*.[31] They examined the histories of four major contenders for the title—KDKA, Pittsburgh; KCBS, San Francisco; WHA, Madison; and WWJ, Detroit—and made their determination on the basis of criteria proposed by R. Franklin Smith.[32] According to these criteria, the station in order to qualify must have provided a continuing if not continuous radio service. (Transmission may not have been continuous due to local or national emergency or act of God.) The service must have been for the general public, not for any one individual or narrowly defined group, and in the form of regularly scheduled programs of music or speech, or both. (Morse code was out.) Finally, the station must have been licensed.

Checking the four stations against these criteria, Baudino and Kittross rule out KCBS on grounds that "the first verifiable documentation of programming (by KQW, which became KCBS) is for January 9, 1922."[33] The researchers recognize the prior existence of Doc Harrold's station, KQW's predecessor, but its service was interrupted by technical and financial difficulties which, they say, cannot be regarded as either involuntary or acts of God. They do not question its right to call itself the first station; they do question its right to call itself the oldest. They decide against WHA because "available evidence indicates that the station started broadcasting weather and market reports to the public by voice, rather than by Morse code, only in January of 1921."[34]

In the case of WWJ, Baudino and Kittross point out that, as 8MK, the station was licensed to the Radio News and Music Company, not to the *Detroit News*.[35] The newspaper did not hold the license until 1921, and then it was a license to operate with the call letters WBL. (WBL became WWJ the next year.) These scholars call the relationship between 8MK and WBL tenuous compared to the relationship between 8XK and KDKA. They say, "It seems clear to us that KDKA . . . deserves the title and honor of being the oldest broadcasting station in the United States."[36]

So it is settled, once and for all? Not quite. Baudino and Kittross quickly add, "We hesitate to say that our conclusion will stand for all time."[37]

Legal Aspects

Such were the beginnings.

Soon hardware stores everywhere were selling variable condensers, transformers, tubes, rheostats, and tuners—everything it took, including batteries, for assembling home receivers. Many sets were put together by teenagers who later found careers in broadcasting. But, more and more, stores were selling sets made by firms like RCA, Fada, Atwater Kent, Westinghouse, Crosley, and Zenith, which boasted it was "the exclusive choice of MacMillan for his North Polar Expedition."[38] Signals from a few transmitters grew in a short time into a great, swelling cacophony of words and music as stations multiplied, caterwauling on identical frequencies until the situation cried for government regulation.[39] So this may be the place to tell how Congress brought regulation about.

Congress did not start by assigning frequencies. The first federal legislation relating to radio was the Wireless Ship Act of 1910, which required large ocean-going vessels to be able to send and receive radio signals over a distance of at least a hundred miles. The law applied to ships of foreign as well as U.S. registry that might "leave or attempt to leave any port of the United States."

In two years, with more than a thousand amateur and disaster stations in operation, Congress again acted. The Radio Act of 1912 made it illegal to operate a radio station without a license from the secretary of commerce. Limits were placed on the range of wave lengths on which stations could operate, but neither the secretary of commerce nor anyone else had authority to assign frequencies. As commerce secretary, Herbert Hoover tried to make the law work, but interference—the jumbling of radio signals—made the situation hopeless. Not only had the number of stations mushroomed (more than 10,000, including 571 commercial AM stations, by 1925), but stations competing for the nation's ear were constantly switching frequencies and increasing their power. WLW, Cincinnati, outdoing all stations, raised its voice to 500,000 watts.[40] It was chaos, and Congress, recognizing the need for more effective regulation, passed the Federal Radio Act of 1927.

This legislation, signed by President Coolidge, was a comprehensive measure designed to plug all loopholes. The bill contained 41 sections, compared to 11 sections in the Radio Act of 1912. It covered questions of censorship, licensing, and freedom of speech. And there appears for the first time in broadcast legislation the phrase "public interest, convenience, and necessity," borrowed from previous measures governing public utilities.

The act called for creation of a Federal Radio Commission which would have five members appointed by the President, "by and with the consent of the Senate." Not more than three commissioners could belong to the same political party. The commission was to "assign bands of frequencies . . . for each individual station and determine the power which each station shall use and the time during which it may operate." No license for a broadcasting station could be for more than three years.

The phrase "public convenience, interest, and necessity" appeared in Section 9. Interestingly, but not importantly, the phrase in Section 11 read "public interest, convenience, *or* necessity." Both sections said the commission, in granting a license, should take care that these public concerns were served. (In the Communications Act of 1934, the wording again is "public interest, convenience *and* necessity.") From the beginning, the phrase has been associated with a station's performance in informing the public.

Section 18 raised further journalistic questions. It said: "If any licensee shall permit any person who is a legally qualified candidate for any public office to use a broadcasting station, he shall afford equal opportunities to all other such candidates for that office in the use of such broadcasting station. . . ."

Section 29 spoke of censorship. It said: "Nothing in this Act shall be understood or construed to give the licensing authority the power of censorship over the radio communications or signals transmitted by any radio station, and no regulation or condition shall be promulgated or fixed by the licensing authority which shall interfere with the right of free speech by means of radio communication." There was one qualification: "No person within the jurisdiction of the United States shall utter any obscene, indecent, or profane language by means of radio communication." More than half a century later, the qualification still was at issue in the courts.

The sprouting of radio towers across the land was matched by the sale of radio sets—an estimated 100,000 sold in 1922 swelling to almost four million in 1930.[41] Because the Radio Act of 1927 was soon outmoded, Congress passed the Communications Act of 1934, which, with amendments, still governs wire and radio communications in the United States. This legislation was based on the old Radio Act. The commission would continue to assign frequencies. Licenses still would be granted for three years. The ban on censorship, except of language deemed obscene, remained. And, as before, stations were to broadcast in "the public interest, convenience, and necessity," although the precise meaning of the phrase was not defined.

The name of the regulatory commission was changed. The Federal Radio Commission (FRC) became the Federal Communications Commission (FCC). Because President Roosevelt, after three Republican administrations, wanted a Democratic majority on the commission, Congress raised the number of commissioners from five to seven. Now, instead of three, not more than four commissioners could belong to the same political party.

2

Growing Pains . . . and Pleasures

Radio news began with people reading newspaper stories over the air. Ham operators used newspapers simply to have something to read, hoping a fellow ham, far away, would send a penny postcard saying the transmission came in "loud and clear." In the 1920s, few stations hired reporters. They pirated their news from newspapers. If a paper owned a station, as the *Detroit News* owned WWJ, the station naturally had access to the paper's contents. There was, at that stage, little sense of rivalry between the station owners and publishers.

In that free-wheeling, disorganized time, the three news services—Associated Press, United Press, and International News Service—were not too concerned if their stories were aired, especially if they were given on-air credit. Lowell Thomas said the press services kept score. "They would keep track of how many times I'd plugged them, and then they'd call up and scold me if I didn't give as many to them as to someone else." [1]

The twenties were the "sandbox" years. Radio had not grown up. It was fun, and so was most of the news, befitting a prosperous time when America was at peace and many of its people were at play. It was not a perfect world. Famines raged in Russia. There were floods in China. At home, there was bigotry and some fear, as demonstrated by the persecution of Sacco and Vanzetti, and some high-level corruption, as demonstrated by Teapot Dome.

But it was an up-beat time. Each year, the indices of business—auto production, freight car loadings, bank deposits—were up. The sky did seem the limit. And radio was part of the boom. As program offerings increased, sales of receivers rose. To meet the demand, manufacturers made 4,428,000 sets in 1929, twice as many as just four years before.[2]

If a network like CBS—called Columbia then—battled to survive, many stations toward the end of the decade were thriving. Political conventions, Lindbergh's flight to Paris, even the trial of the teacher John Scopes were for the listeners' entertainments. Just tuning in, listening to a program—any program—in a far-off city was fascinating.

All kinds of businesses were getting in on the act. Big department stores like Wanamaker in Philadelphia and Bamberger in Newark founded stations during the year. The Bamberger station, WOR, would become famous. Barnouw notes that WAAF was started by a Chicago stockyard and a laundry started KUS in Los Angeles.[3] A good many stations ran out of money and "died" in a few months. The mortality rate was high.

Universities and newspapers were active founders of stations. The papers saw radio as good promotion. WGN, the call letters for the *Tribune* station in Chicago, stood for World's Greatest Newspaper. (Selling time to advertisers would come later.) How newspapers took to radio is shown by the fact that while they had fewer than a dozen stations in mid-1922, they owned 69 at the end of the year.[4]

Enter Professor Terry

Universities came to broadcasting naturally. Physics teachers experimented with radio waves in university laboratories—they had both know-how and equipment—and educators soon recognized the capability of broadcasting to bring courses within reach of persons unable to enroll and attend class. A good illustration of how such stations came into being is WHA, Madison, Wisconsin, one of the four major claimants to the title "oldest station in the nation." WHA, an educational station, was founded at the University of Wisconsin because of the interest in wireless of two professors, Edward Bennett and Earl Terry, who in 1916 set up an experimental transmitter, 9XM. The station in the basement of the physics building could only send code. However, after "homemade" vacuum tubes were fashioned under Professor Terry's direction, the station found its voice, and it was licensed as WHA in 1922. Today, seven days a week, it offers one-hour courses in subjects as diverse as cultural geography, Russian history, and constitutional law. It also carries news, as does its companion station, WHA-TV.

The first "news" carried by many of the early university stations was weather forecasts, transmitted in Morse code, although the University of Nebraska station, 9YD, began including news bulletins as early as 1914.

On January 3, 1921, the University of Wisconsin station, which also had been using code, switched to regularly scheduled weather reports delivered by voice.[5] Later that same year, it began airing news of what was going on at the university, along with agricultural information. Some kind of mark was reached in March 1922, when the station broadcast an account of a local robbery.[6]

Of Sopranos and Sports

It is curious that broadcasters were so slow to realize that news was a natural for radio. Music and lectures made up almost the entire body of commercial broadcasting in the early twenties. The first broadcasters did recognize the opportunity for publicity in airing major sports events. It was to attract attention to RCA that David Sarnoff bought the idea of broadcasting a prize fight, and he chose a big one, the sensational "Battle of the Century" at Boyle's Thirty Acres in Jersey City between heavyweight champion Jack Dempsey and the French challenger, George Carpentier. The fact that Sarnoff had no station at the time didn't stop him. When he found out that General Electric was about to deliver a powerful mobile transmitter to the Navy, he persuaded G.E. to let him borrow it. The transmitter was dispatched to the Lackawanna Railroad terminal in Hoboken and a telephone line put in to the arena, two and a half miles away. The blow-by-blow account was to be given that day, July 2, 1921, by Major J. Andrew White, editor of *Wireless Age*, but White's voice was not heard. A technician, J. O. Smith, stationed at the transmitter, listened on the telephone and broadcast what was happening. The "studio" was a small structure of galvanized iron sheeting used by Pullman porters for changing their clothes.

Sarnoff got the national attention he wanted. Besides the few thousand listeners who heard the description on their home receivers, thousands more heard it over loud-speakers in theaters and lodge halls throughout the Eastern states. Before the fight, only one newspaper, the *New York Times*, deigned to mention the experiment. Afterward, the whole American and European press trumpeted radio's achievement.

Later that year, it was radio's first World Series, and the broadcast was relayed in much the same Rube Goldberg fashion. In his book, *I Looked & I Listened,* the late Ben Gross told how, after the telephone company refused to lease a line to WJZ, one of broadcasting's first announcers, Tommy Cowan, teamed up with Sandy Hunt, sports editor of the *Newark Sunday Call,* to get the play-by-play on the air. They did it by having a telephone installed in a box at the Polo Grounds, where the Series would be played. Gross quoted from a conversation with Cowan:

> So on the day of the opening game between the Giants and the Yankees, October 5, 1921, Sandy was in the box and we began the first broadcast of a World Series. I sat in our studio in Newark with earphones clamped on as my colleague called the plays into the

telephone. I would repeat each word before the mike, but the strain was so great that I did not have the slightest idea of what I was saying. In fact, at the conclusion of the game, I did not even know which team had won![7]

The Yankees had won, three to nothing. But the Giants came back to take the Series by winning five games to the Yankees' three. WJZ carried the Series again the next year. Thus a tradition was established, and the Series has been broadcast each year ever since.

Now . . . the News

In the beginning, then, it was more sports than news. Thereafter, gradually, more news was reported and announcers covered "legitimate" news events as readily as they did boxing and the dancing in hotel ballrooms. Norman Brokenshire, the son of a Canadian minister, worked with Bing Crosby, Will Rogers, and the Boswell Sisters and covered presidential inaugurations and national political conventions.

In *News by Radio*, Mitchell Charnley writes that in those early years there was no universal pattern of how a newsroom fit into the typical station organization, although it was "fairly common and certainly logical and desirable" for the news department to be responsible solely to top management.[8] Still, this was not the rule. At many stations the program manager performed the duties of news director. News did not make up an important enough part of the broadcast schedule.

Announcers had no authority to edit copy. They read on the air what was given them to read. When they presumed to revise a newscast without consulting someone in the newsroom, they were reprimanded. In some instances, those who persisted in taking liberties were fired. On the other hand, writers appreciated the announcer who, while rehearsing a script, brought mistakes to their attention.

There was an informality in the newsroom which disappeared as staffs grew larger, and salaries and competition for position increased. A popular game was to try to "break up" the announcer while he was on the air. Oldtimers recall scripts set afire by pranksters during actual broadcasts. Garter snakes were draped on microphones. One network announcer[9] was startled to find himself eyeball to eyeball with a praying mantis on the microphone as he began his hourly newscast.

Early broadcasters explored the journalistic possibilities with transmissions from unusual locations. On August 12, 1929, NBC carried the voice of a parachute jumper as he floated to earth bearing a 25-pound two-watt transmitter. CBS did the same thing and claims to have done it first.[10] Robert Trout remembers reading this introduction:

Ladies and gentlemen, tonight the Columbia coast-to-coast network attempts a feat hitherto unknown to the world of broadcasting: a famous girl trio of vocalists presenting their programme of songs with each girl singing in a different place—a studio in a different building—here in Washington. And, in a *fourth* studio, their piano accompanist, Ray Bloch.[11]

The date of this contrived broadcast is lost. But this kind of multiple-point origination, no matter how trivial, helped pave the way for what would become commonplace: more than one live report within a single news program, each report from a different location in this country or overseas.

Nineteen twenty-two saw the first broadcast by an American president as Warren G. Harding dedicated a monument to Francis Scott Key in Baltimore. On November 10, 1923, thousands of listeners were astonished to hear the feeble voice of a dying ex-president speaking to them from the library of his home in Washington. On the eve of Armistice Day, Woodrow Wilson was making his final appeal for entry of the United States into the League of Nations. With prompting from Mrs. Wilson, who stood by his side, he floundered through his talk, then went to lie down. AT&T had arranged a hookup linking WCAP, Washington; WEAF, New York, and WJAR, Providence. Three months later, Wilson's funeral service was broadcast over the same stations.

"Ala-ba-mah Casts 24 Votes . . ."

A signal date for American politics is June 10, 1924. On that day, and for two successive days, a national political convention received broadcast coverage. This had never happened before, and politics in the United States never would be the same.

Two fledgling networks—one patched together by the American Telephone and Telegraph Company, the other by General Electric and the Radio Corporation of America—were carrying the proceedings of the Republican National Convention in Cleveland. AT&T was using its own long lines to link its flagship, WEAF, New York, with 17 other stations. RCA had improvised a similar, smaller chain of stations fed by its New York outlet, WJZ, over lines normally used by Western Union. The reporters for the AT&T group were Graham McNamee and an associate announcer, Phillips Carlin. Chief announcer for the RCA hookup was Major J. Andrew White of *Wireless Age*, assisted by Norman Brokenshire, who circulated among delegates on the floor.

Here is a description of the radio setup, given by Ben Gross, who was there:

> As one assigned to gather brief "human interest" sidelights, I often visited Graham in his little glass-enclosed booth on the stage near the speaker's rostrum. With a switchboard, two telephones, a chair and a table with two microphones, it could scarcely hold two persons. Phil had even more cramped quarters in a birdcage-like contraption hanging high above the floor among the steel girders.[12]

There was not much to report. The Republicans, swiftly and without commotion, nominated Calvin Coolidge to be president in his own right. For vice president, they nominated a successful Chicago banker, Charles G. Dawes. It was a cut-and-dried three-day affair, in sharp contrast with the Democratic convention in the old Madison Square Garden in New York two weeks later.

The Democrats opened their meeting decorously, then turned it into a brawl lasting 17 days. Again, the chief broadcasters for AT&T and RCA were McNamee and White, who, appropriately, had reported radio's first prize fight. Brokenshire, once more, scrambled among delegates for tidbits of news. There was no communication, save sign language, between White in his glass booth and Brokenshire on the convention floor. If Brokenshire got a story, he went to the booth and told White about it.

The delegates, wrangling in almost unbearable heat, were stymied on whether to nominate Wilson's son-in-law, William Gibbs McAdoo, or New York's Catholic governor, Al Smith. The Ku Klux Klan opposed Smith because of his religion, and McAdoo, mindful of Protestant prejudice and the Klan's political clout, was afraid to denounce it. The upshot, after 103 roll calls, was that the presidential nomination went to neither Smith nor McAdoo but to John W. Davis. His running mate was Governor Charles Bryan of Nebraska, brother of William Jennings Bryan, the "silver-tongued orator" who had been the party's candidate for president in three previous campaigns.

There were ugly scenes. One day, Brokenshire, taking over the microphone while White went out to eat, observed a row that got so heated the delegates were using signs to beat each other over the head. WJZ had got the broadcast rights to the convention "on the distinct understanding that no disorders of any kind would be reported."[13] Coverage may have been restricted, but disturbances were not. At one point, William Jennings Bryan, seeking peace, knelt between two delegates who were going at each other and prayed for the Lord to intervene.

This was the convention at which the chairman of the Alabama delegation rose at the start of each futile roll call and bellowed, "Ala-ba-mah casts 24 votes for Oscar W. Underwood!" Gross reports that, after a few votes were taken, spectators in the gallery took up the refrain. Radio picked it up and popularized it, and it became a sort of trademark of the convention and a national joke. The chairman of the Alabama delegation was the governor, Bill Brandon. Some time later, when Gross met him, Brandon said, "You know, I've done some mighty good things as governor, but everywhere I go, all the people seem to remember is that I cast 24 votes for Underwood. Sometimes I wish I had never said it."[14]

Such was the power of radio even then, though candidates made little use of it in the course of the campaign. Coolidge, running on a prosperity platform, made a speech in October that was broadcast, then another on the night before the election. This broadcast, carried over AT&T lines to 26 stations, marks the first election eve address on a radio network. It was, even more significantly, the first major broadcast made purposely to affect the political process.

The next night, scores of stations—not just KDKA and WWJ—were on the air with the returns.

The First Radio Inauguration

Calvin Coolidge was inaugurated on March 4, 1925. Norman Broken-shire reported for the RCA hookup of no more than ten stations; Graham McNamee had the larger AT&T network.

In his memoir, Brokenshire says he had two lines to New York, "one to carry the program, one kept open for instantaneous communication between the studio and me, and to serve also as a spare in case of trouble."[15] And he recalls that in order to scoop McNamee—to get on the air first—he was commanded to start speaking from the Capitol at 9:45 A.M., which meant he had, by his own devices, to fill what seemed a vast, perilous void of airtime until noon, when the inaugural ceremony would begin.

He filled it, describing over and over the weather, the crowd, the history of previous inaugurations, what was scheduled to take place, and finally the arrival of the central figures, Mr. and Mrs. Coolidge and Chief Justice Taft. He writes proudly: "In midafternoon, I knew I had set a record . . . two hours and 15 minutes consecutively filled to the brim with words—and absolutely nothing prearranged to say. I returned to New York feeling like the conquering hero."[16]

The Monkey Trial

The first major trial covered by radio or television was the "monkey trial," so called by H. L. Mencken, that took place in Dayton, Tennessee, in the summer of 1925. The defendant, John Scopes, was a young science teacher charged with violating state law by teaching Darwin's theory of evolution at the local high school. The renowned criminal lawyer, Clarence Darrow, volunteered to join in Scopes' defense when he heard that the even more famous "silver-tongued orator," William Jennings Bryan, would assist the prosecution. Now, despite his advanced years, Bryan felt impelled to fight what he saw as godless doctrine.

With such an issue as the teaching of evolution, and such well-known figures in leading roles, the test case attracted wide attention. In his account of the trial, written long afterward, Scopes says more than two hundred reporters and photographers descended on the small mountain town, while a throng of spectators came, not only from nearby communities, but from out of state. "It was busier than the midway of a carnival," he said. "People on the go from early morning until late at night."[17]

Interest was high in Chicago, 500 miles away. Darrow was from that city, and WGN, the *Chicago Tribune* station, brought a telephone line to Dayton at a thousand dollars a day so portions of the trial could be broadcast. Its reporter was Quin Ryan, who used a microphone that stood alongside the counsels' tables—no participant was adverse to publicity—and a steady stream of live reports was aired. Ryan's only real handicap was the hot weather. Describing it, Scopes says, "The sun baked the sidewalks, and its heat boiled into the courtroom, becoming a constant source of annoyance and discomfort."[18] At one point, the judge moved the whole proceedings outdoors to a spot in the shade. Testimony proved so dramatic that WGN began covering the trial nonstop. The trial ended with a verdict of guilty. Scopes was fined $100 and costs. Bryan had won his case, but he was a broken man. He died a few days later.

"Lucky Lindy"

The first really big moment for radio news, and the most dramatic moment in American aviation history since the Wright brothers, came with the flight of Charles Lindbergh—the "Lone Eagle"—across the Atlantic in May 1927. In his single-engine plane, the *Spirit of St. Louis,* Lindbergh had no radio equipment either for sending or receiving. Alone, he flew with no guidance except from a compass and what he could determine from land and sea below and from the stars.

A small crowd of reporters and cameramen witnessed the takeoff from Roosevelt Field, Long Island, at 7:52 A.M. on May 20, 1927. They saw the tiny monoplane, burdened with all the gasoline it could bear, struggle off the ground, barely miss a telephone wire, and disappear.[19]

For the next 33 hours and 29 minutes, until he landed in Paris, the question uppermost in Americans' minds was: Where is he now? It was radio, swift and ubiquitous, that made them of one mind, and it was to the intermittent, fragmentary reports on radio that they turned to keep informed. For more than eleven hours there was no word, then a radio message from CHNS, Halifax, relayed by radio stations all over America. The white monoplane had been sighted over Cape Race, Newfoundland, flying east in poor weather. The time given was 7 P.M.

There was nothing more that night. The reference to poor weather increased concern. Now more often the question was: Will he make it? In the morning, at WJZ, a young announcer, George Hicks, told his listeners, "As Saturday dawns over the vast Atlantic, the Lindbergh plane is unreported since passing Newfoundland last night."

By now, not just America but a large part of the world awaited word of the airman's fate. People listening anxiously to their radios heard nothing more than what Hicks had reported, but they stayed tuned, believing that they would get the news first on the radio. As more hours passed, fears rose. Had he survived the storm? Had he run out of gas? With no one to spell him, had he fallen asleep and plunged into the waves?

Finally word came that caused everyone to breathe more easily:

> This is Station 2RF, Dublin, calling. The American flier Lindbergh passed over Dingle Bay on the Irish coast at a low altitude at 1:30 this afternoon.

Within minutes the news was broadcast in America. There were cheers in homes and offices all over the country. He had crossed the ocean. He was safe. It looked now as though he was going to make it. Lucky Lindy!

Again, silence. Then word by shortwave from Radio Paris that a ship in Cherbourg harbor had sighted the monoplane over the coast of France. Another wait and at last the Associated Press flash:

PARIS—LINDBERGH LANDED 5:21 P.M.

Newspapers blossomed with extras, but many people, listening to their radios, already had heard what they wanted to know—Lindbergh *had* made it.[20] He had dared and made a fantastic dream come true. The nation rejoiced with him in it.

For another three weeks, Lindbergh was the big story. President Coolidge ordered the flier and his plane brought home on the cruiser *Memphis* and on June 11 welcomed him in ceremonies at the base of the Washington Monument. Not only did NBC broadcast the ceremonies but it went on the air with a special program that began with the roar of airplanes flying in review and ended six and a half hours later with a patriotic talk by George M. Cohan. Two days later came the tumultuous reception in New York City—greetings by Governor Al Smith and Mayor Jimmy Walker and a triumphal ticker tape parade reported by NBC's star announcer, Graham McNamee. The day saw an innovation in the coverage of such events—the multiple pickup. Some broadcasters, after reporting what they could see from their vantage point, passed the story along to a colleague farther up the parade route, much as runners in a relay pass the baton.

Five years later—in tragedy—Lindbergh again would be the big story.

NBC Is Born

It was natural for RCA to want to set up a permanent network. It distributed home receivers—the little "music boxes" Sarnoff spoke of— and such a program service, by creating demand, would boost sales. RCA arranged to buy WEAF, which today is WNBC, from AT&T for a million dollars, and it became NBC's flagship station in New York. An announcement of the creation of the National Broadcasting Company was published on September 13, 1926. It promised quality programming and said something directly pertinent to journalism: "It is hoped that arrangements may be made so that every event of national importance may be broadcast widely throughout the United States."

NBC's first program on November 15, 1926, was an entrepreneur's dream. For starters, there were the New York Symphony, the New York Oratorio Society, Cesare Sodero's light opera company, the concert pianist

Harold Bauer, and the comedy team of Weber and Fields, all broadcasting from the ballroom of the old Waldorf-Astoria Hotel, where the Empire State Building now stands. Then there was a monologue by Will Rogers from a theater dressing room in Independence, Kansas, then the glamorous diva, Mary Garden, in Chicago, forgoing opera and singing songs like "Annie Laurie" and "Little Gray Home in the West."

The program, which ran past midnight, lasted more than four hours and was carried by 25 stations in 21 cities. Ben Gross, who was there that night as a reporter for the *New York Daily News*, heard a woman tell her husband as they left the ballroom, "My dear, I had no idea! We simply must get one of those radios the first thing tomorrow."[21]

Within two months, NBC was operating two networks: a Red network of 25 stations fed by WEAF and a Blue network of six stations fed by WJZ. NBC engineers used the colors as a means of identification when drafting maps of where each network's programming would be fed, and the colors came into formal usage. (The American Broadcasting Company had its origin in 1943 when RCA, as the result of antitrust action, sold the Blue network to Edward J. Noble, the manufacturer of Life Savers candy.)

Then Came CBS

NBC was not going to have the field to itself. In 1928, William S. Paley, the hustling 26-year-old heir to a cigar fortune, came up to New York from Philadelphia and bought United Independent Broadcasters, a struggling network of 16 stations, for $500,000.

UIB had been an outlet—a radio platform—for concert artists under the management of the celebrated impresario Arthur Judson. It had no studio. It leased its air facilities from WOR in New York, and its offices consisted of four rooms in the Paramount Building, high above Times Square.[22] For a short time, UIB had been called the Columbia Phonograph Broadcasting System because of some funding by the Columbia Phonograph Company (which CBS later bought), and it was under that name that it premiered on September 18, 1927, broadcasting a Metropolitan Opera Company production of *The King's Henchman,* with music by Deems Taylor set to a libretto by Edna St. Vincent Millay.

Although more modest than NBC's extravaganza, the premiere cost enough to wreck the network's already wobbly finances, and that was when young Paley became excited at the prospect of taking it over. There were months of maneuvering, and then, as he writes in his memoir, "On September 25, I closed the deal and on the next day, September 26, 1928, was elected president of a patchwork, money-losing little company called United Independent Broadcasters." He goes on, "I had the gut feeling that radio was on the threshold of a great awakening . . . and that I had come to the medium at the right moment."[23]

The 1928 Election

The first big thing that happened after CBS and NBC came on the scene was the 1928 election. Heading the Republican ticket was Herbert Hoover, an engineer and son of an Iowa blacksmith. Hoover had the aura of a humanitarian, having organized and directed massive relief missions to Europe after the First World War. Moreover, as secretary of commerce he had built up a formidable influence among business leaders and within the party. His Democratic opponent, Al Smith, who had come up from New York City's Lower East Side to become governor of New York, was a more controversial figure. He had been a popular governor, but he wanted to scuttle Prohibition, which still had wide support, and again there was the bogy that had haunted him in 1924: he was a Roman Catholic.

The campaign affected radio in a financial way. NBC had behind it the resources of a giant corporation. CBS was on its own, operating at a loss, so when both parties bought radio time it meant more to CBS than to its wealthier rival. Paley notes that "while NBC got the lion's share, we got the overflow business, perhaps a couple of hundred thousand dollars." It was, he says, a lifesaver.[24]

An announcer joining Norman Brokenshire and Graham McNamee in the front rank at this time was Ted Husing, who had been office manager for United Independent Broadcasters when Paley took over. Paley found the young man impossible as a manager—"He drove me crazy, giving me the wrong answers to everything"[25]—but Husing also did announcing, and in this he excelled, becoming in time what his critic, Paley, calls "the best and most famous sportscaster in the country."[26]

Husing participated in radio's coverage of the 1928 national conventions, which was more extensive than it had been in 1924. An innovation was NBC's switch to Palo Alto, California, for Hoover's statement accepting the nomination. The president of NBC, Merlin Aylesworth, said, as many broadcasters would say after him, that because voters were able, vicariously, to attend the conventions, they received new insight into the democratic process.[27]

The radio reporter who came out of the election with the most glory— and it was glory—was Ted Husing. By himself, speaking into a microphone in the city room of the *New York World*—from eight o'clock in the evening until six o'clock the next morning, between interludes of music— he gave the returns as they poured in over the press association wires. Broadcasting from the heart of that great newspaper, using his own arithmetic and logic, he scooped the paper in reporting Hoover's election by a whole hour. For his performance, CBS received 12,000 telegrams of congratulation. Husing was elated. Years later, he said, "In the annual competition of 1928 . . . we hadn't yet equaled NBC in prestige and grandeur, but we had passed it in reporting news."[28]

It would be difficult to say whether radio helped Hoover win the

election. If he used the medium to get his views across, so did his opponent. If his voice was flat and the delivery of his speeches monotonous, so
that to listen to him was tedious, his opponent's nasal New York accent and
frequent mispronunciations—*radio* came out *rad-dio*—may have served
him no better. Neither was comfortable before the microphone. At the
very start, Al Smith had said, "When I talk to people, I want to see the
whites of their eyes."[29]

The inauguration of Herbert Hoover not only drew a radio audience
estimated at more than 60 million—the largest audience in history up to
that time—but produced the medium's most saturated coverage of a single
event. Applying the experience gained in covering Lindbergh's ticker tape
parade, and producing other remotes, NBC and CBS went all out in
covering each step in the transfer of presidential powers.

3

The Founding Fathers

In entertainment programming, NBC, a year older than CBS, enjoyed a head start. It had "Amos 'n' Andy," possibly the most popular program ever aired, and paraded stars like Elsie Janis, Rudy Valee, Eddie Cantor, and Will Rogers. CBS' William S. Paley was not about to abandon the field to NBC. He went out and "discovered" Bing Crosby, Kate Smith, and the Mills Brothers.[1] But he wanted his network to have a special identity, to excel in an important specific area, and that area, he decided, would be news. He had realized, listening to returns in the 1928 election and the live reporting of Hoover's inauguration, what radio covering such events could do. He perceived what it would mean in terms of public information and what it would mean in terms of prestige for CBS.

The crucial year was 1930. Paley was hiring journalists who would become founders of what, in the early period, was called CBS World News. One was Edward Klauber, a former night city editor of the *New York Times,* who had been associated briefly with the public relations pioneer, Edward L. Bernays. Another was Paul W. White, who came to the struggling network from the United Press.

A tough-minded, soft-spoken Kentuckian educated at the University of Louisville and the University of Pennsylvania, Edward Klauber came to

New York in 1912 as a reporter for the *New York World*. He joined the staff of the *New York Times* four years later. In 1930, when Paley was looking for an assistant, Bernays suggested Klauber, and Paley made him executive vice president. In his memoir, Paley calls Klauber his mentor regarding news. "Our method was to discuss any given problem until we had exhausted the possibilities. . . . Thus we agreed there would be no editorializing during news broadcasts. Commentaries would be kept completely separate from the news itself." There was also to be fairness and balance. "If we gave one side of a controversy, we would give equal time to the other side."[2]

The enforcer of this policy would be Paul Welrose White, a 200-pound Kansan who had been in love with news since boyhood. At 16, rather than attend business school, he ran away from his home in Pittsburg, Kansas, to be a reporter on the *Salina Journal*. He was working as telegraph editor at the *Kansas City Journal* a few months later when he was recognized by a Pittsburg resident, who notified the family. A deal was struck. Young White would be permitted to pursue his dream of newspapering if he attended college. In September 1919, he enrolled at the University of Kansas, where he remained two years before transferring to Columbia University in journalism's highest heaven, New York.

After earning a master's degree in journalism at Columbia, as well as a B.A., White, who was now 22, tried to get on what was then America's most prestigious newspaper, the *New York World*. He was turned down. One can imagine the young man's thoughts as he descended in the elevator in the hallowed *World* building after this rebuff. He was so deep in thought that when the elevator stopped at the third floor, he mistook it for the street floor and found himself in the bustling headquarters of the United Press. It must have been one of the most felicitous mistakes in White's life, as he was hired on the spot.

Paul White was with the United Press for six years, during which he covered the sensational Hall–Mills murder trial and the transatlantic flights of Charles Lindbergh, Chamberlain-Levine, and Ruth Snyder. His "byline" became well known. In 1929, he became editor of UP's United Feature Syndicate.

"It was a screwball era in news," he reflected years later. "If anyone doubts it, let me remind him that my deskmates at various times during those days were Henry McLemore, H. Allen Smith, and Westbrook Pegler."[3]

White joined CBS in December 1930. He had the title of news editor, which is misleading because at the start he had more to do with publicizing Columbia (as the network generally was known) than with the broadcasting of news bulletins. He was, in fact, director of publicity in 1932, a year in which CBS and NBC aired more news than in any preceding year in their short histories.

What was sometimes referred to in public print as the news department actually was the special events department, and the director of special events at CBS in 1932 was a man named Herbert Glover.[4] J. G. "Jap" Gude worked at various times as assistant to both Glover and White, whom he ultimately succeeded as publicity director. He says:

> Glover was what my grandchildren would call a weirdo, and he was generally known to the engineers, with whom he worked very closely, as "Madman Glover." But we got along well. . . . He was married to a very wealthy woman and lived in a very sumptuous house on Long Island's south shore, where he also maintained a sizable cruiser. . . . I believe he was the son of an Episcopal clergyman, was obviously well educated, and had never, to the best of my knowledge, ever worked for a newspaper or press association.[5]

Gude calls the network's news operation at that time "a pretty haphazard affair."

> You have to remember that in those days there was no news department at NBC or CBS, that it was almost all "special events" —speeches, dedications, parades. We did only snippets of news, which came in on the old-fashioned tickers that gave you the stock market quotations. The news was on this paper ribbon, the kind used in ticker tape parades, and you'd paste it up on a sheet of paper for the announcer to read. Pretty soon we got the teletypes, but there wasn't any news department as you know it today, not until Paul White changed it.

Still, he says, "the moving force behind it all was Ed Klauber."[6]

Introducing Lowell Thomas

The first daily network newscaster was Floyd Gibbons, a swashbuckling newspaper correspondent who lost an eye while covering the Battle of Belleau Wood in World War I. He was trying to reach a wounded Marine when machine-gun bullets struck him. The patch over his left eye and the rapidity with which he read the news were his trademarks.

Gibbons' network career began in a strange way. In 1929, he was writing a fictional story in which a reporter radioed his dispatches from an airplane. He didn't know how that could be done and visited NBC to find out. He became interested in how radio operated, and the network became interested in him, and pretty soon he was doing a half-hour program on NBC called "The Headline Hunter." The series began without a sponsor but quickly proved popular, and General Electric snatched it up. Then, within a year, as a 15-minute broadcast, it went to six nights a week. It had a new sponsor now, *The Literary Digest*, although GE still sponsored Gibbons' local show, "House of Magic," which aired Saturday nights on WEAF.

Over at CBS, this success was viewed with some envy. Paley meant his network to be first in news, and he took an action that gave radio a voice heard throughout America for half a century, the voice of Lowell Thomas, so-called "discoverer of Lawrence of Arabia," lecturer *par excellence*. Paley had heard that R. J. Cuddihy, publisher of *The Literary Digest*, was dissatisfied with Gibbons. One reason was that Cuddihy was a teetotaler, staid in his ways; Gibbons not only was a bit too flamboyant for him but also was known to do a good deal of drinking, Prohibition notwithstanding. Paley saw the opportunity. He would find a replacement for Gibbons at CBS. One of Paley's associates said he knew just the man—Lowell Thomas—and Paley persuaded Thomas to do an audition, talking about anything that came to mind. Thomas did not know his words were being piped to a prospective sponsor in another part of the building; Paley concealed that fact from him. But Thomas played a trick of his own. "There were three musicians in the studio," he recalled, "hanging around for a rehearsal, and I got them to give me a little background music in the oriental vein, 'A Persian Garden' and some other stuff, and I talked for the time prescribed about things I saw on this trip I'd just made to India and other spots in the Far East."

The magazine executives liked what they heard. But they wanted another test, a regular news report this time. They would listen to Thomas and then to Gibbons, whose contract still had a few weeks to run, and compare. To insure success, Paley said he would lend Thomas CBS' best brains. Thomas was slightly offended. He was an accomplished speaker— a professional lecturer, a newsman for 20 years—and he failed to see how Paley's "best brains" could help. But he said, "All right, if you're going to lend me your finest minds, why, I'll round up mine, and we'll make it an event."[7]

So these "brains" met to decide what the newscast should be like. They included Paul Kesten and Jesse Butcher, representing CBS, and three of Thomas' friends, Ogden Nash, who was then a manuscript reader at Doubleday; Prosper Buranelli, a feature writer for the *New York World*, and Dale Carnegie, who later would write *How to Win Friends and Influence People*, one of the biggest best-sellers in publishing history. To enliven discussion, Thomas brought three jugs of applejack, a not altogether successful stratagem since the "great minds" soon fell to wrangling over how a news program should begin.

"They were getting nowhere," Thomas recalled, "absolutely nowhere, so Prosper and I went out and bought late editions of all the afternoon papers, rewrote the news we liked, and did the broadcast."[8]

It worked. Thomas got the program, and Paley got Thomas, though he had to share him with NBC. NBC carried the program in the eastern half of the country while CBS carried it simultaneously in the West. Thus, on September 29, 1930, "Lowell Thomas and the News," one of the longest-running news program in broadcast history, was born. It was most unusual for two networks to use the same reporter, and next year NBC had the program exclusively. But in 1947, "the world's most famous newscaster," as Thomas was billed, returned to CBS and stayed for 29 years.

Two of a Kind

Paul White's counterpart—and adversary—at NBC was the formidable A. A. "Abe" Schechter, who, like White, had a newspaper background. After graduating from Boston University, where he majored in journalism, Schechter reported for the *Providence Journal*, then in quick succession for the *New York World,* the Associated Press, and the International News Service (INS), where he was city editor, the youngest in New York City. Six months later (in 1932) he was at NBC.

A big difference between Schechter and White was that while White ran CBS World News throughout the Second World War, Schechter left NBC in 1941 to join the Office of War Information (OWI). Soon afterward, he became special adviser to the War Department's Bureau of Public Relations. As a lieutenant colonel, he supervised radio communications for correspondents covering General MacArthur's campaign in the Southwest Pacific. For expediting coverage of the Philippine invasion, he received the Legion of Merit.

More than anyone else, these two "magnificos of aerial journalism," as Ben Gross called them,[9] were the founding fathers. They founded as they fought each other "with ingenuity, money, and tigerish ferocity."[10] And pretty soon in their battle for scoops they were joined by a third contender, Johnny Johnstone of Mutual.

Now It's Mutual

The Mutual Broadcasting System (MBS) did not come into being until 1934 when independent stations saw an advantage in sharing their programming, including news. Each station helped pay the cost of shared programs. Another "mutual" advantage was that, as a network with increased audience, advertisers could be charged more.

The founding stations were WOR, Newark; WLW, Cincinnati; WGN, Chicago; and WXYZ, Detroit. WXYZ soon left to become affiliated with NBC,[11] but Mutual gained 23 stations in 1936 when it was joined by two regional networks, Colonial of New England and Don Lee on the West Coast. Of special importance, because of news generated by the Federal Government, was affiliation the next year of WOL in Washington.

Mutual's scrappy news chief, G. W. "Johnny" Johnstone, was battling the NBC and CBS news departments with only a small fraction of their budget, and now and then, to the distress of Abe Schechter and Paul White, he was getting scoops. They discovered just how respectable a rival they had when, in reporting Howard Hughes' round-the-world flight in 1936, Johnstone's enterprise put them for a time—albeit a short time—in total eclipse. In his memoir, Schechter says: "As I study the record, I find that Mutual, which originally entered the picture as a sort of distant relation, and was spending practically no money, was doing very nicely, thank you." [12] He was referring to Mutual's coverage of Hughes' flight, but he could have been characterizing Johnstone's aggressive operation as a whole.

There is a nice twist to this. Later, when NBC's Blue Network became ABC, Johnstone would be in charge of ABC's news department. Schechter, back from Army service in World War II, would direct the news operation at Mutual. And while this was happening, White would be a newspaper executive in California.

4

"The World's Most Famous Baby Has Been Kidnapped"

News gained a further hold on the nation's listening habits in 1932 when the infant son of Charles and Anne Morrow Lindbergh was kidnapped from their New Jersey estate and found slain in a nearby woods. The kidnap-slaying of any child arouses strong emotion, and this was the fair first-born son of America's hero, the Lone Eagle.

Everyone climbed on the story, providing what *Broadcasting* called "perhaps the greatest example of spot news reporting in the history of American broadcasting."[1] At CBS, the news caught Jap Gude and Paul White in a late night poker game.[2] The network was "down," and Gude and White, after a quick call to Trenton to confirm the story, got radio engineers to patch a network together. *Broadcasting* reported:

> Just after midnight, CBS interrupted a dance program from Chicago for the news break, necessitating relaying the news over the monitor wire to its Chicago key, WBBM. There, Harlow Wilcox, announcer, picked up the bulletin and read it to the whole network at 12:14 a.m.[3]

By daybreak, CBS had established a special line into Hopewell, near the Lindbergh estate, and Herbert Glover gave one of the first reports. In his classic, *News on the Air*, White says:

> WOR in New York, first with the news at 11:35 P.M., as well as CBS, made a hash out of regular schedules, sent broadcasters and technicians to state police headquarters at Trenton, to New Brunswick, to Hopewell, and even to the edge of the Lindbergh estate. . . . But that night NBC didn't carry the news at all. The story was considered "too sensational."[4]

White's statement regarding NBC coverage is made questionable by the account in *Broadcasting* magazine on March 15, two weeks after the kidnapping.

> At NBC, the entire organization, news and programming was thrown into action on the story immediately after the first flash, carried shortly after midnight. An engineering staff was soon on its way to Princeton and Hopewell to lay wires and set up equipment. From the morning of March 2 until 2 A.M., March 8, a constant vigil was kept, a period of 148 hours, after which normal operating schedules were resumed.[5]

White must have believed what he wrote. How could he have gone wrong? I believe that White, writing to some extent from memory, confused NBC's coverage of the Lindbergh kidnapping with its coverage (or noncoverage) of the birth of the Dionne quintuplets in 1934. NBC's major newscaster, Lowell Thomas, did not report the extraordinary births at the time they occurred because his writer, Prosper Buranelli, withheld the news. "It just did not seem decent," Buranelli explained, "a woman having five babies all at once." He, too, used the phrase "too sensational."[6]

The next evening, in his first broadcast after the kidnapping, Thomas gave the story a big play. Reporting in his personal style, he began:

> I am sorry to say tonight that there is no favorable news about the Lindbergh baby. A frantic search is on. Airplanes have been out hunting. The police have been searching over a wide area.

Then, in a series of short, stark sentences, dramatic for their simplicity, Thomas reported the tragic circumstances: the isolated location of the house, the baby put to bed, then, two and a half hours later, discovered missing; the ladder reaching to the nursery window, the abductor's footprints in the soft ground. Thomas ended by saying, "The world's most famous baby has been kidnapped, and the attention of literally the whole world has been aroused."[7]

A few days later, one of those in airplanes seeking to solve the case was none other than Herbert Glover of CBS. Gude writes:

> [Glover] eventually disappeared from sight. What happened, we found out later, was that he had hired Russell Thaw, son of the notorious Harry [murderer of the famous architect Stanford White], and his privately owned Lockheed plane to go flying around various parts of the country looking for the kidnapper of the Lindbergh baby. That was Madman Glover for you. An incurable ro-

mantic, he finally showed up at 485[8] decked out in flying suit, helmet, and goggles, and looking very mysterious.[9]

In Glover's absence, Gude had charge of making the news assignments in New York; White, according to *Broadcasting*, was in complete charge of the job of getting the news flashes on the air. John Elwood, operations vice president, took charge at NBC. Among those sent immediately to New Jersey to cover for NBC were Ed Thorgersen, George Hicks, and William "Skeets" Miller, NBC's director of special events. Seven years earlier, Miller had won a Pulitzer for his coverage for the *Louisville Courier Journal* of the ordeal of Floyd Collins, trapped for many days in a Kentucky cave. He was now perhaps the most distinguished radio reporter on the scene.

At Hopewell, NBC used an improvised studio in a restaurant, while CBS operated out of a vacant room over a store. Both networks had small transmitters mounted on trucks. "At one juncture in the proceedings," says *Broadcasting*, "[CBS] carried a four-point broadcast, one from the sound truck and one from each of the remote control points."[10] This may have been the first such multiple pickup in broadcast history, forerunner of the ambitious multiple pickups made from overseas during the tense days preceding the Second World War.

One of those reporting for CBS, besides Glover, was Boake Carter, who later would gain national prominence—and not a little notoriety—as a commentator. At this time, working for the *Philadelphia Daily News*, he was doing two five-minute broadcasts a day on CBS' Philadelphia station, WCAU. Carter got his break because the owner of WCAU, Dr. Leon Levy, a dentist, who liked Carter's style, was Paley's brother-in-law.

Boake Carter was an interesting fellow, born in the city of Baku, on the Caspian Sea, where his father appears to have been in business. At the age of 15, he managed to serve briefly in the Royal Air Force. He claimed to have studied at Cambridge, but research shows no record of his enrollment there.[11] In 1921, Carter came to the United States and, after a short time in Oklahoma, settled in Philadelphia. In his WCAU broadcasts Carter had been strongly opinionated; one listener complained of his "outspoken and venomous remarks."[12] Now on network radio, reporting from Trenton, he mixed the hard news with diatribes against government corruption and organized crime, which, as it turned out, had nothing to do with the kidnapping.

In his scholarly work, *News for Everyman*, David Holbrook Culbert writes of Boake Carter:

> He, along with his competitor, Lowell Thomas, established the commercial possibilities of news commentary before anyone else. This pioneering quality should not be overlooked, no matter how much criticism Carter deserves for his unprincipled tirades against whatever the New Deal proposed to do at home and abroad.[13]

Boake Carter was not the only broadcaster who came to national attention because of the Lindbergh case. When in 1935, after three years of fitful rumor and frustration (at one time, 5,000 federal agents were searching), Bruno Richard Hauptmann finally was brought to trial, WOR's man in the courtroom was Gabriel Heatter. He did three broadcasts a day, fed to the newly created Mutual network, and by the time the trial ended he was famous. Heatter not only had the voice for radio and could write, but he adopted an approach to the story which won him wide appreciation. He says in his autobiography:

> I realized that radio had never before broadcast a murder trial and that this was the most sensational of all trials. I began to see Colonel Lindbergh's face on the keys of my typewriter. I seemed to feel him talking straight at me and saying, "Remember, this is a story of a dead baby. My baby." This was no time to sensationalize.[14]

He spoke with a sense of sympathy, and restraint, that stood in contrast with the insistent, dynamic voices of Boake Carter and Walter Winchell, who, besides writing his newspaper column, had started broadcasting for NBC's Blue Network.

The Trial

What may have been the most publicized murder trial in American history was held in a Greek revival courthouse built of native stone in the small town of Flemington, New Jersey. Reporters' activities centered on the courthouse and the four-story Union Hotel across the street. Radio facilities were installed on the hotel's third floor, with an extra bar downstairs to accommodate the rush. (The bar came to be known as Nellie's Tap Room because of a dog, Nellie, that wandered in, developed a taste for beer, and was adopted by the press as trial mascot.) The jury was quartered in six rooms on the fourth floor. Apparently, there was little soundproofing. According to one account, "the fine resonant voices" of broadcasters reporting, and commenting upon, the day's testimony penetrated to the jurors' rooms directly above.[15]

From the day the trial opened on January 2, 1935, until it ended six weeks later, the courtroom was crowded with reporters and photographers. And sightseers. The trial had become a spectacle. Even during recess on weekends the courthouse was thronged. From New York City and Philadelphia, from Newark and Trenton, people came to see the real life drama they had read about in the newspapers and heard about on the radio. Lindbergh, who attended the trial regularly, was the hero and Bruno Richard Hauptmann, the sullen-faced fugitive German felon who had slipped into the country illegally, the perfect villain. The crowds swelled as the trial progressed. State troopers guessed that on February 10, a Sunday, as many as 100,000 may have squeezed into Flemington during the day. Traffic jams were common and immense.

Spectators fortunate enough to make it into the courtroom sat pressed together on pew-like benches and borrowed chairs, while to the rear, in a gallery, 150 reporters were jammed, elbow to elbow, writing their stories at improvised desks of pine boards. Symbolic of the coverage was the spider-web of cable that technicians wove about the temple of justice itself, permitting telegraph operators, keys clicking like a chorus of crickets, to send out a million words a day. Heatter recalled:

> Since no microphones were allowed in the courtroom, I went across the street to a poolroom to meet my engineer. He was bundled up in an overcoat, muffler, and hat, which were pulled together and exposed only his ears. He sat huddled over a tiny oil stove. Day after day, three times a day, that is how WOR and I covered the Lindbergh kidnap trial in January 1935, the first radio reporting of a murder trial in American history.[16]

When all the testimony in the trial was in, and the jury was reaching its verdict, there sat waiting in the courtroom an AP reporter with a strangely bulging briefcase. The briefcase held a small shortwave transmitter. By means of a prearranged signal, the reporter would flash the verdict to an AP telegrapher in the courthouse attic, which is where, all through the trial, the telegraph operators were stationed.

The reporter waited nervously. The jury had retired at 11:21 A.M. Now it was night. From the crowd in the street came a howl, repeated again and again, "Kill Hauptmann!" It was estimated that 10,000 people were out there. One man threw a rock, smashing a courthouse window. The crowd was becoming a mob.

At 10:45 P.M. the jury announced its verdict: "We, the jury, find the defendant, Bruno Richard Hauptmann, guilty of murder in the first degree." There was no recommendation for mercy, and Hauptmann immediately was sentenced to die in the electric chair.

But because the AP telegrapher in the attic misunderstood a signal flashed by his colleague in the courtroom, the wire service lost its scoop. Still worse, the telegrapher had put out word that the jury had recommended mercy, which meant life imprisonment, not death. Now, receiving a second signal, he learned of the death sentence. But it was too late. All across the country newspaper extras were saying Hauptmann had got life. The networks and most radio stations, fed by AP, also had the story wrong. Stations buying the service of an upstart broadcast news organization called Transradio got the story right.

The Execution

Hauptmann went to the electric chair in Trenton, New Jersey, on the night of April 3, 1936.[17] Thirty reporters stood in the death chamber and watched, but the story memorable for broadcasters is the scriptless story ad libbed by Gabriel Heatter, who went on the air expecting to speak for five minutes and, because of a delay in the execution, had to "fill" for 55 minutes.

> I am in a hotel room looking at a certain window . . . as close as I wish to get to a room in which a man is about to die . . . merely waiting for a signal. . . . There will be no reprieve, of that I am certain. . . . [I] wonder what's going on in that room. It wouldn't be a confession . . . no, that silent fellow, lips pressed together, would not confess.[18]

In his autobiography, Heatter wrote:

> By 50 minutes after eight [the governor] evidently decided Hauptmann would never talk. The signal was given. The most sensational murder trial in history was over. There was nothing else to say after 55 minutes of talk and waiting except: "Ladies and gentlemen, Bruno Hauptmann is dead. Good night."[19]

It was a memorable performance because of Heatter's natural talent, because he knew what he was talking about—he had covered the entire trial and succession of appeals—and because of his character. He was sensitive; he could not bring himself to enter the death chamber. And he was right; there was no confession and no reprieve. He had demonstrated a resourcefulness which remains a landmark in on-the-scene, ad lib reporting to this day. The public, recognizing his achievement, sent him more than fifty thousand letters of praise.

Gabriel Heatter had become a big name in broadcasting literally overnight. Five years earlier, for his first broadcasts on WMCA, New York, he had been paid nothing because he had no sponsor. Now Mutual signed him for a Monday-through-Friday series of 15-minute broadcasts and he was on his way to making $400,000 a year.

There is a postscript which affects broadcasting to this day. Because the legal profession was affronted by the circus atmosphere at the trial, the American Bar Association in 1937 adopted Canon 35 of its ethical code. Canon 35 denied photographers access to courtrooms. It did not have the force of law, but it was generally observed. In 1963, Canon 35 was amended to include radio and television.

And so, with Hauptmann, the stage was set for prolonged debate on two fundamental principles: The right of the defendant to a fair trial (Sixth Amendment) and the sometimes conflicting rights of a free press (First Amendment). The struggle of broadcasters to achieve First Amendment parity with publishers, and gains made in that struggle, will be treated in a separate chapter.

"Get This, Charley! It's on Fire!"

If Hauptmann's was the first murder trial to get heavy radio coverage, the burning of the German dirigible *Hindenburg* was its counterpart among air disasters.

The date was May 6, 1937. The voice was that of Herbert Morrison, staff announcer for WLS, Chicago, who had the idea that, for his station's library of electrical transcriptions, an eyewitness account of the arrival of the *Hindenburg* at Lakehurst, New Jersey, even after 11 successful transatlantic crossings, would be a good thing to have. So, as an experiment, the station sent him and a radio engineer, Charles Nehlsen, to Lakehurst to make a disc recording of the event.

Morrison, standing beside a WLS sound truck, described the scene as slowly, majestically, the *Hindenburg,* filled with seven million cubic feet of highly inflammable hydrogen, came in for docking. The world's largest airship—Hitler's pride—had almost reached its mooring tower when it burst into flames.

"Get this, Charley! Get this, Charley!" Morrison shouted to Nehlsen inside the sound truck. "It's on fire!"

Nehlsen *was* getting it, so psychologists had text for an experience in shock and grief they have been studying ever since. Morrison is almost incoherent. His voice as he tries to describe what is happening is high-pitched.

> It's crashing! Oh, my! Get out of the way, please. And the folks—. Oh, it's terrible! This is one of the worst catastrophes in the world. . . . Oh, the humanity! All the passengers! All the people screaming around here. . . . I'm going to step inside where I can't see it. I tell you it's terrible. Folks, I must stop for a minute. I've lost my voice. It's the worst thing I've ever witnessed.

He was gone only a few moments. He spoke more calmly now.

> Ladies and gentlemen, I'm back again. . . . It's still smoking and flaming and crackling down there. And banging down there. I don't know how many of the ground crew were under it when it fell. There's not a possible chance for anyone to be saved.

Morrison kept on, reporting the futile effort of fire crews and the call for ambulances. He speculated on the possible cause—a spark perhaps that set off the hydrogen gas—and interviewed survivors, for he was mistaken in saying no one could be saved. Of passengers and crew, 36 died. Miraculously, 61 survived. He and Nehlsen stayed on the scene more than two hours, filling three discs and part of a fourth with 40 minutes of talk. A plane put them in Chicago early the next morning. WLS scrapped its normal schedule and played Morrison's eyewitness report again and again to a spellbound audience.

NBC was first to report the disaster with a bulletin flashed over the Red and Blue networks at 7:45 P.M., New York time, minutes after the airship caught fire.[20] But it did something more significant. With Morrison's story, NBC broke its long-standing rule, shared by CBS, against broadcasting recorded material. This was a start toward what is taken for granted today, the prerecorded program or report.

Herbert Morrison's broadcast is notable for another reason. Like Morrison, today's reporters "going live" are often confronted by the unexpected and must make spur-of-the-moment judgments. They edit themselves as they speak. It seemed to Morrison, seeing the huge airship collapse in flames, that no one could survive. The appearance—the awful sight—misled him, just as appearances mislead today.

In May 1967, 30 years after the *Hindenburg* disaster, an ABC correspondent, Bill Brannigan, narrated a special radio program marking the anniversary. Inevitably, the highlight of the broadcast was Morrison's emotional report. Brannigan has told me:

> I remember telling someone in the control room that I didn't see how anyone doing a story could get quite that excited. I soon found out. I was in Vietnam that summer, in Danang, when the base had its first real heavy rocket attack. I ducked under the wing of a plane with a tape recorder—a Phillips, I think. Bits of metal were flying all around. I taped my report right there, and later I got a letter from a listener saying I sounded as excited as Morrison.[21]

Morrison stayed with reporting. After serving in the Army Air Corps in World War II, he became the first news director at WTAE-TV in Pittsburgh. He died in 1989 in a nursing home in Morgantown, West Virginia. He was 83. The burning of the *Hindenburg* was his big story. Fifty years would pass before another air disaster, the explosion of the space shuttle *Challenger,* would so grip the American people and other millions abroad.

5

The Press–Radio War

The appetite for radio news was growing. It had not become what it would be with the crises leading to the Second World War, but radio coverage of events like the Hauptmann trial not only fascinated an increasingly large body of listeners but attracted advertisers who, abandoning newspapers, bought time on the air.

And that, more than anything else, led to the Press–Radio War.

In *News on the Air,* Paul White starts his account of that bitter feud with an understatement. "It hasn't always been possible," he says, "to get newspaper publishers and radio station operators to agree that the two media are supplementary."[1] Which is like saying that the Hatfields of the Kentucky hill country did not always get along well with the McCoys.

The "war" lasted more than ten years. The first skirmish occurred in 1922. On February 20, the Associated Press asked its 1,200 member papers to stop letting radio stations use their stories. The AP was then, and still is, a cooperative association of newspapers. Much of the news distributed by AP comes from these papers. According to association bylaws, these stories are AP property; hence, it reasoned, radio had no right to them. "Apparently," says Mitchell Charnley, "the impulse behind this request [back in 1922] was not a desire to hamper the development of a competing agency, but rather an attempt to protect what was, in effect, commercially valuable merchandise."[2]

The embargo had little effect. Radio stations and networks got their stories from the United Press and Hearst's International News Service.

In 1924, AP retreated slightly when it allowed broadcast of its baseball scores. But it fined the *Portland Oregonian* for broadcasting AP election returns on its radio station. The fine—$100—was meaningless, not only because the *Oregonian* could well afford it, but because with the laissez-faire attitude of UP and INS, it was impossible to stop the flow of news over the air. So again AP retreated. It would allow the broadcast of news bulletins based on its service, but the bulletins could not exceed 35 words. And they had to be "of transcendent importance."[3]

By 1925, the self-interest of newspapers, as well as that of the AP, was involved. With the introduction of commercials, radio was now competing with newspapers for the advertiser's dollar.[4] Reacting to this new competition, the American Newspaper Publishers Association decreed at its 1925 convention that, henceforth, member papers no longer would give free publicity to sponsored programs, to the likes of "The Happiness Boys" and Paul Whiteman, "The King of Jazz." At the same time, it gave broadcasters an unsolicited piece of advice: If you keep on interrupting your programs with sales messages, you may destroy yourselves. People will turn you off.

The advice was ignored, and people stayed tuned. Between 1925 and 1929, the sale of radio sets doubled.[5]

Individual newspapers—those not owning stations—also fought back. Some refused to publish program schedules except at regular advertising rates. Others cut back on radio-related stories, regardless of reader interest. Newspaper groups passed resolutions denouncing the upstart medium, accusing it, among other things, of "destroying the surprise value of news."[6] Radio had become, as Abe Schechter said, "the prize exhibit in American journalism's doghouse."[7]

Election Night, 1932

Full-scale war did not break out until after the 1932 presidential election. Radio so outdistanced newspapers in reporting election returns that the major wire services, under pressure from publishers, cut off all service to the networks.

It happened this way. CBS decided to scrap its entire evening schedule and report the Hoover–Roosevelt race, nonstop, from start to finish—the first time on network radio that this had been done. The marathon broadcast would be based primarily on returns filed by the United Press. Under terms of a contract, CBS would pay a thousand dollars for the service.

But just before the election, a telephone call came from Karl Bickel, president of UP, saying the deal was off. The flak from newspaper interests was too great. Paul White rushed to Bickel's office to protest what he regarded as an indefensible abrogation of contract.

I threatened to sue. Bickel suggested that I do so and asked me how I would prove any damages. Finally, realizing that a raised voice and a flushed face weren't going to accomplish anything constructive, I pleaded for mercy.

No mercy was shown. Bickel said that with newspapers in the mood they were in, UP stood to lose too much if it fed CBS the returns. White says, "I retired defeated, both bloody and bowed."[8]

In the end, because of a confused, almost comical series of events, White was not defeated. Kent Cooper, general manager of AP, did not know that UP's contract with CBS had been cancelled. So to outdo UP, he told CBS and NBC they could have AP's service for nothing. When UP heard this, it reconsidered. It did not want to provoke the newspapers it served, nor did it want AP to have the broadcast field to itself, so it sneaked its returns to CBS. Because of the original agreement, UP had installed teletypes in the CBS newsroom, and early on election night these machines "mysteriously" began feeding returns.[9] INS, not to be left out, also supplied its service.

It marked the first election in which Robert Trout—today the dean of network newscasters—reported returns in a presidential contest, and it was soon apparent that Franklin Delano Roosevelt had swept the country as he had swept New York State for the governorship two years before.

> This is Robert Trout at our election headquarters in our newsroom in New York. The results of the 1932 election now appear certain. The ticket of Roosevelt and [John Nance] Garner has won a clear-cut majority over the ticket of Hoover and [Charles] Curtis. And so the United States has a new president.[10]

Never in history had there been such swift and complete election coverage. It was a triumph, not just for CBS and NBC, but for radio, which in a single night had demonstrated that the newspaper extra was passé.

A Declaration of War

It was the equivalent of Fort Sumter. At the annual meeting of the AP on April 24, 1933, the publishers, up in arms, passed a resolution directing "that the Board of Directors shall not allow any news distributed by the Associated Press, regardless of source, to be given to any radio chain or chains." Two days later, the American Newspaper Publishers Association, at its annual meeting, recommended that radio program listings be published only when paid for. After some hesitation, UP and INS followed AP's lead. As far as news was concerned, NBC and CBS were on their own.

The most ambitious reaction to the news embargo was Paul White's. By late September he had organized the Columbia News Service, the first network news-gathering organization, with bureaus in New York, Washington, Chicago, and Los Angeles, and stringers, who worked on newspapers, in most of the country's large cities. Coverage by the Columbia News Service was surprisingly comprehensive. In *Dateline: Washington,* Ted Koop relates that on its first day the service strove for an exclusive story to show what it could do. What it got was an interview with Senator William E. Borah, the influential foreign affairs leader, on the issue of U.S. recognition of the Soviet Union. CBS' jubilation, Koop says, was multiplied when the *New York Times* put Borah's statement on page one and credited CBS. "No longer," he says, "was radio news a stepchild." [11]

At NBC, Abe Schechter, busy on the telephone, was the network's own one-man news service. His chief concern was the Lowell Thomas program, which aired five nights a week. Winchell's program was heard only on Sunday and consisted mostly of gossip, though occasionally the dynamic ex-vaudevillian and newspaper columnist came up with an important story obtained through his own sources.

Thomas enjoyed telling how it was when the wire services imposed their embargo.

> They thought it would be the end of me. Instead, they merely put new life into what we were doing. Abe set up telephones in the hall, and after we'd read the New York papers and seen the stories we wanted, he would call the senator in Washington to get it direct. Or he'd call the sheriff in California if there was a crime story out there, and he'd get the personal story right from the sheriff. It personalized the whole broadcast and made it stronger than ever before. [12]

In his memoir, Schechter says that by saying he was calling for Lowell Thomas he could get practically anyone to talk.

Local stations gathered news in much the same way. Stations with ties to newspapers had a relatively easy time. WGN, Chicago, for example, could use the *Chicago Tribune* news service. Actually, for most stations at that time news was not an important part of their programming, and the ban on wire service copy, though strongly resented, was not hard to take.

Inevitably, as 1933 progressed, the news embargo turned sour. Neither network was hurting, but each still wanted news from the big press associations. UP and INS, on the other hand, missed the revenue from radio subscribers. AP papers owning radio stations were unhappy. The war—in particular, the suppression of news—was unpopular, and peace feelers were exchanged, culminating in a peace conference at the Hotel Biltmore in New York.

These, briefly, were the peace terms, effective March 1, 1934:

CBS would give up its news service, and a Press–Radio Bureau financed largely by the networks would be established. The bureau would receive news from the press associations free of charge. Editors in the bureau would rewrite the news in summary form for broadcast, but there would be severe restrictions on how these summaries could be used. The bureau could send out only two five-minute summaries a day. The morning summary could not be broadcast before 9:30 A.M., the evening summary not before 9:00 P.M. in order to "protect" the morning and evening papers. No story could exceed 30 words. Each summary had to end with the line: "For further details, consult your local newspaper." If there was news "of transcendental importance," the bureau could issue bulletins for immediate release, but they were "to be used in such manner as to stimulate public interest in the reading of newspapers." None of this news could be sold to advertisers. Sponsorship of commentary, however, would be allowed.

The bureau operated out of a small suite of offices on the 18th floor of the French Building at Fifth Avenue and Forty-fifth Street. Its boss was James Barrett, former city editor of the *New York World.* The staff consisted of three or four writers, a secretary, and a couple of part-time teletype operators. The writers' task was to take the wire service copy and make it more readily understandable for radio listeners who, depending on their ears, would have no opportunity to reread. One of the writers was Henry Wefing, a former desk man at the *New York American,* who later became an executive at CBS News. Wefing says:

> I think Barrett was one of the first to realize that news for the air has to be written differently. We were all ex-newspapermen, and he quickly taught us how to adapt our style to the new medium. He edited every story we wrote, eliminating the old newspaper clichés and making our copy listenable. He was one of the real pioneers in broadcast news style.[13]

The networks and the few independent stations subscribing to the bureau's service all received the same teletyped copy. They also received bulletins simultaneously, so there was little incentive for one station to beat another.

Enter Competition

The "treaty" setting up the bureau, White said, was about as satisfactory as Versailles.[14] And, like Versailles, it didn't work.

It failed, not because of lack of competence on the part of James Barrett and his staff. It failed because it was wrong—a violation of press freedom—and because it was unworkable. There was no way in a free society that the dissemination of news in peacetime, by so important a medium, could be controlled. It flouted the very provision under which stations were licensed, that they should serve "the public interest, convenience, and necessity." It was irresponsible, and it was impossible.

In the end, competition did it in. Services that could rival, and frustrate, Press–Radio seemed to spring up everywhere. In Boston, Richard Grant, former political writer for the *Boston Transcript,* set up a service at WNAC for the eight stations of the Yankee Network. On the West Coast, the radio news service founded by KMPC in Beverly Hills was expanded, and KFI in Los Angeles established a news service. So did WLS in Chicago. Other new organizations supplying news to radio stations included the

American Radio News Service, the Continental Radio News Service, and the American Newscasting Association, all based in Washington.

But Press–Radio's biggest competitor was Transradio Press, founded by Herbert Moore, a former United Press reporter who had worked for the Columbia News Service as a writer. Moore staffed bureaus in ten cities, including New York, Washington, Chicago, and Los Angeles, and claimed to have engaged more than 500 stringers. In 1934, much of Transradio's foreign news came from the French news agency Havas, but this coverage was improved the next year by agreement with Reuters. By 1935, Moore was providing between 5,000 and 50,000 words a day to 150 stations. Even newspapers began subscribing to his service, which did not shut down until 1951.

The more Transradio succeeded, the more Press–Radio relaxed its rules in order to compete. No longer did radio have to wait until after most people had read their morning and evening papers before airing the news summaries. And stories were allowed to run longer. The bureau released a veritable torrent of words on the Hauptmann trial.

Still, in March 1935, there were more than 350 stations that did not subscribe to the Press–Radio service. UP and INS saw the potential market and in April served notice that they would exercise their right to sell news to radio "if competition so required." Not surprisingly, they found that competition did so require. They went in the business, competing with Transradio. Practically speaking, the press–radio treaty, not much more than a year old, was dead.

Another big step was taken in 1936 when UP inaugurated its radio wire, which transmitted news summaries written specifically for broadcast. These summaries moved throughout the day. They could be aired any-time. And, like the news distributed by Transradio—and this was impor-tant—they could be sponsored. AP began allowing newspaper-owned sta-tions to use its news in 1939 but did not begin moving news on a special radio wire until two years later.

The Press–Radio Bureau went out of business early in 1939 when the networks withdrew their support. They didn't need it anymore. "Now," said Paul White, "we are beginning to go places."[15]

6
"The First Fine Careless Rapture"

During the years that broadcasters and publishers were battling, radio reporters and engineers were having a lively time discovering further what radio, as a reporting tool, could do. NBC introduced "studios on wheels" when it sent a mobile unit on a tour of the Bronx Zoo. The naturalist William Beebe did a broadcast from a bathysphere 2,200 feet under the surface of the ocean, and radio listeners heard Auguste Piccard speak from a balloon ten miles above the earth. Senator Clarence Dill of Washington State made a broadcast from a speeding train. Channing Pollock, the playwright, sent him a telegram that read, "Congratulations on your moving address."

Lowell Thomas claimed the first "'news broadcast" from an airplane. He said, "It was one I did from a Curtiss-Condor in 1930. Shortwave, of course. Even so, we had to circle the antenna at the top of the Empire State Building, or the experiment would not have been a success." Soon afterward, he did a radio piece from inside a coal mine in Bluefield, West Virginia.

If ever there was a peripatetic reporter, it was Thomas. Under special arrangement with NBC, and later with CBS, he could originate his nightly radio program anywhere he pleased, from Alaska to the Antarctic. He did innumerable first broadcasts from ski areas, "one even from the ladies' room in the Canadian Pacific railway station at Mont Tremblant in the Laurentians."[1]

Local stations emulated the networks, assembling mobile units and striving for on-the-scene reports. Reporters at KDKA, Pittsburgh, chased fires in a touring car with equipment weighing half a ton. The *Detroit News* station, WWJ, had what it called a radio and photographic car used by still photographers as well as radio personnel.

Perry Morison Reports

In the 1930s, local newscasts often originated in newspaper offices. For stations owned by newspapers it was a natural development, but the arrangement also existed between newspapers and independently owned stations. Then it was a good symbiotic relationship, an even swap. The newspaper got on-air publicity; the station got news. It cost nobody anything.

Typical was the arrangement in the late thirties between WHKC in Columbus, Ohio, and the *Columbus Citizen*, a member of the Scripps-Howard chain.[2] From its own stories and stories moved on the United Press wire, the newspaper's labor reporter, Perry Morison, prepared a 15-minute broadcast aired at 7:30 A.M. The program originated in the city room of the newspaper; there was no studio. Morison sat at a wooden desk on which were a microphone and a small electric light. When the light went on, he started reading. On the far wall was a Western Union clock. When the minute hand reached 7:45—there was no second hand—Morison signed off. Simplicity itself.

The News Directors

At this time, in the late thirties, the term *news editor* for a supervisor of news broadcasts was more common than *news director*. Before that, neither term had existed in radio because the program director, station manager, or owner decided what news to carry. In some instances, the chief announcer who read the news made the selection. By the 1940s, however, most large stations had either a news editor or news director.

In 1946, when the news editors and news directors decided to form a national organization, there was debate over what to call it. The founding president, John Hogan, proposed that it be called the National Association of Radio News Editors. But when the organizing was over, and officers elected, the name finally adopted was National Association of Radio News Directors. Retired Professor Jack Shelley of Iowa State, a charter member, says the word *directors* was substituted for *editors* in order to emphasize that a clearly identifiable professional person would in fact direct the news operation and would report, not to the program director, who had little or no competence in journalism, but to management.[3]

Today, it is the Radio-Television News Directors Association. The goals of RTNDA, stated in its constitution, are "the achievement of high professional standards of electronic journalism and the fostering of principles of journalistic freedom to gather and disseminate information to the public."[4] RTNDA also has a Code of Ethics, which says in its preamble: "The responsibility of radio and television journalists is to gather and report information of importance and interest to the public accurately, honestly, and impartially."[5]

From 68 charter members in 1946, the association grew to 3,600 members by 1990. Behind the growth was dedicated leadership. In 1952, Rob Downey of Michigan State University's radio station, WKAR, agreed to serve as executive secretary on a temporary, volunteer basis. He served 27 years. While RTNDA's headquarters remained in East Lansing, Theodore F. Koop, formerly of CBS and supposedly retired, ran a small "branch office" in Washington, where he acted energetically on questions before the Federal Communications Commission and Congress.

In 1976, the headquarters moved to Washington. Len Allen, a former NBC executive, took charge, concentrating on First Amendment issues. Five years later, when Allen died of a heart attack, the board of directors chose Ernie Schultz, who had long been active in the organization, to succeed him.

RTNDA was now the country's largest, most influential organization devoted to the concerns of broadcast journalists. Aided by its counsel, J. Laurent Scharff, it had filed *amicus curiae* briefs in almost every major First Amendment case of that period. It had fought on the front lines—before the FCC, in Congress, and in the courts—for repeal of the Fairness Doctrine and the opening of the nation's courtrooms to microphones and cameras. It established scholarships for college students and offered awards to promote excellence in news programming.

The association had become so active it no longer was possible for its elected presidents to hold office for a year and at the same time serve their stations as news directors. In 1986, the presidency of RTNDA was made a full-time salaried position, and again Schultz was the board of directors' unanimous choice. Schultz held the newly created office until July 1989, when he was succeeded by David Bartlett, an NBC vice president with wide experience in both radio and television news. Other RTNDA officers are elected. Board members, representing 14 regions, serve two-year terms. The chairman and treasurer are elected annually.

Today, news directors face new challenges. Instead of dealing as much with news at first hand, they are preoccupied with hiring and firing, purchasing equipment, and drawing up—and defending—budgets. In the words of Paul David, a former president of the Society of Professional Journalists and part-time president of RTNDA, "A news director must be a journalist, a business manager, a personnel administrator, electronic wizard, jailhouse lawyer, and talent scout."[6] Because of this expanded role, stations have hired assistant news directors to lighten the load. In 1980, in cooperation with the National Association of Broadcasters and the Wharton School of Business, RTNDA offered its members a series of management training courses.

According to a survey conducted by Dr. Vernon A. Stone of the University of Missouri, the typical news director in 1987 had been in the job only two years. While news directors may be fired for various reasons, including poor ratings, the survey found that most leave the stations for better positions.[7] Walter Cronkite has decried what he terms "the startling turnover" of news directors, reasoning that a person who chooses to make a career in a given community is likely "to give a great deal more in enthusiasm and dedication and interest" than someone passing through.[8] Some news directors are indeed long-tenured. As this is written, Steve Murphy has been news director at WOWT, Omaha, for 20 years. Claude Dorsey was news director at KMBC-TV, Kansas City, for 24 years, and Jack Hogan headed the news operation at WZZM-TV, Grand Rapids, for 25 years. The record may have been set by Ralph Renick, who had charge of news at WTVJ, Miami, for 35 years, which translates to more than a third of a century.

The Good Old Days

Radio news in the early days was simpler. Staffs, even at the networks, were small; everyone knew everyone else. There was an intimacy, a family atmosphere impossible in large news organizations today. This is not to say that the excitement has evaporated, or that enthusiasm is lacking. But as Eric Sevareid has noted, "What Paul White called the first fine, careless rapture of the early radio days is gone."[9] It was all so new then, for the people in news so much less a business.

And, in the real sense, there was less news. In 1930, there existed on the networks only one 15-minute newscast, that of Lowell Thomas, which was heard throughout the week. For the most part, news was special events —athletic contests, ship christenings, and talks. Some of these broadcasts were simply stunts. In 1936, there was a radio conversation between announcers on two trains, one traveling between Boston and Providence, the other between Hamburg and Berlin. No winner was declared.

There were dream assignments, right out of the newsreels, like being told to sail with the *Queen Mary* and the *Normandie* on their maiden voyages. Such noncataclysmic events were covered with remarkable thoroughness. When the *Queen Mary* sailed for the United States in 1936, each network—CBS, NBC, and Mutual—had a man on board, and each day, as the palatial liner steamed westward, they broadcast over the ship's transmitter, interviewing passengers and describing the luxurious accommodations.

In his autobiography, Gabriel Heatter recalls that, while working for Mutual, he covered New York's reception for the *Normandie* from the roof of a skyscraper, despite his paralyzing fear of heights. For the best view he had to climb out on a ledge, and for him, he said, doing that was "like fighting a lion with my bare hands." But he did it. "I talked about the river and the great ship and how . . . Robert Fulton first came sailing along that same river, and the 15 minutes, oddly enough, went by in a hurry."[10]

In 1937, George Hicks, who was aboard the *Normandie* for NBC, was sent half way around the world to Canton Island in the South Pacific to cover the longest eclipse of the sun in more than a thousand years. The next year, NBC managed to do a series of broadcasts from Pitcairn Island of *Mutiny on the Bounty* fame. In June 1939, two network newsmen, Hicks of NBC and Robert Trout of CBS, made broadcasts from Pan American's *Atlantic Clipper* on its maiden flight from New York to Lisbon. Trout was arrested and held briefly by Portuguese authorities for failing to obtain a visa—there had been too little time before takeoff for that formality.

Scuttling of the *Graf Spee*

One of NBC's famous exclusives came early in World War II: the live eyewitness account of the self-immolation of the German pocket battleship *Graf Spee*. The swift, heavily armed ship had been a deadly prowler in Allied sea lanes. It was a ship Hitler liked to boast of. But finally British cruisers caught up with her off the coast of South America and inflicted heavy damage. She limped into Montevideo Harbor, at the mouth of the Rio de la Plata. Crewmen were starting to patch the shell holes in her sides when, on December 15, 1939, the government of Uruguay, uneasy over the warship's presence in its waters, gave her 72 hours to leave. Outside the harbor, the posse of British cruisers waited.

On December 17, rather than see the *Graf Spee* captured, the captain, Hans Langsdorff, decided to scuttle her. After evacuating the crew, he stood off from the ship in a motor launch and pressed a button. As a series of explosions wracked the ship, an NBC stringer, James Bowen, went on the air with the war's first major exclusive. Through binoculars he saw a livid explosion topple the aft turret, and millions tuned to NBC heard him say:

> Evidently the powder magazine caught fire. She is going down. She is going down by the stern. The stern is now completely under water. Flames are shooting into the air, and there are great clouds of smoke. . . . Now she seems to be settling. . . . She is down in the shallow water to its full depth.[11]

Years later, Paul White wrote that he could not look back on that day "without feeling anew a sense of unutterable anguish."[12] Schechter, on the other hand, found the broadcast and the reaction to it exhilarating—"It is a matter of record that we scooped the world."[13] It was true. Newspapers in London and Paris, and throughout America, rushed into print with Bowen's account.

From Berlin, Hitler radioed orders for the *Graf Spee* captain to kill himself and, with a bullet in the head, Langsdorff obliged.

". . . Is Fear Itself"

The inauguration of Franklin Delano Roosevelt as thirty-second president of the United States marked a watershed in American history. For decades to come, until Ronald Reagan tried to turn it around, the federal government would assume social responsibilities borne until that time by private welfare and the states.

In 1932, the economy—society itself—was crumbling. The five million unemployed of 1930 had more than doubled to twelve million. To an extent difficult to imagine today, people were frightened. In desperation they turned to Roosevelt, and when on March 4, 1933, he moved haltingly on his braced legs to take the oath of office, radio was there.

The announcers—they still were not called correspondents—stopped talking, and from loudspeakers across the country came the strong voice of a president exuding confidence: "This great nation will endure as it has endured, will revive and will prosper. So, first of all, let me assert my firm belief that the only thing we have to fear is fear itself—nameless, unreasoning, unjustified terror which paralyzes needed efforts to convert retreat into advance."

Thanks to radio, the people heard. Thanks to the old-fashioned newsreels, it is a scene with which every generation of Americans since then is familiar.

The Fireside Chat

Eight days later, on a Sunday evening, Roosevelt used the medium a new way. To stop a rush on the nation's banks, he had closed them. A banking holiday, it was called. Now, when it appeared safe to reopen the banks, the new president believed he should speak again to the American people, more personally this time. He wanted to assure them in plain language, as a trusted friend, that their savings were safe.

A White House aide, Charles Michelson, wrote the draft of a speech, which was reviewed by Treasury experts. Then Roosevelt went over the speech, giving it his own imprint. In his history, *The Coming of the New Deal*, Arthur Schlesinger, Jr., says Roosevelt dictated a good bit of what he wanted to say.

> With Grace Tully taking his words down, the President looked at the blank wall, trying to visualize the individuals he was seeking to help: a mason at work on a new building, a girl behind a counter, a man repairing an automobile, a farmer in his field, all of them saying, "Our money is in the Poughkeepsie bank, and what is this all about?"[14]

It was the answer to this question that Roosevelt sought to give his listeners in simple terms. That, and confidence that, working together, the future was secure: "Let us unite in banishing fear. . . . It is your problem no less than it is mine. Together we cannot fail." Robert Sherwood said, "Those of us who heard that speech will never forget the surge of confidence that his bouyant spirit evoked."[15] Will Rogers said the president had taken a complicated subject, banking, and made everybody understand it, even the bankers.[16]

On that day, March 12, the two "presidential announcers," as they were called, were Carleton Smith of NBC and Robert Trout of CBS. Trout recalls the historic broadcast:

> Ted Church [T. Wells Church of CBS] and I walked to the White House and went in the big front door. It was, I think, something of a false step. At later broadcasts we always entered through the doorway of the executive offices in the West Wing. But we were made welcome and shown downstairs.

For this first broadcast, Roosevelt used the Lincoln study. On his way down, Trout noticed large trunks and packing boxes with the boldly lettered address, THE WHITE HOUSE, WASHINGTON, D.C., standing in the upstairs passage, still to be unpacked. In the study, radio engineers had set up their equipment. The president was seated on a sofa talking to his close adviser, Louis McHenry Howe.

> When we told the president that it was time for him to take his seat at the table where the microphones were, for the first time I saw him go through the routine of clicking the braces, his legs held straight out, then maneuvering to his feet and walking stiff-kneed and so slowly. We broadcasters became so accustomed to that slow walk at public affairs that we came to feel that that was the way a president *should* walk, with measured dignity.
>
> That night, for the first time, our microphone said "CBS." At last, we had abandoned the Columbia signs. They didn't show up well in the pictures. Instantly, on sitting down, President Roosevelt wanted to know what CBS was. He was used to Columbia. I was impressed by this interest in broadcast matters. Then he lit a cigarette and called for his script.
>
> It could not be found. A search began throughout the living quarters as the clock ticked on. Everyone was anxious, agitated, except FDR. If he was, he didn't show it. At the last moment someone produced a mimeographed press copy of the speech. The staples were pulled out, and we went on the air. That is the copy the president used. After we had left, they found the script—in bed, where the president had been reading it.
>
> FDR read the talk while holding a burning cigarette in one hand. No holder. As it burned nearer and nearer to his fingers, we all began to show signs of nervousness. No need. Just before it

burned him, Mr. Roosevelt, without pausing, simply stabbed the cigarette out in an ash tray. Simple stuff now, from a simpler time. But we weren't used to performers like that, especially not a performer who also happened to be the President of the United States.

In press releases, CBS attributed the origin of the phrase "fireside chat" to Trout. But the credit, Trout says, belongs to Harry Butcher, CBS' first manager in Washington, and it happened like this:

> We proposed two introductory scripts. One was formal, stating the facts coldly. The other was more folksy. It said that what President Roosevelt wanted to do was to come into people's houses by radio as if he were really able to visit them in person (these were not the actual words but the spirit of it), sit down with them and have a fireside chat. That two-word phrase, fireside chat, was put into the copy by Harry Butcher, ex-Iowa farm boy. It was absolutely typical of his way of thinking and talking. . . .
>
> Harry Butcher sent both introductions to the White House. As I recall, it was on the Friday before the [Sunday] broadcast that Marvin McIntyre [who with Steve Early handled press relations] telephoned WJSV [17] to tell Harry (I didn't call him that then!) that the folksy intro was the one the president liked. So, of course, it was the one I used. [18]

It was natural because of its origin for NBC to regard "fireside chat" as a CBS term. More than a year passed before it swallowed its pride and used the phrase on the air.

During his presidency, Roosevelt held almost a thousand press conferences. None was carried by radio. Rarely was direct quotation permitted; reporters had to paraphrase what the president said. But Roosevelt discarded Hoover's policy of requiring them to submit their questions in advance. He enjoyed the give-and-take. Not until 1982 did it become widely known that Roosevelt recorded 14 of these press conferences, along with several private conversations. [19]

For "selling" his New Deal policies, Roosevelt made effective use of the presidential press conference, but his innovation was the fireside chat which enabled him to speak directly to the American people over the heads of reporters and their editors, a stratagem adopted by every future president.

Wisely, Roosevelt rationed his "chats." He knew that if he gave them often they would lose their effectiveness. There were 30 in all, an average of one every five months.

A Skirmish Won

All this while, radio was barred from the Senate and House press galleries, as well as from all of Roosevelt's early press conferences. The galleries, functioning as newsrooms, provided newspaper reporters with wire service facilities, telephones, and typewriters. But except for the visitors' galleries, broadcasters had no workplace in the Capitol.

Newspapermen argued that letting radio into the press galleries would overcrowd them. Broadcasters, led by Fulton Lewis, Jr., fought back, charging violation of their rights, and separate galleries for radio were established in 1939. When the Congressional Radio Correspondents Association was formed, Lewis, in recognition of his leadership, was made president.

In the battle for equality in covering Congress, radio had won an important first skirmish. But the battle would be long.

7
The Oracles

Now come the commentators, radio's first oracles. Commentary is wide-ranging. A case might be made that the comedian Mark Russell is a commentator on television, that in his monologues he comments as a cartoonist comments—in caricature—working not with ink but in a whacky, exaggerated way with words. Before him on radio, operating in similar fashion, was another comedian, Mort Sahl. Their comments were trenchant, slashing into personalities and issues, making the human condition laughable.

Lowell Thomas was not a commentator although, embroidering the news, he made personal asides. He was fundamentally a radio reporter with a flair. In his 15-minute broadcast, Thomas might include a dozen stories; the authentic commentator often restricted himself to one subject, though it was more usual with programs of that length to discuss three or four.

Edwin C. Hill was no more a commentator, in the strict sense, than Thomas. Two years after Thomas entered radio, Hill, an ex-*New York Sun* reporter, signed a contract with CBS to broadcast "The Human Side of the News." The program content fit the name. Hill told stories about people—humorous, heartwarming, tragic—reminiscent of the "people" programming on television today. He had Thomas' gift for story-telling. He knew how to employ language with dollops of humor and pathos to evoke feeling. His voice was rich, comfortable, and warm.

Edwin C. Hill was an important broadcaster and attracted a large audience. But he was no oracle.

Eleanor Roosevelt was more of a commentator than either Hill or Thomas, championing causes ranging from school lunches to human rights. In December 1932, one month after her husband's election to the presidency, she began a 12-week series of talks on NBC's Red Network, sponsored by Pond's skin lotion. Her fees went to charity.

Will Rogers made his dry-wry observations not just in newspapers but over the air on NBC. Rogers supported the New Deal. Soon after Franklin Roosevelt began his first term, Rogers said in a broadcast, "That bird has done more for us in seven weeks than we've done for ourselves in seven years. He's the Houdini of Hyde Park." He called the bonus marchers in Washington "the best behaved of any 15,000 hungry men ever assembled anywhere in the world."[1] Will Rogers, who said he never met a man he didn't like, was on the side of the poor.

Boake Carter has already been introduced.

The earliest commentators were a fascinating lot. Here there is space for only brief "bios."

H. V. Kaltenborn

Most of these voices were first heard in the early 1930s. H. V. Kaltenborn was one of the exceptions. In 1923, while associate editor of the *Brooklyn Eagle,* he began doing weekly commentaries on WEAF. A year earlier, in a "one time only" broadcast, he had analyzed developments in a coal miners' strike and social experiments taking place in Britain over the Army Signal Corps station on Bedloe's Island in New York Harbor. This appears to have been the first commentary ever heard by a radio audience. Kaltenborn later referred to it as radio's first "spoken editorial."[2] The historic date was April 4, 1922.

Listeners marveled that they could hear him so clearly. The truth is that Kaltenborn spoke in such an authoritative way, in precise King's English, that his comments had rather the sound of pronouncements. Apparently there was nobility both in language and in blood, for the commentator was born Hans von Kaltenborn, son of Rudolph von Kaltenborn of Hesse. The father, who claimed he was a baron, had migrated to the United States and settled in Milwaukee, which is where the mother died on giving birth to Hans in 1878.

Kaltenborn's first news job was at the *Merrill* (Wisconsin) *Advocate.* He was a teenage reporter, having dropped out of high school, and the pay was five dollars a week. With the outbreak of war with Spain, he enlisted in the Fourth Wisconsin Volunteers, but never got closer to Cuba than the army camp at Anniston, Alabama.

After the war, Kaltenborn went back to the *Advocate* as city editor, but he was restless. After a few months he was off for Europe, working his way as nursemaid to 500 young steers on a cattleboat. For the next two years he toured England, Germany, and France, much of the time by bicycle. He attended the Paris Exposition, but the highlight of the trip was a visit with relatives in Berlin.

In 1902, he became a reporter for the *Brooklyn Eagle*. Working in a competitive environment and interviewing important people, Kaltenborn realized how handicapped he was with a schooling that had ended in high school. He entered Harvard as a special student, transferred later to regular student status, and graduated with honors in political science. One of his classmates was Maxwell Perkins, Scribner's famous editor. Another student was Walter Lippmann.

In 1907, Kaltenborn went to Europe as secretary to a Harvard professor, and on shipboard, coming back, he met a young baroness, Olga von Nordenflycht. Two years later, they married. Kaltenborn was back at the *Eagle*, and in 1914, with the onset of the First World War, he became the paper's "war editor" in charge of copy dealing with the hostilities. It was now, with sentiment against Germany running high, that the Teutonic-sounding byline Hans von Kaltenborn became H. V. Kaltenborn. And so it would remain.

After the war, Kaltenborn continued to travel, conducting foreign tours sponsored by the newspaper. Then, in April 1922, came that talk on the Army Signal Corps station, followed the next year by the regular series of weekly commentaries over WEAF. He kept his associate editorship—the *Eagle* was his sponsor—but in 1930 the break came. CBS hired him for $100 a week.

Frederic William Wile

When Kaltenborn began commenting on current events from a CBS studio in New York, Frederic William Wile was doing a weekly 15-minute broadcast for CBS from Washington. Wile's program had the unwieldly title "The Political Situation in Washington Tonight" and was an appraisal of what had happened in Washington the past week.

Wile had been an editorial writer for the *Washington Star* but, like Kaltenborn, was an "old hand" at broadcasting, having done radio commentary from time to time since the beginning of the Coolidge administration. In February 1929, he signed an exclusive contract with CBS, where his first political analysis—on Sunday evening, March 3, 1929—dealt with the inauguration of Herbert Hoover the next day.

Wile was CBS' first foreign correspondent, however temporary. In January 1930 he and William Hard of NBC accompanied the United States delegation to the five-power naval disarmament conference in London, an assignment lasting several weeks. Wile participated in, and arranged, many of the 32 broadcasts CBS carried dealing with the conference.

The commentator's association with CBS was relatively brief. In 1934, he joined the Young & Rubicam advertising agency as manager of radio publicity. During the Second World War he was associate director of information for the War Manpower Commission and on active duty with the Navy. Later, he became vice president of radio and television production at NBC.

"Baukhage Talking"

NBC's earliest commentators in Washington were H. R. Baukhage and David Lawrence. Baukhage was heard on the radio for 18 years. Lawrence's principal endeavor was the founding and editing of *United States News*, incorporated later as *U.S. News & World Report*. He also wrote a syndicated newspaper column.

Baukhage was one of Lawrence's colleagues at *United States News* and in 1934 began doing a daily stint on NBC's "National Farm and Home Hour," for which Lawrence had been reporting. This was Baukhage's entry into broadcasting, and Theodore F. Koop, who was a CBS vice president, tells how it came about:

> Because it was evident even in those experimental days that an announcer could not impart the understanding and authority of a reporter, [Lawrence] offered one of his own reporters, H. R. Baukhage, to read the news on the air. Here was the exact combination NBC was seeking: Baukhage had been an actor before he progressed (if that is the word) to reporter. He went on the show, and 'Baukhage talking' became a familiar self-introduction year after year.[3]

In 1942, after NBC's Blue Network became ABC, Baukhage went with the new company as a commentator and stayed with it until 1951. Then he spent three years with Mutual. His was a career that bridged two world wars. As a reporter for *Stars and Stripes,* Baukhage covered the Versailles peace conference in 1919, and he did a radio report from Berlin when Hitler sent his armies into Poland. He died in 1976.

Walter Winchell

Walter Winchell was "Peck's Bad Boy" on commentators' row. While most commentators impressed listeners as learned father figures, Winchell, brash and highly opinionated, used the language of his favorite street— Broadway—as readily in discussing foreign relations as in reporting a sensational murder or divorce. Excited, almost maniacal in delivery, Winchell was an ex-vaudeville hoofer of scant education who, driven by ambition and an unreasonable sense of insecurity, became for a time the most listened-to radio commentator in the country.

"Walter Winchell's Journal," a radio version of his widely syndicated newspaper column, premiered on NBC's Blue Network on December 4, 1932, and was a Sunday night staple on NBC, then on ABC and Mutual for more than twenty years. Crouched at the microphone, belt loosened, pounding (incoherently) a telegraph key, wearing always a gray felt hat, he charged frenetically into his 11½-minute spiel with "Good evening, Mr. and Mrs. America and all the ships at sea!"[4]

Winchell was a gossip columnist, and he seasoned his radio reports of the 1930s and 1940s with the same spice. A fierce enemy of the Nazis— "the Ratzis"—and harsh critic of Harry Truman, he was a booster of Franklin Roosevelt, Joe McCarthy, and J. Edgar Hoover, his long-time friend, and of the Stork Club, the nitery where Grace Kelly gave him his scoop that she was engaged to Prince Rainier.

Drew Pearson

Walter Winchell and Drew Pearson were born the same year, 1897, Winchell of impoverished parents in Harlem, Pearson of a professor of public speaking and his college-educated wife in Evanston, Illinois. Both were syndicated columnists before they were broadcasters. Both, in their columns and in their commentaries, were incorrigible disturbers of the peace.

In Washington, Pearson did in a more urbane way what Winchell did in New York. If Winchell's style was Broadway baroque, Pearson's was the style of the scholar-reporter whose sources seemed everywhere in the federal government. Each in his way made enemies. In his memoir Winchell writes that when "any politico attacked me [or he them] we went to each other's rescue. 'The Katzenjammer Kids of Journalism,' I label'd our act."[5] The "act" broke up on the issue of McCarthyism. Pearson detested McCarthy, Winchell's knight errant, and debunked him.

A grammar school dropout, Winchell grew up in vaudeville. Pearson attended Phillips Exeter Academy and graduated as valedictorian from Swarthmore College, where he edited the campus paper. He worked for two years with the American Friends Service in Serbia, helping to rebuild that Balkan country devastated by war. In 1923, he crossed the Pacific as an ordinary seaman in order to keep a series of speaking engagements in Australia. Continuing around the world, he sold free-lance articles—one was based on an interview with Mussolini—earning enough to return to New York first class on the *Aquitania*. He lectured briefly at Columbia University, then was off for China (1925), the Geneva naval conference (1927), a Pan American conference in Havana and the signing of the Kellogg-Briand Pact in Paris (1928), and the five-power naval conference in London (1930).

He was now a full-fledged newspaperman, foreign editor of *United States Daily*, which would become *U.S. News & World Report*, then diplomatic correspondent for the *Baltimore Sun*. He also had married the 19-

year-old daughter of Eleanor Medill "Cissy" Patterson, publisher of the *Washington Times-Herald*. The marriage ended in early divorce, but Pearson and Cissy Patterson remained friends, and she helped start his column, which had its debut in 1932. The widely syndicated column, "Washington Merry-Go-Round," was written by Pearson and Robert S. Allen, who had been Washington bureau chief for the *Christian Science Monitor*. In time, Pearson bought out Allen, making the column his own. Starting in 1947, one of his legmen was a young reporter, Jack Anderson, who inherited the column upon Pearson's death.

The radio program went on the air for the first time on the evening of July 8, 1940. At first, Pearson and Allen each did commentary, but soon Pearson had the show to himself. His sponsor during much of the life of the program was Adam Hats, which gave it up when McCarthy called for a boycott. From May to November 1952, he also did a weekly commentary (with not always accurate predictions) on ABC Television. From December 1952 to March 1953, he did a similar program for DuMont Television.

Drew Pearson died in 1969. To the end he was what today is called an investigative reporter, though he might have looked askance at the phrase. He could be mean—Truman called him an S.O.B.—but he helped keep Washington honest.

David Lawrence

Since Drew Pearson worked for a time for *United States Daily*, precursor to *U.S. News & World Report*, this may be the place to mention David Lawrence, the publication's founding publisher—mention, not more, because Lawrence, one of America's notable, most durable journalists, did radio commentary for a relatively short time. Although he was a syndicated columnist for four decades, he broadcast regularly for only four years.

A disciple of Woodrow Wilson, Lawrence came to the Associated Press bureau in Washington from Princeton in 1910. After five years with the AP, he began corresponding from Washington for the *New York Evening Post*. And he began doing something that was new in those days: he started *interpreting* what was happening. The *Post* liked his interpretations and began syndicating them. From 1919 on, he syndicated the column himself.

Lawrence started doing his Sunday evening commentaries on NBC in 1929. He was a strong conservative. Raymond Swing once told me, "I read Lawrence for guidance. If I find myself agreeing with him, I know I'm off the beam."[6]

Raymond Swing

Raymond Swing was a liberal. He attended Oberlin College, the first college in America to admit students born white, black, or female. He once wrote: "Just being a part of Oberlin gave me an innate sense of the political equality of men and women, all men and all women."[7]

Swing did not graduate from Oberlin. The college fathers suspended him at the end of his freshman year for playing too many pranks, like mounting baby carriages on chimneys. He cut so many classes his grades were inauspicious. It was his last association with the college until, 35 years later, Oberlin honored him with a Doctor of Laws degree and elected him to its board of trustees.

His first job, at 18, was working as the cashier in a barber shop in Lorain, Ohio. After a few months, he went to the *Cleveland Press* for $10 a week. In quick succession, he moved to the *Cleveland News*, the *Richmond* (Indiana) *Evening Item*, the *Indianapolis Star*, the *Cincinnati Times Star*, and the *Indianapolis Sun*, where he was managing editor at the age of 23. Shortly before the First World War he married a young Frenchwoman studying at the University of Chicago. Their honeymoon was a year in Europe, paid for by Swing's uncle, George Mead, who taught at the university. The marriage did not last.

The war found Swing in Berlin. He was chief of bureau for the *Chicago Daily News* and was the first—perhaps the only—American correspondent allowed to roam freely behind the German lines as the war got under way. He was eyewitness to the Battle of the Dardanelles, survived the torpedoing of a ship on which he was a passenger, and smuggled out the story that the Germans had a huge cannon, a monster piece of artillery pulled by 36 horses. This was the cannon called "Big Bertha," and it was a sweet exclusive for Swing, scooping big-name correspondents like Richard Harding Davis and Irving S. Cobb.

In 1921, Swing remarried. His bride was Betty Gram, a militant feminist, who refused to take his name unless he would take hers, so for most of his career as a broadcaster he was known as Raymond Gram Swing. Years later, when they were divorced, he dropped the *Gram*, but she kept his name for the rest of her life.

Swing spent ten years after the war as head of the London bureau of the *Philadelphia Daily Ledger*. In 1935, he began speaking regularly on foreign affairs on CBS, but Ed Klauber, the network official overseeing the program, complained of his voice, which was slight and low-pitched. Then occurred one of the most curious turns in the history of broadcasting. Since Klauber respected Swing's attainments, he offered him the position of director of talks. In that position he would line up prominent people—authors, scientists, statesmen, educators—for CBS discussion programs. Because he wanted to be on the air himself, Swing turned down the offer. An aspiring young man with no experience on newspapers or in broadcasting, who had been working at the Institute of International Education, took the job. His name was Edward R. Murrow.

In 1936, Swing went to WOR, key station for the Mutual network, where—for $40—he did a weekly broadcast. The broadcasts were expanded to two, three, four, and five times a week as the European crisis grew more grave. By now Swing, sponsored by White Owl cigars, was heard on the full network and making big money. And he was doing something else. At the invitation of Sir John Reith, whom he knew from his London days, Swing was reporting regularly over the BBC. He says in his memoir:

> There was nothing else quite like it. I, an American, was permitted once a week to explain my country and its policies to the British . . . and . . . at a time when they approached and then faced the most severe test in their history.

Swing called the BBC assignment, which lasted for nine years, "the most gratifying of my whole broadcasting experience."[8] Because Swing was heard weekly throughout the British Empire, as well as each weekday in the United States, it is likely that during those years he had the largest audience of anyone on the air anywhere. Certainly he had the most global audience.

Dorothy Thompson

Dorothy Thompson and Raymond Swing were good friends. In 1928, when she married Sinclair Lewis, he was one of the select few invited to their wedding. Like Swing, she worked for a time in prewar Germany. She hated Hitler, and Hitler expelled her because her hatred showed.

Although she had a newspaper column and wrote magazine articles and books, Dorothy Thompson ranks as the foremost woman commentator of her time. She started her syndicated column, "On the Record," in 1935. Her radio work began in 1936 when NBC engaged her as a commentator for the Democratic and Republican national conventions. Her articulate, perceptive comments and the quality of her newspaper writing resulted in a contract for a weekly series of radio commentaries on NBC, then on Mutual. Her strong anti-Hitler, anti-dictator-anywhere views were heard by six million listeners. Here is a sample from her broadcast of November 14, 1938:

> When the dictators commit what to the rest of the world are crimes, they say there is a higher justice. They claim the justification of national necessity and emergency. We do not think that such justice is higher. We think it low.

She also was outspoken on domestic politics. When Roosevelt ran for a third term, he sought and won her support after it became known that she was leaning toward Wendell Willkie. She was a force.

Fulton Lewis, Jr.

To say that Fulton Lewis, Jr., was a vigorous defender of Joe McCarthy —which he certainly was—places the radio commentator in the 1950s, but he had been broadcasting regularly since 1936. Back then he was equally vigorous in attacking Franklin Roosevelt and the New Deal.

Lewis was that rare broadcast personality, a native Washingtonian— the family's summer home stood on the hill where the National Cathedral now stands. His birth date was April 30, 1903. He enrolled at the University of Virginia but dropped out after three years. In 1924, he entered the George Washington University School of Law, dropped out again, and got a job as reporter for the *Washington Herald.* Now he was in his element. In three years he was city editor, then Washington correspondent for Hearst's Universal News Service, which later became the International News Service (INS). At the Chevy Chase Country Club he met Alice Huston, daughter of Claudius Hart Huston, former chairman of the Republican National Committee. President and Mrs. Hoover attended their wedding.

From 1933 to 1936, Lewis wrote a newspaper column. "The Washington Sideshow," syndicated by King Features. It was through resourcefulness and imagination that Lewis got his first job in broadcasting. In 1936, when a Washington newscaster went on vacation, Lewis, volunteered his services. The man he was substituting for, in a format that can only be regarded as quaint, always stopped halfway through the program to read a poem. Lewis not only skipped the poetry but dared, on the first day, to originate from the State Department, where he got a scoop. This kind of enterprise impressed William Dolph, general manager of Mutual's Washington outlet, WOL, and he asked Lewis to do a series of radio talks. Two months later he was on the Mutual network, coast to coast.

While favoring a strong national defense, Lewis vehemently opposed U.S. entry into the Second World War. In the days before Pearl Harbor, when Murrow's broadcasts from London were building bonds of sympathy for Britons under the Blitz, Lewis tried to offset Murrow's effect by saying the situation was not so bad as one might imagine. If windows were being blown out under the bombing—well, it meant more business for the people who made glass.[9] He lined up Charles Lindbergh, the most celebrated of isolationists, for an exclusive broadcast. When Lindbergh asked that CBS and NBC also be allowed to carry his remarks, Lewis was chagrined— after all, it had been his idea—but at least Lindbergh spoke from a Mutual studio.

Like Walter Winchell, Lewis flunked television. Although well-spoken, he appeared on the screen as dour and ill at ease. Somehow under the lights of the television studio his dynamism was lost. The syndicated column was incidental; radio was his primary medium. In the 1940s, his commentary was carried by more than 350 stations. In 1943, he received the first Alfred I. duPont award for "aggressive, consistently excellent and accurate gathering and reporting of news." By the 1950s, when he was supporting Joe McCarthy, both audience and influence had dwindled.

Lewis, whose fierce, pervading tenet was freedom of enterprise, died on August 21, 1966. Four days later, Mutual announced that Fulton Lewis III would succeed his father, broadcasting Monday through Friday at the same hour, 7 P.M. When the son was asked if he had the same conservative outlook as his father, he said they both favored "a Jeffersonian form of government and the right of people to govern themselves. But," he added "it may be that I am more modern and progressive in my views."[10]

So the torch was passed.

Elmer Davis

When Elmer Davis died, Murrow said, "No man ever used a microphone with less fear or greater faith in the Republic."[11]

Davis was a brave and eminent broadcaster who was born in Aurora, Indiana, on January 13, 1890. He attended Franklin College, near Indianapolis, then studied at Oxford as a Rhodes Scholar. In 1914, he became a reporter on the *New York Times,* where he knew Ed Klauber, who was best man at his wedding. Besides reporting, Davis wrote light novels. A serious book among the 16 he wrote[12] was a history of the *Times.* He had risen to the position of editorial writer when, in 1924, he left the newspaper to devote himself to writing.

In 1930, CBS invited Davis to make a radio talk on the purposes of a college education. He spoke intermittently on CBS for the next several years, but his real break into broadcasting came in August 1939 with the signing of the German–Soviet pact, which raised the spectre of imminent war. CBS needed a commentator—Kaltenborn was in Europe—and Paul White telephoned Davis: Would he fill in? Davis was deep in a writing project and wanted to finish it—but as he wrote in *Harper's* magazine, "The old fire horse turned out to pasture rears up his head and sniffs the breeze when he hears the alarm bell; big news was breaking, and I wanted to be in on the story."[13]

Davis took the assignment with some trepidation. To substitute for Kaltenborn in such a crisis, he said, was "a little like trying to play centerfield in place of Joe DiMaggio."[14] He need not have feared. His news analyses, as CBS insisted on calling them, were well received, and in addition he soon was broadcasting a five-minute news summary each night.

William J. Dunn, an early member of the CBS News staff, recalls his first meeting with Davis:

> I came into the office and saw a fellow sitting over in the corner, a grey-haired, rather nondescript-looking person, I should say, in tweed suit and black bow tie pounding on the typewriter, and I said, "Who's that?" Paul White said, "That's Elmer Davis." I said, "Who is he? I don't know him." And Paul said, "He's a damn good analyst, and we needed somebody, so here he is."[15]

On CBS, Elmer Davis became a national figure. His nightly summary —aired at 8:55, New York time—attracted a large, faithful audience. When the program first went on the air, CBS refused to sell it to a sponsor. Indeed, the news (and Davis) were so respected in that critical period in world affairs that CBS made it almost impossible for an affiliated station to schedule a commercial immediately preceding the program. The network did this by cutting the 30 seconds normally provided for a station break down to 15 seconds. In time, the program was sponsored. Interruption for a commercial, however, never was allowed.

If the longer commentaries gave Davis opportunity to display his wide knowledge and wit, they also revealed, after 1939, his nonobjectivity on the issue of American intervention on behalf of Britain and France. He had believed in the beginning that America should stay out of the war, but after the German invasion of the Low Countries on May 10, 1939, he changed his mind, declaring on the question of convoys for Britain that it was true some shooting might result, "but if Hitler should win this war, there's likely to be some shooting afterwards on the other side of the Atlantic."[16] But he never orated. The plain, compact sentences delivered in flat, mater-of-fact Hoosier accents conveyed just the right sense of competency and calm for those times.

The man who felt uneasy taking the place of Kaltenborn—the Joe DiMaggio among commentators—had turned out to be a superlative pinch hitter, and Kaltenborn, on his return from Europe, knew he had a rival. Dunn says Kaltenborn resented Davis:

> White tried his best to play it down the middle, and he was fairly successful, but Hans never quite got over the idea that Elmer Davis had moved into his territory just at the time he'd hit the peak and was really going great guns.[17]

Davis' presence may have been an annoyance to Kaltenborn, but it was a delight to other associates. Despite his black bow tie, intimidating horn-rimmed glasses, and crisp white shirt, Davis was warm and unassuming, as Robert Skedgell, a former CBS News executive, recalls, "the complete gentleman." Skedgell, who was a newly hired page at the time, says:

> He had that most admirable manner which made you feel as though you were the greatest person in the world. I remember someone came with a package that was to be delivered to me, and Elmer said, "Mr. Skedgell? Right over there." I was a kid, you know. I just beamed and beamed.[18]

Davis was as liberal as Fulton Lewis, Jr., was conservative, a believer in Franklin Roosevelt from the beginning. And no one, not even Edward R. Murrow, attacked McCarthy more forthrightly than he.

Other commentators of the early period:

Earl Godwin. He was anti-New Deal and did a nightly program on the Mutual network. His sponsor was Ford.

William J. Cameron, blessed with a splendid sonorous voice, sounded the very epitome of Big Business on CBS' "The Ford Sunday Evening Hour." In 1935, when the Supreme Court declared a series of New Deal measures unconstitutional, Cameron exulted, "Every attempt to subjugate our citizens as vassals of the state has failed."[19]

Jay Franklin has been a reporter for the *New York Times* and an economics specialist in the State Department. Pro-New Deal, he had a program on NBC called "The Week in Washington."

Cedric Foster, who had been a broadcaster in Boston, went to Mutual in 1940. He claimed to be the first commentator heard daily coast to coast in the daytime.

John B. Kennedy was a commentator on NBC. Once, Edwin C. Hill got permission for Kennedy to substitute for him on CBS. The unusual substitution was allowed with the understanding that it was for one time only.

Another early commentator for NBC was Clifton Utley. A native of Chicago, Utley graduated from the University of Chicago, then did graduate work at the Universities of Munich, Algiers, and Mexico City, studying foreign languages and developing an expertise in foreign affairs. He was the first director of the Chicago Council on Foreign Relations and during the early 1930s made frequent lectures. This led to employment as a commentator on NBC's Chicago station, WMAQ. He was the network's first television newscaster in Chicago. NBC Correspondent Garrick Utley is his son.

These commentators devoted almost all their attention to events transpiring in the United States and Europe. Latin America and the Far East were almost totally neglected. David Holbrook Culbert observes that with the exception of Raymond Swing, "those who depended on radio news would not have known that the Chinese Communist Party even existed. . . . No commentator questioned whether an embargo might make the Japanese consider war with America the alternative to national dishonor."[20]

Such neglect was not benign.

More to Come

The stories of some of these earliest commentators are to be continued. Today the name H. V. Kaltenborn is closely associated with the Munich crisis of 1938, which he reported—and interpreted—in a series of marathon broadcasts which belongs in *The Guinness Book of Records*. Elmer Davis is best known for his stand against McCarthy and his service as director of the Office of War Information (OWI).

Great reporters like William L. Shirer and Edward R. Murrow, who also did commentary, wait in the wings. They belong to the second generation of radio pundits, along with Quincy Howe, Morgan Beatty, Edward P. Morgan, Joseph C. Harsch, and Cecil Brown. Then, after them, people like David Brinkley, Eric Sevareid, Bill Moyers, John Chancellor, and Howard K. Smith. With rare exception, Walter Cronkite confined his views to radio. It is as a television anchorman and reporter that he is remembered.

The generations overlap. Nor is the list complete.

8

"Time Marches On!"

Oldsters looking back to radio in the 1930s are apt to remember it as a time when they first heard the songs of Bing Crosby and the wisecracks of Bob Hope. But there was, besides the entertainment, commentary, and straight news, a wide variety of other programming to which journalism was closely related.

The most important series in this genre may have been "The March of Time." With Howard Barlow's 21-piece orchestra and an arsenal of 7,000 sound effects, it certainly was the most ambitious. Among the distinguished cast (at different times) were Agnes Moorehead, Kenny Delmar, Martin Gabel, Arlene Francis, Everett Sloane, Orson Welles, Nancy Kelly, and Dwight Weist. Weist was especially busy in the role of Adolph Hitler, but he also played characters as dissimilar as Fiorello LaGuardia and John L. Lewis. A contemporary writer observed, "The aristocracy of actors are brought into the show, for it is no easy job to portray Winston Churchill one moment and Emperor Hirohito the next."[1]

The half-hour weekly program, hatched from a sustaining quiz show, was the brain child of David Frederick Smith, a former director and chief announcer at WLW in Cincinnati. Smith convinced Roy Larsen of *Time* that radio dramatizations of current events, sponsored by the magazine, would boost circulation. The program was produced by the New York advertising agency of Batten, Barton, Durstine and Osborne, and had its premiere—Barnouw says "erupted"[2]—on the CBS network on the evening of March 6, 1931.

John Shaw Billings, a *Time* editor who witnessed the performance, wrote in his diary:

> Drove down to the [Henry] Luces on 49th Street for dinner. Other guests were Tom Palmer and his wife, Bill Whitney and wife, Marcia Davenport, Washington Dodge and others. Halfway through the dinner we all dashed out and drove up to the Columbia Broadcasting studio on Madison Avenue to watch "The March of Time" from a glass-fronted cubicle. . . . I was amazed at the number of performers—20 or 25. Then back to the Luces for ice cream and coffee.[3]

The earliest narrator was Ted Husing, followed briefly by Harry von Zell, but *the* "voice of *Time*" during most of the program's 14-year run belonged to a onetime Annapolis middy, Westbrook Van Voorhis, who, sounding like God, solemnly pronounced "Time marches on!" at the conclusion of each program segment, a phrase repeated so often, and so profoundly, that even today it is surpassed only by Ovid's "Time flies" as comment upon the passage of time.

Subjects covered during the first year included the election of "Big Bill" Thompson as mayor of Chicago, the death of Thomas Edison, and the repeal of Prohibition. In the reenactment of events like the Hauptmann trial and the abdication of Edward VIII, whole scenes were invented. What did happen often was sensationalized. Trumpets heralded segments; drums rolled. There were fanfares and flourishes. Listeners "attending" a beheading heard a cantalope fall into a bucket of sawdust. It was brash, entertaining stuff, not unlike the television simulations raising questions of journalistic ethics today.

There was, at the same time, a paradoxical striving for accuracy. Once the question arose as to whether London's Big Ben sounded in the key of E or G. Research disclosed it was low E, and that is precisely how listeners to the program heard it. Another broadcast required researchers to determine whether a Siamese or Maltese cat has a higher pitched meow, and the result of that research, alas, is lost. This meticulous care gave the program authenticity.

With the outbreak of World War II, "The March of Time" depended less on dramatization. For hard news as well as incidental information—like the mannerisms of a prime minister or the description of a uniform—producers of the program could turn to *Time*'s 200 correspondents stationed around the world. Two of the best known who contributed were Robert Sherrod and Theodore H. White. Though much of the program was still drama, the newsmakers themselves began participating. Wendell Willkie and Admiral Chester W. Nimitz played themselves. When the U.S.S. *Franklin* limped home from the Battle of Okinawa, it was the carrier's chaplain, Father O'Callahan, who described the crew's heroic effort to save their ship.

Throughout most of its life, "The March of Time" was sponsored by *Time,* but during those relatively short periods when the sponsors were Remington-Rand (1933–1935) and Wrigley's Gum (1936), *Time* retained full editorial control. In 1937, the program moved to NBC; then, in its final days, to ABC.

In 1935, a film version was shown in motion picture theaters and ran for 16 years. It was revived on television in 1966, but this syndicated series, developed by Wolper Productions, lasted for only eight installments. The narrator in this final version was William Conrad.

"The March of Time" was the first important documentary series on radio. With its unparalleled financial and editorial resources, it gave the public a provocative, expertly executed weekly report on current events. Not content with reenactment of those events, the producers often manipulated them in order to produce a story line, or plot, for editorial as well as dramatic effect. These were subjective productions reflecting the views of Henry Luce, *Time*'s editor in chief.

The film version, produced by Louis de Rochement, not only revolutionized the newsreel but represented a model for television documentarians of the future. As the great Scots filmmaker John Grierson, who coined the word *documentary*, said of "The March of Time":

> It gets behind the news, observes the factors of influence, and gives a perspective to events. Not the parade of armies so much as the race in armaments; not the ceremonial opening of a dam but the full story of Roosevelt's experiment in the Tennessee Valley.[4]

That "The March of Time" was not an objective report did not bother Grierson. It pleased him that it had "something of that bright and easy tradition of freeborn comment which the newspaper has won and the cinema has been too abject even to ask for."

Lots of Talk

The thirties saw the arrival of the panel show, the kind of public affairs broadcast represented today by programs like "Washington Week in Review" and "Meet the Press." Outstanding was "The University of Chicago Roundtable," which stayed on the air almost 25 years. On its tenth anniversary in 1943, NBC called it the oldest "continuous" educational broadcast. The program, it said, had maintained its purpose of bringing listeners "spontaneous free discussion of current topics by men and women who are authorities in their special fields."[5] The panel usually was made up of university professors and politicians, but other people, like Prime Minister Jawaharlal Nehru of India and William Allen White, were panelists, too. During the discussions, coffee was served.

Among other important nonentertainment programs of the thirties were "America's Town Meeting of the Air" hosted by George V. Denny, Jr. (NBC), "The American Forum of the Air" moderated by Theodore Granik (Mutual),[6] and "The Columbia School of the Air" supervised by Sterling Fisher and Lyman Bryson (CBS). Bryson also moderated the CBS program "People's Platform," on which he and guests discussed current events. In the forties, he was best known as moderator of "Invitation to Learning," a panel program devoted to the discussion of literature.

On a lighter note, there was "Information Please," featuring the delightfully knowledgeable newspaper columnists Franklin P. Adams and John Kieran and pianist and composer Oscar Levant. Clifton Fadiman, book reviewer for *The New Yorker,* served as moderator. The show was first heard on NBC's Blue Network in 1938. It was seen briefly on CBS-TV in 1952.

Obviously, a mainstay of public affairs programming in the 1930s was talk. The kind of talk offered in those years is reflected in the radio highlights listed in *The New Republic,* issue of July 7, 1937:

> President Roosevelt and Lord Tweedsmuir, Governor-General of Canada, are chief speakers on a program commemorating the seventieth anniversary of the founding of the Canadian Federation, Thursday, July 1, 10:00 P.M., CBS.
>
> William Hinckley and others speak at the annual convention of the American Youth Congress, Saturday, July 3, 2:30 to 3 P.M., NBC-Red Network.
>
> Harold B. Butler, director-general of the International Labor Office, reports the international labor conference in Geneva, Sunday, July 4, 1:45 P.M., CBS.
>
> Special session of America's Town Meeting of the Air, with Senator Nye of North Dakota and Clark M. Eichelberger, president of the League of Nations Association, discussing the question, "Can America Remain Neutral?" Thursday, July 8, 10 to 11 P.M., NBC-Red Network.

The Martians Are Coming

On a Sunday evening, October 30, 1938, Orson Welles' Mercury Theater of the Air presented "The War of the Worlds," a one-hour drama based on the H. G. Wells fantasy, which because of its realism—interrupt bulletins and switching about for up-to-the-minute reports—sent millions of Americans into a panic. Many listening to CBS believed that hideous creatures from Mars had landed in New Jersey and were spreading death with a mysterious poison gas. Police, as well as radio stations, were swamped with telephone calls. People fainted. Others fled their homes.

"War of the Worlds" demonstrated that in that year, 1938, the nation's nerves, strained by Nazi crises, were too taut for such fictionalizing. And it demonstrated the credibility of radio journalism. Radio had become a true journalistic medium, taken so seriously that make-believe news bulletins in radio drama were foresworn for years to come.[7]

These Others Things Were Happening

Radio's most popular comedian, Ed Wynn, announced that he would start a third network called the Amalgamated Broadcasting System. Commercials, he said, would be limited to 30 words at the beginning and end of each program. The network started with 100 affiliates and died for lack of advertising within a year.

NBC moved from 711 Fifth Avenue into new studios in Radio City. NBC News no longer occupied a couple of rooms. It had suites and studios couched on massive springs to avoid vibration from the subway trains rumbling under Sixth Avenue. As part of Rockefeller Center, Radio City lorded over the smaller, no less functional CBS Building at 485 Madison Avenue, where on the 17the floor a constantly expanding news department was located.

CBS carried a series of weekly broadcasts from Little America, Rear Admiral Richard Byrd's base camp in the Antarctic. Buenos Aires relayed the broadcast to New York, which relayed it to London, so that the programs were heard throughout both North America and Western Europe.

Franklin Roosevelt was elected to a second term. It was a landslide victory over Alf Landon, governor of Kansas, and radio, more swiftly than ever, reported the returns. In front of the golden figure of Prometheus in Rockefeller Plaza, NBC erected a huge map of the 48 states. When a state went to Roosevelt, it lit up green. When a state turned amber, it meant the state had gone to Landon. At the end, the only amber states were Maine and Vermont.

The next year, 1937, a 26-year-old sports announcer named Dutch Reagan left WHO, Des Moines, to become a movie actor and, ultimately, president of the United States.

On July 20, 1937, Guglielmo Marconi died, and as *Broadcasting* magazine noted at the time, radio—his own creation—flashed the news of his passing. He was 63.[8]

For the funeral of King Albert of the Belgians, CBS and NBC joined forces. César Saerchinger, CBS' man in London, got the idea of using two shortwave circuits, one for "natural sound"—the solemn music and successive booming of cannon—and another over which, listening with earphones to a Brussels commentator, he could describe in English what was going on. Saerchinger was elated by the result. He wrote in his memoir, "For once, two networks had beaten as one for the benefit of all.[9]

9

"Hello, America, London Calling . . ."

César Saerchinger *was* CBS in London. Paley says, "Some would call him CBS' first foreign correspondent."[1] Actually, Saerchinger's job was to line up people to talk about European affairs. Today, he would be called a producer. He got on the air in 1930 because Frederick William Wile, in London covering the five-power naval conference, needed someone to carry on the assignment. The conference aimed at reducing the navies of the United States, Britain, France, Italy, and Japan had dragged on, and Wile had to get back to Washington.

NBC's man at the conference was William Hard, whom Saerchinger describes as "a brilliant and fearless commentator on political affairs." He says:

> Short-bodied, long-headed Bill Hard, with shrewd, kindly eyes; rotund and white-haired Fred Wile, a hard-hitting go-getter of benign countenance, were . . . two personalities peculiarly fitted by destiny for a pioneering job.[2]

No American broadcaster had covered an international conference on such a sustained basis. Open sessions, including speeches by Ramsey MacDonald, the British prime minister, who was president of the conference, and Henry L. Stimson, the U.S. secretary of state and chief American delegate, were broadcast from St. James Palace, the conference site. For broadcasters of that time, this was exciting. In writing eight years after the event, Saerchinger still felt the thrill. "The microphone could pick up, from the conference table direct, the speeches, the rumble of voices, even the whispers and the rustle of papers."

The network correspondents spoke from what amounted to little more than a telephone booth in a building of the British Broadcasting Corporation about a mile from the place. Again it is interesting to observe Saerchinger's feeling for the pioneer effort when he says, "They talked, not into an ordinary telephone, but into that amazing instrument, the microphone, which reproduced and magnified their voices so as to carry, besides the meaning of their words, a projection of their personalities."[3] He had observed a characteristic of broadcasting which has been noted and much discussed to this day.

Saerchinger claims he was inveigled into broadcasting by Wile, but one suspects that he found the medium enticing. By his own account, he was so fascinated by the first broadcast he witnessed that he thought it was all a dream. He had been European correspondent for the *Musical Courier*. When the naval conference opened, he was working with Raymond Swing, the future broadcaster, in the *Philadelphia Public Ledger*'s London bureau. Swing was chief of bureau.

Saerchinger's understanding when he took over for Wile was that he would protect CBS from the competition on an informal part-time basis. It was not to be. A few days later, just before leaving England, Wile showed Saerchinger a cable from New York. "You may not know it," Wile said, "but until further notice you are our London representative."[4] The result was that Saerchinger gave up his newspaper career and served CBS in London with distinction for the next seven years.

They were busy years. Saerchinger covered, or supervised the coverage of Italy's conquest of Ethiopia, the civil war in Spain, the abdication of Edward VIII, and the coronation of George VI. His title was European director for the Columbia Broadcasting System. He was the network's representative in London and, as such, not only reported and arranged talks but ran all kinds of corporate errands.

For almost two years, Saerchinger had the field to himself. Then in 1932 he was joined in London by NBC's counterpart, Fred Bate, who proved a formidable, though friendly competitor. A slightly older man, Bate had lived in Europe since 1912. He had the services of Max Jordan, one of the most fascinating, most competent, and, today, least known figures in American journalism. Jordan, who spoke at least four languages and was as at home in the capitals of Western Europe as he was in London and New York, was born in Italy. He came to America and, after becoming a naturalized citizen, went into newspaper work in Berlin in 1910. NBC hired him away from Hearst, and for a decade he was the reporter in Europe that CBS kept a wary eye on, lest it be scooped.

NBC, during most of those years before World War II, was a double threat in the area of foreign news because while CBS depended on Saerchinger and whatever correspondents for American newspapers could be induced to broadcast, Jordan, headquartered in Berlin, served as an additional full-time member of NBC's European staff. It was a situation that lasted until August 1937, when Edward R. Murrow, Saerchinger's successor in London, hired William L. Shirer to report from Berlin. Even then, Jordan was a reporter to reckon with. He enjoyed good relations with the Germans and outscored CBS on several occasions early in the war. Perhaps his greatest coup came in 1945 when—in Switzerland—he scooped all media with the news that Japan had surrendered, thus ending the Second World War.

Later, in New York, Jordan directed NBC's religious broadcasts and co-produced the highly regarded educational program "University of the Air." On leaving NBC after 20 years, he became a monk in the Benedictine order. By the time death came in 1977, he was a legend, one of the most remarkable men broadcasting had known.

Those Overseas Talks

In the early 1930s, it was the job of these pioneers in Europe to bring to their microphones renowned novelists, playwrights, politicians, premiers, and kings—anyone Americans tuning in might like to hear. Rarely were these personages interviewed. Just to put them on the air sufficed. It was not even necessary for the speaker to know English. Max Jordan's first broadcast for NBC was on December 31, 1931, when he translated a speech by Paul von Hindenburg, the aged German president.

NBC's prize speaker in that time was Italy's dictator, Benito Mussolini. He was writing a series of articles for the Hearst papers, which offered NBC the talk as part of their promotion. Mussolini took a cram course in English but still was difficult to understand.

Most of the speakers were paid. Jordan beat out Saerchinger in getting the famous balloonist, Professor Jean Piccard, just before one of his ascents because CBS could not match the NBC bid. "Then, five months later," Saerchinger says, "I walked away with King Christian of Denmark, and I felt we were square."[5] Once they shared a talk. Albert of the Belgians spoke on both networks, with Jordan doing the introduction and Saerchinger the close.

Of all the talks arranged, none exceeded the interest—and uproar—of the one that George Bernard Shaw made on October 11, 1931. That Saerchinger had been able to persuade the famous playwright to speak to America on CBS was no small thing in itself. Shaw was shy and suspicious. Being disposed toward the Soviet Union, he feared he would be censored; he had sharp words to say. Saerchinger insisted he would be free to say anything he pleased, which Shaw did. And it was a shocker.

> Hello, America! Hello, all my friends in America! How are all you dear old boobs who have been telling one another for a month that

I had gone dotty about Russia? . . . Russia has the laugh on us. She has us fooled, beaten, shamed, shown up, outpointed, and all but knocked out. We have lectured her from the heights of our modern superiority and now we are calling on the mountains to hide our blushes in her presence.

The blushes, he made plain, were due to the "collapse" of Western industry and agriculture in the Great Depression.[6]

Americans were indignant, and CBS, practicing the Fairness Doctrine long before its formulation, gave time to the Reverend Edmund A. Walsh, vice president of Georgetown University, to reply to this paean to a godless state.

Although much time was spent lining up speakers, the networks did cover a mixed bag of foreign events. Few were of grave concern. One day it might be tennis at Wimbledon and, another day, a nightingale singing in a garden in Surrey[7] or wine harvesting in southern France. For Europe, it was a relatively peaceful time that would soon end.

Saerchinger recalls that he tried a live "man in the street" program from Piccadilly Circus just as the theaters were emptying. No such broadcast had ever been done in England because the BBC was afraid language might be used that would cause offense. Now its fears were confirmed. All went well until Saerchinger asked a certain gaudily dressed young woman what she thought of Britain's economic plight. "Oh," she exclaimed, "is *that* all you wanted, dearie."[8] The crowd around Saerchinger loved it, but the proper BBC forbade repetition of the experiment.

A King Abdicates

It was practically a running story that began on January 20, 1936, with the death of King George V, continued through the abdication of Edward VIII for love of Wallis Simpson, and ended with the coronation of George VI. The voluntary abdication was without precedent in English history. By radio, the whole world heard Edward's own dramatic announcement that he had given up the throne. But Saerchinger was first with the story. How he did it makes a good story.

The affair between the bachelor king and the twice-divorced woman from Baltimore had been no secret, but not until December 3, 1936, did the British press mention Mrs. Simpson's name in connection with the crisis. Even then, the BBC remained respectfully silent. In America, as a result of the agreement in the press–radio war, broadcasters were limited in what they could take from the press services, so the network news chiefs, Schechter and White, deluged their representatives in London with pleas for material. They found the limitations on what they could take from AP, UP, INS especially galling because American newspapers, operating under no restriction, were filling their columns with what H. L. Mencken called "the greatest story since the Resurrection."[9]

The pressure on Fred Bate and César Saerchinger to come up with reports from London during the final days of crisis is described by Saerchinger, who speaks of "the downright torture of nervous tension and physical fatigue" experienced in satisfying New York's demands. "Day after day, night after night, we kept it up—with almost no sleep—hunting news, hounding speakers, sometimes telling them what to say and how to say it, and dickering about terms."[10] And all the time watching the other network man as a cat watches a mouse. "If we booked a transatlantic circuit at 11:30, the opposition would counter at 11:15, scooping us on time if not on facts." He says, "The New York–London telephone rang and rang. Finally, it just rang to make sure I was still awake—or alive."[11]

On the morning of December 11, the House of Commons debated Edward's message of abdication. As members spoke, the press stood by. Every available channel of communication to America, cable and wireless, was tied up by the big newspapers, press associations, and broadcasting chains all waiting for word whether the abdication had gone into effect. Most of these news organizations had a system of private signals by which they hoped to be first with the news. Saerchinger does not reveal his own secret plan. He says,

> I hardly know myself except that I had scouts at three locations, and one of them "came through." The essential fact is that at precisely 3:32 P.M. in London my telephone outside our Broadcasting House studio rang, and a voice, having identified mine, announced the fact of resignation. The terminus of the open circuit to America was but three yards away, and I shouted for the air. . . . For 20 minutes the world outside knew through my words alone that King Edward was king no longer. For once, radio had scooped the world.[12]

That evening, at 10 P.M. in ancestral Windsor Castle outside London —5 P.M. in New York—Edward sat before a radio microphone and read the speech that began, "At long last, I am able to say a few words of my own." The best-remembered words are:

> But you must believe me when I tell you that I have found it impossible to carry the heavy burden of responsibility and to discharge my duties as King, as I would wish to do, without the help and support of the woman I love.

In his broadcast that night, Lowell Thomas called it "the greatest broadcast of all time, a truly extraordinary thing in power, pathos, and simplicity."[13] An exaggeration. But it was, as Robert MacNeil has said, the broadcasting age's "first global sensation."[14]

10
Radio's First
War Correspondents

The story of radio and war correspondence goes back to what Lee De Forest called "the Japanese expedition." [1] He referred to the time when, in 1904, Lionel James of the *London Times*, assisted by two American wireless operators, used de Forest's transmitter to scoop the entire world press on progress of the Russo-Japanese War. Enterprisingly, the operators had installed the wireless equipment on a small Chinese ship from which by Morse code various actions, including the sinking of the Russian battleship *Petropavlovsk*, were reported.

James' dispatches created a sensation, but it would be 28 years before Americans heard the actual voice of a correspondent reporting from a war zone. That happened on January 20, 1932, while Floyd Gibbons was covering Japan's conquest of Manchuria. In a half-hour broadcast over NBC he interviewed Shigeru Honjo, the general commanding the Japanese forces. The broadcast originated in Chinchou in southern Manchuria, was relayed to Mukden by telephone line and from Mukden to Tokyo by shortwave, then radioed across the Pacific to San Francisco. It was the first news broadcast ever to reach the United States from mainland Asia.

The signal was surprisingly good. Edward Gibbons says in the biography of his famous brother, "Sitting snugly by a blazing fire in my lodge, I could hear Floyd's staccato voice with his rapid-fire method of delivery as clearly as if he were in New York."[2]

This seems to have been Gibbons' only broadcast from Manchuria.[3] Radio coverage of Italy's invasion of Ethiopia in 1935 and the civil war the next year in Spain was more sustained.

Calling Addis Ababa!

In Ethiopia, CBS used a stringer, John T. Whitaker of the *New York Herald Tribune,* who had reached the war zone by steamer up the Nile, then by mule, camel, and airplane. The airplane was a bomber piloted by Mussolini's accommodating son-in-law, Count Ciano. Whitaker's competitor, representing NBC as well as INS, was none other than Floyd Gibbons. He, too, was flown about by the count, who sought publicity for Rome's latter-day "conquering legions" wherever it could be found.

As it turned out, Gibbons made only two broadcasts. In the middle of the second broadcast he collapsed because of the thin air at 8,000 feet. He had suffered a heart attack two years earlier. The risk in covering a war at such an altitude was too great, and, after a period of convalescence, he returned to New York.

At the start, the broadcasts were made from Asmara, across the frontier in Eritrea and more than 400 airline miles from Addis Ababa, the Ethiopian capital. The only shortwave transmitter inside Ethiopia was located near the capital but mustered a pitiably weak signal of one kilowatt.

The problem was solved partially when Ernest Hammar, a Swedish engineer employed by Emperor Haile Selassie as communications director, improved the signal so it could be picked up in London for relay to America. Reception was further improved when a Paramount newsreel team, arriving in Addis Ababa, let Hammar have one of its "modern" dynamic microphones.

The first correspondent to use the station, once it found its voice, was Robinson McLean of the *Toronto Evening Telegram.* In that broadcast, made for CBS on October 16, 1935, McLean's sympathies in the war are evident.

> Of course, it's not a real war, because these brown men haven't got tanks and airplanes and because nobody has declared war. Of course, getting excited over a little Italian skirmish in the African mountains is rather childish. But . . . so far as I can see, it doesn't really matter much when men, women, and children die whether they are killed in a real war or merely a glorious little expedition to bring civilization to a savage tinpot kingdom lost in the African hills.[4]

McLean had taken Whitaker's place as a broadcaster for CBS, and he worked with Josef Israels, a CBS employee who had arrived on the scene and taken charge. It was Israels who arranged for the emperor to make a radio appeal to the American people to boycott Italian goods.

The broadcasts from Addis Ababa went on for two months. The American public, so avid for information at first, became bored. CBS decided to call it quits. "Consider we have exhausted broadcastable material," it wired César Saerchinger in London.[5]

In April 1936, after the rainy season, the Italian forces launched their final offensive. The Ethiopians, armed with rifles and spears, were no match. Selassie fled the capital. In June, he made a personal appeal before the League of Nations not to lift its sanctions against Italy. He was ignored.

In Rome, Mussolini had King Victor Emmanuel proclaimed emperor. So again there was a Roman emperor. And it had all happened in about nine months.

Death in the Afternoon

Spain, in the civil war between Loyalists and insurgents led by Francisco Franco, was a testing ground. Germany and Italy, supporting Franco, tried out their new bombers and tanks. Ernest Hemingway tested his ability to describe the tragedy. Without knowing it, radio in a rehearsal for World War II tested what it could do in covering military actions extending at times over a thousand-mile front.

For broadcast journalists, the war is notable for the reporting of H. V. Kaltenborn and, to lesser degree, Floyd Gibbons. Print journalists did occasional pieces for the American networks; they played an important part.

The war began in July 1936, and Kaltenborn, who happened to be in Europe, arrived at the scene of fighting within two weeks. To obtain military passes from the opposing forces he used a circular identifying himself as a lecturer on foreign affairs. Because it featured a photograph of him taken with Hitler, it helped him with the rebels. When he went over to the Loyalist side, the commander "took one look at the picture, sputtered an angry stream of Spanish and summoned an immediate conference of his staff." Kaltenborn suddenly remembered there was a picture of him with a Soviet commissar in the same circular and got his pass.[6]

Although Kaltenborn was in Spain through the rest of that summer and made many broadcasts, it was his reporting of the battle for Irun which captured attention. The city of Irun is just inside Spain, so near the French border that it was possible to be in France and still observe the hostilities. An especially good view could be obtained from a farm which, because of a sharp bend in the Bidassoa River, actually jutted into Spanish territory.

Kaltenborn wrote:

> As the battle for Irun began and shells and bullets whizzed over this French farm I conceived the idea of broadcasting a battle description punctuated by battlesounds. A French radio engineer, who was keen on the idea, located a telephone line in the aban-

doned farmhouse that stood between the two battle lines. To get the best sound effects we ran a long cable from the house to a small haystack located at an ideal vantage point to both see and hear the artillery shells. . . . I was determined to make the first actual battlefield broadcast in radio history.

Kaltenborn's report would be carried by telephone line to Bordeaux, Paris, London and Rugby (!), thence by shortwave to New York. When on September 3, 1936, Kaltenborn finally got through to CBS from the haystack, he was told: "Stand by. Too many commercial programs just now. Will call you later."[7] It was not until 9 o'clock that night that Kaltenborn was heard in the United States. He spoke for 15 minutes. What follows is a small part of what he said:

> In a moment or two, when the machinegun which has been barking all evening sounds again, I will stop talking for a moment in order that you may get something of the sound of this civil war as it continues even through the night. . . . *(Sound of rifle fire)* Those are the isolated shots which are being exchanged by the frontline sentinels. . . . Directly in front of me as I look through the dark of this midsummer night is a bright line of fire rising from the most important single factory in the city of Irun. Late this afternoon, we watched a rebel airplane circling overhead and dropping bombs.[8]

Kaltenborn made several reports from this vantage point. In other broadcasts, he discussed military and political implications, France's problem in caring for refugees, and the bravery of fighting men—and women—on both sides. He spoke repeatedly of the high casualties and what seemed to him contempt for death.

The first broadcast by an American correspondent from Madrid had been made by Floyd Gibbons on August 23, 1936. The NBC file on Gibbons shows the program listed as "Impressions of War-torn Spain." That is an understatement. Gibbons had just witnessed a battle on the outskirts of Madrid. He had no time to submit his copy to a censor, but according to Edward Gibbons' account, soldiers in the studio were instructed to shoot him if he said anything against the Republic.

His report began: I just arrived from the battlefield outside Madrid, and in order to get to this studio I had to step across the bodies of 20 dead Spanish students lying out in the square." At that point, the transmission stopped. Edward Gibbons, who was listening to the broadcast, tells what happened next:

> With that ominous silence, my heart stood still. A moment later the American announcer in New York broke in, saying, "Due to a mechanical breakdown, we are unable to get Mr. Gibbons' Madrid broadcast. . . ." That "mechanical breakdown" explanation didn't sound true to me, and for almost 50 minutes I sat, with beads of perspiration standing on my brow.[9]

The studio had cut him off. He was not shot, but the rest of his script was heavily censored.

After a month in Spain, Gibbons came home, and three years later, on September 24, 1939, he died in the same bed in which he had been born. World War II, the big one he would have liked to cover, was three weeks old.

11
Munich

The momentum was toward war. In 1935, two years after coming to power in Germany, Hitler scrapped the Versailles Treaty and ordered the building of a new army, navy, and air force. The next year, his troops occupied the Rhineland bordering France in defiance of the Locarno Treaty, which declared the region a demilitarized zone.

And in March 1938 he seized Austria.

When the coup occurred—there was no war with Austria—the Nazis barred William L. Shirer, CBS' correspondent in Vienna, from broadcasting. "Here I sit on one of the biggest stories of my life," he lamented in his diary. "I am the only broadcaster in town. Max Jordan of NBC, my only competition, has not yet arrived. Yet I cannot talk."[1] He had argued with the Nazi authorities until finally, after midnight, they removed him from the broadcast building at bayonet point.

CBS had two men in Europe: Shirer, formerly of the *Paris Herald* and Hearst's Universal Service, and Edward R. Murrow, who had never broadcast a news story from overseas although, in the States, he had done some radio talks. Shirer had been hired the year before by Murrow. Universal had just folded and Shirer was without a job, but incredibly on the same day that he learned of his unemployment, he received a wire from Murrow inviting him to dinner at the Adlon in Berlin.[2] Shirer says that as he walked up to Murrow in the hotel lobby he was taken aback by his handsomeness —"Just what you would expect from radio, I thought," But soon the impression changed; there was "something in his eyes that was not Hollywood."[3]

After chatting about mutual friends—one was Raymond Swing—Murrow asked Shirer if he would be interested in working for CBS; the network needed an experienced correspondent on the Continent. Shirer was interested. He did a trial broadcast and, despite his soft, whispery voice that was the antithesis of the traditional golden-throated announcer's voice, Shirer was accepted by New York. But only after Murrow battled the New York brass, arguing that what was required was a first-rate, level-headed journalist, not a mellifluous-sounding announcer. It was a decision CBS would not regret. Even as Murrow came to prominence in London, Shirer distinguished himself as CBS' man in Berlin.

Cedar Rapids to Paris to Berlin

William Lawrence Shirer was born in Chicago on February 23, 1904, the son of a lawyer and a mother who "had a remarkable tolerance for us children and what she considered our wild schemes and our unruly ways."[4] The father died in 1913, and Shirer did most of his growing up in Cedar Rapids. The three children practiced the work ethic. After school, Shirer delivered newspapers and in the summertime pitched tents on the Chautauqua circuit. While attending Coe College he got a part-time job as sports reporter on the *Cedar Rapids Republican.* He was editor of the college paper. Life had taken a journalistic turn.

On graduation with honors (Phi Beta Kappa), Shirer worked his way to Europe on a cattle boat sailing from Montreal. He was fed up with life in what he saw as Babbitt country, a region of "bigotry and banality." He wanted to go "where a man could drink a glass of wine or a stein of beer without breaking the law."[5] He wanted to see the world.

Specifically, he wanted to see Paris, the City of Light that for the young man from Cedar Rapids was Camelot. He thought he might work for one of the English-language papers if he was lucky—very lucky—but for a few days he simply enjoyed the heady atmosphere of Paris, strolling its boulevards, poking about in bookstalls, sipping *apéritifs* at the Café du Dôme.

After a week of intoxication that came from just being there, he went around to the offices of the *Herald* and the Paris edition of the *Chicago Tribune,* only to be told by the editors that all they could do was add his name to a long list of earlier applicants. No word came until late summer. On the day he was going to leave Paris, and start back for Cedar Rapids, a note came from David Darrah, the *Tribune* editor, telling Shirer to drop by if he still wanted a job. He did indeed. He was assigned to the copy desk, where two of his colleagues were James Thurber and Elliot Paul. The pay was 1,200 francs a month or, translated, $15 a week.

How did this miracle come about? With all those applicants, it had to be more than luck. Malcolm Cowley says: "Something about him—his youth, his eagerness, his friendly smile, his enterprise combined with a hint of Midwest solidity—must have impressed Darrah, who had to be a judge of men."[6]

After a year, Shirer became head of the *Chicago Tribune*'s Vienna bureau, competing with the likes of Vincent Sheean, Dorothy Thompson, and John Gunther, who became a lifelong friend. In 1931, he married Theresa Stiberitz—Tess in his diary—a Viennese painter. In the same year, he went to India and met Mohandas Gandhi.[7] He was a foreign correspondent for the *Tribune* until 1932, when, in a skiing accident in the Alps, he lost the sight of one eye. He and Tess spent the next year in a fishing village near Barcelona, a carefree sabbatical year lived "exactly as we dreamed and planned, beautifully independent of the rest of the world."[8]

Then it was back to the *Paris Herald,* a job to pay the bills. Not what Shirer wanted. What he wanted was a post in Berlin, and he got it a few months later when he became a correspondent in Berlin for Universal News Service. Hearst disbanded the agency in 1937. That was when Murrow sent Shirer the wire and he joined CBS.

Ed Murrow

Egbert Roscoe Murrow was born the youngest of three sons on a farm in Guilford County, North Carolina, on April 25, 1908. His father was of Lord Chesterfield's persuasion that all he had to teach his boys was to ride and shoot and try to tell the truth. His mother, a devout Quaker, was God-fearing to the extent that she never let her husband raise tobacco. The boys learned the Bible from her, and there are echoes of it in Murrow's prose.

The family moved out to Washington State when Murrow was five, settling in Blanchard, a sawmill town on Puget Sound. The father became a locomotive engineer. He hauled logs from the cutting site, and young Murrow, when not in school, worked as a donkey-engine fireman at the age of 14. While attending college he still spent his summers in lumber camps. He enjoyed outdoor life, the companionship of strong men, and the smell of fresh-brewed coffee in the woods. In 1954, in commenting on a move to place the coffee exchange under federal legislation, he strayed with this nostalgic note:

> The proper way to make coffee is in a five-pound lard pail over an open fire at least 20 miles from the nearest highway or railroad. You let it boil over three times, then hit it with a dash of cold water to settle the grounds—and you have coffee.[9]

Murrow worked his way through Washington State College (now Washington State University) but he found time for extracurricular activities. He was a member of the debating team and the dramatics society, president of the student council, and cadet commandant of the ROTC. "I took a bastard course," he said once, "everything from philosophy to animal husbandry." His system for getting good grades, he confided, was to read books besides those used in class. "You're so knowledgeable, the teacher is impressed." [10]

The teacher Murrow impressed most was a brilliant young woman, Ida Lou Anderson, an instructor in speech. She was a cripple, victim of infantile paralysis, and if Murrow admired her, she took great pride in, and may even have fallen in love with, her most promising student. After she died in 1941, the college published a collection of tributes. In it, Murrow wrote: "The margin between mediocrity and mastery of the spoken word was measured in terms of her confidence, example, and inspiration. She demanded not excellence so much as integrity." [11] He said he had no words adequate to express his indebtedness.

Murrow's campus activities led on graduation to his election as president of the National Student Federation. His life now—in 1930—had taken a direction. Part of Murrow's job as federation president was the arranging of student tours to Europe, and Murrow himself, that first year, visited five European countries. The next year he was back in Europe, traveling from Paris to Bucharest by car, learning at first hand the physical and political geography of the Continent, a knowledge that soon would stand him in good stead. In 1932, on a train, he met Janet Brewster, president of the student council at Mount Holyoke. They were married in 1934. (By this time he had changed his first name from Egbert to Edward.)

After two years with the student federation, Murrow became assistant director of the Institute of International Education. Stephen Duggan, head of the institute, formed a committee to rescue noted scholars from Nazi Germany and place them in American universities. One was the theologian Paul Tillich. Murrow, who became a workhorse on the committee, practically running it, later called the experience "the most personally satisfying undertaking in which I have ever engaged." [12] He often arranged for these émigrés and other distinguished members of academe to speak on the radio, and that is how he came to the attention of executives at CBS.

Murrow joined CBS as director of talks and education in 1935. Through his contacts, he lined up prominent speakers. He was doing this at the annual meeting of the National Education Association in 1937 when he received a long-distance call from Ed Klauber and was offered a post in London. The title would be European director. While NBC had two veterans, Fred Bate and Max Jordan, on the increasingly ominous scene, CBS had only César Saerchinger.

Murrow took the assignment and was in Europe in early March 1938 when Hitler grabbed Austria for his Thousand-year Reich.

The First News Roundup

On March 11, the day the German army marched into Austria, Ed Klauber telephoned William S. Paley to say that authorities in Vienna were refusing to let Shirer go on the air. Paley knew the Austrian in charge of the state radio and called him by transatlantic telephone.

The official was distraught. "I am sorry, Mr. Paley," he said. "I am no longer in charge here. I cannot do anything." Paley heard the man sobbing. Then the phone went dead.[13]

If a report from Austria was impossible, certainly a broadcast could be made from some other country, and as Paley considered this, he thought: Why not a special program consisting of a whole series of reports from European capitals? How were they reacting to Hitler's takeover? Klauber checked with radio engineers, who said it could not be done on such short notice. Paley insisted. They said they would try.

When Murrow got the word, he was in Warsaw arranging the broadcast of a boys' choir. After checking with Paul White in New York, Murrow advised Shirer to get to London as quickly as possible and broadcast his eyewitness story from there. He would go to Vienna. He would fly to Berlin, then catch another plane. But in Berlin Murrow found all flights to Vienna cancelled, so, in an early display of Murrow enterprise, he chartered an airliner and flew, as sole passenger, to the Austrian capital. The bill for the 300-mile flight was a thousand dollars.

Meanwhile, Shirer found all flights to England completely booked; the only way was via Berlin. He arrived at London's Croyden airport, rushed to the BBC, and there, after no sleep for 36 hours, gave the first uncensored eyewitness report.

> When the radio announcement came over the loudspeaker [that a plebiscite to decide Austria's future had been postponed indefinitely] . . . it was the signal for the Nazis to come out and capture the streets of the capital. And yet, as late as 6 P.M., the picture had been quite different. I was walking across a large square just a block from the Opera at six just as two lone policemen were driving a crowd of 500 Nazis off the square without the slightest difficulty. A half-hour later you would not have recognized Vienna as the same city.[14]

Buildings everywhere suddenly were flying swastika flags. Shirer could not help wondering where the flags had come from so fast.

The next day, at five in the afternoon, he received a telephone call from Paul White: "We want a European roundup tonight. One A.M., your time."[15] It was to be a half-hour show with Shirer reporting from London, Murrow from Vienna, and American newspaper correspondents from Rome, Paris, and Berlin. They had eight hours to set it up—for 1 o'clock on a Sunday morning, London time!

Shirer got on the telephone and lined up three newspaper friends, Edgar Ansel Mowrer of the *Chicago Daily News* in Paris and two INS men, Pierre Huss in Berlin and Frank Gervasi in Rome. White also wanted a member of the British Parliament on the program, and Shirer got Ellen Wilkinson of the Labor Party. Murrow called, saying he would arrange the transmissions from Vienna and Berlin.

That was just the beginning. Huss and Gervasi could not participate unless INS in New York gave its permission. The permission was slow coming because of the difficulty in reaching executives on a Sunday, but it came. Speaking fluently in German and French, Shirer struggled with making the necessary shortwave arrangements. Again, because of the weekend, there was difficulty locating the right people. He discovered Paris had no shortwave transmitter capable of sending a clear signal to America, so he brought a telephone line from the Paris studio to a transmitter that was powerful enough. Then New York wanted to know what wave lengths the transmissions would be on, and he had to find out. What were the cues? Timing was crucial. New York, with Robert Trout at the microphone, would call in all points live.

Somehow it worked. At 1 A.M., London time—8 P.M., New York time, the program went on the air, and from Vienna the steady, competent voice of Murrow was saying:

> I arrived here by air from Warsaw and Berlin only a few hours ago. . . . From the air, Vienna didn't look much different than it has before, but nevertheless it has changed. . . . Young storm troopers are riding about the streets, riding about in trucks and vehicles of all sorts, singing and tossing oranges out to the crowd. Nearly every principal building has its armed guard, including the one from which I am speaking. . . . There's a certain air of expectancy about the city, everyone waiting and wondering where and at what time Herr Hitler will arrive.[16]

Hitler entered Vienna the next day.

The broadcast was not the first multiple pickup from Europe; it had been done at least once before. But then there had been plenty of time for preparation, what Shirer calls "months of fussing over technical arrangements."[17] This was the first *news* roundup from overseas. It changed forever the way foreign news was reported. Henceforth, events occurring in other countries would have an immediacy newspapers could not provide. "This," says Sydney W. Head, professor of communications at Temple University, "was the start of a broadcast journalism tradition that eventually brought the Vietnam War into America's living room."[18]

Until this time, network people overseas were regarded as the arrangers of foreign broadcasts. Murrow was not sent to London as a reporter. In the beginning, Shirer, despite his qualifications, was not supposed to go on the air but was to enlist some foreign correspondent for an American newspaper or wire service. In his diary, he wrote: "Silly, this CBS policy that I must not do any reporting, only hire others to do it."[19] It was not an inflexible policy, which NBC shared with CBS. Occasionally on minor stories, or even on as important a story as Edward VIII's abdication, the network man was heard. But these were exceptions. Now events in Europe were so scary, and moving at so fast a pace, the policy was being scrapped. The mind-bind had been broken.

The first roundup was so successful that a similar program was carried the next night, and other nights. The evening broadcasts, "News of the

World" with Morgan Beatty, heard on NBC Radio, and CBS Radio's "World News Tonight" with Douglas Edwards, were offspring. During the Second World War, a 15-minute roundup was heard each morning on both NBC and CBS. Dallas Townsend anchored the CBS morning program, network radio's longest-running news broadcast, for 25 years. ABC Radio has its roundup, "News Around the World." In fact, the morning and evening news programs on network television, with their anchormen and women, are all descendants of that first "impossible" roundup that Robert Trout anchored, making him first in a long line.

William J. Dunn, who was an editor in the CBS newsroom at the time of the first roundup, says of the new programs:

> Nobody thought of them as a permanent adjunct to the news except Paul White. Paul had tasted blood. But for a while after the excitement of *Anschluss* [the annexation of Austria] died down the idea of international pickups died with it.[20]

Will It Be War?

Hitler's next move—in the summer of 1938—was against Czechoslovakia. He didn't want the whole country, he said, just the part called the Sudetenland. The Sudetenland, with an area of 9,000 square miles, lay on Germany's southeastern flank and had a large German population. The Czechs were adamant in refusing to yield the territory, and German forces, infantry and tanks, massed on the frontier.

On September 15, in an effort to avert war, Britain's prime minister, Neville Chamberlain, flew to Germany. Meeting Hitler at Berchtesgaden, he said that if Hitler would be satisfied with cession of the Sudetenland to Germany, he would try to get France and Czechoslovakia to agree to it. Hitler assured Chamberlain he would be satisfied. Three days later, France accepted the formula. On September 21, the Czechs, abandoned by their allies, went along, believing they had no choice.

But the relaxation in tensions was short-lived. Chamberlain had thought an international commission would draw up new boundaries, that Germany and Czechoslovakia would sit down and negotiate. As a result he, and many others in the West, were jolted when Hitler demanded that the Sudetenland be given up at once. The Führer not only set the date, September 28, but the precise hour, 2 P.M.

Europe was close to war. Correspondents—anyone—could smell it. Czechoslovakia had mobilized its army, Britain its navy. France was calling up its reservists. Then, almost in the final hour, as Europe stood on the brink, Hitler condescended to extend his deadline and confer in Munich with Chamberlain and Premier Daladier of France. Mussolini also would be present.

The four chiefs of state met shortly after noon on September 29. They talked far into the night and signed an agreement which not only gave

Germany the Sudetenland but opened the way for Hungary and Poland to take other parts of Czechoslovakia. The next afternoon, the Czech government announced acceptance of the agreement because, it said, "any other decision today is impossible."

Use of multiple pickups from Europe was revived during these critical days. Regular programming was interrupted continually for bulletins and longer special reports. If the news from Europe was grave, it also was bewildering. It cried for interpretation. During the Munich crisis CBS became preeminent as a broadcast news service, not so much because of hours of news aired, or number of reporters assigned, but because it possessed men like H. V. Kaltenborn, Elmer Davis, William L. Shirer, and Edward R. Murrow, who not only could report but could explain as well. Thanks to his long sojourn in Germany and his connections, NBC's Max Jordan enjoyed an advantage over Shirer; he had, for the time being, more access to information. But neither NBC nor Mutual could match the CBS team. And if the coach of that team was Paul White, its star player in New York was Kaltenborn.

During the 18 days of crisis, Kaltenborn did 85 broadcasts from Studio 9, which called "the one heart and center of the entire organization." Just outside the studio were the press association tickers, pounding out a continuous flow of bulletin material. In *I Cover the Crisis*, Kaltenborn tells how he worked.

> Every word [of this material] had to be reviewed in order to get the complete picture in my mind. Queries had to be cabled out to our own men in Europe on this and that gap in the news which had not been filled. . . . Their responses had to be read and digested.[21]

And then, while reporting the events, Kaltenborn would interpret. He not only had a great gift for speaking extemporaneously; he knew the territory. He had often visited the countries involved, he knew the leaders of those countries, and in the case of Britain, France, and Germany he knew their languages. Many of Hitler's harangues were beamed to the United States by shortwave. Kaltenborn could listen to them, take notes, and be on the air with his own translation and interpretation while the wire services were starting to file their bulletin matter. He analyzed everything. Once he incurred Murrow's ire by analyzing Murrow's analysis from London. White says, "The height of something or other was reached one afternoon when, in a fervor of commentation, he even analyzed a prayer by the Archbishop of Canterbury!"[22]

Kaltenborn says every one of his 85 broadcasts—"easily a record for continuous broadcasting by an individual"—was "entirely unprepared, being an analysis of the news as it was occurring."[23] How do all those analyses, delivered off the cuff, stand up? David Holbrook Culbert recalls the analysis of the Archbishop of Canterbury's prayer but also finds more serious lapses. He cites Kaltenborn's statement, after Hitler's speech of September 26, that each time he heard Hitler he detected "an absolute sincerity there." Culbert notes that during the whole crisis Kaltenborn "never discussed what the dismemberment of Czechoslovakia might mean to the long-term chances for peace."[24]

When the Munich agreement was announced, Kaltenborn told his listeners: "One wonders whether it is peace or whether it just may not be the prelude to other demands and other concessions and then finally to the type of demand which no concessions can satisfy."[25] Yet he starts *I Broadcast the Crisis,* published only a month later, by saying: "We were saved from war, I am convinced, by the mobilization of world opinion for peace."[26] He was right the first time.

Of course, Kaltenborn was not the only person going on the air for CBS News in New York. Elmer Davis and two announcers, Warren Sweeney and Robert Trout, who would become a correspondent, did frequent newscasts. (Boake Carter, who had said that *Anschluss* might right the wrongs of the Versailles Treaty, was dropped by CBS in August 1939, just before the crisis. Apparently his outspoken antilabor, antiadministration views pushed the network too far.)

At NBC, at least 460 newscasts were logged during the 18 days. Its principal broadcaster in New York was Lowell Thomas. Announcers handled many reports, and Fred Bate and Max Jordan, and enlisted newspaper correspondents, came up from overseas during all hours of the day and night. In *I Live on Air,* Abe Schechter relates that, during a period of atmospheric disturbances that plagued shortwave transmission over the North Atlantic, NBC sometimes beat out CBS with a usable signal. His assistant, Jack Hartley, had thought of relaying reports across the South Atlantic to Buenos Aires and from Buenos Aires to New York.[27]

But NBC's major coup has to be credited to Max Jordan, who scooped CBS and the entire world press with the text of the Munich agreement. In a letter to Schechter,[28] Jordan told how he had gotten his exclusive story:

> When the dramatic hour came and the final protocol was to be signed, I strolled down the main lobby [of Hitler's headquarters where the conference had taken place]. . . . I noticed a group of British diplomats leaning against the staircase railing. A friend pointed out to me Sir William Strang of the London Foreign Office. He seemed to be my man, so I approached him, asking for his help to secure the official English text.

Strang agreed, and Jordan rushed to an upstairs studio to tell NBC in New York to stand by. By the time he returned to the lobby, the British diplomats had disappeared. They could have taken any one of several exits, but instinct, Jordan said, led him to where Chamberlain and his party were waiting for cars to take them back to their hotel. In the party he saw Strang and Sir Horace Wilson, who was carrying press releases of what had been decided. They were to be distributed later, but Jordan asked for one, A discussion ensued in which Strang explained the broadcaster's needs. Jordan wrote:

> These seconds seemed years. Then Sir Horace Wilson . . . turned around pleasantly and personally handed me the first copy of the

conference protocol, which up to that moment nobody had seen except for the closest advisers of the Big Four. I dashed upstairs to my microphone in record time.[29]

In *Berlin Diary,* Shirer calls Jordan's scoop "one of the worst beatings I've ever taken." In defense he says the NBC veteran was allowed exclusive use of the studio at Hitler's headquarters, "while I stayed close to the only other outlet, the studio of the Munich station."[30] NBC was 46 minutes ahead of CBS with the English translation. Murrow, reporting from London, was first with word that an agreement had been signed.

Back in England, speaking from the balcony at 10 Downing Street, Neville Chamberlain told a cheering crowd, "I believe it is peace in our time." The dangerous moment which history would call the Munich crisis was over. But in his diary, Shirer wrote:

> Ed Murrow as gloomy as I am. . . . We agree on these things: that war is now more probable than ever, that it is likely to come after the next harvest, that Poland is obviously next on Hitler's list . . . and that we ought to build up a staff of American radio reporters.[31]

Building the staff was the next step.

12
"Steady, Reliable, and Restrained"

The first reporter Murrow hired, after Shirer, was Eric Sevareid. Like Shirer, as well as Davis and Kaltenborn, Sevareid was a product of the Middle West, a native of Velva, a prairie town in the bend of a river in North Dakota, where "on the mercy of the wheat depended the presence of new geography books in the red brick schoolhouse, a new Ranger bicycle from Montgomery Ward's, good humor on my father's face."[1]

The father was Velva's banker, whose own father had come from Norway, and the brick schoolhouse was where the boy who one day would cover Washington and a world war first studied United States history and the geography of foreign lands. When drought broke the bank the family moved to Minneapolis, and Sevareid graduated from Central High School there in 1930.

In an unbelievable, backbreaking summer adventure, Sevareid and a friend—Walter Port, president of the graduating class—paddled a canoe 2,200 miles, by way of the Red River of the North, Lake Winnipeg, and Gods River, from Minneapolis to Hudson Bay. For Sevareid's account of the trip the *Minneapolis Star* paid a hundred dollars.

Sevareid had set out on the road to journalism even before that, editing his high school paper. Now he landed a job running copy on the *Minneap-*

olis Journal. At night he attended classes at the University of Minnesota, but at this point it was newspapering, not studying, that inspired him. Long afterward he would recall the delicious smells of the city room and the thrill of hearing "the finale by the great presses below the street."[2]

After six weeks he was promoted to reporter. Covering accidents and crime, he learned about life in the raw. One of his scoops was an interview with Katherine Hepburn. He got in to see the actress, after she refused to talk to reporters, by posing as a waiter and serving her breakfast in bed. He was 19 and making 15 dollars a week.

The next summer he hitchhiked to Seattle, visited an uncle, and traveled by bus to California's High Sierra, where he joined unemployed men scavenging in mountain stream beds and abandoned tailings with the hope of finding gold, ending up, he reports, with "about 80 cents' worth of gold flecks in black dirt."[3] Then back to Minneapolis, hopping freights along the Union Pacific tracks. Not box cars all the way. "I arrived at my father's house with my face black from the coal dust of a locomotive tender, my berth during the final roaring, kaleidoscopic night of clinging to a passenger express."[4]

That fall he began attending the university full time, majoring in political science, though he took some journalism courses. He was an editor of the undergraduate newspaper, a member of the exclusive Jacobin Club, and president of the journalistic honor society. As a campus activist he helped abolish compulsory military training at the university. "I was the naïve liberal," he says, "still feeling somehow that truth could defeat a Hitler."[5]

While still a student, Sevareid had worked for one summer for the *Minneapolis Star*. On graduation, however, he went back to the *Journal*. He stayed only a few months. Europe lured him—the Europe on the verge of a cataclysm of unknown dimensions—and in 1937 he went over on a freighter loaded with Virginia apples.

Two years later, he was one of the busiest young Americans in Europe, working on the *Paris Herald* in the daytime and for the United Press at night. Hugh Baille, president of the UP, had just visited the Paris bureau and offered Sevareid a promotion when Murrow called from London and asked if he had an appetite to try radio. Sevareid recalls his saying:

> I don't know very much about your experience, but I like the way you write and I like your ideas. There won't be pressure on you to provide scoops or anything sensational. Just provide the honest news.[6]

Sevareid was impressed. An audition was arranged. He thought he would be reading a story on closed circuit for a few CBS executives to hear but shortly before the broadcast learned that his words would be carried over the entire network. He speaks of "my hands shaking so violently that listeners must have heard the paper rattling."[7] Again, as in the case of Shirer, New York was unhappy. Again Murrow explained the priorities, and Sevareid became the Paris correspondent.[8]

Sevareid had a predecessor in Paris. His name was Thomas Grandin. CBS had taken him on as a special correspondent in 1938 to help cover the Munich crisis. Grandin was a political scientist who, after graduation from Yale, had studied at the Ecole des Sciences Politiques in Paris and the University of Berlin. Before CBS hired him, he worked for the Council for Foreign Relations and at the Rockefeller Foundation's research center in Geneva. He and Sevareid collaborated for a time. Later, he was a war correspondent for ABC.

In part, Sevareid left newspapering because the excitement of radio appealed to him. It was the first new form of journalism in more than 300 years. And then there was Ed Murrow. He had met Murrow the year before. They talked far into the night, and it seemed to Sevareid that Murrow possessed "that rare thing, an instinctive, intuitive recognition of truth."[9] He was someone whom Sevareid, entering territory strange to him, felt he could trust.

Other Luminaries

Larry LeSueur had been working for the United Press for seven years when Murrow hired him in London in October 1939.

LeSueur—first name Laurence—is a third-generation journalist born in New York City on June 10, 1909. His paternal grandfather published newspapers in Iowa, the first in the small town of Tama, midway between Des Moines and Cedar Rapids. He was agent for the Indian reservation there and published a newspaper at the same time. A son, Larry LeSueur's father, was a correspondent in France for the *New York Tribune.*

The broadcaster tells how, after the war, he received a long distance call from Hollywood. "It was Joan Crawford. She called a couple of times after that. Her surname was LeSueur, and her family, like mine, came originally from Texas. Probably we were related, but it was distant."

LeSueur studied at the Speyer School, an academy for gifted children run by Columbia University. He attended Evander Childs High School, also in New York City. His father died in 1927, the year he entered New York University.

"I was an English major," LeSueur says. "I studied a lot of English literature, so got interested in the literary magazine and was a contributing editor. That's the closest I got to journalism then, but I always hankered to get into news."

In junior year, the Depression set in, and LeSueur took a job as floor walker at R. H. Macy's department store on Saturday afternoons. He says, "When I graduated, work was still hard to come by, and the nice bosses at Macy's took me on full time."[10]

From Macy's he went to *Women's Wear Daily.* He was reporting now and within a year was working for the United Press.

Charles Collingwood was next to join the elite group that became known as "Murrow's boys." And, hired at 23, he was the youngest. His father, an authority on forestry, taught at Cornell. Both parents appreciated the classics and exposed their six children to the works of Shakespeare, Emerson, and Thoreau.

The family moved about. Although Collingwood was born in Three Rivers, Michigan, he attended high school in Washington, D.C., where he was president of the student council. He won a scholarship to a school in California which had 20 students taught by five professors under the Oxford tutorial system. He attended the school for three years before entering Cornell in the fall of 1937. At Cornell, he took courses looking toward a career in law. He was active in athletics—baseball, swimming, and tennis—and during summer vacations worked for the U.S. Forestry Service in the mountains of western North Carolina. One of his bosses was Albert Maxwell of Morganton, North Carolina. Half a century later, Maxwell said, "Charles was one of the best, brightest fellows I ever had on a crew. I followed his career, and I was proud."[11]

Collingwood graduated from Cornell in 1939. He was named a Rhodes Scholar but did not go to England immediately; instead, he got a summer fellowship with the Students International Union in Geneva. One day the U.S. consul in Geneva suggested that in London he might drop by to see Wallace Carroll, a friend of his at the United Press. Collingwood did call on Carroll with the result that during his first months at Oxford he was taking assignments from the UP. When the Rhodes committee said it had to be one or the other—studying or reporting—Collingwood wrote his family:

> The immediacy of the War is beginning to work on me. I am finding it harder and harder to care about medieval law with the war coming closer and closer. . . . I have never wanted knowledge for its own sake. I have always wanted it for a purpose.[12]

So it was full-time employment with the UP until March 1941, when Murrow hired him.

Collingwood had gone around to the CBS office in Hallam Street to see a Mr. Merrill, because that was the message left for him. There was something in the correctness of Murrow's Savile Row attire, and in his bearing, that made Collingwood, himself a "good dresser," uncomfortable in his orange-colored Argyle socks, so he tucked his feet under his chair. But the interview went well. Murrow discovered that the ex-Rhodes scholar, like himself, once worked in the woods, could even "throw" a surveyor's chain,[13] and it was the beginning of a friendship that lasted until Murrow's death.

Thirty-five years later, Collingwood said that Murrow, at that time, could have recruited almost any journalist in London he wanted. There was a certain glamor to radio, and, compared to radio, the wire services were paying correspondents a pittance.

> I was a very young, very raw correspondent for the United Press who had only recently been raised from five pounds to the princely

wage of 35 dollars American a week. Sometime after I was hired, I mustered courage to ask Ed why on earth he picked me. "Well," he said, "you seemed literate enough, and I wanted someone who had not been contaminated by print." By that he meant I hadn't been around the UP long enough to be contaminated by the conventions of printed journalism, the standard lead and development of a story, which was hardly then, and is hardly still, the way you tell it in the more intimate and colloquial medium of radio.[14]

Murrow had other reasons for hiring Collingwood. Besides having read Collingwood's dispatches, he knew his scholastic achievements. And, listening to Collingwood, he knew the fellow had a pleasant, well-modulated voice, one that would finally please those voice-conscious people back in New York. But just to make certain they would accept Collingwood, who was very young, he raised the recruit's age from 23 to 24, a fib that caught up with Collingwood later when notice of his parents' 25th wedding anniversary appeared in several newspapers. To observant readers it seemed that Collingwood's birth was, as the British might say, a bit irregular.

Murrow was delighted to have the "very young, very raw correspondent" on his staff. As for Collingwood, he wrote in a home letter:

> This is the kind of job I like, and I think I can do it. I will be entirely on my own and can do a job of straightforward reporting, giving facts as they are, my own limitations and censorship permitting.[15]

Unabashedly, in plain sight of everyone, Murrow mined the United Press lode. (The only UP man he wanted and did not get for a war correspondent was Walter Cronkite, who joined CBS in 1950.) After recruiting Sevareid, LeSueur, and Collingwood from the wire service, he went after, and got, Bill Downs and Howard K. Smith. Another "Murrow boy," Richard C. Hottelet, had been with UP but was working for the Office of War Information in London when Murrow took him on the team in 1944. A non-UP recruit was Cecil Brown, Rome correspondent for Hearst's International News Service (INS), whom CBS engaged in 1940.

Murrow hired William Randall Downs, Jr., away from the United Press in 1942, after the fall of France. He liked the 27-year-old reporter's aversion to pretense—what Churchill called varnished nonsense—and his quick grasp of what stories were at their heart. At the same time, Murrow recognized in the plain farm belt speech patterns a voice suited for reporting a war in which America was now taking part.

Downs was born in Kansas City, Kansas, and graduated from the University of Kansas in 1937. He reported for Kansas City papers—this was a *real* Kansan—and, joining the United Press, worked in the same *Kansas City Star* building in which Hemingway had worked as a cub. The UP transferred him to London in 1940. He and Murrow met during the Battle of Britain.

Like Charles Collingwood, Howard K. Smith was a Rhodes Scholar.

He was CBS' man in Berlin for a year after Shirer returned to America in December 1940.

Howard Kingsbury Smith, Jr. was born in Ferriday, Louisiana, a town small enough to be served by a couple of churches and rowdy enough for at least one shooting on Saturday night. His father was a railroad conductor. His mother, daughter of a Mississippi River steamboat pilot, gave the future broadcaster a special appreciation for Mark Twain.

Upon graduation from Tulane University in 1936, Smith, "a student in spirit still,"[16] took off for Europe to make a study of Nazi Germany. He worked his way to Bremen as a deck hand on a freighter loaded with lumber and spent two months—one at Heidelberg University—filling notebooks with his firsthand impressions. Everywhere he saw throngs of young men in uniform. Despite the friendliness of the people, "a terror like that which paralyzes a child alone in the dark took hold of me."[17] Germany was preparing for war.

He returned to New Orleans as he had come, earning his way on a freighter, and began working as a rewrite man on the *New Orleans Item*. But he kept thinking of Germany. He had become fascinated by the drama unfolding in Europe and in 1937 applied for a Rhodes scholarship. He won it and went back to Germany that summer. In Berlin, he called on Fred Oechsner, head of the United Press bureau, who was a native of New Orleans. He began hitchhiking, saw the country up close, and found Hitler more frightening than ever. During a quick side trip into Denmark he bought copies of an anti-Nazi paper to take back to friends in Germany. On returning, he was searched by German border guards, arrested, and held for three days in a Flensburg prison. A Gestapo officer noticed Oechsner's card in his passport, apologized, and set him free. He enrolled at Oxford in the fall.

Two years later, on the same day that Hitler invaded Poland, Smith quit Oxford and joined the United Press in London. Because he spoke German, the UP assigned him, after a stint in Copenhagen, to Berlin. There, in 1941, he joined CBS.[18]

Working with Smith in the UP bureau in Berlin in 1940 was Richard Curt Hottelet. British night bombers had begun raiding the German capital, and because Hottelet wanted to see what damage they inflicted, he often went out after the raids to check. This, and his unconcealed abhorrence of Nazism, led to his arrest in March 1941 on charges of espionage. The same night he was arrested the Gestapo called on Smith, who had relieved Hottelet in the UP office and was staying late. He was questioned at length but not arrested. The office files were ransacked.

After four months of confinement in the notorious Alexanderplatz and Moabit prisons, Hottelet and an American newsman arrested in Occupied France were exchanged for two German journalists held for illicit activities in the United States. The exchange was made in Lisbon in the course of repatriating American diplomatic personnel in the German-occupied countries.

Hottelet, a native New Yorker, was born on September 22, 1917. He received a B.A. in philosophy from Brooklyn College and was doing graduate work at the University of Berlin when he joined the United Press. He says:

> After a few months [at the university] it became apparent that the nazification of the faculty ruled out serious study, and when my German had become fairly fluent, it was suggested that the UP might be looking for a young body. It was the turn of the year [1939]. Hitler was getting his outfit into shape for war. . . . I was called in by Bureau Manager Frederick Oechsner, a first-class journalist and a man of unbendable principle, to lend a hand, and I stayed.

It was while reporting for the UP in Berlin in 1938 that he met a young Englishwoman, Ann Delafield, who worked at the British consulate. They married in 1942, shortly before Hottelet joined the OWI in London. "In December 1943," he says, "I felt that government service was not for me and asked Ed Murrow for a job. He was thinking about building up the staff for the events of 1944, and in January I joined CBS."[19]

Murrow's gift for recognizing journalistic talent is demonstrated by the long distinguished careers of these men. Downs was an active reporter until he died in 1978 and Collingwood until he retired in 1982. Hottelet, LeSueur, Sevareid, and Smith also kept on into the 1980s. Shirer, who left broadcasting early, became a historian and is still writing.

On March 13, 1958—20 years after the memorable overseas roundup that reported *Anschluss*—Murrow said in a special anniversary broadcast:

> In putting together our crew in Europe I tried to concentrate on finding people who were young and knew what they were talking about, without bothering too much about diction. . . . There were occasional complaints from the home office on this score, which were generally answered by saying we were trying to collect a group of reporters who would be steady, reliable and restrained, even though they might not win any elocution contests.[20]

Arrival of Eve

Among these pioneer broadcasters were women: Mary Marvin Breckinridge and Betty Wason for CBS, Margaret Rupli and Helen Hiett for NBC, and Sigrid Schultz for Mutual. Of the five, only Schultz was a truly experienced foreign correspondent. She had reported from Europe for 20 years and was working in the Berlin bureau of the *Chicago Tribune* when Mutual hired her late in 1938.

Shortly before joining Mutual, Schultz had participated in one of the unusual broadcasts to come out of prewar Europe. On September 20, at the height of the Munich crisis, Paul White asked Shirer to do a broadcast from the train taking American correspondents from Berlin to Godesberg, where efforts were being made to save the peace. The program was to consist of the reporters' views. There was no broadcast from the train— impossible, the Germans said—but they cooperated in doing the program from the Friedrichstrasse station, and among those interviewed were Ralph Barnes of the *New York Herald Tribune,* Webb Miller of the United Press, and Sigrid Schultz—all of whom showed up *after the broadcast had begun.* But it worked. Shirer caught the train as it moved out of the station.

In his diary, Shirer calls Sigrid Schultz "buoyant, cheerful, always well informed."[21] A native of Chicago, she graduated from the Sorbonne in 1916 and, three years later, was secretary to Richard Henry Little, the *Chicago Tribune* correspondent in Berlin. In 1925, she became the paper's chief correspondent for Central Europe. She interviewed Hitler as early as 1931. It is no wonder Shirer was impressed by her knowledge of European affairs.

In his paper on radio's first women correspondents, David Hosley says: "Schultz was a dedicated reporter for Mutual, and she broadcast fairly regularly, about once a week, between September 1938 and the end of 1940."[22] In August 1940, she was wounded covering a British bombing raid on Berlin, but continued as a Mutual correspondent until she contracted a typhus infection and returned to the United States in February 1941.

Mary Marvin Breckinridge was the first woman employed by CBS as a foreign correspondent. The war had just started. She was working in London as a free-lance photographer in the tradition of Margaret Bourke White, and Ed Murrow hired her.

Breckinridge and Murrow had known each other earlier. They first met at a meeting of the National Student Federation, of which, like him, she had been president. In 1937, when Ed and Janet Murrow sailed to England on the SS *Manhattan,* Breckinridge and her parents were fellow passengers. Like Murrow, she knew Europe. Not only had the well-to-do parents taken her abroad frequently as a child, but as an officer of the student federation she had attended conferences in half a dozen European capitals. And at Vassar she had majored in the right subjects: history and foreign languages.

In September 1939, when Germany invaded Poland, Breckinridge had gone to Switzerland to cover the Lucerne music festival for *Town and Country.* Compared to war, such an assignment seemed frivolous, and she returned at once to London, where Murrow learned that she was doing a picture story, later sold to *Life,* on the effect of war on a typical English village. He proposed that she do a radio report on the subject, which she did with what has been described as "a natural radio voice and a gift for reporting."[23] Murrow may have thought the story appropriate for a woman, but soon afterward she did a report from Dublin on Irish neutrality, no Woman's Page story. She says, "Before the broadcast, he gave me just one instruction: 'Keep your voice low.' But Murrow did say something else. He said, 'Remember you're American and speak like an American.' He meant America was neutral and I shouldn't take sides."[24]

These first broadcasts were tryouts. The people in New York seemed satisfied, and Breckinridge became a staff correspondent. She took Shirer's place in Berlin for six weeks in February and March 1940, but mostly she reported from studios near Amsterdam. Sevareid says, "She did a marvelous job that first year of the war. I remember in particular a broadcast she did on the Nazi leader in Holland, a fine broadcast that caused an uproar in the Dutch parliament."[25] In early spring, she reported invasion rumors and measures taken for defense. After the Dutch surrender, she radioed several reports from Paris.

In all, Mary Marvin Breckinridge made 50 broadcasts for CBS. She resigned in June 1940 to marry Jefferson Patterson, a U.S. Foreign Service officer who, as the representative of what was still a neutral country, inspected German prisoner-of-war camps for compliance with the Geneva Convention. Years later, he served as ambassador to Uruguay.

Betty Wason had worked on stations in the Midwest and covered the Munich crisis for Transradio, the news service founded during the press–radio war, when Shirer recruited her as a stringer in Norway. She made her first broadcast for CBS on April 12, 1940, after Hitler invaded Norway. Some kind of milestone was passed on April 30 when CBS carried a program on which the only foreign correspondents heard were two women, Wason from Stockholm and Breckinridge from Amsterdam.

After that, Wason reported from the Balkans, where she saw frontline action, but her association with CBS was brief. Network officials complained about her voice—"too young and feminine for war news"[26]— though no fault was found with her reporting. Hosley says that Wason's voice was not so low-pitched as Breckinridge's. "She sometimes ran out of breath and stumbled more often." But Hosley says her writing was excellent.[27]

CBS wanted a man. And, ironically, Wason chose her replacement, Winston Burdett, a *summa cum laude* graduate of Harvard who would be a foreign correspondent for CBS News for 37 years.

It was through the American legation in Amsterdam that NBC, in January 1940, came to hire Margaret Rupli. Max Jordan had told members of the legation that he needed a correspondent, and Rupli had called the legation for a job. So both needs were met.

Margaret Rupli was NBC's first woman correspondent. She was a well-traveled young woman with a gift for foreign languages, a Phi Beta Kappa graduate of Goucher who had spent junior year at the University of Paris and had worked as a researcher in Geneva for the National Council for the Prevention of War. She also lived briefly in Berlin. Her husband was a British newspaperman, David Woodward, but when broadcasting she used her maiden name.

Rupli's and Murrow's paths crossed in Amsterdam a few days after Rupli was hired. She and Breckinridge were staying at the same hotel. He was talking with Breckinridge and, according to Rupli, called over to her to join them. She recalls Murrow reminding the two recruits—and himself —of the strength in language that is restrained. "When you report the invasion of Holland, or I report the invasion of England, understate the situation. Don't say the streets are rivers of blood. Say that the little policeman I usually say hello to every morning is not there today."[28]

Rupli did little broadcasting until April, when she began coming up regularly. One of her longer reports was done live from the frontier with Germany. Using a mobile transmitter provided by the state radio, she interviewed a captain of engineers who explained that water diverted from the Rhine was being used as a barrier against possible German invasion. She could not use the officer's name or tell where the interview was taking place. Dutch soldiers also were heard singing.

On May 10, when the invasion began, Rupli stood by in the Hilversum studio, outside Amsterdam, as German bombers passed overhead. Bombs began falling. They could be heard on the talk-back circuit to New York, but Dutch censors did not clear her script before she had to leave. Because her husband was a British citizen, she fled with him across the Channel on a coal barge crowded with downed British fliers and members of the Sadler's Wells Ballet company.

By the time Rupli reached London she had written a graphic eyewitness account of the invasion. Hosley says:

> But by then interest had shifted to Belgium, and she was put on the air only because a scheduled report from Brussels could not be aired. Rupli was delighted that Murrow, who was monitoring the NBC feed, heard her report and phoned to compliment his one-time student.[29]

Later that month, when Margaret Rupli returned to New York, NBC had little to offer her and she began working for the government in Washington, first at the Department of Labor, then for the War Manpower Commission, and finally as a Foreign Service officer in the State Department. She retired in 1962.

Helen Hiett began working in NBC's Paris bureau in mid-May when Mary Marvin Breckinridge, who had left Amsterdam two days ahead of the Germans, also was working there. Hiett and Paul Archinard were a broadcasting team in the same way that Breckinridge, Sevareid, and Grandin were for CBS.

Like most foreign correspondents in the new medium, Hiett had excelled in her college studies and knew Europe. She graduated from the University of Chicago in three years, then, on a scholarship, spent the next year studying at the League of Nations in Geneva. At the same time, she began writing articles for her hometown paper, the *Pekin* (Illinois) *Daily Times*. She visited Italy in the summer of 1936. After returning briefly to the United States, she embarked on a Ph. D. program at the London School of Economics. With the coming of war she gave up graduate study and, in October 1939, did some broadcasts to America over Radio Mondiale, the French government service. One of her assignments was to read the English translation of a short story by Victor Hugo. It was, she felt, a wasted opportunity.

She began writing a newsletter called *Paris Letter* in which she included reports on life in wartime France and letters from soldiers at the front. In April 1940, she started out on a lecture tour in America, but broke it off on May 10, the day Germany, violating the neutrality of the Low Countries, launched its full-scale invasion aimed at France.

Her last lecture was in Rochester, New York, and that same week, in New York City, she saw the news directors of CBS and NBC about becoming a war correspondent. CBS' response was negative. At NBC it was different. Max Jordan happened to be with Abe Schechter when she had her appointment. Jordan was impressed by Hiett's knowledge of Europe and her ability to speak four languages; he was, himself, a linguist. But it was five days before Schechter gave his answer. Yes, she should go back to Paris, via Lisbon, and help Archinard, who had been doing five or six reports a day and was hard pressed. She reached Paris on May 21 and began broadcasting at once.

Still a Girl

Women were making a breakthrough on the home front as well. Just as the war gave women jobs on the assembly line, it gave them jobs in radio newsrooms. But even for that time an unusually large number were employed at CBS News. This is because Paul White taught a course at the Columbia Graduate School of Journalism. There, among women students, he found six writers, about a third of his writing staff. The first who convinced him of their professionalism were Patricia (Pat) Lochridge and Margaret (Peg) Miller. Later, from Columbia, he recruited Ruth Ashton, Jane Dealy, Beth Zimmerschied, and Alice Weel.

Ashton notes that she did not wait for a master's degree before going to work:

> In my autobiography [which White required from each student] I had written, "I was born and raised in Southern California, and hope to live, work, and die there." A month later, during a tea at Columbia, White handed me a telegram. It was from the news director at KNX, Los Angeles, saying I had a job whenever I wanted to report. Meantime, White said that if I chose to go with CBS, he would like to have me start in New York and work part time until I graduated—writing for Bob Trout!

In April 1944, a month into her second semester, she accepted "that great opportunity."[30] Full time. After the war, she did go back to Southern California—to KNX—married, and continued her successful career in radio and television.

How did they fare, these women who through ability and fortune of war became pioneers?

Pat Lochridge received her master's degree in 1938 and joined White's staff the same year. Unlike the others, Lochridge had newspaper experience. A writer-producer, she shuttled frequently between New York and Washington. She was the first woman at CBS to work solely in news.

In the early forties, Peg Miller was perhaps the most active woman in the news documentary field. A graduate of Wellesley, class of 1938, she received her master's degree and joined CBS as a news writer in 1940— local news at first, then news for the full network. For about a year, she wrote a program called "News for Women."

In 1942, Miller and Bill Slocum, director of special events, began writing the documentary series "Report to the Nation." In the 1944–45 season she also wrote the weekly documentary program "Dateline." She married Paul White. At that time, CBS had a rule prohibiting the employment of close relatives, so White took his wife off the CBS payroll and gave her a separate contract. Later, she went to the radio division of the Associated Press as a staff writer.

Jane Dealy wrote hourly news summaries and married a magazine writer. For several years, Beth Zimmerschied wrote hourly broadcasts; she then married Warren Sweeney, the veteran CBS announcer.

Alice Weel, who died in 1969, worked with distinction at CBS for 25 years. She was the first writer assigned to CBS-TV's evening news and became a television producer responsible for scores of special reports. In 1962, she married Homer Bigart, the Pulitzer Prize-winning correspondent.

Paul White took pride in the women he brought to broadcasting. He called their presence in the newsroom "a constructive force in office morale." Sex, he said, had "reared its competent head."[31]

News chiefs at the networks, as well as at newspapers, took on women as "copy boys." (In most cases, the euphemism in broadcasting was, and still is, desk or editorial assistant.) Two desk assistants hired at CBS during the Second World War were Rosalind "Roz" Gerson and Shirley Lubowitz. Gerson became a writer and after the war married Bill Downs. Lubowitz married Joseph Wershba, a writer who later became a producer for "See It Now" and "60 Minutes." She wrote news at CBS and NBC, became a producer for "The MacNeil-Lehrer Report" on PBS, and returned to CBS as a producer in 1982.

A woman who pioneered in special events coverage, principally in Washington, was Ann Gillis. After marrying Bill Slocum,[32] she worked for many years as a producer at NBC.

The most important position in the public affairs area, as differentiated from the news area, at CBS in Paul White's time was held by Helen Sioussat, who succeeded Ed Murrow as director of talks. A handsome, raven-haired woman who had attended Goucher College, then business school, Sioussat once toured the country as the partner of an adagio dancer, Raphael Sanchez. She entered upon a business career and, working in Washington for the Pure Oil Company, met the veteran actor-producer, Phillips H. Lord. He was about to produce a series of radio dramas based on actual cases in the FBI files.[33] Sioussat became his assistant. She says, "J. Edgar Hoover gave me an office next to his, and I'd go through these files and send story ideas up to New York."[34] She not only did research for Lord's successful "G-Men" and "Gangbusters" series but helped with the casting and got the shows into rehearsal. Occasionally, when a part fit her, she turned actress. She also wrote, and rewrote, scripts.

In her book, *Mikes Don't Bite,* Sioussat says the pressures began to tell on her. "Thriving on work, [Lord] toiled all day and thought up ideas all night, and I, of softer clay, was weakening under the strain . . . until one day I walked out into the April sunshine, bound for NBC and another job."

But she never reached NBC. She says: "I crossed 52nd Street and started down the avenue toward Radio City. I had gone only a few steps when I found myself in front of CBS. That gave me an idea. I suddenly decided to check this possibility off my list first." She went in to see Murrow, who, she was told, was being inundated with work and needed an assistant.

> "Only for a minute," they warned me, as he was then overdue at the Astor for the award luncheon of the Women's National Radio Committee. I crossed the threshold and there before me stood one of the handsomest creatures my eyes had ever beheld . . . and there I sat like an overgrown schoolgirl while Ed Murrow spoke of the benefits and inadequacies, and presented me with as graphic a picture of what the job entailed as the few minutes allowed. . . . Thus it was that I came to CBS and found the kind of work for which I unconsciously had been searching.[35]

A year later, in 1937, Murrow sailed for London as European director, and Helen Sioussat took over his responsibilities. In its issue of March 1938, *Good Housekeeping* named her "Girl of the Month."

"A Whiz Bang Lady"

A precursor to Helen Sioussat in public affairs programming was Margaret Cuthbert of NBC, who entered radio in 1925 when she joined the staff of WEAF as "receptionist, program arranger, announcer, and maid of all work."[36] Within a year, because of her ability and the scheduling of more and more talk programs, she was placed in overall charge of lining up speakers. In 1926, when NBC bought WEAF, she became director of women's activities for the network, which meant producing programs of interest to women. Sixteen years later, responsibility for children's programs was added. She insisted that children's stories "reflect respect for law and order, adult authority, good morals, and clean living."[37] By the time she retired in 1952 she was supervising all public affairs programs on the NBC radio network.

Among the radio series identified with Cuthbert are "Echoes of History," "Gallant American Women," and "The NBC University Theater of the Air," which in 1949 became "NBC Theater." This, the most successful of her programs, received a George Foster Peabody Award for excellence in the adaptation of modern novels, including *Of Human Bondage, Arrow-smith*, and *A Farewell to Arms*. She founded "Consumer Time," the first long-running network program devoted to consumer interests.

In 1936, the New York League of Business and Professional Women cited Margaret Cuthbert as "A Woman of Achievement." In 1946, the Women's National Press Club honored her for her pioneer work. She was, in the words of one authority, "a whiz bang lady."[38]

13
War
The People Listened

Germany invaded Poland on September 1, 1939, one month short of a year after the agreement for "peace in our time." In Berlin, Hitler addressed the Reichstag, saying Polish troops had dared fire upon Germans and declaring, "Since 5:45 A.M. we [seven German armies!] have been returning their fire." Max Jordan and Bill Shirer, listening to the fairy tale, translated for the NBC and CBS networks. H. R. Baukhage, the NBC commentator, happened to be in Berlin and also went on the air.

For correspondents in London the question was: What would Britain do? Unofficial reaction—and prediction—were the substance of stories reaching the United States for the next 48 hours. In his scholarly study of Edward R. Murrow, the late R. Franklin Smith recreates the scene in Studio B-4 of Broadcasting House in the early hours of September 3.

> At the peak period for the evening spot, about 2 A.M. (9 P.M. in New York), the American correspondents came to the microphone one after another, each giving the same message—reasonably deduced, one could suppose, from past experience—that, once again, England would back down. As [they] proceeded to deliver that message in the form of a prediction, there was one notable excep-

tion. One man, after nearly three years on this tiny island, had read the British character differently. Ed Murrow filed his analysis last with Cecilia Reeves [the British censor]. She recalled that he handed her his text and asked, "Am I right in this? I've got to be right!"[1]

Here, in part, is what he said:

> Some people have told me tonight that they believe a big deal is being cooked up which will make Munich and the betrayal of Czechoslovakia look like a pleasant tea party. I find it difficult to accept this thesis. I don't know what's in the mind of the government, but I do know that to Britishers their pledged word is important. . . . I believe that Britain in the end of the day will stand where she is pledged to stand, by the side of Poland in a war that is now in progress.

Still, Murrow could not be sure. At the end he said, "But those of us who've watched this story unfold at close range have lost the ability to be surprised."

But, for Morrow, there was no surprise. Later that day, which was a Sunday, Great Britain honored its defense treaty with Poland and declared war on Germany. France went to war a few hours later.

It was *blitzkrieg*, lightning war. Within a month, before Britain or France could act effectively, Warsaw fell and the Polish Army was crushed. On September 17, in league with Hitler, Stalin had invaded Poland from the East. Now, like two jackals, they divided the country—their carrion—between them. On NBC, Lowell Thomas said, "The surprise is how much of Poland Soviet Russia gets, half of the ill-fated nation."[2]

With the outbreak of hostilities, Americans, including millions descended from immigrants from the warring nations, listened to the news as never before. As television would make the Vietnam War what Michael J. Arlen called "the living room war,"[3] radio brought the Second World War close to an earlier generation. For six years, from the German invasion of Poland to the final Japanese surrender on the battleship *Missouri*, air raid sirens, gunfire, and correspondents' voices were heard in the intimacy of American homes. Here the cliché about being "glued" to the radio was born.

A War Policy

At the start, broadcasters made a genuine effort to report the war objectively. On September 5, Ed Klauber issued a four-page memorandum on CBS' war coverage. There would be, it said, no basic change in policy.

> This policy has been to deal honestly, accurately, and fairly with the news and with public discussion. Columbia's announced policy of having no editorial views of its own and not seeking to maintain

or advance the views of others will be rigidly continued. . . . Columbia, as an organization, has no editorial opinions about the war. . . .
Those, therefore, who are its voice in presenting or analyzing the
news must not express their own feelings. This does not preclude
informed appraisals of the meaning of facts.

The heart of CBS policy regarding commentary, which the network
for many years insisted on calling news analysis, is found in the seventh
paragraph of the memorandum. It said:

> What news analysts are entitled to do and should do so to elucidate
> and illuminate the news out of common knowledge or special
> knowledge possessed by them or made available to them by this
> organization through its news sources. They should point out the
> facts on both sides, show contradictions with the known record,
> and so on. They should bear in mind that in a democracy it is
> important that people not only should know but should under-
> stand, and their function is to help the listener to understand, to
> weigh, and to judge, but not to do the judging for him.

The rest of the memorandum dealt with specifics. It listed the network's news sources, the three press associations—AP, UP, and INS—as
well as its own news bureaus. Dramatics were taboo. "An unexcited demeanor at the microphone should be maintained at all times." Rumor must
be distinguished from fact. Listeners should be reminded "that the news
received from many sources is censored and that, therefore, it may be
incomplete and at times inaccurate." There should be balance in news
presentation. It said:

> An excellent example of how fair and comprehensive broadcasting
> can be was furnished on Sunday when there were speeches from
> London, from Paris, and from Canada, but none in Germany
> which were available for broadcasting. We succeeded in obtaining
> the text of various Hitler proclamations and statements and pre-
> sented his side perhaps just as well as if he had spoken.

Still the criterion was news judgment. "The point . . . is that if we will
honestly and sincerely try to present the news, regardless of which way it
points, we shall do a much better job than if we merely strive for a sort of
mathematical fairness."

It was a landmark statement. Klauber was laying down a policy of
fairness and balance the sense of which would be written into federal law
as the Fairness Doctrine and argued over to this day. CBS was not alone in
this; NBC had a similar policy. CBS simply made more of it. Objectivity
befitted America's neutrality; millions of Americans wanted to stay out of
this one. It was, they said, Europe's war.

The principle of objectivity—of balance—was so deep-rooted that
Lowell Thomas could say as late as 1939, before the outbreak of war but
after Munich:

> Radio has to be impartial. If it has a broadcast from the democracies, it must have another from the totalitarian countries. It must balance Chamberlain [prime minister of Great Britain], with Hitler, Daladier [premier of France], with Mussolini.[4]

When Dorothy Thompson, a week after the invasion of Poland, denounced Nazi aggression in her commentary on NBC, the network's St. Louis outlet, KWK, cut her off the air. The isolationist *New York Daily News* said it could not help wishing her son were 19, instead of 10, because then she "might perhaps be somewhat less hysterical in her public utterances."[5]

The style of reporting from Europe at the start of hostilities probably was dictated as much by the character of the two principal network correspondents in London as by decree from New York. These two men were Fred Bate and Ed Murrow. John MacVane, who became NBC's chief war correspondent in Europe, says, "Gray-haired, lovable Bate and chain-smoking, sardonic Murrow . . . agreed there should be no sensationalism in their war coverage. The war was sensational enough." MacVane says that when he and Larry LeSueur joined them during the Battle of Britain, "we joyfully adopted their broadcasting philosophy, and so grew a tradition which only now and then was broken."[6]

Eric Sevareid would add the name of Elmer Davis. He says:

> The great war had started, and a few men like Ed Klauber and Ed Murrow and Paul White saw immediately that among the potential casualties of war were truth and the language. We needed someone who knew in his bones that the only way to confront a wild world was, as Churchill saw it, with tolerance, variety, and calm. The country needed Elmer then.[7]

Assignment: War

With the coming of war, Abe Schechter and Paul White commanded dozens of foreign correspondents who were giving the public what it wanted most, the latest, most accessible word on what was happening in the new world war in which the United States might become involved. They commanded not only the correspondents but, to large extent, the airwaves as well. Generally if they wanted airtime for an overseas report, they simply took it. Explanations, routinely accepted, came later. CBS management, from Paley down, was committed to covering the war. White had a mandate. So did Schechter. And after Schechter left for government service in 1941, his successor, William J. Brooks, a veteran of the AP, could count on support from John F. Royal, supervisor of all NBC programming. Royal had also been a newspaperman. In 1905, as a youthful reporter for the *Boston Post,* he helped cover the Portsmouth, New Hampshire, conference ending the Russo-Japanese War.

The Listening Posts

CBS and NBC began eavesdropping on the shortwave broadcasts of the belligerents, especially those emanating from Radio Berlin. The idea originated with Paul White during the Munich crisis. He suspected that Hitler might signal his next move with verbal attacks, as he had in the case of the Sudetenland. So he set up a small monitoring unit composed of linguists who listened to Radio Berlin around the clock, recording and transcribing what was said in all languages.

After the crisis, the listening post seemed unnecessary and was abandoned. Bill Dunn says:

> When the Germans marched on Poland, we were so busy that apparently nobody remembered the listening post. Not until the midst of the Sitzkrieg, after the conquest of Poland, did I happen to remember Paul's previous idea. I walked into his office one day and said, "Paul, don't you think it would be a good idea if we set up that listening post of yours again?" His reaction was immediate. "Absolutely," he said. "I'm sorry we haven't done it sooner."

While radio engineers were installing equipment for the monitoring service, and the staff was being reassembled, White sent Dunn around to the wire services to propose that CBS, at its own expense, put printers in their newsrooms and on them, from time to time, report what shortwave stations in Europe were saying. Dunn recalls:

> My first two stops were INS and UP, and their reaction was totally positive. They wanted it and agreed to give CBS credit for anything we could produce that they could use to their advantage. At the Associated Press, however, it was a completely different thing. I don't remember who it was I got hold of, but he couldn't see the idea at all. The Associated Press under no circumstances would disseminate news broadcast by a foreign radio station. I couldn't get the point through to him that we weren't trying to sell him that. I practically got thrown out of the office. But White wasn't worried a bit—"They'll be over. Don't worry."[8]

And almost as soon as UP and INS began using the service they were. It was an ideal arrangement. The service promoted CBS and gave—literally *gave*—the press associations news they needed. Everyone was pleased except Abe Schechter, over at NBC, who immediately set up a similar service. It was a valuable supplement to the news, provided by both networks with listening posts on both coasts until the end of the war.

Two Stories from Norway

On November 30, 1939, Russia invaded Finland, and for more than three months the Finnish army, aided by terrain and frightful cold, held off superior Soviet forces. The courageous stand of outnumbered Finns on the Mannerheim Line across the Karelian Isthmus—the door to Finland —won worldwide admiration. But defeat was inevitable. On March 1, 1940, Lowell Thomas reported, "The Mannerheim Line is being broken."[9] A few days later, "little Finland" was overwhelmed.

Now it was Hitler's turn. In a single day, April 9, 1940, he took Denmark and, in quick, audacious thrusts by air and sea, invaded Norway. Betty Wason produced a scoop for CBS when, on April 12, she reported how the Norwegian royal family escaped a German bombing attack. She said a man in the street saw a German plane approach the house where the court was staying and "gave the one and only air raid alarm with his automobile horn. Down the road ran King Haakon, Crown Prince Olaf, the British and Polish ministers, and all the other government officials. They had to stand waist-deep in snow beneath fir trees while bombs crashed."[10]

It was not the first beat scored by CBS' women correspondents. In February, a British destroyer had intercepted an armed German merchantman, the *Altmark,* in Norwegian waters and, in a small battle, freed 303 British seamen it was taking to Germany to be interned. The rescued seamen had come from freighters sunk by the German pocket battleship *Graf Spee.* Mary Marvin Breckinridge rushed to the scene through a blizzard and not only boarded the *Altmark* but got a live interview with the ship's captain. Here are excerpts of her broadcast describing what she saw:

> I climbed down on an iron ladder from the main deck. . . . The holds had no portholes but had some artificial ventilation, and there were pipes along the iron walls for heating, electric lights, and a mirror in each hold, where about 60 men lived. The iron floors were covered with thick rugs taken from ships that were to be sunk, and the men slept on them, wrapped in blankets close together. Each hold was about 10 yards square. . . . The officers' hold had two tables and two benches, otherwise there was no furniture. Homemade checkerboards were left about. . . . Under the gangway, along the middle deck, I saw a line of frozen blood and a lump of flesh which fell through the slats into the snow where a German sailor was fatally shot. A little later, the [ship's] doctor was walking there when a searchlight from the *Cossack* [the British destroyer], then alongside, caught him and a bullet whizzed by his ear. He could hear some of the rescued Englishmen now on board the *Cossack* shout, "Don't shoot! That's the German doctor!" The firing stopped immediately. So there lies the *Altmark,* grounded in a lonely little Norwegian fjord, its rudder and screw broken, some of its men dead, the others confined to their ship, its captives gone, its future uncertain, and the ultimate effects of its adventure still unknown. I return you now to Columbia, New York.[11]

After Norway

The Allies, principally Britain, sent help to Norway, but it was ineffectual. Aided by Fifth Columnists—the Quislings, named for Vidkun Quisling, leader of Norway's Nazi party—Hitler forced Norway's capitulation in precisely two months. It was from Stockholm, reporting the occupation of Norway, that Winston Burdett made his first broadcast for CBS. He was not a staff correspondent. He had been free-lancing in Norway and Sweden and did not join the network until 1941, when he was reporting from Ankara. He became perhaps CBS' most controversial reporter; certainly he was one of its most distinguished.

A native of Buffalo, New York, Burdett attended Harvard, where he graduated *summa cum laude* in three years. After postgraduate study in romance languages at Columbia, he went to the *Brooklyn Eagle* as a reviewer of motion pictures and books. At the time he came to CBS he was a secret member of the Communist Party. Years later, he told a Senate committee he spied for the Russians in Finland and Yugoslavia before quitting the party in 1942. He testified that soon after he broke with Communism, his first wife, Leah, an Italian journalist, was shot to death by Soviet agents. He said she had never been a Communist.[12]

CBS also acquired Cecil Brown from the INS bureau in Rome. It was only a question of time—four months, as it turned out—until Italy came into the war, and in the Mediterranean theater CBS was understaffed. A graduate of Ohio State University, Brown had worked for the *Pittsburgh Press* before joining INS.

In October 1940, Mussolini attacked Greece from bases in Albania and was thrown back. Hitler came to his rescue, invading Yugoslavia and Greece. Brown was in Yugoslavia on April 6, 1941, when German planes bombed Belgrade at not much more than rooftop level and killed 17,000 people. In Greece, another CBS correspondent, Leigh White, suffered an ugly leg wound from an explosive shell and had to return to the United States.

Brown went to Ankara, where he met Winston Burdett. In his book, *Suez to Singapore,* he describes Burdett as an intense person possessed of "a great energy and willingness."[13] Brown had been unable to broadcast from Belgrade after the bombing. Now, using the Ankara transmitter, he got out a nine-minute uncensored report of the raid. Paul White cabled congratulations on a "noble" piece of reporting.[14] It was only the second broadcast Brown had done for CBS, and he was elated.

Sitzkrieg

Until May 1940, the Western Front was quiet. Except for small probing actions, German and Allied forces—British and French—simply waited, facing each other across the Rhine. It was called the *Sitzkrieg* or "the phoney war." Correspondents searched for stories. Abe Schechter got the idea of a Christmas broadcast in which French and German soldiers, confronting each other in the Maginot and Siegfried lines, would sing carols. The French refused to participate in a program with the Germans, so instead of one broadcast there were two—one German, one French—four hours apart.

The German broadcast began, "Hello, NBC, Max Jordan calling from Bunkershausen! My listeners won't find this name listed on any map, for it's located in what you might call No Man's Land." He described the bitterly cold winter night and how he could see about him "pill-boxes and fortifications of all kinds." He introduced the Germans inside the bunker by saying, "Now we enter the chamber. I think you can hear the soldiers singing."[15]

That same Christmas, Eric Sevareid went inside one of the forts in the Maginot Line to broadcast a Christmas Eve service from a munitions room turned into a temporary chapel. It took weeks of wrangling with French authorities to arrange the broadcast. Then, at airtime, someone threw the wrong switch and none of that part of the program was heard. The portion originating from the Mannerheim Line in Finland, which William L. White "anchored," did get through and inspired Robert E. Sherwood to write his play, "There Shall Be No Night," in which an American radio reporter plays an important role. Lynn Fontanne and Alfred Lunt were the stars.

News—all of it censored—still came out of Germany. Network correspondents, along with wire service correspondents and representatives of major newspapers, kept reporting what they could about Germany at war. From September 1939 to December 1941, radio correspondents regularly made their way through the Berlin blackout to the *Rundfunk*, or state radio center. It behooved them to start for the studio early; British bombers came over at night, and if caught in a raid, you waited in a shelter until the all-clear.

On the first day of war, NBC broadcast what it identified as sirens responding to an air raid alert in Berlin. Max Jordan had heard the wailing of sirens just as he was about to go on the air. "Hurriedly I opened the windows of the studio, instructing the engineer to do his best to pick up the sound." Jordan thought he had broadcast the Allies' first raid on Berlin. "[But] afterwards it was found that the air raid had been no air raid at all and only a rehearsal for meeting one."[16]

NBC corrected its earlier statement.

Later, when air raids did take place, German engineers tried to keep the sirens from being heard in the United States. Windowless studios were used, and broadcasters had to speak close to the microphone, which was turned down in order to eliminate as much extraneous sound as possible.

The censorship was thorough. Scripts were checked by a military censor and by censors representing the interests of the German Foreign Office and the Propaganda Ministry. The Propaganda Ministry censor had lived in the United States and watched for slang expressions that might go by someone else. Scripts had to be submitted at least a half hour before the broadcast, but, when they could, correspondents turned in their copy even earlier so as to leave time for arguing about what they could say.[17] They had to have two copies of their script so that a fourth censor in the control room could have one. The idea was that if the correspondent should stray from the approved script, the "watchdog" in the control room would know and cut him off the air.

Despite the watchful censors, correspondents occasionally slipped information past them. Mary Marvin Breckinridge recalls that Shirer, describing the scene on Hitler's birthday, said, "A crowd of about 65 persons was massed outside the Chancellery." The words *crowd* and *massed* caused censors to overlook the small, revealing figure, 65. Breckinridge herself, reporting from Berlin, got away with a devastating line. She was talking about the official Nazi newspaper, the *Völkische Beobachter,* and said, "The motto of the paper is 'Freedom and Bread.' There is still—bread."[18]

The broadcasts originated from a studio scarcely large enough for a table and two chairs. When the network correspondents reported for programs aired at the same time, they took turns going first. Since there were only seconds between the time one correspondent finished and the other started, it was a scramble getting in and out of the small studio without knocking someone down.

The Fall of France

The *Sitzkrieg* ended on May 10, 1940, when German armies, making a massive end run around the Maginot Line, invaded the Netherlands, Belgium, and Luxembourg on their way to France. America was stunned. As in 1914, the invasion of the Low Countries was in direct violation of treaty. Was history—Verdun and the other horrors of the First World War—to be repeated?

It was night in New York when the news broke. All the networks and almost every independent station on the air interrupted their programs when the flash came in. As part of its coverage, CBS lined up the eminent Dutch writer, Hendrik Willem Van Loon, to speak in its New York studios about what was happening. At NBC, Abe Schechter thought of Dr. Alexander Loudon, the Netherlands minister to the United States. A call to the Dutch legation in Washington disclosed that Loudon was in New York. But when Schechter tracked him down, Loudon refused to comment on the situation, saying he had almost no information.

That gave Schechter an idea. "You tell me you have very little information," he said. "We're beginning to get some details, and as fast as there is additional news, we'll get it." So with information as the bait, he got Loudon to come to the NBC newsroom.

That was step one. For step two, Schechter persuaded the diplomat to make a transatlantic call from the newsroom to the Dutch Foreign Office at The Hague. When the call went through, the Foreign Office advised Loudon that he should make a statement expressing the indignation of his government, which had declared itself in a state of war with Germany. It briefed Loudon on the latest that was happening, and Loudon in turn briefed Schechter, who relayed the information to his news desk. In no time, the wires were quoting NBC.

While Loudon was preparing his statement, Schechter, who must have been reveling in the situation, took step three. "I notified the press that Dr. Loudon was in my office and would shortly issue a statement, and soon the reporters and photographers came swarming into the NBC newsroom." Mutual asked if it could send over a reporter. "Sure," Schechter said, "send him." Paul White was not ready to go *that* far. However, CBS did ask Loudon whether he would be willing, after making his statement, to come over and be interviewed by Van Loon. The Dutch diplomat demurred, saying, "Everyone is very nice to me here."

Some news directors would have stopped there. Not Schechter. NBC had been unable to raise Margaret Rupli, its correspondent in Amsterdam, so Schechter asked Loudon for still another favor. Would he, acting through officials at The Hague, see if she could be located? As it turned out, Rupli and her British husband were fleeing the country, but the Dutch found another woman to take her place. She was Louise Wight, the wife of an American banker, who reported that some German parachutists were landing in Dutch uniforms.[19] Air raid sirens sounded as she spoke, and her sign-off was: "And now I've got to clear out of here! Goodbye!" On the cue channel, Schechter told her, "You were swell." He believed it was the first news broadcast from the Netherlands after the invasion began.[20]

Over at the Mutual studios (at WOR) there was a dramatic moment involving good taste. A more important moment than it may have seemed at the time, for a precedent was set. Raymond Gram Swing calmly informed WOR that he would not do his evening broadcast. It was revolt. The 15-minute program was sponsored by White Owl cigars, and Swing explained that serious discussion of the German assault on the Low Countries and interruption for a blatant cigar commercial were incompatible. What Hitler had done was "something that had to be discussed with solemnity and sadness."[21] WOR executives, after consulting the sponsor, told Swing the station was authorized to drop the middle commercial that evening; he was not to regard it as a permanent arrangement.

But so far as Swing was concerned, it was permanent. No middle commercial was again included in any of Swing's sponsored programs. And, seven years later, when Ed Murrow began his nightly 15-minute broadcasts on CBS, Campbell Soups made the same concession.

Hitler took Western Europe in six weeks. The German parachutists landing near Rotterdam and The Hague, joined by reinforcements, breached the Dutch line. German divisions crossed the Maas (Meuse), while swarms of dive bombers—the Stukas—and heavy tanks paced the attack. Then came a breakthrough in the Ardennes, as General von Rundstedt's armored forces raced for the Channel coast. Liège fell on May 12. Rotterdam was bombed with casualties in the tens of thousands on May 14, the same day the Dutch army, without hope of further assistance, gave up the fight.

British, French, and Belgian forces, disrupted by the unorthodox war of movement, found themselves no match and fell back.

Eric Sevareid had sent a letter to White containing a code made up of nonsensical sentences, one sentence for an Allied victory, another for a big German breakthrough. Now Sevareid, with Ralph Heinzen of the UP, was returning from Cambrai, near the Belgian frontier, with a trainload of refugees. He recalls:

> During one stop we saw the distant flashes of big guns to the northeast, then heard their thunder. We timed the intervals between sight and sound, and figured out the distance. . . . So I sent the silly sentence in a cable after reaching Paris. It lay on White's desk in New York puzzling and irritating everybody until White remembered. . . . Elmer [Davis] went on the air and said, as I inexactly recall it, that CBS had learned from a usually well-informed source that the Germans had broken the main Allied defense line inside France.[22]

Belgium surrendered on May 28, to the dismay of France. Mary Marvin Breckinridge came up from Paris.

> There is important news today. The premier of France, Monsieur Paul Reynaud, made a speech on the radio at 8:30, Paris time. In it he announced that France could no longer count on the support of the Belgian Army since four o'clock this morning. The Belgian decision was made by King Leopold himself without consulting either the French or British governments, and it was taken against the unanimous wishes of his responsible ministers. This leaves the entire British Expeditionary Force and several French divisions commanded by General Blanchard cut off in Belgium. Their sole source of supplies is Dunkerque [Dunkirk].[23]

This is believed to be the first radio report of Belgium's capitulation to reach the United States. There was one break. Von Rundstedt's armor stopped short of the port of Dunkirk, and in eight days and eight nights a ragtag armada ranging from destroyers to small fishing boats evacuated more than 300,000 Allied troops.

On June 10, the French fell back across the Marne, and the fate of the Third Republic was sealed. That night, shortly before midnight from the radio studio in Montparnasse, Sevareid made his last broadcast from Paris until after the war.

> I don't know how many more radio broadcasts I'll be making from this Paris studio. If there is an interruption, we will try to continue with facilities installed in other towns further south. The Minister of Information said he still is expecting to see us many times in the future in his present office. He said the situation was better today, but he said he could not give any specific reasons why he thought

so. I do not think there was any deliberate attempt to hide the real state of affairs from the people of Paris. They are a fatalistic people. There is this quality which makes Frenchmen stand half-naked in this wilting heat, feeding their red-hot guns until literally crushed out by German tanks.[24]

Paris fell on June 14. American correspondents, including Sevareid, had joined the mass exodus from the city. A quarter century later, reminiscing on a radio program with Robert Trout, he described the mood of Paris shortly before the Germans arrived.

> That last day I was in Paris there was a cloud of black smoke away to the north creeping toward Paris. I think some oil dumps or something had been set on fire. This was very symbolic. The whole horizon began to darken and close toward the city and, looking up the Champs Elyseés, that great boulevard, there was hardly a car left. I noticed one waiter out, putting the chairs of a café back inside, no one sitting there. The life just simply ran out of the city like a beautiful woman lying in a coma, the life blood draining out of every vein, every street.[25]

Correspondents joined ranks of refugees streaming south, Paul Archinard with Helen Hiett, Sevareid with Edmund Taylor, who had become his temporary assistant, succeeding Grandin. The two CBS men, in a Citroën, moved slowly on clogged roads, past cars that had broken down and horses, dead and dying, that had been dragged to one side. At Tours, where they managed several broadcasts, they had the luxury of a hotel room. But in Bordeaux, Sevareid spent one night in an attic, another in the back seat of his car.

In Bordeaux, the NBC correspondents set up headquarters in a small dilapidated building "that seems to have served until recently as a combined coal bin and chicken coop with odoriferous vestiges of the stable it was in its prime."

> The desk is a dirt-encrusted board that sagged precariously under the typewriter's weight until a kind captain drove a reinforcing nail under it. . . . I've managed to squeeze a disequilibrated chair behind the desk and the wall behind. For a footstool I've a pile of cinders and broken glass. . . . I've lettered "NBC" on a piece of writing paper and applied it with a rusty nail to the shanty wall. O tempora! O prestige of the Radio Corporation of America![26]

A lot was happening. Italy had entered the war against Britain and France on June 10, and, four days later, the Germans entered Paris. On June 16, Sevareid received a tip that Premier Reynaud had resigned and that Marshal Pétain, France's hero from the First World War, was taking over the government. When Sevareid saw the names of pro-German civilians Petain was naming to his cabinet, he knew the aged marshal was planning surrender.

Paul Archinard also had the news that Petain was heading a new government and, beating Sevareid to the broadcast studio, got the word out first on NBC. Sevareid was crestfallen until, talking with Archinard outside the studio, he discovered, to his immense relief, that his competitor had missed the story; Archinard had said in his broadcast that the new cabinet was formed for the purpose of continuing the struggle. Sevareid immediately reported on CBS that, in fact, France was preparing to capitulate. In his excitement, Sevareid forgot to clear the broadcast through censorship. He could have been jailed for it, but no one seemed to notice, though engineers in the studio were appalled. "All work ceased, and they gathered in the corridor, staring at us and one another, unable to speak their thoughts."[27] Pétain spoke on the radio the next day, confirming France's defeat.

An armistice was not arranged until June 20, and the Germans bombed Bordeaux, provisional seat of the French government, on June 19, the day after it was declared an open city. Here is a portion of Helen Hiett's broadcast of that date:

> They started all of a sudden. . . . When you hear the whistle that precedes the bomb, it means it's pretty close, too close to make light of it. Then came the machine guns, a sound impossible to confuse with anything else. The roaring planes then were low, very low, but the close-range bursts of fire made it difficult for us to tell whether the tumult was being made by German planes machine-gunning the streets or whether French fighter planes and German bombers, locked in battle, combined to make the din.

The "din" must have been considerable, for when Hiett emerged from the emergency shelter, a coal bin in the cellar of the studio building, she was surprised to find the building unscathed, "the nearest bombs having apparently gone across the street."[28]

From Bordeaux, Hiett went to Spain, where she scored a scoop on the bombing of Gibraltar and as a consequence became the first woman to win a National Headliners Club Award. Paul Archinard went to Vichy, seat of Pétain's puppet government, from which he continued to broadcast. Sevareid came home to America and after a few months took charge of CBS' Washington bureau.

The Surrender

The formal surrender took place on June 21 in the forest of Compiègne in the same railway car in which Marshal Foch, 22 years earlier, had dictated France's terms to Germany. Hitler, in his hour of triumph, even sat in Foch's old chair.

Max Jordan missed the surrender ceremony; he was in New York conferring with NBC officials on future coverage of the war. His place was taken by William Kerker, who with William L. Shirer shared a half-hour broadcast direct from the surrender site. Not a single representative of an American wire service was present. Believing that first word of the armistice would come from Berlin, the AP, UP, and INS correspondents had flown back to the German capital.

Here is how Shirer concluded his portion of the pool broadcast:

> The French delegates returned to Compiègne Forest this morning. About 10:30 A.M. we saw them filing into Marshal Foch's old Pullman coach. They remained for an hour, and then General Keitel arrived. Through the windows we could see them talking and going over various papers. At 1:30 P.M. there was a recess so that the French could contact their government in Bordeaux for the last time. And then came the big moment. At 6:50 P.M. the gentlemen in the car started affixing their signatures to Germany's armistice conditions. General Keitel signed for Germany, General Huntziger for France. It was all over in a few moments.

The facilities for the broadcast were arranged by German Army technicians who, on short notice, put in a special broadcast line, rather than an ordinary telephone line, from Compiègne to Brussels and from Brussels to Cologne. The correspondents' microphones and amplifying equipment, supplied by German engineers, were set up less than 50 feet from the railroad car. Because they reported live shortly after the ceremony, the two radio correspondents not only beat the wire services but Berlin Radio. The official Berlin broadcast, which was prerecorded, was delayed because it had to be approved by the German High Command. Incredibly, the American radio audience had the news before the German people.

14
Ankara to Singapore

In 1941, Turkey was a good spot for correspondents who wanted a front seat. To the west, Hitler had occupied Romania and was overrunning Greece; to the south, in northeast Africa, German forces under Rommel were driving for the Suez Canal; to the east, the British battled an Axis-inspired revolt in Iraq, with that country's rich oil resources as the prize. Turkey itself was a potential flash-point. A big question mark was whether it would side with Germany.

American correspondents gathered in Ankara included, besides Cecil Brown and Winston Burdett, Martin Agronsky of NBC and Robert St. John of the Associated Press. Later, St. John would be one of NBC's ablest correspondents. Brown gives a thumbnail description of Agronsky at age 27:

> He is a jet-haired, zealous correspondent . . . who gets almost all his information from the British Embassy. He works very hard . . . and he and Burdett are busy cutting each other's throat to achieve what are euphemistically known as "scoops."[1]

Agronsky's first job on graduating from Rutgers University had been with the *Jerusalem Post*. He felt uncomfortable on the paper; it was published by an uncle and he wanted to make it on his own. So he took off for Paris where, after a period of free-lancing, he found work with INS.

In April 1940, the *New York Times* offered him a foreign assignment; it was what he had always wanted. But that same day, NBC's Max Jordan offered him $250 a week, plus expenses, to report from Greece. In one of the most painful decisions he ever made, he chose NBC. Now he was in Turkey for the same reason that Cecil Brown was. The Balkans were lost to Hitler, and Ankara was the best observation post in the Middle East.

Brown soon left for Cairo, where he teamed up with Edward Chorlian, a CBS stringer who also worked for the Egyptian state radio. He had scarcely arrived before German parachutists invaded Crete, and the battle for Crete was the subject of his first broadcast from Cairo. He based his report on the eyewitness story given him by a British officer: "The parachutists came down with tommy guns in their hands, their belts bulging with hand grenades. A great number of parachutes failed to open, and those Nazi troopers came down like stones, screaming." [2] He described how the king of Greece, who had fled to Crete, narrowly escaped death. Sigma Delta Chi, the journalistic society, deemed it the best radio report from abroad in 1941.

Hitler took Crete in 12 days, then on June 22, 1941, invaded Russia. CBS had no correspondent in Moscow and persuaded author Erskine Caldwell, who was there, to broadcast on a daily basis. CBS had similarly recruited William L. White in Helsinki, and NBC would recruit John Gunther, whose "Inside" books were to make him famous, to report from North Africa, Sicily, and the Middle East in 1943. Brown, who would have liked the Moscow assignment, went up to the British frontline, west of Cairo. He saw small battles and sent stories back to Cairo for Chorlian to read on the air. Two weeks later, on assignment from White, he was on his way to Singapore.

NBC took similar action, sending John Young down to Singapore from Tokyo. The assignments were appropriate. It was suspected that Japan might enter the war on the side of Germany, and Singapore was Britain's major naval base in the Far East. Compared to Brown, Young was an old hand in radio. He was also sociable and smart, and one of the first things he did on reaching Singapore was call up Brown and suggest that the two of them meet and have a drink. Throughout Brown's stay in Singapore, they were friendly competitors working together for better broadcasting facilities and battling censorship.

Brown got a bad first taste of that censorship on August 11, 1941. It took him two and a half hours of wrangling with two censors, each second-guessing the other, to clear his two-and-a-half-minute script. One minute of frustrating argument for every second aired. Brown's style of reporting, as well as the military situation, is shown by the first few sentences:

> This is Singapore. The British in the Straits Settlements consider themselves on the verge of war with Japan. Reinforcements of

troops and aircraft have been pouring into Singapore. This island fortress is bristling with guns and noisy with aircraft overhead. It is now in a state of unofficial emergency. Only the home guard defense force remains to be called up.[3]

General Wavell, who had commanded British forces in the Middle East, arrived on an inspection in November. When Brown tried to cable news of his arrival, every word of the cable was killed although the story had been broadcast in India the day before. When Wavell met with reporters, Young was barred on grounds that he had not been accredited by the War Office in London. Frustrated, he left for Rangoon, and soon after that, Agronsky took his place. A partial list of correspondents complaining of the censorship reads like a page from a *Who's Who* of journalists of that period: Hallett Abend, *New York Times;* Frank Gervasi and Martha Gellhorn, *Collier's;* Bob Casey and Leland Stowe, *Chicago Daily News;* Carl Mydans, *Life;* John Martim, *Time.*

On December 7, Brown reported strong indications that a Japanese invasion of Thailand was imminent. A few hours later, he heard the sound of Japanese planes bombing Singapore. Then he learned that Pearl Harbor, too, had been attacked. Incongruously, the next day he sent Paul White a five-word cable that read, OUTTOWNING FOUR DAYS SWELL STORY.[4]

It would be the biggest, most tragic story he would ever cover. Two correspondents, one American, one British, had been invited to spend four days at sea with a squadron including the magnificent new battleship *Prince of Wales* and the battle cruiser *Repulse.* Brown and O'Dowd Gallagher of the *London Daily Express,* the lucky two, were aboard *Repulse.* They put out on the evening of December 9, Singapore time. Two days later, both the *Prince of Wales* and *Repulse,* proud symbols of British naval strength, lay at the bottom of the South China Sea.

On the first day at sea, at 5:30 in the afternoon, a Japanese plane is sighted in the distance. A half-hour later, the captain of the *Repulse,* William Tennant, announces that the ship is being shadowed by enemy aircraft; gun crews should be alert. The mission was to intercept and destroy a large convoy of Japanese troopships coming down along the Malaya coast. At 9:05, Captain Tennant pipes over the loudspeaker that the mission is being abandoned. They have lost the element of surprise. The *Repulse* and her sister ships, the *Prince of Wales* and three destroyers, turn back toward Singapore.

At 10:30 the next morning, Brown writes in his diary: "Fifteen enemy aircraft are reported southeast, but are not in sight. All kinds of signals are being flashed back and forth." At 11:15, nine Japanese planes make a run over the *Repulse.* Brown writes: "I see the bombs coming down. . . . There's a magnetic, hypnotic, limb-freezing fascination in that sight. It never occurs to me to try and duck or run."

The ship is hit, and there is the cry of "Fire below!" Stokers come up on deck for first aid. "They are very calm but wild-eyed. . . . The skin is hanging from their hands and faces like tissue paper." The *Prince of Wales* is also hit, and torpedo planes strike at the ships in waves "like moths around our flaming guns."[5] Two feet above Brown's head, the smokestack is drilled with Japanese machine-gun bullets. He moves to another position.

Shortly after noon, a torpedo tears a hole in the cruiser's port side; another strikes from starboard. She begins to heel over. Gallagher and Brown are together, Brown with a camera around his neck, notebook in hand. Over the loudspeaker comes the calm voice of the captain: "All hands on deck. Prepare to abandon ship." A pause, then: "God be with you."

There is urgency among the crew, but no panic. Everyone is blowing up their lifebelts. Life rafts are being tossed over the side. Brown looks over toward the *Prince of Wales* and sees that she is going down, too. He says in his book, "My mind cannot absorb what my eyes see. It is impossible to believe that these two beautiful, powerful, invulnerable ships are going down, but they are."[6] And he starts taking off his shoes. When he jumps, the camera with all the wonderful pictures he had taken is still dangling from his neck.

The water is warm, but oil gets into his eyes, nose, and mouth. He sees the *Repulse* disappear stern first and fights the suction and survives. Among the debris is a small wooden table. He crawls onto it. The current carries him toward a crowded life raft, and he is hauled into it by a royal marine. Two men on the raft die and are slipped overboard to make room for more survivors. The camera is still strapped around Brown's neck, and in his bush jacket is the precious notebook, "every page water-and-oil-soaked but still legible."[7]

Before dark, a destroyer picks them up and returns them to base, where Brown discovers that Gallagher is safe. Instead of returning to his hotel, he takes a taxi to the cable office and, with an unsteady hand, writes out a 700-word dispatch to be relayed to New York through Manila. He finishes at 4:35 A.M., goes to bed at five, and is awakened at eight with delivery of a cable from CBS advising him that transmission via Manila is uncertain. So he rushes back to the cable office and asks that his story be sent to New York by way of London as well.

In three days, he has had less than six hours of sleep, but he writes another 2,000 words and goes to a Kodak store to see if his camera can be salvaged. It can be. On top of that, he receives six congratulatory cables—two from Paul White and others from William S. Paley, Frank Gervasi of *Collier's,* Joseph Phillips, managing editor of *Newsweek,* and Bennett Cerf of Random House, who says he looks forward to publishing Brown's story.

On December 13, he makes two broadcasts. He suffers pain in his chest and ears. He attributes this to oil poisoning and sees a doctor. Gradually he recovers.

The Censorship Bugaboo

As Japanese forces came down the Malaya Peninsula toward Singapore, censorship became increasingly tight. An example: Brown wanted, in his broadcast of December 18, to report the absence of air cover for British troops fighting the rearguard action. The closest he was allowed to come to reporting this was that there had been "a strange absence of dogfights in the air thus far."[8] Penang, more than halfway down the peninsula, had been evacuated, but he could not report that either.

On December 21, Brown cabled White, asking if he could go to the front. (The reply was negative.) On December 22, Bill Dunn, who had been broadcasting for CBS from Chungking, in unoccupied China, flew into Singapore on his way to Java. Martin Agronsky, the NBC correspondent, arrived from Ankara the same day, and Brown introduced him to the people he needed to know. Brown says that when Agronsky expressed surprise over this cooperation with a competitor, he told him, "When bombs are dropping, you don't have time to worry about scoops."[9]

Increasingly, the question was being asked: Can Singapore hold? On December 25, Brown's broadcast began: "It is now Christmas Day in Malaya. It's a grim Christmas, with not much joy, and people knowing they may hear the whistle of bombs at any moment. The greeting 'Merry Christmas' has an empty sound. Singapore is fighting for its existence, and with great odds against it.".[10]

The next week, Brown and Agronsky, who had been staying at the Raffles Hotel, moved to the residence of friends outside the city. They moved the same day martial law was declared, and again there was censorship trouble. Correspondents could not report the declaration of martial law unless they transmitted the entire 400-word text of the order. For Agronsky and Brown, with the brief radio reports they had to make, this was impossible.

There were two degrees of censorship: the censorship applied to foreign correspondents and even stricter censorship applied to Singapore newspapers. On January 3, Brown and Agronsky learned that, henceforth, CBS and NBC would be subject to the same censorship as the local press. Their protests were to no avail. The official reasoning was that their broadcasts might be heard by people in Singapore and damage morale. Five days later, Brown received notice from the Malaya Broadcasting Corporation that the British would no longer permit him to broadcast. He went to Sir George Sansom, in charge of press relations, who said it was a decision made by military intelligence. Brown protested to military intelligence. The decision stood; he was silenced even though Agronsky and other correspondents argued strongly on his behalf.

It was the view of some correspondents that the aim was to intimidate them and that the British chose to make an example of Brown because he was the most outspoken. It was several days before censors permitted Agronsky to tell Americans listening to NBC that Brown had been barred from broadcasting. The possible precedent, Agronsky said, "is regarded by his American colleagues with real concern."[11] From New York, Paul White protested in cables to London and Singapore.

Nothing changed, and on January 19, Brown obtained a visa for the Dutch East Indies. Two days later, a cable came from his wife saying that White was cabling him to go to Australia or come home. White's cable had not come the next day when he decided, without waiting further, to fly to Batavia,[12] capital of Java, where General Wavell was supposed to set up headquarters for the British Far East Command. Singapore was doomed. There seemed no point in staying in a city from which he could not report. On January 23 he flew to Batavia on British Airways' next-to-last flight out.

Agronsky lingered for a firsthand look at the fighting upcountry. He ultimately made it to Australia and from there reported Japan's conquest of the Dutch East Indies and the Philippines. In 1943, he became a Washington correspondent for NBC's Blue Network, soon to become ABC.

When Cecil Brown arrived in Batavia, Bill Dunn was already there. He had the title of Far Eastern manager for CBS. Sid Albright, United Artists representative in southeast Asia, who was doing his first broadcasting, was covering for NBC. Again, Brown was stymied. The Dutch said they had an agreement with the British not to provide facilities for anyone whose accreditation had been revoked in Singapore. He still wanted to go home. He said he was exhausted, but White wanted him in Australia, the next important origination point for news out of the Far East. Hopes that Java would hold were not high. So he hitchhiked on U.S. military aircraft to Sydney, where he joined George Folster, CBS' reporter who soon would switch to NBC.

At once, as in Singapore, Brown and the censors became locked in battle. White sent Brown a tactfully worded rebuke.

> SOMEWHAT AFRAID YOU UNWITTINGLY TAKING CRUSADING ATTITUDE YOUR BROADCASTS. CERTAINLY HAVE NO INTENTION GLOSS OVER INEFFICIENCY DISPLAYED BY ANY ALLY BUT FEEL IN VIEW SINGAPORE BAN GENERAL PUBLIC WILL FEEL YOU ARE PAYING OFF OLD DEBTS. THUS PLEASE EXERCISE CAUTION REGARDING FAULTFINDING EXCEPT WHERE IT IS NECESSARY IN ANY OBJECTIVE NEWS REPORTING. THINK OVERDOSE HARSH CRITICISMS WHICH FAIRLY EASY FIND ANYWHERE IN WORLD THESE DAYS WOULD TEND EVENTUALLY DETRACT YOUR WORTH AND PLACE IN PUBLIC CONFIDENCE.[13]

Brown cabled a promise to be more careful and that same week received the Overseas Press Club's annual award for best radio reporting. Nevertheless, the question of objective reporting would arise again and ultimately lead to Brown's departure from CBS.

On February 28, he again asked permission to return to America. On March 6, he sailed for San Francisco on the freighter *Moormacstar* and by the end of the month he was home.

"Continue Filing Until Further Notice"

For most of the war, CBS' big man covering the Pacific, literally and figuratively, was Bill Dunn, the same William J. Dunn who had been editor for CBS News at its creation. Dunn not only served as the network's chief correspondent with General MacArthur in his campaigns across the Southwest Pacific to the Philippines, but was a bustling, dependable, towering reporter of more than 200 pounds. When Cecil Brown left to write his book [14] and broadcast from New York, it was Dunn, down from Java, who alone carried the CBS load.

Paul White had sent Dunn to the Far East in April 1941. Dunn says:

> It was more than China's struggle against Japan. White knew we would get into the war—all his instincts told him that—and he told me, "Your job, Bill, is to go out there and survey the place. See what broadcasting facilities there are, get the attitudes of the people, and, when you can, make regular reports." [15]

Dunn's first stop was Manila, where broadcast facilities were first class, but news from Hong Kong had to be sent by cable. The same in Saigon. Tokyo had excellent radio facilities. In Manila and Tokyo, he lined up stringers. In Chungking (Chongqing), the Chinese state radio put out a reasonably good signal—"that is, when it wanted to." [16]

Chiang Kai-shek had made Chungking, in the mountain fastnesses of Szechwan (Sichuan) Province, his refugee capital after the fall of Nanking (Nanjing). The overcrowded, ill-smelling, black-tiled city stood on the upper reaches of the Yangtze, a thousand miles inland, and was safe from Japanese land forces though not, as was repeatedly demonstrated, from enemy planes. With many times its prewar population, it spread over hillsides like an ugly mold.

Dunn says, "For anyone who thought the life of a foreign correspondent was nothing but a round of cocktail parties, Chungking was the answer." He stayed in a three-story hotel called Chialing House, "held together by some miracle, having been the object of scores of Japanese bombings." His room was on the first floor. "When it rained, water came through the roof and into my room without any seeming interruption." The roof of the press hostel, rebuilt after being bombed, did not leak, but there was no flooring—"You walked on dirt the minute you walked in." [17]

American correspondents picked up their cables at the studios of Radio Chungking. All mail came in care of the U.S. Embassy situated on an eminence on the south side of the river. Dunn, with his girth, cursed the logistics. The studios were three or four miles from Chialing House and the embassy even farther. To reach the embassy he had to walk five miles to the main street of Chungking, descend 492 stone steps to the riverbank, and take a ferry. Next, he had to climb 300 steps to the embassy. Then he had to come back. He dared not rest on the steps. He tried once, and a crowd gathered to find out what was wrong.

It was a good time to be in Chungking. Besides the opportunity to witness the courage of a pummeled population, comparable to that of Londoners under their bombing, there were Chou En-lai, serving as liaison between the Communists and Chiang's nationalist government, and Chiang and Madame Chiang themselves. The three best-known journalists in Chungking at this time were Vincent Sheean, Leland Stowe, and Edgar Ansel Mowrer, who three years earlier had participated in the first "World News Roundup" on CBS. Theodore H. White had been there and had just left.

Like other correspondents, Dunn attended new briefings and press conferences. While he was in Chungking, Chiang met with American correspondents twice, with no real news in either meeting. Dunn had lunch one day with Madame Chiang and Madame Kung, wife of H. H. Kung, Chiang's finance minister, at which the importance of American aid was stressed. Out of that luncheon came a broadcast interview with Madame Chiang, one on one. The Chinese official who most impressed Dunn, as he did most foreigners, was Chou En-lai. An interview with the cultivated future prime minister, shared with three other American correspondents, took place in a clandestine atmosphere necessitated by the Nationalist government's effort to keep foreign correspondents from seeing Chou.

> It was to be about midnight, and we went through a lot of Sax Rohmer dark alleys and doorways. They didn't blindfold us, but they did almost everything else. Eventually we ended up in a small room with Chou. One thing about him: He certainly was a genial and warm personality. We didn't learn a great deal—the questions and answers were very bland—but we did get a chance to inspect the Communist leader up close.

Before leaving Chungking, Dunn signed up a free-lance writer, Jim Stewart, to string for CBS. Stewart did several broadcasts. The son of missionary parents, he had lived in China much of his life.

Dunn left in late November 1941. He rode in a convoy down the Burma Road, crossing into Burma at Want'ing. At Lashio, about 130 miles south of Want'ing, he caught a plane to Rangoon. After registering at the Strand Hotel, the first thing he did was take a shower, than a tub bath. "It was the first hot and cold running water I had seen in two months. And, boy, was it beautiful!"

The euphoric feeling was short-lived. The next morning—December 8, Rangoon time—he got the news: Both Pearl Harbor and Manila had been bombed by the Japanese. No broadcast facilities were available to correspondents in Rangoon; everything went out by cable. So Dunn flew, via Singapore, to Batavia, which not only had excellent facilities for radio transmission but was where there was to be an Allied headquarters.[18] Two hours after Dunn took off, Rangoon was bombed for the first time. He congratulated himself on his timing, but soon afterward, as he was walking across an airstrip on the outskirts of Batavia, two Japanese light bombers came over the field.

> They were headed straight at me. I fell on my face, ate a lot of dirt and did a lot of praying, but fortunately I was straddled by the string of bombs and not hit. However, I never took a shortcut across an airfield again during the war.[19]

Java was doomed. Hong Kong and Singapore had fallen. The Philippines were lost. If the Allies could take comfort in the Battle of Macassar Strait, in which four Japanese transports were sunk, it was quickly cancelled by losses in the Battle of the Java Sea. Japanese ground forces, closing in, made landings in Sumatra to the west and Borneo to the north. Shortly before the landings, the Allies, feeling the pressure, had moved their headquarters inland from Batavia to Bandung, and Dunn followed. So did the Mutual stringer, Frank Cuhel. Albright, the NBC stringer, left for Australia. British press officers had located a ship leaving for Australia and were urging all correspondents to get out as quickly as possible.

Cuhel, a former All-American football player at the University of Iowa, had been a trader representing American and Dutch firms in Java. He had had no news experience but caught on rapidly. For some reason, Mutual made little use of him during the last critical days so that, for radio, Dunn had the Dutch East Indies story virtually to himself. Moreover, because of the swiftness of radio, he beat the press services on both the invasion of Java on February 28 and the Battle of the Java Sea.

Dunn did two broadcasts on Sunday, March 1, when the Japanese were coming ashore at three points. He and Cuhel planned to leave on Monday.

> But the Air Force, which we had counted on to supply a plane to get us out, didn't send the plane, and here we were caught, a half dozen of us, with no transportation. Well, Cuhel and I, and Winston Turner of the Associated Press and George Weller of the *Chicago Daily News*, got into Cuhel's car and started for Tjilatjap, a little port on the south coast of Java, making almost all the run after dark. When we got there, much to our dismay, the harbor was empty. There wasn't a soul around.

Around midnight they learned that there would be another ship in the morning:

> Actually, two ships showed up. One of them was the MS *Janssens,* and that's the one we were put on board. Two correspondents were put on the other ship, and the following morning that ship was sunk off the coast of Sumatra, trying to get to India. One of the correspondents, Whit Hancock of the Associated Press, was drowned, and William MacDougall of the United Press managed to survive and spent the rest of the war in a concentration camp in Sumatra.[20]

Dunn learned later that out of five merchantmen leaving Java that week, the *Janssens* was the only one that was not sunk.

On March 11, on orders from President Roosevelt, General MacArthur left the Philippines, where the situation was hopeless, and proceeded to Melbourne, to become supreme commander of Allied Forces in the Southwest Pacific. After several months, MacArthur moved his command up the east coast of Australia to Brisbane. He was now hundreds of miles closer to the scene of action. However, for network correspondents the change was an aggravation. Brisbane had no transmitter with a signal capable of spanning the Pacific. They were stuck in Sydney, halfway between Melbourne and Brisbane. They appealed for a line linking Sydney and Brisbane so that they could broadcast from Brisbane, but were refused.

The aggravation would remain until MacArthur began his long, arduous, island-to-island, stepping-stone drive toward Japan.

15
The Battle of Britain

The air battle for Britain began on July 10, 1940, three weeks after the fall of France. Hitler's aim at the start was annihilation of the Royal Air Force, since for invasion of England he needed control of the sky. In this stage, England's airfields and Channel ports were heavily bombed. Hitler hoped that British fighter planes, rising to defend these targets, would be destroyed by his own fighters, which outnumbered British aircraft two to one. But the Spitfire proved superior to the Messerschmitt—German losses far exceeded British losses—and Hitler switched tactics. Starting in September, he tried through repeated bombings to smash London and break Britain's will.

It was the radio reporting from London, more than any other reporting, which brought the Battle of Britain into the consciousness of America. And it was Edward R. Murrow, more than any other radio reporter, who caught the listeners' attention. Radio had dimensions—instantaneity and sound—which newspapers did not have, and no reporter in radio could match Murrow, working in the medium for which he seemed to have been made. There were the childhood Bible readings that taught him the power of language, the rich, controlled voice trained in college, the study of military science and history, varied radio experience, and wide travel.

Intelligence, seemingly inexhaustible energy, complete dedication to what he was doing, and the integrity which inspired trust also helped make him, poet and pragmatist, the foremost broadcaster of his time.

Murrow and Fred Bate of NBC attended the same briefings, visited the same airfields, witnessed the same bombings, saw many of the same dead. Both were so highly respected by the British that they alone, with John MacVane, who succeeded Bate, were allowed to broadcast live without prior censorship. Bate was a strong competitor. He had been overseas longer than Murrow. He knew many of Britain's leaders personally, ranging from Edward when he was king to General Harold Alexander, commander of British forces in North Africa and the Middle East. He, as well as Murrow and MacVane, attempted rooftop broadcasts during bombing raids. Yet it was CBS' coverage which captured America's attention. The difference, Bate said afterward, was that CBS had Murrow.[1]

There was a spirit of camaraderie among American correspondents in London in those dangerous days. The MacVanes, John and Lucy, would visit the Murrows in their flat on Hallam Street. Traveling to an airfield or training camp, Bate might catch a ride with Murrow in his open roadster.[2] MacVane taught Larry LeSueur how to play tennis. James Reston of the *New York Times* shared quarters with Bate and occasionally, early in the war, did broadcasts for NBC under a different name. There was little competition for the exclusive story. The whole thing was too big. Too all-encompassing. Also, the British discouraged exclusives, making it a point wherever possible to grant equal opportunities. If the NBC correspondent was cleared to go out on a mine sweeper, so was the correspondent for CBS.

Certainly the danger was shared equally. Every reporter could, and probably did, talk about his close call, how he chanced not to be in the building when it took a direct hit, or how something, some instinct, told him to stay in a doorway and not go into the street. Murrow advised LeSueur that the correct if undignified posture to assume when caught outdoors during a bombing was to lie flat in the gutter head down, mouth open, hands over the ears. It was advice Murrow himself took five times in a single night. He had given up going into bomb shelters except for stories, reasoning, "Once you start going into shelters, you lose your nerve."[3] Again and again, Murrow took risks. LeSueur has recalled dining with Murrow at a Mayfair hotel—under a glass roof—while bombs fell in the vicinity. Murrow, he said, seemed completely unperturbed and continued eating.[4] MacVane says in his memoir, "I do not think any of us really expected to live through the war."[5]

The CBS and NBC offices were damaged repeatedly, perhaps because they were close to the BBC, which was a prime target. Murrow said in one broadcast, "These words were written on a table of good English oak which sheltered me three times as bombs tore down in the vicinity."[6] It was a rare reference to his own danger. Most of his pieces were written by dictation. He marshaled his thoughts, arranging them in his head—all the thoughts and all the facts—then dictated his piece to Katherine Campbell, the capable young Scotswoman who was secretary. His business, he knew, was the spoken word.

From September to December 1940, there were 90 continuous days of raids on London. On December 8, both network offices and Broadcasting House were badly damaged by a magnetic mine that was dropped by parachute. Fred Bate, caught in his office, suffered head and leg injuries and burns. When he got out of the hospital, NBC furloughed him, and John MacVane carried on alone until Bate returned from the States months later.

It was during this time that MacVane, battling exhaustion, came up on NBC three, four, maybe five times a day to become one of the best known of all the war correspondents. A graduate of Phillips Exeter Academy and Williams College, he, like Charles Collingwood and Howard K. Smith, had studied at Oxford and been a print journalist, starting with the *Brooklyn Eagle* and then working in England for the *London Daily Express* and INS. "He struck me," LeSueur says, "as the typical Scotsman, a hard-working, very sincere sort of guy."[7] In 1942, MacVane was the only network correspondent to go on the disastrous seaborne expedition against Dieppe on the French coast. Of the 6,100 who embarked on that hit-and-run raid, only 2,500 returned. Less than half. The rest were killed or captured.

Kuybyshev Calling

In October 1941, the Germans were closing in on Moscow, and the Soviet government moved beyond the Volga to Kuybyshev, 600 miles to the southeast. NBC's Moscow correspondent, Robert Magidoff, moved with it. For its Moscow broadcasts, CBS had been using a stringer, Denis McEvoy of the *Chicago Times*. Now, to match NBC, it decided to send Larry LeSueur.

LeSueur sailed from Scotland with two other American correspondents, Walter Kerr of the *New York Herald Tribune* and Eddy Gilmore of the Associated Press. Their rusty freighter, loaded with munitions, was part of a five-ship convoy bound for Archangel, just below the Arctic Circle. It took three weeks for the convoy, running a gauntlet of German submarines, to reach Russia, then another 17 days for the correspondents to reach Kuybyshev by train.

Because of the nine-hour time difference between Kuybyshev and New York, many broadcasts had to be made at 4 o'clock in the morning. Le Lesueur developed a routine.

> I would write the broadcast in the early evening, make the three-mile walk back and forth to the censorship office through the snow, drop off a copy at the radio station for their scrutiny, and return to the hotel to go to sleep. The station phoned me at three in the morning.[8]

Then he would go to the station and make his broadcast in a studio soundproofed with magnificent rugs from Bokhara and Turkestan. The director of Kuybyshev Radio was a Russian who had been an exchange student at Columbia University. In 1941, the correspondents found the Russians stern but civil. In 1942, after the United States entered the war, the relationship turned warm. "Ah, Americanyits," Russian sentries would say on seeing the American passport, and smile.

LeSueur reported from Russia for more than a year. He came back to America to write a book about his experiences, then returned to England to cover the Normandy invasion. Magidoff stayed on.

"There Are No Words . . ."

Broadcasting House, headquarters of the BBC, was a fairly new, stone-faced building in Portland Place, in the heart of London. Studio B-4, where the reports to America originated, was located in the subbasement, but the tremor of bombs could be felt there, and once, when the building was hit, the plate glass between the control room and studio was shattered. Because of the five-hour difference between New York and London, many broadcasts came in the early morning hours. Sometimes, as a correspondent spoke into the microphone, another would be nearby, asleep on the floor. It was from this room, night after night, that Murrow made his reports starting, "This . . . is London," always pausing after the first word as suggested by Ida Lou Anderson, his speech instructor at Washington State, who kept in touch.

Here is what Murrow's reporting was like:

> I talked with pilots as they came back from Dunkirk . . . the cream of the youth of Britain. As we sat there, they were waiting to take off again. They talked of their own work, discussed the German air force with all the casualness of Sunday morning quarterbacks discussing yesterday's football game. There were no nerves, no profanity and no heroics. There was no swagger about those boys in wrinkled and stained uniforms. The movies do that sort of thing much more dramatically than real life.[9]

> This afternoon I saw a military maneuver that I shall remember for a long time, a company of women dressed in Royal Air Force blue marching in close order. Most of them were girls with blond hair and plenty of make-up. They marched well, right arms thrust forward and snapped smartly down after the fashion of the Guards. They swung through a gate into an airdrome that had been heavily bombed only a few hours before. Some of them were probably frightened, but every head was up.[10]

> We crossed the river and drove up to a little plateau, which gave us a view from the mouth of the Thames to London. . . . Up toward London we could see billows of smoke fanning out above

the river, and over our heads the British fighters, climbing almost straight up, trying to intercept the bombers before they got away. . . . The fires up the river had turned the moon blood red.[11]

Today I went to buy a hat. My favorite shop had gone, blown to bits. . . . I went to another shop to buy flashlight batteries. I bought three. The clerk said, "You needn't buy so many. We'll have enough for the whole winter." But I said, "What if you aren't here?" There were buildings down in that street, and he replied, "Of course we'll be here. We've been in business here for 150 years."[12]

The next week, he said in a broadcast, "There are no words to describe the thing that is happening. . . . These things must be experienced to be understood."[13]

The network correspondents wanted to broadcast the description of a bombing raid while it was in progress. For months, Murrow and Fred Bate sought permission in vain. The BBC did offer to pipe the sounds of battle down to Studio B-4 to be mixed with their reports, but neither Bate nor Murrow believed that would be quite honest. To demonstrate that they could make such eyewitness broadcasts of London under attack without compromising security, they made recordings from the rooftop of Broadcasting House during several raids. Ultimately, after an appeal to Churchill, permission was granted. But, perversely, whenever the overseas circuits were ready, and New York said, "Go ahead, London," the German bombers vanished.

Murrow wrote better than he ad libbed, but his broadcast of September 22, 1940, from the roof of Broadcasting House is a classic. This was a moment he wanted, and there was so little, it seemed to him, that he could say. Reading the transcript of that broadcast, one can almost hear the pauses between sentences as he searched, very effectively, for something to say.

I'm standing again tonight on a rooftop looking out over London, feeling rather large and lonesome. In the course of the last 15 or 20 minutes there's been considerable action up here, but at the moment there's an ominous silence hanging over London. But, at the same time, a silence that has a great deal of dignity. Just straightaway in front of me the searchlights are working. I can see one or two bursts of antiaircraft fire far in the distance. Just on the roof across the way I can see a man wearing a tin hat, a pair of powerful night glasses to his eyes, scanning the sky. Again, looking in the opposite direction, there is a building with two windows gone. Out of one window there waves something that looks like a white bed sheet, a window curtain swinging free in this night breeze. It looks as though it were being shaken by a ghost. There are a great many ghosts around these buildings in London. The searchlights straightaway, miles in front of me, are still scratching the sky.

Soon after that, in November 1940, Murrow returned to America on a three-month furlough. His replacement in London was Robert Trout. Janet Murrow, who made occasional broadcasts for CBS and the BBC, had gone on ahead of him to campaign for Bundles for Britain, a relief agency. Four years earlier, on leaving for London, Murrow had been little known. Now he was famous. Never had so many newspaper reporters wanted to interview a radio reporter; seldom had there been so many requests for any reporter to lecture.

On December 2, CBS held a dinner in his honor in the great ballroom of the Waldorf-Astoria Hotel, at which the speakers, besides Murrow, were William S. Paley and Archibald MacLeish, the librarian of Congress. Paley, in paying tribute to Murrow, urged preservation of freedom of speech, which for broadcasters, he said, was freedom of the air.[14] Murrow reported that the British people—"the world's greatest civilian army"—was determined to fight on. "The flame of courage is high." But they are tired, he said. They believe

> that unless the United States enters this war, Britain may perish or at best secure a stalemate peace. . . . No one who has lived and worked in London for the last three years can doubt that the important decision, perhaps the final decision, that will determine the course of human affairs will be made not in front of Moscow, not on the sands of Libya, but along the banks of the Potomac. General headquarters for the forces of decency is now on Pennsylvania Avenue.

MacLeish, when he spoke, said that Murrow through his broadcasts had "accomplished one of the great miracles of the world." He told Murrow, "You destroyed a superstitition . . . the superstition that what is done beyond 3,000 miles of water is not really done at all. . . . You burned the city of London in our houses, and we felt the flames that burned it. You laid the dead of London at our doors."

MacLeish concluded by saying that so long as the American people were told truthfully what they had to face, they would not be afraid and would face it. What the American people had to face five days later was the Japanese attack on Pearl Harbor.

16
"We Interrupt
This Program . . ."

It was Sunday. Many Americans were relaxing after dinner when, at 2:25 P.M., Eastern Time, the United Press flash moved on news printers across the country.

> WASHINGTON—WHITE HOUSE ANNOUNCES JAPANESE HAVE ATTACKED PEARL HARBOR.

A minute later, Mutual's flagship station, WOR, interrupted its broadcast of the Dodger–Giant football game with the UP flash. The news went out over the NBC Red and Blue Networks at 2:28. Not until three minutes later did John Daly, with more than the bare announcement, break into the CBS network.

> The Japanese have attacked Pearl Harbor, Hawaii, by air, President Roosevelt has just announced. The attack was also made on naval and military activities on the principal island of Oahu. The news came in just after the two Japanese envoys in Washington made the appointment to call at the State Department and follows reports from the Far East that Japan was ready to launch an attack on Thailand.

CBS switched to Washington, where its chief of bureau, Albert Warner, said the attack meant the President would ask Congress for a declaration of war and that there was no doubt that such a declaration would be forthcoming. In the midst of his report, at 2:39, Warner interrupted himself to say, "And just now comes word from the President's office that a second air attack has been reported on Army and Navy bases in Manila."

The next switch was to London and Robert Trout, who said that it was too early to give the British reaction—he had just heard the news from Daly—but that Churchill's government had "made plain what would happen if America became involved in a war with Japan." They would stand together.

At 2:47, CBS raised its Manila stringer, Ford Wilkins, but he was cut off the air, presumably because of censorship. Other attempts to call in Wilkins failed, though Daly was able to report on a telephone conversation with KGMB, the CBS affiliate in Honolulu, which said the raid was still on.[1] At 3:30, he also talked by telephone with John Raleigh, CBS' man in Batavia, and reported that while there was no news of a Japanese invasion of the Netherlands East Indies, police were rounding up Japanese residents. (The invasion came in January).

Swiftly, at all networks, skeleton weekend staffs were reinforced. NBC rang its fourth chime, alerting its news staff and all affiliated stations to the breaking story, a device inspired by the then familiar three-note chimes marking station breaks. The signal, to be sounded only for news of utmost importance, was first used when the Hindenburg exploded.

Art Feldman, NBC's special events supervisor, heard the first news at home. Before taking a cab for Radio City, he telephoned the NBC switchboard and told it to put in overseas calls to KGU and KZRH, the NBC stations in Honolulu and Manila. At the same time, he ordered up shortwave circuits. As a result, NBC had a direct, on-the-air telephone report from Honolulu at 4:06. After two minutes, the circuit was taken over by the military, but NBC got it back at 4:46 for an eyewitness report. Also that afternoon, NBC listeners heard Bert Silen, manager of KZRH, describe the Philippines raid. Sidney Albright came up from Batavia.

In Washington, President Roosevelt immediately called an emergency meeting of his cabinet, and for the first time radio reporters were permitted to bring their gear into the White House press room and broadcast. One of the first reporters to go on the air—he claimed to be the first—was H. R. Baukhage of NBC, who said his microphone was set up before the others. According to his obituary in the *Washington Star,* it was the beginning of a marathon broadcast that lasted more than eight hours. He may have got the break, the newspaper said, because of his friendship with Steve Early, the White House press secretary.[2]

By 4 o'clock the networks' news operations were in high gear. Bulletins, read as fast as they came in, supplemented radio pickups from all over the free world. And in the evening, the networks put on special programs summarizing and interpreting what they knew up to that time. Shortly before midnight, CBS resorted to summarizing the lead editorials of 29 representative morning newspapers. It was CBS' view that, having denied itself an editorial position in conformity with its firm policy against editorializing, it could nevertheless "swiftly and impartially canvass the editors of the nation." It found the consensus to be: "War is here; let's win it."[3]

Ed Murrow was in suburban Washington playing golf when the news broke. He did a broadcast at 7:20, observing that in the American capital he saw the same calmness and determination that the British had shown when war came to them. After the broadcast he hurried to the White House, where he and Janet had a dinner appointment with President and Mrs. Roosevelt.

Roosevelt did not come down for dinner but sent a message for Murrow to wait. He was waiting in the hall just outside the Oval Office when Harry Hopkins, Roosevelt's most intimate confidant, greeted him and asked what he was doing there. Murrow said he was waiting for the President but perhaps he had better leave. Hopkins told him to stay and invited him to come to his White House quarters for a drink.

It was a half hour past midnight when the President sent for the reporter who, more than any other, had brought the Battle of Britain home to the American people. Roosevelt started the conversation with a series of questions: How were the British people reacting to their bombardment? Did they still believe in ultimate victory? How did they feel toward the United States? When the President was through with questions, he gave Murrow a complete picture of what had happened at Pearl Harbor, including casualties and number of American planes destroyed on the ground. Roosevelt stressed the phrase "on the ground," betraying his chagrin that they had never got into the fight.

For Murrow this was a tremendous scoop. Our losses at Hickham Field and Pearl Harbor were not announced until long afterward, and here, less than 24 hours after the attack, the President had given him this vital information. Later that night, back in his hotel room, Murrow paced the floor. One biographer, Alexander Kendrick, quotes him as anguishing, "The biggest story of my life. I can't make up my mind whether it's my duty to tell it, or to forget it."[4]

He forgot it. Another fine reporter, Bill Lawrence, says in his memoir, "Murrow was that kind of conscientious and patriotic reporter."[5]

Today it seems incredible that the networks, reporting the latest information on the Japanese attacks, which clearly meant America's entry in worldwide war, continued at the same time with their usual programs, no matter how often interrupted. CBS, for example, persisted with its New York Philharmonic concert in progress in Carnegie Hall, "The Prudential Family Hour," "The Ford Sunday Evening Hour," and the Gene Autry show.

Never before had broadcast journalists had to handle so big a story. They were learning. In that time, to delay or interrupt commercial programming throughout an entire afternoon and evening showed enterprise, even daring. The only time it had been done on anything approaching this scale had been during the Munich crisis of 1938 and the outbreak of war in Europe. *Broadcasting,* in its issue of December 15, praised radio's performance, saying the networks had "swung smoothly into 24-hour wartime operation with a minimum of confusion." In *Dateline: Washington,* Theodore F. "Ted" Koop says:

> On that "day of infamy" . . . radio news cast off its adolescence. No longer did its voice break with uncertainty or emotion; it spoke firmly, confidently. Years of experimentation, of trial and error had brought results.[6]

On Monday, President Roosevelt went before a joint session of Congress to ask for a declaration of war. Within an hour, his request was granted. (The radio audience could hear the clerk of the House read the enabling resolution, though it did not hear the vote.) Great Britain declared war on Japan the same day. In a rare joint broadcast, John MacVane of NBC and Charles Collingwood of CBS reported the action as it was taking place in the House of Commons.

On the evening of December 9, Roosevelt sat down before six microphones—two for each network—for one of his most important fireside chats. He told the American people, "We are now in this war. We are all in it—all the way." The war would be hard, he said, but it would be won, and so would the peace. According to the C. E. Hooper rating service, 90 million people—the largest audience up to that time—heard the President. Two days later, when Germany and Japan declared war on the United States, Congress responded in kind. The battle was joined.

On December 16, Roosevelt established an Office of Censorship and drafted Byron Price, executive editor of the Associated Press, as its director. Ted Koop, the future CBS vice president who had worked for the AP, became Price's deputy.[7] A broadcaster, John Harold Ryan, who one day would become president of the National Association of Broadcasters, had charge of radio. This censorship on the home front was voluntary; news stories were not passed by a censor unless a newspaper, radio station, or network asked that they be checked. Under the censorship code, disclosure of vital information such as troop movements was prohibited. So were forecasts of the weather, which might aid enemy submarines lurking off the coast. Sports announcers were not to say whether a game was being called because of rain. And there were to be no more man-in-the-street interviews. A spy might participate and broadcast a code message.

Voluntary censorship was a gamble, an expression of confidence in the patriotism and good sense of the people who handled news. And, for the most part, it worked. Erik Barnouw relates that, in a Mutual broadcast, Pasco, Washington, was mentioned as the site of atomic research. The broadcaster did not know the military significance of this information. There were demands that henceforth military censors screen all broadcasts, but the voluntary system was preserved.[8]

Those Rebellious Commentators

With America's entry into the war, the networks issued a joint statement reminiscent of Ed Klauber's policy statement of 1939. No broadcaster was to express his personal views or try to sway opinion. At the same time, Paul White issued a new, detailed set of instructions for CBS personnel.[9] Like Klauber, he prescribed an unexcited demeanor at the microphone and sound editorial judgment. But he scarcely mentioned the role of news analysts, possibly because that was covered in the joint network statement, and whereas Klauber stressed objectivity, White promulgated an editorial tack—a slant—his staff should take. After saying it was more important than ever for Americans to be well informed, he said:

> This is a war for the preservation of democracy. The American people must not only always be kept vividly aware of this objective, but of the value of every man, woman, and child in the nation of preserving democracy.

White had not, at this point, abandoned his stand against expression of personal opinion—CBS did not, in his phrase, "opinionate" the news.[10] Yet now CBS News, like the nation, had abandoned neutrality. White had given it a cause, a mission which was to keep the public "vividly aware" of the need to preserve democracy.

White's memorandum included these work rules:

> If a report emanated from an enemy source, "its precise nature and origin should be carefully pointed out."
>
> Although it was good to be first with the news, competition must not "betray us into recklessness or irresponsibility."
>
> It was more important than ever not to use "improper" sound effects in connection with news broadcasts; particularly, there should be no use of sirens.

The memorandum ended with the statement that now every news editor, writer, reporter, announcer, and analyst was a war correspondent, "just as much as if they actually were at headquarters near the front lines."

CBS' demand for non-opinionated commentary, which it insisted on calling news analysis, ultimately raised a storm. The storm broke in the mid-1940s, but it was brewing in 1940 when H. V. Kaltenborn, chafing under CBS restrictions, bolted to NBC. Although disagreement over editorial policy was not the only reason for Kaltenborn's departure—NBC offered a more favorable broadcast time—certainly he was not one to make sober, objective assessments. He said on the air that he had no use for British imperialism and used subjective phrases like "If I were responsible for our foreign policy."[11] In 1939, when Catholic listeners objected to his attacks on the Church of Spain, and threatened boycott, he lost for himself, and CBS, a lucrative contract with General Mills. CBS found a certain relief in his departure; nor did his predilection for personal pronouncements make for entirely smooth sailing at NBC, from which he retired in 1958. His reporting of the Munich crisis was the high point.

In 1941, commentators formed an Association of Radio News Analysts (later the Association of Radio and Television News Analysts) with Kaltenborn as its first president. The name, Erik Barnouw points out, was a concession to the networks, but members held themselves to be commentators, free to express their educated views.[12]

When Elmer Davis left CBS in the spring of 1942 to direct the Office of War Information, Cecil Brown succeeded him on the popular 8:55 P.M. news. In addition, on a rotation basis with William L. Shirer and Albert Warner, he did news analysis in the late evening. To Paul White's annoyance, Brown was opinionated in these broadcasts. The showdown came after a broadcast Brown made from Indianapolis on August 25, 1943. In his news analysis—not the 8:55 broadcast—Brown discussed the summit meeting in Quebec between President Roosevelt and Prime Minister Churchill on future conduct of the war. He accused the two leaders of failing to dramatize their war aims and said that because of this failure "any reasonably accurate observer of the American scene at this moment knows that a good deal of enthusiasm for this war is evaporating into thin air."

This sounded to White like the broadcaster's opinion, a clear violation not only of CBS policy but of the Mayflower decision of 1941. In this decision against the Mayflower Broadcasting Corporation, the Federal Communications Commission had barred broadcasters from editorializing. Specifically, on grounds of "limitations in frequencies inherent in radio," it prohibited the broadcast of editorials. "The broadcaster," it said, "cannot be an advocate."[13] (The FCC lifted its ban in 1949, but CBS adhered to its policy of objectivity. A radio piece by Eric Sevareid, regarded as "just too editorial," was killed in 1957,[14] and two of Murrow's radio commentaries were killed for the same reason, one in 1950, the other in 1961.

Reacting to the Indianapolis broadcast, White wrote a letter to Brown saying: "These policies [against editorializing] are in no sense capricious. They have been formulated for the protection of the public, and to me it is vital that they be enforced if we are to achieve any genuine freedom of the air." He said if Brown could not conform, CBS would be glad to release him from his contract.[15] On September 2, Brown asked to be released, and his resignation was accepted.

The Brown affair received wide publicity, with Max Lerner, Dorothy Thompson, Walter Winchell, and John W. Vandercook among the well-known names rallying to Brown's defense. In a program devoted to discussions of the issue on CBS, Vandercook said:

> We . . . agree with CBS on just one thing—we, too, seek to tell the truth. But this is the great difference: each of us out of his experience, out of his personal knowledge and out of his constant study of all available opinion, out of all available so-called facts, seeks to tell you, his listeners, that truth as he sees it in his own way. . . . We

believe in each citizen's liberty to agree with us or not to agree with us, in his right to listen or tune us off. We don't think that the decision of what and whom you can hear can be made by anyone but by the individual himself.[16]

On September 15, Kaltenborn presented an argument that is used today. "No journalist worth his salt," he said, "could or would be completely neutral or objective. . . . Every exercise of his editorial judgment constitutes an expression of opinion."[17] In *News on the Air,* White conceded that Kaltenborn had raised an important point. He said:

> Complete journalistic objectivity is only an ideal, but the fact that it is difficult if not impossible to attain does not seem to me to impair the ideal itself, or excuse the broadcaster from a constant and vigilant effort to try for it. The Golden Rule is unattainable, too.[18]

There are postscripts, highly ironic. Cecil Brown continued his career as a commentator and in 1966 received the Alfred I. duPont Award for his "thoughtful, forthright opinions based upon many years of personal observation of, and involvement in, the major events of our time."[19] He was at this time broadcasting over KCET, the educational television station in Los Angeles. He was still giving his opinions.

Paul White himself delivered editorials for KFMB AM-TV, San Diego, in which he fought fiercely for civic improvement. In 1954, when Ed Murrow was under fire for his "See It Now" attack on Senator Joseph R. McCarthy,[20] *Newsweek* cited White's insistence on impartiality in news presentation. When White saw this, he sent a telegram to *Newsweek,* which said in part:

> An eleven-year-old quotation on the emasculation of commentators' opinions on radio or television has returned to haunt me. I have since changed my mind and have recanted publicly on several occasions. My nightly broadcast is proof that I no longer subscribe to that 1943 viewpoint. In that year I also thought that Soviet Russia was a valuable ally, that nuclear fission was impossible and that, after the war and with rationing and controls removed, steaks would be plentiful and cheap. I am perturbed only because some readers may think I am now in disagreement with Ed Murrow. I am not. He is still my favorite bleeding head if not bleeding heart. During the war a British censor once advised me from London that Murrow was not immediately available to answer a question I wanted to put to him. "He's about somewhere," said the censor, "wearing his customary crown of thorns."[21]

Perhaps the most powerful editorializing of the whole early war period was done by Murrow, and he knew what he was doing. Writing to his parents, he said:

> I remember you once wanted me to be a preacher, but I had no faith, except in myself. But now I am preaching from a powerful

pulpit. Often I am wrong, but I am trying to talk as I would have talked were I a preacher. One need not wear a reversed collar to be honest.[22]

Murrow's "preaching" derived from the fact that freedom was at stake, from conviction that Great Britain and America had common cause, and from knowing what, in terms of human dignity, a Nazi victory would mean. In a broadcast of December 3, 1940, he said that there had been a time when some believed the United States would be more help to Britain as a nonbelligerent than as a full-fledged ally, but he no longer heard that thesis expressed. It was, he said, "a dead and dynamited fish." Later in the same broadcast:

> There are no indications that any British minister is going to urge you to declare war against the Axis, but you must expect repeated references in the press and in public statements to the British belief that a democratic nation at peace cannot render full and effective support to a nation at war, for that is what the majority of thinking people in this country have come to believe.[23]

Murrow said he was simply reporting the belief, not evaluating it "in terms of personal approval or disapproval." The caveat, however, is transparent. He shared the view of "the majority of thinking people."

On March 9, 1941, he made plain, again, that Britons wanted the United States to come into the war as "a fighting ally." They were afraid, he said, that the United States was making the same mistakes that Britain had made.[24]

Nine months later, with the attack on Pearl Harbor, the die was cast.

17
Into North Africa and Italy

Hitler gave up the idea of invading England and invaded Russia. In November 1942, U.S. and British seaborne forces landed in Morocco and Algeria, the beginning of a long campaign to drive the Germans out of North Africa and move on to Italy. These Allied forces were under the direct command of General Dwight D. Eisenhower, who now had Harry Butcher, CBS' former vice president in Washington, as his chief naval aide, a circumstance that inevitably raised suspicions of partiality in the minds of NBC correspondents. However, one gathers from the entry in Butcher's diary for July 15, 1942, that few favors, if any, were granted. He wrote:

> Lunch at the Connaught Hotel with Ed Murrow, Bob Trout, and Charles Collingwood, all former CBS associates. Helped train Bob from a pup at WJSV [in Washington]. As might be expected from good radio reporters . . . they phrased questions to get an expression from me as to when and if there would be a second front. For instance, Bob was wondering whether he ought to plan to stay in London or return home. My answers were of necessity evasive. . . . Am afraid they thought CBS lunch money wasted.[1]

Woodrow Wirsig, writing in *Esquire* magazine, tells how news of the invasion of North Africa came to CBS News headquarters in New York.

At 6:30 P.M. the telephone rang. "This is Sevareid in Washington," said the voice. "The President's called a news conference at the White House. Scheduled for 8:30. Looks like a story will break about 9."

"London's coming up on the cue channel!" shouted a copy boy. "Hello, New York," said London. "This is Murrow. Tell White to give me the air from London at nine." White told the engineers to route all CBS network shows through Studio 9 for the rest of the night. This way, programs could be interrupted. . . .

When the flash came over the wires at 9 P.M., a rewrite man typed off the brief sentence: "The White House announces that American troops are now landing in North Africa. Further details will be announced shortly." White himself grabbed the paper, raced into Studio 9. At 9:02 the announcer read the big news. A brief two-minute summary was wrapped up for another "Hit Parade" interruption. Then, at 9:45 P.M., a five-minute report. By this time, White was already concentrating on a special news show at 10:15.[2]

The network correspondents covering the landings in North Africa were Charles Collingwood of CBS and John MacVane of NBC, soon joined by Mutual's Arthur Mann. Fred Bate was now working in New York, and MacVane's place in London had been taken by Robert St. John. Stanley Richardson, formerly of the AP, ran the NBC in London and did not broadcast. (Walter Cronkite, reporting for UP, covered the landings and returned to New York with the first uncensored account.)

The invasion force met half-hearted resistance from French troops directed by the puppet government of Marshal Pétain in Vichy. Admiral Jean Darlan, successor designate to the aged marshal, "happened"[3] to be in Algeria and ordered a cease-fire. Hitler, in a countermove, rushed reinforcements to Tunisia, next door to Algeria, and it was in Tunisia that the heavy fighting of the next five months took place.

There was a political complication. The Allies made Darlan, the Nazi collaborator, French high commissioner in North Africa. He was chosen over General Henri Giraud, who commanded the Free French forces, and American correspondents saw the choice as unprincipled, a betrayal of the ideals for which the war was being fought. For his first broadcast from Algiers, MacVane had written:

> It is pointed out as a choice of expediency. We had to have the Vichy officers on our side. . . . One of Darlan's first moves was to arrest hundreds of fighting Frenchmen who have worked against the Axis for the Allies and French freedom. General [Mark] Clark [Eisenhower's deputy commander] is keeping his hands off. . . . French honesty and courage aren't getting any rewards in North Africa tonight.

This paragraph was killed by Clark personally after the censor thought he should see it. Collingwood was as concerned as MacVane, who says that in those first weeks they both covered the unsavory political story, often in the same way, "although neither of us knew what the other was going to say until we got before the microphone."

On December 3, MacVane, reporting that Darlan had assumed the prerogatives of a chief of state, was allowed to say:

> As far as is apparent on the surface, the American occupation made hardly a ripple in the control of civil and military affairs in North Africa. The same people that ran the show for Vichy are still flourishing.[4]

The *London Times* published the entire piece. It also was picked up by the BBC.

The American deal with Darlan was highly unpopular in Britain. Eric Sevareid, in Washington, did a broadcast in which he noted the rift. This upset Cordell Hull, secretary of state, who complained that the British press was carrying on a campaign against him. Churchill responded that Britain had a free press; it could say whatever it wanted on the subject. The British information minister, Brendan Bracken, tried to patch things up by denying the existence of differences between the State Department and the Foreign Office in the Darlan matter. Murrow reported that if that was so, it was a "new development."[5]

It was in this context of expediency versus ideals that, on Christmas Eve, a young Frenchman approached Darlan at his office and shot him to death, saying he had "brought justice to a traitor."[6]

Now there was a scramble by correspondents in Algiers to report the story. Network correspondents, as well as the military, used a captured transmitter outside Algiers. At first, broadcasts to America were beamed to London for relay to New York, but then New York found it could pick up an excellent signal direct. Neither NBC nor CBS had a satisfactory way of monitoring the Algiers transmitter for the pickups; there was no two-way conversation. Consequently the networks, using Greenwich time, cabled a precise schedule for twice-a-day transmissions. The correspondent would give a one- or two-minute "talk-up" and count down so his report could be inserted in the news broadcast.

On the day Darlan was shot, radio correspondents did not wait with the news until their prearranged times. They went on the air "blind," hoping fervently that New York would hear them. Because the longer the signal went out to New York, the more likely it was to be picked up, Collingwood let the other correspondents, including MacVane, take the microphone ahead of him; he would go last. He says:

> We all, as you will imagine, had cabled our offices saying when we would come up, but it seemed to me that those cables would be very unlikely to get through, what with official communications and heavy press traffic. . . . I knew Paul White or someone at CBS had been trying to rig up a network of ham radio operators and to encourage them to call CBS if they picked up any transmission of

ours on any odd frequency from any odd place and alert it to our presence on the air.

Since I was last and under no compulsion to hurry, I made as sure as I could that someone was listening. So I took the mike and went into a long spiel saying, "This is CBS in Algiers. If anyone is hearing this signal, will he please call CBS collect in New York at Plaza 1-2345 and say that Charles Collingwood in Algiers has an important story for them? I repeated that about 15 times. . . . Then, knowing that this would involve interrupting a regularly scheduled broadcast, I said that this was big enough to interrupt for and that I would begin "in five minutes from now." Then I called the hams again, repeated my advice to interrupt, and went into a two-minute countdown.[7]

MacVane had got through, interrupting the Bob Hope show, but Collingwood's story captured more attention. The *New York Times* published it—with a by-line—and White bestowed a $500 bonus. Collingwood also received the prestigious George Foster Peabody Award for Best Broadcast of 1942.

The young assassin, Bonnier de la Chapelle, a monarchist, was tried, convicted, and executed by a firing squad, all within 38 hours. General Giraud succeeded Darlan, and there were rumors that he, too, would be assassinated. Confusion was so great that Eisenhower imposed censorship on all political news from Algiers for six weeks. Ultimately, Giraud was succeeded as leader of the Free French by General DeGaulle.

A big story out of North Africa in 1943 was the Casablanca conference attended by Roosevelt and Churchill. It was here that the United States and Britain agreed to move on Italy before mounting a cross-Channel invasion of France. With the final, hold-for-release communiqué on the meeting in hand, the network correspondents dashed back to Algiers because the transmitter there was more reliable. For security reasons, the communiqué contained little "meat," but they had significant sidelights— DeGaulle and Giraud shaking hands for photographers like two boxers before a bout and Roosevelt's statement that the Allies would accept nothing less than Germany's unconditional surrender. The print media worried that radio would scoop them, as it had with Darlan's assassination, and asked for permission to file their stories first. Permission was denied, but network reporters were frustrated nonetheless.

The transmitter was shut down due to an air raid and, like the wire service correspondents, they had to get their stories out by cable.

The Battle of Britain had been won. London was quiet, and Murrow flew down to Tunisia to join Collingwood. His reports from North Africa bear the same stamp as his reporting from London—lean, sinewy language and telling detail. Here he reports from the front, near Pichon:

Along the whole front the guns rave and roar, more than a hundred of them. Up on the left the 25-pounders are being worked so fast that a steady stream of fire seems to fan out toward the German positions across the valley.

Of the aftermath, he says:

> You begin to meet ambulances coming back. They are taking the dust as drivers nurse them carefully over those terrible roads. You can see them lift the wheel, trying to ease the shock for the wounded back behind. . . . Where the road cuts down to meet the stream there is a knocked out tank, two dead men beside it and two more digging a grave. A little farther along, a German soldier sits smiling against the bank. He is covered with dust, and he is dead.

He links the war front with the home front.

> The other day I saw a long line of tank carriers moving over narrow mountain roads. . . . They looked grand, each tank on a trailer wearing 24 rubber tires, and the truck pulling it had 10 tires, and I thought: that's where the tires of American automobiles have gone.[8]

"A Kind of Orchestrated Hell"

It was seven months after that broadcast, on December 3, 1943, that Murrow made his "orchestrated hell" broadcast, the account of what he saw on a night bombing raid conducted by the Royal Air Force on Berlin. He rode—one of four or five correspondents, each in a different bomber —in an armada of four-engined Lancasters. Murrow was in "D for Dog" with a crew of six, including Jock, "the finest pilot in Bomber Command." As the bomber fleet approached Berlin

> Jock observed, "there's a kite on fire dead ahead." It was a great golden, slow-moving meteor slanting towards the earth. . . . And then, with no warning at all, "D-Dog" was filled with an unhealthy white light. I was standing just behind Jock and could see all the seams on the wings. His quiet Scots voice beat into my ears, "Steady, lads. We've been coned." . . . It seemed that one big searchlight, instead of being 20,000 feet below, was mounted right on our wing tip. "D-Dog" was corkscrewing. As we rolled down on the other side, I began to see what was happening to Berlin.
>   The clouds were gone, and the sticks of incendiaries from the preceding waves made the place look like a badly laid out city with the street lights on. The small incendiaries were going down like a fistful of white rice thrown on a piece of black velvet. As Jock hauled the "Dog" up again, I was thrown to the other side of the cockpit, and there below were more incendiaries, glowing white and then turning red. The cookies—the 4,000-pound high explosives—were bursting below like great sunflowers gone mad.

Repeatedly, "D-Dog" was caught by enemy searchlights and escaped. It dropped its bomb load, then its incendiaries. "I looked on the port beam at the target area. There was a sullen, obscene glare. The fires seemed to have found each other. . . . Berlin was a kind of orchestrated hell, a terrible symphony of light and flame.[9] Altogether, in defiance of orders from Paley, who deplored the risk, Murrow flew 25 missions—bombers, fighters, transport, reconnaissance. He found it impossible, in good conscience, to report the war from a safe place.

Murrow was disobedient in another respect; he broke the networks' rule against the use of recordings in radio reporting. NBC had used WLS' recording of the Hindenburg disaster, but no one knew the dirigible would explode. The recording had not been planned as news. To Murrow, the reporter, not to use this new tool made no sense. So with a radio engineer he put together a montage of the sounds of London in wartime, a broadcast that included not only sirens, antiaircraft fire, the footsteps of people retreating wearily, without panic, to their accustomed shelter, but also the merrymaking in a night club and the minstrelsy of a barrel organ giving forth with "A Soldier of the Queen."

There was in Murrow's voice, in the narration with these sounds, a rare sense of accomplishment, but New York said he must have misunderstood: the ban on recordings—except for sound effects!—still held.[10]

North to Rome

After driving the Germans out of North Africa and Sicily, the Allies invaded Italy and in a slow, costly campaign pushed north along its mountainous spine toward Rome. The first landings—the Americans at Salerno, near Naples, and the British at Reggio di Calabria, on the toe of Italy— occurred in September 1943. In January, an Anglo-American force landed at Anzio, the birthplace of Nero, behind the German defense line. The Allied force was trapped there for almost four months.

It was not until May 24 that the Anzio group broke out of its pocket and linked up with the U.S. Fifth Army moving up the coast. This was big news because now the Allied forces in Italy were united and advancing in a single unbroken line. John W. Vandercook got word of the linkup before Eric Sevareid, but Sevareid got on the air before the NBC correspondent simply because he was doing a broadcast at 2 p.m., which was the release time for the announcement. In his memoir, Sevareid writes:

> When an excited telegram of congratulation reached me from CBS in New York, I felt obliged, more from embarrassment than from modesty, to reply by asking them not to gloat publicly over our scoop. It was all a silly, childish affair, but it was the way news beats very often occur.[11]

Since September 1943, the Allies had been fighting only Germans. Mussolini, thoroughly discredited, was out, and King Victor Emmanuel, who took over Italy's armed forces, had concluded an armistice. Marshal Badoglio became premier; democracy was being restored. On November 14, 1943, NBC's Don Hollenbeck, reporting from Naples, was able to say, "The broadcast this morning marks an historic occasion, the first time in a long time that free speech has been heard from the continent of Europe."

Rome was liberated on June 4, 1944, two days before the Allied invasion of Normandy. Partisan fighters caught up with Mussolini and killed him. On May 2, 1945, all the German forces in Italy surrendered.

From Out of the Blue

The war was more than half over when the American Broadcasting Company came into existence. The FCC had found NBC's operation of two networks, the Red and the Blue, monopolistic, so the NBC Blue Network, with 155 affiliated stations, was put up for sale. The purchaser, for $8,000,000 was Edward J. Noble, who had made a fortune with Life Savers candy. Although the name chosen for Noble's new network was the American Broadcasting Company, it continued for two years—until 1945—to identify itself as the Blue Network.[12] This was because of litigation over the right to the initials ABC, which had been adopted by the Arizona Broadcasting Company.

Settlement of the suit produced an amusing situation in London, where Donald Coe was ABC's bureau chief. Coe was told to start identifying himself as an ABC correspondent, not as a Blue Network correspondent as he had been doing. He says:

> I explained to our lovely British office manager, Doris Hoskins, the value of ABC identification. She had always answered our phone "Blue Network." But now she drew herself up and told me in no uncertain terms that she would never say "This is ABC" because in London the initials were best known for a chain of bakery shoppes called the Associated Baking Company. So it was "This is the American Broadcasting Company" for Miss Hoskins in the broadest of English accents until her early death in 1953.[13]

The first head of ABC News with the title of director was the same Johnny Johnstone who, at Mutual, had battled Abe Schechter and Paul White. Second in command was Thomas Velotta, formerly of the Red Network, who had charge of special events. He tells how they started out:

> Some of us younger fellows, figuring the old fogies running things at the Red would be there forever, went with the Blue. . . . All we had at first were the wire service printers. Johnstone and I would look at them to see what was going on. We didn't produce anything. A couple of news summaries and any special events thing we wanted were produced by the NBC newsroom under our direction. The only program really ours was a 15-minute show George

Hicks did. He interviewed servicemen and got them to tell their stories.[14]

Johnstone sent Hicks to London to set up a bureau. After that, Hicks was in Italy. In October 1943, he went down to Algiers, headquarters for the Mediterranean theater, to hire a stringer. Broadcasting facilities were poor in Italy, and Hicks needed someone to relay his reports over the Algiers transmitter. That was when he talked to Donald Coe, then a United Press correspondent who had once written Esso Reporter broadcasts for WGY in Schenectady. Coe says:

> After a test transmission to New York and a few pointers from Hicks, I was hired. So while Hicks was in Italy, I would get his copy sent by courier plane from Naples, cleared by the censor, and then read it live to New York. It was a strange reversal of roles; listeners would hear *me* reading *his* copy. I also reported the daily communiqué, which was still given out in Algiers.[15]

In March 1944, a new transmitter was ready in Naples. By this time, Gordon Fraser[16] had arrived in Italy and also was reporting for the Blue Network. Coe had been reporting for the United Press and the Blue, but now the UP wanted to assign him to the Mediterranean Fleet. If he went with the fleet, he could no longer report the daily headquarters story for radio. He had to choose and chose radio.

Meanwhile, Hicks had returned to London to prepare for the Normandy invasion, and after Coe became a full-time correspondent for the Blue Network, Fraser went off to London, too. That left Coe alone, as far as the network was concerned, to cover what soon came to be called the Forgotten Front.

18
And Into Normandy

The invasion was imminent. For months, American G.I.s had been pouring into England, joining British and Canadian forces and other Allied contingents. Guns, planes, tanks, all manner of equipment, were amassed for the most ambitious assault across water in military history. It was coming, and everyone waited: the Allied armada, the Germans, the correspondents. The network "invasion teams" were in place.

Even the presidents of both CBS and NBC were in London. William S. Paley had flown over in January 1944 to take charge of broadcasting in the Psychological Warfare Division, Supreme Headquarters, Allied Expeditionary Forces (SHAEF). Earlier, he had supervised the establishment of radio communications in North Africa and Italy. One of his new responsibilities was the announcement, worldwide, that the cross-Channel invasion was under way. He held the rank of colonel. So did David Sarnoff, who was Eisenhower's special assistant on communications. (Later he made general rank.) It was Sarnoff's job to set up a coordinated communications system, not only for the expeditionary forces, but also for news coverage in the battle areas. This involved mobile transmitters and the creation of an Allied Forces Network.

Preparations in New York included a series of meetings between the network news directors and high-ranking public information officers of the army and navy. These conferences, held as often as twice a week, were attended by Paul White of CBS, Bill Brooks of NBC, John Whitmore of Mutual, and Thomas Velotta, successor to Johnny Johnstone, for the Blue. Besides such matters as accreditation and censorship, they discussed pool broadcasts. The networks agreed to pool all material obtained by their correspondents during the invasion period.[1]

In February, White had issued a seven-page memorandum to his staff "for our domestic coverage of the prospective invasion of Western Europe." His instructions, summarized in his own words, were:

1. No matter what the general tenor of the news, keep an informative, unexcited demeanor at the microphone.
2. Give sources. Be sure to label every report that is not officially released.
3. Be careful in the choice of words. For instance, "Allied forces today *rolled* toward X." "The German defenses of Z today were *pulverized*." The underlined words in those sentences are apt to be exaggerations and breed a dangerous optimism.
4. When we don't know, let's say so.
5. Always aim for the listener's confidence and remember that winning the war is a hell of a lot more important than reporting it.

He concluded:

> Please remember that those who are listening to us are the mothers, fathers, wives and sweethearts of the men participating in this story. The crisis of covering fast-breaking news is a minor crisis compared with that faced by the families of the men in action. But the biggest crisis of all, of course, confronts the men who are actually in the front lines. About the only way that we can help them is to report factually, soberly and intelligently their fight for the freedom of us all.[2]

It was, *Time* said, "a memo which radio and the press in general might well take to heart."[3]

The Little Switch

For D-Day, White had a special switch installed on the wall of Studio 9, just inside the door from the newsroom. The switch caused a good deal of excitement because, by simply pressing it, anyone could interrupt the network coast to coast. The switch and emergency "flash" microphone were housed in a small, unfinished pine cabinet. Every member of the news staff was briefed.

> Do NOT waste time writing a bulletin. And don't waste time in looking for an announcer. After you have pushed down the key,

give the bulletin clearly and concisely. Then say you're taking the microphone to our teletypes in the CBS newsroom for more details. The mike has an extension cable. Carry it into the newsroom and read more of the news as it comes in over the teletypes. . . . It will be speed and not a polished and professional manner at the mike that will count. . . . Of course, have someone call Production and get an engineer and announcer to Studio 9 as quickly as possible. If there is no one else around, make the call yourself, even realizing the public is listening in. It will all make for additional color.[4]

Joel Tall, the radio engineer assigned to Master Control during this time, relates that he was monitoring the network one day, listening to the "feeds" going out to affiliated stations across the country, when suddenly all the loudspeakers fell silent. Then he heard a man's anguished voice exclaim, "Oh, my god!" An instant later, normal program resumed. According to Tall, the voice belonged to another engineer, Frank Orth, who was showing some VIPs the CBS facilities. He says, "I picture Frank escorting the visitors from the newsroom into Studio 9, showing them the emergency switch, saying, 'And if you just press it, like this—.' "[5]

This untoward interruption must have occurred in the brief interval between installation of the switch and the time a padlock was attached to prevent just such an accident. Or sabotage. Eleven persons had keys.

And then appeared what became known as "Paul White's piano," a gray-painted, push-button panel for speaking by transatlantic shortwave with correspondents overseas. The panel, about eighteen inches high, rested within easy reach on White's desk. He could talk to correspondents over a desk mike and hear them over a loudspeaker on the wall. Besides buttons labeled AT&T, RCA, and Press Wireless, there was a button for signaling the Studio 9 control room and controls for hearing whatever program was on the air. For example, if a London circuit had been ordered, he would press the AT&T button.

Long after the war, "Paul White's piano" was still used for bringing in live reports on "The World News Roundup." It was an ingenious device.

On May 17, CBS stations were told that "any day now," in the midst of a program, they might hear three beeps "like a baby chick."[6] The beeps meant important news would be coming up at the end of the program. If the stations heard five beeps, it meant that the program in progress would be interrupted. NBC, as in the past, would alert its stations with the four chimes.

No one knew where the Allies would strike. Paul White gave his New York staff individual assignments based on possible invasion points. Each staffer had a section of the French coast to research as to population, economy, coastal features, inland terrain, and whatever was known regarding German defenses. These "fact sheets" were ready before D-Day, so when the landings came in Normandy, between Cherbourg and Caen, CBS had detailed information with which to flesh out the first bulletins.

The networks hired more people to monitor foreign broadcasts and more teletype operators so that news picked up from the broadcasts could be delivered faster to the press associations. Besides their shortwave listening posts in New York and San Francisco, CBS and NBC, in a sense, had listening posts in Switzerland, where Howard K. Smith and Max Jordan were stationed. Glen Stadler was reporting for CBS from Portugal, which also was neutral. Stadler had won a Pulitzer Prize as a United Press correspondent, but his reporting for CBS was cut short by illness. Later, he did commentary for WCCO in Minneapolis and became owner of a string of radio stations.

One That Got Away

A United Press correspondent in London who attracted CBS attention was Walter Cronkite. Earlier in his career, Cronkite had worked on stations in the Southwest and been disillusioned. Their treatment of news, he thought, was superficial. Now, with the invasion coming, CBS needed another good reporter, and Murrow made Cronkite an offer. Cronkite was making $57.50 a week, and Murrow offered him $120, plus commercial fees.[7]

Cronkite accepted the offer and went back to Harrison Salisbury, then foreign editor in the UP bureau in London, and told him he was leaving. Cronkite recalls Salisbury's distress.

> He said, "Oh, God, you can't do that! I just haven't got around to telling you, but I've been authorized to give you the biggest raise that's ever been offered to anybody in the history of the UP overseas—25 dollars." So I said, "Well, gee, I'm dumbfounded. That's the greatest thing that's ever happened to me. I appreciate it, but I've already given my word." Whereupon I get this phone call the next day from Hugh Baille [president of the UP], and Hugh said, "God damn it, you're ticketed to be president of the United Press some day," and he gave me all this big talk and raised me another 12.50 to $95,
>
> Actually, it was very flattering, and the raise kind of backed up the flattery. I did like the United Press, and my previous experience with radio never had been totally satisfactory, so I stayed. . . . I think Ed never did quite forgive me for that. I think he thought I had reneged and used him as a bargaining thing. I hadn't really meant to.[8]

Another reason he stayed, which he did not mention, was loyalty. He did not join CBS until 1950.

D-Day

There was the false report of June 3. At 4:39 P.M., Eastern War Time, the Associated Press said the invasion was under way. It took 15 seconds for CBS to interrupt Ted Husing's account of the Belmont Stakes with the news. Only it was wrong. AP killed the story at 4:41, and immediately CBS, and the other networks, reported the mistake. Somehow, in London, the punched tape of a practice flash had been fed into a live teletype. It took hours for the excitement to die down.

The first true word of invasion came shortly after midnight on June 6, and it came from the enemy. Again, the report appeared on the AP wire. No flash this time, just a bulletin:

> LONDON TUESDAY JUNE 6 (AP)—THE GERMAN NEWS AGENCY TRANSOCEAN SAID TODAY IN A BROADCAST THAT THE ALLIED INVASION HAS BEGUN.

Was this another false alarm? NBC waited four minutes, then, at 12:41 A.M., interrupted the musical trio, The Three Suns, to quote the German news agency. At CBS, the night editor, Jesse Zousmer, telephoned Paul White, who, because the invasion was imminent, was staying at a nearby hotel. Shortly, when the same story moved on INS, White ordered, "Get it on the air!"[9] At 12:48 A.M., CBS newsman Ned Calmer broke into a dance program from the West Coast.

> We are interrupting this program to bring you a special bulletin. A bulletin has just been received from the London office of the Associated Press which quotes the German Transocean News Agency as asserting that the invasion of Western Europe has begun. This report, and we stress it is of enemy origin with absolutely no confirmation from Allied sources, says that American landings were made this morning on the shores of northwestern France.

Calmer warned that the report might be a German ploy. In any case, he said, the CBS news staff was standing by.

Now the German radio said Le Havre was being bombed; Allied paratroopers were being dropped into northwestern France. The networks began waking, and calling in, their people. They came in by taxi, subway, elevated train, and ferry. One NBC engineer, in desperation, hitched a ride on a milk truck. In Cincinnati, the news caught WLW staffers winding up a farewell party for the station's promotion director, Chick Allison, who had enlisted in the navy. In 15 minutes, they were in the WLW newsroom after a mad dash across town. In Atlanta, an engineer on all-night duty at WSB alerted the news staff. The Germans might be playing some kind of trick, but no one was taking a chance.

In Washington, WMAL's news director, William Neel, was rounding the Lincoln Memorial on his way home when he heard the news on his car radio. He swung around the memorial and back to the station, where he was joined by Jack Edmunds, program director, and Bryson Rash, director of special features. WMAL belonged to the Blue Network, and Rash began coordinating for the network the in-studio reports of Martin Agronsky and H. R. Baukhage and reports by Ray Henle from the Pentagon. Earl Godwin was told to stay home and get some sleep; he would be needed later as relief.

The first gleam of confirmation came at 1:26 A.M. when the BBC warned residents of France's coastal region to move inland and stay off the roads. The War and Navy departments in Washington said they had no information. At 2:55 A.M., a bulletin from London reported many planes —the most ever seen in the air at one time—sweeping southward toward the Channel. At 3:15, NBC interrupted: "Radio Berlin says Allied forces are being landed from the sea and dropped from the air near Cherbourg and Le Havre. . . . We may be approaching the fateful hour."

Now the networks received a call from the War Department: "Stand by for an important message over Army Signal Corps channel at 3:32:00." Then it came, the text of Communiqué No. 1 of the Supreme Headquarters of the Allied Expeditionary Forces: "Under the command of General Eisenhower, Allied naval forces supported by strong air forces began landing Allied armies this morning on the northern coast of France." One sentence. That was all. From NBC's New York studios, Robert St. John said, "Men and women of the United States, this is a momentous hour in world history. This is the invasion of Hitler's Europe, the zero hour."

A few minutes later, the increasingly large radio audience heard Eisenhower's order of the day. It was read by Ed Murrow at the general's choosing.

> Soldiers, sailors and airmen of the Allied Expeditionary Force: You are about to embark on a great crusade. The eyes of the world are upon you, and the hopes and prayers of all liberty-loving peoples go with you. We will accept nothing less than full victory. Good luck and let us all beseech the blessing of Almighty God upon this great and noble undertaking.[10]

The assault was along a 70-mile strip of French coast from Quinéville, near Cherbourg, to the mouth of the Orne, near Caen. The Allies went in with five divisions: the U.S. 4th Infantry at Utah Beach in the west, the U.S. 1st Infantry at Omaha Beach in the middle, and the Canadian 3rd Infantry and British 3rd and 50th Infantry in the east. Covering the landings were 702 warships. Counting minesweepers, ammunition lighters, landing craft, and tugs, the armada totaled more than 9,000 vessels.

Of the 500 American correspondents in England, only about 50 represented broadcasting stations or networks. And only a handful of these accompanied the assault force. The first eyewitness report, pooled for all networks, came at 4:17. The voice belonged to Wright Bryan of WSB, the NBC affiliate in Atlanta. He had just returned from France, where paratroopers were dropped from a C-47 nicknamed "Snooty." His report began, "I rode with the first group of planes from a troop-carrier command to take our fighting men into Europe." It ended:

> "Are you all set?" asked the colonel. "Get this thing hooked for me," he said as he took his own place closest to the door. They blinked as the pilot threw his switch, and before I could look up they began jumping. . . . The paratroopers shoved each other so

swiftly and heavily towards the open door that they jolted against the door frame. One man . . . was thrown into the back of the cabin and was dazed. The men behind shoved him aside and went on jumping. Before the unhappy soldier could get to his feet our plane was well beyond the drop zone, and in a matter of minutes it was back over the water and setting a course for home.

In the NBC studio in New York, H. V. Kaltenborn talked about the possible effect of the paratroop landings. At CBS, Robert Trout began reading bulletin material from the teletypes lining two walls of the CBS newsroom, the cable from Studio 9 trailing as he walked from printer to printer. Trout, anchoring in New York, would be on the air almost continuously for ten hours. *Broadcasting* called his performance "a masterful job of maintaining a running report of 'the greatest news story ever told'."[11] At NBC, Don Hollenbeck and Don Goddard took turns anchoring through the day and far into the night.

Because of the importance of the story, the networks broke their rule against the use of recordings. Not always with success. Lugging a bulky wire recorder—"It must have weighed 50 pounds or more"[12]—John MacVane interviewed soldiers preparing for embarkation, only to learn later that the batteries were run down and nothing could be used. The D-Day report that stirred the most interest was one that was recorded. George Hicks on board the communications ships *Ancon* used a Navy sound film recorder to describe an air attack. Hicks did his eyewitness report as men were going ashore in the first morning light. He was standing in an exposed position above the signal bridge of the *Ancon*, describing what he could see, when the ship became a German target.

> It's planes you hear overhead now. They are the motors of Nazis coming and going. *(Sound of Crash)* That was a bomb hit, another one. . . . Flares are coming down now. You can hear the machine-gunning. The whole seaside is covered with tracer fire . . . going up . . . bombs . . . machinegunning. The planes are coming ever closer, firing low. . . . Smoke, brilliant fire down low toward the French coast a couple of miles. I don't know whether it is on the shore or is a ship on fire. . . .
>
> It's quiet for a moment now. If you'll excuse me, I'll just take a deep breath and stop speaking. . . . Here we go again! Another plane has come over, right over our port side. Tracers are making an arc over the bow now, disappearing into the clouds before they burst. . . . Something burning is falling down through the sky. *(Voices Cheering)* They got one!. . . . The lights of that burning Nazi plane are just twinkling now in the sea and going out.

The voice-on-film was sent to London for processing. After screening by military censors, it was broadcast simultaneously on the four major networks. Despite static which made some words indistinguishable, it was one of the war's most vivid reports. The Blue Network repeated it three times the next morning; NBC, CBS, and Mutual rebroadcast it at least once. Of the D-Day coverage, *Broadcasting* said: "Perhaps the most significant development—and the one destined to influence future operations— was the use of transcribed reports of radio war correspondents over all networks." The magazine suggested that, as a consequence, CBS and NBC might scrap their recording ban.[13] Within the decade they had done so.

MacVane was at Omaha Beach, where Americans suffered the heaviest casualties. Enemy fire was heavy, so heavy MacVane says the water alongside his landing craft suddenly turned "frothy white, as though someone were flogging it with a gigantic cat-o'-nine-tails." Then he realized the froth was caused by machinegun bullets." I saw dead men floating by us in their inflated life belts. . . . Other men were swimming . . . and I wondered what had happened to their landing craft and how far out they had been hit."

The narrow beach, under a cliff, had been subjected to intense mortar and machinegun fire, but when MacVane, weighted down by wet clothes, typewriter, and trenching tool, reached shore the firing had stopped. He spent the night in a trench dug, he says, with only one thought, "to get as deep into the ground as I could."

The next day he hunted for a mobile transmitter. Ultimately he found one—four had been destroyed—and got into London with a perfect signal. He felt he had the scoop of the war, but "a bunch of bureaucratic desk officers" said the frequency was wrong. Besides, no correspondent was supposed to come up from the beachhead that soon! Two days later, MacVane broke his ankle and got shipped back to England. The result was that the first invasion broadcast heard in America from Normandy was done by Bill Downs. MacVane heard the broadcast in London. He was, in his phrase, "not happy."[14]

Getting the Story Out

Reports from mobile transmitters in France soon were flooding into London at the rate of 10,000 words a day. On June 18, Murrow did a broadcast describing the setup.

> All the American networks are operating from a basement here in London.[15] It wouldn't be big enough for a vice president's office, back in New York. The noise is indescribable. Old newspapermen accustomed to the roar of a city room have put their heads in the door and shuddered. There's a shortage of telephones. I can get through to our New York office in less time than it takes to telephone a man upstairs. There are three small studios, each about big enough to hold a Shetland pony or a couple of broadcasters. Occasionally a burst of gunfire or the roar of a falling bomb sweeps through the room where we do our writing. . . .
>
> The control engineer says, "New York is calling you on Channel A, and the beachhead transmitter is up and testing." You go in and

flip switches, listening first to Bill Downs on the beachhead and then to New York. Downs' watch is two minutes slow. You tell New York to delay the switch and start talking about future schedules. . . . These conversations go on for hours each day. You don't hear them. Probably that's as well since we aim to keep confusion off the air. The other night I walked into a studio and found three people down on the floor. Someone said, "The knob came off." The switch on the recording gear was on the floor. We found it and went ahead on time. . . . The engineers are the ones who slave away without recognition.[16]

He ended by saying, "Over on the far shore, the boys stumble through the dark to reach their camouflaged transmitters. They speak their stories. Sometimes they get through, and sometimes they don't."

On August 15, in a giant pincers movement, the U.S. Seventh Army invaded southern France. To the north, as Allied forces pushed for Paris and beyond, and soldiers died, there was a toll among correspondents, too. Wright Bryan was wounded. His NBC colleague Tom Treanor, with the Third Army, was killed. Larry LeSueur, riding in a Jeep with Bill Stringer of Reuters, saw Stringer, sitting beside him, killed instantly by a German antitank gun.[17] One thinks of the testimony of John Gilbert Winant, U.S. ambassador to Britain. Of such correspondents he wrote: "They accepted discomforts and risked life cheerfully in their determined effort to keep the American people informed."[18]

Paris Is Liberated

Correspondents entered Paris on August 25 with a French armored division attached to the U.S. First Army. John MacVane was convinced that he and Wright Bryan were the first American correspondents in the city—they had tried to stay at the head of the French columns, sometimes under fire—"but it was useless to try to convince 100 other correspondents good and true that they were all mistaken."[19] He had opportunity to use a transmitter operated by the French Resistance, but says he did not take it because, as a war correspondent, he was pledged to submit his broadcasts to Army censorship, and he had no censor.

MacVane was in for another disappointment. The Hotel Scribe had been designated as a headquarters for correspondents. He went there and, after a long wait, got a censor to approve his copy, the first copy after the liberation to bear the censor's stamp. His lead was: "This is the first broadcast from liberated Paris." Later that day, when broadcasts were being made and he was waiting to go on the air, another correspondent heard him rehearsing and told him he was wrong; others had broadcast ahead of him. And he named some of them.

"But that's impossible," MacVane said. "My script was the first through censorship."

"Censorship!" the other correspondent said scornfully. "Who cares about censorship tonight?"[20]

MacVane had one comfort. He was carrying a wire recorder when the bells of Notre Dame pealed exultantly in celebration, and this time his recorder was working. The next day the sound of the bells was heard throughout the United States.

Now the big goal was Berlin.

19
Victory in Europe

The largest airborne operation of the war took place on September 17, 1944, when more than 20,000 men riding in 478 gliders and 1,544 transport planes landed in Holland, near Arnhem. The objective was to hasten Allied victory by outflanking the Siegfried Line. Murrow rode a C-47 carrying paratroopers to the drop zone. He speaks into a recorder:

> Bob Masell of the Blue Network is sitting here working on the recording gear just as calm and cool as any of the paratroopers, but perhaps both of us should be because they're going to jump and we aren't. . . . There's a burst of flak. . . . It's coming from the port side, just across our nose, but a little bit low. . . . Nine ships ahead of us have just dropped and you can see the men swinging down.

Then the men with him go.

> I can see their chutes going down now, every man clear. They're dropping just beside a little windmill near a church, hanging there. . . . They seem to be completely relaxed, like nothing so much as khaki dolls hanging beneath a green lampshade. . . . The whole sky is filled.

Murrow ended his report by saying, "That's the way it was," antedating Walter Cronkite's famous sign-off, "And that's the way it is," by 19 years.

Cronkite, still with the United Press, went in as pool correspondent with the 101st Airborne, crash landing in a glider. Two days later, during heavy fighting, he ran into Bill Downs of CBS, attached to the British Second Army. When bombs began falling, they ducked into a woods and somehow got separated. When Cronkite called and got no answer, he feared Downs had been hurt—besides the bombs, the area had been mined—and made a desperate search, shouting until he was hoarse. Finally, believing Downs had been killed or captured, he left.

He worried about Downs for days. Then one night he went into the Hotel Metropole in Brussels and there, laughing with friends at the bar, was the man he had looked for. He felt hurt. "I thought you'd been killed," he said. "I went through the woods calling your name." Downs was sorry about that. "But I couldn't go around calling *your* name," he said. "They'd think I was shouting in German." [1]

To a degree remarkable for that time, the war was covered by individual radio stations. Besides Wright Bryan, who not only reported for NBC and its Atlanta affiliate, WSB, but also for the *Atlanta Journal*, there were others, Ray Clark of WOW, Omaha; Howard Nelson of WDAY, Fargo, North Dakota; Howard Chernoff of WCHS, Charleston, West Virginia; and Jack Shelley of WHO, Des Moines. These correspondents were handicapped. Whereas newspapers and networks could send reporters overseas with no time limit on their accreditation, the accreditation of correspondents from individual stations expired automatically after three months.

There was another catch, which Shelley discovered when he arrived in London. He, and reporters like him, could spend only a month on the Continent where the action was. Shelley argued it was hardly worth coming. The military said that with the communications facilities available at the front it was impossible to accommodate everyone. "They did say I could choose any one of the three months I wanted, and I said I wanted to go at once, which was a lucky choice because I was able to report one of the great battles of the war."

That was the Battle of the Bulge. It began December 16, 1944, when three German armies—25 divisions—struck the Americans' thinly held line in the Ardennes Forest region of Belgium. It lasted more than a month and was the fiercest, most desperate battle fought on the Western Front in World War II.

Shelley describes the logistics involved for one group of correspondents covering the battle:

> It was the custom for the "press camp," which moved with the army headquarters, to be provided with a pool of Jeeps and drivers. Customarily, a war correspondent who intended to go into one of the fighting areas would notify the public information officer's office in advance. He would be assigned a Jeep and a driver, and the driver would pilot the correspondent wherever he wanted to

go, then bring him back to the press camp where transmission facilities—and military censors—were available.[2]

Shelley covered the German offensive with the U.S. First Army.

Not all reporting of the war was from up front. In a broadcast, Charles Collingwood told how some correspondents got their news at the Hotel Scribe in Paris.

> Before the war, the Scribe was just a normal big hotel, much like any other modern hotel in a big city. Today it is like no other hotel in the world. The whole place has been turned upside down to serve as a base of operations for SHAEF correspondents. There are rows of desks and typewriters in the lobby. Great, clacking telegraphic machines have been installed, offices have been set up, radio studios put in. . . . Every day there are press conferences—there's one coming up half an hour from now. Before these conferences, the two briefing officers, one British and one American, telephone each of the army groups for the latest news. By the time we get it, the news is generally about six hours from the time it happened, which is pretty good going.[3]

By early summer 1945, the American forces were advancing toward the heart of Germany. The agony of the Bulge was behind them. The Rhine was crossed. It was "On to Berlin!" and Gabriel Heatter, speaking on the Mutual Network, led the nation in prayer: "Merciful God, watch over these men. They march in a crusade for humanity and freedom. . . . They fight to give all the children of men peace on earth."[4]

The Germans, in their final throes, rocketed London, killing more than 8,000 people. These rockets—the V-1 and the deadlier supersonic V-2—represented a new, revolutionary development in warfare. The rocket attacks on London, and later on Antwerp, lasted from June 1944 to March 1945. "It would be a mistake," Murrow warned, "to make light of this new form of bombardment. Its potentialities are largely unknown."[5] He was appalled by the prospects, though these German rockets carried no nuclear load.

Horror Beyond Words

Murrow was reporting the Holocaust as early as December 1942. In stark language, he said:

> One is almost stunned into silence by some of the information reaching London. Some of it is months old, but it's eyewitness stuff supported by a wealth of detail and vouched for by responsible governments. What is happening is this: Millions of human beings, most of them Jews, are being gathered up with ruthless efficiency and murdered.

He did not generalize. He described what was happening in Norway, in Poland, in the Netherlands, where Anne Frank, unknown to him, was writing in her diary. He spoke of concentration camps, which in reality, he said, are extermination camps—"They are exterminating the Jews." He said, "When you piece it all together, you have a picture of mass murder and moral depravity unequaled in the history of the world. It is a horror beyond what imagination can grasp."[6]

On April 12, 1945, Murrow saw the horror at first hand. He was with the U.S. Third Army when it liberated Buchenwald, one of the largest concentration camps in Germany. Three days later, in a Sunday broadcast, he tried to describe it.

> As I walked down to the end of the barracks, there was applause from the men too weak to get out of bed. It sounded like the hand-clapping of babies, they were so weak. . . . As we walked into the courtyard, a man fell dead. Two others—they must have been over 60—were crawling toward the latrine. I saw it but will not describe it. In another part of the camp they showed me the children, hundreds of them. Some were only six. One rolled up his sleeve, showed me his number. It was tattooed on his arm. D-6030, it was. The others showed me their numbers. They will carry them till they die. . . . Men kept coming up to touch me, professors from Poland, doctors from Vienna, men from all Europe. Men from the countries that made America. . . .

Murrow did not see the crematorium. He was told "it wouldn't be very interesting because the Germans had run out of coke some days ago and had taken to dumping the bodies into a great hole nearby." An inmate said perhaps Murrow would care to see one of the courtyards.

> [In it] were two rows of bodies stacked up like cordwood. They were thin and very white. . . . All except two were naked. I tried to count them as best I could and arrived at the conclusion that all that was mortal of more than 500 men and boys lay there in two neat piles. . . . I have reported what I saw and heard, but only part of it. For most of it I have no words.

On April 12—the same day Buchenwald was liberated—President Roosevelt died in Warm Springs, Georgia. Murrow reported that at Buchenwald "many men in many tongues," unaware of Roosevelt's death, blessed his name. "For long years, [it] had meant the full measure of their hope."[7]

D. G. Bridson, a BBC producer, saw Murrow make the Buchenwald broadcast. He says Murrow was shaking with sorrow and rage by the time he finished.[8]

Death of a President

Franklin Roosevelt was the first president to understand radio's usefulness as a political instrument, and he was the first to die in office after radio came of age. Radio had reported the death of Warren G. Harding in an elementary, fragmentary way. There were no networks in 1923, no broadcast journalist of note. But in 1945, recovering itself after the first bulletins, radio reported the passing of Franklin Roosevelt in full.

INS was first with the flash a few seconds before 5:47 P.M. In the CBS newsroom, Lee Otis, hearing the bell on the INS machine clamoring for attention, saw what is perhaps the shortest news flash in history: FDR DEAD. Within two minutes, "Wilderness Road," a radio series based on the life of Daniel Boone, was interrupted and John Daly was on the air.

> We interrupt this program to bring you a special news bulletin from CBS World News. A press association has just announced that President Roosevelt is dead. All that has been received is that bare announcement. There are no further details as yet, but CBS World News will return to the air in just a few moments with more information as it is received in our New York headquarters. We return you now to our regularly scheduled program.

Within seconds, NBC and Mutual interrupted their programs. At 5:51, AP confirmed the INS report. UP flashed its confirmation at 5:58. At 5:51:30, Daly was back on the air reporting the cause of death and the fact that Mrs. Roosevelt had asked Vice President Truman to come to the White House. At 6:07, the BBC announced solemnly: "It is with deep regret that we report the death of President Roosevelt. He died suddenly this afternoon from cerebral hemorrhage." Minutes later, the news was broadcast to American GIs in Europe by ABSIE, the U.S. Army network. So the word spread.

By now the networks and most stations had scrapped their regular schedules. Commercials were dropped; appropriate music filled the interludes when there was no news. Much of the early special programming consisted of tributes by military, political, and religious leaders. Reporters were called in from all around the country and overseas to report reaction. Some correspondents reacted personally. Robert Trout recalled the night Roosevelt made his first "Fireside Chat." There were memories of his travels with the President, who, he said, "was interested in the technical equipment and the intricate arrangements often necessary when he addressed the nation from remote places." The President, he said, was a battle casualty. "He died in the war."

Another correspondent with special memories of the President was Richard Harkness of NBC. It was Harkness who, as Washington correspondent for the *Philadelphia Enquirer,* had suggested that Roosevelt include freedom from fear in his "Four Freedoms" speech before Congress in January 1941. The other three freedoms were freedom of speech, freedom of worship, and freedom from want. From 5:49 P.M., Thursday, until sign-off at 1 A.M., Friday, NBC broadcast 72 reports related, one way or another, to the President's death.

Douglas Edwards was in London. What marked reaction there, he said, whether from a GI or a commuter in Paddington Station, was shock and disbelief. Alistair Cooke, in New York for the BBC, reported the stunned reaction at Radio City and St. Patrick's Cathedral. In Rockefeller Plaza, he saw small groups of strangers. "They looked sullen, and then, because there was nothing they could do, they drifted helplessly apart." [9]

CBS' Don Pryor came up from Admiral Turner's flagship off Okinawa. Supreme Court Justice William O. Douglas spoke on ABC of the President's devotion to freedom. Someone at Mutual played one of Roosevelt's favorite songs, "Home on the Range."

On Friday, when the President's body was returned to Washington from Warm Springs, all major networks followed the funeral cortege from Union Station to the White House. At one point an NBC announcer lowered his microphone to street level just as the caisson bearing the flag-draped coffin rattled past. Millions of radio listeners heard the horses' hooves and the clattering iron-bound wheels of the caisson. It was a powerful moment. Paul White, checking on what his competition was doing, heard it. "The announcer," he noted, "had sense enough enough not to speak." He found it an emotional experience no words spoken or printed could have provoked. [10]

Among those covering the procession was Arthur Godfrey, a friend of the President. Godfrey had been a radio entertainer in Washington before joining CBS in New York. [11] He dared kid commercials—Fred Allen called him "the Huck Finn of radio"—and he was immensely popular. As the procession turned into Pennsylvania Avenue, near the White House, he reported:

> The drums are wrapped in black crepe and are muffled, as you can hear. The pace of the musicians is so slow. Behind them, these are the Navy boys. And just now, coming past the Treasury, I can see the horses drawing the caisson. . . . And behind it is the car bearing the man on whose shoulders now falls the terrific burdens and responsibilities that were handled so well by the man to whose body we are paying our last respects now. God bless him—President Truman. [12]

Godfrey was crying. He could not go on.

Visit to Berlin

Two weeks after Roosevelt died, the U.S. First Army, driving into the heart of Germany, met Soviet forces on the Elbe. John MacVane described the historic meeting in a broadcast from the First Army press camp at Naumberg;

> This is John MacVane in Germany. I saw American and Russian soldiers meet. I saw them meet and embrace, swap trinkets, drink toasts—and it still didn't seem as though it could really be true. I had waited for days on our front line, heard their voices on the

radio. To meet them, I crossed 30 miles of ground that hadn't been occupied by us or by the Red Army. I rowed twice across the Elbe River in a skittish racing rowboat to go to the Russian command post. . . . The Germans had blown the bridges.

There were English as well as American correspondents at the command post, where MacVane talked to a Red Army lieutenant named Dimitri.

> He asked me to tell what I saw, to try to describe the happiness of the Russian officers and men. They were happy all right. Breakfast had turned into lunch. Bottles of vodka and white wine were getting emptier as toasts were drunk in the Russian fashion, bottoms up to both our armies, to allies, to Marshal Stalin, and to the late President Roosevelt. . . . One officer said to me that in '41 and '42, no Russian man hoped to live. He only hoped to kill a lot of Germans before he died. . . . He pressed me to take a glass of white wine and, lifting it, he said, "To both of us—and to the future." I thought of that as I rowed back across the Elbe in the afternoon sunshine. The future. We can all think of that now.[13]

The Russians had battled their way into the suburbs of Berlin on April 23. They were still mopping up on May 4 when MacVane and Richard C. Hottelet of CBS decided to drive up to Berlin to see for themselves what was happening. It was against orders, but if they got lost in the strange countryside and found themselves in Berlin, could they help it? In this mad adventure they were joined by two print journalists, Bob Reuben of Reuters and Victor Bernstein of *PM,* and an Army press officer, Jack Hansen.

Unchallenged—indeed, saluted—they rode into Berlin in a Jeep sandwiched between two Red Army trucks, part of a supply column. They spent the night with Russian officers and a correspondent for *Izvestia.* The Russian correspondent had good news: Wright Bryan, wounded in the leg, had been liberated from a prisoner of war camp and sent to Moscow for medical treatment.

MacVane believes they were the first American correspondents in Berlin. But, fearing loss of acccreditation, they made no mention of Berlin in their reports; they simply had been with a unit of the Red Army. It had taken five days to get back to the American lines. Two tires blew out on their Jeep. Then they were held—politely but firmly—by the Russians, who wanted to make sure they were what they said they were. When they finally got back on May 8, the war in Europe had ended. It was V-E Day— "V" for victory, "E" for Europe.

Actually, the European war had ended the day before when, in a schoolhouse in Reims, France, General Jodl, Germany's chief of staff, signed the instruments of surrender. Correspondents were to withhold this momentous news. At Stalin's request, the surrender was not to be reported until May 8, when it would be announced simultaneously by the heads of government in Washington, London, and Moscow. Stalin wanted his moment.

It didn't work. An Associated Press correspondent[14] broke the embargo, so that at 9:35 A.M., Eastern War Time, May 7, Robert Trout went on CBS to say:

> The Associated Press has just sent a flash from Reims, in France, and this is the flash: "The Allies officially announce that Germany has surrendered unconditionally." This flash has just come into our Columbia news headquarters here in New York on the Associated Press machine. Why it should come from the town of Reims . . . we don't yet know. Perhaps some sort of negotiations have been going on in that city.[15]

They had indeed. With Hitler gone—dead by his own hand—German representatives had been negotiating with Eisenhower in Reims since May 5. They tried to stall, hoping to surrender to the western allies instead of the Russians. Eisenhower said he was making no deal and declared a 48-hour ultimatum. It was to be German surrender on May 7, unconditional and simultaneous, on all fronts.

Charles Collingwood was one of 16 pool correspondents who witnessed the surrender. He gave his report the next morning. These are fragments:

> Here's this room, not a very large room as rooms go. The walls are covered with maps in bright reds and greens almost up to the ceiling. On these maps is all the information General Jodl would have traded an army group to have had a week ago: Our battle order, our communications system, our supply network, our casualties and, perhaps most important of all, the Germans' own hopeless position clearly marked out.

After describing the arrival of the Allied representatives, he says:

> Then the Germans come in. Jodl's face is like a death mask, drawn, unnatural looking, and with every muscle in it clenched. . . . Both Jodl and his aide have the double red stripe of the German general staff on the side of their cavalry breeches. They reach the table, bow in unison, and wait. General [Bedell] Smith [Eisenhower's chief of staff] motions them to sit down. Everyone sits down.

Jodl signs the surrender at 2:41. Then, after him, the representatives of the Allied powers, as the Germans sit "stiff, unblinking, tasting to the bitter dregs their cup of humiliation."

> Then came the most dramatic moment of all. . . . Colonel General Jodl, chief of staff of the German Army, asked General Bedell Smith's permission to speak. He stood up stiffly, like a man holding himself in against some unbearable pain. In a strangled voice, like a sob, he said: "With this signature the German people and the German armed forces are, for better or worse, delivered into the

victor's hands. In this hour, I can only express the hope that the victor will treat them with generosity." . . . When General Jodl sat down after that, it was all over.[16]

President Truman had already spoken from the White House, reminding the nation by radio that it should remember in its "solemn but glorious hour" that the war against Japan remained to be won. The networks followed Truman with recordings of a speech by Churchill and continued their intense coverage through the day and into the night.

Most of these reports, domestic and foreign, consisted of reaction. But there was, on all networks, a variety of programming that held an audience the Hooper rating service found to be the largest since the U.S. declaration of war on December 8, 1941. There were radio messages from Eleanor Roosevelt, Eve Curie, and King George VI, and prayers by religious leaders. The NBC orchestra, with Arturo Toscanini conducting, played Beethoven's Fifth Symphony, which had been the victory theme in the war. While NBC presented a one-hour dramatization of America's role in the war, CBS offered Norman Corwin's "On a Note of Triumph," with special music by Bernard Herrmann. From London, Mutual brought listeners the Westminster Abbey choir. And over shortwave came the voice of General Douglas MacArthur, saluting the victors in the West "as we rededicate ourselves to the task which lies yet ahead in the East."

The grim battle for Okinawa was in progress as he spoke.

20
The Other War

For scores of war correspondents, Germany's surrender meant reassignment, an about-face from the spent battlefields of Europe to active fronts in the Pacific. Among these were Merrill Mueller (NBC), Bill Downs (CBS), Jack Hooley (ABC), and Paul Manning (Mutual). H. V. Kaltenborn and Lowell Thomas, both of NBC, were in and out of the Pacific theater, just as they had toured the fighting fronts of Europe. CBS' Eric Sevareid had a narrow escape. He had left Washington for an extensive tour of the Far East when, on August 2, 1943, he disappeared. All New York knew was that he had taken off from India on a military flight to Chungking (Chongqing) and that the plane was missing. It was four weeks before word came that Sevareid had survived after parachuting into a part of the Burma jungle inhabited by headhunters.

A few stations sent their own reporters to cover the climactic phase of the war. These included Howard Pyle of KTAR, Phoenix; Ross McConnell of KOMO, Seattle; William Winter of WOL, Washington; and Jack Shelley of WHO, Des Moines, who had reported from Europe in 1944. Mutual's Boston commentator, Cedric Foster, went to the Pacific on a two-month assignment, during which he was accredited to the Navy.

Some movement was in the opposite direction. ABC's Clete Roberts, who had been wounded in the Philippines campaign and awarded two Bronze Stars, was transferred to European duty. WOL sent Kathryn Cravens to Europe to cover its postwar recovery problems, claiming she was "the first woman to go overseas for an individual radio station."[1] WCAU, Philadelphia, sent over Katherine Clark to report on the food and clothing needs of people in the liberated areas. CBS' Douglas Edwards, normally in New York, went to London, then Paris on temporary assignment.

In Praise of the Apache

An unsung heroine of the war with Japan was a rehabilitated old ship, the *Apache,* which served as a floating transmitter for reporting the reconquest of the Philippines. For a year before General MacArthur's return to the Philippines, the Army had been rebuilding the *Apache* for her new role. The ship already claimed three careers. As a Coast Guard cutter, she had hunted icebergs off Newfoundland; she had served as a reception boat at regattas and been McKinley's presidential yacht, which says something about her age. Now the 158-foot ship was refitted and so crammed with communications gear that the crew had to sleep on deck.

The *Apache,* with a small monkey named George as mascot, carried two transmitters, shortwave and medium wave. She had an air-conditioned control room, photographers' dark rooms, and special equipment for transmitting still pictures by radio. To expedite coverage, there was both telephone and teletype communication with MacArthur's headquarters. The radio engineer in charge of equipment was Lieutenant Luther Pierce, formerly of WABC (now WCBS), New York. In overall charge was Abe Schechter, founder of NBC News, now a colonel on MacArthur's staff.

Refitted in dry dock in Sydney, the *Apache* made her way to Leyte, in the Central Philippines, by way of New Guinea. The original plan for retaking the Philippines called for invasion of Leyte in December 1944. Abruptly, in September, the invasion date was advanced to October 20. Because of this new schedule and the necessity of approaching the Philippines under complete radio blackout, there was no real test of the *Apache*'s facilities until she stood off Leyte and the battle for the island began.

After the American forces landed, it was Lieutenant Stanley Quinn of Pelham, New York, who read General MacArthur's first communiqué to millions of listeners back home. Broadcast facilities aboard the *Apache* had worked.

"Believe It Or Not, We're Back!"

Two years and eight months after leaving the Philippines in February 1942, MacArthur waded ashore. The beachhead had barely been secured. From down the beach rifle and machinegun fire could still be heard. From a Signal Corps truck, Bill Dunn made the pool broadcast.

This is William J. Dunn reporting for the joint networks of America. Only a short time after the first wave of American troops hit the beach, here on this Central Philippines island of Leyte, General Douglas MacArthur waded ashore from a tiny landing barge, escorting through the knee-deep surf President Sergio Osmena, rightful leader of this free commonwealth.

I accompanied the general. . . . When the landing barge drew alongside the flagship to carry us onto the beach, he showed the first faint sign of inward excitement which must beset a man when he faces the realization of his greatest ambition. He took his place on the stern of the boat with General Sutherland, his chief of staff who had accompanied him from Bataan, seated beside him. And as the tiny craft rocked away from the great warship, he fixed his eyes on the distant beach and smiled quietly. Then, slapping General Sutherland on the knee, he exclaimed, "Believe it or not, Dick, we're back!"

The Japanese sent reinforcements into Leyte, and hard fighting lasted into December. During the two-month battle almost all broadcasts originated from the *Apache*.

A memorial sculpture was erected on Leyte to commemorate MacArthur's return. Dunn saw it in 1977 when he went back for the dedication. "It was the most amazing experience of my life," he says, "looking at those bronze figures and seeing, amongst them, a nine-foot statue of myself. There they were, bigger than life, in this huge reflecting pool."[2]

As American land forces invaded Leyte, U.S. naval forces won a decisive victory in the Battle of Leyte Gulf, taking such a heavy toll that never again would Japan's warships put to sea as a fleet. U.S. Sixth Army troops invaded and reconquered the principal Philippine island of Luzon. Manila was liberated, and who should come back on the air for NBC but Bert Silen, former manager of KZRH, who had been silenced by the Japanese takeover three years and one month before. "As I was saying when I was so rudely interrupted," he began.

Now the war was coming close to Japan's home islands. In March 1945, the Marines took Iwo Jima, less than 700 miles from Tokyo. In April, the U.S. Tenth Army invaded Okinawa. In an Easter Sunday broadcast over all networks, Admiral Chester Nimitz, commander in chief of the Pacific Fleet, declared: "The capture of Okinawa will give us bases only 325 miles from Japan. . . . Our final, decisive victory is assured." From bases in the Marianas, B-29 bombers stepped up their attacks on Tokyo itself.

Then one airplane, carrying one bomb, changed the history of the world.

Hiroshima

No network, no wire service, had been advised to stand by for the announcement. No background material had been given to any of the media on the usual hold-for-release basis. So it was without warning that at 11:15 A.M., Monday, August 6, 1945, a CBS staff announcer broke into the network to say:

> We interrupt this program to report a bulletin just received from Washington. President Truman has announced that an "atomic bomb" has been used against Japan for the first time, with power equal to 20,000 tons of TNT.

The news all day was of the event that would be debated for decades to come. By late afternoon enough details were known so that Harry Marble, on the CBS program "Feature Story," could report, however inadequately, the dimensions of what had happened.

> The forces from which the sun draws its power has been loosed against those who brought war to the Far East. . . . By 1942, we knew the Germans were working frantically to find a way to harness this power, but they failed. We may be grateful that we have now won the battle of the laboratories as we have won the other battles.

Marble quoted from the statement that Truman, still at sea on his way back from the Potsdam Conference, had issued. Truman spoke of the possible peacetime use of atomic energy. He was going to recommend to Congress the establishment of "an appropriate commission to control the production and use of atomic power in the United States." Normally, the United States would share this scientific knowledge. It would not do so now, "pending further examination of possible methods of protecting us and the rest of the world from the danger of sudden destruction."

Truman had already left for Potsdam to confer with Churchill[3] and Stalin when the first atom bomb was successfully tested in the New Mexico desert on July 16. This epochal news was withheld until after the Hiroshima raid, although the President had confided in reporters traveling with him to Potsdam. But one correspondent, Morgan Beatty of NBC, claimed special knowledge. According to Beatty, it came to him during a poker game. They were aboard the cruiser *Augusta* on their way home. Truman was enjoying the game when an aide brought him a radio message. The President then asked for a map, and Beatty, facing Truman at the table, watched closely as the aide pointed with a pencil at a Japanese city. A bright light behind Truman made the map almost transparent. Beatty could see the name of the city. It was Hiroshima, and Beatty guessed it would be the world's first atomic target. There was no way to get the story out, even if he had wanted to. And, after all, it was only a guess.

The bomb that would change history weighed five tons. At its core was a package of Uranium 235 about the size of a football. Within nine seconds after the explosion, it had turned ground zero into a gridiron with temperatures rivaling those of the sun. An estimated 100,000 people died in Hiroshima that day, or were doomed to die.

At 8 o'clock that evening, New York time, Webley Edwards of CBS reported from Guam, where the plane that carried the bomb was based. He and other correspondents had talked with Paul W. Tibbets, the pilot.

> He named the plane after his mother, Enola Gay—that was her name—but there was no gaiety about Tibbets. He was deadly serious and quiet spoken. . . . As the historic bomb was away, Colonel Tibbets said they executed a classic maneuver, "Let's get the hell out of here," and he banked sharply and left. Then they looked. He said, "It was kind of hard to see what we did see through the smoke. Below and rising rapidly was a tremendous smoke cloud that covered almost the entire city.

The weaponeer on the plane, Navy Captain William Parsons of Chicago,[4] told Edwards, "[O]ne of the crew members said 'My God!' when he saw what had happened. For what had been Hiroshima was a white mountain of smoke, and when we saw it at first, the smoke already was up to 20,000 feet." In describing the "mountain of smoke," Parsons used the word *mushroom*. "It was," he said, " a tremendous, awe-inspiring sight."

The second and last atomic target of the war was Nagasaki, which was struck on August 9. That evening, speaking from the White House, President Truman said:

> Having found the bomb, we have used it. . . . We have used it in order to shorten the agony of war, in order to save the lives of thousands and thousands of young Americans. We shall continue to use it until we completely destroy Japan's power to make war. Only a Japanese surrender will stop us.

Surrender

Russia, in keeping with the Potsdam agreement, had entered the war against Japan on August 8. Despite the Soviet move and America's awesome new weapon, Japan's leadership on August 9 remained split on whether to surrender unconditionally or seek conditions, such as a proviso that Japan would not be occupied. Finally, it was Emperor Hirohito who decided. Japan must bear the unbearable: unconditional surrender.

Americans got the news on the morning of August 10. At 7:36:30 A.M. (in broadcast competition, seconds counted) Allan Jackson of CBS broke into Arthur Godfrey's early morning program. Quoting the United Press, he said: "The press association has picked up a Domei News Agency dispatch broadcast on the Tokyo radio. The broadcast reports that the Japanese will accept the Allied terms if the sovereignty of the emperor is not compromised."

Over at NBC, Don Goddard was delivering his regular morning newscast. At 7:39, he interrupted himself, saying: "Here is a bulletin. NBC monitors in San Francisco have just picked up a Tokyo broadcast which said that Japan accepts the Allied surrender ultimatum."

The networks began giving the story full treatment at 8 o'clock when, during their regularly scheduled roundups, they called in correspondents from Washington and overseas. Typical was the report of CBS' Bill Downs from Manila: "There has been no official confirmation here yet of the sensational surrender reports from Tokyo Radio. But there's a smell of victory in the air at General MacArthur's headquarters."

Nowhere confirmation; everywhere a sense that, at last, the struggle was coming to an end. CBS and ABC resumed normal programming at 10:30 A.M., when President Truman denied official knowledge of the Japanese offer. NBC and Mutual stayed with the story. Not until 7 o'clock that evening did Washington—and then it was the State Department—confirm that it had received a peace proposal from the Japanese. Later that night it became known that the United States had drafted a reply, setting forth terms for surrender. The next morning, the White House revealed the terms. They dealt with such details as cessation of hostilities, yielding up of arms, and transport of Allied prisoners of war and internees to places of safety. The emperor could stay, but he would be subject to General Mac-Arthur, who would be in charge of the occupation.

All this had to have the approval of Great Britain, Russia, and China. Japan had made its initial offer on a Friday. The diplomatic minuet continued through Saturday, Sunday, and Monday. At 4:18 P.M. on Tuesday, August 14, NBC's Max Jordan came up from Berne, Switzerland, which had been a relay point for communication with Japan. He had the word everyone had been waiting for.

> Within approximately two hours from now the White House in Washington will have the complete transcribed facts of the Japanese reply to the last message of the Allies. . . . The general impression [is] that Japan has accepted the terms of the Allies in principle and that the war is over.

Two hours and 43 minutes after Jordan began his report, it was confirmed on the United Press wire.

UP193
    FLASH
    WASHINGTON, TRUMAN ANNOUNCES JAPS ACCEPT SURRENDER TERMS.

MW701P

To make the announcement, Truman had called a news conference for 7 P.M. Among reporters crowded into the Oval Office were Jim Gibbons of ABC, Fulton Lewis, Jr., of Mutual, Richard Harkness of NBC, and Bill Henry of CBS. Henry, as did others, had the prepared statement. As soon as Truman started reading it, he dashed from the room and across the White House lawn to a mobile transmitter in Lafayette Park. At Occidental College, Henry had been an all-round athlete. He could run. Now, as he ran, he could hear Robert Trout's voice coming from a loudspeaker.

Trout, microphone in hand, was broadcasting from beside a teletype machine in the New York newsroom.

> The Japanese have accepted our terms fully. . . . This, ladies and gentlemen, is the end of the Second World War. The United Nations on land, on the sea, and in the air, and to the four corners of the earth are united and are victorious.

At 7:03, Trout called in Washington, and Henry read the President's statement.

> I have received this afternoon a message from the Japanese government in reply to the message forwarded to that government by the secretary of state on August 11. I deem this reply a full acceptance of the Potsdam Declaration. It specifies the unconditional surrender of Japan. . . . Meantime, the Allied armed forces have been ordered to suspend offensive action. The proclamation of V-J Day must wait upon the formal signing of the surrender terms by Japan.

The proclamation might have to wait, but the celebration of victory did not. NBC's veteran announcer, Ben Grauer, in the midst of a surging crowd in Times Square, had difficulty holding onto his microphone. Looking down from the balcony of the Hotel Astor, Charles Shaw of CBS called the scene impossible to describe, then tried to describe it. Speaking from the corner of Forty-second Street and Fifth Avenue, Larry LeSueur said, "New York has been liberated. People are shouting from the tops of [double deck] buses, shaking hands, kissing, embracing."

In Washington, CBS' Tris Coffin went on the air from Lafayette Park, using the same mobile transmitter Henry had used.

> A moment ago, the President walked down to the fence, saw one of his old friends, a photographer, waved to him and said hello. The President was very deeply moved, the crowds out there just cheering him, the streets littered with confetti. A major who fought the New Guinea campaign just proudly says, "Beautiful. It's the most beautiful thing I've ever seen."

The Signing

The date is September 1, 1945, 14 years to the month after Japan began its conquest of Manchuria and six years to the day after Germany invaded Poland. More than three hundred correspondents are on hand for the surrender ceremony aboard the USS *Missouri* in Tokyo Bay. The battleship is so crowded with reporters and military and diplomatic representatives of nine nations that its mighty forward guns have been raised, pointing to the overcast sky, in order to provide room.

So that radio will not beat newspapers, there will be no live coverage.

Instead, the Navy will record the eyewitness reports of Merrill Mueller and Webley Edwards and release their pooled broadcast an hour and a half after the historic event. Mueller is chosen from correspondents attached to General MacArthur's staff, Edwards from correspondents who have been with Admiral Nimitz. They will be speaking from an antiaircraft gun mounting, behind and above the Allied signatories and facing the Japanese. The recordings will be made simultaneously on magnetic wire and acetate discs. A destroyer will rush the discs to Radio Tokyo, which is now under Allied control; the wire recordings will be delivered to the communications ship *Ancon* standing nearby.[5]

It is nighttime in the United States. Twenty-five seconds after 9:30, the pooled report by Webley Edwards and Merrill Mueller comes in on a clear circuit. Edwards is heard first.

> Attention, peoples of the world! World War II is about to come to its official closing. We are on the Pacific Fleet flagship, USS *Missouri,* in Tokyo Bay, for the signing of the surrender of Japan. . . . Oh, here comes, here comes the supreme commander of the Allied forces, General of the Army Douglas MacArthur, and with him Admiral of the Fleet Chester Nimitz and other dignitaries.

As prearranged, Mueller cuts in, "General MacArthur," he says, "is now facing the microphones. He's about to start his speech, which explains the signing of surrender—." He stops abruptly as MacArthur starts to speak. The general expresses his hope for the future—peace without malice— then calls on the representatives of Japan to sign the instrument of surrender. The first to step forward is Shigemitsu, the Japanese foreign minister, who will sign on behalf of the emperor. Now Mueller is speaking.

> He's coming up to the table. He pulls the chair back and he's . . . having a little trouble sitting down because of his wooden leg. He takes off his silk top hat, pulling off his gloves, his long yellow gloves. His assistant is helping him with the papers. . . . This is going a little slower than planned.

Moments later, there is further delay when it is discovered that Shigemitsu has no ink in his pen. Eventually, the surrender document is signed by all parties, with Mueller and Edwards, in turn, describing what is taking place. The last words from the battleship are Edwards'. "And now from the Pacific, ladies and gentlemen of the world, as if God himself approves, the clouds have broken away and the sun has come out in these first moments of peace."

Speaking solemnly in his flat Missouri twang, President Truman pays tribute to the servicemen and women who died for the victory. He speaks hopefully of the future, expressing confidence that a free people capable of producing an atomic bomb "can use the same skill and energy and determination to overcome all the difficulties ahead."

For Keeping the Peace

Even before the war ended, the United Nations organization had been founded as a new world body to keep the peace. Although each wire service had its own correspondent on the train carrying Truman to San Francisco to address the 46-nation conference, the sole radio correspondent allowed to travel with the President was William Hillman of Mutual, who had won the drawing to represent the four networks.

The nine-week meeting, opening on April 25, 1945, was the most heavily covered event to take place in the United States up to that time. Altogether, more than 2,500 applications for accreditation were approved. Of these, 487 went to radio. As newly elected president of the Radio Correspondents Association (now the Radio and Television Correspondents Association), NBC's Richard Harkness led negotiations with the State Department for their accreditation.

Some fifty stations as well as foreign and domestic networks, had reporters on the scene. For special commentary, KFWB, Hollywood, engaged Eleanor Wilson McAdoo, daughter of President Wilson, and Bruce Bliven, editor of *The New Republic.* Radio, said *Broadcasting,* had demonstrated "the industry's capacity to meet heavy responsibilities in handling momentous world affairs."[6]

21
A New Day

In war, radio served the nation well. "I salute America's broadcasters," President Truman said.[1] Now for broadcasters it was a new day. With the lifting of the freeze on station allocations, the FCC was flooded with AM and FM applications. There was a boom in car radios as well as home receivers. While only a few car radios were on the market in 1945, 150,000 were sold in 1946.[2]

Development of television, stymied by the war, got a fresh start. RCA introduced an improved TV camera tube, and before 1945 was out, a coaxial cable linked New York with Philadelphia, which already was linked with Washington. CBS and RCA began their long battle over systems for receiving television pictures in color, which RCA eventually won in 1953.

In war coverage, CBS had been the winner. As early as 1941, *Time* had said that CBS provided "the most efficient and adult news service in radio."[3] And much later, in 1978, the *Chicago Tribune* critic, Gary Deeb, was referring to CBS as "the company that created radio news."[4] The reporting by other networks had been praiseworthy, but CBS' corps of correspondents, led by Edward R. Murrow, was preeminent. There was a remarkable durability about these correspondents. Thirty years after the war, Charles Collingwood, Eric Sevareid, Richard C. Hottelet, Bill Downs, Robert Trout,

Howard K. Smith, and Larry LeSueur were still on the air. Few names in broadcasting were more distinguished, and Murrow's name still appeared in almost every statement of what broadcast journalism should be.

In looking back, it is easy to slight what Sevareid calls "the organizational and editorial genius of Paul White."[5] For such reputation as CBS enjoyed there had to be a mastermind. The mastermind was White, and CBS' coverage of the Second World War was his masterwork.

With the war behind them, the networks took a new approach. It was time, they decided, to pay less attention to foreign news and more attention to what was happening at home. After all, the war was over. Economic and political convulsions might be taking place in Europe and civil war in China, but people were tired of foreign news. For more than a decade, ever since Hitler began making trouble, there had been so much of it. The networks would not ignore major foreign stories—the overseas bureaus were busy—but the new emphasis would be on what happened here.

On September 17, 1945, two weeks after Japan's surrender, Paul White dispatched a memorandum marked "Urgent" to the entire CBS News staff. For emphasis, it was typed on red paper.

> I listened to a great number of news programs over the weekend, and it seems to me that we still have too much of a foreign fixation. I do not mean to imply that foreign news is not important, but I think that we should cover such domestic events as reconversion, the hurricane and the Detroit labor troubles with the same intensity and good writing that we cover the collapse of Japan and the meeting of Big Five ministers in London.

In 1946, CBS introduced a 15-minute weekday program called "News of America," which restricted itself almost entirely to domestic developments. Just as correspondents reported from various foreign capitals on the "World News Roundup," reporters at stations affiliated with CBS told what was happening around the country. The program was first anchored by Don Hollenbeck, who had come over from NBC, and then by Bill Shadel. *Pathfinder* magazine called Hollenbeck "the first newscaster to put the spotlight on drama from small towns."[6]

At NBC, William F. Brooks served notice: "Our news staffs will have to get out of their chairs, and we will have to pay more attention to local news in all our newsrooms."[7] NBC did not start a daily program like "News of America" but did introduce a 15-minute weekend program called "Report on America." The program's chief correspondent, W. W. Chaplin, traveled about the country reporting political, agricultural, and industrial developments. At the same time, NBC's important nightly broadcast, "News of the World," began stressing domestic stories.

And local stations covered more local news. Jack Shelley, who had become news director of WHO, Des Moines, warned:

> The people who are going to get hurt most in this transition period are those who abused the "get rich quick" possibilities of the war

boom in radio news. . . . They are the people who sold every news-cast they could cram into the schedule because any sponsor would buy news. They're the people who filled their shows with nothing but war news because it was so easy to use up 10 or 15 minutes with a couple of nice long roundups off the wire.

He said, "We're going to have to become reporters again."[8]

A survey found that 76 percent of the stations in the country broadcast more local news in 1946 than in any other year in their history.[9] WIND, Chicago, inaugurated a 15-minute program called "Today's News in Chicago." In Boise, Idaho, KIDO launched "Operation Idaho," in which business and civic leaders were taken on an airplane tour of the state to acquaint them with its industrial and recreational resources. The project resulted in a series of radio programs.

Another station emphasizing local coverage was WLIB, New York, which doubled its schedule of broadcasts with a 10-minute program every hour on the hour. WSTP, Minneapolis-St. Paul, in effect made all its employees news people by offering them money for tips on local stories. In 1947, WFOY, St. Augustine, boasted that it had aired an average of 450 minutes of local news a week.

Neither stations nor networks had to "manufacture" this news. Demobilization and removal of wartime restrictions had created problems. Millions of G.I.s were looking for work. The price of food was soaring. Houses were in short supply. So were automobiles. There were strikes and not enough classrooms. In many ways, it was one big story—how the nation would adjust to peace.

In his story of radio news, Mitchell Charnley takes a typical 50,000-watt affiliated station of the mid-1940s and describes the composition of its news staff. At such a station, he says, there might be three commentators, six writers, a wire recorder specialist, and a "newsroom director," who today would be called "news director." Besides serving the station, the director often reported for the network when a story broke in his area. Charnley reports the weekly pay scale as follows:

> Commentator, $150
> Wire recorder specialist, $150
> Writer, $100

He does not report the salary of the "newsroom director," which probably was in the neighborhood of $175. As for the broadcast schedule, the typical affiliated station, in addition to network feeds, aired 11 news programs, all 15-minute newscasts except for one running 5 minutes and another 10 minutes.

Both staff and salary at a small, 250-watt station of that time are in sharp contrast. Charnley's research found that it "might have a news staff of one man who is paid $55 a week."[10] Charnley's small station schedules seven news programs a day, in addition to network newscasts. As many as five of the seven local shows run 15 minutes. The trend toward shorter newscasts on the hour or half-hour, or both, was to come later.

Critic and Conscience

To the surprise of many people, Elmer Davis did not return to CBS after the war. Instead, when the Office of War Information expired, he went to ABC. He had been one of CBS' luminaries. On leaving CBS to head the OWI, he had sent William S. Paley a note saying that CBS had been the "most pleasant" place he had ever worked.[11] But Paley was against expression of personal opinion, and Davis believed in saying what he, personally, thought. On Thanksgiving Day, 1945, he said in a letter to Murrow:

> I understand Jap Gude[12] has advised you that I am not to have the privilege of working for you. Sorry. I shall miss CBS in many ways, but there are certain working conditions that seemed reasonable to me and did not seem reasonable to Col. Paley, so we had to agree to disagree.

At ABC, Davis felt freer to speak his mind And speak it he did, starting with his first broadcast on December 2, 1945, when he chided Congress for timidity. Members kept holding investigations instead of acting on legislative proposals of the President, he said, "because whichever way a man votes on them, he might make some enemies." Summing up the events of 1945, he led by saying, "A truly great man died this year, wearing himself out in winning the war and trying to win the peace." He was speaking of Franklin Roosevelt, and he spoke of how Roosevelt and Jefferson were hated. He said: "Both men were hated for various reasons, but basically they were hated because they tried to give the average man a break."

It was the language of a liberal. Inevitably he would speak against McCarthy. That story later.

Davis' 15-minute commentaries were heard on Sunday, Monday, and Tuesday. Raymond Gram Swing took over on Wednesday, Thursday, and Friday. No network could boast more erudite observers. After 1947, when Swing left ABC in order to have more time for writing and lecturing, Davis was heard on ABC Radio throughout the week. For health reasons he gave up his nightly broadcasts in 1953, but he did appear on ABC Television during 1954, when he was seen on Sunday, sitting relaxed in an armchair, dispensing good sense plainly in his Hoosier accent. He died, struck mute by a stroke, on May 18, 1958.

The day after Davis' death, Ed Murrow said on his radio program:

> Elmer Davis brought to this medium wisdom, maturity, a fierce faith in democratic processes, and an unequalled ability to condense news without distorting it. He never knowingly did violence to the truth. He was at all times a responsible man. Those of us

who worked with him, and those who listened to him, are alike in his debt.[13]

David Holbrook Culbert, the historian, has said that Elmer Davis' greatest contribution "came from his ubiquity during the 20 months before Pearl Harbor. He broadcast more often and over stronger affiliates than any other commentator."[14] Surely Davis' writings in magazines and newspapers during that period must also be counted, but it was by radio that he reached the largest audience. Like Murrow, Davis before Pearl Harbor never explicitly advocated the involvement of American armed forces, but, as Culbert notes, "his summaries of the news [on CBS] subtly led listeners to look favorably on such a point of view."[15]

In 1970, Eric Sevareid gave the fourth annual Elmer Davis Memorial Lecture at Columbia University. "I can hear it now," said Sevareid, "that twangy, salty voice from Indiana." And what he heard the voice saying was:

> The first and great commandment is: Don't let them scare you. For the men who are trying to do that to us are scared themselves. They are . . . afraid that the principles on which this Republic was founded and has been conducted are wrong. They will tell you that there is a hazard in the freedom of the mind, and of course there is, as in any freedom. In trying to think right, you run the risk of thinking wrong. But there is no hazard at all, no uncertainty, in letting somebody else tell you what to think. *That* is sheer damnation.[16]

During his last illness, Elmer Davis was replaced on ABC Television by Gerald Johnson, a friend of H. L. Mencken's who had been editorial page editor of the *Baltimore Sun.* Johnson came to the network with credentials in broadcasting, though the association was short-lived. His commentaries on WJZ-TV, the Westinghouse station in Baltimore, had earned him a Peabody Award in 1954. He also received the duPont and Sidney Hillman foundation awards.

Like Davis, Johnson had a scholarly mind. As a young man, he taught journalism at the University of North Carolina. By the time of his death in 1980, he had written more than thirty books on historical and biographical subjects.

The Shuffle

By the end of the war, Abe Schechter was head of the news operation at Mutual. William F. Brooks, who had taken Schechter's place as director of NBC News, received the title of vice president. Robert Kintner, in charge of news at ABC, had the same title. Paul White did not. At CBS, the title went to Edward R. Murrow, who returned from London in March 1946 to become vice president of news and public affairs, while White, serving under him, remained director of news. Wells "Ted" Church was assistant director. Everett Holles, White's former assistant, had become a commentator at WBBM, the CBS-owned station in Chicago.

Murrow's promotion jolted White. Among network news chiefs he was preeminent; he had reason to believe he might get the top spot. One imagines that although White found the situation hard to take, he understood it. Circumstances had conspired against him. In London, not only had Paley had the opportunity to appreciate Murrow's stature, his charm and easy association with ambassadors and prime ministers, and his reporting ability, but they had become friends. Murrow fit his picture of the man who should be in charge.

And White hurt himself. He was brash, competitive, rough-hewn. He lived news and found the meetings called by other executives boring, a waste of time. When he skipped a meeting called by Paley, he sent a note:

Dear Mr. Paley,
   I am very sorry, but my little boy, Paul, cannot be at your meeting today as he is down very bad with his syphilis.
                                                        Mrs. White[17]

There was, besides Paley the corporate genius, Paley the collector of fine paintings, who recoiled from crudity. This able newsman who had contributed so much to CBS and to journalism could not be to Paley's taste. Years later, Margaret White, his widow, said of Murrow: "He had an air that gave quality to any position he held. Those who appreciated Ed recognized this and could understand his choice for the post."[18]

When, in 1946, Robert Trout succeeded Douglas Edwards as anchor of "The World Today," it became the most highly budgeted news program up to that time. The program was so important that White wanted to speak when it premiered. This was a fateful decision. Ever since Murrow's promotion, White had been drinking heavily. There had been embarrassing scenes, some in public, and the situation was becoming intolerable. Now on this night, perhaps to overcome the nervousness that speaking into a microphone invariably caused him, he went again to the bottle. He may not have drunk a great deal—his tolerance was low—but he obviously was intoxicated, and Murrow fired him. So ended, tragically, a brilliant 15-year career at CBS, a period in which the mold for much of broadcast journalism was cast.

White had always wanted to write a novel. Now, with free time, he wrote one. It was about a celebrated radio correspondent—a fictionalized Murrow?—but by the time it was written, then rewritten, television, not radio, held the public's fancy. The novel seemed outdated and was never published.

In 1947, Harcourt, Brace did publish *News on the Air,* the informative, anecdotal work that is a collector's item today. In the same year, the Associated Press engaged White to make a study of its radio wire and propose ways to make it serve broadcasters better. He stayed two months at the University of Iowa, trying out his textbook and advising the university radio station, WSUI, on how to spruce up its news operation.

The Whites settled in San Diego, where Margaret had been born. She writes:

> At about that time, John A. Kennedy, who owned a West Virginia network of CBS-affiliated stations, bought the *San Diego Journal*. Howard Chernoff, Kennedy's business manager, took over management of the paper. When he learned that Paul was in town, he asked him to come to the *Journal* as chief editorial writer.[19]

White went to the paper and felt at home there. Margaret White says, "After the gruelling years of network radio, he loved the romp of working for a newspaper with a competent staff in a smaller town."[20]

When the *Journal* folded in 1950, Kennedy bought KFMB-AM-TV in San Diego, and White wrote and delivered editorials for both stations. He still believed in objective reporting but saw nothing wrong with opinion if it was confined to commentary and his "Editorial Page of the Air." This was completely contrary to the view he had held and so vigorously enforced in the 1940s. He admitted this publicly in 1954, as already noted.[21]

Early in 1952, Thomas Velotta of ABC asked White if he would direct that network's coverage of the Republican and Democratic national conventions. With the exception of John Daly, ABC's anchorman, he would be dealing with a staff he had neither assembled nor trained. It was a challenge, one he found irresistible. He got a leave of absence from KFMB and returned to the wars with enthusiasm. Velotta says that, at the conventions, White asked no favors. "He was there to deliver, and he did. He was quite a guy."[22]

Paul White died in 1955, ravaged by emphysema, heart disease, and cirrhosis of the liver. He was 52. Ed Klauber had died the preceding year. Ed Murrow would die ten years later. They were, as John Daly says, "a hell of a triumvirate."[23]

Meanwhile, at NBC . . .

In its annual review for 1946–1947, NBC News boasted of "a brilliant trio of early evening news programs heard over the network five times a week." These were Morgan Beatty's "News of the World," heard at 7:15 P.M., and the popular Lowell Thomas and H. V. Kaltenborn programs heard at 6:45 and 7:45. NBC's other daily news programs were "The World News Roundup," anchored by John MacVane at 8 A.M., Robert McCormick's news and analysis at 1:30 P.M., and Richard Harkness' report at 11:15 P.M. The Harkness program originated in Washington; MacVane and McCormick did their broadcasts from New York, where MacVane also covered the United Nations. (MacVane would soon switch to ABC, where he would be covering the U.N. in competition with his wartime rival, Larry

LeSueur. And this was the last year Lowell Thomas would be heard on NBC; he returned to CBS in September, to stay.)

Henry Cassidy had now become NBC's European director, based in Paris. Merrill Mueller went to London as bureau manager. Other assignments included John Donovan to the Middle East and Robert Reuben to the Antarctic to report on the latest expedition led by Admiral Richard Byrd. César Saerchinger, who had been CBS in Europe in the early days, was doing an NBC program called "The Story Behind the Headlines."

And there was a new writer at NBC News named Julian Goodman, who one day would head the news organization, then become president of NBC, then chairman of the board.

Vintage Years

For radio news, this was the Golden Age. Reading issues of *Radio Daily* for 1948, one gets a sense of how, since then, the scene has changed.

> Henry J. Taylor left Los Angeles last night on the *Super Chief* and is slated to arrive in New York Saturday. He'll resume his "Your Land and Mine" series over Mutual next Monday.
>
> Arthur Godfrey tomorrow will fly to Cleveland in his own plane and will assist in the CBS coverage of the National Air Races. He'll return Sunday.
>
> Larry LeSueur sailed today aboard the *America* for Paris, where he'll cover the United Nations General Assembly.
>
> Bill Stern sails tonight aboard the *Mauretania* for England, where he'll cover the Olympics for ABC. Mrs. Stern is with him.
>
> John MacVane, United Nations correspondent for NBC, yesterday left for Germany on an Air Force junket to report on the Berlin airlift. From there, he'll go on to Paris.

The U.N. General Assembly now meets in New York, not Paris. The crack train, the *Super Chief*, no longer makes the run from Los Angeles to Chicago. The Cleveland Air Races have passed into history—the modern jet is much too fast for racing over a local prescribed course. And foreign correspondents no longer travel on liners like the *America* and *Mauretania* for their overseas assignments; they fly and report as they recover from jet lag.

For correspondents who worked in places like London, Paris, and Rome, these were the last halcyon years. Their stories dealt with national elections, diplomacy, the Marshall Plan—the cold war. They lived on expense accounts in luxury apartments to which they invited leaders of government for dinner. They ate in the best restaurants. Traveling, they stayed at the best hotels.

"It was," said Charles Collingwood, who reported from abroad in that time, "a hell of a good life."[24]

These elite reporters broadcast from their European bases virtually every day. England and the Continent were building a new economic order, the Common Market, and a new defense system, NATO, and these efforts and other developments were reported in detail. Much of this was unsensational, even dull, but networks assumed it was something Americans should know.

The correspondent had the foreign capital for his beat; he seldom chased stories in other countries. He did not have ponderous television equipment, ground stations, or production crews to worry about. Because he was not spread thin, he had more time to dig into stories. He became an expert on his country, spoke its language, wrote books about it. He was an authority, and people in high places in Washington listened for what he would say.

Today, foreign correspondents are peripatetic. The Paris correspondent may be dispatched to cover an earthquake in Yugoslavia and the London correspondent to Germany to interview the chancellor. More than one network correspondent has been given all of Africa as his beat — 11 million square miles.

Before his death Collingwood expressed concern that the present-day correspondent, through no fault of his own, may be ill-informed. He reasoned, "You simply cannot be a seismological expert one day, an Islamic scholar the next, and a specialist in the history of Afghanistan the next."[25] It is a concern shared by John Chancellor of NBC. More "reflective" journalism, he says, is needed. Foreign correspondents dash about responding to crises for which the public is unprepared.[26] Peter Jennings of ABC says: "The trouble with television is that it thinks that reporters' minds work at the same speed that electronic newsgathering equipment works. So you end up in Dublin trying to do a one-day story when you should have a week and in East Berlin the next day."[27]

Exceptions are to be noted: CBS' Morley Safer reporting from Vietnam in the 1960s, ABC's Pierre Salinger from France in the 1970s (and later), and NBC's John Cochran from Poland in the 1980s. There are others, able foreign correspondents assigned to the same beat long enough to be expert, but not nearly as many as in the Forties and Fifties when network correspondents dashed about less often and had more opportunity to think.

22
Radio's Revolution

It took less than ten years for radio's dominance of the air waves to evaporate. The medium that in 1946 basked in popularity—and profits— had become a faltering complement to television by 1956. People were not listening to radio in the evening; they were watching the Ed Sullivan show or laughing with Milton Berle, so celebrated he received the sobriquet "Mr. Television." Radio cut its advertising rates. Still, revenue fell perilously. In 1951, the CBS Radio Network, which had thrived with Jack Benny and Bing Crosby, went into the red. Such high-budget shows as "Lux Radio Theatre" and "Kraft Music Hall" disappeared. Then other entertainment programs. Radio's future seemed dim.

Two staples, music and news, remained. Newscasters like Edward R. Murrow, Gabriel Heatter, Lowell Thomas, and Fulton Lewis, Jr., were still heard on radio. Some of them preferred radio to television. It was so much simpler—no makeup, no cameras, no hot lights. You sat in front of a microphone and reported. Murrow worked in radio until 1961. Thomas' program, ultimately reduced to six minutes, lasted into 1976 (he was back in the CBS fold after having left NBC in 1947).

Ever since the days of the Munich crisis, when peace hung in the

TABLE 22.1. **The Network News Schedule (Radio) as of August 1952**

	ABC	**CBS**	**NBC**	**Mutual**
6:00 P.M.	George Sokolsky (Sunday only)	Allan Jackson	Bob Warren on Monday, Tuesday, Wednesday and Saturday. Lionel Ricau on Thursday and Friday	
6:45 P.M.		Lowell Thomas	Three-star Extra	
7:00 P.M.	Headline Edition		News Time	Fulton Lewis, Jr.
7:15 P.M.	Elmer Davis			Report from the Pentagon (Saturday only)
7:30 P.M.			News of the World	Gabriel Heatter
7:45 P.M.		Edward R. Murrow		Mutual Newsreel
11:00 P.M.	News	News	News	Baukhage Talking

balance, the five-minute news summary on the hour had been a fixture in radio. Of these "hourlies," CBS' Charles Osgood once wrote:

> The stuff that news is made of
>   keeps happening each day,
> Relentlessly occurring in
>   the most peculiar way,
> So that always some development
>   develops, as it were,
> To create enough anxiety
>   and cause sufficient stir
> In the avenues of influence
>   And corridors of power
> To lead the news on radio
>   Each hour on the hour.[1]

During the war, and for a short time afterward, most of these summaries were read by staff announcers. With the arrival of television, radio executives saw news, along with music, as an area in which they could remain competitive. To make the hourlies more attractive, it was decided that they should be aired by experienced reporters with names listeners recognized.

This was done at all networks, but CBS Radio went a step further. On November 28, 1960—three days after its last soap opera departed for television—it expanded its news schedule, ordering up 10-minute summaries on the hour, instead of five minutes. It also introduced its "Dimension" series, which consisted of five-minute informational inserts on the half hour. Subjects ranged from politics and science to health. Joel Heller was executive producer.

A bigger step was taken by NBC, which pioneered with a radio magazine called "Monitor." The program was another brainchild of Sylvester "Pat" Weaver, who had become president of the network in 1953. He created the "Today" show, and "Monitor" was, in effect, the weekend radio edition.

"Monitor" premiered on June 12, 1955. Jim Fleming, the first newscaster assigned to "Today," was its first producer. Two of the first anchors, who had the fancy title "communicators," were Frank Blair and Hugh Downs. An intriguing mixture of news, music, interviews, dramatic sketches, and sports was scattered through the weekend. Gene Shalit, who later would appear on "Today," did occasional film reviews. During the series' first six years, the comedy team of Bob Elliott and Ray Goulding—Bob and Ray—did live routines, but most segments were prerecorded. "Monitor" was radio's most effective answer to television at the time, and it ran until 1975. Weaver had made radio exciting again.

ABC Radio introduced "New Sounds," a weekday evening series patterned after "Monitor," but it never matched the original's success.

"All News, All the Time"

Radio stations, like radio networks, felt the heat from television and, as advertisers deserted them, fought back with new formats. Demographics, a word of respectable Greek origins, became a new important word for programmers. It meant scheduling for specific audiences according to education, income, and age. For years, there had been foreign language stations; now there were stations for racial groups, such as Hispanics and blacks.

This produced unparalleled diversity. No longer, to use Jack Gould's phrase, did a radio station broadcast "a mixed bag of a little of this and a little of that."[2] A station's programming was all of one kind. If it was a music station, it had its own sound, which might be beautiful music, middle of the road (MOR), or rock. "Top 40" stations played the hits. There were country music stations. Classical music stations catered to listeners in a higher socioeconomic group. Stations specializing in two-way telephone conversation made the listener–broadcaster relationship intimate.

Some stations originated late night programs from restaurants or night clubs where guests were interviewed on subjects ranging from the national divorce rate to Nikita Khrushchev. The most popular late night interviewer on radio today is Larry King, but Barry Gray of WMCA, New York, was top "call-in" host for more than three decades.

Finally, there is the all-news station. KFAX, San Francisco, adopted the format in 1960. Each hour began with 25 minutes of hard news, updated as the day progressed. The rest of the hour was filled with business news, all kinds of features, and sports. It tried to be a "newspaper of the air." The attempt failed after four months. There weren't enough advertisers.

The first commercially successful all-news station was located in Tijuana, Mexico, and began operating on May 5, 1961. With a powerful 50,000-watt transmitter, it beamed its news—in English—at the large Los Angeles market. It had been XEAK, a rock and roll station. Its new operator, Gordon McLendon, changed the station's call letters to XETRA and, dropping the "E" in XETRA, began broadcasting what he called XTRA News.[3]

Joshua Mills of New York University, who has made a study of all-news operations, says McLendon went to great lengths to disguise XETRA as a Los Angeles station.

> XETRA's jingles would say, "The world's first and only all-news radio station, in the air everywhere over Los Angeles," or "at 690 on your Los Angeles radio dial." The only address ever announced was the Los Angeles sales office. The station was required by law to give its call letters and location every hour. McLendon handled this by having them done in Spanish in a soft, feminine voice, backed by Mexican music and followed by a description in English of Mexico's tourist attractions. He made it all too easy for listeners to assume that they were hearing an ad for Mexico, rather than the call letters of a Mexican station.[4]

McLendon had no reporters. He aired no editorials, offered no commentary. The station carried only hard news from the Los Angeles City News Service and the AP and UPI wires. At first, the news was recycled every seven minutes, but this became every half-hour when McLendon realized how many commuters, listening to their car radios, took that long to get to work.

The first successful all-news station in the United States, founded in 1964, was McLendon's WNUS, Chicago, which had operated as WYNR with a rhythm and blues format. News on WNUS followed the XETRA pattern. Although WNUS was in the black by the second year, it never gained a dominant share of the market and, after four years, returned to broadcasting music. Later, the call letters WNUS went to an all-news station in West Springfield, Massachusetts.

The next radio station to adopt an all-news format was Westinghouse's WINS in New York. The day it began broadcasting—April 19, 1965—it proclaimed in a *New York Times* advertisement, "All news, all the time—News as it happens direct from where the action is." Since the station had no network affiliation, it played up local news. Stories were repeated but updated each half-hour. And, unlike McLendon's stations, it had a strong reporting staff.

Richard Pack, editor of *Television Quarterly,* was a Westinghouse vice president in charge of programming in 1965. He tells the inside story. At the same time that WINS was trying to come up with a successful format,

Westinghouse was moving KYW-AM, Cleveland, to Philadelphia and also looking for a new format. Pack says:

> Our radio manager was a great and wonderful young man, the late James Rayburn Lightfoot, a reformed Texan, nephew of the redoubtable House Speaker Sam Rayburn. One day, just about the time the manager of WINS had come up with a third or fourth new format, one based on another variation of pop music, Jimmy came to me very excited. "Hey," he said, "I've got a great idea!" Jimmy and I worked so well together I sometimes thought we had our own ESP. "What about?" I asked. "For KYW when we get back to Philly." "Don't tell me," I said. "I know it, the same idea I have for WINS."

The idea was all-news radio. The next step was for the two of them to sell the idea to the top brass.

> The next day I set up a meeting with Don McGannon, our chairman, and Larry Israel, another rare and splendid broadcast exec, and told them Jimmy and I wanted to meet with them very privately, very confidentially, outside of the building. So one afternoon we met in a rather crummy but large room at the Hotel McAlpin. Jimmy and I made our pitch, explained why it would work and how we would set up a small task force within the company to get the operation rolling. And that was the beginning. We didn't have flip charts, graphs, any fancy projections, but we had eloquence and conviction and two guys to hear us out.[5]

Two years later, WCBS, the CBS-owned radio outlet in New York, followed WINS' lead. Among its first reporters were Charles Osgood and Ed Bradley, who would become well-known network correspondents. Under the supervision of Joseph Dembo, vice president and general manager, WCBS was the first network-owned station to go all-news. After that, scores of stations across the country adopted the daring all-news format—daring because of the risk in higher costs. Besides a large editorial staff, the all-news station in a major market may have suburban bureaus, even a small bureau in Washington. A helicopter for traffic reports is often a must.[6]

From 1975 to 1978, three radio stations in the Washington area—WRC, WTOP, and WAVA—were all-news. One of the syndicated commentators on WAVA was Ronald Reagan. The weatherman heard most often on WRC was Willard Scott. Three all-news stations operating in the same market could not possibly succeed. WRC switched to news–talk and WAVA to gospel, then adult rock. But in March 1977, when Hanafi Moslem gunmen seized three buildings in Washington and held more than a hundred persons hostage, the stations were still all-news. Their coverage was aggressive and virtually nonstop. "It was," said WTOP's news director, Morry Alter, "the height of live radio."[7]

In 1976, WEBR, Buffalo, broadcasting 13 hours of uninterrupted news a day, called itself the nation's first noncommercial all-news radio station, though it scheduled music at night. In its first year, WEBR's reporters received four first-place awards from the AP. For national and foreign news, the station relied on AP Radio and National Public Radio.

As all-news radio spread, Richard Fagley of Westchester County, New York, found a novel use for it. He discovered that a radio receiver tuned to an all-news station and left overnight in his garden fended off raccoons. Music, he found, only whetted their appetite.

By the mid-1970s, all-news—news all the time—was the fastest-growing concept in commercial broadcasting. But it grew too fast. Some station owners, trusting the wide appeal of news, went in over their heads. They had to give up news around the clock and return to lower-budget of programming. While about 50 radio stations were all-news in 1985, the number had dropped to 28 in 1990.[8] The trend was to combine news with talk and call-ins. Talk has wide appeal. And it is cheap.

Many stations that remained all-news have modified the format. For a time, the all-news stations owned by CBS carried "Mystery Theater." Professional baseball, football, and basketball games are heard today on stations that say they are all-news. They include more features, everything from health hints to child guidance. They have a different sound.

A few television stations have experimented with the all-news format. In 1980, KAUT, a UHF station in Oklahoma City, tried broadcasting news in a seven-hour block, rotating two anchors in three-hour shifts. (The news director anchored a one-hour shift.) Because of poor ratings, the station gave up after 10 months.

The story of Ted Turner's all-news cable network will be told in another chapter.

NBC's News & Information Service

In June 1975, NBC took a big gamble. Hiring a staff of 300, it established what it called the News & Information Service (NIS). The product was 47 minutes of national and international news every hour, 24 hours a day, seven days a week. It was the first attempt at all-news radio on a coast-to-coast basis. Announcing the service in an extravagant eight-page advertisement in *Broadcasting*, NBC hailed it as "the biggest news in radio history."[9]

It looked like a good bet. All-news stations in large markets would have a new substantial source of stories. Stations in small markets would have the means to go all-news; they could report world events and sports, and developments in business, science, medicine, motion pictures, and music in a way they never could manage on their own. In each hour, stations were entitled to 14 commercial minutes. They could take as little as 25 minutes of the hour, though at stated times. This arrangement enabled NIS to sell and guarantee time to national advertisers. NBC gambled that it could be to radio clients what AP and UPI were to newspapers, a national news service.

It didn't work. Advertisers held back, waiting to see how the service would fare, and not enough stations subscribed. The service cost stations from $750 to $15,000 a month, depending on the size of the market, and for too many stations that was too steep. NBC also had underestimated competition from the other established networks and the AP and UPI audio services. UPI alone was servicing more than 900 stations. Only 62 stations, instead of the 150 expected, were buying the NIS service when NBC gave up. In two years, trying to make the experiment work, it had spent $20,000,000.[10] John Thayer, president of NBC Radio, said, "[The stations] know we did the best we could."[11]

There would be nothing like NIS until 1982, when Ted Turner created CNN Radio, a 24-hour news service that updated stories in 30-minute cycles. Until mid-1983, it was mostly the audio portion of CNN's Headline News, a video service. Since then CNN Radio has branched out with its own long-form news and editorial staff.

An Explosion in Networks

Specialization in radio programming was demonstrated most dramatically when ABC, in a bold venture approved by the FCC, split its radio network into four networks of distinctly different character. It seemed an act of desperation. The radio network had been operating in the red; there was talk that ABC might abandon it, even drop out of radio altogether. But now suddenly, on January 1, 1968, ABC had *four* radio networks:

Contemporary Network. Fast-paced programming appealing to young people. Rock music. News in brief.

Entertainment Network. Popular music, news, and features for Middle of the Road (MOR) stations. Emphasis on personalities.

FM Network. Four minutes of news on the hour. Radio magazine called "Listen Closely." Music.

Information Network. Five minutes of news on the hour, except 15 minutes at 8 A.M. and 10 P.M. and nine minutes at 6 P.M. Commentary. Sports.

At one time, Paul Harvey's programs were heard on all four networks, making him the most listened-to newscaster in the country.

In the first year, these demographic networks lost close to eight million dollars. It took four years for them to break even, then another year to turn a profit. Afterward, they did so well that 1982 saw the expansion of the four networks to six with the creation of the Rock Radio Network and the Direction Radio Network. Direction was aimed at adult listeners interested in not only "what's happening in the world today but how it will affect their lives."[12] Besides news and sports, its features included reports on science, physical fitness, and medical research.

Other networks adapted in similar fashion. CBS' "RadioRadio" service, inaugurated in April 1982, is designed for young adults. Emerson Stone, who was then vice president in charge of radio news at CBS, said it represented a new approach. Anchors would report the news, using the information gathered by CBS correspondents and other sources; only in case of important breaking stories would they switch to correspondents. Insert material would be confined almost entirely to the actual sounds and voices of events.[13] Besides two-minute news summaries each hour around the clock, RadioRadio offers music and an assortment of features, including reports on life-style trends and health.

Late in 1982, CBS Radio launched "Byline Magazine," a syndicated package of news features. It also inaugurated a documentary series called "Newsmark," which has received both Peabody and Overseas Press Club awards. In 1990, CBS took a new marketing approach by merging its CBS Radio Network and RadioRadio to form the CBS Spectrum Radio Network. The news line-up was not changed.

NBC's most distinguished series in this period was "Second Sunday," which received a Peabody Award. An example of the thoroughness of this documentary series is provided by the 90-minute program of August 14, 1977, which examined the pervasive problem of carcinogens.

For eight years (1979–1987) NBC Radio had a young adult network called The Source. Its reports were wide-ranging. Its subject might be the price of rock concerts one day and views on creation of a Palestinian state the next. In 1987, when Westwood One, a California-based company, bought NBC's radio networks for 50 million dollars, it got The Source and Talknet, a call-in service.

National Public Radio (NPR)

Adventuresome. The adjective fits National Public Radio, where listeners hear the most profuse, varied, and informative programming heard anywhere.

NPR was created with the financial support of the Corporation for Public Broadcasting in 1969 when public radio stations decided they needed a national program service. Unlike PBS, its counterpart in public television, NPR produces many of its own programs. It distributes these programs and cooperates with member stations in the national distribution of programs that they produce.

Incorporated as a nonprofit organization with headquarters in Washington, NPR began transmitting programs to 93 member stations, mostly in the FM band, on April 19, 1971. Membership soon grew to more than 200 stations receiving a potpourri of cultural and informational programming: music, drama, satire, news. In 1979, it became the first radio network to distribute its programs by satellite. PBS had scored a first for television a year earlier when it started linking its stations via Westar I.

From the beginning, NPR has been news-oriented. Its first program consisted of live gavel-to-gavel coverage of a Senate hearing.[14] Its earliest hit was a 90-minute newsmagazine, "All Things Considered," hosted by Susan Stamberg and Bob Edwards. Here, on a single afternoon, listeners could hear interviews about a baseball ruling, astrological medicine, a hookers' convention, and the intricacies of Lebanese politics. By 1977, the program, produced in the early years by Jim Russell, had won Peabody, duPont-Columbia, Ohio State, and Headliner awards.

"Morning Edition," heard Monday through Friday, premiered in 1979. At the start, Bob Edwards hosted the program with Barbara Hochter; later, he became sole anchor. As 1989 ended, "Morning Edition," with almost five million listeners, had edged ahead of the evening showpiece, "All Things Considered." "Weekend Edition," a Saturday version of the morning program, was added to the schedule in 1985 after NPR weathered a financial crisis which resulted in major cutbacks in both programming and personnel. Among those departing was Frank Mankiewicz, NPR's dynamic president, who had expanded the news operation and done much to win it recognition. With further recovery, NPR began carrying "Weekend Edition" on both Saturday and Sunday.

In 1989, NPR expanded its news programming by presenting five-minute news summaries each day, seven days a week, from 5 A.M. to 10 P.M. Insight on national and international events was provided by the weekly documentary series "Horizons" and commentary by Daniel Schorr and Rod MacLeish.

NPR makes good use of reports from member stations. It maintains foreign and domestic bureaus, though not on the scale of the commercial networks, and has a first-class corps of Washington correspondents. It was one of these, Nina Totenberg, who broke the story that Supreme Court nominee Douglas Ginsburg, while teaching law, was smoking marijuana. Another, Linda Wertheimer, scooped her competition with the first live broadcast of a Senate debate. That was in 1978 when the Senate was enacting the Panama Canal Treaty. As 1990 began, 26 correspondents and reporters, not counting program hosts, were based in the Washington headquarters. At the same time, it was feeding its programs to more than 370 stations.

The audience, though growing, is estimated at no more than 13 million. It is, however, a fiercely loyal and influential audience. A Harris poll conducted in 1986 found 57 percent of top corporate executives listened either "very often" or "somewhat often." The reason for this following may be found in a duPont-Columbia University survey of broadcast journalism published in 1982. The survey said that NPR in its brief life had

> delivered some of the nation's most consistently intelligent coverage of breaking news as well as literate commentary, criticism, and the sort of documentary essays that had all but disappeared from network radio with the advent of TV.

There was nothing on commercial radio, it said, comparable to NPR's commitment to news.[15]

Although the Corporation for Public Broadcasting still provides funding, NPR is supported increasingly by subletting space on its Western Union satellite and the sale of audiocassettes, as well as by corporate underwriters. Its principal income, however, comes from fees paid by member stations.

NPR is governed by a board of directors consisting of 25 members, 12 of whom are elected by the stations. Twelve are selected from the general public. The public members have included Janet Murrow, widow of Edward R. Murrow; Reuven Frank, former president of NBC News, and Richard Salant, former president of CBS News. The president of NPR (Douglas Bennet in 1990) serves as ex-officio member and vice chairman of the board.

American Public Radio (APR)

NPR has a competitor in American Public Radio. APR, founded in 1982, is based in St. Paul. It won attention as the service distributing Garrison Keillor's "A Prairie Home Companion" and since then has been providing various types of programming, including news, to a growing number of stations. A current hit is the daily half-hour business report called "Marketplace," which, while covering the day's developments on domestic and world markets, includes numerous off-beat features. It is business news with a sense of humor. As the host, Michael Creedman, reports the latest trading figures, the listener may hear the tune "We're in the Money" in the background.

"Marketplace" is produced at KLON-FM, Long Beach, California, by Jim Russell, who once produced "All Things Considered."

Radio News and Deregulation

Radio, the first broadcast medium, has never stopped growing. As of October 1990, there were 10,717 radio stations, more than three times as many as in 1950 when television began its inroads on radio's evening audience. Fourteen million radio sets were sold in 1950. Thirty years later, three times as many were sold.[16] By 1981, the number of radio stations had grown so large and become so competitive that the FCC issued an order that, to a large degree, deregulated the radio industry. A radio station no longer had to devote a minimum amount of time to news and public affairs. Similar deregulation was extended to television in 1984.

In 1986, Dr. Vernon A. Stone of the University of Missouri conducted a national survey which indicated that deregulation had not affected either news or public affairs programming at most commercial radio stations. About 8 percent of the 362 respondents had cut back either in news presentation or staff, but another 5.3 percent said they had upgraded their news operations. Projecting these figures, Stone estimated that about 82 stations were doing less in the area of news. The net effect of deregulation, according to the survey, had been cutbacks in news at roughly one of every six major market radio stations.[17]

Some observers, like John Kittross, professor of communications at Temple University, viewed these findings with concern. Although most stations had not cut back on either news or public affairs, he noted that stations in larger markets seemed to be cutting back more than stations in smaller markets and that public affairs seemed harder hit than news. He saw in this a possible unhealthy trend.[18] (In the vocabulary of broadcasting, public affairs encompasses programming such as panel discussions, editorials, political debates, and documentaries, whereas news consists of reports of what is happening.

But the revolutionary change—more than a trend—in radio had been the custom tailoring of program content for different audiences. As *Broadcasting* observed, "From progressive rock, to country, to Top 40, to classical, to all-news, radio proved itself flexible enough to compete [with television] through diversification."[19] In technology, a landmark was passed in 1984 with the networks' transition from landlines to satellites for distribution of their radio programs. FM radio was overtaking AM radio in popularity. Nothing was standing still.

23

Edward R. Murrow, V.P.

The spring of 1946 found Ed Murrow in the executive suite, no longer reporting but trying to determine the direction radio news should go. He gave television news little thought. What he thought about, and acted upon, was ways to make radio, the medium dominant at that time, more than a source of entertainment and revenue.

Murrow made the eighteen months he served as vice president of news and public affairs a productive period. He started a series called "As Others See Us," a report on what publications in other countries were saying about the United States, and he pioneered in media criticism by creating "CBS Views the Press" with Don Hollenbeck. In the same year, 1946, he founded a documentary unit at CBS. NBC produced occasional documentaries but did not go for them as heavily at the start. It did break ground in 1948 with a documentary series called "Living," which ran until 1951. These half-hour radio programs, aired on Sunday afternoons, dealt with a wide variety of subjects ranging from air pollution—yes, air pollution—to the Olympic Games.

CBS' documentary unit, the first in broadcasting, was headed by Robert Heller. Among the producers were Lane Blackwell, Robert Lewis Shayon, and Ruth Ashton Taylor. Taylor recalls, "Ed told us, 'I want you to choose a subject closest to your heart. Take as long as you need to research and write it, and we will preempt the top show on the air to put it on.' " [1] Shayon's choice was juvenile delinquency, and his documentary, "The Eagle's Brood," was widely praised. A. William Bluem, in his *Documentary in American Television,* says, "Hailed as a 'new documentary,' this and subsequent efforts of the CBS unit represented a final departure from the 'stagey' drama of an earlier time." [2]

Sound effects may have been muted, the crashing music not so crashing, but use still was made of actors—after all, "The Eagle's Brood" featured Hollywood's Joseph Cotten. Over the years, actors' participation did become less frequent—nonexistent in many documentary series—but it never disappeared and today, with its resurgence, is hotly debated.

Another early CBS documentary was "The Sunny Side of the Atom." The producer-reporter for this program on the beneficial aspects of atomic science was Ruth Ashton Taylor, who years later could still express excitement over the broadcast. "It took me around the country and through memorable experiences with Einstein, Oppenheimer, and Seaborg. Agnes Moorehead played me, and one night it was put in place of Lux Radio Theatre." [3]

Quite naturally, the atom at the dawn of the Atomic Age was a popular subject. NBC offered a series of four documentaries on the relationship of atomic discoveries to society. Mutual carried a four-part series titled "The Atom and You," and ABC marked both the first and second anniversaries of the dropping of the atom bomb on Hiroshima with documentary-type specials. The person in charge of documentaries at ABC was Robert Saudek, who later produced the distinguished television series "Omnibus."

A popular program introduced during Murrow's vice presidency was "CBS Is There." The series recreated historical events such as the French Revolution with CBS correspondents speaking as though they were on the scene at the time. Because this was simulation, the series has been cited in the journalism ethics debate over creation of events in news programming today. It is hard to see how the interview of a correspondent with an actor playing Louis XVI can be mistaken for reality. Still, Murrow was against airing the program. On principle, he didn't like correspondents in simulated situations. Paley, however, gave the go-ahead. The program was a hit and later came to television as "You Are There."

Tape, the New Tool

"One World Flight," produced by Norman Corwin and Lee Bland, is notable not only because it was the most ambitious documentary series of the late 1940s, but because of its use of magnetic tape, the new reporting tool. For "On a Note of Triumph" and his other broadcasts promoting global unity, Corwin had received the Wendell Willkie-Freedom House "One World Award." The award consisted of a trip around the world, dramatizing Willkie's concept of one world. Before accepting the award,

Corwin consulted Paley, saying he would make the trip only if he could use it to report the postwar aspirations of people everywhere in a series of radio broadcasts. Paley urged Corwin to accept and offered whatever equipment and staff he would need.

The two-man team, Corwin and Bland, took off on their four-month journey on June 15, 1946, carrying a cumbersome 115-volt General Electric wire recorder, an inverter for powering the recorder from storage batteries, hundreds of spools of wire, and a tool kit for emergency repairs. Traveling in primitive airplanes, mostly DC-3s, the two men flew 36,000 miles on eleven commercial airlines and sundry military aircraft to seventeen countries on four continents. Interviews were conducted with writers, peasants, and prime ministers. They returned to New York with 400 hours of recordings.

The first task, back at home base, was to transcribe the interviews so Corwin would have a full text. Next, the difficult-to-edit wire recordings were transferred to discs and simultaneously to the new recording medium, magnetic tape, which had been unavailable when they set out. The tape recording was done on a Brush Soundmirror, a troublesome process because of voltage and cycle problems encountered in foreign countries. Moreover, the machine proved erratic. Sometimes, in putting the program together, Joel Tall, the CBS engineer who became an international authority on magnetic recording, had to regulate playback speed by pressing his thumb on the tape as it ran past. Finally, because of the unreliability of the tape, which was made of paper and frequently broke, the half-hour broadcasts, thirteen in all, were made from discs. Nevertheless, tape had been used in the production of a major broadcast for the first time.

The Shirer Affair

While engaged in these adventurous pursuits, Murrow also was making dreary decisions involving budget allocations and personnel. For him, administrative duties could be depressing. "Who am I to be firing people," he wondered, "the Almighty Himself?"[4]

Paley sensed Murrow's frustration. He asked the thwarted reporter if he would like to return to broadcasting, but Murrow insisted he was happy. There was, says Paley, a stubborn streak in Murrow. He had accepted a challenge; it was not in his nature to give up, especially after so short a time. But when Paley ordered him back on the air, he obeyed cheerfully.[5]

The firing of Paul White had been unpleasant, but Murrow found his role in William L. Shirer's departure rending. Shirer was his own special correspondent, the first reporter he had hired, a man whose broadcasts early in the war, like his own, earned superlatively high marks. The two had respect, even affection, for each other. The break between them, the way it happened, would haunt them the rest of their lives.

Shirer had come home from Germany in December 1940. Since then he had lectured, done commentary for CBS, and written his first best-seller, *Berlin Diary*.[6] The blow fell on March 10, 1947. He was told that the J. B. Williams Company no longer would sponsor the 15 minutes of news analysis, or commentary, he did on Sunday afternoons. Not only that. The ad agency said he was being dropped from the program. Shirer was dismayed. He went to Murrow, who confirmed it. The program would be done by another CBS commentator, Joseph C. Harsch, and Shirer would be assigned a new slot where, for the time being, he would have no sponsor and consequently earn much less.

It was something Shirer would not accept. After his final Sunday broadcast on March 30, he told reporters he was leaving CBS, that it was plain his usefulness there was over. He didn't like being taken off the program, but the important thing, he said, "is that a soap company can decide who cannot be heard on the air." On this issue he was resigning.[7]

Murrow issued a statement denying sponsor pressure. Sponsors had no right to dictate content; he did believe they were entitled to choose their programs.[8] In Shirer's case, J. B. Williams, which didn't sponsor Harsch either, wanted something different from commentary; news no longer was the drawing card it had been. Shirer, on the other hand, suspected that the company, if not CBS itself, objected to his liberal views. And he let his suspicions be known.

Newspapers grabbed the story. Was CBS letting sponsors decide who would do the news? Did Shirer's liberal views do him in? If so, was this not a violation of the First Amendment? The CIO Political Action Committee said the FCC should investigate. A telegram signed by notables like author Dorothy Parker, actor Gregory Peck, and playwright Arthur Miller decried what had happened as "a shocking blow to those who had faith in the freedom of the airwaves."[9] Other celebrities picketed the network's Madison Avenue headquarters. "It is hard," Harrison E. Salisbury says, "to imagine the firestorm Shirer's dismissal touched off."[10]

Shirer had spoken out against the Chinese Nationalist leader, Chiang Kai-shek, and questioned the wisdom of President Truman's policy for containing Communism in Greece. But this, CBS maintained, was not why the sponsor dropped him or why he was reassigned. Harsch in Washington and Howard K. Smith in London had been expressing similar "liberal" views. Harsch, Murrow said bluntly, was being assigned the Sunday spot in order "to improve Columbia's news analysis in this period."[11] There it was. Shirer had forced Murrow to say it. To the proud commentator, says biographer Joseph Persico, the words must have felt "like being stabbed through the heart."[12]

Through it all, Shirer felt betrayed. He felt it from the start when Murrow, intentionally or unintentionally, left it up to the ad agency to tell him he was being taken off the program. In not getting to Shirer first and explaining the change to him, Murrow mishandled the situation. Janet Murrow says, "Much later on, Ed said to me, 'If I'd realized that Bill thought he *owned* that time, I suppose I might have broken the news to him more gently.' "[13]

In the matter of "owning" a time period, a contradiction exists between the position Murrow took with Shirer and the position he took later with his own radio broadcast. In 1950, Campbell Soup, sponsor of his 7:45 P.M. news, wanted to replace it with a musical program. Murrow protested, and Paley supported him. The 15 minutes was Murrow's to use, just as Shirer had contended the 15-minute Sunday slot was his. Campbell Soup dropped its sponsorship, but Murrow, with new sponsors, kept on reporting at the same time. Kendrick writes in his biography, "If any blush was brought to Murrow's cheek by memory of the Shirer case, it was not noticed."[14]

Network time, of course, belonged to neither Murrow nor Shirer; it belonged to the network. The difference in what happened lay in what management wanted.

Shirer went from CBS to Mutual, where he did commentary for eighteen months, then found himself unemployable in network broadcasting. It was no help to him at that time, or later in the McCarthy era, that like other concerned Americans he had once signed a petition against the blacklisting of Hollywood writers on charges of Communism. So he began writing books, including his masterwork, the 1,245-page *Rise and Fall of the Third Reich.*[15] The hurt from his CBS experience was still there. In one of his three novels[16] a radio reporter turned network executive fails to stand by a broadcaster with liberal views.

By 1971, Shirer started work on his memoirs, which have appeared in three volumes. In the last, *A Native's Return,*[17] he reports in detail what he calls Murrow's effort to "finish me off at CBS."[18] Murrow cannot respond, but there are survivors who tell a different story, and their testimony should be entered.

Shirer says that before his last broadcast on CBS, Ted Church and Dallas Townsend, the editor on duty, told him they were "under pressure from Murrow to read carefully every word of my script." During the broadcast, he says, "Ed's henchmen" stood by in the control room to see that he was cut off if he said anything he shouldn't. He recalls that Townsend was in the control room with them.[19] Townsend says:

> I certainly don't remember telling Shirer that Ted Church and I were "under pressure from Murrow" to go carefully over every word. No such admonition would have been necessary in any case. That's what editors are there for. . . . I also don't remember being in the control room during the broadcast. If I followed standard operating procedure, I was in the newsroom where I should have been, and that's where I think I was.[20]

According to Shirer, Murrow never made a "definite" offer of another time period. He writes that Murrow, speaking vaguely, suggested scheduling him between 11 and 11:30 p.m., "after most listeners had gone to bed."[21] This sounded definite enough to discourage Shirer and is a period in which Eric Sevareid later provided commentary following the radio network's 11 p.m. news. Larry LeSueur testifies that Murrow made what he certainly regards as a hard offer. He says, "Ed offered him *my* time. I was doing this show at 6:45 p.m. on Saturdays, and I was a bit put out."[22]

This may be the spot Shirer is referring to when in his memoir he says, "Ed at one stage said CBS would create a period for me on Saturday afternoon." But, says Shirer, Paley quashed the idea.[23]

Shirer, building his case that he was removed from the Sunday program because of opinions he voiced, stresses ratings. He reasons that if his ratings were good, removal must have been due to his liberal views. He says his program enjoyed the highest Hooper rating of any daytime Sunday broadcast.[24] That is not saying much. Audiences for daytime Sunday programs are relatively small, and Shirer's ratings fluctuated. His highest rating, achieved once, was 6.9. The Sunday before that it was only 3.8.[25] He says Murrow never complained about his ratings.[26] It is unlikely he would. The quality of the commentary, not size of audience, was what most concerned Murrow; it was out of concern for quality that he had advised Shirer to get out from behind his desk and do more firsthand reporting. The reassignment of Shirer, as biographer A. M. Sperber says, was due to dissatisfaction with performance brought finally to a head by the sponsor's cancellation when the usual thirteen-week option was up.[27]

Former colleagues testify that Shirer, to a considerable extent, was coasting on his reputation. Helen Sioussat, who was director of talks at CBS at the time, says Shirer was lax in his approach to the Sunday program. "There were events he should have gone out and covered, but he was quite content to use the reports of others. He was lazy."[28] Joseph Persico, in his biography of Murrow, quotes Charles Collingwood as saying Shirer had become "a stuck whistle. He wasn't analyzing the news. He just kept preaching his beliefs over and over."[29] Eric Sevareid, another contemporary, says outright, "His commentaries were terrible; there wasn't a thing in them. Ed felt betrayed."[30] It is hard not to take seriously so much testimony.

Still, there is no question Shirer commanded respect. As he points out, he received the George Foster Peabody Award only days after leaving CBS.[31] The award was for "outstanding interpretation of the news in 1946" and "for the truth he told us about Hitler and Germany despite the opposition of censors during those crucial years, 1938–1941." In other words, Shirer was being honored for his early reporting from Germany as much as for his more recent commentary.

Two months after receiving this award, *Billboard*'s annual poll of newspaper radio editors found Shirer "the most interesting news commentator on the air." Shirer cites this. But the Hooper ratings service reported that for radio listeners in general, Walter Winchell was by far the most interesting, followed by Lowell Thomas. Shirer placed eighth, with one-fourth as many listeners as Winchell.[32]

Murrow rode out the storm, but the atmosphere was such that CBS asked its employees to sign loyalty statements declaring whether they belonged to the Communist Party, not a question any Communist agent was likely to answer truthfully. (Actually, there was a Communist mole in a low-level, off-the-air position at CBS News. The fellow went undetected until suddenly he surfaced at the Soviet-run radio station in East Berlin.)

Quincy Howe, the historian-commentator who broadcast for CBS, called Shirer's departure "a sad occasion for all."[33] Shirer says the experience

> not only destroyed a close friendship but my career in broadcasting. As it turned out, this was a blessing in disguise. It drove me to writing books, which is what I wanted to do all along. The broken friendship was never healed, nor could it be. Ed did invite me over for a day on his farm shortly before he died. It was sad to see him nearing the end. We had a good talk, but I steered it off our break[34]

Shirer's estimation of Murrow's work never changed. "He was," Shirer says, "the best broadcaster of us all."[35]

At the heart of the affair smouldered an ethical issue, the right of sponsors of news programs to select who would do them. Even before this, Jack Gould, the *New York Times* critic, had denounced the practice. It is this, says Persico, that makes the question whether Shirer had grown lax "almost beside the point. . . . Gould was saying that the news should be totally divorced from sponsor influence. Murrow the broadcast journalist would have agreed. But Murrow the corporate executive was not free to say so."[36]

In theory, Murrow the journalist might agree. But a few months later, when as journalist he went back on the air, and Campbell Soup preferred him to Robert Trout, who had been doing the broadcast, he gladly went along.

This . . . Is the News

The program "Edward R. Murrow With the News" was heard for the first time on Monday, September 29, 1947, taking the place of "The News Till Now" anchored by Trout. The 15-minute time period had, abruptly, become Murrow's province. Trout, deeply hurt, left to work at NBC but returned to CBS in 1952. Still later, as respected dean of newscasters, he reported for ABC in a career stretching to the time these words are written.

The sponsor of the Murrow program in 1947 was still the Campbell Soup Company. The budget was the largest for any radio news broadcast up to that time, allowing Murrow a staff of three secretaries, including Kay Campbell, who had worked with him since he first went to London, and two writer-producers, Jesse Zousmer and John Aaron. Zousmer's assignment was to put together the news summary—roughly six minutes—that preceded Murrow's commentary, which the network called news-analysis and which Murrow called his "think piece." The program closed with a 23-second postscript, "The Word for Today," written by Aaron, whose principal assignment was research.

"The Word" was a gimmick. Murrow would not allow interruption of the news for a middle commercial. The compromise was an opening commercial and a commercial after the news summary and commentary, at which time the announcer would say, "Mr. Murrow will be back in a moment with his 'Word for Today.' " "The Word" was a sort of tease, or tidbit, to hold listeners for the third and final commercial. It always included a quotation by a person of some stature—it could be Thomas Jefferson or Will Rogers or anyone else—which tied in with the commentary.

Writing the news summary for the first time, Zousmer did not know what Murrow would say at the beginning, whether he wanted to start by saying "Good evening," or "This is Ed Murrow" or what. The decision was made by Murrow at the last moment. As he sat before the microphone, with seconds to go, he wrote across the top of the page: "This is the news." He read it just as he had read "This is London" in wartime, with a pause after the word *this*. From time to time, during the twelve years the program was on the air, Murrow was criticized for this opening line. Listeners said he had delusions of journalistic grandeur, thinking that in fifteen minutes he could give all the news, so one night he began by saying, "This is *some* of the news." It had been, he said, some of the news all the time.[37]

In his first broadcast, instead of commentary, Murrow had a personal word. He read the section of his contract which said that news programs are broadcast "solely for the purpose of enabling listeners thereto to know facts, so far as they are ascertainable, and so to elucidate, illuminate and explain facts and situations as fairly as possible to enable the listener to weigh and judge for himself." He called this (and there was a good deal more) "pretty complicated language, the kind that lawyers like to write." His own interpretation, he said, was that

> this program is not a place where personal opinion should be mixed up with ascertainable facts. We shall do our best to identify sources and to resist the temptation to use this microphone as a privileged platform from which to advocate action.

He allowed, at the same time, that to be completely objective is an impossibility. He would try to remember, he said, "that the mechanics of radio which make it possible for an individual voice to be heard throughout the entire land don't confer great wisdom or infallibility on that individual."[38]

It was the old thing about CBS insisting on the highest degree of objectivity possible, not only in reporting, but in "elucidation." It was a commandment Murrow broke. There was no way, being what he was, that he could resist expressing himself, either directly or by implication, on what he took to be wrong and what he took to be right if he believed the issue to be important.

The examples are not hard to find. In October 1947, the House Un-American Activities Committee was conducting hearings on Communist infiltration of the Hollywood studios. Then, more than six years before his indictment of McCarthyism on "See It Now" and only a month after going back on the air, he said in his radio commentary:

[I]t may be assumed that this internal tension, suspicion, witch hunting, grade labeling—call it what you like—will continue. It may well cause a lot of us to dig deep into both our history and our convictions to determine just how firmly we hold to the principles we were taught.[39]

Again in 1949 on the subject of coping with subversive activity:

That there is danger of Communist espionage and infiltration cannot be denied. That there is need for legal, constitutional methods of protection would seem to be equally obvious. . . . But the fact is that the climate for the development of Communism in this country is less salubrious than any other in the world. . . . We sometimes forget that the thing that makes this country what it is isn't our size or our racial mixture or anything else (sic), but the fact that this is a nation that lives under law.[40]

He spoke often in this vein. It is a mistake to suppose he waited until the "See It Now" broadcast of March 9, 1954, to speak his mind. In violation of the CBS commandment, he delivered editorials. He got away with it because of his prestige and because, deep down, enough people knew he was right.

It was too good to last.

24
The Greatest
Political Show on Earth

The technology that would change forever the way presidential candidates are chosen was introduced at the Republican national convention of 1940. The introduction was on so small a scale it scarcely was noticed. Scenes from the Philadelphia meeting, piped by coaxial cable to New York, were transmitted by NBC's experimental station, W2XBS, to an audience of no more than a few thousand viewers. Some of the convention program also was carried by W3XE, the Philco station in Philadelphia. When the Democrats held their convention in Chicago, NBC flew newsreel film to New York for W2XBS to use the next day—it was as primitive as that. On election night, among those present in NBC's television studio, watching as a huge, unwieldy camera scanned returns coming in on a teletype machine, was Leo Rosenberg, the same man who had made history at KDKA on election night 20 years before (see chapter 1).

In 1944, television again played a negligible role. It was radio that Franklin Roosevelt and Thomas E. Dewey used in their campaigning, and there was no live coverage of the conventions because of equipment shortages caused by the war.

If television didn't play a starring role in politics until 1952, it did have a good dress rehearsal in 1948 when the Republican national convention became the first to be covered by a hookup of television stations. The Democratic convention the next week was the second and the Progressive Party convention right after that the third. Coverage was made easier by the fact that all three conventions took place in one city, Philadelphia. The ponderous television equipment, far more cumbersome than today, would not have to be moved. The same temporary studios could be used.

A major reason for choosing Philadelphia was that it was tied into a primitive TV system serving Baltimore, Washington, New York, and Boston. During the conventions it was linked by cable with 14 eastern states. But in the cities served there were fewer than 400,000 television receivers.[1] It was still primarily a radio show.

The two TV anchormen at the 1948 conventions were Douglas Edwards for CBS and John Cameron Swayze for NBC. At that time, no such word as *anchorman* existed in broadcast parlance. Sig Mickelson, president of CBS News, coined the word when he needed a term for Walter Cronkite at the 1952 conventions. In his book *From Whistle Stop to Sound Bite*, Mickelson says:

> I visualized the "anchorman" as the best-informed person at the convention. All our communications lines would terminate with him. Reporters on the floor, in the wings, or in downtown hotels would transmit to a desk that would screen information to be relayed to him. The studio where we stationed him would be the heart and brain of our coverage.[2]

The term stuck. *Anchorwoman* and *anchor* are variations.

In 1948, most coverage originated in improvised studios in Philadelphia's Convention Hall. Swayze describes the conditions under which NBC operated:

> We worked in a studio high among the rafters, in a place that had been thrown together. The two-by-fours were raw wood with the butt end of nails protruding where they hadn't been fully hammered in. There was a swinging door that could have come from a saloon.
>
> Philadelphia was murderously hot that summer, and we had an air conditioning unit of sorts. We had a few chairs we used for interviews and also to sit on when we ate. There were some cutouts of a donkey and an elephant, as well as some blow-ups of leading politicians. Those were put on the wall when appropriate for an interview.[3]

Sometimes, without notice, a floor reporter would send a dignitary up to be interviewed. Then it was up to the interviewer to get rid of the person at that moment being interviewed, recognize the newcomer, introduce him, and carry on. Swayze tells how embarrassing it could be:

> There, approaching me through the door, was a well-known face, but I couldn't think of his name. It was a hell of a spot. I was a

reporter. He was an important politician. I held out my hand. "How do you do, sir," I said. "Won't you introduce yourself to our audience?" Without batting an eye, he swept off his hat and proclaimed, "I am Mayor James Curley of Boston." Grasping his hand, heartily, I almost shouted, "Thank you, Mayor Curley. I'm sure our audience recognized you even before you spoke."[4]

Among those working with Swayze at the convention were Ray Henle, Richard Harkness, Robert Trout, Clifton Utley, David Brinkley, Kenneth Banghart, W. W. Chaplin, Jim Hurlbut, H. V. Kaltenborn, Alex Dreier, and John MacVane. William F. Brooks, head of NBC News, was in overall charge.

Then, as today, reporters' hours at national political conventions were long. The sessions in Philadelphia often ran past midnight, and Swayze was doing NBC Radio's news roundup at 8 o'clock in the morning, as well as anchoring in the daytime and at night. Douglas Edwards, who was doing most of the anchoring for CBS radio and television, had a similar schedule. The CBS floor reporters included John Daly, who says:

> It was hot work. Not only were there the lights but, working on the floor, I'd carry this 30-pound pack on my back with an engineer behind me turning the dials. I was so sodden with perspiration, I used two seersucker suits. I wore one suit in the afternoon and then, before the evening session, I would go back to the hotel, shower, soak the suit I'd just worn and change into the other.[5]

Other CBS personnel at the conventions included Charles Collingwood, Richard C. Hottelet, Howard K. Smith, Edmund Chester, Lee Otis, Lowell Thomas, Larry LeSueur, Joseph Wershba, Griffing Bancroft, Bill Leonard, who one day would be president of CBS News, and Don Hewitt, a dynamic young director who, 20 years later, would be executive producer of "60 Minutes." Commentators for the network were Edward R. Murrow, Eric Sevareid, and Quincy Howe. Ted Church, as news director, had overall supervision.

More than 50 persons were accredited to represent ABC News. Along with technicians, they included Earl Godwin, Martin Agronsky, Walter Winchell, John B. Kennedy, H. R. Baukhage, George Hicks, Drew Pearson, and Elmer Davis. They were supervised by Robert Kintner, executive vice president of ABC, and Thomas Velotta, vice president in charge of news and special events.

Mutual's man in charge was Abe Schechter. Because Mutual was all-radio, it had a simpler time. The same with the struggling DuMont network, which was strictly television and in Philadelphia enlisted the help of reporters from the *New York Herald Tribune* and *Newsweek* in order to compete.

Women helped cover the 1948 conventions. NBC's Nancy Osgood reported the so-called women's angle. Shirley Lubowitz of CBS, who would marry Joseph Wershba and, like him, become a network producer, went to

Philadelphia as a writer. Ann Gillis was an NBC producer at all three Philadelphia conventions. Ruth Ashton Taylor worked as a producer for CBS. From the print media Mutual recruited Doris Fleeson and Dorothy Kilgallen. The sole woman on the broadcasters planning committee was Rosella Donohue of WLW, Cincinnati. Pauline Frederick, reporting for ABC, received her first major television assignments.

Local stations sent scores of reporters. Among these were Dave Driscoll of WOR and Don Goddard of WINS; Grant Holcomb of KQW (now KCBS), San Francisco; Joe McCaffrey of WASH, Washington; Sig Mickelson, another future president of CBS News, from WCCO, Minneapolis; Clete Roberts of KFWB, Los Angeles; and Ron Cochran of WCOP, Boston. In all, more than a hundred independent AM and FM stations covered the Republican and Democratic conventions.

For the first time, audiotape was used for covering a political convention. There was no air conditioning in many areas, and frequently the tape machines became overheated. Joel Tall recalled:

> This resulted in distortion. When the recording head is hot, it won't accept as much magnetism. Then I had an idea. I got ice packs and piled them around the machines. It worked! Engineers from other networks said, "Joe, your sound is perfect. What did you do?"[6]

The Republicans for the second time nominated Governor Thomas E. Dewey of New York. He chose Governor Earl Warren of California as his running mate. It was an orderly convention. By contrast, the Democrats were a bunch of rowdies. Roosevelt's former secretary of agriculture, Henry Wallace, had revolted and formed the Progressive Party. Other liberal forces, including Americans for Democratic Action, thought Truman had weaseled on equal rights for blacks. They wanted a strong civil rights plank in the party platform. Millions of Americans tuned to radio and television heard a little-known politician, Hubert Humphrey of Minnesota, fight for unequivocal language, declaring in a ringing speech, "The time has arrived for the Democratic Party to get out of the states' rights and walk forthrightly into the bright sunshine of human rights." Suddenly the whole country knew who Hubert Humphrey was.

Stronger language was approved, causing a bloc of southern delegates, led by Strom Thurmond of South Carolina, to bolt the convention. One of Mutual's commentators at the convention was Gabriel Heatter, who had witnessed the nominating process since 1932. At the first conventions, he said, the crowds—the roar—frightened him. Now he was enjoying himself. "I found myself smiling. It was democracy at work."[7]

Despite the disarray, Truman won nomination on the first ballot. Senator Alben Barkley of Kentucky was nominated for vice president. Because Truman issued no advance copies of his acceptance speech, the country's newspaper editors got it first from the broadcast media. "A clean beat," said *Broadcasting* proudly. "One of radio and television's greatest days in history."[8]

Three days after the Democratic convention, the States' Rights Party, meeting in Birmingham, nominated Thurmond for president and Governor Fielding Wright of Mississippi for vice president. The Progressive Party, as expected, nominated Henry Wallace. Its vice presidential nominee was Senator Glen Taylor of Idaho.

It was inevitable that addition of sight to sound in convention coverage would alter the political institution. The first significant signs of change appeared in Philadelphia in 1948. Looks became important in a way they never had before. WFIL, Philadelphia, in cooperation with Max Factor of Hollywood, set up a makeup room as a special service for candidates and other national figures after station executives noticed that some notables facing the cameras could use a bit of touching up. NBC brought in its own makeup specialist.

At the Republican convention, which preceded the Democratic convention, television had shown delegates drowsing during long-winded speeches. Others were reading newspapers—and worse. Recognizing the vulnerability of his own people, Kenneth Fry, radio-television director for the Democratic convention, issued a warning to delegates that television has "a merciless eye."[9]

The convention programs were not tailored for radio and television to the extent that they are today, but managers of the Republican convention obviously had the broadcast media in mind when every predictable major event was scheduled for an evening session.

Specifically, they learned how to use television. From a hat box India Edwards, executive director of the women's division of the Republican Party, released a toy balloon representing inflation, then brandished a steak over her head to show how, under the Democrats, the price of food had risen. From now on, *Broadcasting* said, each party will be "anxious to make the convention not only a vehicle for choosing nominees but also the initial step in putting those nominees into office."[10]

The radio audience at each of the two major party conventions was estimated at more than 60 million, or six times the number tuned in on television.[11]

Public reaction to the television coverage was enthusiastic. Swayze says it was apparent in all the letters, telephone calls, and telegrams received from viewers.

> We were working hard in a new medium and didn't know who was seeing us. To find there was a friendly audience out there, seeing as well as hearing the conventions because of our labor, was encouraging, even comforting. We were pioneers and what we were doing was worthwhile.[12]

At the various network headquarters in New York, news people who did not go to Philadelphia gathered before small, indistinct but revolutionary images on tiny television screens to see what was going on. In newspaper city rooms, and at AP, UP, and INS, others did the same. The print media, from which newscasters had borrowed for so long, now borrowed from television. Decisions were still made in hotel rooms, out of camera range. Deals could be made in secret among delegations on the convention floor. But henceforth, to most that transpired the country would be eyewitness.

And convention planners would act accordingly.

The Campaign

Television had arrived, but Truman, the first president to see his opponent nominated on television, decided against making much use of the broadcast media in his campaign. Whereas Roosevelt made a distinction between the anti-New Deal press and the neutral radio networks, Truman lumped the two together. So he went to the people in person, making his campaign train the symbol of what has been called "the most colorful and astonishing political campaign in modern American history."[13]

Starting in Crestline, Ohio, Truman whistle-stopped the country, giving the Republicans hell in 356 speeches along the way. "Give 'em hell" was Truman's own phrase picked up by enthusiastic crowds at railroad sidings where the train pulled in, and it typifies the down-to-earth, aggressive Truman approach. Favorite targets were the "do-nothing" Republican Congress and the pollsters, who said Dewey would win in a walk.[14]

By contrast, Dewey, conducting a high-level, aloof campaign, seemed almost to be delivering lectures, many of which were broadcast. Some of his campaigning fell into the category of what today is called a "media event." In a memorandum, Truman noted: "Dewey synthetically milks cows and pitches hay for the cameras."[15] Truman might have used radio more if he had had more money. On October 6, his radio speech in Philadelphia was cut off the air to avoid runover costs.

Throughout the campaign, the networks carried special programs. CBS' Helen Sioussat produced a weekly series called "Presidential Timber," which was simulcast—carried on both radio and television—and gave presidential and vice presidential candidates of all parties a platform for presenting their views. During the last six weeks, CBS Television aired an innovative program called "Presidential Straws in the Wind," hosted by Lyman Bryson. What made this program different was that it featured a pollster, Elmo Roper, who reported how, according to his surveys, people felt about issues and candidates.

In future campaigns, pollsters would play an ever larger role.

The Election

It was the last time that, in reporting a national election, radio would be king.

CBS' radio coverage originated in Studio 22, a remarkable studio because, to quote *Broadcasting*, it was "patterned on the basic principle of a fine violin, with walls lined with resonant panels made of woods similar to those of master violin makers."[16] On a platform, seated at one end of the studio, were CBS' heavy artillery—Ed Murrow, John Daly, Eric Sevareid, and Lowell Thomas. Other correspondents in New York and Washington included Allan Jackson, Richard C. Hottelet, Don Hollenbeck, Griffing Bancroft, Joseph C. Harsch, Quincy Howe, and Bill Shadel.

Special telephone circuits connected Studio 22 with other reporters, most of them stringers, who, supplementing the wire services, phoned in returns from all 48 states. The phones were manned by recruits from all over CBS, ranging from important program executives to secretaries and accountants. Separate desks were set up for compiling returns in the presidential, gubernatorial, and congressional contests. There were no computers, only adding machines commandeered from the accounting departments. Totals were chalked up on a large blackboard, from which they were read.

As usual, there were guests in the studio. On this night they included James A. Farley, former postmaster general; David Selznick, producer of *Gone With the Wind;* and actress Jennifer Jones, whom Selznick would soon marry. They sat below the correspondents' platform, facing the blackboard, and it is likely that the compilers of returns found them quite as interesting as the celebrities found the broadcasting of election results.

At the Hotel Roosevelt, Governor Dewey and his supporters were preparing to celebrate the sure victory. Dewey's press secretary, Jim Hagerty, said, "We may be out of the trenches by midnight."[17] President Truman was at a hotel in Excelsior Springs, Missouri, 32 miles from Kansas City. Fresh from a Turkish bath, he ordered a ham sandwich and a glass of buttermilk and settled down to listen to the returns. He didn't listen long. Before midnight, after a bit of bourbon, he fell asleep.

For Dewey, the early returns were encouraging. He quickly captured New York, New Jersey, and Pennsylvania. Truman was taking Massachusetts and all the border states, but this did not worry the Republicans. So far, it was mostly the city vote. Confident of strong support from rural sections of the country, Alf Landon, speaking on CBS, said flatly, "Thomas E. Dewey is certain to be the next president of the United States." Over at NBC, H. V. Kaltenborn was almost as convinced. He said: "I am inclined to think that while it is a very close race, on the basis of the figures as they now stand on our board, Dewey has the best chance." It was a typical rambling Kaltenborn sentence delivered in Kaltenborn's typical clipped style. Out in Missouri, President Truman awoke just in time to hear it.

CBS' commentators were more cautious. John Daly says:

> The first inkling I had Dewey might not win was around 8 o'clock when the returns from Connecticut came in and Jim Farley said to me, "You be careful, John. These returns are cockeyed. They're not what was expected." Farley didn't say Dewey wouldn't win. He just said be careful. He smelled something in those returns.[18]

Truman went ahead in the popular vote, but there were Ohio and California, each with 25 electoral votes, which were expected to go to Dewey. Returns from those states and Illinois were still coming in when CBS called it a night and closed down. In a room next to the CBS studio, a sumptuous breakfast was served for those who had toiled until the small hours. The mood was more than one of disappointment; it was morose. On orders from high up, these people had been forced to stop reporting a tremendous unfinished story. Ed Murrow, who only a year before had been in command, had protested the decision to shut down, calling it inexcusable. The meal was cheerless. Years later, Daly referred to "that unpleasant night."[19]

As it turned out, Dewey was unable to carry California, even though his running mate was governor of the state. Nor did he take Illinois. Finally, after it became definite that Ohio was lost to him as well, he conceded. Truman entertained reporters that morning with an imitation of Kaltenborn prophesying his political demise, a ribbing Kaltenborn took good-naturedly and seemed to enjoy the rest of his career. A small drama took place in the ABC studio when Walter Winchell went on camera wearing the gray felt hat he traditionally wore when speaking over the radio. When the telephone switchboard was swamped with demands that he take it off, he complied. But other callers insisted he put it back on, claiming that the reflection from Klieg lights on his baldness made viewing difficult. His compromise was to alternate—hat on, hat off.

As in Philadelphia, some television stations covered the election independent of the networks. Many of these stations recruited reporters from the print side. Typical was the coverage provided by WPIX, the station owned by the *New York Daily News*. There the newspapermen turned broadcasters included Lowell Limpus, the paper's U.N. correspondent, and its "inquiring fotographer," Jimmy Jemail. Two of the experienced broadcasters going before the cameras that night were Carl Warren, head of the station's news department, and John Tillman, who did news for the station and had been a radio announcer at CBS. Political writers for the paper, like John O'Donnell and Ruth Montgomery, came on as commentators. A reporter giving the returns on WQXR, the *New York Times* FM station, was one of the paper's White House correspondents, Bill Lawrence, who in 1961 moved to ABC News and became one of broadcast journalism's elite.

President Truman's inauguration on January 20, 1949, was the first covered by television. Networks pooled their facilities; later, as in all else, they would compete.

The pollsters had said the next occupant of the White House would be Dewey, not Truman. In his nightly radio broadcast, Murrow ventured that perhaps the country, besides electing a president, had learned a lesson about polls. He said:

> We know now that during recent months many of us were taken in
> by something that wasn't true. We had almost come to believe that

the hopes, the fears, the prejudices, the aspirations of the people who live on this great continent could be neatly measured and pigeonholed, figured out with a slide rule. What has happened is that a bit of current mythology has been destroyed.[20]

He thought it was a good thing. "We are not robots," he said later. "The individual is not predictable, and in the area of what he believes he is still sovereign."[21]

Meanwhile, Overseas. . . .

Despite the presidential election, there was no danger of underplaying foreign news in 1948. Gandhi was assassinated, Italy almost went Communist, Israel was founded, and the Russians blockaded Berlin. For all these stories the networks supplemented their regular news with special reports. But the Berlin Blockade, threatening to precipitate a third world war, got the most play.

The blockade of Allied-controlled sectors of the city began in April 1948 and ended in September 1949. During those 18 months, British and American planes airlifted 2,343,315 tons of food and other supplies into West Berlin, sustaining some two million German civilians and thousands of U.S. and British army personnel. It was the first dangerous confrontation with Russia since the war. Stalin wanted the Allies out of Berlin; Truman said, "We are going to stay."[22]

The networks sent in their war-experienced reporters. Among them were Bill Downs of CBS and John MacVane of NBC. When Soviet military police besieged the Berlin city hall, ABC's Lyford Moore, who was trapped inside for 43 hours, had an exclusive report. In the same broadcast, he gave an eyewitness account of the kidnaping of 19 Western Sector police.

H. V. Kaltenborn flew into Berlin with his wife and 10 tons of coal. Twice, between Frankfurt and Berlin, their plane was buzzed by Soviet fighter planes. Ed Murrow could not resist and, like Kaltenborn, arrived in a C-54 stacked with coal. He radioed:

> The approach to the field is over a graveyard, and that 50-mile gust that they reported is accurate. As you come in, the co-pilot laughs and points to the graveyard and says, "That would be a fine place to end up, all because you're carrying coal. . . . Right now, at midnight, the sky is heavy with the rumble of motors. The coal and flour and all the rest continue to come in.[23]

The airlift lasted 324 days. It broke the Soviets' land blockade. West Berlin remained free.

Last Full Measure

On May 16, 1948, the body of a young American was found floating in Greece's Salonika Bay, a bullet hole in the head. The body belonged to

CBS' chief Middle East correspondent, George Polk, who had been missing for a week.

Greece was in the midst of a civil war with Communist guerrillas in the mountainous north seeking to wrest control of the country from the rightist regime in Athens. Polk had been reporting both sides, sparing—in Murrow's phrase—"neither the corruption, inefficiency and petty political maneuvering of the Greek government, nor the vacillation of American policy, nor the atrocities committed by the Communists."[24] Along with Homer Bigart, Pulitzer Prize-winning correspondent for the *New York Herald Tribune,* Polk was regarded by Greek government officials as a thorn in their side. The State Department, which was buttressing the anti-Communist regime with aid under the Truman Doctrine, also was unhappy.

For many, the question of who killed George Polk never has been satisfactorily answered. The Greek government insisted it was the work of Communists. In late summer, a Salonika newspaper reporter, Gregory Staktopoulos, made a confession. He had promised, he said, to guide Polk to the guerrillas but instead delivered him to two Communists who killed him. Staktopoulos, convicted as an accessory, received a life sentence. The two other men were sentenced to death in absentia. Twelve years later, Staktopoulos was released from prison. In 1976, he recanted, saying that he had confessed after two months of torture. Other evidence surfaced casting suspicion on the oppressive regime then in power.

When George Polk died, Howard K. Smith said, "The murder of a good reporter is more than the death of one man. It is the murder of truth."[25] Today, celebrating both courageous reporting and truth, there is the George Polk Award administered annually by Long Island University.

25
The Roving Eye

I t was a German, Paul Nipkow, who in 1884 had the idea of transmitting images over an electric wire by using a perforated scanning disc. Twenty years later, a Russian scientist, Boris Rosing, experimented with transmitting images by cathode ray. One of his assistants was Vladimir Zworykin, who came to America in 1918 and invented the iconoscope. No longer was there a mechanical element, the revolving disc. Zworykin translated varying intensity of light into electronic signals. An American, Philo T. Farnsworth, worked on a similar all-electronic system for transmitting images and eventually held more than 150 patents. His major contribution was the orthicon tube, which produced a brighter, sharper picture.[1]

RCA's first television station, W2XBS, was opened in 1930 with an antenna mounted on top of the Empire State Building. The subject shown on NBC's first experimental telecast was a toy model of Felix the Cat, a cartoon character as popular in that day as Garfield today. Its image appeared on screens the size of playing cards. On May 17, 1939, the station carried a baseball game between Columbia and Princeton, with action covered by a single camera perched on a wooden platform behind third base. It was the first sports event ever televised in the United States and one of the first television remotes. The announcer was Bill Stern.

The NBC station had made an even more historic broadcast two weeks earlier, on April 30, when it telecast the speech delivered by President Roosevelt at the opening of the New York World's Fair. This was the first presidential address on television.[2] A few months later, the Sun Oil Company (Sunoco) became the first sponsor of any regularly scheduled television program when Lowell Thomas' program on NBC's Blue Network was simulcast on W2XBS.

CBS' experimental station, W2XAB, went on the air on July 21, 1931, with a stellar program that included George Gershwin, the Boswell Sisters, and Kate Smith, who sang her radio theme song, "When the Moon Comes Over the Mountain." In the same year, 1931, CBS introduced television's first regularly scheduled news program.[3] Its anchor was William Schudt, Jr., and the program consisted largely of interviews with reporters, much along the lines, decades later, of public television's "Washington Week in Review." Its unpretentious title was "Bill Schudt's Going to Press." In a rudimentary way, the station gave returns on election night, 1932.

The station's program director, starting in 1937, was Gilbert Seldes, who describes what may have been CBS' classiest primordial experiment:

> After the radio programs went off the air at night . . . CBS transmitted pictures. One of the programs—it wasn't so much a program as a transmission—carried the scintillation and brightness of a collection of diamonds. The reason I remember this is that the report I read made much of the protective guard which accompanied the diamonds from Cartier's to the CBS studios.[4]

On July 1, 1941, CBS began a regular television service totaling 15 hours a week, using a studio in the Grand Central Terminal Building and a transmitter on top of the Chrysler Building. It had adopted new call letters, WCBW, while the NBC station, the first commercially licensed television station, began calling itself WNBT.

The CBS station was now televising two 15-minute news programs a day, Monday through Friday. One was at 2:30 P.M., the other at 7:30 P.M. Richard Hubbell was the reader for both programs. Robert Skedgell was the writer. They were the entire news staff. Skedgell, now retired from CBS, says:

> The newsroom, if it could be so called, was an open space just large enough to hold two desks, one UP radio wire, and a couple of filing cabinets. It looked like an insurance office. . . . Dick and I would confer in the morning as to the line-up for the afternoon broadcast and then would meet with Rudy Bretz, a graphics artist who would supply the only visual components then available to us —symbols of tanks, planes, bomb bursts, sinking ships, and so forth—no film, no switches anywhere.

Before airtime, Skedgell's script would be checked by Seldes or in his absence by Adrian Murphy, the station president. After the first months, Skedgell wrote in the main newsroom at 485 Madison Avenue, where he had access to stories moved by AP and INS as well as UP. At 485, as it was called, Skedgell's scripts were copyread by the editor on duty, either Matt Gordon or Jesse Zousmer, or sometimes by Paul White. Then he returned to Grand Central for broadcast.

Although the station had never done a news show on Sunday, Skedgell knew when he heard Pearl Harbor had been attacked that there would—had to be—one on this day. Hubbell knew it, too. So did Seldes, and they no sooner reached the television studio before Adrian Murphy called, saying that he was putting the station on the air and that it was to stay on the air for as long as it took to tell the story.

The result was television's first "instant special." Skedgell says:

> I believe we were on the air at about 3:30 and continued non-stop until 1:30 the next morning. I don't mean that Hubbell went non-stop. Much of the time was taken up by such as George Fielding Eliot [CBS' military analyst] and Linton Wells and various other regular radio correspondents when they were not in demand at 485. I remember there were panel discussions with Helen Sioussat and sportsman Bob Edge acting as moderators. I don't know if it was technically possible, but we aired no radio reports from overseas.
>
> There was not very much hard news that Sunday night, so much of our report was speculative: where the Japanese fleet was, what the Japanese intentions were, where the U.S. fleet had gone, how much damage it had suffered. Of course, the maps were brought into considerable use, along with our usual graphics, during the long hours.[5]

On December 8, when President Roosevelt went before a joint session of Congress to ask for a declaration of war, CBS had no video line to Washington. Its television coverage consisted of an audio feed with a camera focused on an American flag. The flag rippled in a breeze from an electric fan.

WCBW kept its weekday schedule of two newscasts a day until February 1942, when general programming was cut back and regularly scheduled news was abandoned altogether.[6] For momentous events like the Allied invasion of Normandy and Germany's surrender, there were news specials on the television stations operated by CBS and NBC, as well as on Allen B. DuMont's New York station, WABD.[7] On V-E Day, WNBT provided 14 hours of uninterrupted coverage, including the celebrating throng in Times Square. It was on this program that Eleanor Roosevelt made her first television appearance, warning the country against apathy. The war against Japan was still to be won.

Although hampered by wartime shortages in manpower and material, the NBC station pressed ahead with a variety of television offerings. It carried programs for training New York air raid wardens and sporting events from Madison Square Garden for veterans' hospitals. In 1944, film from the battle zones was used for a series called "The War As It Happens."

These were not the only commercial television stations of the early 1940s. Ten were on the air as early as May 1942. Six continued to broadcast during the war.[8] Not until after the war were channels assigned for noncommercial educational purposes.

Dress Rehearsal

With the surrender of Japan, television was ready to take off. The electronics giant, RCA, joined DuMont and others in manufacturing television receivers, and five million television sets were in use by 1950. The FCC, deluged with license applications, soon discovered the few VHF channels totally inadequate to meet demand and issued a freeze order on the issuing of commercial station licenses. In 1952, it lifted the freeze, expanding the number of UHF channels and setting criteria for operation within the VHF spectrum to reduce interference. This permitted an explosion in commercial television stations from 97 in 1950 to 439 in 1955.[9]

Like radio in the 1930s, television began demonstrating how it could cover what was happening, however clumsy these "demonstrations" may appear by today's standards. What follows is a sampling.

The first television outlet in New England was the Westinghouse station, WBZ-TV, Boston, which went on the air on June 9, 1948. Its newscaster that day was Arch Macdonald. In 1978, when the station celebrated its thirtieth anniversary, the *Boston Globe* reported that carpenters were still hammering away on the set at airtime. Macdonald yelled, "Quiet!" and delivered the news seated on a keg of nails behind a temporary plywood desk.[10]

In August 1948, the *New York Daily News* station, WPIX, scored what may have been the most dramatic video coup up to that time. When a Russian school teacher, Oksana Kosenkina, leapt from a window of the Soviet consulate, a WPIX cameraman, Lester Mannix, got footage of the woman as she lay, broken-boned, in the paved courtyard, along with footage of consulate staff members bundling her off inside. Other cameramen had caught the scene, but WPIX was first with it on the air. Delivery, processing, editing, and scripting had taken "only" three hours and 10 minutes.

It was now (1947–1948) that the television networks came into being. In news, these networks were taking tottering first steps. In May 1947, NBC sent Ben Grauer and a camera crew to Brazil to cover a total eclipse of the sun. Six months later, in cooperation with the BBC, the network televised a filmed account of the wedding of Princess Elizabeth and Philip, duke of Edinburgh, in Westminster Abbey. Though shown two days afterward, it was still, for that time, an exciting television event. The same year, 1947, saw the arrival on NBC of television's oldest network program, "Meet the Press."

NBC Television was proving itself more aggressive than either ABC or CBS in the journalistic field, although all TV networks would soon be covering such events as President Truman's inauguration and important U.N. sessions. CBS-TV, trailblazing in other areas, presented the distinguished drama series "Studio One" and, early in 1948, Eugene Ormandy and the Philadelphia Symphony Orchestra, the first concert of its kind on television. Concerts by the NBC Symphony, with Toscanini conducting, were only months away. (Just to keep things in perspective, other newcomers to network television in 1948 were "Texaco Star Theater" with Milton Berle, Ted Mack's "Original Amateur Hour," Ed Sullivan, Gene Autry, and Bert Parks. "Howdy Doody" and "Kukla, Fran, and Ollie" had arrived the year before.)

Genesis of the Evening News

It was a small beginning, recalling the biblical cloud no larger than a man's hand. In 1946, there were only two regularly scheduled news programs on network evening television. NBC-TV offered a film package called "The Esso Newsreel"—15 minutes on Sunday, 10 minutes on Monday and Thursday. The script was read by Paul Alley. In 1947, the program was cut back to one day a week and its name changed to "The Esso Reporter."

In 1946, CBS-TV had the other news program. It aired Thursday nights and was sponsored by Gulf. (Interesting that oil companies attended the creation.) The CBS program was anchored by Milo Boulton, host of "We, the People." Its editor was Henry Cassirer. When a Saturday newscast was added early in 1947, Douglas Edwards was persuaded to anchor.[11] Persuasion was required because, at that time, correspondents regarded television as a pesky stepchild. Radio was where the audience was, where the exposure was. John Daly recalls:

> Back then, if you were on television, you were talking to yourself. Radio was booming, and there were only a few thousand TV sets in the whole country. So we senior broadcasters weren't much interested in working in television, and at CBS it fell to a junior broadcaster, Doug Edwards, to do most of the anchor work. Really, none of us dreamed what television would become.[12]

Nineteen forty-eight was a landmark year. Not only did it see television play a major role in a presidential election, but in that year—and the year after—emerged the prototype of the network evening news that 40 million people now watch on a weekday night. Starting in August 1948, Douglas Edwards came on with "The CBS-TV News" every weekday evening. This was network television's first quarter-hour news program scheduled across the board.

The key word here is *quarter-hour*. In February 1948, six months earlier, NBC-TV had launched a 10-minute Monday-through-Friday program with John Cameron Swayze. The show was called "The Camel News-reel Theater." Swayze had read copy over film; he had seldom appeared on camera as Edwards did until—unbelievable title—"The Camel News Caravan" premiered in February 1949. Like the CBS program, it was 15 minutes in length. Since time would be sold to advertisers, it seemed logical throughout television to adhere to the 15-minute, half-hour, and one-hour pattern established in radio.

The Edwards program aired at 7:30, Swayze's at 7:45. On the wall behind Swayze loomed a large map of the world, and there was an ash tray on his desk—after all, the program was sponsored by the manufacturer of Camel cigarettes. "No smoking" signs were *verboten* in film used on the program. No one, save Churchill, could be shown smoking a cigar. On Edwards' desk stood a world globe. Behind him on the wall, instead of a map, were clocks showing the time in New York, London, and Tokyo. Television news was to embrace the planet.

ABC-TV went on with its nightly program, "News and Views," in August 1948. Combining hard news and commentary, it used two broadcasters, H. R. Baukhage and Jim Gibbons. Pauline Frederick had a 15-minute show on Sunday. "News and Views" was revamped in 1951 and given a new name, "After the Deadlines," but it lasted only a year. The replacement was an ambitious one-hour program called "All Star News," with Gordon Fraser, Pauline Frederick, Leo Cherne, and Bryson Rash. Content ran the gamut from hard news and commentary to interviews and short documentary-type reports, making the program the granddaddy of Robert MacNeil and Jim Lehrer's "NewsHour" three decades later.

ABC began the series with one-hour programs in prime time on Monday, Wednesday, and Friday, and a half-hour edition on Thursday. After five months, there was only a Sunday night edition. Then, after a few weeks, no edition at all. "All Star News" was doomed from the start. Not only was it aired at irregular times—at 8 P.M. one night, at 9 P.M. another—but it was pitted against such hit shows as "Arthur Godfrey and His Friends" and "I Love Lucy." Although to air such a program would have been daring for any network, it was especially enterprising for ABC, which, next to DuMont, possessed the least resources.

Sobered by this experience, ABC adopted the 15-minute evening news format employed successfully at CBS and NBC. In 1953, it chose John Daly, the former CBS war correspondent and moderator of the popular quiz show "What's My Line?," to anchor its 7:15 P.M. news. The nightly program, "John Daly and the News," had its premiere on October 12, 1953, and ran for seven years. His contract allowed him, at the same time, to play host on "What's My Line?" on CBS-TV. At CBS, such free-ranging careers were frowned upon. It was one of the reasons Daly had left.

The struggling DuMont network got into news programming in 1947 with "The Walter Compton News." The short-lived program is notable because it was the first news series on a television network to originate from Washington. DuMont's principal offering, starting in 1948, was "Camera Headlines," a 15-minute film package of domestic stories carried at 7:30 P.M., Monday through Friday. "INS Telenews," a Hearst production, consisted largely of newsreel footage from abroad and aired at 7:45 p.m. on Tuesday. A weekly interview show was conducted by Ernest K. Lindley, a senior editor of *Newsweek*.

"Camera Headlines" was dropped in 1949, and there was no regularly scheduled evening news on DuMont until the fall of 1953. But the new program, anchored by Morgan Beatty, was a last gasp. Within two years, the DuMont network ceased to exist. Two people who worked at DuMont came over to CBS News. David Lowe, director of news and special events, won distinction as a producer of documentaries for CBS Reports. He died in 1965. Marian Glick also went to CBS, where he had a distinguished career as an editor.

Introducing in This Corner. . . .

It took more than twenty years for ABC to get its act together. Until the 1970s, wags said ABC stood for the Almost Broadcasting Company. Its television network had too few (and too weak) affiliates, which meant too few viewers and not enough advertising revenue. So the prime contenders in the evening news arena at the start were John Cameron Swayze of NBC and Douglas Edwards of CBS.

A Kansan, born in Wichita, Swayze attended the University of Kansas. After studying drama for a year in New York—he thought of being an actor—he worked as a newspaper reporter and as a broadcaster (KMBC) in Kansas City, Missouri, where he knew Walter Cronkite, who was working for the United Press. Looking back to 1937, Cronkite says:

> Swayze was doing an early morning news broadcast for a Kansas City station which was billed as emanating from the city desk of the *Journal-Post*. He'd come puffing up the three flights of stairs to the UP office and grab the carbons of the overnight report off the spike on my desk. It would be only a couple of minutes until air time, and I would then race across the building to the city room with him, briefing him on the top stories as we went. Swayze would slide into his chair in front of the microphone just as the red light came on and recite, with that amazing memory of his, almost verbatim what I had told him.[13]

It was a memory Swayze relied on when he began anchoring "The Camel News Caravan." He tried then to deliver the news without reading from a script and largely succeeded. He had a formal look, always a fresh carnation in his lapel, but for comfort, out of sight behind the anchor desk —and they really were desks in those days—he might be wearing a pair of old sailing pants. Just as Dan Rather came to wear an assortment of sweaters, Swayze tried each evening to wear a different tie.

He spoke briskly. His opening was formal—"Ladies and gentlemen, a good evening to you!" But toward the end of the program, when he reported a hodgepodge of short items, he would say, "Now let's go hopscotching the world for headlines."[14] His ending was: "Well, that's the story, folks! This is John Cameron Swayze, and I'm glad we could get together."

There is a lingering impression among some critics that Swayze was more performer than journalist. Les Brown has called him "essentially a news reader . . . before it mattered that the presenter of the news was not a journalist."[15] But in 1949, when he began anchoring "The Camel News Caravan," Swayze had been a journalist for more than twenty years, a newspaperman, newscaster, and director of news for NBC's western network. He had not been a "reader" at the 1948 conventions; his work at these conventions was one reason why he was selected for NBC's most important news program. Cronkite, who in Kansas City came to appreciate Swayze's editorial judgments, calls him "a complete newsman."[16]

Swayze held down the anchor position for seven years. A staff writer on the program at one time was Reuven Frank, who would serve two terms (1968–73 and 1982–1984) as president of NBC News. There was no producer. Clarence Thoman was production supervisor; Ralph Peterson directed. The news editor was John Lynch. One film editor, David McCruden, was assigned to the program. As late as March 1952, this was the entire staff.

Douglas Edwards, who reported news on network television longer than anyone else, was born in Oklahoma, but it was in Troy, Alabama, that, at the age of 15, he began his broadcasting career. The part-time job was at WHET (now WAGF in Dothan), where he was a kind of junior announcer. He attended the University of Alabama with the idea of becoming a doctor, but left after two years because of the lure of radio.

Like a lot of announcers, he "moved around." After another short stint at WHET, he went in 1935 to WSB, the *Atlanta Journal* station, and soon, in addition to doing three newscasts a day, was editing the *Journal*'s radio page on Sunday. When the paper's radio editor was away, he wrote the daily column.

When he was 21, Edwards moved north. He joined WXYZ, Detroit, where, besides news and special events, he sometimes did dance band remotes. A major sponsor was the Cunningham Drug Company, and Edwards found himself sharing "Cunningham News Ace" chores with another future CBS newsman, Mike Wallace. Edwards recalled:

> In the fall of 1940, WSB offered me a bit more money than I was making in Detroit to return to Atlanta as assistant news editor. I would also do three news reports in the afternoon and the feature evening report at 10:15. But by this time I had my sights set on CBS, and on December 1, 1942, came to the big town on a gamble to take a staff announcer's job until such time as I got really lucky and had exposure to Paul White on the news side.[17]

It was good timing. The United States was in the war. Correspondents were being drawn from New York to cover events overseas, and early in 1943, when John Daly left for North Africa, Edwards got a three-year contract to take his place. Edwards' first assignment for CBS was to anchor the early evening program, "The World Today." There were other important broadcasts, all from New York, and Edwards was wondering if he would be trapped stateside for the rest of the war. Then in March of 1945, when it seemed hopeless, he received orders to report to Murrow in London.

> My assignments were to have been six-week stints on each of the western fronts to allow the regular types to go to London for R. and R. As it happened, the war was winding down. A bit frustrating, but Murrow, sensing my disappointment, reminded me, "There's nothing intellectual about being shot at." After London, Paris for 10 months as correspondent there with plenty of opportunities for travel. Then back to New York in May 1946.[18]

Up to this time, Edwards' experience had been in radio. Now, with John Cameron Swayze across town, he entered the new world of television.

They quickly became the hottest competitors in television news. Edwards' less breezy style could he characterized as CBS traditional. Like Swayze, he spoke with authority, but his sentences were leaner, less extravagant. To think of Edwards "hopscotching" for headlines was impossible. And there was in his voice a warmth that seemed a carryover from the Deep South, even though he had shed the accent.

The show, renamed "Douglas Edwards with the News," had four directors. These four—Fred Rickey, David Rich, Don Hewitt, and Franklin Schaffner—took turns directing during the week. Edwards said:

> In short, there was no continuity of direction, and although I appreciated and admired the work of the others, there was no doubt that the man for the Monday-through-Friday job was Don Hewitt [with whom Edwards had worked at the Philadelphia conventions]. I went to Edmund Chester, the over-all boss of radio and TV news at this point, and requested that Don be assigned across the board. Got it![19]

Today, Hewitt is executive producer of "60 Minutes," the most widely viewed news program in television history. Schaffner directed other television programs, then went on to Hollywood, where he won worldwide recognition for his direction of such films as *Patton* and *Planet of the Apes*.

Early television news was a hybrid obtained by the crossbreeding of radio and film. If early television had a newsreel look, it was understandable. Most of the film came from newsreel companies. NBC bought 35mm footage from Fox-Movietone. Telenews, an arm of Hearst-MGM News of the Day, sold 16mm film to CBS. The result was a preponderance of fashion shows, ship arrivals, and fires. These stories gave camera crews time to set up their cumbersome gear. Live reports were rare. It was considered a breakthrough in 1951 when RCA developed a portable camera-transmitter weighing "only" 53 pounds.

There was a great deal of improvisation. In 1957, when Russia sent its first Sputnik into orbit, Don Hewitt illustrated the feat with an ordinary world globe, a wire coathanger, and a pingpong ball stuck with toothpicks to represent Sputnik's antennae. The coathanger, straightened out, was bent around the globe, the pingpong ball suspended at one end. When the globe turned, viewers had a realistic picture of the satellite circling the earth.

Edwards told of a July day when most of the country was sweltering in a record heat wave.

> Don and I were trying to come up with something a little different for a closing piece acknowledging the weather and perhaps easing it a bit for imaginative viewers. So we bought a 75-pound block of ice and at some expense had it moved from the ice truck through a couple of union jurisdictions into its proper posture on the set. On the show, we took a shot of this steaming block of ice as I said something like, "Well, take a look at this, folks. Perhaps it'll help cool you off a little."

There's a postscript to this.

> A few minutes later, on the way to catch our respective trains in Grand Central, Hewitt looked at me and began to laugh. "Doug," he said, "what idiots we are. We could have taken an *ice cube,* gotten a tight close-up of it, and had the same effect." [20]

A lot of trial and some error. There was no electronic wizardry like that available today.

Hewitt, dissatisfied with easel shots of still photographs or Edwards holding them in his hand, went to rear projection (RP), the process by which images are projected on a screen behind the anchor person. These images, consisting more often of slides than film or videotape, underscore the anchor's story. They may be schematic: an artist's drawing of billowing factory smoke and a Union Jack to accompany a story about high industrial production in Britain. On occasion, they show key words from a newsmaker's statement or put a label on a report. Pioneering in this field was Ben Blank, the first graphics artist assigned to the CBS program. Later, at ABC, he became the dean of television news artists.

The lone woman on the CBS evening news staff at the start was Alice Weel, a writer who helped Hewitt with production of the program and later became a respected producer in her own right. Weel, a newswoman as gifted and conscientious as she was kind, died in 1969.

Whereas the Swayze program originated where it was produced, in Radio City, the Edwards program in its first years was put together at Grand Central but broadcast from facilities in Liederkrantz Hall, 13 blocks uptown, requiring a mad dash by taxi for everyone before airtime. "Imagine what that sort of arrangement did to us," said Edwards, "especially when we had to cope with late-breaking news." [21]

Early on, Swayze captured and held onto a ratings lead. Rapturous writers acclaimed him "mighty monarch of the air." [22] Nevertheless, competition was keen. As in the days of Abe Schechter and Paul White, it was a rivalry that permeated both news departments. ABC-TV had such a small news department, it didn't count. Or so they thought.

Tragedy at Sea

A big disaster story in the early days of television news was the sinking of the Italian liner *Andrea Doria* off Nantucket on July 26, 1956. The beautiful ship collided in morning fog with the Swedish liner *Stockholm,* which survived. Fifty-one persons aboard the *Andrea Doria* died.

Reporters from all media rushed to Quonset Naval Station, Rhode Island, where information from the Coast Guard and other sources was being pieced together. Don Hewitt, Douglas Edwards, and Tony Petri, a CBS cameraman, were late arriving on the scene. Hewitt recalls:

> Everybody had finished shooting and were rushing back to New York to get their film on the air. We were even pondering whether to give it up when a Coast Guard pilot recognized Doug and said, "Hang around. That thing's going down in five minutes." And he was right. In about five minutes the ship turned over like a big dead elephant, and all of a sudden it wasn't there."[23]

With the cameraman, Hewitt and Edwards had gone up in a seaplane and filmed the liner's final moments, and that night "The CBS Evening News with Douglas Edwards" was the only program with actual footage of the sinking. "And the thing was," said Edwards, "if we had got there 10 minutes earlier, we would have missed it."[24]

Television had demonstrated that it could take the public to the scene of a major story more effectively than any other news medium. This was an ability—a power—it would demonstrate again and again in such disparate places as Vietnam, Tiananmen Square, and the moon. Henceforth, events caught by television's roving eye would be perceived in a way they never had been before. Less importantly, it showed how an anchor's celebrity status could help. Edwards was immediately recognized—"Hello, Mr. Edwards"—and the seaplane placed at CBS' disposal. The stars might find themselves getting in the way of stories at times. But often, as when seeking interviews with world leaders, identity eases their way.

There were television pictures. And there were words. Edwards said:

> Our philosophy was to put on a real news show, news being just that, whether in cuneiform or smoke signals, print or picture. This was TV, and we hoped to use pictures where it was appropriate, of course. But keeping in mind one of Ed Murrow's observations that you can't always put ideas into pictures, we set out to tell the news of the day in picture if possible but with the "talking head" if necessary. . . . We knew that gradually our tools would improve and so would our output.[25]

In the early 1950s, with a larger budget and its own photographers and better tools, "Douglas Edwards with the News" caught up with, then overtook, "The Camel News Caravan." In 1956, John Cameron Swayze was replaced by network television's first co-anchors, Chet Huntley and David Brinkley.[26] But Edwards' audience kept growing. In the second week of December 1957, Nielsen gave the CBS program an 18.6 rating against an 11.4 rating for "The Huntley-Brinkley Report." This meant that, each evening, Edwards was being watched in roughly seven million homes while Huntley and Brinkley were being watched in four million homes.

Variety took the figures, translated them, and came up with a front-page story that began:

> The world's largest single news medium is now a network television newscast, CBS-TV's "Douglas Edwards with the News." The news show, which has strong audience gains this season, now reaches 14,156,400 viewers per day and 33,975,360 per week, topping the leading journals in the daily newspaper and magazine class.[27]

It was the first published recognition that a television news program had a larger "circulation" than any newspaper or magazine in the world.[28]

26
Era of Fear

It was November 18, 1951, a Sunday afternoon. Viewers tuned to CBS' first "See It Now" program were about to see a memorable performance—a stunt—opening a new chapter in television news.

Ed Murrow was sitting in a swivel chair in the control room of Studio 41. Behind his right shoulder, Don Hewitt, the director, sat at a console facing four monitors, a primitive setup which, as *Newsweek* said, today suggests a Model T dashboard.[1] All a viewer could see of Hewitt was the back of his head. When the second hand of the studio clock reached 3:30 straight up, Ed Murrow, turning, locked into the camera and explained that he was in the control room because that was where it was happening.

What was happening was a technological miracle for that time. A high-frequency coaxial cable, buried in the soil of 12 states, now connected the East and West coasts. Harry Truman, addressing the Japanese peace treaty conference in San Francisco, had inaugurated live transcontinental television that September, an event recalling completion of the transcontinental railroad in 1869. "This is an old team," Murrow said, "trying to learn a new trade," and then he asked technicians to "bring in" the Atlantic and Pacific oceans so that they appeared simultaneously, live, on the control room monitors. "We are impressed," said Murrow, "by a medium in which a man sitting in his living room has been able for the first time to look at two oceans at once." Fred W. Friendly, who produced the program, said years later:

> We thought that a medium capable of doing this was capable of providing reporters with an entirely new weapon in journalism. We stated that we were going to try to learn to use it, that we hoped we would never abuse it, and that we would not get too big for our britches. There are those who will testify that we have done all three things.[2]

CBS had bought a full page of the *New York Times* to advertise the series premiere. The advertisement announced with an assurance bordering on bravado:

> Edward R. Murrow, broadcasting's most respected reporter, brings a new dimension to television reporting today. In his new half-hour program, "See It Now," you will see the exciting potential of television as a news gatherer. You will watch a scrupulously edited report of the week's significant events, some of it on film, some of it happening before your eyes. You will meet, face to face, kings and commoners, soldiers and scientists, politicos and plain people who are the masters—or the victims—of events that affect us all. From your own armchair, you will witness the world.[3]

The promise was not vain. "See It Now" not only was the first news magazine on television but was for seven years the most provocative and innovative documentary series. No other program of the 1950s carried its impact.

"See It Now" was a descendant of "March of Time." More immediately, it was the offspring of the radio show "Hear It Now," which got its title from the best-selling record album "I Can Hear It Now." The television series, the radio show, and the album—all daring ventures—had as their creative, driving force one man, Fred W. Friendly, who had as his voice and conscience broadcasting's most distinguished reporter, Edward R. Murrow. Their collaboration left an imprint which remains, to this day, uneffaced.

Friendly, like Murrow, came to journalism without credentials as a reporter. After attending business college, he worked for a short time in a department store, then with a company making tire retreads. In 1936, he talked the unenthusiastic management of Station WEAN, Providence, into taking him on staff. A year later, he was producing and narrating a series of five-minute radio biographies of famous people in history called "Footprints in the Sands of Time." He was making $35 a week. For each broadcast, the sponsor of "Footprints" gave him an extra five dollars.

Fred Friendly was called into the Army in September 1941. Because of his radio experience, he was assigned to the Information and Education Section, where with characteristic enterprise he sold the Army on a novel way of testing soldiers on what they learned in basic training; GIs would answer questions in a competition called "Sergeant Quiz."

After he had spent two years setting up the training quiz at Army camps and lecturing on why America was fighting, the Army sent Friendly, master sergeant, to the China–Burma–India theater of operations. There, besides lecturing, he corresponded for the Army newspaper. This led to a tour of Pacific bases and flights with the first B-29s to bomb Japan. He covered the Normandy invasion, and it was with special interest, and gratification, that in 1964 he produced "D-Day Plus 20 Years," a memorable CBS Reports program in which General Eisenhower and Walter Cronkite visited the invasion beaches and reminisced.

Friendly, who was full of ideas about how the war should be fought, communicated them up the line as a matter of course, so that he may have been the only noncom in the CBI who advised generals, including "Uncle Joe" Stilwell, on what to do. He was lecturing in India when an explosion tore through a Bombay dock. Without orders, Friendly assumed charge of removing the dead and injured and salvaging supplies. The pier and ships alongside had caught fire and there was danger of new explosions, but he stayed, directed rescue operations, until the job was done. For his bravery Friendly received the Soldier's Medal of Heroism. Before discharge in 1945, he also was awarded the Legion of Merit and four battle stars.

It was with a quiz program that Friendly got back into broadcasting, and this time it was television as well as radio. After making the rounds fruitlessly for two years, peddling all sorts of ideas, he sold his concept of a panel show called "Who Said That?" to NBC. Panel members were given a quotation from the week's news and asked to identify its source. Panelists included, at different times, John Cameron Swayze, June Lockhart, Oscar Levant, Kitty Carlisle, Quentin Reynolds, and Al Capp.

"Who Said That?" had a seven-year run, starting in 1948. At first, it was carried on both radio and television, then only on television. The moderator at the start was Robert Trout, who had left CBS with bruised feelings after being replaced on the Campbell Soup news program by Ed Murrow. When Trout returned to CBS, his emcee role was taken over by Walter Kiernan.

Meanwhile, Murrow and Friendly had got together, introduced to each other by Jap Gude, the original CBS newsman turned agent. Again, it was a case of Friendly having an idea, which really was an outgrowth of his early radio program, "Footprints in the Sands of Time." Why not collect the recorded voices of historical figures of the past 10 or 15 years—Will Rogers, Huey Long, Al Smith, Franklin Roosevelt, Churchill, Hitler, and the rest—and put them in an album? And how about bringing it out in time for Christmas? It might sell.

The album was called "I Can Hear It Now." It got its name as the result of an argument over whether Churchill had made a certain statement. When a member of the production staff insisted, "I know he did. I can hear it now," Friendly exclaimed, "That's it! That's the title—'I Can Hear It Now'."[4]

As finally pressed, the Columbia album (10 sides) carried 46 voices, including those of six radio reporters: Herbert Morrison, Elmer Davis, William L. Shirer, John Daly, George Hicks, and Robert Trout. The range was impressive, from Roosevelt's declaration that America had "a rendez-vous with destiny" to Lou Gehrig's farewell to baseball. It was, the jacket copy said, "the history of an era spoken by the men who made it."

It was an unprecedented undertaking. The production team listened to more than five hundred hours of radio broadcasts, of which a hundred hours were put on magnetic tape, then distilled to 45 minutes. Joseph Wershba tracked down raw material. Friendly joined in the writing and editing. Murrow narrated. Producer's credit went to Gude, who oversaw the operation.

Sale of the album exceeded all expectations, and a second album covering the years 1946–1948 was produced as speedily as possible, then a third, still more up-to-date album in which newsmakers acted out their parts. For example, Supreme Court Justice Robert Jackson came to the recording studio and read his summation from the war crimes trial at Nuremberg. Plans for a fourth album were abandoned. As his share of the royalties, Friendly received some $100,000.[5]

The big thing about the "I Can Hear It Now" albums, technologically, was magnetic tape. Tape made them feasible. Three CBS engineers, Max Weiman, Arthur Buckner, and Joel Tall, transferred the voices from wire recordings and acetate disks onto tape, then edited the tape with scissors. (The Editall block, invented by Tall, and the Gem blade came later.) Many technicians shunned tape. One told Wershba, "If I wanted to be a tailor, I'd cut out dresses."[6]

It was while Friendly was working on the second album that CBS induced him to leave NBC, where, in addition to his quiz show, he had just produced a four-part radio documentary on development of the atomic bomb. It was this documentary, "The Quick and the Dead," which accord-ing to Friendly "convinced the CBS management that a permanent Mur-row–Friendly partnership might be productive."[7] And so came about the most productive, most influential partnership in the whole history of broadcast journalism.

Their first effort for broadcast was "Hear It Now," a radio newsmaga-zine compiled from audiotape.[8] Use of tape in summarizing the week's news was not new. A year earlier, Murrow himself had anchored such a pilot program. Because advertisers were not interested, it never got on the air. But in 1950, when "Hear It Now" debuted, the United States was at war in Korea, and news was salable. The program ran a full hour in prime time, and this in a period when nighttime radio still outdrew television.

"Hear It Now" was ambitious, more than a mere recitation of events. It was reminiscent of Paul White's "Report to the Nation" program of a decade before, but instead of using actors and sound effects, the sounds on "Hear It Now," ranging from artillery fire in Korea to the start up of the world's most powerful atom smasher at the University of Chicago, were authentic. Events were placed in their context. And there was independent reporting, of which the following is typical: "Earl Warren had yet to indicate his position on the debate [over President Truman's recall of General MacArthur]. We called Governor Warren and asked him what conclusions he had been able to reach."[9] The call was warranted since Warren, then governor of California, was a possible Republican nominee for President.

Murrow and Friendly collaborated in the writing but still played different roles. Murrow biographer Alexander Kendrick, explains:

> Friendly was responsible for the close, meticulous editing of the program—wasting no words, playing upon ironic contrasts, and not suffering fools gladly, unless of course their foolishness made a point—and Murrow was the reporter, the practical cogitator, and the consummate narrator.[10]

They complemented each other. Friendly had the gift of creativity. His enthusiasm and dramatic sense contributed substantially to the program's success. But in journalism the same attributes can also do harm. When Friendly was in danger of being carried away, Murrow, the careful journalist, brought him back. Murrow gave Friendly his bearing. Twenty years later, Friendly said it was "the Murrow bearing against which the profession measures itself and occasionally corrects its course."[11] He said that in 1971, and it is still true today.

The series, carried on 173 stations, brought a new dimension to radio. NBC imitated it with "Voices and Events" and ABC with "Week Around the World." But it was "Hear It Now" that made the mark, setting the pattern for radio news specials forever after. It won a Peabody Award almost immediately, and there is no question about its effectiveness. A single broadcast tracing delivery of a pint of blood from the United States to a wounded soldier in Korea caused listeners to volunteer 500,000 pints of blood. Nevertheless, the program went off the air after one season. Murrow and Friendly were absorbed with a similar series for television. They would add sight to sound.

"See It Now"

In television, Ed Murrow and Fred Friendly were learning a new trade, and their teacher was Palmer Williams, who knew documentary film. As Friendly has said, "[He was] our pathfinder as we ventured down an unmarked trail."[12]

Williams was a New Yorker who, growing up in Greenwich Village, loved movies. By the age of 18, he no longer paid to see them. In that day, motion pictures had to be approved by the National Board of Review, and Williams was one of its junior reviewers. At 19, he was working as a researcher in *Newsweek*'s stage and screen department. After the outbreak of World War II, he gathered stock footage for "Why We Fight," the now famous Army series produced by Frank Capra.

Williams had gone to work with the Office of War Information when he was drafted and helped Anatole Litvak with a service film called "The True Glory," which won an Academy Award. Shortly after the war, while Williams was employed at Film Associates making documentaries, he met Burgess Meredith. They became friends, and Meredith hired him as production manager for New World Films. After John Houseman joined them it became Media Productions, which made movie shorts for television. Williams says:

> After listening to the first "I Can Hear It Now" album, John and I went to Jap Gude to see if he, Fred and Ed would be interested in doing the album on film. Eventually they declined. Seven or eight months later . . . I went to Barbetta's [a restaurant popular with writers] and heard that News of the Day had just signed a deal with CBS to provide camera crews and library footage for Fred and Ed. So I called Fred, went in to see him, and got hired in September 1951.

Although the challenge presented by a television program as ambitious as Friendly described appealed to Williams, he had no idea that such a series with the pressure of weekly deadlines could last. In fact, after the first program he told his wife he had to find a new job. "When they see how tough it's going to be," he said, "they'll fold."

But they didn't fold. Williams relates that after the series had run for 40 or 50 weeks, he and Murrow were talking and the subject of some difficulty with the program came up. Williams says Murrow gave him a long baneful look and said, "You son of a bitch, you *knew* how tough this was going to be and didn't tell us."[13]

"See It Now" became CBS News' showpiece and Palmer Williams its director of operations. Friendly, with awesome energies matching his six-foot-two frame, was its engine, Murrow its editor. Williams, the knowledgeable puller-together of loose ends, made it work. Friendly writes in his introduction to *Due to Circumstances Beyond Our Control:*

> At a moment's notice Williams could not only tell you the time and flight number of the next plane from Karachi to New Delhi for a film shipment, he could also diagnose the editorial flaws of footage on Bertrand Russell or the Polaris submarine. In a way, he was as much my teacher as was Murrow.[14]

"See It Now," the first major documentary series on television, had a production budget of $23,000 a week, more than CBS allocated for its nightly news. Frequently the cost of a single program exceeded $100,000. Not once during the four years the program was sponsored by the Aluminum Company of America did SIN, as internal memoranda referred to it,[15] operate out of the red.

At the start, the film for "See It Now" was shot by cameramen employed by Hearst-MGM's News of the Day. This contract arrangement proved unsatisfactory and, on Williams' recommendation, topnotch cameramen were hired: Martin "Marty" Barnett and Leo Rossi, and Charles

Mack from News of the Day. As film editors "See It Now" hired Gene Milford from Columbia Pictures, William P. Thompson from the Capra unit, F. Howard "Bucky" O'Neill, and Mili Lerner, whose credit after her marriage read Mili Bonsignore. These people were used to working with 35-millimeter film, not 16-millimeter, and Friendly, convinced that 35-millimeter film produced brighter, sharper pictures, kept it that way. In the screening room on Ninth Avenue were two 35-millimeter projectors operated by a union projectionist. Originally, only two reporters, Joseph Wershba and Edmund Scott, served the series full time.

Of the early days, Williams recalls, "There were fights, howls of laughter, a great comraderie, always the pride of accomplishment." [16]

The shows they produced were the best of the genre in their time. "The admixture of radio people and film people was what did it," says Williams. "Radio people, not knowing what could not be done, tried everything. Film people knew what could not be done but tried to do it anyway." [17]

It was a great team—this band of brothers, as Friendly would often say—and he drove it, and himself, hard. It was not unusual for persons working on the Sunday program to disappear into the film center on Friday and not be seen for 48 hours as they fought the deadline—editing, screening, writing, filming, recording, wrestling with timing, and transcribing for two days and two nights, subsisting on sandwiches and coffee—and adrenaline—and catching catnaps as opportunity allowed.

One Saturday night, with apologies, Friendly slipped away to the theater. He had tickets for a hit musical, but he was back in half an hour. During the overture he had thought of how to solve a production problem and left his wife to see the show by herself. Reports of Friendly's rages at ineptitude, real or imagined, are not exaggerated. But he was one with his people. They had more than his enormous talent; they had his devotion. And he had their respect.

"Somebody Certainly Has to Take a Stand"

People who remember "See It Now" are apt to visualize a one-hour documentary series treating highly controversial subjects. The series began, however, as a half-hour program distinguished by its immediacy and imagination, not by its bite. Even when, in April 1952, it moved from Sunday afternoons to early evening, its topics were largely noncontroversial.

The first "See It Now" program set the pattern. The "stunt" showing the Atlantic and Pacific oceans simultaneously, live, was only part of the broadcast. There were also reports from Washington by Eric Sevareid, from Paris by Howard K. Smith, and from Korea by Robert Pierpoint, who sat through an anxious night with Fox Company as it braced for an enemy counterattack. Also in that first program Murrow interviewed Senator

Robert Taft on his presidential ambitions, and viewers, via film, saw and heard an aging Winston Churchill deliver a Guildhall speech.

Occasionally, the program was devoted to a single subject. If it dealt with more than one subject, they were apt to be contrasting subjects. On the broadcast of September 29, 1953, an interview with Prime Minister Jawaharlal Nehru of India was followed by an interview with Chuck Dressen, manager of the Brooklyn Dodgers.

The variety of subjects was striking. Topics in the first two years included the restoration of Williamsburg, mental health, wire tapping, floods, the part coffee plays in American life, the Korean War, atomic research, the European Common Market, Italian land reform, coal mining, Passover in Berlin, and President Eisenhower's inaugural ball. One senses in the use of this new tool television a rare excitement, an appetite to tackle every subject of interest under the sun.

It was toward the end of the second year, on October 20, 1953, that Murrow and Friendly took on the most controversial subject—McCarthyism. Milo Radulovich, a lieutenant in the Air Force Reserve, had been declared a security risk. Although his loyalty to the United States was not questioned, he was asked to resign. He refused.

The charge was that he "maintained a close, continuing association" with his father and sister, who were suspected of being communistic. The father denied being anything but a good American, saying that he read a Serbian-language newspaper because he came originally from Serbia. The sister said her political beliefs were her own affair. Radulovich, who was studying at the University of Michigan, said he was fighting the security risk label because, in the existing political climate, "if the Air Force won't have me, who will?"

Joseph Wershba went to Radulovich's home town of Dexter, Michigan, and talked to the American Legion post commander, the town marshal and a former mayor, all of whom supported the lieutenant in his stand. Murrow ended the report—one of television's first investigative reports —with what was tantamount to an editorial:

> We believe that "the son shall not bear the iniquity of the father," even though that iniquity be proved, and in this case it was not. But we believe, too, that this case illustrates the urgent need for the armed forces to communicate more fully than they have so far done, the procedures and regulations to be followed in attempting to protect the national security and the rights of the individual at the same time. . . . It seems to us . . . that this is a subject that should be argued about endlessly.

Five weeks later, on November 24, the secretary of the Air Force, Harold Talbott, said on "See It Now" that he had reviewed the case and did not regard Radulovich as a security risk and had "therefore directed that he be retained in his present status in the United States Air Force."

If "See It Now" had a theme, it was the safeguarding of individual liberties under the Constitution. On the same program on which the secretary of the Air Force appeared, Murrow reported that pressure from the American Legion in Indianapolis had made it almost impossible for people who wanted to organize a chapter of the American Civil Liberties Union to find a meeting place. They finally met in the social hall of St. Mary's Roman Catholic Church.

The priest, Father Victor Goosens, said:

> When the climate is such that so many people are so quick to take the law into their own hands, or rather, I should say perhaps, to ignore the law and to deny to others the right of peaceful assembly and free speech, then somebody certainly has to take a stand.

The producers gave Father Goosens the last word.

The Radulovich and Civil Liberties Union broadcasts were Murrow and Friendly's opening salvos against McCarthyism, and McCarthy knew it. Shortly after the Radulovich program, an investigator on Senator McCarthy's staff, Donald Surine, approached Wershba and said, "What if I told you Murrow was on the Soviet payroll in 1934?"[18] That year, the Institute of International Education had sponsored a student seminar in Moscow, and Murrow, as assistant director of the institute, took part in the planning. Surine told Wershba that although he was not calling Murrow a Communist, it appeared that he was part of the Communist conspiracy.

It was blackmail. Exaggerated stories of Murrow's role in the seminar had appeared in the Hearst press, but, so far, McCarthy had been quiet. The threat only strengthened Murrow's resolve. McCarthyism was evil; he had only begun to expose it.

On February 9, 1950, in a speech in Wheeling, West Virginia, Joe McCarthy had whipped a sheet of paper out of his pocket and said it was a list of 205 people "known to the secretary of state as being members of the Communist Party and who nevertheless are still working and shaping policy in the State Department." It was an absurd charge. Recognizing the absurdity, McCarthy within 24 hours reduced the number to 57. Later, he would reduce it still further. Reporters were not shown the "lists," but that did not keep them from bruiting the accusations throughout the land. McCarthy loved the headlines. With a bit of scheming he had stumbled upon the Communists-in-government issue on which he would thrive.

It was an era of fear. "The idea seemed to be that every liberal was a socialist, every socialist a Communist, and every Communist a spy," says Eric Sevareid, who had to have his telephone disconnected because of threatening calls.[19] Names of supposedly suspect persons appeared regularly in the weekly newsletter *Counterattack*. *Red Channels*, a report from the same publishers—three former FBI agents—provided a list of 151 persons from the radio-television industry who, it said, were associated with a variety of Communist causes. The common phrase at the time was "left-wing connections," which could mean almost anything. As organization called Aware, Inc., issued similar reports.

A few victims sued. One who did so was Joseph Julian, a radio actor whom Murrow and Collingwood had come to know in London during the war. Both testified on his behalf. Without public knowledge, Murrow contributed $7,500 to John Henry Faulk, a CBS radio personality who had been smeared by Aware, Inc., so that he could hire Louis Nizer, one of America's most prominent attorneys. Faulk won his libel suit but only after a six-year struggle.

Fear of Communism was fed by the outbreak of war in Korea and intensification of the Cold War. McCarthy's victims, besides broadcasters, included newspaper reporters, teachers, government workers, and well-known Hollywood actors, producers, and directors. It was a nightmarish time. Alistair Cooke wrote:

> If we [the United States] are now baited in every direction by the Russians, it does not satisfy Americans to say that this is the turn of history. It must mean that somebody entrusted with our welfare has blundered. . . . In such a nation no man's honor is above suspicion.[20]

The climate was becoming intolerable. How far in pursuit of scapegoats, and power, would McCarthy go?

Day of Reckoning

For months, Ed Murrow and Fred Friendly had planned a "See It Now" program on the dismaying tactics of the junior senator from Wisconsin. Crews under the direction of Palmer Williams and Joseph Wershba filmed or recorded on audiotape virtually every public statement he made. By late 1953, even as they presented the case of Milo Radulovich, they had 50,000 feet of film showing McCarthy in action.

The highlight of this self-incriminating evidence was McCarthy's gross questioning of Reed Harris, director of the Voice of America, whom McCarthy accused of having written a Communist-inspired book when he was an undergraduate at Columbia. Also "placed in evidence" was the senator's snickering reference to Adlai Stevenson as "Alger." This, after Alger Hiss, a former State Department official, had been convicted of perjury in a case involving espionage.

The success of the Radulovich program strengthened its producers' determination to take on McCarthy. They agonized over how to do it. And when. They knew they would be attacked, that nothing would be the same for them again. Later, interviewed on the BBC, Janet Murrow said: "I knew [they] had been working on this program for a long time. Chills went up and down my spine because I knew that about anything could happen as a result of it."[21]

The program would be carried on March 9, 1954, from 10:30 to 11 P.M.[22] McCarthy would be speaking the next week—there might be raw material in that—and they still had not found either film or audio-tape of the Wheeling, West Virginia, speech. But they were going to go ahead anyway. Friendly says, "Ed and I knew that the timing of this broadcast was crucial. If we waited much longer, history or McCarthy—or both— might run us down."[23]

On March 7, the program, despite numerous cuts, was still seven minutes too long. More cuts were made. That night, at counsel's suggestion, each person in the "See It Now" unit was asked if there was anything in his or her background that would play into McCarthy's hands, for he was certain to strike back. A member of the unit said he had once been married to a Communist, but she was his first wife, and that was years ago. Still, the atmosphere was tense. Murrow observed, "The terror is right here in this room."[24]

On the morning of the broadcast, William S. Paley, CBS' board chairman, telephoned Murrow to say, "I'll be with you tonight, Ed, and I'll be with you tomorrow as well."[25] In his memoir, Paley says that when Murrow asked if he wanted to see the program before it was aired, he asked Murrow if he was sure of his facts. On being told there was no question about the facts, Paley's response was that he would wait until everybody saw it. "That," says Paley, "was meant as a vote of confidence and was received by him as such."[26]

But CBS declined to advertise the program, and the producers placed their own local ad—minus the CBS eye—saying simply, "Tonight at 10:30 on 'See It Now' a report on Senator Joseph R. McCarthy over Channel 2." One day Friendly would remark on the irony that 20 years later, when CBS rebroadcast the program, and it no longer was dangerous, the network did advertise. "If Murrow had lived," said Friendly, "he would have gotten a kick out of that."[27]

At the start of the program, Murrow offered McCarthy opportunity to reply. Both Paley and Frank Stanton, president of CBS, had suggested that the offer be made, though it is likely Murrow would have done so anyway. Except for Murrow's opening and closing statements, the program was pure McCarthy the witchhunter in film clips as public speaker and Senate committee chairman, browbeating, sniggering, ruthless, demagogic, evil. The producers had not been sure it would play. There were things McCarthy had said and done, examples of his excesses, for which there was no footage. They wondered whether the patchwork would hold together, if the impact could be sustained. To ensure that the danger that McCarthy represented for the country—the point of it all—would not be missed, Murrow delivered in conclusion what is probably the most forceful editorial ever delivered on radio or television.

> No one familiar with the history of this country can deny that congressional committees are useful. It is necessary to investigate before legislating, but the line between investigation and persecuting is a very fine one, and the junior senator from Wisconsin has stepped over it repeatedly. His primary achievement has been in confusing the public mind as between the internal and external threat of Communism. We must not confuse dissent with disloy-

alty. We must remember always that accusation is not proof, and that conviction depends upon evidence and due process of law. We will not walk in fear, one of another. We will not be driven by fear into an age of unreason if we dig deep in our history and our doctrine and remember that we are not descended from fearful men, not from men who feared to write, to speak, to associate with, and to defend causes that were for the moment unpopular. . . .

As a nation we have come into our full inheritance at a tender age. We proclaim ourselves, as indeed we are, the defenders of freedom—what's left of it—but we cannot defend freedom abroad by deserting it at home. The actions of the junior senator from Wisconsin have caused alarm and dismay amongst our allies abroad and given considerable comfort to our enemies. And whose fault is that? Not really his. He didn't create this situation of fear, he merely exploited it and rather successfully. Cassius was right: "The fault, dear Brutus, is not in our stars but in ourselves."

Murrow signed off with his usual "good night and good luck" and slumped in his chair, exhausted. He had given the reading everything he had. The strain had been both physical and emotional. He had taken on one of the most popular figures in American politics and he had broken CBS' most holy commandment, the long-standing rule against editorialization, the very rule that had brought the departure from CBS of H. V. Kaltenborn and Cecil Brown. He simply had to speak out. Paley reasons that it was the CBS policy that caused Murrow to hold back from attacking McCarthy as long as he did.[28]

Even as Murrow was speaking, the impact of the broadcast became obvious. Switchboards of CBS-owned and affiliated stations were swamped. Telegrams began arriving at CBS headquarters in New York—more than 4,000 of them—and there is no accurate count of letters and postcards. Most of the responses were favorable. Among callers offering their congratulations were former President Truman and Bishop Bernard Sheil of Chicago. Albert Einstein, theologian Reinhold Niebuhr, and George Meany, president of the American Federation of Labor, wrote, expressing gratification. Some of the unfavorable reaction was threatening as well as obscene, and a guard was assigned to protect the Murrows' son, Casey.

The Hearst press denounced the broadcast. Jack O'Brian, writing in the *New York Journal-American* the next day, called it a smear. In the *New York Times,* Jack Gould said the program represented "crusading journalism of high responsibility and genuine courage."[29] The *New York Herald Tribune* said Murrow had presented "a sober and realistic appraisal of McCarthyism and the climate in which it flourishes."[30]

A week later, on March 16, "See It Now" returned to the attack by devoting its half-hour to the case of Annie Lee Moss, a black woman employed in the Pentagon. Mrs. Moss, suspected on hearsay evidence of being a Soviet spy, had appeared five days earlier before McCarthy's permanent subcommittee on investigations, generally referred to as the Mc-Carthy committee. Assisted by Joseph Wershba, Charles Mack had filmed the proceedings.

The coverage was protective. Friendly did not expect the hearing to produce anything especially noteworthy. Although he and Murrow were thinking a good deal about what McCarthy might say when he took over the "See It Now" spot to make his reply, their main attention was directed to a program they were preparing on the coming of commercial television to Great Britain and France's troubles in Indochina. But the Moss hearing provided such a demonstration of McCarthy's methods that the program was put off until March 23 and the revealing hearing footage run instead on March 16.

McCarthy, questioning Mrs. Moss, demanded to know how she happened to work in a Pentagon code room. She said she never had been in the code room, which seemed a verifiable statement. Her name, McCarthy said, had appeared on a list of dues-paying Communists. She said she never had been a Communist, and it turned out that at least three women named Annie Lee Moss were living in Washington.

"Did you ever hear of Karl Marx?" asked Senator Stuart Symington, a committee member.

"Who's that?" she said.

The hearing was proving an embarrassment, and McCarthy excused himself, saying he had an appointment. His assistant, Roy Cohn, took over. The hearing ended with Symington offering to help Mrs. Moss, who had lost her Pentagon job, find employment.

It was exquisite use of the "little picture" to illustrate a large issue. The guilt or innocence of Annie Lee Moss was never proven, but McCarthy's use of congressional hearings to convict on hearsay evidence was.

Predictably, when McCarthy gave his reply to Murrow on April 6, he resurrected the old charge that Murrow had supported Communism when he served with the Institute of International Education, a reference to the Moscow University summer seminar for which the institute helped select American students and teachers. By innuendo, he associated Murrow with the Soviet secret police. He called the eminent broadcaster "leader of the jackel pack which is always found at the throat of anyone who dares to expose Communists and traitors."

It was a clumsy production. Although aired on CBS—an affirmation of the Fairness Doctrine before the doctrine was formally established—the broadcast was produced independently. McCarthy's makeup was so bad Friendly worried that CBS might be accused of sabotaging the senator's effort. CBS paid the cost of production, $6,336.99, and issued a statement expressing its confidence in "the integrity and responsibility of Mr. Murrow as a broadcaster and as a loyal American." Murrow appreciated the network's support; he did not appreciate the payment.[31]

On the next "See It Now" program, April 13, Murrow stated the role of the institute in relation to the Moscow seminar, explaining that it made arrangements for American students to attend summer sessions in many foreign countries, not just the Soviet Union. He noted that John Foster Dulles, the secretary of state, had been a trustee, and that the advisory council included Robert Hutchins, president of the University of Chicago, and Frank P. Graham, president of the University of North Carolina. The institute, he pointed out, was largely financed by the Carnegie Corporation and the Rockefeller Foundation. Hardly a Communist-front organization.

By 1954, when Murrow and Friendly took on the senator, several prominent broadcasters already had spoken out. Among these were Martin Agronsky and Elmer Davis. Davis took a stand against McCarthy as early as 1950, when he said on the air that in his assault on the State Department McCarthy had proved nothing. It would be best, Davis said, before convicting to see the evidence.[32] At another time, he said:

> I regret that I have to mention McCarthy; I regret that he exists. But he does exist, and not to mention him would be as if people in a malarial country refused to mention the anopheles mosquito.[33]

Davis was speaking on ABC, the same network on which Agronsky was doing daily radio commentary. Agronsky received a George Foster Peabody Award after making McCarthy his target in 1952. The citation read: "In this uneasy period of insecurity and fear, he has consistently and with rare courage given voice to the preservation of basic values in our democratic system." He lost sponsors, but Robert Kintner, president of ABC, stood by him.

Some newspapers also had attacked McCarthy's methods. In his broadcast of March 9, Murrow could quote editorials from eight influential papers.

"Until This Moment, Senator . . ."

In his encounter with Murrow, McCarthy wounded himself; in the Army–McCarthy hearings, he committed political suicide.

The hearings began in the Senate Caucus Room on April 22, 1954, and ran for 35 days. McCarthy accused the Army of lax security practices. (It had promoted a dental officer while his loyalty was questioned.) McCarthy, in turn, was accused of exerting improper influence to obtain preferential treatment for an Army private, G. David Schine, who had been his assistant. Ultimately, the hearings became a test between McCarthy and President Eisenhower, who finally had found the senator's arrogance intolerable.

CBS and NBC, which had lucrative daytime programs, carried digests of each day's session at night. Only ABC and DuMont broadcast the hearings live. Since the DuMont network had so few stations, the primary public service was performed by ABC. Robert Kintner, ABC's president, had made John Daly, formerly of CBS, head of ABC News. Daly tells how the ABC coverage came about.

In those days, we had no money. We could make our place in the sun only if we did something new and very special, so when I heard they were scheduling these hearings, I went in to Kintner and said, "We have a chance here to make a mark. CBS and NBC aren't covering this, so why don't we go in there and clobber them on this hell of a story?"

Kintner said he'd think about it and give me an answer by 5 o'clock. At 5 he called and said ABC would cover the hearings live from start to finish. That, in our financial straits, took more guts than I've seen anywhere else in this business. We are the people who destroyed Joe McCarthy. It was the most courageous thing done in the early history of television news, and Kintner has never gotten the credit he should for that.[34]

The chief ABC correspondent covering the hearings was Gunnar Back, whose perceptive reporting enhanced the network's reputation for news and public affairs.

No one person, or act, destroyed McCarthy. But Kintner did show courage. The network was losing money, and coverage of the hearings cost ABC half a million dollars.[35]

The climax of the Army–McCarthy hearings came as a thunderbolt on June 9, after McCarthy attacked the patriotism of a young Boston attorney named Fred Fisher. Joseph Welch, the Army's counsel at the hearings, knew Fisher and had affection for him, and when he heard the promising young lawyer's reputation being soiled, he responded with devasting eloquence, interrupting McCarthy, asking if he had no decency.

Until this moment, senator, I think I never gauged your cruelty or recklessness. If it were in my power to forgive you . . . I would do so. I like to think I am a gentle man. But your forgiveness will have to come from someone other than me.

Welch's words were greeted with a storm of applause. At that point, the demagogue, unmasked, was doomed. In December, the Senate passed a resolution censoring McCarthy, stating that his conduct was "contrary to senatorial traditions and is hereby condemned."

On May 2, 1957, he died.

27
The Electronic Politician

In the movie *The Verdict*, James Mason, playing a high-powered lawyer, discusses strategy for winning a case through the media. "Television," he says. "You got to have television."

Politicians got to have television. Television has changed forever the ways in which they gain and wield power. To a lesser degree, so did radio. Both media allow politicians to address voters directly, bypassing the press. In presidential campaigns, they have enhanced the role of the state primary, dethroned the city bosses, and made the national conventions ceremonial occasions at which delegates rubberstamp candidates who have, in effect, already been nominated. The candidates' progress through state primaries, month after month, tempts reporters to concentrate on the race —who's ahead—rather than on the calibre of the candidate and where he or she stands on the issues. Inevitably, because campaigns are prolonged, the cost escalates. And voters become bored.

Robert Kennedy said he would rather have "30 seconds on an evening news program than coverage in every newspaper in the world."[1] Because of the intensity of television and its mass audience, the managers of presidential candidates schedule events with the network evening news in mind. They set up press conferences early enough in the day so that they can make these top-rated shows. They know that unless it is of extreme importance, the candidate's statement made shortly before airtime is not likely to get on. The candidate is advised not to ramble, to plant in the statement a sentence or two—a quotable quote—that network producers, because of its succinctness, will find hard to resist.

The TV consultant tells the candidate how to project those qualities people look for in someone aspiring to the presidency, so the candidate appears before the crowd in shirtsleeves to show he is one of them, leaps onto the platform to demonstrate what good shape he is in, and appears without a topcoat in freezing weather to prove that if John F. Kennedy could do it, he can, too. Because of the camera's eye, and the importance of image, the politician in search of office becomes, more than ever, an actor.

Advance men, appreciating television's hunger for pictures, concoct photo opportunities. These are not new with television. Long ago, newspapers carried publicity shots of Herbert Hoover fishing and Calvin Coolidge in Indian headdress. But with a medium as powerful as television the photo opportunity takes on new importance. It not only gets the candidate on the tube but reinforces his message. For television producers it illustrates the story. Thus, when addressing the issue of unemployment, the candidate may visit a factory that is about to be shut down. To make his policy statement on food price supports, he may go to an Iowa farm. During the 1984 presidential campaign, Walter Mondale got in a jibe at Reagan by saying he would rather be photographed in a barn in 110-degree heat answering farmers' questions than on a stage in Nashville singing songs, as Reagan had done the preceding week with Minnie Pearl.[2] It was a rare instance of a candidate comparing his photo opportunity with an opponent's photo opportunity for political advantage.

If a candidate goes abroad, all the better. Scenes of him conferring with heads of foreign governments suggest statesmanship. And, at the same time, he is accumulating footage that can be used in forthcoming political commercials. The *New York Times* critic John Corry observed that Reagan "looked great" traveling abroad during the 1984 campaign. "There he was at the DMZ in Korea, peering through binoculars. There he was in Normandy, talking to the boys of Pointe du Hoc." Reagan seemed, said Corry, "to be running for the title role in *Patton*."[3] The classic case of a foreign journey paying political dividends was Nixon's historic trip to China in 1972. It assured his reelection.

Any newsworthy politician has control. He chooses where to deliver a speech, which Sunday panel show to appear on, to whom to grant an interview, when to hold a news conference, and which questions to answer. The photo opportunity is his production. He can be confident that because he is a newsmaker, microphones and cameras will cover these events of his choosing. No one can be more confident of this than a president. Robert Pierpoint, who covered six presidents for CBS, says, "Presidents plan photogenic activities because television will provide coverage, and television provides coverage because the president has planned photogenic activities."[4] Broadcasters concede that it is a symbiotic relationship but believe that somewhere in covering these staged events they should draw a line. CBS correspondent Eric Engberg says, "Editors have to be a little bit tougher, have got to be willing to give up some of those good pictures and give up some of those color stories by saying, 'This event has no substance to it—it is a dog-and-pony show—let's write it out.' "[5] ABC's Peter Jennings speaks of the instinct of politicians to substitute theater for debate and warns, "Our willingness to go along is a trap."[6]

Presidents, in the age of television, have not forgotten radio. President Nixon made frequent radio talks when he was running for reelection in 1972, in part because his managers wanted to avoid overkill on television. With his Saturday radio talks President Reagan campaigned persistently for his policies. Both presidents knew that radio not only gave them millions of listeners but newspaper coverage the next day. Radio did carry the responses of Democratic spokesmen, but no opposition spokesman could possess the aura, or speak with the same authority, as the president.

Presidential Debates

The modern presidential debate is the creature of television, going back to the series of four debates between Nixon and Kennedy in 1960. Presidential debates, and most other debates on television, are not true debates but resemble panel discussions in which journalists put questions to opposing candidates. They resemble debates only in that candidates are limited as to the time they have to state their positions. The time allowed for rebuttal, for give and take, is lamentably limited.

Congress made the first presidential debates possible by temporarily suspending Section 315 of the Communications Act, which would have required the networks to grant equal time to the dozen or more minor party candidates. The format called for a panel of journalists and a moderator. The networks took turns producing the debates, with CBS producing the first in the studios of its Chicago station, WBBM-TV, on September 26. Don Hewitt was the producer and Howard K. Smith served as moderator.

The role of image in electronic politics was never more apparent. Nixon's managers demanded that he not be photographed from the left. They objected to the pale color of the set—not enough contrast with their candidate's gray suit—so the set was repainted. Hewitt, wisely, advised Nixon to wear makeup, and Nixon, foolishly, declined. "The atmosphere," wrote Robert Lewis Shayon, "was clearly that of a prize fight: the referee (producer) instructing the champ and the challenger (the candidates), the seconds (advisers) milling around, and the 'come out fighting' handshake."[7] The feeling of television viewers was that Kennedy, who gave an impression of youthfulness and vigor, had won the debate and that Nixon, who appeared haggard and ill at ease, had lost. Radio listeners, on the other hand, thought Nixon had won. Because more people saw the debate on television than heard it on radio, it is quite possible that Nixon lost the election because of the perception of viewers that one night.

The big thing about presidential debates is that the entire nation is witness. Reporters are not telling what they saw; the people are seeing it first hand. Commenting on this democratizing of the election process, the critic William A. Henry III says the Nixon–Kennedy debates "surely marked the end for old-fashioned punditry; voters did not need the entree of the columnist . . . but instead could walk in themselves."[8] This is true. Voters will have seen and heard what the pundit has seen and heard, will have become participants. But it would be rash to say public opinion is unaffected by what reporters say about a candidate. Thomas E. Patterson, professor of political science at Syracuse University, holds that a favorable assessment from reporters helps a candidate more than an agreeable manner or good looks. He is convinced, for example, "that many voters in 1976 came to regard Carter as personable and sincere because [at those times when he was ahead in the campaign] reporters constantly said Carter possessed these qualities."[9]

"A Curse and an Abomination"

Computers revolutionized the way elections are reported. Exit polls—the polling of people who have just voted—may produce miraculously early reports on who won, but neither they nor the projections devised earlier by using early returns from bellwether precincts would have been possible without the computer printout.

The networks experimented with computers in covering the 1952 presidential election, but it was not until 1962 that procedures were improved sufficiently for the computer to replace the adding machine and become the principal tool. Two major changes came with the congressional elections of 1962. The networks and press associations, AP and UPI, agreed to pool the raw vote. They no longer would compete in collecting returns but together would compile and make available to each other the returns provided by precinct and county officials around the country. They called the new operation the News Election Service (NES).

The other big change was a new method of predicting the outcome of races. With the help of pollster Lou Harris, CBS figured out a computerized system for making early calls on the basis of returns from sample precincts, which were used as a microcosm for the state as a whole. Selecting these key precincts required months of research, but the procedure on Election Night was simple. Harris and Bill Leonard, head of the Election Unit, working from printouts, compared how the precincts had gone in past elections with returns coming in. Thus, although early returns might show Candidate X winning, if precincts that normally would go to him had switched to Candidate Y, Candidate Y was declared the winner. CBS called its system Vote Profile Analysis (VPA).[10]

In reporting the 1964 election, all networks made their projections on this basis. NBC made the first presidential call, declaring Lyndon Johnson the winner over Barry Goldwater at 6:48 P.M., Eastern time, four hours and 12 minutes before polls closed in California. ABC and CBS also projected Johnson as elected while people on the West Coast were still voting. These early calls were based not on exit polls but on votes actually cast and counted. In the 1990 congressional elections, the network, CNN included, began pooling exit poll informations and projections.

The networks experimented with exit polling as early as 1968. It did not become basic procedure, however, until 1980 when NBC, using exit polls, declared Ronald Reagan the next president of the United States at 8:15 P.M., Eastern time. Faced with this call, and convinced by his own information that he had lost, President Carter conceded defeat at 9:50 P.M., Eastern time, more than an hour before polls closed in the Far West. It was a bombshell. For the presidential candidate of a major party to concede before the polls closed in California, with its 45 electoral votes, was unheard of. CBS, playing it safe, waited to call the race until 40 minutes after Carter's concession.

Members of Congress protested such calls, saying that people in Western states, knowing the outcome of national races, were discouraged from voting. They said it was bound to affect contests for local and state office. Newspaper critics joined in the outcry. John Corry of the *New York Times* called the projections "a curse and an abomination," serving only the pride of network news departments.[11]

Network executives responded by saying they could not withhold from the public reasonable conclusions that the candidates themselves and other insiders already had reached. Nor, they said, had it been demonstrated to their satisfaction that the early calls had any appreciable effect on voter turnout. But they made a concession. In the 1986 congressional elections, they would not use exit polls to project winners in any state until after the voting places in that state closed. As a long-term solution the networks advocated federal legislation that would have voting places throughout the country, with the exception of Alaska and Hawaii, close at the same time. It was a solution pressed by CBS' president, Frank Stanton, in the 1960s. Twenty years later, Congress still had not enacted it into law.

A voter's participation in exit polling is voluntary. On a confidential basis—questionnaires are unsigned—the person who has just voted answers a series of questions. Besides "Whom did you vote for?" there are questions designed to provide detailed demographic information that may explain why a candidate, or party, lost or won. In the 1984 election, for example, the form used by CBS News in exit polling in Massachusetts included 22 questions. These ranged from age, sex, and race through occupation and income to whether the voter was of Italian descent, information the network sought because of the candidacy of Geraldine Ferraro for vice president on the Democratic ticket. It is the answers to such questions, compiled by computer, that make it possible for the person on the anchor desk to say, for instance, "Candidate X failed to get the support expected from blacks," and "Candidate Y appears to have won, thanks to the Yuppie vote."

With results available so early, the reasons for those results—the why —takes on new importance on Election Night.

"Mr. President!"

Woodrow Wilson held the first regular news conferences in the modern sense in 1913. He abandoned them with America's entry in World War I, and they languished until Franklin Roosevelt began meeting reporters on a semiweekly basis 20 years later. Roosevelt's news conferences were cozy affairs with perhaps a hundred reporters crowded around his desk asking questions. Since they could only paraphrase what he said—direct quotation was prohibited—he could deny having made the statement if it proved ill-advised. (Eleanor Roosevelt was the first "First Lady" to hold news conferences, and she restricted them to women.)

The direct quote came with President Eisenhower, whose news conferences were filmed. His press secretary, James Hagerty, trusting Eisenhower's personality as well as competence, saw broadcasting of the conferences as a means of building public support. The trust was not unlimited. The White House reserved the right to edit the film before it was released.

While Eisenhower may be credited as the first president to allow what he said at a news conference to be quoted directly, an exception must be noted. On May 24, 1951, President Truman broke precedent by letting CBS Radio include excerpts of his in a newscast. The excerpts, highlights of the conference on audiotape, were from an official recording obtained by Charles Collingwood, who was CBS' White House correspondent. Another aberration occurred with the first live broadcast of a presidential news conference. It originated not in Washington but in San Francisco, site of a Republican national convention. The date was August 22, 1956. Harold Stassen, onetime candidate for president, had been working for the nomination of Governor Herter of Massachusetts as Eisenhower's running mate. It would have meant dumping Vice President Nixon. In a 17-minute session with reporters, carried on radio and television, Eisenhower said Stassen not only had given up his fight for Herter but wanted to second Nixon's nomination for vice president. The broadcast was historic and, for Eisenhower, one of a kind.

Live coverage on a regular basis did not come until John F. Kennedy established it five years later. Commenting on Kennedy's first live conference of January 25, 1961, the Associated Press said:

> President Kennedy looked fresh and poised and sounded decisive and self-assured. He took on all questions posed by a large roomful of reporters for more than 30 minutes. . . . From the moment he stepped before the large gathering to announce the release of two

U.S. fliers held by the Russians to the final "Thank you, Mr. President," the conference ran smoothly. ... It was more than fascinating viewing; it was an important forward step in public enlightenment.[12]

Max Lerner, a journalist who had attended Roosevelt's news conferences, said Kennedy would now be able to use his news conferences to project "the image of an alert, resourceful, literate, and activist leader," which is exactly what he did.[13]

> A journalist probing at a president and his policies employs a powerful weapon, but it is a double-edged sword and, if wielded improperly, can be deflected to wound the user. The worst experience for a correspondent is to be turned aside either by a presidential quip or have the president say, "I'm glad you asked that." Pressure is greatest when you stand up during a news conference and for one intense moment the reporter and the president spar one on one.[14]

The sparring correspondent risks public rebuke. The classic example is a response Dan Rather gave President Nixon at the height of the Watergate investigation. Nixon was holding a news conference in connection with an annual meeting of the National Association of Broadcasters in Houston. NAB members, as well as reporters, were asking questions. When Rather, who had the reputation of being tough on Nixon, rose to ask his question, he was greeted by a mixture of boos and applause.

Noting the applause, Nixon asked him, "Are you running for something?"

"No sir, Mr. President," said Rather. "Are you?"

Rather was strongly criticized for what some saw as disrespect for the high office. Later, he acknowledged that, given more time to think, he might have responded differently. "I didn't feel then that my words were disrespectful."[15] A more typical example of reportorial bluntness in a presidential news conference is the question ABC's Sam Donaldson asked President Carter toward the end of his administration. "Do you recognize," said Donaldson, "that there is this charge of incompetence that settles over you?"[16] It seemed a rough question, but UPI's veteran White House correspondent Helen Thomas says that in inquiring into the handling of government affairs, "There are no unacceptable questions, only unacceptable answers."[17]

Through the news conference, the president at his choosing can command an audience of millions. Although networks, exercising news judgment, may decline to carry a presidential address, they invariably carry presidential news conferences. The president, assured of this "bully pulpit," can make any announcement he wishes and duck any question. He can learn from questions put to him what is on the public mind. Correspondents, in turn, serve as unelected representatives of the people, asking questions the people might ask. It is ironic that Ronald Reagan, the Great

Communicator, made so little use of this forum. Whereas Ford averaged twenty formal news conferences a year and Carter fifteen, Reagan averaged only six, the same number as Nixon.

Unlegitimatized by act of Congress, the presidential news conference has become an institution serving both the chief executive and the people. It forces the president to account for his actions in much the same way that Britain's prime ministers are forced to defend their actions in the House of Commons. A president holds news conferences at his pleasure; he dare not abandon them. Public expectation growing from media coverage, in particular, the coverage accorded by radio and television, has made them an institution of government.

A Matter of Hearing and Seeing

More than any publisher's editorial or broadcaster's commentary, it was the succession of shocking mirror images on "See It Now" and the 187 hours on ABC television in the course of the Army–McCarthy hearings that brought McCarthy down. It was not the first time ABC had televised a congressional hearing. In 1951, over as much network as it could muster, it had carried the Senate Crime Committee hearings conducted by Senator Estes Kefauver of Tennessee. These were the hearings in which big-time gambler Frank Costello's nervously moving hands were shown repeatedly in close-up because he testified on condition his face would not appear.

Ratings by the Hooper service showed that at times the committee's proceedings captured New York City's entire viewing audience. Daytime soap operas on other networks were forsaken for this "show" in which real mobsters and the svelte gangster's moll, Virginia Hill, appeared live in an atmosphere of suspenseful courtroom drama. The hearings made Kefauver a contender for the Democratic presidential nomination in 1952 (he won an Emmy but not the nomination) and propelled the committee's chief counsel, Rudolph Halley, into presidency of the New York City Council. If the Army–McCarthy hearings showed how television can destroy a politician, the crime hearings showed how television exposure can help, a lesson politicians quickly learned.

Radio microphones and television cameras might be allowed at public hearings in the Senate, but in the House Speaker Sam Rayburn banned their presence at committee hearings, contending that radio-television coverage was distracting. It was a ruling broadcasters, seeking parity with the print press, fought unsuccessfully for years to come.

The Electronic Candidate

Television, which had poked its nose under the tent at the national political circuses of 1948, performed boldly in center ring at the national conventions in 1952. This time, the "tent" would be the International

Amphitheater in Chicago, close by the sprawling, less than aromatic stock-yards.

Again, broadcasters were helped by the fact that Republicans and Democrats met not only in the same city but in the same hall. But there were fresh benefits. News staffs were beefed up and more experienced. Audiotape had arrived, permitting playback. NBC had a new portable camera nicknamed the "walkie-lookie" after the "walkie-talkie." In fact, almost all radio and television equipment was more sophisticated.[18] But, most important, there was now a coaxial cable linking television stations coast to coast. A speaker on the rostrum in Chicago was heard simultaneously in all states.

The Republicans opened their convention on July 7, but not before a bitter row between broadcasters and GOP managers, who excluded radio and television from preconvention sessions. The blackout was instigated by forces backing Senator Robert Taft of Ohio against the war hero, Dwight Eisenhower. Taft's supporters were battling to have as many pro-Taft delegates seated as possible, not the kind of intraparty wrangling they wanted on the air. When the fight in the Credentials Committee was over and cameras were admitted, *Broadcasting* observed:

> One cannot avoid the suspicion that the politicians' attitudes toward television are founded almost exclusively on self-interest. . . . It is time that politicians were made to quit courting broadcasting when it serves their personal purposes and kicking it out the door when it doesn't.[19]

To which now, about four decades later, one might ask, "So what else is new?"

In his book, *The Electric Mirror*, Sig Mickelson, who was head of CBS News at the time, reports that his people hid microphones in the Credentials Committee room and eavesdropped. Sixteen years later, an NBC producer caught "bugging" was charged with invasion of privacy. But in 1952, says Mickelson, "such ethical and legal considerations were a matter of slight concern."[20]

Two weeks later, when the Democrats met, Martin Agronsky got exclusive coverage of a Louisiana caucus meeting in similarly unorthodox fashion. A wide-angle camera lens peeking through a large crack in the wall took in the entire proceedings. There was no audio, but Agronsky described, over the picture, what was going on.

These Chicago conventions were the first covered by local stations on a large scale. News from the various state delegations was fed to hometown audiences live and recorded throughout the day and night. *Broadcasting* reported:

> Stations . . . took part in a pool arrangement at $250 each, with an additional $200 for line costs. . . . Stations frequently found it advisable to cancel regularly scheduled local commercial commit-

ments and, in any event, saturate their schedules with convention news and extend their broadcast day.[21]

Many stations sent their own reporters. WEEB, Southern Pines, North Carolina, boasted that it was probably the smallest station in the country to send a correspondent. He was Arch Coleman, who fed reports for WEWO, Laurinburg, and WGWR, Asheboro, as well as for WEEB. WPIX, New York, may have provided the heaviest coverage among independent television stations. It carried summaries at 2, 8, and 11 P.M. each day, using still pictures and newsreel film. WLWT, Cincinnati, claimed to be the only independent television station originating a roundtable discussion program from the Republican convention. Moderator was the station's veteran newscaster, Peter Grant. His two panelists were Bill Henry and Ben Grauer.

More than 2,000 broadcast personnel—reporters, engineers, photographers, directors, producers—worked at the two conventions. Among network people present were Paul White, masterminding ABC's coverage at his last political convention, and Walter Cronkite, broadcasting at his first. Although Cronkite for more than a decade had been a distinguished correspondent for the United Press, few knew his name. After broadcasting from Chicago for two weeks, he was recognized by millions.

There were about twenty-five fewer news writers at the Republican convention than at the Democratic convention because the Writers Guild of America had called a strike against ABC, CBS, and NBC. The issue was the writers' right to a commercial fee—that is, additional payment if the news program was sponsored—a fee from which announcers reading the news prepared by staff writers had profited handsomely for years. The strike, the first of its kind in the industry, was settled to the satisfaction of the writers by the start of the Democratic convention on July 21.

The Democrats appear to have been more TV-minded than the Republicans. They provided the networks with shooting scripts before each session and even had a room at the Conrad Hilton Hotel where they monitored the proceedings and telephoned critiques on the speakers' performances to the convention hall. Delegates were warned to take care what they did—they might be seen on television. Sam Rayburn's bald head was made up, and all back-of-the-head shots discouraged.

Those were the first conventions at which television was king and the first to be heavily sponsored. Admiral paid ABC two million dollars. NBC got two and a half million from Philco and CBS three million from Westinghouse. It was at these conventions that a former stage and screen actress, Betty Furness, extolling the attributes of a refrigerator in a Westinghouse commercial, became a national celebrity, and later a reporter on consumer affairs. Still, with expenses totaling almost ten million dollars,[22] the networks lost money.

They did, however, earn a new status. As, indeed, did radio and television as a whole. The electronic media, *Broadcasting* declared, had become the dominant news media. With audiences estimated at 60 million, it said a new age in American politics had dawned.[23]

Television's potential was demonstrated in an unusual way in the 1952 campaign when Nixon appealed to voters, and to the Republican leadership, in the famous Checkers speech. In this speech, Nixon, who was Eisenhower's running mate, denied impropriety in the use of a "slush" fund provided by California supporters. He also said he was not giving back a cocker spaniel named Checkers sent to him by a man in Texas. "And you know," he said, "the kids, like all kids, love that dog, and I just want to say this, right now, that regardless of what they say, we're going to keep it."[24] He went on to say that he did not believe he should quit, and neither was his wife a quitter either. "After all, her name was Patricia Ryan, and she was born on St. Patrick's Day, and you know the Irish never quit."

Nixon asked his nationwide audience to wire or write the Republican National Committee, saying whether he should get off the ticket. The overwhelming response was that he should stay, and soon afterward, at a political rally in Wheeling, West Virginia, Eisenhower told him, "You're my boy!"

What Nixon accomplished by his Checkers speech could only have been achieved through radio and television. He needed instantaneous, impressive reaction from a mass audience. The speech that helped Eisenhower most in the 1952 campaign was the one broadcast on October 24 in which he promised, if elected, to "concentrate on ending the Korean War." It would require going there, he said, and he added, "I shall make that trip. . . . I shall go to Korea."

This statement, the inspiration of one of his speechwriters, carried tremendous impact. The public wanted peace, and he was going to Korea to get it.

28
Korea

It recalled Pearl Harbor. Again, there was no declaration of war. Again, the attack came on a weekend. And, again, broadcasters had the breaking story to themselves since there were no afternoon papers on Sunday. Actually, the story did not break; it sort of oozed out. For days, dispatches had told of skirmishes along the frontier, North Korean patrols probing South Korean positions along the 38th parallel. These limited actions were so frequent that when the first sketchy reports reached CBS News that Saturday night, June 24, 1950, it was decided not to lead with them on the 11 P.M. broadcast.[1]

By the next day, the operation was recognizable for what it was—full-scale invasion of South Korea by the Communist North—and the networks scrambled to get their Tokyo-based correspondents on the air. None was in Korea. NBC, with George Folster, was the only network with a staff correspondent in Tokyo. ABC was being served by John Rich of INS. CBS' stringer was Robert "Pepper" Martin. Its full-time Tokyo correspondent, Bill Costello, who had just returned to the United States, started back posthaste.

President Truman's response was immediate. At first, he committed only air and sea forces. Then, as North Korea pressed its attack, the United

States introduced a resolution in the United Nations Security Council urging freedom-loving members to help in what Truman called a police action. The Soviet delegate, who had power of veto, was conveniently absent—Moscow had been boycotting the sessions—and the resolution passed with a stipulation that all forces contributed by member nations would serve under American command. Truman gave the command to General MacArthur with authority to employ whatever U.S. ground forces were available in the Far East. As of that date, June 30, the United States was engaged in undeclared war.

ABC's Drew Pearson was first with Truman's decision to commit American forces. Official word from the White House came an hour later. Mutual scored a beat on Monday when it arranged a broadcast by U.S. Ambassador John J. Muccio direct from Seoul, the South Korean capital. On Wednesday, the North Korean invaders took Seoul. Throughout the first days, the air was filled with bulletins and half-hour special reports.

In a televised speech, Truman explained what was at stake. The United States had no choice but to move, with others, against Communist aggression. The overrunning of South Korea could set off a disastrous chain of events. Radio commentators agreed. On ABC, Elmer Davis said, "This is where we came in," referring to 1938 "when the pattern of totalitarian aggression became clear."[2] On CBS, Ed Murrow said, "We were caught in a position where we had to shoot or put down the gun. . . . If South Korea falls, it is only reasonable to expect there will be other and bolder blows."[3] He pointed out in another broadcast that the United States had commitments to Iran and Turkey—and to Indochina—as binding as those to Korea. He said, "We have drawn a line, not across the [Korean] peninsula, but across the world."[4]

For Indochina, read Vietnam.

Representatives of the communications industry met with government officials in Washington in an all-day session. Among the network representatives were Bryson Rash and William R. McAndrew of NBC, Earl Gammons and Theodore Koop of CBS, and Hollis Seavey of MBS. Their talk centered on how news would be handled should all-out war ensue.

Throughout the first weeks of the invasion, television cameras at United Nations headquarters were kept hot. Sessions in the Security Council and in the General Assembly made dramatic viewing. Live television coverage of the U.N. debate totaled more than a hundred hours. Some radio stations like WFIL, Philadelphia, played back the daytime sessions for nighttime listeners.

The Voice of America, raising its voice, reported what was happening in 24 languages, including Korean. The programs, divided equally between hard news and commentary and features, included President Truman's orders to the armed forces and congressional reaction. At the same time, Radio Free Europe expanded its programming for countries behind the Iron Curtain. Although long retired, Mary Pickford offered her services for foreign broadcasts.

NBC made the first live television broadcast from the Senate Radio

Gallery on July 19. Correspondents Robert McCormick, Richard Harkness, and Earl Godwin commented on a message President Truman had just delivered to Congress on the Korean situation. The 15-minute program was microwaved from Capitol Hill to NBC's Washington outlet, WNBW, now WRC-TV. During this early "instant analysis" other correspondents were seen bustling about in the background.

As during World War II, the public turned to radio for late-breaking news. According to a Hooper survey, news ratings for the radio networks in the week ending July 11, 1950, compared to the same week in 1949, jumped 63 percent. All networks expanded their news schedules. Besides adding a daily 15-minute broadcast, ABC News devoted its weekly "Town Meeting" program to discussion of Korean developments. CBS Radio changed its daily feature program "You and —" to "You and Korea." NBC Radio's 11:15 A.M. newscast became "Report on Korea." NBC Television started a late evening program, "Report from the Pentagon," featuring the daily briefings by Pentagon spokesmen. Major George Fielding Eliot, who had been CBS' military analyst during World War II, returned with his commentary on the Mutual network, which carried special reports on Korea nightly at 11 and 11:55.

Stations also expanded their schedules. WMCA, New York, doubled its news time with reports every half hour as well as on the hour. WOR added 56 news summaries a week to its 110 previously scheduled newscasts. Immediately after Truman's announcement of support for South Korea, WAVE, Louisville, aired a documentary, "The 38th Parallel," explaining how Korea had become divided. CBS' radio affiliates carried a series of half-hour programs on America's role in the war. Matching this expansion of news programming was a mounting demand by sponsors for available news spots. For the first time, Proctor & Gamble sponsored a newscast, Murrow's weekday radio program, on 31 stations in the Midwest. In the East, the program was sponsored by the American Oil Company. Quaker State sponsored it in the West.

Another Dunkirk?

The North Koreans, spearheaded by Soviet-made tanks, moved south crushingly, in superior strength. Lines of defense were drawn and demolished among scenes of heroism, disorder, and retreat. With so much confusion, correspondents had trouble assessing the situation. CBS' Bill Downs, in a cable to New York, reported the need for censorship and briefings for correspondents trying to evaluate what was happening. "If war correspondents in Korea have exaggerated American losses," he said, "it was [because] GHQ found neither the time nor opportunity to reply to requests to expand the picture."[5] The situation became so grave in July that a contingency plan was drawn for a last-ditch perimeter at the southern port of Pusan, similar to the beachhead the British had at Dunkirk in World War II.

Murrow made three trips to Korea, none lasting more than a few weeks. Setting out the first time in July, he said:

> I am going to spend my vacation doing some traveling with light baggage and a heavy heart. During nine years in Europe I had thought to have seen enough dead men and wounded buildings; of fear and high courage in the air and on the ground.[6]

If the face of war was familiar to Murrow, so to listeners was his style of reporting in time of war. Visiting the First Cavalry Division, he talked to a sergeant from Texas who had just been across the Naktong River on patrol.

> He said the patrol lost one American and two South Koreans. Another sergeant carried a wounded G.I. for nearly 800 yards under fire. The boy had come back from the hospital only yesterday morning. He was 20 years of age. He'd been recovering in the hospital from a minor wound and had volunteered for the patrol. They brought him back to this side of the river and there he died.

It was like a scene out of M*A*S*H.[7]

By August 1950, there were 200 correspondents in Korea. Representing the American networks were John Rich and Ray Falk of INS, Jimmy Cannon of the *New York Post,* and Peter Kalischer of UP, using the pseudonym Peter Murray, for ABC; Murrow, Downs, Pepper Martin, Jack Walters, and Bill Costello for CBS, soon to be reinforced by George Herman, Robert Pierpoint, Lou Cioffi, and John Jefferson; George Folster, W. W. Chaplin, Leon Pearson, and Bill Dunn[8] for NBC; and Cedric Foster, Bob Stewart, Walter and Edith Simmons of the *Chicago Tribune,* and Pat Michaels and Jack Reed of INS for Mutual. Directing the coverage from New York were Thomas Velotta, ABC's vice president in charge of news and special events; T. Wells "Ted" Church, succeeded by Edmund Chester as director of news at CBS; A. A. Schechter, Mutual's vice president for news, and William F. Brooks, vice president for NBC News.

Not all broadcast coverage was for the networks. Robert Schakne of INS, who later would join CBS, reported on a stringer basis for WLW, Cincinnati. George Grim of the *Minneapolis Tribune* reported for a time for WCCO. And there were others.

A Close Call

An often-told story that desperate summer of 1950 was how Ed Murrow and three other correspondents were taken prisoner by U.S. Marines. It happened when Murrow and Bill Dunn of NBC, James Hicks of the *Afro-American Press,* and Bill Lawrence of the *New York Times* wanted to contact a Marine unit recently landed at Pusan. For the trip, they had a truck and a small escort of South Korean troops. None of them had the password.

It was night. Approaching the Marine position, they were challenged in the darkness by a sentry who refused to believe they were American newsmen. "He said if we moved, he'd shoot," Dunn recalled years later. "He sounded scared as hell."[9] Other sentries, warned to be on guard against infiltrators, were equally edgy. The correspondents were shadows in the dark. They could hear the clicking of rifle bolts. "I thought they intended to shoot us," Lawrence said.[10] Instead, along with the South Koreans, they were held until an officer recognized Murrow and apologized.

Before the night was over, two Marines had been killed by "friendly" fire.

"Mighty Lonely This Christmas"

"See It Now," more than any other documentary series, showed the nature of the war. Its two most ambitious, historically most important reports were carried by CBS on December 28, 1952, and December 29, 1953. For the 1952 broadcast, 15 reporters, cameramen, and soundmen were moved into Korea for a single week of filming. The scope of the 1953 broadcast is demonstrated by the correspondents' assignments: Murrow speaking from a liaison plane, Robert Pierpoint at a Marine outpost, Ed Scott on the flight deck of a hospital ship, Lou Cioffi (later wounded) with a mortar unit, Larry LeSueur with a French unit, and Joseph Wershba on a C-47 showering propaganda leaflets on enemy territory.

More than anything else, the program was an album of the faces and voices of members of the U.S., British, French, Australian, New Zealand, South Korean, and Ethiopian forces joined in the struggle. More than fifty individual faces were seen. Thirty-three servicemen and four nurses were heard, most of them saying in different ways that they wished they were spending Christmas at home. Many, with encouragement from the correspondent, gave messages like "Hi, honey!" and "Merry Christmas!" to loved ones in the States. "Mighty lonely this Christmas," Nurse Alice Emery told her husband, assuring him that next Christmas they would be together.

The program was poignant. Nurses and servicemen yearned for home. There was a brooding sense that you could get killed, but it was something that happened off camera.

The CBS newsman reporting the Korean War for the longest period was George Herman, who arrived in late August 1950 and stayed for the next two and a half years. A graduate of Dartmouth, Herman had studied at the Columbia University Graduate School of Journalism and worked in local radio before joining CBS in 1944. He went quickly from writer to editor, then got on the air as a reporter. When he asked for assignment overseas and nothing came of it, he offered to go at his own expense. The result was that in 1949, equipped with a CBS camera, he went off to Asia to show what he could do.

The timing was good. The French Army was being bloodied in Indo-china, Communist guerrillas were engaged in jungle warfare in Malaya, and, in bordering raids, the North Koreans were threatening South Korea. Herman reported on all these actions. According to a CBS News release, his were the network's first sound-and-film reports received from abroad.[11] When the Korean War broke out, he was a natural choice to cover it.

Herman returned to Korea in time to report General MacArthur's master stroke at Inchon. It was old strategy, simple and audacious. The main enemy force was deep in South Korea, preoccupied with trying to drive the battered American and Republic of Korea (ROK) divisions off the peninsula into the sea. With the enemy concentrated in the south, MacArthur would land a large amphibious force behind the Communist lines at Inchon in the north.

The operation was opposed at first by the Joint Chiefs of Staff. Inchon, the port city for Seoul, has some of the most formidable tides in the world —as high as 30 feet—and mud flats in which vehicles and men could become hopelessly mired. MacArthur timed the landing to minimize these hazards and on September 15 poured an assault force of 70,000 men into Inchon. He quickly liberated Seoul and, five weeks later, took Pyongyang, the North Korean capital.

With Seoul recaptured, radio correspondents had access to a powerful RCA transmitter that could reach 7,000 miles across the Pacific to Oakland, California. Broadcasts originated in a small studio in the Communications Ministry, linked by FM to the transmitter in a nearby town. Still, there were frustrations. Herman recalls how, when the FM link deteriorated, a driver from GHQ took him by Jeep every night to the transmitter:

> The driver insisted I carry a carbine and watch for ambushes, so I got one. After two weeks of riding shotgun to the driver, I tested the carbine on the range and found it wouldn't fire. I'd been carrying a carbine with a broken firing pin.

On one occasion, Herman got an eyewitness account of a battle as far as Oakland, only for it to be lost, inexplicably, crossing the bay to CBS in San Francisco.[12]

Debacle

With the North Koreans on the run, MacArthur acted rashly. China had warned that if American forces moved north of the 38th parallel dividing North and South Korea, it would intervene. MacArthur underestimated the warning. He resolved to liberate all of Korea, which meant advancing up the peninsula to China's border. The miscalculation resulted in catastrophe. More than 300,000 Chinese troops entered the war, driving United Nations forces south over the same roads on which they had advanced confidently only a few weeks before.

CBS' John Jefferson, who had been a Navy intelligence officer in

World War II, was one of the few correspondents accompanying the Marines on their painful 50-mile retreat from the Chosin Reservoir to the port of Hungnam, where in a "little Dunkirk" they were evacuated by ship. His stark eyewitness reports of the Marines, hungry and frostbitten, harassed by murderous flank attacks, carrying their dead in temperatures that froze carbines and automatic rifles, were picked up by the wire services and published nationwide. There his career as war correspondent ended. The military transport in which he was riding crashed, and a badly splintered leg took him out of action.

By the middle of December, the Eighth Army, made up of United States and United Nations forces, had been knocked back down below the 38th parallel, a "withdrawal" of more than 120 miles as the crow flies, the longest retreat in American history.

"This Is a Dying City"

It was apparent that the Communists would take Seoul once again. On January 3, 1951, George Herman made his last broadcast from the capital as all around him station employes packed in wooden cases the equipment they hoped to save. He spoke quietly.

> This is a dying city. Outside in the streets there are no pedestrians who are not refugees. . . . Planes have screamed overhead much of the morning, and there has been intermittent artillery fire in the distance but not so far away as it was yesterday. It's hard to say just how far away the enemy is at the moment. . . .
>
> A few lonely trolley cars are still running, and when a fire broke out in a string of tenement houses this morning the fire department arrived and managed to get it under control after only four houses had burned out. . . . I'd like to say more. The technicians are ready now to pull the switch. They have brought in a packing case for the apparatus over which I'm speaking.

Herman finished his broadcast at five minutes before two in the afternoon. One minute later, the station went dead. But only for the time being was it the CBS correspondent's "last broadcast from Seoul." He and the other radio correspondents would be back.

Censorship

There was no military censorship in Korea for the first six months. Correspondents withheld information they regarded as being of possible use to the enemy on a voluntary basis. Predictably, disagreement arose over what was legitimate news. In mid-July, two correspondents, Tom Lambert of AP and Peter Kalischer of UP,[13] were ordered out of the war zone for reporting soldiers' complaints, an order that was rescinded after protests from the wire services and other organizations, including the National Association of Radio News Directors, now the Radio-Television News Directors Association.

It was during this early period that a Murrow broadcast was killed, not by the military, but by CBS. The date was August 14, 1950, a time when it appeared that the Communists might push the outnumbered American force off the peninsula. Murrow prepared an eight-minute broadcast critical of the deployment of American troops. He quoted unidentified officers, "some of them wearing stars," as calling MacArthur's strategy "folly." When CBS executives received a transcript of the broadcast Murrow wanted to make, they decided to kill it on grounds that the Communists might use it as propaganda. John Aaron, coproducer of the Murrow program, fought the decision to no avail. On this occasion, the most respected broadcast voice of World War II was not trusted.

On December 21, 1950, MacArthur imposed full military censorship. In his book, *The First Casualty*, Phillip Knightley writes:

> No correspondent dared ask whether MacArthur had overextended his forces by miscalculating China's reaction and the strength of her intervention, probably because the supreme commander had already expelled some 17 correspondents from Japan for having criticized his policies.[14]

In April 1951, President Truman removed MacArthur from all Far East commands, replacing him with General Matthew Ridgway. Despite repeated instructions not to advocate war policy without clearance from Washington, MacArthur had publicly advocated fresh approaches, including the bombing of air bases in China. Truman saw it as a constitutional issue. He was upholding the principle that the President, a civilian, is commander in chief.

Two months later, MacArthur received a Caesar's welcome in New York. Ed Murrow went out to cover the parade but soon returned, disgusted that an officer who had obstinately disobeyed his commander in chief was being accorded such a reception. It was estimated that in the four days from MacArthur's takeoff from Tokyo to his New York appearance before addressing a special session of Congress, more than forty million viewers tuned in to some part of his triumphal return. It was more than adulation for conduct of the war in Korea; this was the four-star general most closely identified with victory over Japan.

Stalemate

Under General Ridgway, U.N. forces moved back up the peninsula, and by June almost all of South Korea, including Seoul, was rid of the enemy. Once more, the battle line stretched along the 38th parallel. This was where, a year earlier, it had all started. It seemed to both sides, after suffering casualties totaling almost two million, that the time had come to talk peace.

Cease-fire negotiations in the small village of Panmunjom, near Seoul, dragged on unmercifully with a mounting toll of dead and wounded for two years. A corps of correspondents representing all networks stayed on to cover the on-and-off-again talks, as well as an exchange of prisoners of war. Most of the coverage was for radio. Television crews came and went. Not until July 27, 1953, was a cease-fire agreement signed and the border between North and South Korea reestablished at the 38th parallel.

Summing Up

At considerable cost, the United States had thwarted North Korea in its aggression, and North Korea and China had thwarted the United States in its attempt to overrun North Korea. In three years, one month, and two days of fighting, the United States had lost 24,965 killed in action and 12,939 missing and presumed dead. South Korea suffered 46,812 killed and 66,436 missing and presumed dead. Other U.N. nations that sent reinforcements to Korea lost 2,597 killed and 1,925 missing. With oppressive heat in summer, sub-zero Siberian winds in winter, and mountainous terrain, the war equaled in ordeal any that American forces had ever fought.

The Korean War was the first covered by television and the last covered without benefit of communications satellites. Film shipped by air to New York might take three or four days. Air battles between American Sabrejets and Soviet-made MIGs were commonplace, but film showing the action was rare. Producer Av Westin tells how CBS made do with stock footage of fighter jets in comparable action. The footage was used over and over with copy that might read, "Sabrejets like these today fought fierce dogfights over the Yalu River." Westin says, "We did the best we could with what we had."[15]

Still, even in adolescence, television's role was significant. It had pictures. It showed G.I.s eating, waiting, praying, responding to mail call, going out on patrol. The pictures showed faces and on them the tediousness, loneliness, and fear. Natural sound played as important a part as ever, not just the stereotyped crackle of machinegun fire and firing of artillery pieces but, as in "See It Now," the bright, metallic sound of lead, taken from the body of a wounded man, dropped into a stainless steel pan, and the scraping of a shovel as a G.I., preparing for enemy counterattack, tries to dig a foxhole in frozen ground.[16]

Television showed a country ravaged. Bill Downs stood beside the rubble of a peasant's home, and as he described what had happened—the whole village had been laid waste—he wept. While he fought to control his voice, the camera showed an old man walking down what had been a street. The old man was holding a child's hand. "This," said Downs, "is the side of war we don't see very much of, but probably it's the most important part of all."[17] The unpretentious video, the old man and child, provided powerful accompaniment to Downs' words. Television was learning how to cover a war.

For the most part, it was still radio. Early in the war, radio correspondents battled for time on the sole military telephone line that was accessible for relaying their reports to Tokyo. The alternative was to fly there with their reports. There was an apocryphal story that CBS' Lou Cioffi tried using barbed wire as an antenna for getting his stories out. In July 1951, after U.N. forces had been thrown back toward Pusan for the second time, correspondents managed to rig up their own emergency transmitter. Later, with Seoul recaptured, the communications situation improved, but many correspondents still flew to Tokyo with their stories. Hal Boyle of the Associated Press wrote: "Never since and including the Civil War have correspondents had so few of the facilities vital to their trade."[18]

For the first time, war correspondents could use audiotape. Most recorders—the Stancil-Hoffman was popular—had no playback and with batteries weighed as much as 70 pounds, no mean weight to carry up a hill under fire. And they were frail compared to today's recorders; after a bumpy Jeep ride they often would not work. George Herman of CBS collaborated with technicians who happened to have some old hand-wound phonograph motors. With these they came up with a hand-wound recorder that not only was lighter, with no heavy power pack, but enabled tape to be played back.

Although audiotape was available, it was not a part of daily reporting. Little tape was used in programs such as hourly newscasts. "Combat recordings," as "Hear It Now" called them,[19] were used primarily in longer news specials and documentaries.

And how, covering the war, did radio and television do? Looking back, George Herman says:

> I think we did a good job. We invented ways of getting stories out under great technical odds and gave Americans a clear picture of the war. Film was black and white, shot in newsreel style rather than in the intimate close-up style TV later developed, so the horrors of war were not brought into the living room. Radio, too, was more in the cool, factual style of World War II than in the personal suffering style of Vietnam. We were more Ed Murrow than Ernie Pyle.[20]

29
Time Out for Ratings

After several of his favorite programs had been canceled, Goodman Ace, one of broadcasting's most gifted writers, said, "Actually, it wasn't the Lord who took them away. It was a power much higher. It was the Nielsen ratings."[1] Because it is impossible to talk about broadcast news without talking about ratings, this may be a good place to summarize what ratings are, how they are obtained, and what they mean. The subject will be coming up more often as we go on.

Ratings are based on population samples. The samples vary in size, but all are relatively small. The sample used by the A. C. Nielsen Company for measuring a nationally televised program is roughly 4,000 households. For many years, to measure the size of audience, Nielsen employed a patented device called an Audimeter, which, placed in a household, recorded the channel that was turned on. Nielsen also used diaries kept by selected viewers. Arbitron, the other major rating company, used diaries and telephone calls. It concentrated, and still concentrates, on local station audiences, radio and television. Nielsen gave up measuring radio audiences in 1964.

Broadcasting saw a ratings revolution in 1987 with the arrival of the peoplemeter, a way of measuring the demographics of audiences as well as their size. Members of selected households are interviewed as to age, education, income, and ethnic origin. These data, including sex of the interviewee, are stored in the system's central computer, and each household member receives a number keyed to that information. For example, the father in a family may have the number 3 and his 12-year-old son the number 6. Turning on the television set, the father presses button 3 on a small hand-held device. Later, the son, turning to a different program, presses button 6. If they act responsibly, the service knows not only how many people are watching a given program but also their age, income, and everything else, precisely the kind of information advertisers want.

The peoplemeter was pioneered by Audits of Great Britain and introduced in this country by its subsidiary, AGB Television Research, commonly referred to as AGB. After successful tests by AGB in Boston, the new approach was tried out nationally in the 1987–1988 season, with both Nielsen and Arbitron scrambling to implement their own peoplemeter systems. By July 1987, Nielsen was boasting that it had installed peoplemeters "in all kinds of households and neighborhoods across the country."[2] Two months later, both Nielsen and AGB began daily delivery of prime-time numbers derived from peoplemeters. Nielsen stopped using Audimeters as all three traditional networks and the new Fox network subscribed to its peoplemeter service.[3] Arbitron launched a local peoplemeter service called Scan-America. Since then, AGB has discontinued its service.

In television, the peoplemeter is now the standard for audience measurement, although its accuracy has been questioned so that it may be revised or a whole new system introduced. One possibility is a system that would require no effort on the part of viewers. It would involve a computerized "image recognition" sensor for identifying automatically not only how many members of a household are watching but which members. The sensor, about the size of a VCR, would store the facial features of each member of the household and become activated when the set is turned on. If a member is absent, or isn't watching, the sensor will know. Orwell, are you watching?

There are "ratings points" and there are "shares." Take the ratings race for primetime programs in the week ending July 1, 1990: "60 Minutes" came in seventh, just ahead of "Golden Girls," with a 13.2 rating and a 30 share. The 13.2 rating means that, according to Nielsen, 13.2 percent of all television households in the country had turned to channels carrying "60 Minutes." The 30 share, on the other hand, is the percentage the program had, not of all households with television, but of those that had their sets turned on. In short, its share of the actual viewing audience.

Broadcasters charge advertisers according to the size and composition of audience. Since ratings measure audience, and audience determines revenue, commercial broadcasters, not surprisingly, pay the ratings charts close attention. For a network program, each rating point, small as it may appear, represents 921,000 households. Since advertisers buying 30 seconds of prime time in 1988 might pay $84,000 for each thousand of these households, obviously revenue in the millions of dollars is involved.

For broadcast journalists, the "tawdry" ratings system has been both friend and foe. Low ratings have killed good programs, with casualties tragically high in the field of the network documentary, where an audience of a few million is taken as failure. Low ratings have killed off one NBC magazine show after another.

In pursuit of higher ratings, some programmers have taken television news, which inevitably has show business aspects, and made it show business, pure and simple. Abetted by consultants, who are paid to improve ratings, they offer what entertains and excites, rather than what viewers need to know. Other more responsible programmers have achieved high numbers by convincing viewers that if they want to know what of significance is going on, theirs is the channel to watch. Most stations, keeping their viewers informed, try to do it in the most interesting, imaginative way.

The news operation with high ratings—and high revenue—is more likely to receive support from management, which translates into money for new equipment, a computerized newsroom perhaps, and a larger, more competent staff. Therefore, although a race for ratings can mean more reporting of what is sensational, even salacious, it also can benefit. It was in part ratings competition that spurred the introduction on network television of the half-hour evening news.

A sidebar: For years, newspaper critics, ignoring their own dependence on circulation figures, gibed broadcasters for the attention they paid to ratings figures. Jack Gould called the few thousand people in ratings samples, representing the whole country, "the cathode aristocracy."[4] He frowned on it. But, in 1978, the *New York Times,* recognizing public as well as industry interest, began publishing a boxscore of the top-rated programs each week.

Television ratings had become fit to print.

30

The Alarm Clock War

There never had been anything on television quite like the program born on the morning of January 14, 1952. NBC called it "Today." Critics predicted death in infancy, but it lived, grew up, and became rich.

The immodest birth announcement, published that morning in major dailies, read:

> Before you leave home in the morning, even before you finish your second cup of coffee, you are going to become an ear and eye witness to every major world event—as it happened while you slept, as it happens *now*. . . . This is the program that *entertains* as it informs. This is the morning briefing session that will arm you with information to meet the day more fully than any citizen has ever been armed before.

"Today" was the brainchild of NBC's innovating programmer, Sylvester "Pat" Weaver, who a year later would become network president. He was the creator of NBC's other big money-maker, "Tonight," which bowed in 1954 with Steve Allen. After Allen came Jack Paar. Whereas Allen conducted what amounted to a variety show, Paar built the program on interviews. Among the most frequent guests were Dody Goodman, Alexander King, and Zsa Zsa Gabor.[1] After five years, Paar was succeeded by Johnny Carson, the longest-running late night act on television. Once, when Carson threatened to quit, David Brinkley quipped that Carson's wanting to leave "Tonight" was "like George Washington asking to get off the one-dollar bill."[2]

"Peace!"

The first host of "Today" was Dave Garroway, former NBC page whose popular "Garroway at Large" program had originated in Chicago. Garroway worked casually and effectively. Deeply philosophical, he would raise his right hand at the end of each program and, looking solemnly into the camera through horn-rimmed glasses, say, "Peace!" He said it quietly, pronouncing a benediction. Tom Shales, the *Washington Post* critic, called Garroway "the least grating, the most seemingly trustworthy, and one of the most assuring intruders ever to enter millions of American homes."[3]

With Garroway at the start were Jack Lescoulie, who did sports; Jim Fleming (succeeded by Frank Blair), who gave news summaries on the hour and half-hour; and Estelle Parsons, the production assistant who became an on-air personality and Oscar-winning actress, the first in a long line of "Today" women that included Betsy Palmer, Lee Meriwether, and Helen O'Connell. Even Barbara Walters, when she first appeared on the program, was regarded as another of the "girls"—all talented—who came, contributed charm, and were gone. Joe Garagiola took over sports when Lescoulie left in the late 1960s. (Garagiola left the show in 1973, but to the surprise of everyone, including himself, was back in 1990. How it happened later.) Gene Shalit of the overbearing moustache began coming on the program occasionally in 1958, reviewing books and motion pictures, then became a permanent fixture as critic-at-large. Edwin Newman did play reviews for a while, as well as interviews.

During the months of planning that preceded the birth of "Today," when its working title was "Rise and Shine," the man in immediate charge was none other than Abe Schechter, founder of NBC News. Schechter, the program's first executive producer, soon left to set up the public relations firm A. A. Schechter Associates. His successor was Richard Pinkham, a former newspaper executive who, with producer Mort Werner, guided the program through the first crucial years.

Theirs was no easy success, and it says something about television—and society as a whole—that it took J. Fred Muggs, a chimpanzee, finally to lift "Today" out of the red. The program was a year old, and the chimp only a few weeks old, when viewers tuned in and discovered the adorable rascal cuddling with Garroway one moment, scattering his notes another, and scampering about the studio the next. The ratings skyrocketed. In his story of the "Today" show, Robert Metz tells how young viewers played an important part in saving the program:

[They] guarded the TV dial like goalies protecting the nets at Madison Square Garden, threatening tears or mayhem if a parent tried to change channels. Consequently, parents who had shunned "Today" . . . became involuntary regulars. Though captive at first, many became fans, discovering that "Today" was a good news show.[4]

J. Fred Muggs costarred with Garroway for four years. It was only after his personality change, when he took to nipping people and tossing furniture, that he was let go.

Garroway remained the host—"The Communicator," Pat Weaver called him—for nine years. Between 1955 and 1958, he also hosted "Wide, Wide World," a Sunday afternoon program that covered a broad range of subjects, heavy and light. He died July 21, 1982, of a self-inflicted gunshot wound after undergoing heart surgery. Garroway was a true pioneer. Part entertainer, part journalist, he entered unknown regions. "There was," he told Jane Pauley on the 30th anniversary show, "so much to talk about and do."

Among the program's early writers were Alan Smith, Bud Lewis, Richard "Ric" Ballad, and John Dunn. News editor on the show was Gerald Green, the future novelist. When Green resigned, Dunn took his place. Metz calls Dunn, who died in 1976, "the conscience and residential intellectual for the show for most of its history."[5] Another veteran was Paul Cunningham. He appeared on the premiere broadcast and was reporter-at-large on the program for more than twenty years.

Almost everyone else came and went. Executive editors for relatively short periods after Pinkham, who left the show in 1956 for a vice presidency at the Ted Bates advertising agency, were Robert Bendick, Robert "Shad" Northshield, and Fred Freed. Al Morgan, another soon-to-be novelist, served for six years, starting in 1961. He was followed by Stuart Schulberg, son of Hollywood producer B. P. Schulberg and brother of the novelist Budd Schulberg. Schulberg produced the program for a record eight years and was succeeded by Paul Friedman. Joe Bartelme became executive producer early in 1979, followed by Steve Friedman, who now produces the "NBC Nightly News with Tom Brokaw."

This turnover in producers reflects NBC's concern over competition from ABC's "Good Morning America" program,[6] which for a time overtook "Today" in the Nielsen ratings and is back in front today. In May 1979, NBC engaged Phil Donahue to do interview segments on "Today," but the three-day-a-week feature later was dropped. In March 1980, the "Today" cast was joined by Willard Scott, an inherently friendly, clowning weatherman from WRC-TV, the NBC-owned station in Washington, D.C. Admittedly no meteorologist, Scott's chief function has been simply, through robust neighborliness, to loosen things up. No other network weatherman plugs cucumber festivals and, along with rain showers, predicts how far you can throw a tongue depressor, and congratulates people on their 100th birthdays. One suspects that by now no other would dare.

But the stars of the "Today" show were, and always would be, the hosts, the anchors and co-anchors who presided at the big desk. Garroway was succeeded briefly by John Chancellor, then by Hugh Downs (1962–1971) and Frank McGee (1971–1974). When McGee died of bone cancer in April 1974, his successor was a fellow Oklahoman and friend, Jim Hartz (1974–1977). It was at the start of Hartz' reign that, for the first time, "Today" had a cohost. A woman.

Five-Million-Dollar Woman

It had been a struggle, this battle of the poor little, very bright girl from Boston who became the best-known woman in network news. The daughter of a night club owner—tourists crowded his Latin Quarter in New York—Barbara Jill Walters knew very soon after graduation from Sarah Lawrence that she wanted to make it in broadcasting and make it big.

Being the daughter of Lou Walters helped her land a series of jobs, one as a writer for CBS' morning show, which was trying to compete with "Today." A further irony was that she was turned down at ABC, which one day would want her so badly that it gave her a million dollars a year.

Her first real break came in 1961 when Fred Freed hired her as a freelance writer for "Today." Freed's successor, Shad Northshield, impressed by her conscientiousness and hustle, began to give her film assignments. In 1964, when Maureen O'Sullivan left the show, Hugh Downs backed her as a replacement, and that is when Walters became an on-camera regular, no "girl" but a genuine journalist asking guests the tough questions that have become her trademark. *Newsweek* observed at the time that she got away with impertinent questions viewers would never hear from Hugh Downs. The magazine gave these early examples: "She asked Ingrid Bergman, 'What's it like for great beauties to grow old?' With Truman Capote it was: 'Were you made fun of as a child because you were different?' "[7]

Walters became what the Associated Press called "the reigning monarch of morning television"[8] when she and Jim Hartz took over as cohosts of "Today" in 1974. Hartz, who had an ingratiating personality and experience in anchoring, handled the assignment competently, but Walters possessed a drive—a star quality—that made her dominant. And with her ascendancy, the ratings for "Today" also rose. Hugh Downs called her, with her uncommon combination of intelligence, toughness, and femininity, "without question the best find the 'Today' show ever had."[9]

Only months after Walters became cohost of "Today," ABC on January 6, 1975, launched its own high-budgeted morning show, "AM America," with Stephanie Edwards and Bill Beutel. The two-hour broadcast, heavy on feature material, was fine-honed to cut into the "Today" audience. It failed. After 10 months, Beutel and Edwards were dropped. The program got a single host, David Hartman, and a new title, "Good Morning America." The revamped program took off with an audience gain in its first year of about 60 percent, while the "Today" audience declined about 20 percent.

At this point, Walters had been involved with "Today" for 15 years. As early as 1969 she told an interviewer that sometimes, with the heavy schedule starting at 4 A.M., she was "so bone-tired" she could cry.[10] Now she was weary, not only physically, but weary of the routine. She had been on the show such a long time and had achieved her goal. There was nowhere higher to go except the "Nightly News" anchor desk, and John Chancellor, who presided there, would not soon share that position or be replaced. With "Today" slipping in the ratings, she was more restless than ever. Roone Arledge, president of ABC News, gauged her mood and invited her to do the ABC evening news with Harry Reasoner.

No woman had ever anchored the evening news regularly, Monday through Friday, on a television network.[11] Moreover, Arledge offered an unprecedented contract. ABC would give her a million dollars a year— double her NBC salary—for five years. For that she would co-anchor the evening news, produce four prime-time specials a year, and appear occasionally on other programs. *Newsweek* called her "the five-million-dollar woman."[12] *Time* saw it as "the biggest talent raid since CBS grabbed Jack Benny from NBC."[13] Walters saw it as the biggest barrier-breaking opportunity any woman in broadcast news had ever had. The industry came to perceive it as the precedent for all the multimillion-dollar salaries star anchors would receive in years to come.

Brokaw at Daybreak

At "Today," the show went on. Tom Brokaw, assigned to the White House since 1973, succeeded Jim Hartz, who left to anchor at WRC-TV, Washington. Brokaw could have hosted "Today" years earlier but had refused to read commercials and so was passed by.[14] Now, in 1976, he was sole anchor.

NBC releases referred to Jane Pauley, the new woman on the program, as "featured panelist." Pauley, a debater in high school, was only four years out of Indiana University, where she had majored in political science. Her brief experience in broadcasting had been at WISH-TV, Indianapolis, where she was a reporter, and at WMAQ-TV, the NBC station in Chicago, where she co-anchored the nightly news. No woman had been a television anchor in Chicago before. Early in 1976, when the "Today" show originated in Chicago and Walters was out of the country on assignment, Pauley filled in. "If it hadn't been for that," she says, "I don't think the NBC people would have noticed me when Barbara left the network."[15]

Although "Today" led in audience, ABC's morning show was closing the gap. To counter the threat, NBC in 1977 made substantive changes in "Today." It added frequent special reports from Eric Burns and Jack Perkins, backed by production units in Chicago and Los Angeles. New emphasis was given to life-style subjects such as home decorating, money management, and physical fitness.

Still, "Good Morning America" kept gaining and in 1979 overtook "Today" in the ratings for the first time. It was clearly ahead in 1982 when "Today" again changed its lineup. Brokaw left to co-anchor the "Nightly News" with Roger Mudd, and Pauley was joined by two new regulars, Bryant Gumbel and Chris Wallace. Gumbel, one of NBC's most popular sportscasters, cohosted with Pauley in New York. Just as Walters had broken ground on "Today" as a woman, Gumbel broke ground as the program's first featured black. Wallace, son of CBS' Mike Wallace, had been covering the House of Representatives for NBC and was now the show's news anchor in Washington.

Soon there would be more changes. After an audience survey, Gumbel was made principal host, leaving Pauley in a secondary role. "People want a leader," explained Reuven Frank, president of NBC News.[16] Chris Wallace was shifted to the White House, and Judy Woodruff took his place. Then she went to the new MacNeil-Lehrer program on PBS, and John Palmer took *her* place. It was no wonder viewers were confused.

Trouble in Paradise

But in Gumbel, Pauley, Palmer, and jovial Willard Scott, "Today" had found the winning formula. It took back the lead from "Good Morning America" and seemed unbeatable until February 1989, when it became known that Gumbel had written a four-page internal memo knocking most of his colleagues, including Scott, whose behavior, he said, "is killing us."[17] He didn't mention Jane Pauley, but she got a shock in August when Deborah Norville, who had been anchoring "NBC News at Sunrise," not only replaced John Palmer as the deliverer of hard news, but sat down alongside Gumbel in the studio, apparently as her equal.

Viewers loyal to Pauley asked themselves, "What's going on here?" Pauley asked herself the same question and decided that thirteen years of getting up in the middle of the night to go to work was long enough and left the show for other projects, including a new magazine program.

"Today" no longer projected the picture of a happy family. Its ratings slipped, then the slipping became such a slide that in January 1990, after four years as runner-up, "Good Morning America" retook first place. Marty Ryan, paying the price, was out as executive producer and Tom Capra was in. When that didn't help, management's cure was to expand the cast. It brought in Faith Daniels from CBS and Katherine Couric, one of NBC's own, as national correspondent. And among the new faces on the program was an old face, that of Joe Garagiola, onetime catcher for the St. Louis Cardinals, who had been part of "Today" back in the halycon days when Hugh Downs was host.

Still the show floundered. And it had done it to itself.

CBS Morning News

In 1954, two years after "Today" premiered, CBS bravely launched a two-hour imitation with Charles Collingwood and Dorothy Doan. After two years, Collingwood was joined by Walter Cronkite, the ex-United Press correspondent who had excelled as an anchorman on local television in Washington. He and Collingwood handled the news. The show went heavy on entertainment; publicity pictures show Cronkite posed with a puppet, a lion named Charlemane. Jack Paar soon took on the show, along with Collingwood, who still read the news. Singer Betty Clooney and Pupi Campo's band supplied music. When Paar couldn't make a dent in "Today," CBS engaged Dick Van Dyke, then Will Rogers, Jr., who said he would not try to be a humorist like his father. They also failed.

In 1957, the program was cut back to an hour, starting at 7 A.M., and the title changed from "The Good Morning Show" to "The CBS Morning News." It was now, as the title suggests, basically a news program with a distinguished correspondent, Richard C. Hottelet, as its anchor. Hottelet brought respect to the program—he conducted it for four years, longer than anyone else—but viewers preferred the lighter mix on NBC. It hadn't worked.

CBS responded to this disappointment by presenting something entirely new. This was a woman's program called "Calendar," strategically rescheduled for 10 A.M. to avoid the formidable competition of "Today." Its co-anchors were Harry Reasoner and Mary Fickett, the actress daughter of Homer Fickett, a radio director who had worked with many of CBS' early correspondents, including Edward R. Murrow. She had played Eleanor Roosevelt in "Sunrise at Campobello," for which she received a Tony Award nomination.

There was a spirit of camaraderie between the hosts that made the program enjoyable. Going into her conversation with the shapely exercise instructor Debbie Drake, Fickett could say with perfect naturalness, "Harry is a little bit jealous today—it's because he couldn't get to interview our next guest."[18] Invariably, the program dealt with one or more serious subjects as, in this broadcast, physical fitness and the off-year election.

The program lasted two years. During the first year, the writer for the program was Andy Rooney, who later became well known as the sardonic essayist on "60 Minutes." Reasoner wrote his own "end-pieces," many of which reappeared in his book *Before the Colors Fade*.[19]

Mike Wallace took over as sole anchor in 1963. More attention was given to hard news, and the title of the program—still a half hour—reverted to "The CBS Morning News." Wallace anchored the program until 1966, when he left for reporting assignments and Joseph Benti was brought in from KNXT, Los Angeles, to take his place. On March 31, 1969, the show was lengthened to an hour. *Variety* called it "the first regular newscast on the webs to so expand . . . a trial balloon for the hour-long nighttime strips to come in networking."[20] But as this is written, the long-anticipated one-hour evening newscast still has not arrived on any of the "Big Three" networks.

Benti anchored until 1970. After him, CBS tried with various two-hour formats to achieve a respectable rating for the show. The anchors were:

John Hart and Nelson Benton (1970–1973)
Hughes Rudd and Sally Quinn (August 1973–December 1973)
Hughes Rudd (1974–1975)
Hughes Rudd and Bruce Morton (1975–1977)
Hughes Rudd and Lesley Stahl (October 3, 1977–October 28, 1977)
Lesley Stahl and Richard Threlkeld (1977–1979)
Bob Schieffer (1979–1980)
Charles Kuralt (1980–1981)
Charles Kuralt and Diane Sawyer (1981–1982)
Bill Kurtis and Diane Sawyer (1982–1984)
Bill Kurtis and Phyllis George (January–June 1985)
Phyllis George and Forrest Sawyer (July–August 1985)
Forrest Sawyer and Maria Shriver (1985–1986)
Harry Smith and Kathleen Sullivan (1987–1990)
Harry Smith and Paula Zahn (1990–   )

For 32 years, ever since 1954, CBS had been trying to produce a morning news program that was competitive. In 1986, it gave up. It canceled "The CBS Morning News" and replaced it with a combination entertainment-information program, which had a stand-up comedian. Mercifully, the show lasted only a few months. In 1987, the news division regained the time period and tried once more with "CBS This Morning." Again, news is taken seriously. Charles Osgood contributes hard news summaries and special reports. Co-anchors Kathleen Sullivan and Harry Smith work well together and, with Faith Daniels, interview intelligently. The result has been a modest increase in ratings.

In at least two instances CBS handled morning anchor assignments badly. In 1973, in choosing Sally Quinn of the *Washington Post* to anchor with Hughes Rudd, the network not only engaged a woman totally inexperienced in television but outdid itself ballyhooing her arrival. An attractive, talented writer, Quinn might have made the grade with more rehearsal. After four months she went back to the *Post,* where between assignments she wrote a book about her misadventure.[21] In 1985, CBS was guilty of monumental miscasting in pairing a former Miss America, Phyllis George, with Bill Kurtis. At least Quinn had had solid journalistic credentials. George not only lacked knowledge of current events but proved herself a mistress of the infelicitous remark. Her only previous experience had been her tour as hostess of the "NFL Today" pregame show. A final word on the debacle in chapter 48.

Always on Sundays

"Sunday Morning" debuted on CBS in 1979. It was an ambitious 90-minute news program with Charles Kuralt as anchor and Shad Northshield, one of television's most honored documentarians, as executive producer. The whole style of the program, wrote *TV Guide*'s reviewer, Robert MacKenzie, is set by Kuralt's "benign, articulate presence." [22] John Carman wrote in the *Minneapolis Star:* "He has a *voice* like Sunday morning. Deep, at ease, reassuring." [23]

Kuralt, a graduate of the University of North Carolina and the *Charlotte News,* is one of television journalism's rare low-key stars. Viewers did not really become conscious of him until, in a three-month experiment in covering "non-news," he set out with cameraman Jimmy Wilson in a camper rented from the National Geographic Society to do a series of "On the Road" pieces for "The CBS Evening News With Walter Cronkite." The first "On the Road" report, aired on October 26, 1967, dealt with the beauty of autumn in rural Vermont. "It is death," he wrote, "that causes this blinding show of color, but it is a fierce and flaming death."

The idea of driving along the byways of America, catching the significant in the ordinary, grew from conversations between Kuralt and Richard Salent, head of CBS News. They felt there was something to be said for reminding viewers once in a while "that many people live in peace with their neighbors and that, beside the world of headlines, there is another world of people trying to get their kids off to school on time, who live the ordinary life of the country." [24] So he told of fiddle makers and gandy dancers, of a priest in the Alaska wilderness and of the farm couple, struggling in poverty, who made sure that each of their seven children got an education. Such "reminders" gave assurance to a people engaged in a rupturing war in Vietnam. When he became host of "Sunday Morning" in 1979, Kuralt had traveled more than 500,000 miles and reported his neighborly stories from all 50 states.

"Sunday Morning" was conceived by Salent and brought on under the stewardship of Bill Leonard, who succeeded him. It airs from 9 to 10:30 A.M. in the East and an hour or more earlier elsewhere. The present executive producer is Linda Mason.

"Good Morning America"

ABC-TV did not enter morning news competition until January 6, 1975, 23 years after NBC and 21 years after CBS. Its first attempt, "AM America," did not fail for lack of commitment. Besides Bill Beutel from the network's New York station and Stephanie Edwards, who had been cohost of "Ralph Story's AM" in Los Angeles, management had recruited Peter Jennings to report hard news from Washington and Sam Ervin, the Watergate hearings figure, and John Lindsay, New York's former mayor, to do political commentary. The program had a weather segment, a "people" segment, a coping segment, and its own musical theme.

The show, for all this, was a disaster. Edwards left after four months; the program died in less than a year. It was not Beutel or Edwards that caused the death; it was the program's chirpiness, the whole misguided, overdone light approach. It was an $8,000,000 gamble based on being pleasing—"as determinedly innocuous as Musak," said *Newsweek*[25]—and it failed.

The replacement, premiering on November 3, 1975, was "Good Morning America," subtitled "The Friendly Awakening." Edwin Vane, ABC's director of entertainment programming, described the show as "people oriented." Since the CBS and NBC programs stressed news, "Good Morning America" would stress information and entertainment—"infotainment"—"with a distinct, friendly, comforting tone."[26] No dull news. "We're not looking to fill the show with interviews with senators," Mel Ferber, the program's first executive producer, said.[27]

There would be one anchor, David Hartman. The principal woman on the show, Nancy Dussault, was identified in ABC advertising as "David's sidekick."[28] Other regular participants, so numerous as to recall Cecil B. deMille's casts of thousands, were Helen Gurley Brown, Erma Bombeck, Jack Anderson, John Lindsay (politics), F. Lee Bailey (law), Rona Barrett (Hollywood gossip), John Coleman (weather), Howard Cosell (sports), Storm Field (science and medicine), Sylvia Porter (money) Bruce and Christie Jenner (couples), Dr. Lendon Smith (children), Joan Lunden (products), Al Ubell (household hints), Geraldo Rivera (people), and Margaret Osmer and Steve Bell (hard news).

By the second year, Dussault, Osmer, Field, Jennings, and Christie Jenner were gone. Jennings asked to go back to regular reporting. Sandy Hill, who had worked at the ABC and CBS stations in Los Angeles, succeeded Dussault as Hartman's "sidekick," and then Joan Lunden succeeded Hill. Dr. Timothy Johnson came on the program with medical advice.

David Hartman led "Good Morning America" to supremacy over "Today" and dominated the program for a decade. He left in 1987, replaced by Charles Gibson, who had been ABC News' congressional correspondent. A solid journalist, Gibson had worked in broadcasting since his undergraduate days at Princeton, where he was news director of the university radio station.

News in the Night

The three networks are not just competing among themselves; they have a strong fourth competitor in CNN, and it was in large part because of this round-the-clock competition that NBC and CBS in 1982 began offering television news during the night. NBC led off in July with a low-keyed show called "NBC News Overnight" with Lloyd Dobyns and Linda Ellerbee. Critics applauded the 1:30–2:30 A.M. effort. The *New York Times*' John J. O'Connor called it "one of the classier new acts in television news."[29] *Time* found it to be "TV's wittiest, toughest, least snazzy news strip."[30] Most scripting for the program was done by Dobyns and Ellerbee themselves, two capable, irreverent writers. Herb Dudnick was executive producer. (After the first months, Dobyns left to work on NBC's prime-time magazine show, "First Camera." His replacement was Bill Schechner of NBC's Atlanta bureau.)

"NBC News Overnight" attracted a small but devoted audience, which was dismayed when the show died after 17 months due to lack of advertiser support. NBC received an estimated 10,000 protests. A monk wrote that he had watched the program "religiously." Some people sent money, hoping their contributions would save the show. In 1984, the broadcast was honored posthumously with an Alfred I. duPont-Columbia University Award for excellence in television news.

Three months after the debut of "NBC News Overnight, CBS introduced "Nightwatch," a pioneering program which ran from 2 to 6 A.M. The co-anchors, who often did field reports and interviews, were Harold Dow, Christopher Glenn, and Karen Stone. The executive producer, Bob Ferrante, came from public television. For 11 years he had been an award-winning producer of public affairs broadcasts at WGBH-TV, Boston. Because of budget cuts, the amount of live reporting on "Nightwatch" was reduced in 1983 to two hours. It remained a four-hour program, however, since material used in the first two hours was repeated with live updates.

In the same year that CBS and NBC launched their overnight programs, all three networks began carrying news at 6 A.M. These were "ABC News This Morning" (quickly changed to "World News This Morning"), "CBS Early Morning News," and "NBC News at Sunrise." The programs are important not only for themselves but from a ratings standpoint because viewers tend to stay tuned for the two-hour shows that follow.

31
Magazines of the Air

When Jane Pauley left the "Today" show to anchor her new series, "Real Life with Jane Pauley," she really was leaving one kind of magazine program for another. Magazine programs, like morning programs, delve into a potpourri of subjects, heavy and light, at greater length than regular newscasts. Normally, on network television, they are an hour in length. Local magazine shows usually run a half hour.

The first popular magazine of the air was "March of Time," created for radio in 1931. It was still a hit in 1936 when Heinz Foods sponsored a CBS program called "The Heinz Magazine of the Air," presided over by Delmar Edmondson, who had the title of editor. The show lasted only a year.

A burst of morale-lifting programs of the magazine type came with America's entry in World War II. Outstanding was "The Army Hour" produced by the Army and NBC. In 1943 alone, the program carried pickups from 102 Army posts, 10 war plants, and 21 military hospitals, plus scores of reports from bases overseas.

CBS' newsmagazine, "Report to the Nation," also covered the activities of servicemen and women, though to a lesser degree. Walter Cronkite made his network debut on "Report," participating in the program as a

United Press war correspondent. "The subject," he says, "may have been the burning of the troopship *Wakefield* in the summer of 1943, or it could have been the invasion of North Africa in November of that year."[1] The program went off the air in 1944.

A six-week series heard on CBS in the summer of 1942 was "An American in England," produced by Edward R. Murrow and written by Norman Corwin, both located in London. The half-hour program aired at 10 P.M., New York time, which meant 3 A.M. in London, and involved more than a hundred actors, musicians, and technicians. In the premiere broadcast, Corwin, played by Joseph Julian, reported his impressions of wartime London.[2] This was the first live dramatic series to originate overseas and be heard in the United States.

Some programs were pure propaganda. The Office of War Information offered the series "This Is Our Enemy" and "You Can't Do Business With Hitler," which the radio networks could, and did, pick up as a patriotic service. Together, the networks and government produced a 13-week series titled "This Is War," with scripts by such renowned writers as Maxwell Anderson and Stephen Vincent Benet. Other propaganda programs for stateside audiences were produced in cooperation with the Air Corps, Navy, War Shipping Administration, U.S. Maritime Commission, and American Red Cross. In 1943, NBC's Red and Blue networks were carrying, on a sustaining basis, 23 so-called war service programs.[3]

No sharp line can be drawn between the magazine and documentary forms. Ray Carroll of the University of Alabama has defined the difference by saying that whereas the documentary usually provides the big picture, the magazine tends to report a part of that picture. "For example," he says, "where the traditional documentary might examine the United States' military preparedness, a magazine segment would more likely focus on a single aspect, say the reliability of U.S. Army tanks."[4]

A television magazine comparable to a "slick" in the print magazine field was "Omnibus," which debuted in CBS in 1951. The host of this highly acclaimed Sunday program was Alistair Cooke. Its producer was Robert Saudek, who had left ABC to direct the Ford Foundation's radio-television workshop. In its last year, 1956, the series ran on ABC. "Omnibus" was a rare experimental program, underwritten by the Ford Foundation, to demonstrate on commercial television the potential of non-commercial television. Subjects ranged from origins of the Constitution, to original drama by William Inge, to the comedy of Bert Lahr.

NBC's "Wide, Wide World" also was well received by the critics. From it, ABC derived inspiration for its "Wide World of Entertainment" and "Wide World of Sports." "Wide, Wide World," with Dave Garroway, pioneered in using long-distance pickups and filmed and audio-taped inserts.

In 1954, Eric Sevareid was hosting a Sunday afternoon program on CBS television called "The American Week," which approached today's magazine format. So did "David Brinkley's Journal," an NBC program scheduled on a weekly basis from 1961 to 1963 and intermittently for several more years.

ABC-TV's early entry in the magazine field was the half-hour "Reasoner Report," which aired for three years (1973–1975) in the period that Harry Reasoner was away from CBS. The *New York Times* rated the series, produced by Ernest Leiser, "generally good, occasionally excellent."[5] Still, it succumbed to low ratings.

CBS introduced a daytime show called "Magazine," featuring subjects of special interest to women. Typical was the program of October 21, 1975, which consisted of a profile of Cornelia Wallace, wife of Governor George Wallace of Alabama; an interview with a woman propelling her 12-year-old daughter toward an acting career, and a report on genetic engineering. Producers of the monthly program were John Sharnik and Grace Diekhaus.

NBC experimented with "Now," hosted by Linda Ellerbee and Jack Perkins. What made the short-lived magazine different was its use of shorter segments, none running more than eight and a half minutes. The executive producer was Stuart Schulberg, former producer of "Today."

The First Public Magazine

Public television's first major effort in this genre came from the Public Broadcast Laboratory (PBL), founded in 1967, the year Congress passed the Public Broadcasting Act. The measure created the Corporation for Public Broadcasting (CPB) as a conduit for federal money for program production. Distribution of programs was the job of the Public Broadcasting Service (PBS).

The Public Broadcast Laboratory came into being shortly before this landmark legislation became law. With a two-year grant of $10,000,000 from the Ford Foundation, the laboratory launched a television magazine designed to show what exciting and worthwhile programs noncommercial television could provide in the area of news and public affairs. Fred Friendly, who had left CBS and was consultant to the foundation, conceived the series. Edward P. Morgan came on as senior correspondent. Av Westin was executive director.

Westin, like Friendly, came from CBS News, where he had started as a copy boy while still a student at New York University. By the time he took charge at PBL, he had won two Peabody Awards as a producer. For a short time, before tiring of administrative duties, Morgan was head of CBS News. He had worked at ABC and done news and commentary on a 15-minute radio program, which, although sponsored by the AFL-CIO, earned respect for its objectivity.

The ambitious weekly program—the first regularly scheduled public television series to be seen nationwide—bowed on Sunday night, November 5, 1967. Advertisements on the eve of the broadcast created high expectations, "PBL," they promised, "will use television as it's never been used before." Free of advertiser influence, it would venture into subjects commercial television had not dared to touch.[6]

The first broadcast, devoted to racial problems, ran two and a half hours. There were reports from Chicago, Boston, and Gary, Indiana, but the centerpiece of the program was a controversial drama, "Day of Absence," by Douglas Turner Ward. The play portrays the consternation of whites in a Southern community when black servants, on whom they have become dependent, fail to show up for work. Because of the play, done with black actors in white face, six noncommercial stations in South Carolina refused to take the program.

Reviews by newspaper critics were mixed. The *Chicago Daily News* called the show "hard-hitting, fearless, explosive."[7] The *New York Times* said the program had shown "flashes of provocative heat but far more moments of journalistic and theatrical ineptitude."[8] After six more programs, *Variety* called the disparity between promise and production "devastating." It said "Day of Absence" had been the last significant modern drama, "explosive or otherwise," it had shown.[9]

Forebodingly, *Time* called PBL's second season its last chance.[10] A two-part documentary dealing close up with birth and death gave the new season a strong start. Another program provided a thorough discussion of the power and purpose of television. The roster of participants, sounding like a who's who in broadcast news, included David Brinkley, Frank Reynolds, Walter Cronkite, Mike Wallace, John Chancellor, Shad Northshield, Reuven Frank, Elmer Lower, and Richard Salant. The moderator, lured to public television from NBC, was Robert MacNeil.

But the season's major coup came by chance. For weeks before the assassination of Martin Luther King, Jr., a PBL camera crew had followed the civil rights leader about the country, so the laboratory had footage for an obituary no station or network could equal. The Venice Film Festival voted it the best television documentary of the year.

There were other good programs, among them an impressive investigative report on the meat-packing industry and a 90-minute examination of the issues surrounding cable television. But after two years, Westin announced that he was going to ABC News, and soon afterward the ambitious experiment was called off.

Several things had gone wrong. While many public stations believed the programming was too avant-garde for their audiences, staff members argued that PBL was, after all, a laboratory and that they should be even more venturesome, an issue never resolved. And there were too many cooks. During the first season decisions were reviewed by an editorial policy board headed by Edward Barrett, former dean of the Columbia University Graduate School of Journalism. It was decided to drop the policy board, but then Westin was joined by Frederick Bohen, who as executive editor had equal say. Not only did PBL now have two heads, but Bohen, a former White House staffer, and Friendly did not get along. At the same time, struggling educational television stations resented the millions of dollars bestowed on PBL by the Ford Foundation. PBL died of dissension.

The program went off the air on May 18, 1969. In his final commentary, Edward P. Morgan said:

The question is not so much what happened to all those Sunday nights PBL was going to save but whether our two-year trial run has strengthened the case for noncommercial broadcasting. . . . We broke a lot of beakers and test tubes and stirred up some experiments smelling like Major Bowes' amateur hour. But if the elixir capable of transmuting the clinkers of TV into a golden age of inspired viewing eluded us, we discovered something else: viewers are hungry for a change.

One hears an echo in the statement by the *New York Times'* John Corry, 15 years later: "The great justification for public television, indeed the only one worth talking about, is that it can offer an alternative to the networks. It can gamble, making excellence its own reward."[11]

The Golden Hour

It was in 1968, a year after the start of PBL, that CBS aired its own magazine, "60 Minutes." Immediately, because of the timing, critics tagged the show as a copy. At CBS News, Vice President Bill Leonard called this nonsense, saying that he, Don Hewitt, and others had worked on the concept for months before PBL went on the air.[12] *Variety,* in a story headlined "PBL's Paternity Case," pointed out that there had been similar shows earlier in Great Britain and Canada.[13] Actually, says Leonard, it was the Canadian show, "This Hour Has Seven Days," that gave CBS the idea.[14]

Mary Ann Lee, critic for the *Memphis Press-Scimitar,* called the new program "the best thing to happen to CBS in a long, long time."[15] In light of what happened, this was understatement. As journalism, the program is respected; in terms of revenue, it is pure gold. Ten years after its premiere, if an advertiser wanted 30 seconds on "60 Minutes," he paid up to $100,000. By 1989 the price had doubled. CBS had the most widely viewed, most lucrative news program in history.

The program was slow catching on. Only after six years did it become what *Parade* magazine called "TV's Red Hot Hour."[16] "The lesson," says Morley Safer, one of its six correspondents, "is that a good program should have a chance. If management hadn't been patient and given us time to build an audience, it never would have happened."[17]

"60 Minutes" began as a biweekly, alternating at 10 P.M. Tuesday with "CBS Reports." The scheduling was suicidal. It was up against "Marcus Welby, M.D.," a hit show, and it almost died. At the start, the correspondents, whom Hewitt, the executive producer, prefers to call "coeditors," were Harry Reasoner and Mike Wallace. Then in December 1970, Reasoner went to ABC, and Morley Safer, CBS bureau chief in London, took his place. Safer liked working in London and joined "60 Minutes" only after it was agreed that if the program failed—a distinct possibility—he could go back to his London post. CBS, for its part, expressed confidence in Safer. "He has style and wit and courage," it said, "all commodities in generally short supply."[18]

In 1971, the program became a weekly series. It no longer appeared in prime time but was seen at 6 P.M. on Sunday, a time almost as bad because it was so often bumped by NFL football. Still, it picked up viewers.

The real gamble came in 1975, when CBS shifted "60 Minutes" to 7 P.M. Sunday, placing it head-on against prime-time entertainment on the other networks, thus flouting what the communication scholar Edwin Diamond has called broadcasting's version of Gresham's Law: "Any entertainment program, no matter how bad, will outdraw any public affairs program, no matter how good."[19] Hewitt and his staff made "60 Minutes" the exception. Gradually the audience grew until in the 1978–1979 season it became CBS' most popular program. Next season, it moved out in front of all series on television, past perennial favorites like "Dallas," "Three's Company," and "M★A★S★H." Incredibly, a news program had beaten everybody.

It was a solid achievement. In the 1982–1983 season, "60 Minutes" again won first place among all series. Since then, in the weekly ratings, it has appeared occasionally in first place, frequently in second and third place, and almost always in the Top 10. The number of coeditors also grew. Dan Rather came onto the show in 1975. Harry Reasoner, back at CBS after an eight-year absence, returned to the program in 1978. ("A Few Minutes With Andy Rooney" became a regular feature of the program the same year). Ed Bradley came on in 1981, replacing Rather, who had begun anchoring the evening news. Diane Sawyer signed on, raising the number of coeditors to five.

In 1989, when Sawyer went to ABC, two correspondents from canceled "57th Street" joined the team. It wasn't a matter of requiring two people— Meredith Vieira and Steve Kroft—to fill Sawyer's shoes. Hewitt wanted to fill the vacancy, but he also wanted to lighten the load borne so long by the other correspondents.

The producers working under Hewitt's direction in 1990 totaled 28. Credit listings show producers, past and present, to include such veterans as Al Wasserman, Igor Oganesoff, Marion Goldin, Russ Bensley, Joseph Wershba, Grace Diekhaus, William McClure, Barry Lando, Paul Loewenwarter, Harry Moses, David Lowe, Jr., Norman Gorin, John Tiffin, and Palmer Williams, senior producer until his retirement in 1984, when he was succeeded by Philip Scheffler. Williams, McClure, Wershba, and Tiffin go back to the old Murrow days and "See It Now." One of the newer producers is Suzanne St. Pierre, wife of Eric Sevareid.

Hewitt believes strongly that, for "60 Minutes," the term *producer* is wrong. He says:

> I really have 34 reporters—Mike, Morley, Harry, Ed, Meredith, and Steve, these six and the 28 people called producers. I've tried

for years to get CBS to let me change that. Darryl Zanuck and David Merrick are producers. *These* are reporters. They do what reporters do, dig out stories. They're great.

The program owes much to the personalities of the on-air correspondents.

Years ago, I said, "People tune in to see what Mike and Morley are up to tonight." I still believe that, only it's six now. They tune in for the adventures of six reporters. It was that way in the '50s with "See It Now." It really was "Let's watch Murrow."[20]

There is this feeling Hewitt has about his correspondents. You catch it in what he said when Ed Bradley joined the show; he said he was "a man on whom God in his infinite wisdom had bestowed Mike and Harry and Morley and Dan, and now Ed." He added that perhaps he also had been blessed with "enough common sense . . . to know how to deal with this precious gift."[21] What he has going for him is one of the most professional teams in television. "What we have going for *us,*" says Safer, "is Don Hewitt."[22]

When he was growing up, Hewitt's idol was not Charles Lindbergh or Lou Gehrig but Hildy Johnson, ace reporter in *The Front Page,* and, impatient for the newspaperman's life, he dropped out of New York University and took a job as copy boy on the *New York Herald Tribune.* He graduated to the Associated Press and was assigned (1943–1945) to the War Shipping Administration, which took him to war zones in Europe and the Pacific, and, after the war, to the AP bureau in Memphis. For a time, he edited a weekly paper. It was as a telephoto editor at Acme Pictures in New York City that his intuitive feeling for the dramatic news picture found expression. The next step was from telephotos, pictures sent over telephone lines, to television, pictures carried by radio waves through the air. In 1948, he found a job—and his medium—as associate director of the evening news with Douglas Edwards at CBS.

Don Hewitt may have more historic credits than anyone else in television news: producer-director of the first Monday-through-Friday evening news (1948); executive producer of network television's first half-hour evening news (1963); producer of the first presidential debate (1960); director of the first "See It Now" program (1951); producer-director of "A Conversation with President Kennedy" (1962) and "A Conversation with President Johnson (1964), both carried by ABC and NBC as well as CBS; director for CBS of more than a dozen national political conventions; executive producer of CBS' ambitious "Town Meeting of the World," a series of live transatlantic discussions with U.S. and European leaders via the Early Bird communications satellite (1965); and then "60 Minutes."

In producing "60 Minutes," Hewitt has it all: superbly skilled technicians, state of the art equipment, a multimillion-dollar budget, and correspondents who are stars. But the driving force, what makes it work, as Safer said, is Hewitt, who does it with imagination, enthusiasm, seemingly inexhaustible energy, and attention to detail. This is the man who, when television was in diapers, and there was no such thing as a TelePrompTer, let alone a VideoPrompTer, suggested to Douglas Edwards that he learn Braille so he could deliver the news without looking down at his script. Amusing, but it was this same imagination that conceived of a way to show an anchorman and a picture over his shoulder, both at the same time, who introduced double-system recording and projection. "He invented the wheel," sums up Av Westin, who when executive producer of ABC's "20/20" was Hewitt's rival at ABC.[23]

Expansion of the evening news from 15 minutes to half an hour gave Hewitt range for his imagination. In 1963, when robbers took $7,000,000 from a train in England, he used footage of the film classic *The Great Train Robbery* to complement the story, for which there was no picture. Soon after that, when a Hollywood actress died, he incorporated highlights from one of her films in the obituary, common practice today but an innovation then when so much in television was being done for the first time.

Besides letters from viewers on "60 Minutes," he wanted commentary, not just one person's viewpoint, someone alone on the screen speaking his or her mind, but a *clash* of opinion. So he engaged a conservative, James J. Kilpatrick, and a liberal, Shana Alexander, two articulate, witty people—man and woman—to attack each other's strongly held views. In time, the segment lost appeal and was replaced by Rooney's commentary of another kind, but it had a good run and illustrates a basic Hollywood tenet: "You don't have to tell them it's information. Let them think it's entertainment and then fool them."[24] Kilpatrick and Alexander provided insight on important issues; they also were a good show.

No one seeing Hewitt in action can doubt his enthusiasm. It is unquenchable and immense. He follows the creation of "60 Minutes" through every second, delighting as a child on Christmas morning in each good sound ("I've always been such a bug about sound"),[25] each quotable quote, each picture with impact. "I look at stuff like this," he said, "and I'm in awe. I sit here the way Harry Winston must have sat when he looked at a diamond."[26] Hyperbole, but true nevertheless.

When "The CBS Evening News With Walter Cronkite" moved from the Graybar Building to the production center on West Fifty-Seventh Street, Hewitt showed me about the new set—his creation. "Here's Walter's place, and here's where you will sit, right next to him. And we'll have the teletypes over there. You'll be closer to them now."

Visiting the new set, my feelings were mixed. I was accustomed to the old setup, comfortable in it. The Graybar Building was convenient to Grand Central, where I caught my commuter train—in fact, they were practically part of the terminal—and the production center was many blocks away, off toward the Hudson River piers. But by the time Hewitt was finished, all that was forgotten. This was, indeed, the most marvelous, most exciting spot on earth. This was where we would all work together, and it would be great fun.

Hewitt's enthusiasm can be manic. In February 1964, network producers met in San Francisco to make arrangements for covering the Republican national convention in July. During a briefing session, Hewitt found himself sitting next to an NBC executive who, foolishly, had laid the network's top-secret plans on the floor next to his chair. After a while, Hewitt left, and then the NBC man discovered his plans were missing. Suspecting foul play, he went to the Fairmont Hotel, where Hewitt was staying and, after some words, got the loose-leaf notebook back.

The case of the purloined papers was played up in the papers. The *Los Angeles Times* called it "gripping melodrama."[27] "A LATE LATE SHOW WHODUNIT," headlined the *New York Daily News*.[28] Twenty years later, when Hewitt was asked about snatching the NBC notebook, he said, "I did anything any red-blooded American boy would do. I picked it up and ran."[29]

"60 Minutes" is not only the most successful news program but the most controversial. It may celebrate Eubie Blake, the late great jazz artist, and tour the White House with Rosalynn Carter, but it may also do a major story on Syria, as it did in 1975, and be scorned by the American Jewish Congress because Wallace, himself a Jew, reported the lot of Jews living in Syria to be not so bad as generally believed.

The program goes for the exposure of evildoers, such as slum lords and crooked health inspectors, and the righting of wrongs. It did a damaging piece on the Pinto when Ford was one of its sponsors, exposed environmental dangers inherent in presticide production, investigated nuclear power plants, helped free an innocent man sentenced to prison for life. "60 Minutes" is television's chief practitioner, if not founder, of confrontation journalism. It plays rough. "In almost any story," Wallace says, "somebody's ox is gored."[30]

Lawsuits have resulted. Don Hewitt says there have been about 40 and that CBS did not lose one of them, although one case, for $5,000, was settled out of court.

The television critic Tom Shales once said that "60 Minutes" is basically "an adventure show about four globe-trotting guys who are all but licensed to kill (in the name of truth, justice, and the American way, of course")."[31] Most of the "killing" is done by meticulous research and by confronting the victim, on camera, with the evidence. Such confrontation worries some people; others see nothing wrong with good guys confronting bad guys—if they really *are* bad guys—with the goods. There are critics who believe attention should be given to larger subjects. David Shaw of the *Los Angeles Times* says, "Exposing a fraudulent antipoverty program is one thing; '60 Minutes' does that. Examining the root causes of poverty and exploring solutions to the problem is quite another; '60 Minutes' doesn't do that."[32] That is the province of the long-form documentary, and it was such a documentary—"Hunger in America," produced by Don Hewitt and Martin Carr—that spurred government into reforming its food stamp program.

A young reporter asked Wallace what words he would choose for his epitaph. Wallace said he had not given it much thought, but he would settle for three words: "Tough—but fair."[33] In the first chapter of *"60*

Minutes": The Power and the Politics of America's Most Popular TV News Show, Axel Madsen details an instance, if not of unfairness, then of inexcusable distortion in reporting a perceived wrong. The program can be tough, aggressively illuminating and redeeming—and mistaken. On errands of mercy it can be unmerciful.

But the program will be remembered for its good works, for solid journalistic achievement as well as for its Guinness Book ratings. Hewitt says:

> My biggest satisfaction is that we have done something they said couldn't be done—no way, they said, can you be good *and* successful. I said we're going to beat them at that, be proud and make money at the same time. And we did.

He laughs. "And there's something else. When you're making money for them, they leave you alone."[34]

Back Into the Fray

In September 1983, an article in the *Washington Journalism Review* asked in its title, "Can ABC and NBC Challenge '60 Minutes'?"[35] The peg for the article was NBC's decision to pit its low-rated magazine, "Monitor," head on against "60 Minutes" on Sunday and plans at ABC News for a new magazine show in addition to "20/20."

"Monitor" long since took the count. ABC's plans materialized with "PrimeTime Live," and NBC, undismayed, is trying once again, this time with Jane Pauley, to duplicate CBS's success. (Its last effort, "Yesterday, Today and Tomorrow," which premiered in 1989 at the same time as "PrimeTime Live," disappeared after only four outings.)

ABC's anchors are Diane Sawyer, lured from CBS by Arledge's offer of more money and opportunity, and Sam Donaldson, a combination compared jokingly by Sawyer to "fixing up Emily Dickinson on a blind date with The Exterminator."[36] Chris Wallace, having left NBC, joined as one of the program's chief correspondents. Richard Kaplan, formerly of "Nightline," is executive producer. The magic hoped for in pairing Sawyer and Donaldson has not materialized, but "PrimeTime Live" lives.

A month after ABC launched "PrimeTime Live," CBS replaced its innovative, fast-paced magazine "West 57th" with "Saturday Night With Connie Chung." The program occasionally used actors, and *Washington Post* critic Tom Shales, while praising the craftsmanship of the production and Chung's performance, wondered in his review "if this is the proper direction for a network news division to take."[37] Walter Goodman of the *New York Times* was rougher. He called such dramatic recreations "the latest, most florid outgrowth caused by the show-biz bug."[38] After less than a year, the program was dropped for a more straightforward, more personalized "One on One with Connie Chung."

Meanwhile, Back at the Beginning

No network, or station, has suffered more knockouts in the magazine field than NBC. Its frustrations began with "First Tuesday," which came on the air in January 1969, only a few weeks after the premiere of "60 Minutes." The NBC magazine ran two hours and, because it aired at 9 P.M. on the first Tuesday of the month, sometimes overlapped "60 Minutes," which was then alternating with "CBS Reports" on Tuesdays at 10. *Time* called trying to catch both shows "a channel flipper's delight."[39]

After two seasons, "First Tuesday" got a new name, "Chronolog," and a new time, Friday night. It remained a two-hour program, even though "First Tuesday" at times had seemed overlong. Friday night, moreover, was a night viewers relaxed, a bad night for informational programming, and so "Chronolog" was scrapped. "First Tuesday" was back in the 1972–1973 season, then was replaced by "Special Edition," which alternated on Tuesdays with "NBC Reports."

NBC's next effort, a major one, was "Weekend," produced by Reuven Frank, one of television's most distinguished journalists. An ex-newspaperman, he joined NBC as a writer for the old "Camel News Caravan" and gained prominence in 1962 with his award-winning documentary, "The Tunnel," which chronicled the harrowing escape of 59 men, women, and children from East Berlin. From 1968 to 1973, Frank was president of NBC News. He enjoyed production, had imagination, and was determined to have "Weekend" work.

He did so to a large degree. With Lloyd Dobyns as the anchor, the program moved at a more leisurely pace than "60 Minutes," and, in the main, the pieces were lighter. Typical was the program of August 6, 1977, which covered skateboard sailing in California; unethical practices used for gaining admission to medical schools; the unusual way in which French gourmands consume the ortolan, a migratory bird; and how the Japanese use hot baths to keep calm. Breaks before and after commercials were spiced with sayings like "Agnostic Chinese: Yee of little faith" and "Caution: I brake for fish." These sayings were not spoken; Frank wanted people to watch. In 1976, the program received the George Foster Peabody Award for its "new and refreshing approach to television programming, providing the viewer with a quality experience."

In 1974, when "Weekend" went on the air, it was seen on the first Saturday of each month. Starting at 11:30 P.M. and running to 1 A.M., it was not reaching for numbers but for a young sophisticated audience. Four years later, that changed. "Weekend" became a one-hour program and shifted to 10 P.M. Sunday. Now, for the first time, NBC had scheduled a magazine the same length as "60 Minutes" on the same day.

They were not alone. "60 Minutes" had demolished the myth that a network could not make money with news, and now ABC was in the competition with its own one-hour magazine, "20/20." No series ever had a more dismal start than ABC's entry—"memorably disastrous," one critic called it.[40] Plans for the new series had been leaking out for months. The executive producer, tapped by Arledge, would be Bob Shanks, who had been in charge of "Good Morning America" and, before that, producer of "The Merv Griffin Show." There would be two hosts, Harold Hayes, a former editor of *Esquire,* and an Australian, Robert Hughes, whom affiliate representatives had said they could not understand because of his accent but who would be hosting anyway. As for the nature of the show, the *Washington Post* published an internal ABC memorandum, which read in part:

> The tempo of "20/20" will reflect an American culture in which most people talk and act—quick, to the point, in shorthand. This is the contemporary American philosophy: jet planes, fast cars, computers, microwave cooking, instant foods, prefab houses, disposable diapers, mobile homes—and 30 years of conditioning to television. . . . yes, the public has a short attention span but can also get the message faster than we think.[41]

In the *Saturday Review,* Karl E. Meyer mused that if the items zipped by too fast, "perhaps Arledge will give us an instant replay."[42]

The première was Tuesday, June 6, 1978, a date that for ABC News has roughly the same meaning as Pearl Harbor Day for the United States. " '20/20' Gets Both Eyes Blackened," headlined *Broadcasting,* which quoted Tom Shales of the *Washington Post* as calling the show "an animated smudge on the great lens of television."[43] Most criticism centered on the program's sensationalism and pace. *Newsweek* cited Geraldo Rivera's exposé about the use of rabbits as live bait for training greyhounds and its "endless footage of drooling dogs mauling the rabbits, with the cameras zooming in for the kill."[44] The news, complained *Variety,* went by so quickly "as to create a void in the mind, and whatever point was being made was lost."[45]

The situation called for major surgery. Within a week the two hosts were gone, replaced by Hugh Downs, a veteran who had anchored the "Today" show for nine years. *Variety* commented:

> True, Hayes and Hughes were not widely experienced as on-camera hosts, and it showed. But they also indicated they could improve with time. The show's major fault was in its selection and handling of stories, areas in which Shanks himself is far more involved than either of the now-deposed hosts.[46]

Within two months, Shanks left. The correspondents, Sander Vanocur, Sylvia Chase, Dave Marash, and Rivera stayed. So did Thomas Hoving, former director of New York's Metropolitan Museum of Art, who reported periodically on the arts. With Shanks' departure, Jeff Gralnick, director of special events broadcasts, began supervising "20/20" in addition to his other duties. Av Westin, who by this time was a vice president at ABC News, took over supervision of the program in 1979 and became its executive producer in 1980.

With these changes, the show improved—it was respectable, no longer ludicrous—but for a year had no set time. Then in May 1979, it got a regular spot—Thursdays at 10—and there, in prime time, found an audience that occasionally has exceeded that of "60 Minutes." Part of this success is due to the reporting of Tom Jarriel, whom Westin brought onto the program, and celebrity interviews by Barbara Walters.

Also, "20/20" was heavily advertised. A newspaper ad for the March 31, 1983, edition illustrates a "mix" of subject matter that remains typical. It also demonstrates that advertising copy for the program leaned toward the sensational.

THE FBI STALKED JOHN LENNON
Why did they deny it?
By Geraldo Rivera

BRITAIN'S MISSION IMPOSSIBLE
What price victory in the Falklands?
By Tom Jarriel

IS THERE ANYONE FINAH?
Dinah Shore reaches for new
success—and her ideal man.
By Barbara Walters[47]

The formula works. "60 Minutes" may lead. It may be formidable. But "20/20" has stayed in the race.

The Longest Search

NBC has entered and quit the race so many times, introducing new programs and dropping them, making so many changes, that even if the right formula for a magazine show had been found, there was no chance for the show to catch on. After "First Tuesday" came "Chronolog," then "First Tuesday" again for less than a year, then "Special Edition" and "Weekend." Even after moving "Weekend" into prime time and bringing on Linda Ellerbee with her writing talent and wit to cohost with Dobyns, NBC discarded the program after only eight months.

In 1979 it offered yet another magazine, "Prime Time Sunday." The host was Tom Snyder, who had been conducting a late night talk show on NBC Television called "Tomorrow." He had been a popular and somewhat flamboyant anchor of local news in New York and Los Angeles. Success of the new program was important to him, he said, "because failure and I are strangers, and I want to keep it that way."[48]

What was new about "Prime Time Sunday" besides Snyder and its producer, Paul Friedman—and its principal correspondents, Chris Wallace, and Jack Perkins—was Snyder's live interviews and its gimmickry. Snyder could inject excitement with his questioning, but the gimmickry, part of which consisted of a disembodied woman's voice counting down to each commercial, became tiresome. John O'Connor of the *New York Times* was unimpressed. He noted that the program originated in a studio control room, which was where "See It Now" started in 1952. "So much," he said, "for innovation and suspiciously bright ideas."[49] In the Nielsen ratings, the program ran smoothly downhill. Twice in November 1979, within months of its premiere, "Prime Time Sunday" was preempted for a movie. By the new year, 1980, it was gone, replaced by "Prime Time Saturday." Snyder was still host, Friedman still executive producer, but soon it had gone as well.

NBC, undismayed, kept trying for a successful prime-time magazine, but Snyder no longer was in its plans. The new entry was "NBC Magazine With David Brinkley." A star of the first magnitude, Brinkley surrendered his commentator's role on "The NBC Nightly News" to concentrate on the program. He made the subject matter more topical. There was more attention to what was happening in Washington and fewer soft features. It was going to be a program, Brinkley said on its premiere, "for people who did not give a damn who shot J.R."[50]

Apparently many people did care. The program ran opposite top-rated "Dallas," and, despite the encouragement of critics, sank to the bottom of the ratings chart. Brinkley left the show and the network for which he had worked for 38 years for ABC in September 1981. For the rest of its short life, the program was just plain "NBC Magazine."

Brinkley and William J. Small, the president of NBC News who had been vice president of CBS News, had not got along. But it was more than that. "I'm leaving," Brinkley told *TV Guide*, "because there's nothing at NBC I really want to do."[51] The magazine program was another factor. It was not being produced to his satisfaction, he did not have as much "say" as he wanted, and he was weary of the weekly commute to New York from Washington, which was his home. Still, he found the break difficult. "I shed a few tears," he told Tom Shales. "I'm not a crybaby, but I did cry a little."[52]

The next NBC magazine was "Monitor," with Lloyd Dobyns back as the anchor, and then, when it failed, NBC introduced "First Camera," again with Dobyns. He would have a new set, less sterile-looking than the last—denlike in appearance with bookshelves and a rug. It was publicized that there would be an investigative unit and that the program's staff reporters would be joined from time to time by no less a correspondent than Marvin Kalb. But what attracted most attention was that NBC had pitted the program directly against "60 Minutes" at 7 P.M. Sunday. Not since counterprogramming Brinkley's magazine against "Dallas" had the network exhibited such daring. Or foolhardiness. "First Camera," which some called "Ninth Try,"[53] never lasted the season.

In July 1984, NBC made still another attempt with "Summer Sunday, USA." Again the show was scheduled opposite "60 Minutes," but NBC announced beforehand that the program was "unabashedly experimental" and would have only a nine-week run.[54] "Summer Sunday, USA" was marked by its live reporting, sophisticated scripting, and its hosts, Linda Ellerbee and Andrea Mitchell, who became the first women in television history to co-anchor a network news program.

Outspoken Ellerbee, whom *Time* dubbed "Queen of Tart,"[55] had come to the summer program from "NBC News Overnight," the innovative, highly acclaimed program the network introduced in July 1982 and cancelled because of low ratings in December 1983. Unforgettable for those who saw it is the feature piece "Overnight" did for Thanksgiving 1982. A man jogging through the woods is followed by his pet turkey, Wilbur, which struggles manfully, wings flapping ineffectually, to keep up. All to the accompaniment of "Chariots of Fire."

NBC has no monopoly on rating failures when it comes to magazines. Early in 1984, CBS ran afoul of ratings with a new prime-time series, "The American Parade." Everything about the series was ambitious. The set may have sported the greatest array of television monitors—almost 200—ever displayed. On camera were Charles Kuralt, Dan Rather, Bill Kurtis, Andrew Lack, and Art Buchwald. Its producers, "Shad" Northshield, Russ Bensley, and Perry Wolff, were no less distinguished. Yet the series foundered after only three months. It had been scheduled opposite NBC's popular "A-Team." That was part of the trouble. But something more basic was wrong. "Parade," *Variety* said, seemed "undecided if its purpose was to inform or entertain, to make the audience think, or just enjoy the trip."[56]

The program was completely done over and reintroduced as "Crossroads." The principal correspondents now were Kuralt and Bill Moyers. The executive producer was Andrew Lack. Gone were the monitors; back was a large old-fashioned desk. John Corry of the *New York Times* praised "Crossroads," calling it an exercise in personal journalism that should be kept on the schedule. Tom Shales of the *Washington Post* said that "Crossroads" looked a lot more like "Cross Purposes." The Moyers and Kuralt styles, to his mind, did not mix.[57]

Kuralt from North Carolina and Moyers from Texas have much in common. Both are quiet-spoken. There is a sense, in their presence, of decency. Both write extraordinarily well and are masters of the interview. Kuralt's subject is what people are up to, and Moyers' is the direction society is going. Each can carry off his own program, as Moyers has demonstrated on commercial and public television and Kuralt demonstrates each weekend with "Sunday Morning." Together on "Crossroads," however, they did not belong.

Sometimes in Moyers' commentary is a hint of sermon; he warns of consequences. But, as John Corry points out, if he "seems to believe in the wages of sin . . . he is careful enough to buttress his moral position with hard reporting."[58] Moyers, in fact, *is* a preacher. Although he showed an early interest in journalism—he was reporting part time for a paper in Marshall, Texas, at age 15—he has a Bachelor of Divinity degree from Southwestern Theological Seminary. This, after graduation from the University of Texas at Austin and postgraduate study in philosophy at the University of Edinburgh.

Few people in broadcasting have Moyers' experience. He wanted to teach, but Lyndon Johnson, then vice president, brought him to Washington as a special assistant. President Kennedy made him deputy director of the Peace Corps. After Kennedy's assassination, President Johnson appointed him press secretary. When Moyers could not conscientiously support Johnson, he became publisher of the Long Island, New York, newspaper *Newsday.* After three years, he entered broadcasting, first at public television with the series "Bill Moyers' Journal," then at CBS, where he was chief correspondent for "CBS Reports." The CBS program aired erratically. Moyers became dissatisfied and went back to public television, only to return to CBS when it offered him a regular weekly program to be called "Our Times With Bill Moyers." It would be carried, he was told, on CBS' new cable service.

CBS Cable was to have been one of Paley's dreams come true. Its programming, CBS said, would be "a celebration of the arts."[59] *Time* called the network's multimillion-dollar bet on Shakespeare and Beethoven, and other high-taste entertainment, "cable's cultural crapshoot."[60] It was a gamble CBS lost. The service had its debut in October 1981 and folded a year later. Consequently, Moyers' series ran on regular television, dealing with such subjects as defense spending and the involvement of organized crime in the disposal of toxic wastes. Corry of the *New York Times* said Moyers "is presenting some of the most substantial journalism on television."[61] "He's so damn sane and decent," said Shales of the *Washington Post,* "it's almost spooky."[62]

The People Epidemic

In 1977, CBS attempted a spin-off of "60 Minutes" with "Who's Who," which profiled celebrities like Jodie Foster and John Wayne, along with other well-known figures like Henry Kissinger. Sometimes the subject would be an unknown, such as the 19-year-old woman railroad engineer who appeared on the first show. Dan Rather was host of the short-lived series, and Charles Kuralt and Barbara Howar the profilers.

Don Hewitt thinks that for "Who's Who" to have succeeded, it would have had "to get a little bit tabloid," and CBS News shied from that.[63] Significantly, the network went outside its news division in 1978 to schedule a weekly entertainment series called "People," produced by Time-Life, publishers of *People* magazine. This television clone, hosted by Phyllis George, had an even shorter run. Lawrence Laurent, veteran critic for the *Washington Post,* said that, instead of "People," it should have been named "Piffle."[64]

NBC succeeded with "Real People." A typical program featured a woman truck driver, a small "mom and pop" television station, and a San

Francisco policeman whose specialty was finding lost pets. Some participants were bizarre, like the Wisconsin lawyer who claimed that he had once had more than 100,000 people stored in suspended animation, all of them an inch tall.

The success of "Real People" spawned similar shows, such as ABC's "That's Incredible!" and the syndicated programs "Wide World of People" and "Couples." Local stations searched their communities for people with unusual ideas or occupations. In New York, WCBS-TV's series was called "Real Life!" The first show featured a window washer at the Empire State Building who sang in a neighborhood bar. A documentary, "Third Avenue," produced for public television, consisted of vignettes of "genuine New Yorkers splendid in their variety and cheerfully willing to pronounce 'oil' as 'earl'."[65] Revived were "Ripley's Believe It Or Not" and "This Is Your Life." Television had discovered people as radio had in the 1940s, only more so. John O'Connor called the rediscovery—and, in some cases, exploitation—"a new kind of populism."[66]

Celebrities are a mainstay of "Entertainment Tonight," the prosperous nationally syndicated program offering news about show business five nights a week. More than a gossip magazine, "ET" often has covered subjects such as drug use in Hollywood and General William Westmoreland's libel suit against CBS. Launched in 1981, the half-hour program was soon being beamed by satellite to stations reaching 90 percent of the television households in the country.[67] Managing editor during its first crucial seasons was James Bellows, who had been editor of both the *Los Angeles Herald Examiner* and the *Washington Star*.

The fast-paced, slickly produced program often appears in the prime-time access period. This is the weekday half-hour—7:30 to 8 P.M.—that the FCC took from the networks and gave to local stations in 1971. The commission's purpose was to encourage local programming. For the most part, it has been a lost cause. Instead of using the time to put on locally produced programs, stations fill the half-hour with syndicated material, such as game shows, "Entertainment Tonight," and Westinghouse's "Evening" and "PM" magazines.

Whereas "Entertainment Tonight" covers breaking stories, the two Westinghouse programs are composed of features. "Evening Magazine" got its start on Westinghouse's San Francisco station, WPIX, in 1976. Within the year, the other Group W stations in Pittsburgh, Philadelphia, Baltimore, and Boston had their versions of "Evening." *Newsweek* observed, "In contrast and tone, the typical Group W edition is to '60 Minutes' what *People* magazine is to *The New Republic*."[68]

"PM Magazine," the name given the series on non-Group W stations, came two years later. These stations had their own hosts and inserted locally produced segments, giving the program a local flavor. Seventy-five stations were taking "PM" in late 1984, when its format changed with the addition of well-known entertainers—celebrities again—speaking on subjects dear to their hearts.[69] Westinghouse also syndicated "Hour Magazine," a five-day-a-week afternoon program.

CBS News produced a one-hour afternoon magazine from 1973 to 1981. It began as a series of specials but became a monthly program the title of which in January became "January Magazine" and the next month "February Magazine," and so on. Sylvia Chase conducted the program until 1977, when she went to ABC. Sharron Lovejoy succeeded her. Typical subjects were hyperactive children, women sports writers, and Caesarean births.

In 1980, RKO's television stations began carrying a monthly magazine, "What's Happening, America?" with Shana Alexander. NBC Radio had a newsmagazine, "The Women's Program," hosted by Ann Taylor. ABC Television hired Phil Donahue to be "editor" of an hour-long magazine called "The Last Word," which aired at midnight. It was short-lived. PBS, in 1977, began carrying "Over Easy," a nightly magazine series for the elderly hosted by Hugh Downs. In the same year, both ABC and CBS had magazine programs for young viewers. There were magazines, it seemed, for every age and every taste.

Despite network offerings and the growth of syndication, scores of stations, commercial and public, produce magazines that are completely their own. In Boston, for example, WCVB-TV pitted "Chronicle" head to head against "Evening" on the Group W station, WBZ-TV. KPRC-TV, Houston, was producing a weekly strip, "Eyes of Texas," as early as 1969. KCRA-TV, Sacramento, had "Weeknight." a daily magazine show, in 1973. In Pittsburgh, KDKA-TV has a two-hour public affairs program titled "Weekend." At KING-TV, Seattle, it is the public service series "This Week." WMAL-TV, Washington (now WJLA-TV), pioneered in 1976 with "7:30 Live!" In 1977, WBTV, Charlotte, switched from hard news at noon to a one-hour magazine, "Top o' the Day," with veteran broadcaster Clyde McLean. WHAS-TV, Louisville, claims a first in having "PM" come immediately after its own magazine, "Louisville Tonight."[70]

Public stations are equally magazine-minded. WNET, New York, was airing "The 51st State" in 1971, making it perhaps the first nightly newsmagazine produced by any television station in the country. Ten years later, the station attempted an ambitious two-hour program, "The Brand New Illustrated Journal of the Arts," with Robert MacNeil introducing scenes from film and stage productions and moderating discussion with people like John Updike and Gore Vidal. It was an experiment and too good to last. A sampling of other public television stations and the year the magazine premiered: "Up Close," KCPQ-TV, Tacoma (1978); "Electronicle," KTCA-TV, Minneapolis (1979); "56 Reports," WTVS, which is Channel 56, Detroit (1979); "Accent," KETC, St. Louis (1980); "New Hampshire Journal," WENH-TV, Durham (1982).

The public magazine that will be remembered, along with "PBL," is "The Great American Dream Machine," which had an exciting, uneven, and, for some, disturbing one-year run. It did everything: essays, drama, music, documentary, satire. From its huffing, puffing, clanking, laboring "dream machine" opening experienced by PBS viewers for the first time in January 1971, to its last regrettable gasp in January 1972, the one-hour program demanded attention. Even in occasional failure, as when comedian Marshall Efron got too cute, it never was boring. As Tom Shales wrote in the *Washington Post:* "Sometimes 'The Great American Dream Machine' seems all oiled up with no place to go [but] it's still probably the best show on television."[71]

"GADM," as it came to be abbreviated in print, dared to be controversial at a time when President Nixon threatened public television because of its liberal positions. At the height of agitation against the Vietnam War, it let one of the medium's best writers, Andy Rooney, a man who had seen war at first hand, go on "GADM" and deliver an essay on war, an essay in which he made statements as challenging as:

> If it is true, as we would like to think it is, that we are more civilized than formerly, we must all agree that it is very strange that in the 20th Century, our century, we have killed more than 70,000,000 of our fellow men on purpose, at war.

And as contrary as: "The Japanese did not attack Pearl Harbor with any sense in their own minds that they were scheming, deceitful or infamous."

The "Essay on War," written and produced by Rooney with archival film to match his words, was broadcast on April 14, 1971, almost half-way in the series' life. It died for want of funding eight months later.

The principal producers of "The Great American Dream Machine" were Al Perlmutter and Jack Willis.

It should be said that in talking about radio and television magazines, terminology is a problem. Series like "Nature" and "Smithsonian World" on PBS, commonly regarded as documentaries, could easily be classified as magazines. "All Things Considered" and "Morning Edition" on National Public Radio are, in a real sense, of the magazine genre. So are tabloid programs like "Hard Copy" and "A Current Affair."

Reuven Frank was about right. "You can call anything a magazine," he said. "If it ever had a meaning, it's been leached out."[72]

32
"In Greater Depth and In Broader Scope"

It was on Labor Day, 1963, that CBS inaugurated the first half-hour evening news on network television. The executive producer was Don Hewitt. Les Midgley and Sandy Socolow were producers. Fred Stollmack was the director. The managing editor and anchor was CBS News' rising star, Walter Cronkite, who had taken over the nightly 15-minute broadcast from Douglas Edwards the year before.

The program set precedent in more than length. It marked the first time an anchor had demanded, and received, the title of managing editor. It marked the first time such a network program originated, not from a studio, but from a newsroom—Hewitt's idea, and it made sense. While Cronkite was on the air, bulletins could be fed to him from wire service machines only a few feet away. For the first time, the evening news offered commentary on a regular basis. Eric Sevareid became the program's interpreter of events, and to underscore the fact that it was his interpretation, Sevareid's signature appeared on the screen as he was speaking, just as David Brinkley's signature appeared 20 years later with his commentary on ABC's "World News Tonight."

Audiotape had been a staple in radio for more than a decade; now videotape was coming into use. Film had to be developed, which took time.

Tape required no developing and sped up the reportorial process. Cronkite demonstrated this on the first half-hour broadcast with his taped same-day interview with President Kennedy at Hyannis Port, the much-quoted interview in which Kennedy said of the South Vietnamese that "in the final analysis [it is] their war. They are the ones who have to win it or lose it." [1]

The expanded broadcast not only allowed stories to run longer but made room for features such as the Kennedy interview. The significance was expressed by Frank Stanton, president of CBS, who said:

> The expansion of the evening news is not just a quantitative matter; it is qualitative as well. We live in a world where a quick scanning of the headlines is no longer adequate, a world of intricate scientific and technical advances, of sensitive and volatile political relationships, of deep and widespread social change. CBS News conceived and developed the half-hour concept in order to report this fast-moving, constantly changing world in greater depth and in broader scope. [2]

And, he might have said, in order to challenge NBC, whose evening newscast, "The Huntley-Brinkley Report," had overtaken CBS' quarter-hour in the ratings. CBS' advantage, in terms of length, was short-lived. On September 9, only a week after the CBS premiere, "Huntley-Brinkley" also went to a half-hour.

None of this happened as suddenly as it might seem. Expanded programs had been in the planning stage at both CBS and NBC for some time, a calculated response not only to competition but to editorial and technological pressures. The public appetite for news had been whetted by the civil rights marches, the Cuban missile crisis, the Soviet and American expeditions into space. The 1960s, to understate it, were not dull. The audience was there, and where the audience was, so were advertisers. Local television stations, already airing half-hour news, demonstrated that.

New technology, as well as economic feasibility, encouraged change. Cameras were smaller and more portable. Communications satellites were coming into being. So was color television. Videotape had arrived. The time was ripe to branch out and expand. Only ABC held back. Lacking the resources required, it did not expand its evening news to a half hour until 1967.

The Most Trusted Public Figure in America

Walter Cronkite anchored CBS News' showcase program from April 16, 1962, to March 6, 1981. In those 19 years he became better known than most Hollywood stars, a personage enjoying both celebrity status and trust. According to a public opinion survey conducted in 1972, he was the most trusted public figure in America. [3] Besides a zest for life—sailing, dancing, auto racing until his wife, Betsy, made him give it up—he had a respect for news that showed on camera. Viewers sensed the seasoning that came from experience. There was authority in what he said.

Following Germany's surrender, Cronkite reestablished the United Press bureaus in Belgium, Luxembourg, and the Netherlands. He covered the trial of top Nazis in Nuremberg and served for two years as United Press bureau chief in Moscow. In 1950, he was covering Washington for a group of Midwestern radio stations, and it was only then, six years after Murrow tried to recruit him in London, that Cronkite went to work for CBS.

CBS hired Cronkite to cover the Korean War. While arrangements were being made to ship him overseas, he filled in as anchorman at a Washington station, WTOP-TV, now WUSA-TV. The money was in radio then, not television, but as the newest man on staff he had to take what no one else wanted. He became a hit on local television. So instead of going to Korea and covering a new war, the ex-war correspondent reported it at a distance, pointing out what was happening on maps. His new career as anchorman had begun.

Cronkite's "And that's the way it is" became as familiar a sign-off as Lowell Thomas' "So long until tomorrow" and Ed Murrow's "Goodnight and good luck." No broadcaster received more awards, including doctorates from more than a dozen colleges and universities. In 1970, on the occasion of its 50th anniversary, the American Civil Liberties Union saluted him for distinguished service in defense of the First Amendment. In January 1981, shortly before he retired as anchorman and signed a long-term contract as special correspondent, Cronkite received the Medal of Freedom, the nation's highest civilian award.

A New Team

Cronkite's successor on the evening news was Dan Rather, son of a Wharton, Texas, pipeline worker and his waitress wife, strong characters to whom he dedicated his autobiography, *The Camera Never Blinks*. His dream of becoming a reporter, he says, came from two sources: his father, who was always reading newspapers and getting upset at what they said, and another strong character, Hugh Cunningham, whose journalism classes Rather attended at Sam Houston State.

"[He] kept preaching experience to us, that you learn to write by writing. . . . I would compose stories and mail them to the *Houston Post*."[4] These were mostly feature stories about someone on campus, like a football player or teacher. He was thrilled when one was published. Cunningham also preached integrity. "Each semester when we returned to school he required us, in class, to repeat aloud the journalist's creed: 'A public journal is a public trust.' "[5]

Rather worked his way through college as campus correspondent for the *Huntsville Item* and general utility man at Huntsville's 250-watt radio station, KSAM. Toward the end he earned money doing sports publicity for the college. For a year after graduating he taught journalism at Sam

Houston, then moved in quick succession to KTRH-AM, Houston, and the *Houston Chronicle*. He became news director at KTRH in 1956 and a reporter for KTRK-TV, Houston, in 1959. Early on, he served six months in the Marines.

The break—the story that made CBS News take notice of Rather—came in September 1961 when he was news director and anchorman at KHOU-TV, the CBS affiliate in Houston. Hurricane Carla was building up in the Caribbean. Rather hustled a mobile unit to Galveston, where the U.S. Weather Service had the most up-to-date radar. On the radarscope he showed viewers the frightening live image of the approaching storm. It may have been a "first" for television, and partly because of the dramatic picture, Galveston was evacuated. Port O'Connor, near Galveston, took the brunt of the storm, but Louisiana and Mississippi also suffered. Forty people died.

Rather and his crew covered Carla nonstop for 72 hours; an amphibious vehicle had to bring them out. For their reporting, Rather and his station won the Headliner and Sigma Delta Chi awards for public service. And CBS, hiring Rather in 1962, put him in charge of its Dallas bureau. That is how he happened to be on the scene when President Kennedy was assassinated, a story he covered so impressively he was made White House correspondent.

On March 9, 1981, when he took Cronkite's place on the evening news —demanding, and getting, Cronkite's title of managing editor—Rather had served as White House correspondent in the Nixon as well as Johnson administrations, anchorman for "CBS Reports," co-editor of "60 Minutes," London bureau chief, and correspondent in Vietnam. He had proved himself. Still, selection of Cronkite's replacement had been difficult.

The difficulty arose because Rather had a competitor for the position in CBS' ace congressional correspondent, Roger Mudd. Mudd had been with CBS slightly longer than Rather and had sat in for Cronkite frequently, and successfully, when the anchorman was away. Because he had been Cronkite's substitute so often—more often than anyone else—Mudd assumed he was heir apparent. Rather, taking nothing for granted, fought for the assignment. When it appeared he might not get in, he exerted pressure by talking to ABC, which hoped he would come over and anchor its evening news. Roone Arledge, president of ABC News, told him he could even have a voice in running the news division.[6] In what *Newsweek* called "the hottest bidding war in the history of broadcast journalism,"[7] NBC dangled a multimillion-dollar contract and, ultimately, the anchoring of "Nightly News."

None of this was to be. Because CBS meant to hold onto Rather, it gave him what he wanted—Cronkite's seat and more than a million dollars a year.[8] Mudd, chagrined, went to NBC as chief Washington correspondent with assurances that when John Chancellor stepped down as "Nightly News" anchor, he would take Chancellor's place.

Seldom, if ever, has a newscaster taken on a more challenging assignment than did Rather in succeeding Cronkite, one of America's most esteemed, most affectionately regarded figures. Comparisons in performance were inevitable. Would the viewers devoted to Cronkite still watch? Rather knew that critics, poniards ready, would pounce on every real or imagined mistake. Would he meet the test?

The ratings did slump. Badly. In the first week of November 1981, the newscast that had outdistanced the ABC and NBC programs in the ratings since 1968, actually came in last. Sandy Socolow, who had worked closely with Cronkite on the program longer than anyone else, was replaced by Howard Stringer. The set was repainted in a new beige color deemed more becoming to Rather. In billboarding upcoming stories, music with a hyped drum beat was added. Bill Moyers was brought in to do commentary. Rather, who had been dressing formally, began wearing sweaters. The ratings turned around. The program went on top and held.

"Goodnight, David. Goodnight, Chet."

The most successful anchor team in the whole history of broadcast news came about by accident. CBS had tapped Walter Cronkite to anchor the 1956 political conventions. NBC had no Cronkite, so it took a chance on pairing Chet Huntley and David Brinkley to anchor its coverage. Brinkley's wit and no-nonsense perceptions and Huntley's contrasting solid, almost sombre reporting made just the right mix. It was sirloin and spice, something so novel and refreshing, as well as informative, that critics gave NBC's coverage rave reviews. CBS tried to recoup at the Democratic convention by pairing Murrow and Cronkite, a disastrous decision since neither correspondent felt comfortable with the other, and it showed.

NBC, heady with its discovery of a winning combination, chose Huntley and Brinkley to take John Cameron Swayze's place on the evening news. "The Huntley-Brinkley Report" debuted only two months after the conventions and had a 14-year run.

The format, at the beginning, remained unchanged. It was still a 15-minute broadcast with every second precious. But the question arose how to end the program. Who would have the last word—Huntley or Brinkley? It had to end somehow, and in such a way that neither seemed to have a more important role. The solution came finally from the program's producer, Reuven Frank. He recalls, "I wrote down 'Goodnight, David; Goodnight, Chet', and they both hated it. I told them that it timed out to one and a half seconds, and if they could do it any better, go ahead."[9] They couldn't, and so the famous sign-off was born.

Neither Brinkley nor Huntley was Eastern Establishment, no matter what Spiro Agnew might say. Brinkley started as a reporter in his home town of Wilmington, North Carolina, working at the local paper while in high school. In 1943, after a stint with the United Press, he joined NBC as a $60-a-week radio news writer in Washington. He broke into television in Washington in the old NBC studios above the Trans Lux theater at Fourteenth Street and New York Avenue, narrating a five-minute television newsreel. He says:

> I remember taking satisfaction getting on the air with a piece of film the same day it was shot, knowing the newsreel company wouldn't get to use it for another week. . . . So there we were, working upstairs over the theater where the newsreels were being shown, a new force that would put the operator of the theater out of business.[10]

Later, he covered Washington for Swayze's "Camel News Caravan." The pieces were marked by good writing and irreverence. When Congress was debating whether Boulder Dam should be named Hoover Dam, he suggested that Herbert Hoover, who was still living, might change his name to Boulder, eliminating the problem. At the same time, covering hard news, he demonstrated that he was hard-nosed. He could, as his friend Art Buchwald said, "cut through all the junk and see things as they are."[11] These talents led to his selection as co-anchor at the 1956 conventions, which was his biggest break.

Chet Huntley was a westerner who, with his 6-foot, 1-inch height and craggy features, could have been the Marlboro Man. He was born in 1911 on a small ranch in what had been Sioux country in northern Montana. His first announcing experience came after his father gave up the ranch to work as a telegrapher for the Northern Pacific Railroad. "Dad would write down the play-by-play reports as they came over the wire. A cluster of people would gather in the waiting room of the station, and I would bellow through the ticket window the play-by-play action of the game."[12]

The real announcing began in 1934 when, during senior year at the University of Washington, Huntley worked as writer, disk jockey, time salesman, and janitor at KPCB-AM in Seattle. The pay was $10 a month, plus free meals in return for on-the-air plugs. He moved on quickly to larger stations in Spokane and Portland, then in 1937 to Los Angeles.

Huntley became known in Los Angeles for his outspokenness on controversial issues. He attacked discrimination against Mexican Americans and racism in South Africa, and instigated the case against George A. Richards, who owned a chain of radio stations, including KMPC in Los Angeles. The stations had standing orders to slant the news, not only against the New Deal, but also against President Roosevelt personally. When Mrs. Roosevelt was in an auto accident, he ordered KMPC to make it seem as if she had been drinking. On behalf of the Radio News Club of Southern California, of which he was president, Huntley sent affidavits to the FCC documenting Richards' policies. Hearings were being held when Richards died. Assured that his practices would be discontinued, the commission closed the case. Huntley drew right-wing fire for his broadcast criticism of the tactics of Senator Joseph McCarthy, and when a listener called him a Communist, he sued and won a $10,000 judgment. He also won the admiration, and friendship, of Edward R. Murrow.

During his years in Los Angeles, Huntley worked for the outlets of all

The first broadcast of presidential election returns on a commercial radio station occurred November 2, 1920, on KDKA, Pittsburgh. For more than four hours, Leo Rosenberg, seated at the box mike, read bulletins provided by the *Pittsburgh Post*.

Credit: Courtesy of KDKA

Don Hewitt, who later would create "60 Minutes," produced and directed broadcasting's first presidential debate. Nixon rejected Hewitt's offer of makeup.

Credit: Courtesy of Don Hewitt

Floyd Gibbons, broadcasting in 1930, became the first newscaster to be heard nightly nationwide. In World War I, a machine gun bullet tore out his left eye.

Credit: NBC Photo/Courtesy of Broadcast Pioneers Library

Lowell Thomas, author, explorer, lecturer, came on CBS with his greeting "Good evening, everybody!" in 1930, shifted to NBC, then returned to CBS in 1947. He was one of the nation's most popular newscasters for forty-six years.

Credit: NBC Photo/National Archives

Gabriel Heatter liked to start his newscasts by saying, "Ah, there's good news tonight." During World War II and the postwar years, he attracted an audience of more than 11 million listeners.

Credit: MBS Photo/David Dary Collection

An ex-vaudevillian, Walter Winchell with his hyped style—"Flash! Lucille Ball and Desi Arnaz are expecting a bundle from heaven!"—made it big on radio in the 1930s and 1940s.

Credit: ABC Photo/Bliss Collection

Helen Sioussat of CBS, first woman to head a network news operation, directs former Republican presidential nominee Wendell Willkie, who used radio to promote his "One World" concept.

Credit: Courtesy of Helen Sioussat

The late Pauline Frederick was the first woman to make network reporting her career. She started at ABC, then served as correspondent for NBC for twenty-two years.

Credit: ABC Photo/American University Archives

Mary Marvin Breckinridge broadcasts for CBS from Hilversum, The Netherlands, shortly before German invasion of The Lowlands in May 1940. She was the first woman to serve the network as a full-time correspondent.

Credit: Courtesy of Mary Marvin Breckinridge

CBS covers the Munich crisis, September 1938. H. V. Kaltenborn is at the microphone. The others (left to right) are: Robert Trout at the typewriter, announcer John Reed King, Paul W. White, news chief, and John D. Fitzgerald, assistant director of special events.

Credit: Courtesy of Broadcast Pioneers Library

Hitler invades Poland. Robert Trout awaits go-ahead cue from Paul White, who is in his office with A. H. Petersen, assistant traffic manager. Elmer Davis stands by. Busy in the CBS newsroom (left to right) are: Robert Gibson, desk assistant (seated); John D. Fitzgerald, assistant director of special events; Lawrence Elliott, announcer; Matthew Gordon, assistant news editor (seated), and Paul Glynn, writer.

Credit: CBS Photo/David Dary Collection

Deep underground, behind gas-proof steel doors, Ed Murrow composes a Battle of Britain report as censors wait. Note two-finger approach.

Credit: CBS Photo/Bliss Collection

Eric Sevareid of CBS (center) and
Edward P. Morgan of *Chicago Daily
News* (right) receive briefing from
General Darrel Daniels, U.S. 3d In-
fantry commander, shortly before
Allied forces enter Rome in 1944.
Morgan later worked at CBS and
ABC.

Credit: Courtesy of Eric Sevareid

During World War II, Combat Correspondent George Fuller, U.S. Ninth Army, conducted more than
500 interviews with GI's for stations back home. He also produced segments for NBC's "Army Hour."
Here, using a wire recorder, he is interviewing an artillery officer near Düsseldorf. Before the war, Fuller
was a newscaster at WFBR, Baltimore.

Credit: Courtesy of Mrs. George Fuller

As a correspondent for WHO-AM, Des Moines, during World War II, Jack Shelley, professor emeritus Iowa State University, became one of the few reporters for a local station to cover action in both the European and Pacific theaters. Here he is interviewing two members of an Army Air Force crew at the time that B-29s were conducting their climactic saturation raids on Japan.

Credit: Courtesy of Jack Shelley

With help from the U.S. Army Signal Corps, William J. Dunn managed in December 1943 to report direct from the New Guinea jungle to CBS New York. Dunn was the only network correspondent to cover the Pacific war from Pearl Harbor Day to the Japanese surrender.

Credit: Courtesy of William J. Dunn

Douglas Edwards anchored CBS-TV's evening news each weekday from 1948 to 1962. This photograph was taken in 1948. Edwards was 15 when he began working part time as an announcer at a 100-watt radio station in Troy, Alabama. Note that anchor desks in the early days were desks.

Credit: Courtesy of CBS

John Cameron Swayze's assignment as anchor for NBC-TV's evening news ran eight years, starting in 1948. The program, sponsored by Camel cigarettes, was called "The Camel News Caravan." The NBC and CBS newscasts were both 15 minutes in length. Not until 1963 did they expand to 30 minutes.

Credit: NBC Photo/David Dary Collection

Co-anchors Chet Huntley and David Brinkley led NBC to ratings supremacy during the national political conventions of 1956, 1960, and 1964. This shows them at the Democratic convention in Los Angeles in 1960.

Credit: Courtesy of NBC

In 1964, "The CBS Evening News with Walter Cronkite" had not yet overtaken Huntley–Brinkley in the ratings. Here, working against deadline (left to right), are: Mervin Block, writer; unidentified person looking over Block's shoulder; Cronkite; Bliss, news editor; Jim Clevenger, associate director, and Sand Socolow, co-producer. Two staffers with backs to camera are unidentified.

Credit: Courtesy of Mervin Block

A distinguished CBS series in the 1950s was "Years of Crisis." Each December, network correspondents from around the world assembled in New York to discuss the year's major events. Here, assembled for rehearsal, is most of the reporting team that gave CBS News its second-to-none reputation at that time. The correspondents (left to right) are Charles Collingwood and Ned Calmer, New York; Winston Burdett, Rome; Eric Sevareid, Washington; Bill Costello, Tokyo; Larry LeSueur, New York; David Schoenbrun, Paris; Howard K. Smith, London; and Richard C. Hottelet, Bonn. Ed Murrow, moderator, is at extreme right.

Credit: CBS Photo/Bliss Collection

In Korea, television had its tryout for covering war. By going there three times, the "See It Now" team tried out more than any other. Here in December 1952 is Murrow (front center) with the crew that would shoot film and record sound. They are (left to right, back row): Charles Mack, John Bockhorst, Leo Rossi, Marty Barnett, Norman Alley, and (front row) Andrew Willoner, Robert Huttenloch, Chick Peden, Donald Geis, and Herb Tice.

Credit: CBS Photo/Wershba Productions

A television original was "Today," which premiered January 14, 1952, on NBC. Dave Garroway, its first host, gives the news as sportscaster Jack Lescoulie (seated) awaits his turn.

Credit: NBC Photo/David Dary Collection

George Herman, CBS, broadcasts from "studio" he and Army technicians jerry-built in the correspondents' billet in Seoul during the Korean War. The walls were soundproofed with seaweed.

Credit: Courtesy of George Herman

Edward R. Murrow and Fred W. Friendly editing CBS Radio's "Hear It Now," which pioneered with audiotape in covering the Korean War. It was the two journalists' first collaboration in a broadcast series. "See It Now" was next.

Credit: CBS Photo/Bliss Collection

Not until 1962 did any network have a black correspondent. The breakthrough came when Jim Hagerty, head of ABC News, hired Mal Goode, a reporter for the *Pittsburgh Courier*.

Credit: Courtesy of RTNDA

During his presidency of CBS (1946–1972), Frank Stanton often served as broadcasting's spokesman before the FCC and Congress, defending the industry's First Amendment rights. Here he is testifying before the Senate Commerce Committee.

Credit: UPI Photo/Courtesy of Frank Stanton

In 1980, when this photograph was taken, Walter Cronkite, "the most trusted man in America," was also the network anchor with the largest audience.

Credit: CBS Photo/Bliss Collection

By 1990 only John Chancellor of NBC was still doing commentary on the traditional evening news.

Credit: Courtesy of NBC

When Ted Turner decided that CNN should have broadcasting's biggest, highest-budgeted investigative reporting unit, he put Pamela Hill, former ABC News vice president, in charge. The unit's first reports appeared in March 1990.

Credit: ABC Photo/Bliss Collection

Zona B. Davis, one of the first women news directors in the country, ran the newsroom at WCRA-AM in Effingham, Illinois, for twenty-nine years. When this picture was taken in 1950, she had been on the air only a few months.

Credit: Courtesy of Plaford Davis

Max Robinson was the first black anchor reporting nightly in network news. The breakthrough came at ABC in 1978.

Credit: Courtesy of Jim Snyder

After thirteen years as co-host of "Today," Jane Pauley in March 1990 began anchoring primetime specials. She also drew favorable reviews as a substitute for Tom Brokaw on the nightly news. Ahead lay a central role in still another NBC effort at magazine programming.

Credit: NBC Photo/Courtesy of Jane Pauley

ABC's "Nightline" with Ted Koppel as permanent anchor premiered
on March 24, 1980. The broadcast marked the 142d day that 63
Americans were held hostage in Iran.

Credit: Courtesy of ABC

In 1983, Fred W. Friendly created a PBS series titled "The Constitution: That Delicate Balance," in which
lawyers, journalists, politicians, and jurists argued crucial constitutional issues. Pictured is a seminar on national
security and freedom of the press that was moderated by Columbia University law professor Benno C. Schmidt,
Jr., now president of Yale.

Credit: Lynn Cates/Courtesy of Fred W. Friendly

Roone Arledge became president of ABC News in 1977. With record budgetary resources, talent raids, and innovative programming he led the news division to parity with its competitors.

Credit: Courtesy of ABC

Elmer Lower upgraded ABC News during his presidency, 1963–1974. Upon retirement, he went into teaching.

Credit: Courtesy of RTNDA

Richard S. Salant ran CBS News eminently for sixteen years, longer than the head of news operations at any other network.

Credit: Courtesy of C

Ted Turner envisioned a cable network devoted solely to news, dared bet everything he had on it, and won. That network, CNN, has grown to become one of the world's major sources of news.

Credit: Courtesy of CNN

William McAndrew directed the course of NBC News from 1951 until his death in 1968. He was a capable, respected, and, for many who worked with him, revered administrator.

Credit: Courtesy of William McAndrew, Jr.

In his long career at CBS News, the late Burton Benjamin may have produced more documentary programs than anyone else in television history. In 1982, he wrote the critical "Benjamin Report" examining CBS' controversial documentary on General William Westmoreland and the Vietnam War.

Credit: Courtesy of C

Early co-hosts of the widely acclaimed National Public Radio program "All Things Considered" were Susan Stamberg and Bob Edwards. Today, Stamberg is special correspondent. Edwards has hosted NPR's "Morning Edition" since 1979.

Credit: Dennis Brack/Black Star

The only network magazine approaching the success of "60 Minutes" on CBS has been ABC's "20/20" hosted by Barbara Walters and Hugh Downs. Both were at one time hosts on "Today."

Credit: Courtesy of ABC

In 1985, Shiite extremists hijacked TWA Flight 847 flying from Athens to Rome. One American passenger was killed. In the finale played out at Beirut Airport, ABC photographer Steve Cocklin got this picture as correspondent Charles Glass interviewed the threatened pilot. Later, Glass himself was held hostage but escaped.

Credit: Courtesy of ABC

There was a moment in 1969 when for everyone listening to radio or watching television time stood still. It was the moment *Apollo 11*'s lunar module, ending the long voyage from Earth, touched down on the surface of the moon. Even Walter Cronkite, for those few seconds, was speechless.

Credit: Courtesy of CBS

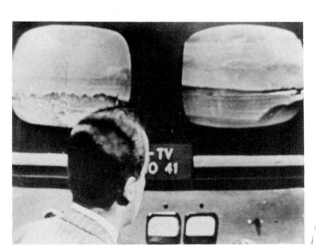

The Atlantic and Pacific oceans appear together, live, on television. Murrow and Friendly used the premiere of "See It Now" on November 18, 1951, to demonstrate the reach of journalism's new revolutionary tool.

Credit: CBS Photo/Courtesy of Fred W. Friendly

A CBS report from Vietnam that affected viewers profoundly was Morley Safer's account of how American forces set fire to peasants' homes in the village of Cam Ne.

Credit: Courtesy of CBS

"The MacNeil/Lehrer NewsHour," with Robert MacNeil and Jim Lehrer, has the distinction of being the first one-hour newscast aired nightly on national television. The program premiered on PBS in 1983.

Credit: Courtesy of MacNeil/Lehrer Productions

Don Hewitt, executive producer of "60 Minutes," broadcasting's most successful program, checks script with Correspondent Morley Safer. "We don't write memos to each other," says Hewitt. "We talk."

Credit: Courtesy of Don Hewitt

One of journalism's unforgettable pictures appeared on television in June 1989, when a Chinese student stood alone before an advancing column of tanks.

Credit: Courtesy of CNN

CNN's Bernard Shaw prepares to go on the air from Tiananmen Square during the pro-democracy demonstrations of 1989.

Credit: Courtesy of CNN

Tom Brokaw has anchored NBC's "Nightly News" since 1982. Before that, he was White House correspondent and host of "Today." When first offered the lucrative "Today" spot, he refused because he would have to read commercials. Two years later, he got to host the show on his own terms.

Credit: NBC Photo by Al Levine

"ABC World News Tonight With Peter Jennings" in 1990 established itself as network television's most popular evening newscast.

Credit: Courtesy of ABC

John Hart, veteran of CBS and NBC, received high marks as anchor for "World Monitor," the *Christian Science Monitor* program seen weeknights on the Discovery Channel.

Credit: Courtesy of John Hart

For CBS News, Dan Rather has been White House correspondent, war correspondent, bureau chief, and anchorman. Rather came to CBS in 1962 from KTRK-TV, Houston. He has anchored the evening news since 1981.

Credit: Courtesy of CBS

ABC News Correspondent Jackie Judd reported the Tiananmen Square massacre and the revolution in Czechoslovakia. From Prague's Wenceslaus Square (above) she filed a report on the secret police that won her an Overseas Press Club citation.

Credit: Courtesy of ABC

Gillett Communications had a reporter-photographer team in Panama soon after the U.S. invasion of December 1989. It was sent to cover a visiting congressional delegation and, at the same time, interview servicemen from markets served by Gillett. Here Gary Nurenberg interviews an M.P., Bart Hayes, of Rochester, New York, for WOKR-TV. The photographer is Gary Westphalen.

Credit: Kenneth Pagel/Courtesy of Gillett Communications

three major networks. NBC brought him to New York in 1955. Then came the 1956 presidential campaign and birth of "The Huntley-Brinkley Report."

When, in 1963, "Huntley-Brinkley" went from 15 minutes to a half hour, following CBS' example, no one was surprised. Competition required it. The surprise was how quickly it was done. A major television program—NBC's journalistic showpiece—had been revamped, it seemed, in seven days. Reuven Frank of NBC tells how it came about:

> The change was not made on short notice, at least in the terms of those days. It had been suggested for some time, but affiliates balked. When the CBS announcement was made, Bob Kintner [president of NBC] used that to force the change through. . . . I [had] spent the summer planning, doing a little hiring, and writing a long memo about what kind of program we expected to have. . . . Every weekend in August we prepared a half-hour program . . . and I commuted between Washington and New York on Friday, Saturday, and Sunday as we tried it out. We established the program's own offices in London and Tokyo, redesigned the look, and physically moved within 30 Rock to larger quarters, never a small matter. This was in sharp contrast to the very beginning of Huntley-Brinkley, where Swayze did his report on Friday and we began ours on Monday with only one dry run on Sunday afternoon.[13]

The pairing of Huntley and Brinkley was one of the most propitious in television history; even their names sounded good together, the syllables matching so well they might have been made up. The only rupture, a temporary one, came on March 29, 1967, when Brinkley refused to work because the American Federation of Television and Radio Artists (AFTRA) was on strike. Huntley, holding that journalists had no business in an artists' union, anchored alone for nine days. All he said was: "David Brinkley is off tonight."[14]

The team broke up in 1970 when Huntley retired. He wanted to develop a recreational area in Montana and died of cancer four years later even as he prepared to dedicate the 25-million-dollar resort, which he called Big Sky.

The night Huntley died, Walter Cronkite saluted his longtime rival on the air and played a tape of the end of the last Huntley-Brinkley program, including the final "Goodnights." A *New York Times* editorial said: "For nearly fifteen years Chet Huntley delivered the news professionally. . . . The Huntley-Brinkley Report . . . was a turning point toward maturity and sophistication in television news."[15]

"Lights and Wires in a Box"

It also was the first big money-maker in broadcast news, and with it broadcast news lost its innocence. In the last year before Huntley's retirement the program, ringing up 34 million dollars, constituted NBC's single biggest source of revenue. It had, in its time, attracted more viewers than any other newscast. Only after four years of slow, steady gains in the half-hour format did CBS' evening news catch up.

With the greening of these two programs, and the expansion of news programming at hundreds of local stations—all profiting from the hunger to know what was happening in a turbulent time—the treatment of news changed. Increasingly, news was packaged to attract larger and larger audiences. Consultants advised broadcasters on giving the public what it wanted, rather than what it needed. More emphasis was placed on pictures —the visuals—and on pace. "Talking heads" were discouraged. And although many broadcasters still acted responsibly, many did not. News had become golden. It was difficult, having a profit center, not to make profit the name of the game.

The trend distressed Ed Murrow as early as 1958, when he told a meeting of news directors, "I am frightened by the imbalance, the constant striving to reach the largest possible audience for everything, by the absence of a sustained study of the state of the nation." It was in this speech that he said television "can teach. It can illuminate. Yes, and it can even inspire. But it can do so only to the extent that humans use it to those ends. Otherwise it is merely wires and lights in a box."[16] The warning is perhaps better known than anything else Murrow ever said.

Hard Act to Follow

When Chet Huntley retired, two New York-based correspondents, John Chancellor and Frank McGee, took his place. Brinkley stayed as anchor in Washington, marking the first time a network news program had three anchors. It proved a clumsy arrangement. Chancellor soon became sole anchor and Brinkley a regularly scheduled commentator on the program. Five years later, Brinkley rejoined Chancellor as co-anchor, but Chancellor was alone again after the 1976 elections. Brinkley was busy with "The NBC Magazine with David Brinkley."

The shuffling continued in 1982. Brinkley had left NBC, after 38 years, for ABC due to restlessness and his bad relationship with NBC News president Bill Small. For the evening news, NBC revived the two-anchor format, this time with Tom Brokaw in New York and Roger Mudd in Washington. Chancellor took over the commentator's role.

NBC hoped Brokaw and Mudd could be another Huntley-Brinkley. After a year, it decided they could not. For the first time, the program trailed its competition on both CBS and ABC, and, in a surprise move, Mudd was dropped. The decision seemed strange in that Mudd had declined to enforce an option in his contract that would have made him sole anchor. Recalling how CBS had chosen Dan Rather over Mudd to succeed Cronkite, *Broadcasting* noted, "For the second time in his illustrious career as a broadcast journalist, Roger Mudd has been painfully rejected by the network for which he worked so tirelessly."[17]

Reuven Frank, then president of NBC News, said the change was no reflection on Mudd, that there was no question of his capability, and that, as senior political correspondent, Mudd would host an expanded "NBC White Paper" series. Mudd, blaming enslavement to ratings, expressed distress at what he saw as a de-emphasizing of Washington news.[18] There was speculation he might go to ABC. He stayed for the time being, however, and, after covering the 1984 presidential election, hosted NBC's new magazine venture, "American Almanac."

"The NBC Nightly News," with Brokaw as solo anchor, attracted enough viewers not only to hold onto second place, ahead of ABC's evening news, but to threaten CBS's news with Dan Rather. In recognition of Brokaw's success, NBC in 1985 renamed its program "The NBC Nightly News With Tom Brokaw."[19]

Poor Kid on the Block

Since ABC, which had been NBC's Blue Network, did not come into existence until 1943, and was poor, it had to play catch-up. The merger with United Paramount Theaters helped, but it was still a pauper network. Inevitably this affected its news coverage.

A major force was Robert Kintner. He became president of the distressed network in 1950, three years before the merger. He was a champion of news, and he was one of broadcasting's giants, a tough, gruff, seemingly indefatigable executive who, through rare insight, could peak both ratings and prestige.

Kintner began his career as financial writer and Washington correspondent for the *New York Herald Tribune*. Other correspondents found him formidable. "He drove you silly with scoops," recalled Joseph Alsop, who, tiring of the competition, made Kintner a partner in writing his syndicated newspaper column "Capitol Parade."[20] During World War II, Kintner served in Army Intelligence, advancing from captain to lieutenant colonel. On discharge, he joined ABC as a publicist. He was executive vice president by 1946 and president four years later.

Kintner tackled ABC's ratings problem with programs like Walt Disney's "Davy Crockett" and "Warner Brothers Presents" and beefed up the almost nonexistent news department with recognized journalists like Elmer Davis and John Daly. In 1953, he made Daly vice president in charge not only of news but also of religious programming and sports. Daly was a busy man. Five nights a week he anchored "John Daly With the World News," a program he had done since leaving CBS in 1949. With this evening broadcast he was pitted against John Cameron Swayze on NBC and Douglas Edwards on CBS. He anchored convention coverage and news specials. At the same time, he hosted the popular quiz show "What's My Line?" on CBS.

The seven years Kintner was president of ABC (before leaving for NBC) were marked by his daring. In the early 1980s, the networks talked of expanding their half-hour evening news to an hour. Affiliates opposed the move because the additional half-hour would bump their syndicated shows. Station owners argued that if the networks really wanted an extra half hour, let them put the program in their own prime time. Largely forgotten was the fact that, three decades earlier, Kintner had experimented with such a one-hour program. News is less expensive to produce than entertainment, and his was a desperate low-budget effort to compete with the rival networks, which had hits like "I Love Lucy" and "Robert Montgomery Presents." The program was born, and died, in one year, 1952. Its reporters were Pauline Frederick, Gordon Fraser, Leo Cherne, and Bryson Rash.[21]

Kintner's coup at ABC was his decision to carry the full Army–McCarthy hearings, while CBS and NBC carried only excerpts.[22] The hearings ran intermittently for two months. Fascinated by the real life drama, as many as twenty million viewers tuned in to the third-place network at a time.[23] Advertisers became interested. It was demonstrated that good journalism is good promotion, that good journalism sells.

In 1956, Kintner got into a policy row with the controlling Paramount group within ABC and was forced to resign. With offers from both NBC and CBS, he chose NBC, where he went from coordinating NBC's color television activities, to executive vice president in charge of NBC Television, to president of NBC, and finally, and briefly, to chairman of the board. He retired in ill health in 1966—drinking was a problem—and died in 1980.[24]

Colleagues in journalism had a friend in Bob Kintner. Daly and William R. McAndrew, head of news at NBC, encountering problems, knew they could count on the understanding of their newsman-president. Kintner established ABC News and, with McAndrew, made NBC the news leader in his time. It was Kintner who saw the potential in an anchor team made up of Huntley and Brinkley. It was Kintner, with his attention to detail, who checked on whether NBC News had a camera ready to cover the transfer of Lee Harvey Oswald from the Dallas jail, so that NBC alone had live coverage of Jack Ruby shooting President Kennedy's assassin. And it was Kintner, with his fierce competitive spirit, who ordered that on any good story NBC stay on it 30 minutes longer than CBS, no matter what.

Kintner benefited from the strength of his head of news, Bill McAndrew. The documentarian Fred Freed said of McAndrew, "When he believed in something, he fought for it. He fought quietly, not in a flashy way. He understood how things work."[25] Julian Goodman, when he was board chairman of NBC, said that he considered himself fortunate, back when he was an NBC newsman, to have known and worked with Bill McAndrew, "who gave himself unselfishly to increasing the capabilities of electronic journalism and tutoring me, and Bob Kintner, who provided the drive and determination to have NBC succeed and excel in news performance."[26]

It was not long after Kintner left ABC that John Daly, missing Kintner's commitment, also left. He continued to host "What's My Line?" on CBS until 1967, when President Johnson appointed him director of the Voice of America.

New Day at ABC News

James C. Hagerty came to ABC as vice president in charge of news, succeeding Daly, in 1961. Hagerty was an ex-newspaperman steeped in politics. A former political reporter for the *New York Times*, he had served as press secretary to Governor Thomas E. Dewey of New York and President Eisenhower. It was Hagerty who had persuaded Eisenhower to allow his news conferences to be broadcast.

Coming to ABC only three days after Eisenhower left office, Hagerty set about shaking up and expanding ABC's entire news operation, adding bureaus throughout the world, including the network's first bureau in Moscow, and hiring a group of journalists that commanded respect. These newcomers included Howard K. Smith and Edward P. Morgan, formerly of CBS; Quincy Howe, the erudite CBS analyst noted for his Boston-accented, flat-out, no-nonsense commentary; William H. Lawrence, the *New York Times* White House correspondent; Bill Sheehan, a fine labor reporter from Detroit, who later would be president of ABC News; John Scali, diplomatic correspondent for the Associated Press; Jules Bergman of CBS, whom Hagerty made television's first science editor, and a bright young Canadian named Peter Jennings.

"I didn't come to ABC to be third," Hagerty said. "I came because I wanted ABC to be first." It was, says Elmer Lower, who would succeed Hagerty, "a declaration that was to serve almost as a company legend."[27]

With Daly's departure from ABC, the name of its nightly news was changed to "The ABC Evening Report." No longer was there a single anchor. Instead, on coming to ABC, Hagerty found seven correspondents rotating as anchors, each anchoring for a week. These "anchors for a week" were: Don Goddard, John Rolfson, Edward P. Morgan, Al Mann, John Secondari, Bill Shadel, and John MacVane.

This game of musical chairs lasted less than a year. For the seven rotating anchors Hagerty substituted William H. Lawrence, anchoring in Washington, and Al Mann and John Cameron Swayze, based in New York. Mann provided commentary, while Swayze came on with a feature story at the end of the program. The setup worked fairly well and lasted until January 1963.

Swayze was dropped. Lawrence and Mann went back to full-time reporting, and "The ABC Evening Report" got a new anchor, Ron Cochran, who had been an FBI agent during World War II and then a reporter for CBS. As an anchor, Cochran had both warmth and presence. The program was renamed "Ron Cochran and the News"—the sales people had argued for personality identification—and Cochran held down the anchor position for two years. Only Daly, with seven years, had anchored longer.

Two Gambles

Hagerty had been at ABC only a short time when the United States, using Cuban exile forces, took the gamble of invading Cuba at the Bay of Pigs. Though all networks covered the fiasco after the fact—the C.I.A. mission was planned and executed in secrecy without benefit of press—there had been on the air in the news blackout one flash of light. In a radio broadcast on April 6, 1961, 11 days before the ill-fated invasion, Stuart Novins of CBS reported that preparations were well underway. Although he identified the invaders as Cubans, he suggested they would have strong U.S. support.

The *New York Times* knew of the impending invasion but played down the story. It eliminated all reference to the C.I.A. and killed the statement that the invasion was imminent. The paper also took the unusual step of removing the story, for policy reasons, from the front page. The Novins broadcast and *Times* story had little effect, in part because the Kennedy Administration put out so much false information, carried dutifully by the press services, undermining their credibility. Kennedy said later that he wished the *Times* had given the story the play it deserved. "If you had . . . you would have saved us from a colossal mistake."[28]

Edward R. Murrow, then director of the United States Information Agency, would have spoken against the invasion plan had he known of it. He was not invited to the April 4 meeting of the National Security Council at which the plan was discussed and approved. This violated the understanding reached when Murrow joined the administration that he would be privy to such planning since he would be obliged in the performance of his office to explain America's actions to the world.

The other gamble, a much bigger one, came a year later.

On October 14, 1962, a high-altitude spy plane, sent by the United States over western Cuba, photographed incontrovertible evidence that Soviet engineers had built facilities for the launching of nuclear ballistic missiles from Cuba and that at least one ballistic missile already was in place. President Kennedy issued an ultimatum to Soviet Premier Khrushchev to remove the missiles, or the United States would go in and remove them. The ultimatum was delivered by radio and television on October 22.

> I call upon Chairman Khrushchev to halt and eliminate this clandestine, reckless, and provocative threat. . . . I call upon him further to abandon this course of world domination and to join in an historic effort to end the perilous arms race and transform the history of man.

Kennedy said that any missile launched from Cuba would be regarded as an attack by the Soviet Union on the United States requiring all-out retaliation.

For Americans, Kennedy calmly spelled out the danger. There was being assembled in Cuba, a scant ninety miles from the United States, an arsenal of

> medium-range ballistic missiles capable of carrying a nuclear war-head for a distance of more than 1,000 nautical miles. Each of these missiles, in short, is capable of striking Washington, D.C., the Panama Canal, Cape Canaveral, Mexico City, or any other city in the southeastern part of the United States, in Central America, or in the Caribbean area.

The possibility of widespread nuclear war, he was saying, was real. Not since Franklin Roosevelt summoned the American people to courage in his first inaugural address and rallied the nation after the Japanese attack on Pearl Harbor had a president used the airwaves so effectively in an hour of crisis.

A broadcast journalist played a key role in averting disaster. Four days after Kennedy's ultimatum, ABC's diplomatic correspondent, John Scali, received an urgent call from an official at the Soviet embassy asking that they meet. They met at a downtown Washington restaurant—the old Occidental, now razed—where the Russian made a proposal. If Khrushchev promised to pull the missiles out of Cuba and never reintroduce them, would Kennedy promise not to invade Cuba? When Scali said he did not know, the official urged him to find out.

Scali checked with the State Department, which said it might be a basis for negotiation. He relayed the word to the Russian later the same day, and within two hours Kennedy received a long cable from Khrushchev saying pretty much what the Russian had told Scali. It was imperative, Khrushchev said, that the situation not get out of hand. There was more negotiation. Soviet ships bringing missiles to Cuba turned back. Missiles already in place were removed, and Kennedy assured Khrushchev that the United States would not invade.

"The Fastest-Growing News Organization in America"

James Hagerty was head of ABC News for less than three years. In 1963, he became vice president of corporate relations, and Elmer Lower succeeded him.

Lower came to ABC with broad experience. He had worked for news-papers, the wire services, *Life* magazine, and for CBS and NBC. He was an innovator. As an executive at NBC News he had replaced old-fashioned adding machines with an electronic system for tabulating election returns. At ABC he dispensed with gavel-to-gavel coverage of national political conventions and instead switched to them as news dictated. Each night ABC summarized the convention proceedings.

Still it was not until 1967, four years after CBS and NBC, that ABC expanded its evening news to a half-hour. The anchor was Peter Jennings, who had taken over from Ron Cochran two years earlier when he was just 26.

Jennings is one of the new generation of anchors, like Tom Brokaw, whose whole experience has been in radio and television. Son of a Canadian Broadcasting Corporation executive who wanted him to go into banking, Jennings began on a small radio station[29] and moved on to co-anchor Canada's first nationally televised news on a commercial network, CTV. He came to ABC in 1964, where his first major assignment was covering the civil rights struggle.

Within a year, Lower made Jennings anchor of the evening news. It was a mistake. He lacked the experience necessary to compete with the likes of Brinkley, Huntley, and Cronkite. He himself was dissatisfied. On leaving the anchor desk, he said he wanted to get out in the field and report, and that is what he did, mostly from Europe, for the next 16 years.

Jennings' successor was Bob Young, ABC's London correspondent, who was succeeded after only five months by Frank Reynolds. A conscientious reporter for 14 years in Chicago television, Reynolds had joined ABC in 1965 and served two years as White House correspondent. He became anchor of the ABC evening news in 1968, then co-anchor with Howard K. Smith in 1969. A year later, Reynolds, who had caused waves by speaking out against President Nixon, was taken off the program and replaced by Harry Reasoner, who had left CBS (temporarily, it turned out) for ABC.

From anchoring, Reynolds went to Washington as special correspondent. In time, both he and Jennings would be back as anchors on ABC's evening news, only then the program would be called "World News Tonight."

"The Evening News with Howard K. Smith and Harry Reasoner," with Av Westin as executive producer, had a five-year run (December 1970 to September 1975), the longest run of two anchors on any network evening news program with the exception of Huntley-Brinkley. The program had been on the air a year when the *New York Times* took note that "the Smith-Reasoner combination, complete with personal and clearly labeled commentary each night, is making itself felt." It quoted Westin as saying, "Getting to be No. 1 may be impossible, but getting to be No. 2 is no longer out of the question."[30]

In 1974, Elmer Lower, like Hagerty before him, went to a vice presidency in corporate affairs. He had run ABC News for 11 years and could justifiably feel a sense of achievement. He had set out to strengthen his organization and had done it. Besides promoting capable people within ABC News, he lured from CBS three of its best producers, Ernest Leiser, Joan Richman, and David Buksbaum, all of whom, like Reasoner, later returned to the CBS fold. He hired Jesse Zousmer, the distinguished Murrow editor, and placed him in overall charge of television news.

Not content with enlarging ABC's bureaus in Chicago and Los Angeles, Lower established new bureaus in Miami, Atlanta, and Dallas. He stopped using newsreel photographers and recruited ABC News' own camera team, hiring Jack Bush, a film expert, away from CBS to impose quality control. Ben Blank, CBS' top graphics artist, also came over. It was he, at ABC, who revolutionized news graphics (before computer-generated graphics) by enhancing the key picture appearing on the screen over the anchor's shoulder. A weekly newsmagazine with Harry Reasoner[31] was added to the Saturday evening schedule. Following the example of CBS and NBC, Lower started a news syndication service. More documentaries were aired. Tailored newscasts went out on the four new networks created by ABC Radio.

An index to the expansion of ABC News during the first years of Lower's administration is the money allocated to it. In 1961, Hagerty's budget was $3,500,000. In 1967, four years after Lower's arrival, it had increased ninefold.[32] No longer was ABC News in disrepute. It had come far enough to boast that it was now "the fastest growing news organization n America."[33]

"I Thought the Time Had Come"

The president of ABC News, after Elmer Lower, was Bill Sheehan, who had been Lower's right-hand man. Sheehan dropped Howard K. Smith as co-anchor on the evening news, restricting him to commentary, after research indicated the program might do better in the ratings with Reasoner as sole anchor. When this didn't work, Sheehan made the most publicized move by a network up to that time. He offered Barbara Walters a million dollars a year, for five years, if she would leave NBC and join Reasoner on the evening news. The offer was unprecedented. No woman had anchored such a program on a regular basis. No woman—no man, for that matter—in journalism history had received so high a salary.

Almost all of Barbara Walters' professional life had been spent at NBC, where she had advanced from publicity writer in 1954 to co-host of "Today." NBC was home. But ABC was opportunity. NBC was willing to match the million-dollar salary but balked at giving Walters what she wanted most at that moment, a position as co-anchor on the nightly news. So she accepted the ABC offer. "I thought the time had come," she told *Newsweek*, "to take the plunge."[34]

The story made the front page of major newspapers, including the *New York Times*. It got two pages in *Time*, three pages in *Newsweek*. Lost to many readers was the fact that the million-dollar-a-year salary was for more than co-anchoring the evening news. Walters also was to anchor a series of prime-time specials, host the public affairs program "Issues and Answers" on occasion, and help with an unspecified number of documentaries.

Still, it was a lot of money. Karl E. Meyer, writing in *The Saturday Review*, said he wished Barbara Walters well; women in television had been treated badly. But the money depressed him. "Quite obviously," he said, "it further blurs the distinction between journalism and entertainment."[35] Richard S. Salant, president of CBS News, found the amount of money "grotesque." "A good journalist is worth more than a baseball player or rock star," he said, "but I'm worried about where it's going." [36]

As Salant, surmised, it was going toward vastly higher salaries for all the big names. Walters, the William Morris Agency, and ABC had shown the way. The course was set. There would be no turning back. And implicit in the money was power.

Reasoner was less than enthusiastic about being paired with Walters. She, however, accentuated the positive, saying, "I think Harry and I will be balanced and spark off good things in each other." [37] ABC went overboard with its blurbs. One advertisement began: "Barbara Walters and Harry Reasoner, the news team America has been waiting for!" [38] Reviews were lukewarm. Tom Shales of the *Washington Post* granted, "It could, indeed, have been worse." [39]

What was worse was that the pairing didn't work. They "sparked off" not good things but tension. Reasoner disliked sharing the anchor desk with Walters, and viewers could see it. Years later, she told *USA Today:* "My whole world fell apart. I knew I was failing. I knew I was drowning. . . . People can say, 'But she was making all that money.' Money is little comfort if you think that your whole career is over." [40]

It was inevitable that with all the publicity and Walters' following, ratings for the program would go up. But then they slipped. Sheehan was replaced by Roone Arledge. Walters appeared on the program only occasionally. She concentrated on her primetime specials, which consistently drew high ratings. "Critics who go around muttering about Barbara Walters' six-figure [sic] salary," said UPI, "just aren't watching the Nielsens." [41]

She had come back.

Wide World of News

Roone Arledge took over ABC News in June 1977. It was Arledge, newly arrived, who had Barbara Walters turn to what she enjoyed most and did best, the personality interview, and who began at once to demonstrate what he was good at doing, which was adventuring in television news in an exciting, yet responsible way.

Responsible performance is not what some expected. Arledge made his reputation as president of ABC Sports, where he had raised computerized graphics, stop action, slow motion, the split screen, and instant replay to a dizzying art. Now he would be president of ABC News *and* ABC Sports, and it was feared he might apply the electronic gimmickry of "Monday Night Football" to news broadcasts. At his first news conference, Arledge tried to allay this fear, vowing he would preserve journalistic integrity. Ratings and credibility are achieved, he said, "by having a good news organization, and that's what I intend to build." [42]

Almost immediately he went on a hiring spree, raiding newsrooms for top talent. From NBC he snatched Cassie Mackin, David Brinkley, Jim Laurie, and Dick Schaap. He persuaded Richard Wald, who had been president of NBC News, to come to ABC from the Times-Mirror Company in Los Angeles. Wald and Arledge had been classmates at Columbia, and Arledge made him a senior vice president in charge of day-to-day operations. (At this point, Sheehan resigned.) He hired James Wooten from the *New York Times*, Brit Hume from columnist Jack Anderson, Hal Bruno from *Newsweek*, Lynn Sherr from PBS, Sander Vanocur, who had previously worked for NBC, from the *Washington Post*, and Carl Bernstein, the ex-*Washington Post* reporter who with Bob Woodward won fame for their revelations in the Watergate scandal. He lined up Pierre Salinger, President Kennedy's French-speaking press secretary, to be ABC's man in Paris.

Arledge's big raid was on CBS, where he got Barry Sarafin, Gary Shepard, Sylvia Chase, Barry Lando, Tony Sargent, Marion Goldin, Jack Laurence, Jed Duvall, Bernard Shaw, Don Kladstrup, Richard Threlkeld, and Hughes Rudd. At CBS' Washington bureau a prankster posted a sign advising: "Will the last person leaving for ABC please turn out the lights." Local stations were not immune. Lured from WTOP-TV (now WUSA-TV), Washington, were Max Robinson and Susan King, along with Bill Greenwood from WCBS-TV, New York; Wallace Westfeldt, former NBC producer, from noncommercial WETA-TV, Washington; and Kenneth Tiven from KYW-TV, Philadelphia.

This hiring cost money, and Arledge had a budget larger than that enjoyed by any of his predecessors. ABC Television in 1976–1977 had experienced its richest season, finishing ahead of both CBS and NBC in prime-time ratings.

The Troika

Arledge set about breaking molds. He used computer graphics and satellites in news production as never before. He added freeze-frame and slow motion. In reporting a slowdown in national productivity, the video-tape of a moving assembly line was slowed down. He beefed up the documentary unit, made more use of portable cameras. He tried to change the role of anchor from news reader to star reporter, as when he sent Barbara Walters to Cuba to interview Castro. He told *Time*, "The concept of anchor people sitting in New York with the news flowing through them is outdated."[43]

When Harry Reasoner left in August 1978, returning to CBS, Arledge acted. He traded the New York anchor desk for three desks, with Frank Reynolds in Washington, Max Robinson in Chicago, and Peter Jennings in London. The Chicago desk—called the National Desk—was ABC's promise that stories from the heartland would not be slighted. It also made Robinson the first black to anchor nightly network news. Arledge changed the name of the program from "The ABC Evening News" to "ABC's World News Tonight," and put Av Westin, who was back after a brief period of independent producing, in charge of the broadcast.

The three-desk format, or "whiparound" as Arledge called it, proved confusing at first. *Newsweek* referred to its "dizzying back-and-forth pace." But then, said *Newsweek,* "the show settled down, and smooth, steady Frank Reynolds emerged as the anchor troika's first among equals,"[44] a position that became obvious when he began opening the program each night and introducing his colleagues with their reports. It took a main anchor to tie the elements together.

And the program improved journalistically. It began beating the competition on stories—a scoop on two Supreme Court decisions caused a small furor—and it added a regular feature called "Special Assignment," which was a copy of the "Segment 3" feature NBC had introduced in its evening program in 1977.[45] Typical "Special Assignment" topics concerned working parents and frauds committed against the elderly. When the program was a year old, *Newsweek* said, "Under Arledge the evening newscast has taken on a crisp, professional edge."[46] The whole news operation, said the *New York Times,* "is both vastly improved and far more competitive."[47]

Competitive it was. "World News Tonight," in the ratings week ending April 20, 1979, outdrew NBC's nightly news. Not by much. The margin was one-tenth of a Nielsen ratings point but enough to cause Arledge to send a congratulatory message to all bureaus. One reason for the new success was that ABC now had more affiliates. Some had come over to it from NBC. But also the commitment in money and talent was showing. It was more than coincidence that in that heartening week in April "World News Tonight" was airing a series ABC called "the most comprehensive and informative look at U.S. military might ever to appear on a nightly network news program."[48]

It was at this time (1979) that Arledge promoted Westin to the newly created post of vice president for program development, a responsibility covering both present and future programs. Jeff Gralnick, executive producer of weekend and special events broadcasts, succeeded Westin as executive producer of "World News Tonight."[49]

By 1980, the program virtually tied "NBC Nightly News" for second place. And then, in 1981, the unheard of happened. It beat CBS' evening news, which had led in the three-way race for more than a decade. The Nielsens showed "World News Tonight" winning the week of July 13–17 by almost half a ratings point, or roughly 300,000 homes. This was only a few months after Dan Rather took over the CBS anchor desk from Cronkite. He was still settling in, proving himself. Soon the CBS program would rebound and again be No. 1.

"Unmistakably Serious About His Craft"

On April 20, 1983, Frank Reynolds, suffering bone cancer, made his last broadcast and entered a Washington hospital. He died on July 20, ending a five-year battle of which few were aware.

Reynolds' principal competitors, Dan Rather and Tom Brokaw, applauded his life and his work. So did his colleagues. Ted Koppel, calling him extraordinary, said, "Frank felt other peoples' pain. He showed everybody's pain but his own."[50] The critic Tom Shales said, "He was unmistakably serious about his craft and its social effects, and though he was hardly tall, he had grandeur."[51]

With Reynolds gone, the tri-anchor format was abandoned. Peter Jennings, now a seasoned award-winning foreign correspondent, returned alone to the anchor desk he left because of inexperience 16 years before. Now he had earned it.

The struggle for dominance went on. In 1985, "The CBS Evening News With Dan Rather" faltered in the ratings. Occasionally, during 1986, "The NBC Nightly News With Tom Brokaw" overtook it. "Brokaw Nipping at Rather's Heels," headlined the *New York Daily News*.[52] "ABC World News Tonight With Peter Jennings" was third. But not for long. By the summer of 1990, in a remarkable recovery, it had moved ahead of both the Brokaw and Rather broadcasts and established itself in first place.

No More Also Ran

It was with coverage of the Iranian hostage crisis of 1979–1980 that ABC News caught up with its network competitors. For years, despite budgetary obstacles, it had been gaining. The gap narrowed impressively in 1977 when its budget was increased and Roone Arledge became president of the news division. Two years later, with ABC News' aggressive reporting of the crisis, the gap disappeared.

The crisis began on November 3, 1979, when Iranian militants stormed the U.S. embassy in Teheran and took its staff hostage. This was a very big story. Arledge, a hustler in the tradition of Paul White, decided to give viewers a nightly 20-minute update on what was happening. He put these special reports, titled "The Iran Crisis: America Held Hostage," on ABC Television at 11:30 P.M., Eastern time, when rival networks were airing old movies and "The Tonight Show With Johnny Carson." At first, Frank Reynolds anchored the specials, but soon Ted Koppel, ABC's State Department correspondent, took over to relieve Reynolds, who was anchoring the evening news. (This was the period in which each night at the end of his broadcast Walter Cronkite was ticking off how many days the hostages had been held captive.)

"The Iran Crisis: America Held Hostage" proved the existence of an audience for late-night news, and with the release of the 52 American hostages in January 1981, just as President Reagan was taking office, it became "Nightline" and Koppel the premier interviewer on television. Until "Nightline" there was no regularly scheduled news that late on any network. Throughout the long crisis, ABC News distinguished itself. As *Variety* said, "ABC's reporting has been just a little quicker, a little more imaginative, and always with more depth than either CBS or NBC."[53]

In the contest between network news divisions, ABC News had scored the tying run.

"The NacNeil/Lehrer NewsHour"

PBS' "MacNeil/Lehrer NewsHour" had the distinction of being the first one-hour newscast aired nightly on national television. Commercial television had struggled with the idea of such a program, but affiliates refused to surrender their lucrative half-hour at 7:30, and the networks balked at surrendering a half-hour, or an hour, in prime time. ABC had experimented with the format only briefly. So it was on public television, on September 5, 1983, that the expanded hour-long evening news, with Les Crystal as executive producer, finally appeared.

The history of "The MacNeil/Lehrer NewsHour" goes back to 1975 and the half-hour "Robert MacNeil Report" on WNET, New York. Jim Lehrer, who had covered the Watergate hearings with MacNeil for public television, reported on the program from Washington. They had a good working relationship, based on mutual respect, and after a year they teamed up to do "The MacNeil/Lehrer Report" coast to coast on PBS. This was the first news program aired nightly on national television that devoted its entire half hour to a single subject, as ABC's "Nightline" would four years later. The executive producer was Al Vecchione.

Although some viewers felt they were being told more about certain subjects than they cared to know, and found the program dull, others praised the in-depth approach. These included critics like Thomas Griffith of *Time* magazine, who said it "consistently provides TV's best discussion of public affairs."[54] Within a year of its premiere, "The MacNeil/Lehrer Report" was being carried by 210 of PBS' 258 stations.

"NewsHour" is produced by the anchormen's own company, MacNeil/Lehrer Productions, of which Vecchione, who spent 20 years at NBC before entering public television, is president. It is the only major evening newscast wholly owned by its anchors. Gannett was once half-owner, but MacNeil and Lehrer took full control in 1986. The company also produces documentaries. The first one was "My Heart, Your Heart," a documentary based on Lehrer's experience when he underwent heart surgery. An early series was "The Story of English," in which MacNeil explored the history of the language and its variations. "The Heart of the Dragon," a 12-part series on China, was produced by another company but hosted by Lehrer and brought to PBS by MacNeil/Lehrer Productions.

Late Entries

1988 saw the arrival of two new entries in the evening news race: "USA Today: The Television Show"[55] and the Discovery Channel's "World Monitor." Both half-hour programs premiered the same day, September 12, and both appeared as television versions of established national newspapers, the *Christian Science Monitor* and *USA Today*.

Each had strong financial backing, 40 million dollars for the first year in the case of the *USA Today* program created by the Gannett Corporation and former NBC chairman Grant Tinker. Its first executive producer was Steve Friedman, who, producing "Today" in the early 1980s, made it No. 1 in the ratings. The new show opened to scathing criticism—Fred Friendly called it "junk news"[56]—and while the frentic pace of the syndicated broadcast was eased, fewer stations took the program. On top of that, there was internal dissension, and in November 1989, 14 months after its premier, the program was cancelled.

"World Monitor," anchored by John Hart, formerly of CBS and NBC, basked in reviewers' praise. The *New York Times* found "the sheer integrity" of the program invigorating.[57] Hart wanted to come to the program, he says, because of the *Christian Science Monitor*'s reputation for "depth, balance, fairness, and thought."[58] Former State Department spokesman Hodding Carter came on as special correspondent. The executive producer of "World Monitor" in its first year was Sandy Socolow, who once produced "The CBS Evening News With Walter Cronkite" and "The CBS Evening News With Dan Rather." He left "World Monitor" in January 1990 to produce with Cronkite a massive television history of the 20th Century.

CNN's entry in evening news competition is reported in chapter 45, which deals with cable as a major news medium.

33

"Let Freedom Ring . . ."

The domestic stories of the century, tearing the country, were the Great Depression of the 1930s and the civil rights movement of the 1960s. Radio covered the first. For the most part, it parroted the wire service reports of measures taken by President Roosevelt's New Deal. The "Fireside Chats," in which Roosevelt spoke directly to the electorate, established a pattern with profound political implications. Henceforth, presidents would address the nation precisely as they wished, unedited by the press.

Radio seldom portrayed the plight of individual victims of the Depression, such as the destitute Dust Bowl farmer or unemployed auto worker. Nothing on the air approached the impact of the story of the Joad family in John Steinbeck's novel, *The Grapes of Wrath*. Radio news was still in its adolescence and would not reach maturity until World War II, when the likes of Paul White and Ed Murrow showed what it could do.

But in the 1960s, radio and television covered the struggles of the civil rights movement as they covered the anguish of Vietnam, uncensored and up close. Listeners heard the snarls of attacking dogs. In their living rooms, people saw, along with battle scenes from Vietnam, the bloodied heads of blacks in places like Birmingham and Detroit. They saw children, because of color, attending school under armed protection. They heard Dr. Martin

Luther King, Jr., proclaim his dream and crowds sing "We shall over-come." Many, seeing and hearing, perceived the sickness, and the percep-tion contributed to cure.

Network coverage of the riots of 1962, when James Meredith broke the color line at the University of Mississippi, and the peaceful assembly of 200,000 people at the Lincoln Memorial, where King in 1963 gave words to his dream, prepared the ground for passage of the Civil Rights Act of 1964. But rights are not secured by law alone. The public must believe in the law, and gradually, through sit-ins, marches, sermons, and media cov-erage, came belief. Not total. Not in every person and place. But wide-spread enough to make segregation unacceptable. The late CBS corre-spondent Robert Schakne recalled:

> I remember we were down in New Orleans, at an elementary school—first- and second-grade kids. Three of them were coming out of this school just integrated—two black kids and one white—and while we were shooting, the mother of this little white girl kept shouting to her, "Say boo to the nigger!" The little girl said, "I want some candy," and the mother cried, "Do you hear me? Say boo to the nigger!" We ran that, and Westbrook Pegler [a syndi-cated columnist] accused us of faking it. But that's what happened. It wasn't staged. It just happened. Imagine that happening today.[1]

Network accounts of what was happening nationalized awareness. Wil-liam A. Wood, who taught at Columbia University's Graduate School of Journalism, says, "Suddenly men and women all over the country were as close as across the street to the crucible of revolution. Whites everywhere were awakened and shaken up."[2] Blacks in out-of-the-way places them-selves became conscious of the scale of the movement. As NBC's Bill Monroe remarked at the time,

> The signals went out from the TV towers . . . to hundreds of thousands of shacks and houses with leaky roofs and unpainted sides—and television antennas on the roof. . . . Negroes in Missis-sippi watched the sit-in demonstrators in Tennessee and the free-dom riders pushing into Alabama. And many of them who couldn't read could watch and listen as Presidents of the United States talked on television about civil rights and registering to vote.[3]

Networks received complaints, some from their own southern affili-ates, that correspondents were biased in their reporting and "stirring up trouble." Harry Reasoner was among the first CBS correspondents cover-ing the civil rights story. In 1959, he reported the showdown in Little Rock, Arkansas, where Governor Orval Faubus refused to allow desegregation of Central High School. After days of ugly confrontation, President Eisen-hower dispatched federal troops to the city to insure integration. In his memoir, *Before the Colors Fade,* Reasoner says the situation demanded fair reporting.

So we always tried to remember that there were 100,000 people in
Little Rock, and that on the worst day not more than a thousand
or so of them were behaving badly in front of Central High—and
a lot of those were from out of town. . . . We tried to remember
that Daisy Bates, the leader of the black effort, and Jimmy Karam
of the White Citizens Council both quite sincerely believed they
were right.[4]

Robert MacNeil has spoken of the "stunning impact" racial segregation
made on him when, in 1963, NBC News sent him into the Deep South.[5]
Correspondents might strive for objectivity, but their prejudice on behalf
of blacks often showed. Even the neutered report—just the facts—could
be an appeal. "Beneath the formal message—so-and-so said this, such-
and-such happened here—there is an informal message: different uncomfortable events are happening, and they involve you."[6] In 1964, the networks pursued the story of three young civil rights workers missing in
Mississippi. After six weeks, their bodies were found in an earthen dam.
The murders, themselves, screamed for involvement.[7]

Reporters risked their lives. Covering the desegregation of the University of Georgia, Schakne was the target of rocks and bottles. NBC's Richard
Valeriani suffered a gash in the back of his head from someone wielding
an ax handle and had to be hospitalized. Dan Rather writes that a National
Guardsman in Mississippi struck him across the side of his head with a rifle
butt, knocking him down.[8] Both he and Robert MacNeil were threatened,
at different times, by men with sawed-off shotguns.

Cameramen were special targets. MacNeil cites the experience of one
NBC cameraman:

George Sozio got attacked one night by an angry crowd and had to
use his Filmo, a very sturdy 16mm camera, as a weapon. A shot of
him about to club someone with it went out across the country on
the wire services. That made Sozio feel it would be healthier for
him to get out of town.[9]

Southern affiliates complained that networks were presenting too negative a picture and not reporting positive aspects of the civil rights story,
such as instances in which schools were integrated peacefully. Racial tensions in the North, they charged, seldom were reported. A complaint,
North and South, was that the networks "built up" militant blacks, no
matter how small their constituency, simply because with their escalated
rhetoric they made better copy. "Television, including me," says veteran
correspondent Dan Schorr, "was involved with the radicalization of the
black community."[10] Robert Schakne said:

It was a testing time, and while we were learning we made some
terrible mistakes. I was at Little Rock the first day, and we'd never
dealt with crowds like that before. I remember the crowd yelling,
but by the time we were ready to shoot the yelling had stopped. I

asked them to do it again, so we could get it. Governor Faubus called us on that, and I realized it was wrong.[11]

Precautions were taken. Networks invoked their evolving guidelines for coverage of violent or potentially violent events, using special lighting, for example, as little as possible; lights turned off whenever the situation was tense. Stations sometimes delayed riot reports to prevent trouble from spreading. News bulletins like "A crowd is gathering at the intersection of Summit and Pine" were discouraged on grounds that people, attracted to the scene, might cause the situation to get out of hand.

The situation did get out of hand, no place more than in the national capital, after Dr. King was assassinated in Memphis on the night of April 4, 1968. Fires lit the skies of many American cities as blacks let loose their rage, looting and burning Whitey's businesses in ghetto areas. Federal troops in full battle dress patrolled downtown Washington. President Johnson proclaimed Sunday, April 7, a day of national mourning for the slain civil rights leader. In an essay on CBS, Eric Sevaried said:

> It is doubtful if this nation has ever before gone into officially proclaimed mourning . . . over the death of a private citizen, and this man was the descendant of slaves. This is not the reaction of a sick society but of a fundamentally healthy society trying desperately to cleanse itself of the one chronic, persistent poison in its body. So the label on his life must not be a long day's journey into night. It must be a long night's journey into day.[12]

The wave of violence did not quickly subside. By April 14 more than forty persons had been killed and 2,600 injured. It was a time when, because of the anger, stations with "token" blacks sent them out to get the story. White reporters entered the riot zones in unmarked cars and otherwise functioned as inconspicuously as possible. At least one station, WMAQ-TV, Chicago, assigned bodyguards to accompany its film crews. In the haste to get on the air, mistakes were made. Broadcasters in Washington reported Army tanks rumbling down New Hampshire Avenue when in fact they were personnel carriers. In Boston, Chicago, and Los Angeles, the city governments set up rumor-control centers where reporters could check with police and fire officials.

Three months after the King assassination, CBS Television aired an ambitious seven-part series entitled "Of Black America," which attempted a purview of racial discrimination in America from Hollywood's "yes, suh" portrayal of blacks in the 1930s to the present. The documentary, produced by Perry Wolff and Andy Rooney, was narrated by Bill Cosby. Also shown was how persistently the role of blacks in American history had been ignored in the nation's classrooms. Sponsor of the award-winning program was Xerox.

Production of documentaries dealing with racial issues was by no means confined to the period following King's assassination. The March on Washington in 1963, the Watts uprising of 1965, and the march from Selma to

Montgomery that same year all spurred the production of documentaries dealing with civil rights. Along with the special programming related to Vietnam, space exploration, and the assassinations of President Kennedy and Robert Kennedy, social turmoil helped make the 1960s the Decade of the Documentary. Even before the March on Washington, in the period from January 1960 to April 1963, CBS Television had carried 75 one-hour documentaries produced under the direction of Fred Friendly. Four dealt with the civil rights belonging to blacks.[13]

One of these programs, "Who Speaks for Birmingham?" helped precipitate in 1961 the departure from CBS of one of its most respected correspondents, Howard K. Smith. He and CBS had been at odds for some time over what the network, always touchy on the subject of opinionated news, regarded as bias in his reporting. The showdown came when Smith wanted to conclude the Birmingham documentary with a quotation attributed to Edmund Burke: "The only thing necessary for the triumph of evil is for good men to do nothing."[14] The idea was that the good white people of Birmingham should work to correct the racial abuses in their midst.

Today, the quotation appears unremarkable. However, in that day emotions ran high, and CBS, because of its racially controversial programming, had just lost several Southern affiliates to the other networks. But it was more than that. Richard Salent, head of CBS News, objected to the approach taken by Smith in other instances. Significantly, "Who Speaks for Birmingham?" soon was followed on CBS by "The Other Face of Dixie," a one-hour report on the progress of integration in four southern cities.

Any list of outstanding documentaries dealing with the volatile racial situation would have to include the NBC White Paper "Sit-in," Irving Gitlin and Al Wasserman, producers, 1960; "Walk in My Shoes," John Secondari, producer, ABC-TV, 1961; "The American Revolution of '63," Robert "Shad" Northshield, producer, NBC-TV; "Ku Klux Klan, the Invisible Empire," David Lowe, producer, CBS-TV, 1964; "The Angry Voices of Watts," Stuart Schulberg, producer, NBC-TV, 1966; "Time for Americans," a six-part series, Stephen Fleischman and Robert Siegenthaler, producers, ABC-TV, 1968; and "The People Are the City," Fred Freed, producer, NBC-TV, 1968.

Many stations, not just networks, appealed to white America's conscience. Typical were WSB-TV, Atlanta, which spoke out against the segregationists' tactics in block-busting, and WDSU-TV, New Orleans, which strove for reconciliation in that city's integration crisis. In 1969, when Boston was embroiled in a bitter, sometimes violent school decentralization controversy, WBZ-AM got white and black protagonists into a studio and let them go at each other verbally, nonstop, for 22 hours. The taped "debate" made 11 hours of what *Newsweek* called "a remarkable study in what communication is all about."[15] In Bogalusa, Louisiana, a radio station, WBOX, took such a strong stand against segregation that advertisers boycotted the station and it had to be sold.

The filibuster against the Civil Rights Act of 1964 brought national attention to a relatively unknown CBS newsman, Roger Mudd. Standing in front of the Capitol, under an umbrella if it was raining or bareheaded in bright sunshine, he reported latest developments in the hard-fought congressional battle as often as seven times a day.

This went on for three months. "His soft Southern accent, along with an affable personality," said *Newsweek,* "has attracted millions of viewers. Several ladies, in fact, have written CBS to express concern about his health, since he had broadcast outdoors in every weather imaginable."[16] The idea for marathon spot coverage of the story by one reporter came from Fred Friendly, president of CBS News at that time.

With the Black Revolution came black news, newscasts in large urban areas anchored by blacks for the black audience. "Black on Black" on KNXT (now KCBS-TV), Los Angeles, was among the first. Many stations simply used the title "Black News." On of the most ambitious of these programs was a daily one-hour show called "Harambee" on WTOP-TV (now WUSA-TV), Washington, which combined entertainment with civic affairs. KING-TV, Seattle, introduced a discussion program, "Face to Face." Broadcasting's first nationally viewed news program for and about blacks was "Black Journal," launched in 1968 by National Educational Television (NET). After two years its producer, William Greaves, was succeeded by another black activist, Tony Brown, who was dean of Howard University's School of Communications. In 1990, the series, renamed "Tony Brown's Journal," was still on the air.

The first black-owned radio network was the National Black Network (NBN) founded in 1972, which presented five minutes of black-oriented news on the hour in addition to live coverage of public affairs and sporting events. That same year, Mutual Radio set up in the Mutual Black Network serving more than fifty affiliates. Sheridan Broadcasting, with a black president, Thomas McKinney, bought the network in 1979. The nation's first black-owned, black-operated television station in the continental United States was WGPR-TV, Channel 62, Detroit, which went on the air on September 29, 1975. (Two television stations were already being operated by blacks in the Virgin Islands.) The first black-owned VHF station was an NBC affiliate, WAEO-TV, in Rhinelander, Wisconsin, acquired by Seaway Communications in June 1979. A CBS affiliate, WHEC-TV, Rochester, New York, became the first black-owned VHF outlet in a major market later that same month. These were not like radio's soul stations, owned by whites who employed black deejays to give their properties a black sound. The black-owned television station offered entertainment but also took news seriously.

Intermittently, white television has returned to the subject of the rightful place of blacks in American society. The instances, which are many, include NBC's "A Country Called Watts" that in 1975 explored the change, and lack of change, in the Los Angeles ghetto since the conflagration of 1965. In 1979, 25 years after the Supreme Court outlawed segregation in the public schools, CBS aired a two-hour progress report, "Blacks in America: With All Deliberate Speed." In 1984, while Bill Moyers was still at CBS, he did a program for public television called "The Second American Revolution," which took stock of the status of blacks in America 100 years after the Emancipation Proclamation.

And the end of the story, and the need for thorough public knowledge of it, are not in sight.

34
"If You're White and a Male, O.K."

The headline appeared in the *New York Times* on December 3, 1972. It called attention to a study conducted by the Office of Communication of the United Church of Christ. According to the study, half the commercial television stations in the country did not employ as anchor, reporter, or producer, let alone as manager, any black man or woman, American Indian, oriental, or Hispanic. Three of every four women employed in commercial television held clerical or secretarial positions. News was being reported largely from the perspective of white males.

Discrimination was not limited to television. A survey made by the *Columbia Journalism Review* and B'nai B'rith in 1968 found that of all employees in the news media, broadcast and print, blacks constituted only 4.2 percent. If the sign in some of journalism's show windows said, "Minorities Wanted," it also said, "Not Too Many, Not Too Fast."

Breakthrough

The first black person to report for a network program may have been William Worthy, a correspondent for the *Baltimore Afro-American*. On a free-lance basis, he made a broadcast for CBS from Moscow. The year was 1954. Two years later, while a Nieman Fellow at Harvard, he obtained a visa to enter Communist China. Defying a State Department ban on such travel, he went to Beijing and again broadcast by shortwave for CBS.[1]

The first network to hire a black reporter was ABC. James C. Hagerty, vice president in charge of news, had discussed the matter with Jackie Robinson, the first black to play major league baseball. Great care was taken. Hagerty first interviewed about thirty people. Then on August 9–10, 1962, he auditioned eight. The final choice was Mal Goode. He had applied, he told *Newsweek*, because he felt, "What the hell, I'm 54 years old. What can I lose?"[2]

Goode had been a reporter for the *Pittsburgh Courier,* a black newspaper, since 1948. He also had done news for KQV, ABC's radio affiliate in Pittsburgh. Hagerty assigned him to the United Nations, but part of his job was giving lectures, not before the general public, but before minority groups such as chapters of the NAACP, on the theme "I did it. You can do it, too."

In having a black newsman, CBS was a close second. It hired Ben Holman, a graduate of the University of Kansas who, after postgraduate study at the University of Chicago, had worked for nine years as a reporter for the *Chicago Daily News.* In 1962, he did commentary for WBBM-TV, the CBs-owned station in Chicago, and the next year became assignment editor for CBS News in New York. Occasionally, he went out on stories.

Holman left CBS in 1965 to take a media relations job in the Justice Department. Three years later, NBC hired him as a producer. It was a short stint. President Nixon appointed him director of the U.S. Community Relations Service, making him the highest-ranking black in the Justice Department. He remained head of the service through the Ford and Nixon administrations.

Although Holman reported for CBS, he never received the designation of correspondent. The first black reporter promoted to correspondent at CBS News was Hal Walker, who ironically had lost to Holman in an audition six years earlier. Walker was reporting for WTOP-TV (now WUSA-TV) in Washington when his coverage of racial disorders in the capital following the assassination of Dr. Martin Luther King, Jr., drew the attention of New York brass. In particular, executives were impressed by a one-hour special, "A Dialogue With Whitey," in which Walker was principal reporter. It was a daring program for that time, produced by the station's newly formed documentary unit headed by Don Harris. *Washington Post* critic Lawrence Laurent applauded the broadcast, singling out Walker's "excellent on-the-scene reports."[3]

Walker, who has been a network correspondent longer than any other black, is a South Carolinian reared in New York City and educated at three universities, Denison, Syracuse, and Yeshiva. His first assignment with CBS was as a reporter in the Washington bureau. After promotion to correspondent in 1969, he covered events, foreign and domestic, including the inaugurations of three presidents. In 1980, he joined ABC News, which he has served as foreign correspondent ever since.

The first black correspondent for NBC News was Bob Teague, hired in March 1963. Typically, Teague came out of a newspaper background, having reported for the *New York Times* before working as a writer in local radio and television. Like Goode and other black reporters in a predominately white society, Teague was constantly reminded of his blackness. In a magazine article, he spoke of making "a getaway of sorts from the ghetto."[4] On Labor Day, 1963, NBC aired a three-hour television documentary called "The American Revolution of '63." Teague reported on the program, and Robert Kintner, who was then president of NBC, said this made him the first black ever to go on camera as a network correspondent covering a story.[5]

In the mid-1960s, the Goodes, Holmans, and Teagues were a rarity. The major stations in New York City, with the largest black population of any city in America, had almost no black reporters. Then came the riots, first in the Watts section of Los Angeles, then in Newark and Detroit, then in the nation's capital with helmeted troops in the streets. How did the violence begin? Why had it taken so many by surprise?

The Kerner Commission, headed by Governor Otto Kerner of Illinois, said it was due, in large part, to the distorted picture newspapers and radio and television had presented of black America. "The ills of the ghetto, the difficulties of life there, the Negro's burning sense of grievance," it said, "are seldom conveyed." It urged that more black reporters be hired.[6]

Broadcasters scrambled for black faces, not solely because of the commission's finding and fear of FCC action; they needed black reporters to cover stories white reporters could not get or covered at their peril. Radio station WLIB in Harlem lost five of its black newsmen to New York outlets overnight. Addressing the annual meeting of news directors in 1981, Lem Tucker said,

> Let's be honest with each other. . . . [S]uddenly you needed us, and it would do you no good to have us as copy boys, producers, production assistants, and in those other positions which were, or led to, jobs of power because the public would not see us. . . . Industry kept us from aiming at the real power. Now our greed, and money and fame [that go with being on camera] keep many of us who now know better from pursuing it.[7]

Lem Tucker was the first black news director at a major television station. WOR-TV (now WWOR-TV) hired him to head up its news operation in August 1970. He already had worked at NBC, and since leaving WOR-TV has corresponded for both ABC and CBS.

Ed Bradley and Bernard Shaw are among this country's most respected, most visible journalists. Shaw, who as a CNN anchor reports nightly to millions of cable subscribers, has had a passion for news since his Chicago boyhood, when he eavesdropped on press conferences at the

Republican and Democratic national conventions. It was then, listening to the radio as a teenager, that he took Edward R. Murrow as his model.

At the University of Illinois, he majored in history. After working at a succession of Chicago stations as news writer, reporter, and anchor, paying his dues, he went to CBS and ABC. In 1980, when Ted Turner was starting up his 24-hour news service, Shaw bet his future on CNN. If he is known for one attribute, it is for taking news seriously. An inveterate reader, he says, "You never know enough."[8]

Ed Bradley of "60 Minutes" was born in a Philadelphia ghetto and earned a degree in education at Cheyney State College. He was teaching sixth grade math when he began hanging around a Philadelphia soul station, WDAS-FM, and got a job spinning records on Saturdays. Then he began going out on stories. He was program manager in 1967 when he left for WCBS-AM, New York, which had just gone to all news.

After three years, Bradley took off for Paris to write The Great American Novel. The novel never materialized, but he worked as a stringer for CBS and when he got the chance to go to Vietnam as a war correspondent, he grabbed it. His place in history is secure because in 1976, by anchoring the "CBS Sunday Night News," he became the first black anchorman on a major network. Bradley is a hard worker. "My mother always worked hard," he says. "My father worked hard. They always made *me* work hard. It's there at the core."[9]

"Why Can't a Woman Be More Like a Man?"

Managers in broadcast news asked the same question as did Professor Higgins in *My Fair Lady*. Women's voices, they said, lacked authority. Women weren't tough enough. Also they got married and had babies. As soon as you trained them, they were gone.

Still, some women were gaining a foothold—or was it a toehold?—in production and direction. Getting on the air was more difficult, and those who did make it to a microphone were supposed to talk about child care, how to prepare a Thanksgiving turkey, and clothes. Although women like Helen Hiett and Mary Marvin Breckinridge had demonstrated in 1940 that they could cover the ultimate story, war, not until a decade later could a woman, Pauline Frederick, establish herself as a correspondent in network ranks.

Pauline Frederick meant to be a lawyer. Her studies at American University were in that direction. She changed course when a teacher convinced her that the world was full of lawyers and she began, in 1931, doing free-lance articles on diplomats' wives for the *Washington Star*—"Her Excellency, Lady Lindsay, small and alert, sat on a settee facing the fire."[10] During World War II she worked as a "legman" for the Blue Network commentator Hjalmar Baukhage. One of her rare early broadcasts was from China's wartime capital, Chungking (spelled Chongqing today). The shortwave report was picked up on a ham radio by a dentist in Ventura, California, who relayed it to the network.

In 1946, after being turned down at CBS and NBC, Frederick got part-time work at ABC doing so-called women's news. Her break came when the network, caught shorthanded, sent her to cover a foreign ministers meeting. She did so well (with her woman's voice) that ABC made her a full-time correspondent. Still, most of the time, she was told to pursue "the woman's angle." Her first assignment was covering a forum on how to get a husband.

It was at ABC that Pauline Frederick began reporting from the United Nations, and she strove for stories—major stories—that no one else had found. The network had to put her on the air with them. It was her strategy for breaking out, at last, from "women's news." The strategy worked so well that in 1953 she went to NBC as its chief United Nations correspondent, an assignment she kept for 21 years.

After mandatory retirement at 65 (she learned of her retirement from the *New York Times*), Frederick served as international affairs analyst and program host for National Public Radio. In 1976, she became the first woman to moderate a presidential debate. She died in 1990.

The first woman to cover the White House for television on a regular basis was Nancy Dickerson. Before her now dissolved marriage to Washington businessman G. Wyatt Dickerson (and before she went to NBC in 1963), CBS viewers knew her as Nancy Hanschman. As Hanschman or Dickerson, she was an aggressive reporter who, like Pauline Frederick, went for the exclusive. One scoop was that President Johnson would choose Senator Humphrey as his running mate in 1964. She had noticed that Mrs. Humphrey was the only senator's wife invited to a tea for Lady Bird Johnson on the eve of the Democratic convention. Twenty-four hours before Johnson planned to announce his choice, with millions watching (and competing correspondents wincing) Nancy Dickerson got him to confirm her hunch. In her memoir, *Among Those Present,* she endorses the view that the woman who achieves as a Washington correspondent has "to work twice as hard and do twice as well as a man." [11]

The first newswoman to achieve the rank of vice president at a network was Marlene Sanders. That was at ABC, where in 1976 she was appointed vice president and director of television documentaries. From 1978 to 1987 she worked as correspondent and documentary producer at CBS. Two honors stand out: In 1975, Sanders was named Broadcast Woman of the Year by American Women in Radio and Television (AWRT). In 1984, the Society of Professional Journalists made her a Fellow, the highest honor it can bestow.

Liz Trotta was television's first woman assigned full-time as a foreign correspondent. The year was 1965. The network was NBC, which knew her from her work as an investigative reporter for WNBC-TV. Trotta was with NBC for 13 years, covering major stories in Europe, Asia, Africa, and the Middle East. She was the only woman to serve three tours as a television correspondent in Vietnam. In 1979, she moved to CBS and reported for that network until 1985, when in a drastic economy wave she and dozens of other news people were dropped. Later, she was Residential Fellow at the Gannett Center for Media Studies.

One of television's first, most important women to cover politics was Catherine "Cassie" Mackin, who broke into prominence in the 1972 presidential campaign. This outspoken ex-Hearst reporter, ex-Nieman Fellow, had been with NBC only a short time when she was assigned to the floor of the Republican national convention. Reviewing her convention performance, Les Brown wrote in the *New York Times* that she came to the assignment well prepared "and was as nimble as any of the floor reporters in pursuing her stories."[12] Translation: As good as any man.

On December 12, 1976, Mackin took over NBC's "Sunday Night News" and so became the first woman to anchor, alone, an evening newscast on any network on a regular basis. She switched the next year to ABC and died of cancer in 1982. Roone Arledge said upon her death, "She was a wonderful woman and a superb journalist."[13] She was 42.

One of the most remarkable women in broadcasting was Dorothy Fuldheim, who at the age of 91 was appearing regularly on her own television news program. The energetic, red-haired nonagenarian began broadcasting in 1947 as a commentator on ABC Radio, but moved within a few months to WEWS-TV, Cleveland. The ABC affiliate had just gone on the air, and she did news and commentary on the station for the next 37 years. Sometimes she covered stories overseas. She was 87 when she flew to Belfast to report on the conflict in Northern Ireland and a year older when she covered the funeral of Egypt's assassinated president, Anwar Sadat. An interview with President Reagan highlighted her last broadcast in 1984.

Here are more pioneers.

ABC's Ann Compton was the first woman to cover the White House on a full-time basis for both radio and television. In December 1974, she joined Tom Jarriel and Steve Bell in providing television coverage. At the same time, she reported for all four ABC radio networks. Philomena Jurey covered the White House for Voice of America for 14 years, starting the same year as Compton. Fay Gillis Wells had the beat for Storer Broadcasting from 1964 to 1977. During the years they worked, the presence of women at presidential news conferences became commonplace. In his book, *At the White House,* Robert Pierpoint remarks that women covering the President have "added both beauty and dignity to our group."[14]

Aline Saarinen, widow of Eero Saarinen, the noted architect, became head of NBC's Paris bureau in 1971, the first woman in television history to hold such a post. An early CBS mainstay was Patricia Bernie, who started in the London bureau in 1954, became field producer and office manager in London, then manager of the Rome bureau. Covering a riot at Rome University, she was shot in the leg. She ultimately was director of European operations for documentaries and "60 Minutes."

Two critically acclaimed documentarians in the 1960s were Helen Jean

Rogers and Lucy Jarvis. Rogers, with her husband, John Secondari, produced the "Saga of Man" series on ABC. Jarvis won top awards for cultural documentaries like "The Kremlin" and "The Louvre."

Jo Moring, as an NBC vice president, was the first woman to head radio news operations at a major network. Joan Richman, who worked her way up from researcher, was the first woman promoted to executive producer of hard news at a television network. She held the title from 1976 to 1982 when she was responsible for the Saturday and Sunday editions of the CBS evening news. In 1976, CBS' Pam Ilott was named vice president and executive producer of religious and cultural affairs broadcasts. No longer in broadcast journalism were the titles vice president and executive producer possessed solely by men.

An early pioneer was Hazel Markel, who reported for several Washington stations, including WTTG when it was part of the old DuMont network in the early 1950s. Marian Glick, who had produced news for DuMont, marked up 30 years as a news editor at CBS. Shirley Wershba, a gofer at CBS News in Paul White's time, in the mid-60s was producing news programs for ABC. Before retirement, she did more production work at CBS and PBS. Grace Diekhaus, who studied journalism at Columbia, was among the first producers to work with Don Hewitt at "60 Minutes."

Any list of pioneering women in broadcast news (and this does not pretend to be a complete list) must include Michele Clark, the first black woman to report from Washington for CBS News. Clark died in a Chicago plane crash in 1972. She was 29 and recognized as one of broadcast journalism's great emerging talents. The Radio-Television News Directors Association established the annual Michele Clark Award in her honor. John Hart, anchor of "World Monitor," speaking at the first presentation of the award, described her as "indeed a journalist of great skill, courage, and sensibility."[15]

Female and Black

It helped stations at licensing time to have a woman on camera, and it helped doubly if the woman was black. And so suddenly, in the 1960s, black women began appearing on television news programs.

Charlayne Hunter-Gault, the first black woman to enroll at the University of Georgia, became an investigative reporter at WRC-TV, then a correspondent for "NewsHour" on PBS. Melba Tolliver, a graduate of New York University's School of Nursing, reported for WABC-TV. Maureen Bunyan anchored at WTOP-TV (now WUSA-TV). Role models at the networks include Carole Simpson, the ABC correspondent who, in 1965, started as a reporter on WCFL-AM, Chicago, and Lee Thornton and Jacqueline Adams, White House correspondents for CBS.

These are just a few.

Hope and a Restrained Hurrah

Women, white and black, have gained more than a foothold. A dramatic demonstration of this came in January 1989 when a woman, Barbara Cohen, resigned as executive producer of NBC's "Meet the Press" to become chief of CBS News' Washington bureau. The appointment made news because she was the first woman ever placed in charge of a network bureau in Washington and because it meant that six of CBS' top news executives in Washington at that time were women. Besides Cohen, they were Mary Martin, deputy bureau chief; Karen Sughrue, executive producer of "Face the Nation"; Susan Zirinsky, senior Washington producer for "The CBS Evening News With Dan Rather"; Deborah Johnson, executive producer of "Nightwatch"; and Deborah Antonellis, director of operations.

Exciting as that may be, reports from the field are mixed. A survey made by Professor Vernon A. Stone of the University of Missouri indicates that, in 1989, blacks and Hispanics working at commercial television stations constituted 17 percent of the news staff, up from 16 percent in 1988. In radio, minorities gained on average only in larger markets.

Another survey by Dr. Stone shows that although the total number of women in radio and television news is virtually unchanged, more news directors are women. In 1988, 18.5 percent of television's news directors were women, up from 14.5 percent in the year before. Smaller though significant gains were made in radio.

Today, women hold about a third of the jobs in broadcast news, a figure that has changed little since the mid-1980s. News operations in general are still dominated by men, which means that men, generally speaking, decide which stories will be covered, who will be promoted, and what policy will be pursued.

35

A Season for Sorrow

Many in network news, as elsewhere, were saying, "Thank God, it's Friday." On the weekend they would find escape from deadlines and the rat race and relax. But early that afternoon it came upon them, and the nation, the news that President Kennedy had been shot. Then, after that, the terrible word: he was dead. During the next four days, until the body of the young president was laid to rest in Arlington, they discovered what working under pressure really was. It was strange how so many, looking back to those days, could recall so little. The extraordinary events had demanded so much and come so fast.

It started as a slow day. Kennedy, seeking party harmony in Texas, was speaking at a Chamber of Commerce breakfast in Fort Worth. Shortly afterward, he would go to Dallas. Europe was quiet. Nor, for the moment, was much happening in Vietnam, where, only three weeks earlier, South Vietnam's President Diem had died in a military coup. By 1:00 P.M., Eastern Standard Time, most people in network newsrooms in New York had gone out for lunch.

In his Chamber of Commerce talk, Kennedy spoke of Fort Worth's contribution to the defense effort in "a very dangerous and uncertain world." Then the short flight to Dallas, where at a luncheon he planned to speak of "the ancient vision of peace on earth." In Dallas, on the way to the luncheon in the presidential limousine—bubble top removed and bullet-proof side windows rolled down because of the pleasant weather and Kennedy's desire to be close to the people—someone fired three shots from an upper floor of the Texas School Book Depository Building. Immediately, the motorcade changed direction and sped toward Parkland Hospital.

UPI's Merriman Smith, riding in the pool car, heard the shooting. He grabbed a radio-telephone and moments later, at 1:34 Eastern Time, UPI interrupted its story about a murder trial to say,

> THREE SHOTS WERE FIRED AT PRESIDENT KENNEDY'S MOTORCADE TODAY IN DOWNTOWN DALLAS.

The teletyped message was not labeled a flash, a bulletin, or even an urgent. But it got attention. One of the first, if not the first, to report the shooting was Don Gardiner of ABC Radio at 1:36.

The flash came three minutes later.

> KENNEDY SERIOUSLY WOUNDED PERHAPS SERIOUSLY PERHAPS FATALLY BY ASSASSIN'S BULLET

The clumsy repetitious wording may well be testimony, not only to haste, but to shock.

At CBS, Walter Cronkite had not gone out to lunch. He was catching up on the news—reading in—and eating a cottage cheese and pineapple salad at his desk, a meal he did not finish. At 1:40 he was on the television network, audio only, saying, "In Dallas, Texas, three shots were fired at President Kennedy's motorcade in downtown Dallas. The first reports say President Kennedy has been seriously wounded by this shooting."

Cronkite was speaking from a converted telephone booth in the main newsroom, down the hall from the combination studio-newsroom from which the evening news originated. The two television cameras in the evening news area were not "hot," nor was there anyone to operate them. For six or seven minutes, until a cameraman came, Cronkite, cramped inside the booth, relayed the bulletin matter pouring in on the AP and UPI wires.

In Dallas, two veteran reporters associated with CBS were trying, out of the confusion, to get the facts. One was Dan Rather, chief of CBS' Dallas bureau. The other was Eddie Barker, news director of KRLD-TV, the CBS affiliate in Dallas.

The big fact was that President Kennedy was dead. Rather was first with the news on CBS Radio, which beat the other networks. How this happened, and how the news got on CBS Television, has been talked about inside CBS, and elsewhere, ever since. In his memoir, *The Camera Never Blinks,* Rather says that when he told the radio editor in New York that according to his information Kennedy was dead, he thought he was talking with Barker. He had been talking on several phones. Barker was still at the

Trade Mart, where Kennedy had been scheduled to speak. Rather was at KRLD. He recalls:

> The radio editor shot back, "Did you say 'dead'? Are you sure, Dan?"
>
> "Right, dead. The President definitely has been shot, and I think he is dead," I said, still believing I was talking all the while to Barker. "That's the word I get from two people at the hospital."

Moments later, because of this misunderstanding, Allan Jackson reported on the CBS Radio Network that the President was dead. This was 17 minutes ahead of anyone else. Rather says that, hearing the bulletin, he felt a chill.[1] What if the President had not died? There was no way to take the story back.

In his memoir, published in 1977, Rather says, "It has never been clear exactly how, and by whom, the signal was given to announce the bulletin."[2] Actually, the "signal" was given by Robert Skedgell, who was in charge of the radio newsroom at the time. Skedgell says:

> I was standing in Paul White's old office. Mort Dank [an editor] was on the phone with Rather, and I heard him ask, "You say he's dead?" Then I took the phone from Mort. I asked, "Are you sure? Are you absolutely certain? He said he was, so I took a piece of yellow copy paper and wrote "JFK DEAD" and handed it to Allan, who then went on the air.
>
> I was driven by the old professional thing about being right and being first. But we knew the President had been shot in the head. All my instincts told me he was dead, and I had absolutely no doubt that Rather was telling me the President was dead—he had got it from a doctor. I had no reason to disbelieve him.[3]

It was after the radio report that Eddie Barker reported on CBS Television that President Kennedy was dead. The network had aired rumors to that effect. Cronkite had responsibly labeled them as rumors. But now, reporting from the Trade Mart, Barker had something that was more than a rumor. He said:

> The word we have is that President Kennedy is dead. This we do not know for a fact. . . . The word we have is from a doctor on the staff at Parkland Hospital who says that it is true. He was in tears when he told me just a moment ago. This is still not officially confirmed, but, as I say, the source would normally be a good one.

The doctor was a friend of Barker's. What he had told the newsman was: "Eddie, he's dead." In reporting his television exclusive, Barker thought his words were being carried only on KRLD.[4] Instead, millions of people had heard.

A minute later, Cronkite, who was now on camera at his anchor desk, said, "We just have a report from our correspondent, Dan Rather, in Dallas that he has confirmed that President Kennedy is dead." He emphasized that there was still no official confirmation.

At 2:37, as news editor, I handed Cronkite a piece of copy from the AP wire. He read it carefully—to himself—then looked up into the camera and said, his voice breaking, "From Dallas, Texas, a flash, apparently official. President Kennedy died at 1 P.M., Central Standard Time, two o'clock, Eastern Standard Time." He looked at the studio clock and added, "Some 38 minutes ago."

The news keeps breaking, and all networks—all reporters, editors, photographers, writers, producers—are trying to keep pace.

Governor John Connally of Texas, who was struck by a bullet as he rode with Kennedy, is expected to live.

Aboard *Air Force One*, Lyndon Johnson takes the oath of office. Jacqueline Kennedy, in a wool suit splotched with blood, stands beside him. Sid Davis of Westinghouse Broadcasting, one of a three-man pool, is the only broadcast journalist present.

Police capture a suspect, a slight, pale-faced man who shot and killed a patrolman trying to question him. The suspect is Lee Harvey Oswald, a high school dropout, twice court-martialed while in the Marines. Detectives find, and question, the suspect's Russian-born wife.

Cameraman Jim Underwood of KRLD-TV gets exclusive footage of Oswald being brought into police headquarters.

Two newsmen from WFAA-TV, Dallas, also score a beat. Police take Tom Alyea and Pierce Allman inside the Texas School Book Depository, now cordoned off, and show them what is believed to be the murder weapon, a 6.5-millimeter Mannlicher-Carcano carbine with telescopic sight. It was hidden behind some cartons on the fifth floor. Three spent shells have been found by a sixth-floor window.

The world, watching, sees *Air Force One* take off for Washington, bearing both President Johnson and the body of the slain president. It is announced that the funeral will be on Monday with burial in Arlington National Cemetery. Correspondents report from Dallas that Oswald has been formally charged with murdering both Kennedy and the patrolman, J. D. Tippit. CBS and Eddie Barker join forces to track down an amateur photographer believed to have shot 8-millimeter film of the assassination. To obtain such footage would be a tremendous coup.

Air Force One touches down at Andrews Air Force Base, outside Washington. It is 5:59 and already dark. The darkness underscores the atmosphere of gloom. Jacqueline Kennedy insists on accompanying the casket in the Navy ambulance. When she has left, the new president goes on the air. He speaks briefly. "We have suffered a loss that cannot be weighed. . . . I will do my best."

The long day ends with special broadcasts—instant documentaries— that try to put together, piece by piece, what has happened. Memorial concerts are scheduled through the night.

The next day, Saturday, Dallas police claim they have an airtight case.

Ballistic tests, they say, prove that the rifle bearing Oswald's fingerprints is the murder weapon. The suspect himself is grilled for hours. Each time he is taken from his cell for questioning, he faces a chorus of reporters' questions. Many of the questions, such as "Why did you kill the President?", presume guilt.[5] In Washington, foreign dignitaries are arriving for the funeral. They include France's Charles de Gaulle, Greece's Queen Frederika, Israel's Golda Meir, Ethiopia's old, embattled emperor, Haile Selassie, and Baudouin, king of the Belgians. In the afternoon, President Johnson receives them and former Presidents Truman and Eisenhower at the White House, where, on camera, they pay their respects.

On Sunday, while Washington is becoming what historian Erik Barnouw calls "a scene of unparallel pageantry,"[6] a new ugly drama is in the making in Dallas. Oswald is to be transferred from City Prison to the county jail. The plan is to bring him down by elevator to the basement, then take him to the jail by armored car. Between forty and fifty reporters and about seventy police officers are crowded in the basement area, waiting to witness the transfer. Oswald, handcuffed to a detective, comes out of the elevator. As he is led toward the car, a short, pudgy man steps forward and fires a pistol shot into Oswald's stomach. Millions of NBC viewers see Oswald grimace with pain and collapse. It is murder, live, on television. The first time.

ABC and CBS don't have it. They are taking the pool feed from Washington, where Kennedy's body is about to be taken from the White House to the rotunda of the Capitol to lie in state. They catch up as best they can by playing back tape of the shooting. The picture is indelible in the mind of every viewer. Nothing comparable to it will be seen until the moonwalk six years later.

Oswald is rushed by ambulance to Parkland Hospital, where he dies of internal bleeding only a few feet from the spot where President Kennedy was pronounced dead two days before. The man who shot him is readily identified as Jack Ruby, owner of a striptease joint called the Carousel. Police know him well because he is always hanging around headquarters, handing out passes to his shows. He is charged with murder in the first degree.

CBS, with the help of the Dallas police, the FBI, and the KRLD staff, has found the man who filmed the motorcade at the instant President Kennedy was shot. He is Abraham Zapruder, a wholesale clothier who, through a lawyer, puts the precious 22-second record of history up for bids. Because of CBS' cooperation in processing the film, Rather sees it first and goes on the air, describing what he saw: Kennedy struck brutally by a bullet in the head. CBS advises him to start the bidding at $10,000 for a one-time showing. Then comes the heartbreaker. When Rather gets back to the lawyer he is told that, in his absence, *Life* magazine has made a preemptive bid. It will pay so much money that further bidding is futile.[7]

Throughout Sunday afternoon and into the night, people, perhaps 250,000, file solemnly past the bier in the Capitol rotunda. The crowd waiting outside is so large no camera can encompass it except from a distance with a long lens. It takes six hours, sometimes seven, to reach the flag-draped coffin, pause in the stillness, and pass.

On Monday, at 9 A.M., the bronze doors of the Capitol are closed, ending the lying in state. Two hours later, after the coffin is mounted on a caisson, the cortege leaves for St. Matthew's Cathedral, where Richard Cardinal Cushing of Boston, who married John and Jacqueline Kennedy, conducts the Requiem Mass.

At 1:30, the procession resumes. It moves to the beat of muffled drums, a throbbing, almost as though the nation's heart can be heard, in offices, hospitals, factories, restaurants, automobiles, homes, aboard airliners and ships. Everywhere. The caisson is drawn by six gray horses, paired, and viewers see, just behind it, the spirited black horse without rider, symbolizing the lost leader. Marching with the military units are the bagpipers of the Black Watch Highland Regiment from Scotland, who only 12 days earlier delighted Kennedy when they played for him at the White House.

Television viewing reaches the highest level ever recorded up to that time—93 percent of homes with television, according to Nielsen, are tuned in. More than half of them stay tuned for 13 consecutive hours. Radio, with its coverage, is demonstrating the peculiar power of sound alone— the sharp, piercing swirl of bagpipes, the muffled drum beat, the clatter of the caisson on the pavement, the long, mournful bugle notes of Taps.

The sight of such solemnity and sadness, and the hearing of such sound, is almost beyond bearing. Men and women covering the story, in newsrooms and on location, are not immune. In Dallas, Robert MacNeil of NBC[8] is preparing a report from the grassy knoll by the Texas School Book Depository, where people, sorrowful and ashamed of what happened in their city, have placed bouquets of flowers. He recalls:

> While we were filming, an old man sat down near us and turned on his transister radio. Over it came the broadcast of the President's funeral in Washington. It was when I heard the lament played by the bagpipes of the Black Watch Regiment . . . that I really understood, with my feelings, what had happened. I sat there in the sunshine with the tears running out of my eyes, aware of how much the salt in them burned because crying was such an unaccustomed thing to do.[9]

Broadcasters along the route of the procession are experiencing similar feelings. Some are fighting tears. All are restrained in their commentary. What is happening has its own eloquence.

"A Chapter of Honor"

In terms of coverage, the funeral presented networks with their greatest challenge since the coming of television. So much had to be done quickly. Telephone and power companies in Washington opened man-holes so underground cables could be strung, carrying pictures from scores of locations to an emergency master control room in the Capitol. Cameras not only transmitted pictures from points along the route but moved with the procession. Other cameras captured the spectacle from aircraft over-head.

ABC, CBS, and NBC pooled their effort. CBS, on toss of a coin, took charge and directed the operation from the Capitol control center, with Arthur Kane as executive producer. NBC had responsibility for transmit-ting the story by satellite to 23 countries, including the Soviet Union. As one American wrote from abroad, "The whole world stopped to cry with us."[10]

Extra cameras were flown in from bureaus as far away as California, more than fifty in all, and stationed along the route from the Capitol to St. Matthew's Cathedral, at the Lincoln Memorial, on Memorial Bridge, along the Avenue of Heroes, and at Arlington National Cemetery. Each network had other cameras for supplementing the pool coverage. ABC, for ex-ample, contributed thirteen cameras to the pool and reserved five to use as it chose. Altogether, the networks deployed more than twenty mobile units. It was, for that time, a total commitment. In the *New York Times*, Jack Gould said, "When the day's history is written, the record of television as a medium will constitute a chapter of honor."[11]

From November 22 through November 25 NBC Television devoted 71 hours and 36 minutes to events surrounding the assassination. The other television networks devoted almost as much time. CBS Films sent footage with a running time of 13 hours by jet transport to 38 countries. Radio's words and "natural sound" brought the tragedy to people whom television's pictures could not reach. In various ways, more than 2,000 network personnel took part.[12] For broadcasters and advertising agencies, the cost exceeded 32 million dollars.[13]

The broadcasts produced a national catharsis. David Brinkley says, "I think we gave people a place to center their grief, rather than being alone."[14] Frank Stanton addressed a memorandum to CBS personnel in which, in thanking them for "a great and memorable accomplishment," he recalled the "wild rumors" and "divisive recriminations" that had followed the assassination of President Lincoln on another Friday a century earlier. Stanton said:

> There have been, of course, many factors in our national growth since 1865 that accounted for our ability as a people to handle ourselves with more wisdom and restraint. . . . It is no exaggeration to suggest that not the least of these was the capacity of electronic communications to bring a shocked people together in common awareness, in common sympathy, and in common rededication.[15]

So it ended.

Only it did not. Questions arose as to whether Oswald, in killing the President, had acted alone. Was he even guilty? He had been presumed guilty and questioned relentlessly without benefit of counsel. In a lead editorial, the *New York Times* said that Dallas authorities, abetted by the press, print and broadcast, "trampled on every principle of justice." They had a duty, the newspaper said, to protect the prisoner. They knew the possibility of an attempt on Oswald's life. Yet, to accommodate television, they decided to transfer him publicly at noontime instead of quietly late at night as originally planned. Now, it pointed out, there could be no trial to determine the truth.[16]

Stanton was right; there was no governmental crisis as in 1865. But accusations and rumors were sufficient for President Johnson to appoint a blue-ribbon commission headed by Chief Justice Earl Warren of the Supreme Court to investigate. In a lengthy report released on September 27, 1964, the Warren Commission concluded that Oswald was solely responsible for the Kennedy assassination. It decried "the regrettable lack of self-discipline" on the part of reporters. Their "uninhibited access" to Oswald, it said, led to "chaotic conditions" which were not conducive to the protection of his rights. Nevertheless, the commission conceded that the news media were less responsible for the congestion at police headquarters than had sometimes been claimed.

Lessons Are Learned

The ugly year 1968 saw the assassination of Dr. Martin Luther King, Jr., on a motel balcony in Memphis and Robert Kennedy in a hotel pantry in Los Angeles. Again, radio and television bound the country together, making it, momentarily, one family in mourning. Something in society seemed to be breeding assassins. "I wished I could have turned off the world by turning off the television," wrote television critic Dean Gysel of the *Chicago Daily News*.[17] "There's something unreal about this," said NBC's Edwin Newman. "Nothing changes—only the name."[18]

But one thing had changed. As the *Washington Post*'s television critic, Lawrence Laurent, noted the day after Robert Kennedy was shot, "The lessons of Dallas have been learned, both by TV reporters and by public officials. Police in Los Angeles make little effort to 'accommodate' the reporters. . . . TV reporters, in turn, refrain from referring to Sirhan[19] as either 'assassin' or 'killer' or 'would-be murderer'."[20] Later, there would be attempts on the lives of George Wallace, Gerald Ford, and Ronald Reagan. The media were having occasion, to society's shame, for becoming ever more adept at assassination coverage.

Two Landmarks in Reporting

Two outstanding assassination series have come from CBS News. The first, with Walter Cronkite and Eric Sevareid, appeared as a four-hour series in 1967. The feeling at CBS was that even if its own investigation supported the findings of the Warren Commission, it still would have performed a public service; so much in the commission report had been brought into question. For example, could Oswald alone have fired three shots within the time span given in the commission report? CBS conducted tests showing it was possible. Further tests were made, angles of trajectories studied. Commission members who had never talked to reporters were interviewed. Altogether, the series cost half a million dollars to produce. Rick DuBrow, the UPI critic, called it "a rare and important experience in television journalism."[21]

Eight years later, in 1975, CBS followed up with another ambitious work, "The American Assassins," which, on four consecutive nights, ran for an hour in prime time. In addition to its own findings and the findings of the Warren Commission, CBS News now had access to an accumulation of articles and books on the subject, as well as insights from the assassination of two more public figures, Robert Kennedy and Dr. King, and from the attempted assassination of George Wallace.

The original Zapruder film was shown during the first two hours devoted to questions persisting about the assassination of President Kennedy. Through the cooperation of Itek, a film analysis organization, CBS provided viewers with a frame-by-frame, split-second examination of the footage, showing in detail the sequence in which both the President and Connally were hit. Dr. James Weston, president-elect of the American Academy of Forensic Scientists, discussed the Kennedy autopsy report. The CIA's relationship to Oswald and his Cuban connection were reported. The final two hours dealt in comparable detail with the assassination of Robert Kennedy and Dr. King and the attempt on Governor Wallace's life.

It was a formidable undertaking, and "The American Assassins" received the George Foster Peabody Award as the outstanding documentary of 1975. The program, the *Washington Post* said, "demonstrate[s] what can happen when a news organization decides to commit a great deal of time and a great deal of money to examine an important subject."[22] "The American Assassins" and the earlier four-part series, taken together, may constitute CBS' greatest achievement, as well as effort, in investigative reporting.

The executive producer of both series was Leslie Midgley. Other producers were Hal Haley, Ernest Leiser, and Lee Townsend, but the only producer to work with Midgley from the start was Bernard Birnbaum. The correspondent for "The American Assassins" was Dan Rather.

36
War:
The People Watched

No matter the thousands of hours of news on radio and television, no matter the millions of column inches in newspapers and magazines, the American people never knew what they were getting into. It happened little by little. Painlessly at first. A long way off. Then one day what was happening was called a war and by that time it was too late.

A region no larger than the state of New Mexico, Vietnam had been a battleground for nine years (1945–1954) as France fought unsuccessfully to reimpose colonial rule. As early as 1950, President Truman assigned military advisers to the French. President Eisenhower sent more advisers and a billion dollars in aid. Vice President Nixon suggested intervention by U.S. combat forces. The debate over how far to go in helping France ended in May 1954 when a Viet Minh army overwhelmed the French at Dienbienphu. France, after suffering 92,000 dead and missing, got out of it. The United States, learning not enough from the French lesson, gradually got in.

Although the United States took part in the Geneva conference that ended France's involvement, it refused to sign the agreements that were reached.[1] One agreement was that the division of Vietnam along the 17th parallel, creating North and South Vietnam, was not to be interpreted as a political or territorial boundary. Few Americans knew that, which is a commentary on the American press, radio and television included. Another agreement was that elections looking toward reunification were to be held in 1956. Ho Chi Minh, the Communist leader who had fought, and defeated, both Japanese and French occupiers of his country, became president of North Vietnam, while Ngo Dinh Diem, a wealthy nationalist who sat out the struggle, headed an anti-Communist government in the South. Diem ignored the elections agreement, which South Vietnam also had not signed. The United States backed him. The fatal commitment had begun.

What it could not achieve through elections, North Vietnam sought— first with guerrilla fighters, then with regular army units—to obtain through force. Ho got help from China and the Soviet Union; Diem got help from the United States, almost two and a half billion dollars between 1954 and 1962 and more military advisers. By 1963 the number of advisers had grown to 12,000.

Diem's ineffectual administration and repression of the Buddhists brought the U.S. aid program into question in Congress. It was then, in September 1963, that President Kennedy told Walter Cronkite that, after all, it was a war for the Vietnamese themselves to win or lose.[2] A week later, interviewed by Chet Huntley and David Brinkley, Kennedy said the United States should not withdraw its aid, but he did want Diem to clean up his act.[3]

On November 1, 1963, Diem was killed in a military coup. The United States denied any hand in it, then quickly recognized the new government. Three weeks after Diem, Kennedy himself was assassinated, and Lyndon Johnson inherited the problem. He doubled the number of advisers, but things still went badly as South Vietnamese governments, one after another, failed to win popular support. Johnson needed an incident that would let the United States teach North Vietnam a lesson.

The Die Is Cast

The incident occurred in August 1964. Two U.S. destroyers, the *Maddox* and *C. Turner Joy,* patrolling the Gulf of Tonkin, radioed that they had been attacked by Communist PT boats. Although the destroyers were operating provocatively close to North Vietman and suffered no loss of life, President Johnson pictured the skirmish as a major incident. On August 5, in a nationwide broadcast, he asked Congress to pass a resolution that would "give convincing evidence to the aggressive Communist nations" that such acts could not be committed with impunity.

When CBS, after only a recap of the President's speech, returned to regular programming, Ed Murrow, dying of cancer, was dismayed. He telephoned Fred Friendly, then head of CBS News, demanding to know how he could have let the critical moment pass without having correspondents assess what Johnson had said. The President had used radio and television to pressure Congress. As Murrow saw it, CBS had the same means—and duty—to examine the speech's implications. He believed fervently that such a large issue warranted debate.[4]

There was almost no debate. Two days later, Congress adopted a resolution supporting the President in "all necessary measures to repel any armed attack against the forces of the United States and to prevent further aggression." Johnson had in his pocket what amounted to a blank check. He would not have to go back to Congress for a declaration of war.

In his crucial broadcast, Johnson misled the country. He gave the impression of unprovoked aggression in the Gulf of Tonkin when actually the destroyers, prowling off the coast of North Vietnam, had been spying on radar installations. There is doubt that an attack on the *C. Turner Joy* ever occurred. But commentators and those who heard them generally approved Congress' action. Underpinning all rationale, says Erik Barnouw, was the sense of "worldwide conspiracy and the argument that 'they' had to be stopped in Vietnam or 'they' would sweep the world.[5] So began America's longest war and television's longest running story.

Deceit was practiced from the start. It was policy. In 1962, long before the Tonkin Gulf incident, the State Department cabled Saigon: "IT IS NOT—REPEAT NOT—IN OUR INTEREST . . . TO HAVE STORIES INDICATING THAT AMERICANS ARE LEADING AND DIRECTING COMBAT MISSIONS AGAINST THE VIET CONG."[6] The cable was sent at a time when the United States had more than 10,000 "advisory personnel" in Vietnam. Not until three years later was the arrival of U.S. combat forces announced.

Correspondents began their coverage of the Vietnam War as believers. They believed in their country's cause and, in the first years, generally accepted official statements at face value. Disillusionment came gradually. Too often reporters, told one thing, saw another. And because there was no censorship—this was an undeclared war—they reported what they saw. Through television, Americans for the first time could see a great deal of what war correspondents were seeing. Opponents of the war, angered by what they saw, demonstrated in the streets. Supporters accused broadcasters of undermining the war effort—how dare they show body bags and so much blood. In fact, what the television viewer saw was sanitized. Producers did go for action footage but routinely cut out the bloodiest scenes.[7] Still, viewers scolded the networks for showing too much.

This was not the first "living room war," as Michael Arlen phrased it, the historic role of television notwithstanding. The first was World War II, brought into American living rooms—and bedrooms and kitchens—by radio. One thinks of Archibald MacLeish telling Murrow, "You laid the dead of London at our doors."[8] But the pictures, what Meg Greenfield calls "those searing television tableaux," did make a difference. If you saw them, you see them still: a nine-year-old girl screaming as she runs naked after a napalm attack; a captured Viet Cong officer executed as casually as a greeting, a bullet in the head; Americans, besieged in their embassy, airlifted from the roof.

Ever since the end of the war, questions have been raised over the pictures. Did they distort? Can a visual medium, relying so heavily on pictures—the more dramatic the better—avoid distortion? Did the pictures harden viewers to violence or heighten feeling? Did they shorten the war or prolong it? Should they have been censored? What of the future? Does the realism of uncensored television make impossible the successful prosecution of war?

The earliest network correspondents in Vietnam came from bureaus in Tokyo and Hong Kong: Lou Cioffi and Charles Arnot for ABC; Murray Fromson, Adam Raphael, Peter Kalischer, and Bernard Kalb for CBS; and Welles Hangen, John Rich, Jim Robinson, and John Sharkey for NBC. No network had a correspondent serving full time in Vietnam until 1964, when NBC's Garrick Utley set up a permanent Saigon bureau. The CBS bureau was established by Morley Safer, transferred from London. ABC followed suit with Malcolm Browne, a Pulitzer Prize winner hired away from AP. In time, dozens of network correspondents arrived, usually for tours of 18 months or less.[9]

In the end, more than two hundred correspondents, producers, bureau managers, soundmen, and photographers worked for radio and television in Vietnam. A few reporters were from stations. Frank Reynolds' coverage for WBKB-TV, now WLS-TV, Chicago, attracted the attention of ABC News, which soon hired him. Bob Schieffer, who would join CBS News, reported from Vietnam for the *Fort Worth Star-Telegram*. The paper owned WBAP-TV, now WXAS-TV. It had Schieffer take along a silent camera, but when he arrived in Saigon, customs impounded it. To serve its stations, Westinghouse Broadcasting set up a Saigon bureau in 1965. Jim Russell did good work for UPI Audio. And, of course, there were others.

The Blackest Day

The blackest day for network newsmen was May 31, 1970, when nine disappeared while covering the invasion of Cambodia by U.S. and South Vietnamese forces. One of them was NBC correspondent Welles Hangen.[10] Two NBC cameramen, Yoshiko Waku and Roger Colne, disappeared with him. Waku was Japanese. Colne, a journalist-adventurer type, was a Frenchman who had once been an architect. Vanishing with them was their Cambodian driver.

CBS lost six men. They were correspondent George Syvertsen, reporter-producer Gerald Miller, soundman Kojiro Sakai, and photographers Tomoharu Ishii, Ramnik Lekhi and Dana Stone. Another who disappeared that day was Sean Flynn, who was writing for *Time*. The son of Errol Flynn, the actor, he was riding up to the front on his motorcycle. The NBC crew was traveling in a rented van. The CBS crew was split up, riding in a battered old sedan and a Jeep. It was a bright Sunday morning when they started out from the Cambodian capital, Phnom Penh, for the village of Takeo, where there was supposed to be some action. Together they made a strung-out convoy headed for disaster.

Eleven years later, it was revealed that CBS had hired a platoon of Cambodian mercenaries in an effort to recover the bodies of the CBS News team. The expedition was led by Gordon Manning, vice president of CBS News, later a news executive at NBC. With him went David Miller, CBS bureau manager in Saigon, and Stuart Witt, who directed the network's financial dealings overseas.

Manning tells what is believed to have happened to the CBS newsmen on May 31, 1970, and how their bodies were recovered:

> [They] went to Takeo that Sunday morning in a French military jeep obtained in Phnom Penh. All were dressed in military khaki. . . . The Viet Cong had infiltrated the village. When they saw the French jeep and what looked like military men aboard, they presumably fired rocket-propelled grenades at the bright, sun-lit target, killing all four CBS staffers.
>
> As we reconstructed the scene later on arrival in Takeo, the V.C. must have searched the bodies and then found they had killed journalists. We surmised, since the jeep was blackened, that they set fire to the vehicle, attempting to leave the impression that there had been an accident and a fire. The four were buried in shallow graves on the grounds of the small farm complex.
>
> Back in Phnom Penh, when neither the Syvertsen party nor the Hangen party returned the following day, they were reported missing. A few days later, a Takeo native reaching the capital brought word of the abandoned NBC car and the burned and riddled CBS car, adding that four bodies had been buried at the scene by the V.C.
>
> The problem, once I arrived in Phnom Penh, was getting down to Takeo with reasonable security to find out what had happened to our men. The U.S. chargé d'affaires in the capital was not interested in helping us. . . . U.S. policy at the time was to downplay the expansion of the war into Cambodia and discourage press coverage.
>
> We waited a couple of weeks, hoping day to day that the area around Takeo would be cleared. Frustrated, we finally went to Major Lon Non, brother of the then Cambodian prime minister, Lon Nol, seeking some mercenaries to provide security for the CBS team bent on learning the fate of the missing crew and recovering their bodies, if indeed they were dead as feared. . . . Fresh in mind was the fact that in order for the families to collect full insurance, the bodies had to be recovered and positively identified. . . . We gave Major Lon an expensive shortwave radio and some sweet talk, and he assigned us a platoon of his special soldiers (30 to 40) and two trucks for the Takeo expedition.

Luckily, the Viet Cong had abandoned Takeo, and the search team had no trouble finding the bodies of Syvertsen, Miller, Lekhi, and their jeep driver. Due to decomposition, identification had to be made from dental records forwarded to Phnom Penh. Witt paid off the mercenaries. According to Manning, it added up to no more than $400. In a postscript, he says:

> In retrospect, one can question the judgment of Syvertsen and the others in going to Takeo that day dressed in khaki and riding in a military jeep. But they were in pursuit of an aspect of an important story, the extension of the Vietnam War into Cambodia.[11]

No trace was found of the CBS newsmen traveling in the sedan or members of Hangen's party. Altogether, 22 representatives of American news organizations were listed as missing in Cambodia and now are presumed dead. A committee of journalists headed by Walter Cronkite sought unsuccessfully for more than five years to learn their fate.

Welles Hangen was a brilliant journalist who had graduated *summa cum laude* from Brown University at the age of 18. Gerald Miller, a 12-year veteran of the Associated Press, had been with CBS less than a year. As a member of the armed forces, he had survived both World War II and the Korean War. Lawrence Lichty, the historian, knew George Syvertsen. He says the CBS correspondent believed fellow correspondents weren't "going out" enough. "He thought that they depended too much on handouts and failed to look beyond."[12]

They died "looking beyond."

Two Reporters, Two Reports

Two of the networks' most frequently decorated correspondents, in terms of awards for Vietnam reporting, were Morley Safer and John Laurence. Safer won the Paul White, George Foster Peabody, and George Polk awards in addition to three Overseas Press Club awards. Laurence won the Overseas Press Club, George Polk, and Alfred I. duPont–Columbia University awards, plus two Emmys.

A Canadian, Safer began his career reporting for newspapers and the Canadian Broadcasting Corporation. He had been with CBS only a year when he opened the network's Saigon bureau in 1965. Laurence worked at stations in Bridgeport, Connecticut; Washington, D.C.; and New York City before joining CBS in January 1965. After he covered the U.S. military intervention in the Dominican Republic, CBS sent him to Vietnam.

Both Laurence and Safer liked to be where the action was. Laurence's experience with an Army patrol resulted in "The World of Charlie Company," one of the most honored documentaries to come out of the war. It showed G.I.s close to mutiny, balking at orders that seemed to them unreasonable. This was something never seen on television before. It was a

349

character study that spoke eloquently, if sadly, of the kind of war that was being fought.[13]

The other report could be datelined Cam Ne, August 3, 1965. Safer's cable to CBS News, New York, began: "FFFYYYIII EYE WAS ONLY CORRESPONDENT TODAYS BURNING OF HAMLET BY MARINES SURROUNDING VILLAGE OF CAM NE RPT CAM NE STOP AGENCIES QUOTING MY REPORTS STOP HEREWITH BRIEF DESCRIPTIVE STOP." Safer told how first with cigarette lighters, then with flame throwers, the Marines burned down more than a hundred dwellings.

> OLD MEN ETWOMEN PLEADING TO SPARE HOUSES WERE IGNORED AND HOUSES BURNED WITH TOTAL BELONGINGS OF PEOPLE STOP PLEAS TO DELAY BURNINGS SO THAT BELONGINGS COULD BE REMOVED ALSO IGNORED STOP ALL RICE STORES BURNED AS WELL STOP ALL ABOVE PERSONALLY EYEWITNESSED BUT SUBSEQUENTLY LEARNED THAT PLATOON ON RIGHT FLANK WOUNDED THREE WOMEN KILLED ONE CHILD IN ROCKET BARRAGE STOP

The Marines suffered two wounded, both by their own fire.

Fred Friendly, in New York, bought a special line to the West Coast so he could screen the film before it went on the air. He and Ernest Leiser, executive producer of the evening news, knew they would be in trouble if they ran it. They also knew, after checking with Safer for accuracy, that they had to. The film showed American fighting men in a bad light, but what it showed had happened. And what had happened was significant. It could be a factor in winning the hearts and minds of the Vietnamese people, a precondition to winning the war.[14]

No sooner had the piece aired before CBS received calls accusing the network of betrayal. The Pentagon wanted Safer out of Vietnam; Friendly stood firm. President Johnson ordered a check on Safer to see whether he was a Communist. When the investigation cleared him, Johnson grumbled, "Well, I knew he wasn't an American."[15]

A Matter of Conscience

In 1966, a Senate hearing on Vietnam precipitated the resignation of Friendly as president of CBS News. The immediate issue was live daytime coverage of the testimony of George F. Kennan, former ambassador to Moscow, before the Foreign Relations Committee. NBC covered the hearing live. Friendly wanted to do so but was overruled by John Schneider, who had come in as head of CBS' Broadcast Group. Schneider contended that Kennan's testimony could be covered adequately with excerpts on the evening news. So instead of live coverage of Kennan, a recognized authority on Communism, CBS aired reruns of "I Love Lucy" and "The Real McCoys."

The larger issue in Friendly's resignation was his inability, in making such decisions, to go directly to either William S. Paley, CBS board chairman, or Frank Stanton, president of CBS, as he and other heads of the news division had been able to do in the past. Lost, said Friendly in his letter of resignation, was the fundamental "concept of an autonomous news organization responsible only to the chairman and the president."[16]

In leaving, Friendly said Murrow would have understood, the Murrow who held that television had a duty to enlighten, the same Murrow who had jumped him for not having correspondents analyze, at once, President Johnson's fateful Tonkin Gulf speech.[17]

Friendly went from CBS to become the Ford Foundation's chief adviser on public television and Edward R. Murrow Professor at the Columbia Graduate School of Journalism. His successor at CBS was Richard S. Salant, the brilliant, gutsy, Harvard-trained lawyer who had run the news operation from 1961 to 1964.

Tet

On January 30, 1968, during the Tet holidays marking the Vietnamese New Year, the Viet Cong, reinforced by North Vietnamese regulars, launched a series of lightning attacks throughout South Vietnam. Only weeks before, General William C. Westmoreland, commander of U.S. forces in Vietnam, had pictured the enemy reeling. Now the enemy seemed to be attacking everywhere, even inside the U.S. Embassy compound in Saigon.

Walter Cronkite had visited Vietnam in 1965. With the surprise offensive it was time, he felt, for another firsthand look. What he saw was disillusioning. Hue was an example. Westmoreland had told him the situation was under control, but when Cronkite got there he found Hue in Communist hands and U.S. Marines in a fierce battle to retake the city. Marines were astonished to see the famous correspondent, in steel helmet, in the midst of the street fighting. "It was almost," says Gary Paul Gates, "as if he wanted to be absolutely certain that what he saw in Hue was truly happening."[18]

On his return to New York, Cronkite went on the air and gave testimony.

> To say that we are closer to victory today is to believe, in the face of the evidence, the optimists who have been wrong in the past. To suggest we are on the edge of defeat is to yield to unreasonable pessimism. To say that we are mired in stalemate seems the only realistic, yet unsatisfactory conclusion.
>
> On the off chance that military and political analysts are right, in the next few months we must test the enemy's intentions in case this is indeed his last big gasp before negotiations. But it is increasingly clear to this reporter that the only rational way out then will be to negotiate, not as victors, but as an honorable people who

lived up to their pledge to defend democracy and did the best they could.[19]

Because of Cronkite's popularity and trustworthiness, his words carried tremendous weight. They shook Lyndon Johnson, who concluded that if Cronkite thought the war was unwinnable, so did much of the country. It was the most telling demonstration of a respected broadcaster's influence since Ed Murrow's McCarthy broadcast 14 years earlier. As Barbara Tuchman saw it, "The nation's uncle had rendered judgment."[20]

The "judgment" was out of character. What had happened to Cronkite's famed objectivity, his commitment to impartial reporting? Years later, Cronkite said he spoke his mind "because of the great confusion the American people found themselves in at the time."[21] He pointed out that he did it, not on the evening news but in a special broadcast, that his comment deliberately was separated from the body of the broadcast by a commercial, and that he specifically labeled what he said as "speculative" and "personal."[22]

One month after Cronkite's broadcast, President Johnson called for peace talks and, addressing the nation, stunned it by saying he would not seek reelection. History had caught up with the macho Texan and shattered him.

At ABC, Howard K. Smith remained a hawk. He not only believed in the American purpose but felt that, properly supported, it could be achieved. Huntley and Brinkley were inclined to share Cronkite's view. Huntley, more objective than Brinkley on television, expressed his doubt most strongly in a *TV Guide* article. He wrote that while he carried no brief for Ho Chi Minh,

> we are in the process of discovering, most painfully, that given the characteristics of the Vietnamese people, given the terrain and the geographical location of Vietnam, and given the enemy's type of warfare, Vietnam may lie beyond the outer reaches of our power.[23]

As solo anchor on a Saturday edition of the nightly news,[24] Brinkley gave what Jack Gould of the *New York Times* called "a sensitive account of how the Vietnamese war bears down on many individuals at home, while so much of society blithely goes its affluent ways." He thought that by "taking a half-hour to detail this divisive contradiction, Brinkley and his colleagues said it better than any number of televised battle scenes." The effect, said Gould, was "an appeal for peace, all the more moving because it was couched in such soft terms."[25]

A Grim Boxscore

It seemed that the war might end soon. In April 1968, two months after Tet and four days after Lyndon Johnson announced he would not seek a second term, North Vietnam agreed to preliminary peace talks in

Paris. Richard Nixon, exuding peace, became president. North Vietnam admitted American reporters to see the damage inflicted by U.S. bombing. Charles Collingwood of CBS, the first network correspondent to go, interviewed the North Vietnamese premier, Pham Van Dong. So did Harrison Salisbury of the *New York Times*. Despite objections from members of Congress, public television aired "Inside North Vietnam," produced by Felix Greene, a British subject who had once worked for the BBC. CBS, underwriter of the production, had carried excerpts.

In January 1969, the Paris talks were expanded to include South Vietnam and the Viet Cong; initially, only the United States and North Vietnam had met. As negotiations continued, so did the fighting. Each week, network anchors, with stark figures behind them on the screen, broadcast the number of American, South Vietnamese, and enemy dead for the previous week. Specifying that these were *reported* figures—that is, figures given out by the military in Saigon—they betrayed skepticism regarding the consistently high figure for enemy dead.

"I Want Them Dead"

Another television "shocker" came in 1969. An Army platoon led by Lieutenant William L. Calley, Jr., killed more than 90 Vietnamese civilians. The place was the village of My Lai, and what happened there became known as the My Lai massacre. An account of the atrocity, researched by free-lance writer Seymour Hersh, had appeared in more than thirty newspapers, but it was not until a broadcast interview by Mike Wallace with a participant in the massacre that the country awoke to the proportions of what had happened.

The interview, carried on both the CBS morning and evening news, was with Paul Meadlo, who had been a private in Calley's platoon. Meadlo said villagers were rounded up and made to squat down "like a little island right there in the center of the village."

> MEADLO: Lieutenant Calley came over and said, "You know what to do with them, don't you?" And I said yes. I took it for granted that he just wanted us to watch them. And he left and came back 10 or 15 minutes later and said, "How come you ain't killed them yet?" And I told him that I didn't think you wanted us to kill them. I thought you just wanted us to guard them. He said, "No, I want them dead."
>
> WALLACE: He told this to all of you or to you in particular?
>
> MEADLO: Well, I was facing him, but the other three or four guys heard it. And so he stepped back about 10, 15 feet, and he started shooting them. And he told me to start shooting. So I started. . . .
>
> WALLACE: And you killed how many? At that time?

MEADLO: Well, I fired on automatic, so you can't—you just spray
the area. . . .

WALLACE: Men, women, and children?

MEADLO: Men, women, and children.

WALLACE: And babies?

MEADLO: And babies.

WALLACE: But how do you shoot babies?

MEADLO: I don't know. It was just one of those things. . . .

WALLACE: And nothing went through your mind and heart?

MEADLO: Many a times. Many a times.[26]

The interview made the front page of major newspapers across the
country. After telephone calls abusing him, Wallace began receiving letters. Of the first hundred counted, "all but two berated me for 'giving that
boy a hard time' or for 'putting words in his mouth' or for 'dishonoring the
Army and the country'."[27] It was a side of the war seen for the first time.
For his part, Hersh found it noteworthy "that television was needed, that
somehow just relying on newspapers to sear the conscience of America
hadn't been working or had been working too slowly."[28] It seemed almost
as though a story had not been told until television told it.

Calley was court-martialed and sentenced to life imprisonment. Later,
the sentence was reduced to 20 years. No charges were filed against Meadlo,
who lost a foot the day after the massacre when he stepped on a land mine.
Hersh received a Pulitzer Prize.

The War Widens

In 1970, President Nixon ordered the invasion of Cambodia. The
objective was destruction of enemy supply depots. It seemed a safe move,
but expansion of the war into the technically neutral country sparked
demonstrations throughout the United States. Television covered the revolt on the nation's campuses, in particular the anguish at Kent State,
where Ohio National Guardsmen fired on a demonstration, killing four
students. Broadcasters became sensitive to accusations that, by their coverage, they were fomenting protest. As a result, on November 15, 1969,
when Washington saw the largest political demonstration in its history—
more than 200,000 marchers—the networks, to the astonishment of many,
provided no live coverage. Only local stations in Washington kept pace
with the events.

The networks made up rules for covering demonstrations. As early as
1963, NBC's Robert Kintner issued a memorandum saying that in reporting events, such as demonstrations,

> it is our obligation to be factually accurate, to exercise responsible
> judgment in the necessary selection of material to go on the air, so
> that the selection is based on newsworthiness and significance of

the material presented, and to avoid "taking sides" by manner or tone of presentation.[29]

By 1978, policy instructions at NBC News had expanded from an occasional memorandum to a codified 73-page looseleaf notebook. Subjects treated included riot coverage, privacy, use of handouts, and the Fairness Doctrine. Since then, instructions dealing with other subjects, such as terrorism, have been added.

Salant had prepared a similar "book of standards" for CBS News. Some highlights:

- Use unmarked cars whenever possible.
- Use lights only when essential for coverage of important aspects of the story.
- If, in your judgment, your presence is clearly inspiring, continuing or intensifying a dangerous or possibly dangerous disturbance, cap your cameras and conceal your microphones regardless of what other news organizations may do.
- Be restrained, neutral, and noncommittal in your comments and behavior.
- Cover any disturbance *exactly* as it happens with no staging whatsoever.[30]

The rules applied to coverage of both the antiwar and civil rights movements.

"The Whole World Is Watching!"

Antiwar agitation made the Democratic National Convention held in Chicago in August 1968 the most violence-ridden in history. There had been disturbances at the Republican convention in Miami Beach, at which Nixon was nominated, but nothing like the turmoil marking the Democratic meeting. Chicago's mayor, Richard Daley, claiming that the city was about to be taken over by 100,000 Yippies, reinforced his police with members of the Illinois National Guard. Actually, between 10,000 and 15,000 demonstrators showed up. An army of security officers patrolled inside the convention hall. Each network was allowed only two correspondents on the floor at a time.

Throughout, Daley was a key figure. When Senator Abraham Ribicoff of Connecticut spoke from the rostrum against Daley's "Gestapo tactics," the mayor, seated down front with the Illinois delegation, signaled for Ribicoff's microphone to be cut off. At one point, city workers waving "We Want Daley" signs filled the galleries. Broadcasters were kept from doing live remotes from Grant and Lincoln Parks, where demonstrators gathered, because of a three-month-old communications workers strike. Without the installation of equipment for pickups, television had to depend on video tape and film for reports from outside the convention hall. There was suspicion that Daley, not wanting coverage of what the demonstrators might do, or the reaction of his police, had discouraged settlement, a suspicion reinforced when the city imposed a parking ban on TV vans.

Reporters were casting Daley as the bad guy, and Cronkite let the mayor, in the CBS anchor booth, give his side of the story. Because Cronkite asked no hard questions—in effect, gave Daley free rein—he himself came under criticism. He purposely had not prodded out of a sense of fair play. But when a plainclothes guard slugged Dan Rather, knocking him down, Cronkite lost his temper, saying on the air, "I think we've got a bunch of thugs down there." The next day, two guards grabbed Mike Wallace and hustled him off the convention floor. And, again, Cronkite spoke his mind.

The convention had opened on Monday, August 26. Skirmishes between war protesters and police occurred that day and Tuesday. Early Wednesday night, after defeat of the "peace plank" that Eugene McCarthy wanted, protesters began moving en masse down Michigan Avenue, a coalescence of Yippies, clean-cut intellectual types, and crazies. At Balbo Street, by the Conrad Hilton Hotel, a large body of helmeted police stood in their way. They hesitated. Then, chanting "The whole world is watching!", they came on the police. A nightmare battle followed, ending when National Guard troops brandishing bayonets and machine guns closed in.

It had lasted, in view of cameras, just 19 minutes. Nightsticks, bottles, fists, bloodied heads, police reacting to a week of provocation—obscenities, human feces, Vietcong flags—protesters striking back in frustration, anger feeding on anger, consuming restraint. Couriers on motorcycles were hustling video tape to the convention hall, out by the stockyards, and soon the street battle, punctuated by exploding tear gas grenades and yells of "Sieg Heil!", was appearing on television screens coast to coast and across the oceans, so that much of the world, it turned out, was watching. Again and again, the picture of what was happening inside the hall—delegates nominating, delegates parading, Daley grimacing—was interrupted by the picture of police clubbing mercilessly and would-be demonstrators running about with blood on their faces as millions watched, not quite believing what they saw.

The interruptions sat poorly with convention managers—nominating speeches were being chopped to pieces—but news executives were in charge of what went on the air, and what was happening in downtown Chicago clearly was news. People were getting their heads busted, and here was tape to show it. Some footage was replayed. At least once the replay was not identified as a replay, and that was a mistake. Nothing was staged.

Scores of marchers were injured, along with more than thirty reporters and photographers, many of whom saw their cameras smashed. Yet, according to polls, most viewers thought television exaggerated the brutality. Later, the Presidential Commission on the Causes and Prevention of Violence did label the incident a *police* riot, demonstrating how widely televised reality and viewer perception of it can vary. Viewers complained that networks gave the bloodletting, and demonstrations earlier in the week, too much play. In fact, during the week NBC televised only 65 minutes of demonstrations as compared to more than 35 hours devoted to proceedings within the convention hall. CBS' coverage totaled 38 hours. Of this, only 32 minutes and 20 seconds was devoted to antiwar protests.

In the end, the Democrats nominated Hubert Humphrey. The ugliness accompanying his nomination, shown on television, may have reelected Nixon, who squeaked to victory by the lowest proportion of the popular vote since Woodrow Wilson in 1912.

There Seemed No End

Nine months after the invasion of Cambodia—Nixon called the bloody episode an "incursion"—South Vietnamese troops, with U.S. air support, invaded Laos, Vietnam's neighbor to the west. This time, the objective was severance of the enemy's supply line in Laos, the so-called Ho Chi Minh Trail.

The operation began under a news embargo. It was only after Hanoi Radio reported the drive that correspondents could report it, which meant the North Vietnamese, in that instance, were better informed than the American people. Not until the fourth week of the offensive were American helicopters assigned to take correspondents to see what was happening. Until then, they had been going into Laos any way they could manage. This was dangerous. Four photographers, including Larry Burrows of *Life* magazine, died, and it became "painfully obvious," as one officer put it, "that we had to do something." [31]

The military's hampering of coverage during the first weeks created suspicion that things were going badly, and later, when the military reported success, correspondents were still skeptical. On ABC's evening news, reporter Don Farmer said:

> When they say things like "We now have cut the Ho Chi Minh Trail," you and I know that's absurd. And that's the kind of statements we're getting, and they're so unbelievable that I think sometimes we're getting slightly paranoid, you know. We start looking for lies where maybe they don't exist. [32]

And so the war went on, one year dragging into another. In March 1972, North Vietnam launched a new offensive. The United States went back to bombing Hanoi, and the Paris peace talks collapsed. Nixon announced the mining of Haiphong harbor, then suddenly, in July 1972, the Paris talks resumed. Henry Kissinger proclaimed, "Peace is at hand," [33] a heartening escalation of repeated assurances that light was visible "at the end of the tunnel." But, six weeks later, Kissinger was saying that the peace talks had failed. There seemed no end.

American ground forces had been withdrawing, turning more and more conduct of the war over to South Vietnam—Vietnamization, it was called—when a peace treaty was signed in 1973. American POWs were released, but there was no peace. The war tormented the Vietnamese another two years before Saigon fell on April 29, 1975.

At the end, among Vietnamese who had worked with the Americans, there was panic. Many of them feared that if taken by the Communists, they would be executed. At Da Nang Airport, CBS' Bruce Dunning reported a scene of horror. He told, and viewers saw, how desperate Vietnamese stormed an evacuation plane—men struggling, shoving women and children aside—and how, even as the plane began to taxi down the runway, people tried to climb aboard.

> Finally, there was room for no more. . . . As the plane strained laboriously into the air, people were still clinging to the wheels and rear stairs. Seven men fell off as the plane reached heights of a thousand feet or more. As the plane reached 6,000 feet, one man was still stuck in the ladder.[34]

The scene was recorded by cameraman Mike Marriott and soundman Mai Van Duc.

After 10 years, most correspondents were leaving Vietnam. All of ABC's people got out. So did the correspondents for CBS. The one NBC correspondent who stayed was Jim Laurie, whose reports on the fall of Saigon earned him a Peabody. Several reporters for AP and UPI Audio also stayed. Mutual had already closed its Saigon bureau.

Official word of Saigon's unconditional surrender came at 10:30 P.M., New York time, while both CBS and NBC were on the air with special broadcasts marking the end of the war. CBS News had preempted two and a half hours of prime time. NBC's John Chancellor was anchoring a one-hour special. The ABC special with Harry Reasoner, which ran for 90 minutes, did not start until 11:30 P.M. Throughout the evening, radio networks aired special reports.

Concluding the television special on CBS, Cronkite said:

> There's no way to capture in one evening's broadcast the suffering and the grief of 30 years of a subcontinent at war. There's no way to capture the suffering and grief of our own nation from the most divisive conflict since our own Civil War. We embarked on this Vietnam journey with good intentions, I think, but once upon the path we found ourselves having been misguided. . . . . And perhaps that is our big lesson from Vietnam: the necessity for candor. We, the American people, the world's admired democracy, cannot ever again allow ourselves to be misinformed, manipulated and misled into disastrous foreign adventures. . . .[35]

And so the misadventure ended.

Aftermath

There had been prophecies. Ed Murrow posted a warning at the edge of the quagmire as early as 1951. On his radio program he cautioned that the United States, supporting the French in Indochina, "might well be involved in an Asiatic war on an even bigger scale than the one in Korea." The possibility, he said, should be carefully considered.[36] It wasn't.

In 1955, one year after the Geneva accords and 10 years before Congress passed the Tonkin Gulf resolution, Eric Sevareid said, "The danger in Vietnam is not believed to be military attack but disorganization in the Vietnam government, continued to a point where Communist penetration and subversion will be unstoppable."[37]

The danger was there in 1955 and all the way to the end in 1975, as one disorganized, unstable regime followed another.

How the media, television in particular, covered the Vietnam War, and the effect of that coverage, will be debated for years to come.

In its Tet offensive, did North Vietnam win or lose? In *Big Story,* his two-volume study of media performance during the battle, Peter Braestrup argues that correspondents so misinformed the American public that it thought the North Vietnamese had won. There are distinguished correspondents who say that, in general, the public was *not* misinformed. Charles Mohr of the *New York Times* concedes that there is room for criticism but asks that it be legitimate criticism. He questions how journalists can be accused of concealing an obvious allied victory when that victory did not seem obvious until months later, "even to officials."[38] Correspondents did err in reporting that Viet Cong commandos had fought their way into the U.S. Embassy. Braestrup makes much of it. John Laurence points out that correspondents got the story from two sources, a military police captain and sergeant on the scene.[39] Peter Arnett, who covered the war for the Associated Press, says he disagrees with Braestrup reluctantly because he finds so much in *Big Story* illuminating. In disagreeing, Arnett cites Braestrup's praise for the performance of more than twenty correspondents during Tet.[40] "My question," he says, "is, if so many newsman for the major media produced superior reporting, how then can they, as he charged, have 'veered so widely from reality'?"[41]

In Tet, the enemy suffered military defeat but won political victory. North Vietnam had demonstrated a resoluteness, a capacity to strike, which mocked the optimism American leaders were wont to express. As Philip Caputo, the Vietnam veteran and author, put it, "The only sin the media committed was to report the carnage and to bring home to the American people that they'd been grossly misled."[42]

Before Tet, did Westmoreland purposely deceive his superiors in Washington by underestimating enemy strength? Seventeen years after Tet, CBS produced a 90-minute documentary, "The Uncounted Enemy: A Vietnam Deception," saying he did. That program, which resulted in a 120-million-dollar libel suit against CBS, and "Vietnam: A Television History," PBS' landmark documentary on the Vietnam War, are subjects for a later chapter.

Were words and pictures decisive in forcing the American withdrawal from Vietnam? Historians will debate the question. No one will know. Still, journalism's impact was great enough so that, as James Reston noted at the time,

> reporters of the press and radio and television are now being blamed for the defeat . . . which is another way of challenging the whole idea of democracy. For in the long, tragic history of the war, the reporters have been more honest with the American people than the officials, and, with all their shortcomings, their contributions should not be despised or forgotten.[43]

The mistake of being in Vietnam was recognized, not so much because of antiwar protests, as because of bodies coming home in boxes and television making the trauma apparent.

Can any nation with uncensored television ever successfully prosecute a war? Alistair Cooke has speculated on what the reaction would have been in Britain if, in 1916, television had shown trenchfuls of corpses after the Battle of the Somme. He speaks of television's capacity, which is also radio's capacity, to reveal what is taking place *now*, not years later in some old soldier's memoir. He finds that capacity "shattering" and wonders "whether any nation not under a dictatorship can ever again fight a war with a steady spirit."[44]

The war in Vietnam was a small, dirty, painful war with lasting consequences for journalism and the conduct of foreign policy. Long after the end of the war, it was being cited in arguments over military involvement in Central America and the war-making powers of the president. Together with Watergate, it poisoned media–government relations, the press ever suspicious of government, government doubtful that the press in any delicate situation, such as the invasion of Grenada, can be trusted.

It's the war that won't go away.

37
Knights of the Camera

Mathew Brady founded the tradition during the Civil War. Photographers like Joe Rosenthal, Margaret Bourke-White and Robert Capa followed in his footsteps in World War II. In Korea, the television cameraman appeared in battle dress for the first time; in Vietnam, his pictures changed the course of history.

Courage and danger have been the common denominators. Erik Barnouw related that, on the Russian front during World War II, the death of a Soviet cameraman was recorded by a second cameraman, who died in the same battle.[1] In 1983, in Lebanon, a CBS cameraman and his soundman were caught in an artillery barrage. Shrapnel shattered the elbow of the soundman, Nicholas Follows, who called for a bandage. The cameraman, Alain Debos, was wounded in the thigh but kept his camera rolling. Viewers of the CBS evening news saw the barrage and Debos' hand offering a bandage. That, observed the *Wall Street Journal,* "was as close as Mr. Debos has ever come to getting on-the-air recognition."[2]

In March 1968, two ABC newsmen, Bill Brannigan (correspondent) and Jim Deckert (cameraman) flew into the Marine outpost at Khe Sanh. North Vietnamese forces were in the hills all around, pouring rocket, mortar, and machine-gun fire into the base. The incoming fire was so heavy the Marines burrowed underground in bunkers. Brannigan says:

> By way of showing casualties, we positioned ourselves at the medical evacuation point at the edge of the runway. First the ambulatory, then the stretcher cases. . . . We were filming, but before any stretchers could be placed aboard the chopper, a round exploded about five yards in front of us. Some of the wounded were wounded afresh. Deckert caught several pieces of shrapnel in his chest. I caught two very small pieces—one in my hand, the other in my knee. Deckert was between me and the blast. There was a tiny fountain of blood spurting from his chest. I grabbed the camera rig from him as he slowly collapsed, just barely conscious. I helped him to his feet and assisted him to the underground sick bay, where the corpsmen took over. About 45 minutes later, he on a stretcher and I ambulatory were on our way out of Khe Sanh on another medivac chopper.[3]

Doctors sent Deckert home. Three months later, he was back in Vietnam with some of the shrapnel still in his chest.

Correspondents, who could hide during a firefight, respected their cameramen, who could not. CBS's Ed Bradley worked with Norman Lloyd in both Vietnam and Cambodia. Of Lloyd he says:

> Norman was always more than just a cameraman. First of all, he is a warm, sensitive human being who always made a special effort to understand the ways of the people wherever we were. He was also a producer for us. . . . He could always search out the little nuance on film that would help to bring the story across. I never hesitated on any story to show Norman the script I had written and get his criticism.

Bradley gives an example of his cameraman's insight.

> We wandered off the road into a so-called No Man's Land along the border of Thailand and Cambodia. While there, we saw a woman who had been abandoned. She was very thin, emaciated. Probably had a number of diseases as a result of what she had been through, and she presented to us a very pathetic picture but not a story—that is, not a piece for the evening news. But Norman said, "Look, let's shoot her and tell her story."
>
> Now this is a woman who spoke Khmer, and we didn't speak enough Khmer to communicate with her. But because of what Norman did, in the way he filmed the woman, in the way he filmed what was going on around her, we were able to portray the plight of many of the Cambodian people at that time.

What Lloyd was able to do with his camera was retell the story of the Good Samaritan. What he showed going on around the woman abandoned by the side of the road, says Bradley, was well-supplied, reasonably healthy people "unwilling to help those who had fallen by the wayside."[4] He showed, too, that although there were thousands of Cambodian refugees in organized camps, more did not have the strength to get to them. The Good Samaritans in the story were Lloyd and Bradley, who saw to it that the woman got help.

The cameraman who shot CBS' celebrated "Charlie Company" was Keith Kay. "When Keith Kay goes to war," wrote Peter Kann of the *Wall Street Journal,* "he carries no weapons. Instead, he lugs a bulky 30-pound movie camera that makes it hard for him to run or duck and in itself presents a fat target to snipers. He usually doesn't wear a helmet because it would block the viewfinder of his camera."[5] John Laurence, the correspondent with Charlie Company, says:

> Kay brought an unusual degree of honesty, individual courage and integrity to his craft as a cameraman. If he suspected that someone was acting out of character because of the presence of his camera, he'd put it away. He always tried to capture the truth of a story by recording it as it happened, naturally.

Laurence says another outstanding cameraman was NBC's Vo Huynh, who "understood the depth and complexity of what was happening and worked, usually at great personal risk, to record the war in all its aspects."[6]

Vo Huynh, using an Arriflex for silent footage, and his brother, Vo Suu, with a sound camera, filmed one of the most shocking scenes ever shown on television. NBC Correspondent Howard Tuckner was with the camera crew. Eddie Adams, an Associated Press photographer, also was present. What they saw happened February 1, 1968, on the third day of Tet. On a Saigon street, near the An Quang Pagoda, a captured Viet Cong officer in civilian clothes was taken to General Nguyen Ngoc Loan, chief of the South Vietnamese, for interrogation. Tuckner remembers the proud, defiant look on the prisoner's face.

> General Loan took one look at him and knew he was going to get no information out of him. . . . There was not a word. Loan did not try to talk to him nor to scare him. He did not wave his gun at his face or his head. He did not put the gun to his temple. He just blew his brains out.[7]

Eddie Adams' still picture of the summary execution appeared on "The Huntley-Brinkley Report" that evening. Adams had recorded the incident in a series of exposures. The picture used was taken the instant the bullet entered the victim's head. It did not show the resulting gush of blood.

The next morning, when Robert "Shad" Northshield, executive producer of "The Huntley-Brinkley Report," received word from NBC's Saigon bureau that it had the story on film, he immediately authorized a satellite feed from Tokyo. In the interest of good taste, Tuckner's report on the shooting was trimmed to 52 seconds, one-fourth its original length.[8]

Another searing picture from Vietnam was of a 9-year-old girl running, naked and screaming, down a road after her clothes reportedly caught fire in a napalm attack. Again the incident was recorded both by NBC and a still photographer for the Associated Press. The picture showed the girl and other villagers fleeing from a wall of smoke and flame. Years later, to support his charge of media distortion, General Westmoreland said he had been told that the girl was burned in an accident involving a hibachi.[9] He could not remember who had told him.

More than correspondents, photographers put their lives on the line. They felt the need, amounting to compulsion, to be out in front. Larry Travis, one of the first NBC cameramen in Vietnam, says, "I think we were really trying to live life as close to the edge as we could . . . to see how far we could push it." This, he says, was not a death wish, and he describes one way he learned for staying alive.

> I covered the aftermath of a really bad ambush, and the lieutenant I was with showed me how the ambush occurred . . . and I could see that it was imperative that almost every step you took, you had to know almost like a baseball player where you were going to run. Because, just like a baseball player, if you have to think about it when it happens, it's too late.[10]

Many of the photographers, like the Vo brothers, were Vietnamese. Some died in action; more were wounded. Nick Ut of the Associated Press, who photographed the fleeing 9-year-old girl, was wounded three times.[11] His brother, who also worked for the Associated Press as a photographer, was killed. Something of the nature of these cameramen is shown in a cable CBS received early in the war from one who decided to stay in a particularly unhealthy situation. Most correspondents and photographers, he said, had left. "Self holding presently. Hope you insured me adequately."[12] This photographer was Ramnik Lekhi, who eight years later died with George Syvertsen and Jerry Miller in their Jeep. Other cameramen were Japanese, including Yoshiko Waku, who disappeared with Welles Hangen of NBC.

Other distinguished photographers were Andrew Pearson, Y. B. Tang, Ron Hedford, Tony Hirashiki, and Terry Khoo, all of ABC. Khoo was killed while covering the war in July 1972. The cameraman who shot Morley Safer's "Burning of Cam Ne" story was Ha Thuc Can. Other CBS cameramen in Vietnam included Kurt Volkert, Jerry Adams, Alex Brauer, P. B. Hoan, Carl Sorensen, Jim Wilson, and Mike Marriott. It was Marriott who, as the war was ending, shot the classic "Last Plane Out of Danang" report voiced over by Bruce Dunning.

And there was Neil Davis, the late respected cameraman who wrote and narrated many of his stories. Davis started with Visnews in 1963, covered the Vietnam War for NBC, and stayed on in the Indochina theater until in 1985, during an attempted coup d'état, the 70-mm shell fired by a Thai soldier killed him. Already, in other actions, he had been wounded twice.

All were very brave.

Because of television, Vietnam more than any other war was a photographer's war. Correspondents wrote about it; photographers showed it. What they showed was burned, day after day, into the minds of viewers. Finally the viewers cried, "Enough!"

They Also Serve

In peace, as well as war, the photographer is the supreme reporter. No words can equal the ghostly image of men walking on the moon, the visual impact of *Challenger* exploding, the lone unarmed Chinese student confronting an advancing column of tanks.

Here are some more memorable contributors.

Mohamed Amin of Visnews alerted the world to the devastating famine in Ethiopia. ITN cameraman Alan Downes penetrated Afghanistan in 1979 and came out with the first film of Afghan rebels harassing Russian convoys. Leaning out of the open hatchway of a Navy plane, Tony Petri of CBS got exclusive pictures of the sinking of the *Andrea Doria*. CNN's Tyrone Edwards covered the bombing of a guerrilla-held town in El Salvador. The civilian casualties were heavy, and Edwards said, "These are the Dachau pictures of the future."[13] Through the years, Isadore Bleckman graced Charles Kuralt's "On the Road" series with his true artist's eye.

When a would-be assassin shot Governor Wallace of Alabama, only Laurens Pierce of CBS got close-up footage, so close his clothes were bloodied. A tour de force was William Cole's hour-long special in which the CBS correspondent, doubling as cameraman, obtained the first filmed interviews with Soviet dissidents to come out of Russia. After the broadcast[14] Cole was expelled. Two early cameramen at CBS were Larry Racies and Patty Kingham. Covering a Missouri River flood in 1952, they provided the first live flood scenes shown on network television.

Douglas Edwards recalled another milestone.

> You remember those walks Truman was famous for. Once, in 1953, he was up in New York, staying at the Waldorf, and one morning Herbie Schwartz was there. He had his camera loaded with sound film and, walking backwards in front of Truman, got wonderful footage of him with all the reporters and photographers trailing along. The sound was great. A cabbie came by and yelled, "Hi, Mr. President!" Truman waved, and you could hear him talking, responding to reporters' questions.
>
> It was the first *portable* sound-on-film ever done. Until then, everything like that was either shot from a sound truck or silent. Herbie got it all on foot.[15]

Schwartz' piece, titled "Truman Takes a Walk," received a first place award from the National Press Photographers Association. (It would be 1962—nine years—before the association elected a photographer in television news as its president. The honor went to James Bennett of KLZ-TV,

Denver. John Faber, NPPA historian, began shooting newsfilm for WAFM-TV, Birmingham, in 1949 while he was secretary. A future CBS cameraman, Charles Mack, became the organization's first treasurer in 1946.)

Workers in television recognize the photographer's worth. When he was producing "See It Now," Fred Friendly said:

> If there is any magic, it is a magic born of the resilience and skill of our four cameramen—[Marty] Barnett, [Charles] Mack, [Bill] McClure, [Leo] Rossi—who have learned the secret of staying on their feet 30 hours at a time in extreme temperatures with 100 pounds of equipment on their backs, without losing their sense of humor or their focus.[16]

NBC's veteran correspondent Frank Bourgholtzer sees a model in Josef Oexle, "who always works harder than any human being should be able to work," and who

> knows how to work with a correspondent, striving constantly to understand what the story is as the correspondent sees it, contributing constantly his own expertise, not only to make the most of the correspondent's idea, but to help the correspondent see all the visual possibilities, oftentimes possibilities the correspondent otherwise would not notice. On top of that, Joe is that rare expert who is willing to try anything, even if he doesn't think it will work.[17]

There are the photographer association awards, national and state. There are the Emmys. Still, public recognition is rare. And technicians, even more than photographers, go unrecognized outside their own shops. They are the men and women who record and edit, plot the graphics, gauge the sound, switch, and set lights. Their credits flash by, and only a quick eye catches the name and role.

When Neil Davis died in the aborted coup in Thailand, Bill Latch, his soundman, died with him. When Don Harris, the NBC correspondent, was killed in Guyana while covering the tragic Johnstown story, the same people killed his cameraman, Bob Brown. Their deaths are a statement that, in broadcast journalism, reporters and those working with them are a team.

Eric Sevareid did not see CBS' headquarters until he returned to New York after the fall of France. Then, he says, "I felt conscience-stricken in the realization that so many men, so much complicated machinery, had been devoted so often to processing the brief, hesitant little speeches I had been giving from the areas of war."[18]

38
Out of This World

Only twice has television's audience approached in size the audience that witnessed the solemn pageantry of President Kennedy's funeral procession. What attracted viewers to an extraordinary degree on the other two occasions were achievements in space: the *Gemini IV* space walk in 1965 and the landing of Neil Armstrong and Edwin Aldrin, Jr., on the moon in 1969, the goal Kennedy himself had set for the country on becoming president. Ninety-two percent of homes with television sets were turned to Edward White's tethered walk in space—he seemed afloat in the vastness like an inflatable man. Ninety-four percent were tuned to catch the scarcely credible moment when Armstrong set foot on the moon.[1]

Space exploration, with the drama of lift-off and recovery, had been superb television ever since Alan Shepard became the first American in space with his brief suborbital flight in 1961 and John Glenn's orbit of the earth in 1962.[2] To demonstrate what was happening when spacecraft were boosted beyond range of cameras, all networks used artist's animations and full-scale models and models made to scale. After the early flights, the astronauts sent back live pictures. One of the first was in 1963 when Gordon Cooper showed how bright and breathtakingly beautiful planet Earth appears in space. Later, the networks engaged astronauts to sit beside their anchor people and help explain what was going on. Commentary in New York was supplemented by reports from correspondents assigned to the Manned Spacecraft Center in Houston. The audience also could eavesdrop on communication between the spacecraft and Mission Control. It was Buck Rogers stuff. And it was all live.

". . . One Giant Leap for Mankind"

President Kennedy's dream of a moon landing within the decade was realized on July 20, 1969. Michael Collins aboard *Apollo XI* in lunar orbit released module *Eagle* carrying Armstrong and Aldrin, and *Eagle*, kicking up moondust with its rockets, settled down gently on the surface at 4:17 P.M., Eastern time. "Oh, boy!" exclaimed Walter Cronkite, who was so relieved, and delighted, he could find little else to say. Six hours and 39 minutes later, after descending a short ladder from *Eagle*, Armstrong stepped onto the moon. This is how Cronkite reported that historic moment:

> CRONKITE: There he is. There's a foot coming down the steps.
> HOUSTON VOICE: O.K., Neil. We can see you coming down the ladder now.
> ARMSTRONG: O.K. I just checked getting back up to that first step. It didn't collapse too far. It's adequate to get back up.
> HOUSTON VOICE: Roger. We copy.
> ARMSTRONG: It's just a little jump.
> CRONKITE: So there's a foot on the moon, stepping down on the moon. If he's testing that first step, he must be stepping down on the moon at this point.[3]

It was then that perhaps a billion people, worldwide, heard Armstrong's words: "One small step for man; one giant leap for mankind." Few understood immediately what he said—reception was fuzzy—but they soon knew, noting that the astronaut, with appreciation for the far-reaching significance of the achievement, did not say "for America" but "for mankind."

"Buzz" Aldrin joined Armstrong on the moon's surface, and the two men, bouncing about in their space suits, busied themselves collecting rock samples and planting the American flag. From a quarter-million miles away, President Nixon talked to them by radio-telephone. The astronauts used a seven-pound television camera, set up on a tripod, to broadcast their activity to a receiving station in Australia, where the black and white picture was relayed by satellite around the world. And all the while, as Armstrong and Aldrin performed their tasks, moving like ghosts on the moonscape, a fear grew malignantly in people's minds. Once these two men reentered *Eagle*, would its rockets fire? Would it return them safely to the mother spaceship? When it did, millions sighed with relief. Cronkite expressed his relief with an exclamation rare in television news—"Hot diggity dog!"[4]

Except for commercials and an occasional film piece, which ran only two or three minutes. Cronkite was on the air continuously for 17 and a half hours—until 3:15 A.M.—when he broke off to get some sleep. The next night, he was on for another nine hours. The *New York Times* called his performance "seemingly effortless."[5] Cronkite admitted he was tired but said, "You don't think about that." He paid tribute to Walter Schirra, the former astronaut who had sat by his side. "Thank God for Wally Schirra," he said. "He had such confidence. It was contagious. He was a wonderful crutch."[6]

CBS and NBC carried the story for 31 consecutive hours, ABC for 30. ABC's anchors were Frank Reynolds and Jules Bergman, assisted by astronaut Frank Borman. Their executive producer was Walter Pfister. The anchormen at NBC were Chet Huntley, David Brinkley, and Frank McGee. With them were two astronauts, Tom Stafford and Eugene Cernan. Jim Kitchell was the executive producer. Robert Wussler was the executive producer for CBS. The television networks, it was said, had provided the single most striking sequence of images of the century, perhaps in recorded history.[7]

Because of the impact of these images, it was easy to overlook the important role of radio. Not only did radio serve as the auditory lifeline between the astronauts and Earth, but, in global terms, radio was the principal source of news of the adventure. In many countries, cheap transistor radios vastly outnumber television sets, so that it was by radio that most earthlings learned of the successful landing. The astronauts' voices had a startling clarity. *Variety* noted that when radio station WINS in New York switched to Pittsburgh for a live remote on public reaction, "the audio quality of that little earthly broadcast seemed [by comparison] from a small closet on Mars."[8]

The scientific knowledge gained by the expedition to the moon was immense. But what else? James Reston said it taught that "the American mind and the American political system seem to need great challenges and clear goals to work at their best."[9] Jack Gould, while praising the networks for their coverage, spoke of the duty to make fundamental issues facing the country no less vivid. He wished they would treat "the reality of life" with more substance and resourcefulness, "not merely as a kaleidoscopic newsreel."[10] Eric Sevareid saw a danger that, in the end, "the chief use of space will be military." He warned that

> history has never proceeded by a rational plan. Not even science knows what it is doing beyond the immediate experiment. . . . It is possible that the divine spirit in Man will consume him in flames, that the big brain will prove our ultimate flaw, like the dinosaur's big body.[11]

A Fire in the Sky

There were seven more *Apollo* missions, five more landings on the moon. In 1973, the United States put up an orbiting space station, Skylab, and, two years later, American and Soviet spacecraft linked up in a remarkable demonstration of international cooperation. The first space shuttle, *Columbia*, flew in 1981. Then came the second and third shuttles, *Challenger* and *Discovery*.

Between the launching of *Discovery* in 1984 and Alan Shepard's pioneering flight in 1961, death had visited America's space program only once. That was in 1967 when *Apollo I* caught fire on the launch pad, killing Virgil Grissom, Roger Chaffee, and Edward White. But on January 28, 1986, death returned, it seemed, in the most terrible way.

By that time, the public, and others who should have known better, were taking safe lift-off too much for granted. With the impressive record of successful flights, and much of the novelty gone, the networks had cut back on live coverage. So it happened that on that January day when *Challenger* lifted off for the tenth time, only CNN's viewers and NBC-TV's audience on the West Coast saw the explosion the moment it occurred.[12] Radio, with its more flexible schedules, fared better. Interest in the flight centered on Christa McAuliffe, a young mother from Concord, New Hampshire, who was to have become the first schoolteacher in space. NASA and President Reagan believed that her participation in the program would inspire students to study science. She was accompanying a cosmopolitan six-member crew that included one of the few women astronauts, a Japanese-American, and a black.

The flight had been postponed five times because of freezing weather and technical foul-ups. During the night of January 27–28 there had been more frost—icicles were found in the engines—but, this time, NASA went ahead. Blast-off came at 11:38 A.M., Eastern time, and the gleaming white shuttle, riding its powerful rockets, rose majestically from the pad. Bob Moon, a radio reporter for the AP, was on the air describing the ascent. One minute and 12 seconds after launch, he saw *Challenger,* 10 miles up, explode in a ball of fire. He said afterward:

> It was at once fascinating and horrifying. Things began to move in slow motion. After covering so many successful launches, there was stunned disbelief at first and a hesitation to sound the alarm. . . . The mind wanted to believe that *Challenger* would somehow emerge attached to one of those pinpoints of flame.[13]

All television networks had videotaped the disaster and quickly broke into their regular programming with the story. Dan Rather got on the air before Peter Jennings and Tom Brokaw, who were attending a White House briefing and had to rush across town to their Washington studios. The networks killed all commercials for the next five hours as they tried, with little help from NASA, to report that had gone wrong.

To show the explosion to viewers just tuning in, and to see if pictures might disclose what had caused it, the television networks kept replaying their tape, sometimes at normal speed, at other times in slow motion. "Replay, slow motion, magnification," said a *New York Times* editorial, "burned the sickening fireball into our brains."[14] The replaying paid off. It showed flames licking along a rocket seam where no flames belonged. And, in the end, that is what a presidential commission investigating the disaster found: fuel from a leaky joint in one of the two booster rockets had ignited, spread, and set off the terrible blast.

Many radio stations, like the networks, cancelled their commercials. The news was too shocking for either the soft or hard sell. Although it lacked pictures, radio followed the story through the day and into the night. Foreign radio picked it up, as did the Armed Forces Radio Network. The next day, radio talk shows were jammed by callers wanting to discuss the disaster.

But it was sight—seeing it—that hit hardest. The crew and the teacher, all exuding confidence, stepping smartly to the spacecraft and their deaths; the rocket exploding, the bits and pieces falling like a grotesque finale on Fourth of July; McAuliffe's parents watching, absorbing the shock of what they were seeing; the faces of the schoolchildren in Concord watching the ascent, their expressions turning from happy, to confused, to stricken, the horror intensified for the millions of viewers because of imaginings of what was happening, right then, to the astronauts, to the teacher, to her parents, to the children. Once more, common sorrow made of the country one community.

Inevitably, when it was over, questions were raised about the space administration's lack of forthrightness in responding to reporters' questions, about the quality of work on the shuttle, about the direction the space program should take. Should there be, for example, this emphasis on manned flight? What about NASA's judgment in giving the go-ahead for the flight in freezing weather? Previous flights had been postponed because of the cold. Had NASA been pressured by reports in the media about all the delays? Had the media been irresponsible in focusing on the delays, which had been ordered in the interest of safety?

Some critics, not many, accused television of playing on people's emotions.[15] Was it ethical for television to replay the tape showing the schoolteacher's parents as they watched and came to comprehend the horror of what was happening? Were all those other replays necessary? When asked that question, Brokaw said, "What else could we do? We couldn't go back to the soap operas. People wanted answers."[16] Most critics agreed with *Time* that, overall, the networks "performed with admirable sensitivity and restraint."[17]

The *Challenger* disaster occurred on a Tuesday. The next Sunday, on "60 Minutes," Andy Rooney did not try to amuse. Instead, he delivered a small essay on bravery. He said:

> Those seven astronauts . . . were genuine heroes, really brave men and women. It isn't brave if you're too dumb to know what the danger is or you don't give a damn about your life. They knew exactly how dangerous their adventure was, and they cared about their lives, too. But they did it, anyway.
>
> I suppose that if no one ever died doing a brave and dangerous

thing, the quality of bravery would cease to exist. These seven people have reestablished the credentials of bravery. Maybe the best thing to say on an occasion like this is that we can all be prouder to be human beings because of what they were.[18]

It would be late 1988 before NASA, reorganized and taking great care, attempted another shuttle flight. Then it would be *Discovery*'s turn again, and this time the mission, crewed by six brave men, met with success.

39
Those Panel Shows

Sunday, October 23, 1983. The stunning news on the wires was that the U.S. Marine barracks in Beirut had been car-bombed. First reports said scores of Marines were killed. Producers of CBS' "Face the Nation" reached Secretary of Defense Casper Weinberger at an emergency meeting of the National Security Council. Would he appear on the program? The answer was yes, he would be right over. Within the hour he was on the air, telling the public that a full-scale effort was underway to find the perpetrators and that the Administration was looking at ways to reduce the vulnerability of U.S. installations overseas. Predictably, what he said made the front pages of Monday's papers.

The longest-running public affairs programs on network television have been the panel shows like "Face the Nation." These programs, which attract relatively small audiences, demand attention because the people interviewed are important and often personally involved in what is happening. Viewers tend to be well educated with higher than average incomes. Many are government officials. In 1966, when Robert Kennedy, then a senator, suggested on "Face the Nation" that the Viet Cong be represented in any coalition government in Vietnam, Vice President Humphrey was watching. Less than two hours later, on ABC's "Issues and

Answers," Humphrey strongly attacked Kennedy's suggestion, thus delighting the producers of both programs. For scheduling the guest who will make news is the name of the game.

The panel program represents a symbiotic relationship between politicians and the press. George Herman, who for 14 years moderated "Face the Nation," says, "They come on, wanting to score points for themselves or some policy, and reporters want to get from them something that hasn't come out before, maybe something they didn't mean to come out. It's a trade-off."[1] On these programs guests have much more time—and it is free time—to express themselves than on the evening news, where what they say may be edited down to 10 or 15 seconds.

"Meet the Press"

"Meet the Press" is the oldest series on network television. It premiered in 1945 as a radio program promoting *American Mercury* magazine, then moved to television in 1947. Its first moderator, Lawrence Spivak, was editor and publisher of *American Mercury,* and although he continued as a panelist, he was replaced as moderator for a time by Martha Roundtree, a free-lance writer who, with Spivak, had created the program. In 1953, Spivak bought out Roundtree's interest. He sold the program to NBC in 1955 and for the next 20 years, until his retirement, served as moderator, permanent panelist, and executive producer.

Spivak did not conduct the program; he ruled it. No guest, or anyone on his staff, could smoke. When Anastas Mikoyan, deputy premier of the Soviet Union, became wordy, Spivak snapped, "Don't filibuster. We have only two minutes left."[2] Frequent panelists in the Spivak era were Jack Bell of the Associated Press, columnist Richard Wilson, and May Craig, Washington correspondent for the *Portland* (Maine) *Press Herald.* Craig's perky flowered hat and tenacious questioning became her trademark. Washington correpondent Bill Monroe succeeded Spivak as executive producer and moderator. The program underwent a major change in 1984 when Marvin Kalb, who had succeeded Monroe as moderator, was joined by Roger Mudd. The term *moderator* was dropped. Kalb and Mudd, NBC said in a full-page advertisement, had become the program's "principal interviewers."[3] The present interviewer is Garrick Utley.

"Face the Nation"

In 1954, CBS launched "Face the Nation," which resembled "Meet the Press" without Spivak's bristling presence. Early moderators were Theodore F. Koop, Stuart Novins, Paul Niven, Howard K. Smith, and Martin Agronsky. Besides the moderator and guest, the format called for two panelists, one from CBS News, the other from a magazine or major newspaper. George Herman moderated the program from 1969 to 1983, when Lesley Stahl, who had been covering the White House, succeeded him. Stahl enlivened the show with political cartoons; also on occasion she has departed from governmental affairs to delve into such subjects as drugs, medical costs, and contemporary art. No longer did a single guest appear but several guests with opposing views. "Face the Nation" has no panel. Stahl, depending on homework and wit, is the sole quesioner.

The program's most historic moment came in 1957 when Daniel Schorr, who was then Moscow correspondent for CBS, arranged for Nikita Khrushchev to be interviewed in the Kremlin. Schorr may have arranged the first interview ever granted by a Soviet premier for American television, but he couldn't get Khrushchev to powder his bald head. "I'm not an actor!" blustered the Soviet leader.[4] The panelists, besides Schorr, were B. J. Cutler of the *New York Herald Tribune* and Stuart Novins of CBS.

Most producers of "Face the Nation" have been women. These include Mary O. Yates, Joan Barone, Sylvia Westerman, Karen Sughrue, and Marianna Spicer-Brooks. Two women, Christie Basham and Barbara Cohen, have been executive producers of "Meet the Press," which was developed in large part by Martha Roundtree. When Bill Monroe was executive producer, Betty Dukert was producer. It was Peggy Whedon, producer of a defunct program called "College News Conference," who created ABC's "Issues and Answers."

"Issues and Answers"

ABC introduced its Sunday panel show, "Issues and Answers," on November 27, 1960, 13 years after NBC and six years after CBS. Peggy Whedon produced the program until "This Week With David Brinkley" took its place in 1981. The permanent panelist during most of that time was Bob Clark, who, joined by another ABC correspondent, questioned a single guest. There were exceptions. One was on March 13, 1977, when Prime Ministers James Callaghan of Great Britain and Yitzhak Rabin of Israel participated in a special one-hour edition. Clark and Peter Jennings interviewed Callaghan; Barbara Walters and Bill Seamans interviewed Rabin. These were the prime ministers' first interviews on American television since their election.

Usually, like "Meet the Press" and "Face the Nation," the program originated in Washington, where administration spokesmen, members of Congress, and other newsmakers are readily available. The need for instant availability was demonstrated dramatically one Sunday morning when Whedon found the program's guest could not appear. Hubert Humphrey agreed to substitute. She says, "He was playing baseball, and I got him on his walkie-talkie about an hour before showtime. He came in wearing his baseball uniform with mud on his knees. We gave him a coat and tie and shot him from the waist up."[5]

"This Week With David Brinkley"

It was a break for ABC that David Brinkley left NBC when he did. At that time, 1981, Roone Arledge, president of ABC News, was wondering how to replace "Issues and Answers" with a livelier, more wide-ranging public affairs program, one presided over by a correspondent with star quality. At that felicitous moment, Brinkley became available. Arledge hired him, gave him an hour, and—not least important—his head. As regulars with Brinkley, Arledge cast the outspoken White House correspondent Sam Donaldson—the program's gunslinger, one critic called him[6]—and the cool, scholarly conservative columnist George Will. These regulars are joined from time to time by other journalists, including Tom Wicker of the *New York Times*, Hodding Carter III, former State Department spokesman, and Jody Powell, former press secretary for President Carter.

"This Week With David Brinkley" starts with Brinkley's summary of the latest news. It then goes into interviews with guests, usually leaders in government, followed by a free-wheeling discussion of the week's major events sparked by Brinkley, who ends the program with a brief, often wry, occasionally irreverent commentary. Sample: "If you turn on your set and see a program in which nothing is happening . . . do not be alarmed. Do not call a service man. You have tuned in the U.S. Senate."[7]

The program, produced by Dorrance Smith, became the pacesetter, overcoming the other Sunday interview programs in both critical approval and ratings.

"Evans & Novak"

The longest-running panel show on CNN is "Evans & Novak." The program, aired live at 12:30 P.M. Saturday, New York time, features syndicated columnists Rowland Evans and Robert Novak. Another weekend panel show on CNN is "Newsmaker Sunday." "Crossfire" bowed in 1982 with conservative Pat Buchanan exchanging salvos with liberal Tom Braden, who has since been replaced by Michael Kinsley, editor of *The New Republic*. The Monday-through-Friday broadcast, live at 7:30, is repeated at odd hours. A latecomer in 1988 was the lively discussion program "Capital Gang."

Washington Week in Review

PBS' public affairs program "Washington Week in Review" first aired in 1967. From the beginning, moderators of the Friday program have been broadcasters, but other participants have come from the print media.

In its first five years, "Washington Week" had four moderators—John Davenport, Max Kampelman, Lincoln Furber, and Robert MacNeil—but in 1974 it settled down with Paul Duke, former congressional correspondent for NBC. An early panelist who contributed to the success of the program was Peter Lisagor of the *Chicago Daily News*. He died in 1977. Other panelists appearing regularly have included Jack Nelson of the *Los Angeles Times*, Haynes Johnson of the *Washington Post*, Hedrick Smith of the *New York Times*, Al Hunt and Michel McQueen of the *Wall Street Journal*, Charles Corddry of the *Baltimore Sun*, and Georgie Anne Geyer of the Universal Press syndicate. Sue Ducat is the producer.

"Newsroom"

To fill the "news hole" left by a strike that shut down San Francisco's newspapers in 1968, KQED, the public television station serving the Bay area, created the program "Newsroom." Its format, like the format for "Washington Week in Review," was simple. Reporters idled by the strike sat around a table with a moderator who guided them in an informal discussion of the day's news. The reporters not only told what had happened that day but gave their informed opinions as to why it had happened and what the effect might be.

The format was adopted by other public stations, but never with the same success. One by one the "Newsroom" programs closed down. Finally, in 1980, the original San Francisco "Newsroom" retitled "Evening Edition," died for lack of funding.

"Agronsky & Company"/"Inside Washington"

A panel show in which the participants challenged not a guest but each other was "Agronsky & Company." The program had its start in Washington in 1969, shortly after Martin Agronsky left CBS to anchor the news on WTOP-TV, now WUSA-TV. Panelists appearing most often on the half-hour weekend program were Washington correspondent Hugh Sidey of *Time*, author Elizabeth Drew of *The New Yorker*, and columnists Carl Rowan and James J. Kilpatrick. Talk on "Agronsky & Company" had the quality of an animated discussion over drinks at the National Press Club, with Sidey and Kilpatrick on the conservative side and Rowan and Agronsky on the liberal side. Drew was the program's moderate voice. Its producer was James L. Snyder, the vice president for news, *Washington Post-Newsweek* stations.

The last program in the series aired on Saturday, January 2, 1988. In taking his departure after 18 years and more than 900 shows, Agronsky said it had been "a responsibility and a privilege." Replacing "Agronsky & Company" was "Inside Washington," which kept most of the same panelists. The new moderator was Gordon Peterson, veteran anchorman at WUSA-TV.

"The McLaughlin Group"

"Agronsky & Company" had competition from "The McLaughlin Group," which offers zippier, rowdier discussion on more than two hundred public and commercial stations. The moderator, John McLaughlin, a former Jesuit priest and editor who served as assistant to both Presidents Nixon and Ford, comes off unmistakably conservative. Among the regulars (who appear in pairs) are reporter Jack Germond, a liberal, and Morton Kondracke, senior editor of *The New Republic,* who falls somewhere in between. Eleanor Clift, Fred Barnes, and Pat Buchanan (definitely conservative) are other participants. "The McLaughlin Group" is a coproduction of WRC-TV, Washington; WTTW-TV, Chicago, and Oliver Productions, Inc.

And Many, Many More

There have been other panel shows. Among them was CBS Radio's "Capitol Cloakroom," produced by Ellen Wadley. The award-winning program, aired on Wednesdays, ran from March 31, 1948, to December 29, 1983. A remarkable 35 years. In 1952, ABC Television aired "Crossfire." The program, moderated by Gunnar Back, was short-lived, as was NBC's "Congressional Report," moderated by Bill Monroe. A distinguished program on National Public Radio was "National Town Meeting," established in 1974 and underwritten by Mobil. Under its format two guests had their say on a selected topic, such as U.S. relations with China, and then fielded questions. Guests over the years included W. Averell Harriman, Senator Paul Laxalt, Senator Jacob K. Javits, Professor John K. Fairbank of Harvard, and Andrew Young.

Fred Friendly's media and society seminars on PBS are panel shows extraordinary both in terms of talent and subjects discussed. For the series, Friendly has succeeded in enlisting law professor-moderstors like Arthur Miller, Charles Nesson, and Benno Schmidt, who is now president of Yale. Panelists have included such figures as retired Supreme Court Justice Potter Stewart, former President Gerald Ford, and Harvard law professor Archibald Cox. Discussions in the Socratic fashion cover fundamental issues ranging from health care to affirmative action to freedom of the press, programs that Nat Hentoff of the *Village Voice* said have cornered people into "actually doing some fresh thinking."[8]

The seminars, conceived by Friendly, are produced by Columbia University in association with WNET, New York, and WQED, Pittsburgh. Friendly is the host.

40
Conversations

That "talking heads" invariably make boring television has been disproven so often that the canard, long dead, should be buried. Whether the talking head excites or puts to sleep depends on who is talking and what is being said. Eric Sevareid's conversation with longshoreman-philosopher Eric Hoffer in 1967 proved so compelling that CBS had Sevareid go back and do another television interview with him in 1969. Mike Wallace's inquisitorial questioning on "60 Minutes" is talking heads, and so have been the popular Barbara Walters specials with subjects ranging from Fidel Castro to John Wayne.

Other conversations have produced more insight than audience. A notable example is the interview conducted in 1968 by Eric Sevareid and Martin Agronsky with Hugo Black, senior justice of the Supreme Court.[1] Here, as Robert Lewis Shayon said, was "the glow of a great legal mind expressing the noblest ideals of a free society."[2] For a sitting justice to talk at length on camera about his interpretation of the Constitution was unprecedented. Still, most viewers switched to another channel to watch France's sex symbol, Brigitte Bardot. Eighteen years later, Chief Justice Warren Burger allowed himself to be interviewed by Bill Moyers. The interview was done the same day Burger announced his intention to retire.

Never before had a chief justice talked candidly for television about deliberations of the high court.[3]

An early highly respected television program was NBC's "Conversations With Elder Wise Men," which premiered May 18, 1952, with a filmed interview with Bertrand Russell at his home in Surrey, England. In 1959, the series title became "Wisdom." Henry Salomon, then Donald B. Hyatt were its executive producers. Throughout its 11-year run, the half-hour program aired on Sunday, though not always on a weekly basis.

By the time this distinguished series went off the air in 1963, Edward Steichen, Ruth St. Denis, David Ben Gurion, Eleanor Roosevelt, Igor Stravinsky, Edith Hamilton, Wanda Landowska, Eamon de Valera, Somerset Maugham, Paul Tillich, Arnold Toynbee, and Frank Lloyd Wright had talked before its cameras. That is a partial list. To this day, no television series has displayed a greater array of world figures.

In CBS News' "Conversations with Eric Sevareid" (1975–1977), Sevareid spoke with such "elder wise men" as George Kennan, Robert Hutchins, Leo Rosten, Dean Acheson, and Willy Brandt. On the same series, he conducted the first television interview with Anne Morrow Lindbergh, widow of the first person to fly the Atlantic alone and a best-selling author in her own right. The program, said UPI's Joan Hanauer, left the viewer "with a deep insight into the extraordinary scenery of her mind."[4]

Of course, talking heads—the interview—always has been a staple of broadcast journalism. It was the basic ingredient of much of "See It Now." Memorable are Murrow's interviews with General George Marshall, former secretary of state and defense; Dr. Jonas Salk, developer of the polio vaccine, and physicist J. Robert Oppenheimer. Oppenheimer told Murrow that while a nuclear war might not spell the end of the human race, "you can certainly destroy enough of humanity so that only the greatest act of faith can persuade you that what's left will be human."[5] For Murrow to interview Oppenheimer required some courage. Only two years earlier, with McCarthyism rampant, the nuclear physicist had been declared a risk to the security of the United States. Later, Presidents Kennedy and Johnson would honor him.

In 1956, Murrow dared interview Communist China's premier, Zhou En-lai. *Variety* called it "one of the biggest journalistic beats in television history."[6] His "See It Now" interview six months later with Marshal Tito of Yugoslavia was less controversial. Nevertheless, CBS followed both interviews with panel discussions of what the "Red" leaders had said.

On June 2, 1957, CBS scored a greater coup when, through negotiation by Frank Stanton, president of the network, and Moscow correspondent Daniel Schorr, Nikita Khrushchev appeared on "Face the Nation," stressing his theme of peaceful competition. With the program, CBS achieved two firsts: it was the first interview with a head of the Soviet government on American television and the first American program filmed inside the Kremlin.

"Person to Person"

"The joint is full of cameras, lights and googly-eyed gear. Millie and I are trussed with special built-in transmitters. My microphone is in my navel. Disaster impends."[7] The renowned newspaper reporter Bob Considine, with only slight exaggeration, was describing what it was like for a CBS production team to descend on your residence for a segment of "Person to Person," back in the 1950s.

This was the series in which Murrow, sitting in a comfortable armchair in a New York studio made to look like a living room, chatted over long distance lines with famous people in their homes. By coaxial cable, song writers, actors, authors, musicians politicians, and comedians appeared as if by magic on a television monitor that seemed to occupy most of the wall of the studio, opposite Murrow. After a few pleasantries—"How is the weather out there?"—these people would ask Murrow if he would like to see their new game room or throphy collection, or meet their children. He would like that very much, so what followed was a conducted tour of their house or apartment and, through Murrow's polite questioning, the story of their lives. It was *People* magazine without sexual references.

The program, aired on Fridays in prime time, proved a hit. Viewers enjoyed looking in on the likes of Elizabeth Taylor, Sid Caesar, Lauren Bacall, the Duke and Duchess of Windsor, Zsa Zsa Gabor, Liberace, and John Kennedy, newly elected to the U.S. Senate, and his handsome wife Jacqueline—all carefully rehearsed because of cameras and lights set up in the right places—showing you their kitchens, boudoirs, swimming pools, and, in one instance, gorgeous bathroom. The program received its highest rating April 8, 1955, when Marilyn Monroe, making her first appearance outside of a dramatic role, talked with Murrow from the home of her friend, photographer Milton Greene. Each program consisted of two segments of contrasting nature. The evening Monroe appeared, the other participants were Sir Thomas and Lady Beecham. When Murrow "visited" Gloria Vanderbilt, he also called on Roy Campanella, catcher for the Brooklyn Dodgers. This variety gave the program wide appeal.

"Person to Person" premiered October 2, 1953, and ran until September 15, 1961. Charles Collingwood took Murrow's place in the last two years. Jesse Zousmer and John Aaron produced the series and, with Murrow, owned and packaged it for sale to CBS. The field producers, responsible for individual segments, were Charles Hill, John Horn, David Moore, Robert Sammon, and Liz Scofield. Nothing quite like the series, employing the latest technology, cambersome though it was, had been done before. The cameras were bulky. Heavy cables ran from room to room. Considine complained, "Loudspeakers and mikes hang like bats from our belfry."[8] But it was live. Anything could happen. And did. Women appearing on the program were asked to wear full skirts so that a battery and microphone (the size of a pack of cigarettes in those days) could be concealed on their person. Monroe insisted on a tight skirt and sweater, so battery and microphone were hidden nearby in some flowers.

The series was more popular with viewers than with critics, who felt that Murrow, in going the celebrity route, was demeaning himself. What was CBS' most presitgious correspondent doing interviewing Marilyn Monroe and Zsa Zsa Gabor? And he asked puff questions. It was so banal.

> MURROW: Marilyn, I saw some pictures of you the other day riding an elephant at the circus. Did you have fun?
> MONROE: Ooh, I loved it. It was wonderful. It was a pink elephant.

Persons close to Murrow knew he accepted "Person to Person" for what it was, entertainment, and that he did not ask tough questions because he regarded himself as a guest of the people on the program and behaved as a guest. If he called on sex symbols, he also called on Margaret Mead, John Steinbeck, Sam Rayburn, George Meany, and Agnes DeMille. There was a touching moment during the call on H. V. Kaltenborn when the dean of newscasters instructed Murrow to stop smoking, or it would kill him.[9] Nine years later, it did.

The idea for "Person to Person" came from Aaron and Zousmer, who still worked with Murrow on his nightly radio newscast. When they asked if he would do this new television program, thereby giving its chances a big boost, he said he would. He agreed for several reasons. Aaron and Zousmer were colleagues; he had high regard for them. He would like to help. He could see, at the same time, that he would be helping himself, and not only financially. Frequent appearances on a popular prime-time program would make him known to more people who might then watch and respond to the serious journalism of "See It Now." Also, there was this fascination with show business. Murrow had acted in plays in college. He enjoyed his contacts with Hollywood and Broadway stars. He got a kick out of people like Sam Goldwyn. And when he had opportunity to appear in "Around the World in 80 Days," he took it. It was a lark.

In believing he could become better known through "Person to Person," and perhaps increase his influence, he was right. In 1957, the program was drawing more than twice the audience of "See It Now." Murrow, in that year, was being rated as no newscaster before or since—not only as television's foremost journalist but as "one of TV's five top-rated entertainers,"[10] right up there with Ed Sullivan and Bob Hope. Six months after the debut of "Person to Person," Ed Murrow and Fred Friendly mounted their formidable attack on the dangerous tactics of Senator Joe McCarthy. As Joseph Wershba, the CBS producer and close associate of Murrow, once wrote:

> It was precisely the popularity of "Person to Person" . . . that made Murrow's attack so powerful in terms of reaching a broad-based audience. For it was inconceivable to these starry-eyed millions that the commentator who had taken them into the boudoirs of Hollywood sexpots could be anything but a true-blood American.[11]

"Small World"

Murrow's "Small World" resembled NBC's "Wisdom" series, though destined to have a shorter run. That it was serious journalism in contrast to "Person to Person" became apparent with the first broadcast when Murrow talked with Prime Minister Jawaharlal Nehru of India, Governor Thomas E. Dewey of New York, and Aldous Huxley, author of *Brave New World,* who talked with each other of war and peace.

At the start, Murrow explained that it would be a four-way intercontinental conversation "dedicated to the proposition that talking over each other's back fences is a good idea, electronic or otherwise."[12] For the first broadcast, Friendly linked North America, Europe, and Asia with 24,000 miles of radio and telephone circuits. Camera crews filmed Nehru in New Delhi, Dewey in Portland, Maine, and Huxley in Turin, Italy. At the same time, what they said was recorded. For broadcast, film and audiotape portions were combined, producing simultaneous sight and sound, an editing effort that communications satellites would soon make obsolete.

Guests on "Small World" experienced the same "equipment shock" as interviewees on "Person to Person." British statesman Harold Nicolson described the scene in one of his diaries:

> In the afternoon, three vans arrive bearing Mr. [William] McClure of the Columbia Broadcasting System, two French electricians and three others, together with vast trunks and suitcases. . . . I am sat down in a chair by the fire, and the lights are turned on and adjusted. . . . I talk to Ed Murrow in St. Moritz, to Mrs. [Clare Boothe] Luce in, I think, Los Angeles, and to Chip Bohlen [former U.S. ambassador to Moscow] in New York. I do not see their faces.[13]

"Small World" ran as a half-hour Sunday program from October 1958 to May 1960. The last broadcasts were done while Murrow was abroad on sabbatical.

A Diplomatic Initiative

Two questions asked by Walter Cronkite in an interview on November 14, 1977, helped shape history. He was speaking via satellite with President Anwar Sadat in Cairo and Prime Minister Menachem Begin in Jerusalem. Technology and journalistic enterprise had brought the two longtime enemies together on the tube. Seizing the opportunity, Cronkite asked Sadat if he would go to Jerusalem and talk to Begin face to face. When Sadat said yes, Cronkite asked Begin if he would talk to Sadat if he came. When Begin said yes, the way was paved for the historic meeting in Jerusalem five days later.[14] That meeting led to peace talks at Camp David and the signing of a peace treaty between Israel and Egypt on March 26, 1979.

A special report issued as part of that year's duPont-Columbia University survey of broadcast journalism said, "The birth of TV diplomacy was a phenomenon variously considered an insufferable intrusion, a public service, or just the latest in a series of media expropriations." It quoted Flora Lewis of the *New York Times* as saying:

> To consider the new technique a matter of show business or personal vanity would be a serious mistake. It has already proven highly effective in the Middle East. And the chances are that it will gradually be taken up for use in other areas. . . . In effect, mass diplomacy has become a tool of negotiations.[15]

The Eliciting Art

Interviewing is an art, and among broadcast journalists there are the recognized artists. Ted Koppel, Mike Wallace, Barbara Walters, Bill Moyers, Charles Kuralt come immediately to mind.

Koppel, Wallace, and Walters play hard ball, can be rough in their probing. On "Nightline" and in "The Koppel Report," Koppel is relentless. He is an unearther of information, and insight, as demonstrated by his "Town Meeting With Nelson Mandela," on June 21, 1990.[16] Mike Wallace's skilled performance on "60 Minutes" is a fascinating study in criminatory questioning. In her ABC specials, Barbara Walters, speaking ever so sweetly, can be a Venus flytrap. With their facial expressions, as well as words, she and Wallace lead on the unwary.

Bill Moyers probes unaccusingly in the manner of your family physician. The distinguishing characteristic of "Bill Moyers' Journal" and his later public television program, "A World of Ideas," is enlightenment. Memorable are Charles Kuralt's visits with folk met "On the Road," visits marked by the reporter's warmth and his subjects' humankindness. Tom Shales, the critic, says of Kuralt, "Maybe he doesn't have a high profile or a ferocious investigative zeal, but he knows a good human story."[17]

The list of expert interviewers is easily lengthened. An interview program marked by the gentleness and wit of its host, and by its perilous existence, was "The Dick Cavett Show," which premiered on ABC-TV in 1968 and still was on the air—on CNBC—in 1990. The late David Susskind's syndicated program "Open End," renamed "The David Susskind Show" in 1967, could be counted on for good conversation, as could Bill Buckley's "Firing Line." On National Public Radio, the conversations between Bob Edwards and Red Barber, dean of sportscasters, are gems. On commercial radio, no one is more expert in the art of interviewing than Larry King and Jim Bohannon.

41
Jewel in the Crown

The television documentary is the child of the picture taker who, as A. William Bluem said of Civil War photographer Mathew Brady, "demonstrated that the photograph could not only record events but penetrate the surface details of reality to make strong and dramatic commentary."[1] Just as Brady showed the grotesqueness of death in battle, so did film maker Robert Flaherty show the Eskimo's reconciliation with a hostile environment in "Nanook of the North" and Fred Friendly and David Lowe stir compassion for migrant workers in "Harvest of Shame." Surfaces were penetrated, the commentary strong and dramatic.

It was not a simple path from Flaherty to Friendly and Lowe. There were newsreels and the radio documentary with its constellation of pioneer producers, which besides Friendly included Norman Corwin, Robert Heller, Irving Gitlin, Robert Saudek, and Robert Lewis Shayon. The progression from the radio version of "March of Time" to Shayon's "Eagle's Brood" to Murrow and Friendly's "Hear It Now" and "See It Now" has been set forth in earlier chapters. The subject here is television's brightest and too rare jewel, the full-length documentary.

The word *documentary* did not exist until John Grierson, an English film producer, coined it in 1926. He wanted a word for motion pictures designed to persuade. Grierson's concept of the documentary as a means of persuasion has been shared by producers to this day. Storms have broken over their heads, raising fundamental issues such as balance in news programming and freedom of the press.

The Compilation Documentary

Documentaries fall into different categories. Bluem speaks of the compilation documentary.[2] This is the documentary like "Victory at Sea," which NBC compiled from footage of naval action in World War II. The "20th Century" programs produced by Burton Benjamin and Isaac Kleinerman, and narrated by Walter Cronkite, are documentaries of the compilation genre. Typical programs in this series, assembled from archival material, are "Trial at Nuremberg" (1958) and "The Plots Against Hitler" (1963). The same is true of the "Making of the President" series on ABC and PBS' "Vietnam: A Television History" (1983). Most compilation documentaries have been historical. Ken Burns' monumental 11-hour series, "The Civil War," on PBS (1990) is a prime example.

The Investigative Documentary

The investigative documentary is the most controversial form. It attacks, provoking counterattack. Most often the person or institution investigated cries foul, charging that the producer, because of bias, was unfair. Two documentaries that raised vehement charges of unfairness were CBS' "The Selling of the Pentagon" (1971) and NBC's "Pensions: The Broken Promise" (1972). More about them later in this chapter. On occasion, the documentary investigates not a person or institution but a situation. Fred Friendly's "The Water Famine" (1961) reported the crisis in the world's supply of fresh water. Fred Freed, concentrating on the problem of water pollution, did "Who Killed Lake Erie?" (1969) and "Pollution Is a Matter of Choice" (1970). Lake Erie is cleaner today, and credit must be shared with Freed.

Another example is ABC's "Asbestos: The Way of Dusty Death" (1982). In it, Phil Lewis, producer, and the late Jules Bergman, correspondent, investigated the question of compensation for victims of asbestos-related diseases. The program cited evidence that for years the industry had known more about the danger than it admitted.

If he were alive today, Bluem might categorize these as "theme" documentaries, his term for the documentary the elements of which "are selected, arranged, and intensified" to present a point of view. In his authoritative *Documentary in American Television*, he says, "The theme documentarist begins with an idea which has created an emotional response within him. It is a personal choice, a personal reaction, which leads him to find the proper subject by which to express his impression of events." The reporting, he says, may be pure, which is to say factual, but in the selection of subject matter the documentary maker pursues his personally chosen theme.[3] Bluem would regard propagandizing by the Pentagon, neglect by the asbestos industry, and water pollution as the producers' themes. The theme documentary is often investigative, an adjective used less widely in Bluem's time than it is today.

The Cultural Documentary

Because of the high drama of the investigative documentary—Exposé! —achievements in the field of the cultural documentary may be slighted. But nowhere have programs been produced with more sensitivity and imagination.

One of the earliest and longest-running cultural series was "Camera Three," a half-hour Sunday show put on by CBS-TV as an experiment in 1953. The series, developed by Robert Herridge, got its name from the fact that it employed three cameras instead of the two usually allowed low-bugeted television programs. In 1978, "Camera Three" received a Peabody for exploring the arts world in such a way that "a retrospective of shows could provide a most fascinating glimpse into the best of our cultural life." CBS dropped the program in 1979. PBS carried it for a few months. John Musilli was the producer at both CBS and PBS.

Another early, highly respected cultural series on television was "Omnibus," which started on CBS on November 9, 1952, but later appeared on ABC and NBC. Fred Rickey succeeded its first producer, Robert Saudek. The host was Alistair Cooke. In subject matter, the program delved unhesitatingly, and in depth, into literature, music, drama, and dance.

The Religious Angle

Some cultural series were short-lived because of low ratings.

It was different with low-budget cultural programs done from a religious perspective. Networks kept them on regardless. ABC News' "Directions" ran for 23 years; CBS News' "Look Up and Live" and "Lamp Unto My Feet" for 25 and 30 years respectively. None of these programs was strictly religious. As the critic Karl E. Meyer said of "Lamp Unto My Feet," "[It has] a misleading title, with its overtones of preachiness. In fact, its spiritual net is cast so wide that even heathens can find nourishment in its fare."[4] A review of its programming finds such diverse subjects as seventeenth-century Chinese artists, abortion, the humanist philosophy of Albert Einstein, and the temples of Nepal. "Look Up and Live" dealt with subjects as varied as disarmament, single-parent families, and sexism in the Bible. Its last program, aired January 21, 1979, was a documentary, "Suffer the Children," which reported on Covenant House, an organization that rescued runaways.

"Look Up and Live" and "Lamp Unto My Feet" went off the air at the same time to make way for "Sunday Morning" with Charles Kuralt. Both programs were produced by Pamela Ilott, the first woman at CBS News to become a vice president. She also created "For Our Times," a similar program hosted by Douglas Edwards. The NBC News series corresponding to these programs and ABC's "Directions" was "Eternal Light." In subject matter, it cast an equally wide net.

People and Places

A popular subject has been the people who enriched life with their works, as in the case of NBC's "Shakespeare: Soul of an Age" (1962) and PBS' "The World of James Joyce" (1983). Edward R. Murrow and several million viewers enjoyed a conversation with Carl Sandburg in CBS' "Visit to Flat Rock." (1954). Producers could illustrate the lives of great painters with their canvasses. For CBS, Martin Carr produced "Gauguin in Tahiti" (1967) and Perry Wolff "Pablo Picasso: Once in a Lifetime" (1982). For syndication, Equinox Films produced "In a Brilliant Light: Van Gogh in Arles" (1985).

Whole peoples have been depicted, among them—both on CBS— "The Italians" (1967) and "The Japanese" (1969). In 1973, ABC broadcast "The Vandals." In NBC's "Greece: The Golden Age" (1963) Lou Hazam focused on the Age of Pericles. A trailblazer for China programs was CBS' "Inside Red China," produced by Don Hewitt and Palmer Williams in 1966. Because Americans could not enter China, Marley Safer was admitted as a Canadian on a tourist's visa. Film was shot by a West German cameraman.

The character of America itself has been the subject of perhaps a dozen cultural documentaries. Two stand out. One is Alistair Cooke's "America: A Personal History of the United States" produced by Michael Gill for Time-Life Films and the BBC. The acclaimed 13-hour series aired simultaneously on NBC and the BBC during the 1972–1973 season, then a year later on PBS. The program was personal in that Cooke, best known as host of "Masterpiece Theater," gave his own interpretation of events. Although Cooke had become an American citizen, some critics expressed chagrin that the best television history of the United States to date was produced by a man from the BBC and written and hosted by a British-born journalist. John O'Connor of the *New York Times* called it "a scathing comment on the imagination and initiative of American television."[5]

The other outstanding program is Peter Davis' six-part study of Americans and their institutions using Muncie, Indiana, as a microcosm. In this 1982 series, which had the title of "Middletown," the life of a Midwestern community is shown, not described. It is the camera that exposes racism when a 17-year-old girl dates a black youth and a cross burns on her front lawn. *Newsweek* applauded the PBS series for its "uncommon emotional power."[6]

Three other classics in the cultural genre are John Secondari's "The Vatican" (ABC, 1963), Lucy Jarvis' and John Sughrue's "The Louvre" (NBC, 1964) and George Vicas' "The Kremlin" (NBC, 1963). Color had come to television, and each of these programs was stunningly filmed. In "The Kremlin," Vicas recreated historical scenes by dramatic use of lighting, sound, and camera movement. Actors playing the murderers of Peter the Great's family are not seen, but the viewer hears their shouts and sees their flaming torches as they rush up the stairs to the family quarters. The camera becomes the viewer who goes up the stairs with the others and, with them, bursts through the door.

In the mid-1960s, Andrew Rooney—the Andy Rooney of "60 Minutes" —produced for CBS a brief series of filmed essays on the often overlooked art of the commonplace. The best of these essays, which Rooney wrote and which with exceptional music and photography constituted a celebration of form, were "An Essay on Bridges" and "An Essay on Doors." In these, and the other essays, Harry Reasoner narrated.

Several of NBC's "Project XX" programs like "The Innocent Years" (1957) and "The Real West" (1961) are in essence cultural. So in ABC's "Saga of Western Man" series are programs such as "I, Leonardo Da Vinci" (1965) and "The Legacy of Rome" (1966). It would be easy to expand the list with cultural programs from ABC's "Close-up" series and from "CBS Reports" and "NBC Reports."

The major networks and many local stations have produced cultural programs of distinction, but none so distinguished as the British series "Civilisation" and "The Ascent of Man," which PBS presented in 1970 and 1975 and later rebroadcast. "Civilisation" was produced by Michael Gill and Peter Montagnon. The man who hosted the 13-part series was the late Kenneth Clark, noted art historian, former director of the British National Gallery, and chairman of Britain's Independent Television Authority. In writing about the series' fascinating review of Western culture, Jack Gould observed that Clark, with his background, appreciated the visual requirements of television and so "uses art, sculpture, and mechanical design to illustrate his essay, reinforced by the color, movement, and music which in knowing hands can make TV a genuinely creative medium of expression."[7]

"The Ascent of Man" was a magnificent 13-hour series, which, like Alistair Cooke's "America," came from Time-Life Films and the BBC. Its creator and host was Dr. Jacob Bronowski, a Polish-born scientist associated with the Salk Institute. The series traced the history of human discovery from prehistoric times to the present, with Bronowski on location in many parts of the world, explaining the significant thing that happened in that particular place. After presentation on the BBC, "Ascent" premiered in the United States on January 7, 1975. Bronowski died of a heart attack shortly before the American premiere. "Ascent" was his great public work.

Instant Specials, News Specials

The so-called instant special is a special, but not all specials are instant. Reuven Frank's "The Tunnel" was labeled an NBC News Special, but it was four months in preparation. The television tours of the White House, starting with President Truman and Walter Cronkite in 1952, have all been specials requiring detailed planning in terms of placement of cameras and lights. Through the years there have been many of these broadcasts called specials for promotional reasons and because they were distinct from other programming.

The instant special is done in a hurry. It generally is produced and aired the same day as the event that promoted it, as on December 2, 1982, when a retired dentist, Dr. Barney Clark, became the first recipient of an artificial heart. CBS and NBC often put on these specials at 11:30 P.M., Eastern time. ABC usually handles the story on "Nightline," while CNN, with its 24-hour format, is more flexible. Whether for radio, television, or cable, the late-breaking story is treated in as much depth as preparation time allows. Questions are raised and, if possible, answered as to how the event came about and what it means. Bluem categorized the form as "somewhere between the full documentary instrument and the hard news story."[8]

The adjective *instant* is used loosely. In the early 1960s, CBS ran an award-winning series of instant specials called "Eyewitness to History," a title later shortened to "Eyewitness," which reviewed the news story of the week. Leslie Midgley produced the Friday night program. Bernard Birnbaum, Midgley's associate, says "Les was so smart he could figure out on Monday or Tuesday what would be the big story so we could have it ready on Friday night. He knew what to do, though sometimes we'd have two or three projects underway to play safe. A very interesting time."[9]

Chet Hagan produced similar specials at NBC, but under less pressure since he did not have to come up with a program each week.

"The National Drivers' Test"

Participatory documentary came to television on May 24, 1965, when CBS aired "The National Drivers' Test." Fred Friendly was so impressed by what he learned in traffic school, to which he had been "sentenced" for speeding, that he set up the one-hour national test, replete with visuals, on the rules for safe driving. Newspapers throughout the country carried forms on which viewers could check their answers. More than 25 million people watched the program. It drew 600,000 letters. Obviously, viewers enjoyed taking an active role. CBS immediately followed with television tests on the responsibilities of citizenship, filing income tax returns, and health. So did local stations. In New York, WNBC-TV offered "The Marriage Test." WABC-TV aired a quiz on viewers' likes and dislikes called

"You Are What You Like." WTBS-TV, Atlanta, tested its viewers on their knowledge of cancer. In St. Louis, KMOX-TV broadcast a four-week series of sports quizzes. It is a format that, though used sparingly, has stayed in style.

Milestones

Your way through these next pages will be marked by milestones in the history of the television documentary. Dozens of other significant programs might be described.

"Victory at Sea" (1952–1953)

In 1951, an NBC producer, Henry "Pete" Salomon, set out to perform an almost impossible task. It was to take the whole global history of the U.S. Navy in World War II and tell it with pictures on television. Salomon, an ex-naval officer, had helped Samuel Eliot Morison prepare his renowned 14-volume history of the Navy's operations. From that work Salomon got the idea for the magnificent "Victory at Sea" series, which remains today the classic compilation documentary, rivaled only by PBS' "The Civil War."

Salomon recruited Richard Hanser to write the script, Leonard Graves to read it, and Isaac Kleinerman to be senior film editor. Donald B. Hyatt, a young Dartmouth graduate with a degree in sociology, came on as Salomon's assistant. Clay Adams directed. Evidence of NBC's commitment to the project is that Salomon was authorized to engage Richard Rodgers, whose Broadway credits included "Oklahoma!," to compose an original score with orchestration by Robert Russell Bennett. Evidence of the quality of the production team is that Hanser, Kleinerman, and Hyatt all went on to become documentary producers of the first rank.

"Victory at Sea" was presented in 26 half-hour installments. Together, they comprised 60,000 feet of film. In selecting that footage from military archives from around the world, the producers screened 60 million feet of film, a ratio of one to 1,000. Much of what was aired had to be declassified.

Salomon, still a young man, lived for only four years after "Victory at Sea" premiered. When he died, the BBC interrupted its programming with a special tribute, a respect it would pay no other American broadcast journalist until the death of Edward R. Murrow in 1965. The production team assembled by Salomon lived on as the Project XX unit, which gave viewers a succession of fine documentaries, including "Nightmare in Red" (1955), an account of the Russian revolution, and "The Twisted Cross" (1956), which with German footage documented Hitler's rise and fall.

"Harvest of Shame" (1960)

The names most often associated with CBS Reports' "Harvest of Shame" are those of Fred Friendly and Ed Murrow, but chief credit for this cele-

391

brated documentary on America's exploited migrant workers belongs to David Lowe. Friendly was executive producer. As narrator, Murrow contributed prestige. But it was Lowe with cameraman Marty Barnett who went out and did the story. Barnett's pictures of miserable living conditions and Lowe's gentle, probing interviews with these toilers in "the sweatshops of the soil" drove home the migrants' predicament.

The documentary aired on November 25, 1960, the day after Thanksgiving, when harvesting and the land's bounty were in people's minds. At the end of the program, in a rare editorial, Murrow called for federal legislation to alleviate the migrants' plight. "The migrants have no lobby," he said. "Only an enlightened, aroused, and perhaps angered public opinion can do anything about the migrants. The people you have seen have the strength to harvest your fruit and vegetables. They do not have the strength to influence legislation. Maybe you do."

The program had little effect. Erik Barnouw believes it "portrayed the plight of migrant workers so vividly that many people simply rejected its truth," that "such poverty and human erosion could not easily be fitted into the world as seen in prime time."[10] Ironically, when Murrow became director of the United States Information Agency, he tried, without success, to keep the BBC from showing "Harvest of Shame" in Great Britain. Pressures existed against exporting the program, but Murrow himself, in his position, had misgivings about showing such a seamy side of his country abroad.

Ten years after "Harvest of Shame," NBC aired "Migrant," which began by saying it was a follow-up to the CBS program, possibly the first time a network ever broadcast a sequel to another network's documentary and came right out and said so. "Migrant" showed the poor housing that growers of Minute Maid oranges provided, with the result that Coca-Cola, owner of Minute Maid, complained. At the same time, the Florida Fruit and Vegetable Association, charging distortion, said it was taking its case to the FCC. After the broadcast, when the association demanded equal time to answer, NBC refused. Coca-Cola told a Senate hearing it would improve working conditions for the migrants but canceled its advertising on NBC. The program was seen in prime time on July 16, 1970. Its producer and principal correspondent was Martin Carr. Chet Huntley narrated.

NBC returned to the subject once again with "The Migrants, 1980," another one-hour documentary which, the *New York Times* said, "demonstrates how time has virtually stood still in the way of improving the lot of the seasonal pickers." The paper wondered who would do the follow-up in 1990.[11] Again, growers protested. The American Farm Bureau Federation said the program, accenting the negative, overlooked improvements, particularly in housing. "The Migrants, 1980" was produced by Morton Silverstein. Chris Wallace was the correspondent.

"Biography of a Bookie Joint" (1961)

No fine line can be drawn between general reporting and investigative reporting—most reporting involves some investigation—but a report requiring weeks, even months, of what might be called police work rates the investigative label. A landmark investigative documentary was "Biography of a Bookie Joint," network television's first full-length report on police corruption. The program in the "CBS Reports" series was produced by Jay McMullen under Fred Friendly's direction as executive producer. Mc-Mullen and Walter Cronkite narrated.

To illustrate the lucrative, largely tolerated practice of illegal gambling and police payoffs, McMullen chose a small key shop in Boston's Back Bay section that operated as a bookmaking establishment. From an apartment window across the street, CBS filmed the parade of bettors, including uniformed police, entering and leaving the shop. On some days, more than a thousand persons came and went. In his narration, Cronkite said it might be one of the busiest key shops in the world. To clinch his case, McMullen took an 8 mm. camera, concealed in a lunch box, into the shop and recorded the placing of off-track bets.

"Biography of a Bookie Joint" aired November 30, 1961, and was rebroadcast on March 20, 1963. At CBS' request, it was not shown in the Boston area at the time of its first airing because of prosecutions pending, in large part, as a result of McMullen's investigation. In a shake-up in the police department, two of Boston's three deputy superintendents were demoted. The police commissioner, who declined an invitation to appear on the program, resigned. The documentary's principal contribution, however, was the light it shed on a corrupting influence in American society. As Cronkite remarked at the end of the program: "At this point, you may be inclined to say, 'Well, those people in Boston certainly have their problems.' Don't deceive yourself. The chances are very great that you have the same problem in your community."

"The Tunnel" (1962)

This NBC News special, produced by Reuven Frank in 1962, was the first television documentary ever named "Program of the Year" by the National Academy of Television Arts and Sciences. Frank had wanted to do a story on the state of mind of East Germans under Communist rule but could not go in to East Germany to do it. So he was looking, he says, "for effects, the sign, the small indicator that you have to find of what was building up inside."[12] He found the sign when Piers Anderton, assigned to NBC's Berlin bureau, told him that some West German students were burrowing a tunnel under the Berlin Wall to help people escape to the West. Moreover, said Anderton, the students were willing to have their effort filmed. (It turned out the students wanted $50,000 but they ultimately settled for less.) Besides Frank and Bill McAndrew, president of NBC News, few at network headquarters knew of the project. No mention of it was made over the telephone. No film went to New York until the last moment, and then Frank brought it out in his hand luggage.

The 90-minute documentary ran in prime time on December 10, 1962, sponsored by Gulf Oil. What it showed besides the patient digging was 26 people, including five babies, escaping to freedom. The sight was so powerful as propaganda the U.S.I.A. showed it abroad. Yet there were questions. It seemed to Jack Gould of the *New York Times* that with "peace hanging by a thread" it was wrong "for adventurous laymen to turn up in the front lines of world tension." He also questioned, as did others, the propriety of paying the diggers of the tunnel.[13]

"Africa" (1967)

ABC-TV launched its 1967–1968 season with a massive assault on public ignorance about Africa. The broadcast took all of Sunday evening, September 10, 1967. It concentrated on Africans occupying the vast region south of the Sahara because, as narrator Gregory Peck said in the opening, "These are the Africans we know least about, strangers whom we need to know better."

The program required feats of organization. ABC never had done a documentary longer than one hour. Now it was about to produce television's first four-hour documentary, which because of complexity of subject, inclement environment, and great distances presented major problems. Camera crews—and there were six of them—had to be inoculated for typhoid fever, cholera, polio, tetanus, yellow fever, and smallpox. It would be a costly operation. The budget was slightly more than one million dollars, a dismaying figure for ABC at that time. But two million was spent. Crews filmed in 39 of the 49 political divisions of Africa then in existence.

To command this effort as executive producer, Elmer Lower, president of ABC News, chose James Fleming, who had worked at all three networks, collaborated with David Susskind to create "Festival of the Performing Arts," and won numerous awards. The producers, foraging for the essential Africa in an area the size of the Untied States, Western Europe, and China combined, were Tad Danielewski, Edward M. Jones, William Peters, and Pierre Streit. They also served, with Richard Siemanowski, as reporters. Howard K. Smith provided commentary. Blaine Littell, who had covered Africa with distinction for CBS, coordinated the far-flung effort. Elmer Lower was impressed that Skeets Kelly, who had filmed much of "Lawrence of Arabia," turned down a chance to shoot a James Bond movie to join one of the camera crews. Everyone, including Gregory Peck, who had a son in the Peace Corps in Africa, was absorbed in the subject. Still, it seemed an impossible task. When it was all over, Lower found in the project's files a memorandum that read in part: "I think you'll agree that we have an excellent chance of falling on our collective corporate face. . . . It can't be done." Then the line: "The problem is that we are now in too deep."[14]

Aram Boyajian, as senior associate producer, directed the editing of 600,000 feet of color film, which meant cutting 270 hours of film down to four hours. Many of the cuts were painful, but structure—the story line— had to be maintained. "As a result," says Boyajian, "many beautiful and exciting sequences were ruthlessly cut down or eliminated entirely, simply because they took the film down a dead-end road. We had to do our best to keep the film moving." [15]

No one expected high ratings with "Africa." It was pitted that Sunday evening against such formidably popular shows as "The Smothers Brothers" and "Mission Impossible." ABC produced the record-long documentary in part to win respect, not ratings, but ended up with both. In the Trendex ratings, "Africa" attracted a surprising 31.3 per cent of the available audience, which pleased 3M, the company that had bought full sponsorship.

"Hunger in America" (1968)

On the evening of May 21, 1968, CBS shocked the nation with a television documentary showing that acute hunger, even starvation, existed in America, not just in places like Asia and Africa. The documentary was "Hunger in America." Its pictures, and prose, were stark. Viewers see a baby in one of the opening scenes. Charles Kuralt says, "He was an American. Now he is dead."

Ten months went into production of the program, which looked into the plight of the desperate hungry in San Antonio, at a Navajo reservation, in Halicon County, Alabama, and in Loudon County, Virginia, horse country where, said the documentary, "hunger is the last thing an outsider would expect to find." [16]

The program charged that while the United States was spending one and a half billion dollars a year to feed the rest of the world, it was slighting its own hungry. Of the 30 million Americans who were impoverished, it said, 10 million were not getting enough food. It criticized the Department of Agriculture's administration of the food stamp program. Public health officers, and victims, testified on camera to the need.

The public response was extraordinary. Before the program was off the air, CBS was receiving thousands of phone calls, many from viewers asking, "What can we do to help?" Then letters began coming. One woman wrote, "It seems odd to thank you for breaking my heart, but I do." [17]

The secretary of agriculture, Orville Freeman, attacked the broadcast as presenting a "distorted, oversimplified and misleading picture." [18] His complaint and protests from several members of Congress led to an investigation by the FCC, which learned that the dead baby seen in the program had died, not from lack of nourishment, but from complications arising from premature birth. In response, producers of the program testified that they had been told by the hospital that the infant had died because its mother was malnourished. The commission exonerated CBS News, saying it had found no evidence of deliberate distortion.

Thirteen days after the broadcast the Agriculture Department announced it was expanding its food distribution program, and later Congress voted an additional 200 million dollars for food relief, a response that brings to mind Grierson's concept of documentary: film designed to enlighten and persuade. On June 16, CBS broadcast an updated version of

"Hunger in America" that included both the criticism and the network's defense.

The documentary's credits are formidable. The producer was Martin Carr, who would achieve distinction as a documentarian at all three networks. Peter Davis participated as associate producer. Davis would go on to produce "The Selling of the Pentagon" and "Hearts and Minds," a controversial theater film on the Vietnam War.[19] He and Carr wrote the script narrated by Kuralt and David Culhane. As executive producer, Don Hewitt had overall charge.

"The Selling of the Pentagon" (1971)

It was the argument of "The Selling of the Pentagon" that the military establishment was spending tens of millions of dollars a year to promote itself in the eyes of the public and that this was improper. The program charged, moreover, that as part of this massive public relations effort, the Defense Department, in violation of regulations, was peddling foreign policy.

The program, produced by Peter Davis with Roger Mudd as correspondent and narrator, had required more than six months of research. It cited military exhibitions at shopping malls and state fairs, and civilian tours of military bases where VIPs were invited to fire machine guns and recoilless rifles. It showed children imitating a Green Beret officer who had demonstrated "killing blows to vulnerable parts of the body." The Pentagon, it said, had a team of colonels who, in lectures around the country, were promoting American involvement in Vietnam. It reported that 12 million dollars a year was being spent by the Defense Department on motion pictures, and that some of these, shown at public gatherings and on television, were pure Cold War propaganda. In conclusion, Mudd noted that President Nixon had ordered a curtailment in the costly PR effort. "But," he said, "to date not a single activity shown on this broadcast has been eliminated."

No documentary up to that time, with the possible exception of Murrow's McCarthy broadcast, raised more furor. Although widely praised by newspaper critics—Jack Gould found it "brilliant"[20]—the program came under heavy attack from powerful figures like F. Edward Hébert, chairman of the House Armed Services Committee, and Vice President Spiro Agnew, who called the program "disreputable."[21]

CBS was made vulnerable by liberties taken in the editing process. In violation of the network's own policy, some quotes were rearranged and patched together.[22] And there were factual errors, as in the composition of "the team of colonels"—the team included a Navy captain and a Foreign Service officer—and regarding the number of offices in the Pentagon.[23] These mistakes fueled attacks on the broadcast's central argument, which was sound.

"The Selling of the Pentagon" was broadcast on February 23, 1971, then rebroadcast a month later with a 20-minute postscript that included

Vice President Agnew's views and rebuttal by CBS News' president, Richard Salant. The audience for the second broadcast was more than half again larger than the audience for the first, one of the few times in television history that has happened.

The controversy became more than a battle of words. On April 8, the subcommittee on investigations of the House Commerce Committee served a subpoena on CBS for all televised and untelevised materials pertaining to the program. On the same day, Frank Stanton, president of CBS, replied that the network would give the committee only material that actually was broadcast. Stanton claimed for broadcast journalists the same First Amendment rights as print journalists, saying: "No newspaper, magazine or other part of the press can be required constitutionally to comply with such a subpoena with respect to material gathered by reporters in the course of a journalistic investigation but not published."[24]

The stage was set for a showdown. Letters and telegrams to the subcommittee chairman, Harley Staggers, who also chaired the full committee, supported Stanton's position. Many protests against the subpoena came from newspapers and such organizations as the American Society of Newspaper Editors and the Association of American Publishers. The publishers' response was typical. The subcommittee's subpoena, it said, "casts a long shadow of government suppression over all the media and will, if allowed to stand, result in an even greater voluntary curtailment of expression by those who seek to avoid controversy."[25]

When Stanton remained adamant, refusing to yield the program's outtakes and producers' notes, Staggers' committee recommended that he be cited for contempt. Stanton still refused, thereby risking a prison sentence. Not a great risk perhaps—he was a widely respected figure—but a risk nonetheless. He was not cited. In an unusual action, the full House, by a vote of 226 to 181, rejected the committee's recommendation.

An assault on press freedom had been repelled. But out of the firestorm of controversy had come, for documentary producers, painful lessons: The danger inherent in oversimplification, in rearranging participants' statements for impact, and the need in documentaries, especially in investigative documentaries, for constant awareness that there must be, in the armor of argument, no chinks. Lessons taught, but, as CBS found 11 years later with "The Uncounted Enemy: A Vietnam Deception," not always remembered.

"Pensions: The Broken Promise" (1972)

On September 12, 1972, when NBC broadcast "Pensions: The Broken Promise," it set off reverberations that echoed through the courts, the corridors of the Federal Communications Commission, and the nation's press for more than three years. At the time, media scholar Ben Bagdikian said the case "may be the most important test yet in the role of the government in regulating broadcast journalism."[26]

Reuven Frank, president of NBC News, had chosen the one-hour documentary to launch a new series, "NBC Reports." Eliot Frankel was executive producer and David Schmerler producer. Edwin Newman opened the program by stating that 25 million Americans were enrolled in private pension plans and that "if experience is any guide, very many of their hopes will prove empty." He cited tragic instances in which long-term employees suddenly found themselves in the street as they approached retirement and qualification for pension benefits. Several victims appeared on camera. Officers of the Bank of America and the National Association of Manufacturers, appearing on the program, presented management's argument that the record, overall, was good. Newman allowed that many pension systems do operate fairly, but a situation that permitted so much injustice, he said, was deplorable.

The conservative organization Accuracy in Media (AIM) complained to the FCC, charging that NBC had presented a "grotesquely distorted picture" on an issue of public importance and that, in so doing, had violated the Fairness Doctrine.[27] The Broadcast Bureau of the FCC agreed with AIM that the Fairness Doctrine had been violated and, ironically, notified NBC of its finding the same day that "Pensions" won a Peabody Award as "a shining example of constructive and superlative reporting."[28] Never before had the FCC applied the Fairness Doctrine to a network television documentary.

A series of appeals followed. NBC appealed the Broadcast Bureau's finding to the full commission, which upheld the bureau and said that NBC, to correct the imbalance in the documentary, must make time available for the expression of opposing views. NBC refused and took its case to the U.S. Circuit Court of Appeals, where it was supported with briefs filed by the Radio-Television News Directors Association, the National Association of Broadcasters, the *New York Times,* and CBS. When the Court of Appeals decided for the network, AIM appealed to the U.S. Supreme Court. The case ended in NBC's favor when the high court, without comment, let stand the Appeals Court decision.

When it was over, Julian Goodman, who had become chairman of NBC, posed two questions:

> What did we win? We didn't really win anything; we maintained a right we believed to be self-evident, that it should be the role of the journalist, and not the government, to decide the fairness of each documentary program. . . . What could we have lost? We could have lost to the government—not just this one, but any future one —the right to judge what is balanced and what is not on each news program we produce. It is a right we should not surrender to anyone without doing all we can to prevent it.[29]

The "Pensions" case, not the fairness issue, was closed.

"The Uncounted Enemy: A Vietnam Deception" (1982)

The most costly battle involving a broadcaster in a case of libel was fought by CBS in defending itself against a four-star general. On January

23, 1982, the network broadcast a 90-minute documentary entitled "The Uncounted Enemy: A Vietnam Deception," which reported "a conscious effort—indeed, a conspiracy at the highest levels of American military intelligence—to suppress and alter critical intelligence on the enemy in the year leading up to the Tet offensive." It sought to show, through interviews, that General William C. Westmoreland, commander of U.S. forces in Vietnam, ordered his subordinates to underestimate enemy strength in South Vietnam and thus mislead President Johnson and the Congress into believing that the war was being won.

The documentary was produced by George Crile. The narrator and principal reporter was Mike Wallace. Samuel A. Adams, a former CIA analyst, not only was heard on the program but served CBS as a paid consultant. It was he who had given Crile the idea for the documentary. In 1975, when Crile was an editor at *Harper's,* the magazine had published an article by Adams charging a cover-up of intelligence reports on enemy strength.[30] All three, Crile, Wallace, and Adams, were codefendants in the ensuing trial.

Four months after the broadcast, *TV Guide* published an article charging that CBS had been unethical in its production procedures.[31] CBS News assigned the late Bud Benjamin, who was then a senior executive producer, to conduct an in-house investigation of *TV Guide*'s charges. What has become known as the Benjamin Report found that CBS News' own guidelines had been violated. Crile had coached "friendly" interviewees, rehearsing their on-camera statements. Answers to certain questions had been made to appear in response to other questions. Viewers were not told when Adams appeared in interviews that he was a consultant for the program, paid by CBS. Benjamin found an inordinate imbalance in presentation. Viewers heard eight persons supporting the documentary's thesis, one person besides Westmoreland who did not, and that one person for only 21 seconds. Also, Crile taped a telephone interview with Robert McNamara, the former secretary of defense, without McNamara's knowledge.[32]

Three months after the appearance of the *TV Guide* article and seven months after the broadcast, Westmoreland sued CBS for 120 million dollars. CBS sought to avoid trial, offering air time for rebuttal, but not in the format Westmoreland demanded. What Westmoreland charged was that statements in the broadcast were made "with actual malice, with the knowledge that they were false, unfair, inaccurate, and defamatory." The phrase "actual malice" derives from the 1964 Supreme Court decision in *New York Times v. Sullivan,* which said public figures must prove not only that a story is false, but also that the news organization acted with actual malice. The court defined "actual malice" as knowledge that the story was false, or reckless disregard for whether it was true or false.

The trial in the United States Courthouse in Manhattan lasted four months and cost the network more than one million dollars a month. Westmoreland's legal costs, borne by the conservative Washington-based Capital Legal Foundation, exceeded two million dollars. In arguing absence of malice and basic accuracy, CBS called 17 witnesses. Westmoreland's lawyers called 19 witnesses. The official trial transcript ran 9,745 pages. Throughout, CNN fought to carry the proceedings on grounds that the federal court rule barring cameras violated the First Amendment guarantee of free speech and free press. After losing in the lower courts, CNN sought review by the Supreme Court, which rejected the petition without comment. (An irony is that while the Westmoreland case received more media coverage than any lawsuit involving television journalism to date, the documentary itself finished last in the weekly prime-time ratings.)

Abruptly, as the case was about to go to the jury, Westmoreland dropped his suit. CBS joined him in issuing a statement, which read in part:

> CBS respects General Westmoreland's long and faithful service to his country and never intended to assert, and does not now believe, that General Westmoreland was unpatriotic or disloyal in performing his duties as he saw them. General Westmoreland respects the long and distinguished journalistic tradition of CBS and the rights of journalists to examine the complex issues of Vietnam and to present perspectives contrary to his own.[33]

Westmoreland said the statement vindicated him, but the fact is that, in the face of testimony favorable to CBS, he withdrew his suit. CBS won, but at a cost many broadcasters cannot afford. Consequently, the case may have a chilling effect on the production of similar hard-hitting reports. On the other hand, the outcome may restrain public figures from suing. It could work both ways. Ed Joyce, president of CBS News, advised his staff: "This is a time for us to feel relief, but not jubilation. . . . I think it is time for us to reflect and then go about the business of good journalism."[34]

"Vietnam: A Television History" (1983)

Dozens of documentaries have grown out of America's experience in Vietnam. A flurry of retrospectives appeared in 1985, the tenth anniversary of the U.S. pullout, but no review had the scope or impact of "Vietnam: A Television History," which PBS aired in 1983. According to Richard Ellison, executive producer, what viewers saw in that 13-part series was the distillation of hundreds of interviews and more than 200,000 feet of film from archives in 11 countries. Fifty-nine persons, scholars and journalists, served at one time or other as consultants. The hope, Ellison says, was that the painstakingly researched series "might contribute to a better factual understanding of what happened and therefore to some resolution of the gulfs that still divide us about the war."[35]

Viewers recognized stock footage: GIs patroling, gunships attacking, tall grass billowing as helicopters land and take off. But combat footage from the enemy side was new, and interviews with military and civilian leaders on both sides provided fresh insights. High-ranking Communist officers, for example, confirmed that for them the Tet offensive was a military failure. Lawrence Lichty, who directed much of the research, says that contrary to the usual practice in documentary production, interviewing was undertaken before in-depth research. "We went for the principal participants. We had to get them. Some already had died."[36]

"In nearly all this," wrote John Corry of the *New York Times,* "the series is determinedly even handed. . . . [It] tried hard not to reach conclusions. On the other hand, some conclusions are simply implicit in the reporting. The foremost one is that virtually all the assumptions about Vietnam were wrong."[37]

Perhaps because of what was implicit, as well as what it charged were serious errors, the conservative watchdog organization Accuracy in Media (AIM) persuaded public stations to air a one-hour denunciation of the series. It was extraordinary counterprogramming financed in part by the National Endowment for the Humanities, which had contributed to the original production. PBS followed the AIM rebuttal with a one-hour discussion of the charges in a special edition of "Inside Story." Broadcasters wondered what kind of precedent had been set.

"Vietnam: A Television History" was a coproduction of WGBH-TV, Boston, and England's Central Independent Television and France's Antenne-2. Stanley Karnow, who had reported from Vietnam for the *Washington Post,* was chief correspondent. Narration by actor Will Lyman was kept to a minimum. The series, which cost four and a half million dollars and was six years in the making, received broadcasting's highest awards. In terms of journalism, it may have been public television's best, most ambitious venture.

"Paul Jacobs and the Nuclear Gang" (1979)

Paul Jacobs was a reporter who had worked in public television and become committed to telling a story at the risk of his life. Jacobs had become deeply concerned over the high rate of cancer among workers in atomic plants and people living in areas of radioactive fallout, as in Nevada where the government had conducted atomic tests. He was pursuing the story in 1977 when, after inspecting several "hot spots," he himself contracted cancer. On February 25, 1979, PBS carried the program, which was Jacobs' last testament.

"Paul Jacobs and the Nuclear Gang," produced by Jack Willis and Saul Landau, was powerful in its intimacy. It showed Jacobs interviewing men and women, stricken by cancer, who had lived near the test sites and been assured it was safe. By the time the program aired, all were dead. Jacobs himself would die. *Variety* said:

> The doomed reporter didn't rave or rant. His calm appraisal of his own situation and the reasons for it were the strongest arguments for a serious study of this country's proliferating use of atomic energy and the people who have been pushing it.[38]

Other Documentaries, Other Makers

Until the 1960s, few documentaries on commercial networks were produced outside their own shops. It was policy, a way for network news organizations to control content. Then a series of developments loosened that policy. First came the quiz show scandals of 1959, revealing that contestants were fed the answers to questions, that the whole thing was rigged. Next, the public learned that disc jockeys were taking "payola"— bribes to plug new records. It was in this climate of disillusionment that Newton N. Minow, newly appointed chairman of the FCC, called television "a vast wasteland."[39] The phrase caught on, plaguing broadcasters. It served as a catalyst, spurring the creation of more news and public affairs programming.

It was the demand for this kind of programming that enabled David Wolper, an independent producer, to break the network barrier and sell documentaries to ABC and NBC. He had attracted attention in 1960 when he succeeded in selling his first documentary, "The Race for Space," to 105 stations. "Hollywood: The Golden Years" aired on NBC in 1961, but Wolper did not achieve distinction until 1963, when he produced "The Making of a President," based on Theodore H. White's book. *The Making of the President, 1960,* for ABC. He produced *National Geographic* and Jacques Cousteau specials for network showing while continuing to produce programs for syndication. In 1977, he hit the ratings jackpot with the docudrama "Roots."

Frederick Wiseman has produced for public television a remarkable series of scriptless films in which a roving, omnipresent, unsparing camera is the reporter. Using this *cinéma vérité* approach, Wiseman focuses his camera on institutions. The first film, "Titicut Follies" (1967), gave viewers a searing look inside an asylum for the insane. His other documentaries include "Hospital" (1970), "Juvenile Court" (1973), and "Primates" (1974). These films shock. They show, unadorned, what is.

Before Wiseman, Robert Drew was using the same candid camera technique. In "Primary" (1960), an intimate report on the crucial primary race between John F. Kennedy and Hubert Humphrey, Drew accomplished with informal, behind-the-scene pictures what Theodore H. White accomplished in campaign reporting with words. Although only a scattering of stations carried "Primary," ABC News was impressed, and Drew produced documentaries for the network, starting in 1960 with "Yanki No!" which documented rising sentiment against the United States in Latin America and became the first program in ABC's long-running, highly respected "Closeup" series.

Although John Secondari and his wife, Helen Jean Rogers, produced many fine documentaries at ABC in the 1960s, the network was unprepared to produce its own "Closeup" programs on a regular monthly basis until 1973. By that time, Av Westin had built up the documentary unit with Phil Lewis from CBS; Paul Altmeyer from Westinghouse Broadcasting; Martin Carr, formerly of CBS and NBC; Brit Hume, former associate of columnist Jack Anderson, and Pamela Hill, widow of Fred Freed, from NBC. Stephen Fleischman and Marlene Sanders were already on staff.

The first program in the new "Closeup" series, "West Virginia—Life, Liberty and the Pursuit of Coal," was produced and directed by Fleischman. The *New York Times* called the documentary investigating the influence of the coal industry on the politics of West Virginia "encouragingly tough and unblinking." The new series, it said, was off to an impressive start.[40] A burst of hard-hitting documentaries followed. Typical was "Fire!" (1973), a report on neglected fire hazards produced and directed by Pamela Hill. The duPont-Columbia citation said ABC had told "a shattering human story exposing a national scandal of major proportions." In its first three years, the new series received 27 awards.

Not coincidentally, the debut of the series came at a time when ABC's income was up. The network could afford expansion in the documentary area. But soon that changed. Profits were down. People were let go, and fewer documentaries were produced. Westin, losing his fight against slashes in the "Closeup" budget, left for Capital Cities Communications, where he again produced documentaries, notably a much praised program on the energy crisis the country was experiencing. Marlene Sanders directed the "Closeup" unit in his place until 1978, when she went to CBS and Pamela Hill took over. Sanders and Hill were the first women at ABC News to become vice presidents, the title Westin had when he was in charge.

Roone at the Top

Enter Roone Arledge. In 1977, this man who in safari jacket and swirl of cigar smoke had created ABC's "Wide World of Sports" and outmaneuvered rival networks to capture three Olympics in a row, became president of ABC News and revived the documentary unit. In 1979, in a New Year's memorandum to all ABC News personnel, he said:

> While other networks were lamenting the demise of the documentary . . . we at ABC News were bringing "Closeup" back again to the edge, contentious as it may be, of television journalism. In the past six months alone, our documentary unit has received by far the greatest critical acclaim afforded ABC News. From the revelations of military unpreparedness in "The American Army: A Shocking State of Readiness" and the insurance scandals associated with the growth of arson as a leading crime in "Arson: Fire for Hire" to the controversial documentary on urban youth gangs, "Youth Terror: The View Behind the Gun," and the hour spent exploring the terrorist motivations of the Palestinian Liberation Organization, "Terror in the Promised Land," "Closeup" has, I believe, regained its position as the leader in this important area of television.[41]

If the series had not become the leader as Arledge boasted, it definitely was close, an achievement in which he and ABC's documentary producers, who now included Richard Richter, Judy Crichton, Helen Whitney, and Richard Gerdau, could take pride. Yet in 1988, nine years after his memorandum praising the accomplishments of "Closeup," Arledge closed the unit down. Pamela Hill left ABC and now heads up a new hard-hitting investigative team at CNN.

"CBS Reports"

"See It Now" was taken off the air, ignominiously, in 1958. The honored program, buffeted by controversy, had been shifted from prime time to a Sunday afternoon slot, and even there it ran irregularly. In an emotional confrontation, its producers, Fred Friendly and Ed Murrow, appealed to Chairman Paley to save it. Friendly describes the meeting as "a blazing showdown," with Murrow fighting for the life of the program and Paley telling Murrow he didn't want "this constant stomachache every time you do a controversial subject."[42]

A year later, CBS, its eye blackened by the quiz shows, resurrected the program in the form of "CBS Reports." No longer did Murrow coproduce; his decision to take a one-year sabbatical made it easy for management to drop him from that role. For a while he did participate in the series as a reporter, rotating the assignment with other distinguished correspondents like Walter Cronkite, Charles Collingwood, and Howard K. Smith. But now, as regards production, Friendly ruled.

In announcing the new series, Frank Stanton said the network was determined "to press the medium to its fullest extent."[43] In the first years of "CBS Reports," the determination showed. These were the years of "The Population Explosion" (1959), "Harvest of Shame" (1960), "Biography of a Bookie Joint" (1961), and "The Silent Spring of Rachel Carson" (1963). "CBS Reports," which started as a monthly series, became a weekly series in its second season with 28 hours of documentaries, including summer repeats. And every program in prime time.

Friendly persevered as executive producer of "CBS Reports," battling the bookkeepers, until 1964, when he became president of the news division. He was succeeded through the years by Arthur Morse, Palmer Williams, Perry Wolff, Burton Benjamin, Andrew Lack, and Howard Stringer, who himself would become president of CBS News and, later, president of the CBS broadcast group.

As this is written, "CBS Reports" lives, but not as it once lived. Not for many seasons has it been an hour of enlightenment available each week on the same night. In his book, *The People Machine*, Robert MacNeil wrote that documentary production reached its peak in the early 1960s. "Since then," he said, "it has lapsed into a period of commercial timidity."[44] He wrote that in 1968, and afterward came "The Selling of the Pentagon," "Pensions: The Broken Promise," and other fine documentaries. Clearly the lapse was not complete. But MacNeil was right about the commercial pressure. Cost, always rising, became an increasingly important factor. Producers had to fight harder for air time. Good things could be done, but not too much of a good thing. Documentary making had changed.

NBC News "White Papers" and "Reports"

NBC News' first "White Paper" was "The U-2 Affair" (1960), a report on events surrounding the crash of America's top-secret spy plane on Soviet territory. Step by step, the program traced developments from the designing of the U-2 to the international repercussions that followed the crash and the capture of its pilot, Francis Gary Powers.[45] The executive producer was the scrupulous, now legendary Irving Gitlin, who recently had left CBS. Al Wasserman produced and directed. Meticulously researched, brilliantly edited, "The U-2 Affair" deserved its numerous awards.

During his eight years at NBC News—he died of leukemia in 1968—Gitlin oversaw a steady, unhurried stream of distinguished "White Papers" that included "Sit-in" (1960), "Angola: Journey to War" (1961), "The Business of Gambling" (1963), and "Cuba: The Missile Crisis" (1964).

The master documentarians who succeeded Gitlin at NBC were Fred Freed and Reuven Frank. Frank went on to become president of NBC News, then executive producer of the magazine program "Weekend," then once more to presidency of the news division. They produced scores of documentaries; Freed himself, before he died in 1974, made 33. Some were "White Papers," but most of them were documentaries in the long-running "NBC Reports" series. "White Papers" tended to examine major issues, such as racial segregation ("Sit-in") and the Cold War ("Cuba: The Missile Crisis"). Other "White Papers" are Freed's massive "United States Foreign Policy" (1965), which aired in three and a half hours of prime time, and "Organized Crime in the U.S." (1966), to which NBC also committed an entire evening. The *New York Times* called his three-hour "White Paper: The Energy Crisis" (1973) "a solid and valuable survey of a staggeringly complicated subject" and Freed himself "one of the most intelligent and talented veterans of the TV documentary business."[46]

When the "NBC Reports" series premiered in the fall of 1972, it was the season's only weekly hour of network news programming in prime time. Soon, like "CBS Reports," the program appeared sporadically. Among the documentaries presented that first season, besides "Pensions: The Broken Promise," were "Guilty by Reason of Race," which concerned the internment of Japanese-Americans at the start of World War II, and "The Sins of the Fathers," a disturbing report on the plight of the children of American GIs in Vietnam.

Besides Irving Gitlin, Fred Freed, and Reuven Frank, any list of most active documentary producers at NBC would have to include Al Wasserman, Lucy Jarvis, Lou Hazam, Donald B. Hyatt, "Shad" Northshield, and Ted Yates, who died of gunshot wounds while covering the Arab-Israeli

War of 1967. Three years earlier, Yates had produced "Vietnam: It's a Mad War," the first NBC documentary to probe behind the official version of what was going on.

The early generation of documentary producers at NBC had the staunch support of William P. McAndrew, who ran NBC News from 1951 until his death in 1968. Fred Freed once said of McAndrew:

> Whenever Bill said to me, "Go ahead and do the show," I could count on him being there to protect me, to fight for me, to take care of the interests of the program in that whole large area of the network, while I was out there in the front line getting the program on. . . . He had a sense of pride in what the network ought to do.[47]

Decline of the Documentary

From season to season, the number of documentaries rose and fell. In the lean 1971–1972 season, grave issues abounded: inflation, drug abuse, busing, unemployment, crime, the Vietnam War. Yet the three commercial networks devoted only 16 of their 51 documentaries to these issues. Many dealt with innocuous subjects like a bird's-eye view of California and Jacques Cousteau's findings on the sea otter. The 51 documentaries averaged out to 17 documentaries for each network, or about half as many as in previous seasons.

Some predict the demise of the documentary. Even Fred Freed, staunch believer in the form, could write in 1978 an article titled "The Rise and Fall of the Television Documentary."[48] But the documentary has not gone the way of the dinosaur. ABC has disbanded its "Closeup" unit, but its moving force, Pamela Hill, is alive and well at CNN. Among public television's highly informative but uncontroversial documentaries, such as those in the recent "Miracle Planet" series, are to be found provocative "Frontline" reports and Bill Moyers specials. It was PBS that aired Henry Hampton's video history of the civil rights struggle for American blacks.[49] The Discovery Channel is producing fine documentaries rivaling those of PBC. Nor have ABC, CBS, and NBC abandoned the form. ABC, for example, went into 1990 with a series of one-hour, prime-time specials under the title of "Peter Jennings Reporting." The documentary is endangered but not extinct.

Surely the journalist's responsibility to probe and report, in whatever length it takes to enlighten, remains. "I think," said Freed, speaking of documentary making in the future, "our problems are not going to be how many programs we do but how well we do them. Not how strongly we take positions but how clearly we point out imperfect alternatives. Not how we give answers but what questions we ask."[50]

42
Nixon vs. the Nets

The wound was largely self-inflicted. The networks knew beforehand that the attack Vice President Spiro Agnew was about to make upon them would be massive, artfully prepared, and probably effective. They had copies of the speech hours before its delivery at 7 P.M., Eastern time, and yet each, acting independently, turned over to Agnew the half-hour in which many stations normally would be carrying the network evening news. At this point—November 13, 1969—the networks were manipulated by the Nixon administration to that degree.[1]

Agnew began his speech with a tirade against the "small band of network commentators," none of them elected, who a week earlier had followed a broadcast by President Nixon on Vietnam with "instant analysis and querulous criticism." Neither Winston Churchill in World War II nor John F. Kennedy in the Cuban missile crisis, said Agnew, had had to contend with such "a gaggle of commentators" swaying public opinion. "What do Americans know," he asked, "of the men who wield this power?"

> We do know that, to a man, these commentators and producers live and work in the geographical and intellectual confines of Washington, D.C., or New York City. . . . We also can deduce that

these men thus read the same newspapers and draw their political and social views from the same sources. Worse, they talk constantly to one another, thereby providing artificial reinforcement to their shared viewpoints.

He decried the networks' "endless pursuit of controversy" and wondered, "How many marches and demonstrations would we have if the marchers did not know the ever-faithful TV cameras would be there to record their antics for the next news show?" Agnew said he was not advocating censorship, but perhaps it was "time that the networks were made more responsive to the views of the nation and more responsible to the people they serve."

Agnew spoke at a regional meeting of Republicans in Des Moines. If the networks had not carried the attack, it would have been heard by a few hundred people in a hotel ballroom, although no doubt excerpts would have been included in later newscasts and newspaper accounts. Instead, virtually the whole country heard the entire speech. The duPont-Columbia survey for 1969–1970 says, "For broadcast journalism it was unquestionably the year's most significant event. . . . With one clever thrust the vice president had shifted the credibility gap, the bane of the previous and now the current administration, from the White House to the Manhattan offices of the television networks."[2]

No matter that much of what Agnew said was nonsense. The commentators he attacked were broadcast journalism's stars, the subject of innumerable newspaper and magazine articles. Americans, despite what Agnew implied, knew them well. And if they worked in the confines of New York and Washington, they came from a cross section of the country, from such states as North Carolina, Montana, Indiana, Missouri, North Dakota, and Louisiana. To people in broadcasting, the picture of Chet Huntley, Frank Reynolds, Walter Cronkite, and the rest "talking constantly to one another" was laughable. Nor was the "instant analysis" to which Agnew referred instantaneous. Not only did network correspondents have copies of Nixon's speech to study for two hours before he spoke, but some had been briefed by Henry Kissinger, Nixon's foreign affairs adviser.

Inevitably, from time to time, correspondents had made mistakes. But that is not what Agnew's speech was about. It was not designed to raise journalistic standards; it was designed to stifle criticism. The networks, bearers of so much bad news—Vietnam, campus unrest, racial strife— were unpopular, and to accomplish his purpose Agnew played on that unpopularity. The network presidents issued statements. CBS' Frank Stanton said Agnew had gone beyond legitimate criticism by trying to "intimidate a news medium which depended for its existence upon government licenses."[3] Julian Goodman of NBC called it "regrettable that the vice president of the United States would deny to television freedom of the press. Evidently he would prefer a different kind of television reporting, one that would be subservient to whatever political group was in authority."[4] ABC's Leonard Goldenson shared the concern but expressed confidence in the public's ultimate judgment.[5]

The public's immediate judgment seemed to favor Agnew. Network and station switchboards were choked with telephone calls supporting his position. "Hate mail" piled up at network headquarters. In general, newspapers were complacent,[6] an attitude that changed a week later when Agnew broadened his attack to include the printed press—in particular, the *New York Times* and the *Washington Post*. He was not proposing censorship of newspapers, he said. "But the time for blind acceptance of their opinions is past, and the time for naïve belief in their neutrality is gone."[7]

Administration officials fell into line. In his book *To Kill a Messenger*, Bill Small, who was then chief of CBS' Washington bureau, cites the case of Dean Burch, chairman of the FCC. Two days before Agnew spoke in Des Moines, Burch said, "I think all of us will agree that the finest hour of television is in its news and public affairs." The public, he said, owed people in broadcast news a debt. After Agnew spoke, Burch said he approved of the vice president's assault on those to whom gratitude was owed.[8]

Network correspondents found Agnew's speech frightening in its implications. The exception was Howard K. Smith, who with Frank Reynolds co-anchored the ABC evening news. Smith told viewers he agreed with much of what Agnew said.

> In fact, I said some of it before he did. We must continue to discipline ourselves to fairness. We must do something to change the negative tradition of all American journalism, reporting mainly what goes wrong in a nation where much goes right.[9]

Reynolds saw Agnew's attacks differently and, in a strongly worded commentary, urged broadcasters not to be intimidated. "There is something much worse," he said, "than a public official attempting to frighten a broadcaster, and that is a broadcaster who allows himself to be frightened."[10]

Reynolds kept counterattacking and paid the price. ABC removed him from his anchor position, replacing him with Harry Reasoner, who had been with CBS for 14 years. Reynolds' farewell from the anchor desk on December 4, 1970, was one of the most audacious utterances ever made by a correspondent on the air.

> This is my last program as anchorman for the ABC evening news. On Monday, Harry Reasoner, whom I respect personally and professionally, takes over. I wish him well.
>
> The standard script on an occasion such as this calls for some breast-beating about how wonderful it's all been, and how much is owed to all the wonderful people who have made it all possible. . . . The truth is it has been wonderful at times, and of course there are many people who have made it possible and to whom I shall

always be grateful. But I am not going to suggest that I'm completely happy. For it is also the truth that I don't like it one bit and see no reason to pretend that I do.

Like most prisoners I was put here against my will, and like most prisoners I would prefer to pick my own time to leave. However, such matters are decided elsewhere, and I have no quarrel with the judgment that it is time for a change. I have given this assignment my best and, I'm sure, my worst. So maybe we're even. I suppose I ought to say I hope I have not offended anyone in the last two and a half years, but that's not really the truth either because there are a few people I did very much want to bother, and I hope I have.

Reynolds said later that he regretted not handling the matter more maturely. "[T]here is no doubt in my mind that I antagonized a great many people, and when ABC saw an opportunity to replace me with a very popular and thoroughly professional reporter like Harry, they did it. . . . I understand the decision but could not pretend I liked it." As for why he fought the administration's's anti-media campaign so doggedly, he said:

> It seemed to me the country was looking for a scapegoat for our very painful problems. The war was awful, but so many people, including some in the highest reaches of our government, tried to spread the notion that it was awful because of the way it was reported. Deep in my bones was the feeling that journalists had to stand against that kind of mindlessness.[11]

For seven years after leaving the program—until Roone Arledge made him principal anchor for ABC News' reformatted "World News Tonight" —Reynolds served the network as national correspondent in Washington. Ironically, in the course of that assignment, he covered the Watergate hearings that forced Nixon's resignation.

With Agnew's attacks, ABC began carefully labeling the televised opinion of its correspondents with the word *commentary*. Paley banned instant analysis on CBS. The ban lasted several months, and although it may have been instituted out of Paley's own conviction, not administration pressure, he was perceived as succumbing to pressure. Agnew had complained in Des Moines that, on television, bad news was driving out good news. In a duPont-Columbia canvas of 123 stations, 115 said they had begun a serious search for more "good news" items.[12]

Cronkite said the campaign of intimidation spearheaded by Agnew went beyond the right of anyone to correct distortion. Agnew was attacking "the qualifications of the press as the single, most powerful monitor of the performance of the people's government." It was a game, he said, "dangerous to democracy in America."[13] Herbert Klein, White House director of communications, said journalists like Cronkite were overreacting. "I have seen no intimidation," he said. "I have seen criticism, and I think we have a right."[14] Years later, William Safire, who had been a speech writer for Nixon, asked rhetorically:

> Was there a conspiracy, as Walter Cronkite of CBS once solemnly charged, on the part of the Nixon Administration to discredit and malign the press? Was this so-called "anti-media campaign" encouraged, directed and urged by the President himself? Did this alleged campaign to defame and intimidate Nixon-hating newsmen succeed, isolating and weakening them politically? . . . [T]he answer to all those questions is, sadly, yes.[15]

The administration pressed its campaign. It promoted harassment by subpoena. It asked to see transcripts of commentaries, hit the networks with antitrust suits,[16] set up a challenge of the *Washington Post*'s television stations in Jacksonville and Miami, and tried to drive a wedge between the networks and their affiliated stations. In this last stratagem, it had Clay Whitehead, director of the White House Office of Telecommunications Policy, warn affiliates that they were responsible for the network programming they carried, including news. If they accepted the networks' "ideological payola," as he called it, they could be in trouble come license renewal time. With this blatant threat, he held out a carrot. His office, he said, was preparing a bill that would extend license terms from three years to five, something the stations longed for and have today.[17]

It was naked use of government power. Fred Friendly called the scheme, capitalizing on the affiliates' hopes and fears, "the most dangerous thing to come along in 50 years of broadcasting."[18] Senator Sam Ervin saw it as nothing less than an attempt at government censorship; affiliates would serve as surrogates of the administration.[19] There was the example of what had happened to Frank Reynolds. When members of ABC's affiliates board demanded his removal, which meant an end to his commentary, he was removed.

PBS was another target. It had carried reports critical of the administration—one on illegal conduct by the FBI[20]—and Nixon tried, by cutting federal funding, to kill all its public affairs programming. He found "Washington Week in Review" especially objectionable. Its producer, Lincoln Furber, went public, asking viewers how they felt, and the response was so positive, the program survived.[21] So did PBS, but with less money than it needed and, for the time being, with fewer muckraking reports.

Spiro Agnew's service as vice president, and Nixon's point man, ended ignobly on October 10, 1973, when he resigned after pleading no contest to charges of income tax evasion. The larger shame was that he had been found a grafter. The tax he owed was on kickbacks received while governor of Maryland.

That night, Cronkite could not forego comment. He said:

> There is no feeling of revenge here, but one of great pity. I first met Spiro Agnew in 1967 and I liked him. . . . Then there came that November 1969 speech that opened officially the Nixon offensive against the news media . . . and because of my strong belief that the free press must fight any attempt to intimidate it, we became ideological enemies. But we would not have wished, even

on Spiro Agnew, the degree in which his reputation, his hopes and dreams are smothered tonight.[22]

Two days after Agnew resigned, Nixon named the House minority leader, Gerald Ford, vice president in his place.

The Unmaking of the President

It began in the early hours of June 17, 1972, with the arrest of five "burglars" in Democratic National Committee headquarters in the opulent Watergate complex in Washington and ended 13 months later with President Nixon's resignation. The House Judiciary Committee had recommended his impeachment in the Watergate affair, in which the press played a leading role.

The cover-up began the first day. John Mitchell, who had resigned as U.S. attorney general to manage the President's reelection campaign, put out a statement that none of those apprehended was "operating on either our behalf or with our consent."[23] But one of the men arrested at Democratic headquarters, then indicted, proved to be James McCord, security director for the Committee to Re-elect the President.

The *Washington Post* had assigned two young reporters, Carl Bernstein and Bob Woodward, to stay with the story. They and reporters from a few other papers, notably the *New York Times* and *Los Angeles Times,* kept digging out evidence in what proved to be the most sensational whodunit in American political history. Day after day, on its front page, the *Post* made new revelations. The networks picked up these stories and gave them national exposure.

It occurred to Cronkite that if the Watergate story was reported piecemeal over so long a period his viewers might be missing its significance—the large picture—and Stanhope Gould, a producer for the evening news, began assembling a two-part series that would wrap up the developments so far and show which members of the administration were involved.

The first segment aired on October 27, 1972. There was little new in the report. What struck viewers was the scope of what seemed to be a conspiracy originating in the White House. Richard Salant, president of CBS News, wondered about the length of the report—14 minutes—in a program that had only 22 minutes for news. That so much time was devoted to Watergate less than two weeks before the election, in which Senator George McGovern was running against Nixon, made the network vulnerable to charges of bias. Paley voiced no criticism, at least not to Salant.

The morning after the broadcast, Paley received a telephone call form Charles Colson, special counsel to the President. Colson attacked the report as one-sided and, in a not so veiled threat, said that if Nixon were reelected, "it would be very hard for them to establish good relations with [CBS]."[24] Paley defended Cronkite's news judgment but then called a meeting of CBS news executives at which he not only again expressed his view that, in proportion to the rest of the program, the Watergate segment had been much too long, but that it was unbalanced and presented nothing new. Paley gave no direct order to Salant, but because of the chairman's strong feeling the second segment on October 31 was shortened to eight minutes. Paley was still unhappy, to put it mildly, but the deed was done.[25]

The deed carried the weight the White House feared it would. No longer could newspaper editors around the country ignore the story or bury it on an inside page, believing, as Ben Bradlee, executive editor of the *Washington Post,* said, that "it was some kind of weird crusade on our part."[26] Once the story captured national attention, irreversible forces came into play. "It was," Theodore H. White said, "as if the church had detected a heresy; the inquisition must pursue the suspects, extract the evidence and then turn the culprits over to the secular arm for punishment."[27]

Before the grand juries, before the special prosecutors, before the House and Senate committees, it was the press that pursued suspects and extracted evidence, and if for its efforts the *Washington Post* was first on Nixon's hate list, CBS was second. Nixon, reelected, protested Dan Rather's hard-hitting reports from the White House and tried, unsuccessfully, to have CBS give him a different assignment.[28] He had no greater liking for Bob Pierpoint, CBS' veteran White House correspondent, who, working with producer Ed Fouhy, had exposed the favorable treatment that Nixon's good friend Charles "Bebe" Rebozo received from the federal government in the savings and loan business. And it was Pierpoint who, in April 1973, scooped all media with the story that presidential counsel John Dean, in a dramatic break with Nixon, would not accept the role of scapegoat in the Watergate scandal.[29]

Nixon's resentment of Pierpoint exploded in the course of a news conference in which he tore into the networks for their "outrageous, vicious, distorted, frantic, hysterical" coverage but added curiously, almost in the same breath, "I am not blaming anyone for that." On being recognized, Pierpoint said, "Mr. President, you have lambasted the television networks pretty well, but you say . . . you don't blame anyone. I find that a little puzzling. What is about the television coverage of you in these past weeks and months that has so aroused your anger?" Then came this exchange:

> NIXON: Don't get the impression that you arouse my anger.
> PIERPOINT: I'm afraid, sir, that I have that impression.
> NIXON: You see, one can only be angry with those he respects.

There were murmurs of shock from the correspondents present. Later in the news conference, Nixon brought the subject up again, saying he did not mean a lack of respect for reporters in general, only the commentator who, knowing the facts, distorts them viciously. "I have no respect for that individual." He named no names.[30]

There was good reason for Nixon to be tense. With reports of intimidation, perjury, and bribes had come Dean's damaging testimony before the Senate Watergate Committee that Nixon had participated in the cover-up almost from the start. Then came revelation of the existence of White House tapes, Nixon's refusal to surrender the tapes, then his surrender of all but two of the subpoenaed tapes. He was losing control. Six days before the news conference, in what became known as "The Saturday Night Massacre," Archibald Cox who was getting close to the truth, had been fired as special Watergate prosecutor. Nixon had tried to get Attorney General Elliot Richardson to do the firing, but, rather than do it, Richardson had resigned. William Ruckelshaus, deputy attorney general, also refused and was dismissed.

Howard K. Smith, who had found merit in Agnew's Des Moines speech, now became the first network commentator to call for Nixon's resignation. After citing the record, he said: "I think it is not excessive to say we have been put through too much. Either the Congress, or the President by his own decision, should relieve us of a burden too heavy to carry any longer."[31]

The end came in 1974. On March 1, seven of Nixon's former aides were indicted in the cover-up. Nixon himself was named as an unindicted coconspirator. On July 24, the Supreme Court said he could stall no longer. He had to surrender the White House tapes, with their incriminating evidence, to Leon Jaworski, who had succeeded Cox as special prosecutor. On July 27, the House Judiciary Committee, in a bipartisan vote, found him guilty of obstruction of justice in lying and concealing evidence, and called for impeachment.

For the first time, a House committee hearing had been broadcast while members debated and voted. Each day, the television networks rotated their coverage. Public television provided complete live coverage day in and day out. So did National Public Radio and CBS Radio. Other networks carried excerpts. But when the vote came, all America heard it—a bill of impeachment, the first offered against any president since Andrew Johnson in the uncertain days following the Civil War.

As the Senate Watergate Committee hearings had made a national figure of its colorful chairman, Sam Ervin of North Carolina, so the House committee's public hearings, aired for 45 hours, popularized chairman Peter Rodino and many other members. Despite the drama inherent in the situation, members, aware of the unusual, even painful responsibility placed on them, for the most part played their deliberative role with restraint. And because they deliberated in full view, in the presence of microphones and cameras, the American people were educated in a special democratic way. They understood. The issue was not a burglary. The issue was the corruption that had spread from it through the highest levels of government with gangrenous effect.

The networks carried Nixon's last public utterances as president. On August 8, the country heard him make his resignation announcement, then next morning take one more jab at reporters in his informal farewell speech. "Let the record show," he said, surrounded by his family and White House staff, "that this is one of those spontaneous things we always arrange whenever the president speaks. And," he added with a smile that was humorless, "it will be so reported in the press." Minutes later, television viewers watched soberly as a helicopter rose from the White House grounds and whisked him away.

43
Electronic Coverage: Congress and the Courts

Live coverage of Congress, so routine today, was a long time coming. It was one thing to broadcast a president's message delivered before a joint session—Coolidge's in 1923 was the first—but quite another to let microphones and cameras pick up and transmit what actually was taking place on the floor in regular session. Six decades would pass, and more than thirty bills and resolutions be fought over, before Congress allowed it.

Members who opposed opening up the House and Senate chambers to radio and television contended that such exposure would encourage grandstanding on the part of some of their number (never themselves) and impede the work of Congress. Some feared that a politically dangerous person elected to Congress—another Huey Long—might use the electronic soapbox to mislead. There also was apprehension, real but less often expressed, that cameras might show members asleep or reading newspapers and a largely empty chamber. Proponents argued that the public's right to be informed on the workings of Congress overrode these objections. Newton Minow, who had called television "a vast wasteland" when he became chairman of the FCC, said:

> Our democratic system's health and strength is founded on an
> informed and concerned electorate. I believe the most useful thing
> television can do in the future is to broadcast the debates of Con-
> gress on the great issues of our time.[1]

Frank Stanton called television "a fact of life." He said to limit its role on
the basis of how members might behave was "a wholly untenable proposition." The burden of responsibility for conduct," he said, "must rest, not
with the instruments that transmit legislative or judicial events, but with
the participants who make those events."[2]

Not until 1979 did the House chamber accept electronic coverage.
Even then, over the strong protest of broadcasters, the House took control.
House employees operate the equipment, restricting what can be broadcast. The cameras do not pan; they lock routinely on a tight shot of the
member speaking or on a wide shot of the rostrum. In the beginning,
cameras and microphones were turned off as votes were taken, but this
restriction was lifted. Seven years later, when the Senate allowed live coverage, it adopted a similar system. Broadcasters settled for what they could
get.

From Gangster's Moll to Joe McCarthy to Impeachment

Long before broadcasts originated from the House and Senate chambers there was live coverage of committee hearings. In 1952, Senator Estes
Kefauver conducted a series of televised hearings on organized crime
which proved a sensation. Millions tuned in to see the gangster's moll,
Virginia Hill, and hear the gravel-voiced testimony of bigtime gambler
Frank Costello. Costello balked at being on camera, so viewers saw only a
close-up of his hands, which, with their nervous movements, presented a
kind of psychological study. Kefauver became a national figure and made
an unsuccessful bid for the Democratic nomination for president.

The Army–McCarthy hearings of 1954 sealed the political fate of
Senator Joseph McCarthy but launched the successful, highly controversial
law career of his aide, Roy Cohn.

It is an understatement to say that radio and television played a prime
role in the impeachment hearings that forced the resignation of President
Nixon. The whole nation, listening to hundreds of hours of testimony
before the Senate Select Committee and the House Judiciary Committee,
was educated in both evidence and process. Government was made more
participatory—more of the people and by the people—and because of
public understanding of the process, and trust in it, the crisis was defused.
Sydney Head of Temple University has observed that the hearings demonstrated not only that members of Congress can behave responsibly in
front of cameras but that "such coverage could have unique value in
helping restore the balance of power within the government," which is to
say between the executive branch and the Congress.[3]

The Rayburn Rule

Microphones and cameras were barred from House committee hearings, public as well as closed, during most of the 1950s and 1960s. This was because of an interpretation of House rules by Speaker Sam Rayburn. On February 25, 1952, he stated:

> There is no authority and, as far as the chair knows, there is no granting the privilege of television in the House of Representatives, and the chair interprets that as applying to these committees or subcommittees, whether they sit in Washington or elsewhere.

Eight months later, Republicans won control of the House. The new speaker, Joseph W. Martin, Jr., ignored what Rayburn had said and authorized the broadcast of committee hearings that were open to the public. As far as Martin was concerned, it was a matter for the committees to decide. However, within two years the Democrats regained control. Rayburn, back as speaker, had not changed his mind. "Television in the House?" he said, responding to reporters' questions. "Hell, no!"[4] And again he ruled that no House committee could allow broadcast of its proceedings.

It was thought that John W. McCormack, who succeeded Rayburn, might open up the committees. But in 1962, when proponents of broadcast coverage raised the issue, McCormack upheld the so-called Rayburn Rule, and the ban remained in force. Representative George Meader of Michigan, who fought for electronic coverage, complained of "a horse-and-buggy Congress in a jet age."[5]

The breakthrough came in 1970 when the House Rules Committee voted to allow broadcast of public hearings. The full House then approved by the narrow vote of 96 to 93. The fact that Senate hearings were televised provided the winning margin; House members wanted the same exposure. Still, there were restrictions. No more than five cameras would be permitted at a hearing. Sponsorship was prohibited, and subpoenaed witnesses had the right not to have their testimony broadcast.

Coverage a Plus

Live coverage of proceedings on the House floor began on March 19, 1979, after a trial period in which debates were piped by closed circuit into the offices of various House members. After a similar test, television on June 2, 1986, began covering floor action in the Senate. (Live radio broadcasts from the chamber had started in March.) "Today," said Majority Leader Robert Dole, "the Senate catches up with the 20th Century."

Although some members were still apprehensive, the general atmosphere was festive. As a joke, Senator John Glenn came on camera and powdered his balding head. A party was held for Howard Baker, the former majority leader who championed electronic access. Eight weeks later, on July 29, the Senate voted to continue radio-television coverage of its proceedings on a permanent basis.

From the start, C-SPAN has been the service providing gavel-to-gavel coverage of floor debate in the House and Senate. The complete feed may be seen on cable, while excerpts are used by individual stations and networks. The effect has been positive. There have been more speeches and some "playing to the cameras," as when a congressman opposed to a lame duck session held up a rubber duck and wrung its neck.[6] But such posturing was not unknown in the days before television, and the public is better informed. What is said is what people hear, not what the *Congressional Record,* which accepts revision, claims was said. And television provides an extra dimension. "It can," as James Reston said, "put a face and a voice to the words."[7]

A practical advantage for members is that, working in their offices, they can monitor what is happening on the floor and so themselves be better informed. The political benefit is obvious. Speeches are directed more to the radio-television audience than to fellow members; not just a few lawmakers but millions out there are listening. Phil Jones of CBS' Washington staff finds that as a consequence the speeches are better written and more to the point. Ann Compton of ABC notes that radio-television coverage has added to the prominence of congressional leaders like Robert Dole and Robert Byrd—and of red neckties.[8] Former House Speaker Thomas P. "Tip" O'Neill, who once regarded such coverage as a disaster, has said that members would raise "a hue and cry" if it were cut off.[9]

State legislatures were more ready than Congress to grant access. By the time the House allowed broadcast of its debates, 44 of the nation's 50 legislatures already were permitting it. Forty of them, unlike Congress, were letting broadcasters handle the operation. Cable systems, seeking franchises, offered to cover city council meetings, and the offers were accepted. In 1978, Governor Pierre du Pont of Delaware broke precedent by delivering his annual message, not before the General Assembly, but from the studios of noncommercial WHYY-TV in Wilmington.

Increasingly, at all levels, the broadcast media were performing not just a reportorial role; they were becoming integrated to a significant degree with government.

Coverage of the Courts

During this whole time, broadcasters were battling on another front to get their microphones and cameras into the courts. They contended that they had the same right to enter courtrooms with their reporting tools as newspaper reporters did with their pads and pencils. It was a tough, uphill fight. The principal opponent was the American Bar Association (ABA). Its position was stated in Canon 35 of the Canons of Judicial Ethics, adopted by the association's House of Delegates in 1937 because of the circus atmosphere surrounding the trial of Bruno Hauptmann in the Lindbergh kidnap case. In 1952, the ABA amended Canon 35 to include a prohibition against broadcasting court proceedings. It reads in part:

> Proceedings in court should be conducted with fitting dignity and decorum. The taking of photographs in the courtroom . . . and the broadcasting or televising of court proceedings are calculated to detract from the essential dignity of the proceedings, distract the witness in giving his testimony, degrade the court, and create misconceptions with respect thereto in the mind of the public and should not be permitted.

Although Canon 35, so full of damning language, was not law, it carried great weight. The first state to dare ignore it was Texas, and KWTX-TV, Waco, may have been the first station in the country to provide live coverage of a murder trial. The date was December 6, 1955. The next state to allow microphones and cameras in its courtrooms was Colorado, where the rule was that the trial judge was to decide whether, with the consent of all parties, the proceedings could be broadcast.[10] An early trial covered for television was held in LeMars, Iowa, in 1956. KTIV, Sioux City, sent one of its reporter-photographers, Ben Silver, to LeMars with a Bell & Howell picture camera and a Polaroid still camera. Silver says:

> It was a murder trial held in a state court, and we covered it from the first day. We weren't the only crew there. KCAU, our competitor in Sioux City, also sent a photographer, but we had it to ourselves for the first couple days. The film was strictly silent, and I don't remember any problems.[11]

In 1962, the Radio-Television News Directors Association (RTNDA) and the National Association of Broadcasters (NAB) proposed to the bar association that a series of trials be covered by radio and television on a limited, experimental basis. They suggested using trials in cities of varying size and location, either on a closed circuit basis or on the air. It would be a fair test.[12] But on February 5, 1963, the bar association's House of Delegates voted to keep its ban on broadcasting and the taking of pictures by newspaper photographers.

Broadcasters received a further setback in 1965 when the Supreme Court, in a free press–fair trial decision, reversed the conviction of Billie Sol Estes, who had been found guilty of fraud by a Texas court. The Supreme Court ruled, 5 to 4, that due to disruption caused by broadcast of the proceedings, Estes had been deprived of his right to a fair trial.[13]

Broadcasters persisted in attacking the unreasonableness of Canon 35 and were joined in the fight by such influential organizations as the American Society of Newspaper Editors, the Reporters' Committee for Freedom of the Press, the National Press Photographers' Association, and the Society of Professional Journalists, Sigma Delta Chi. They argued the First Amendment and new technology—miniaturized cameras and faster film—which would make coverage less intrusive. Trials, it was pointed out, could be covered on a pool basis, further reducing congestion in the courtroom.

More states began allowing broadcast coverage, notwithstanding the ABA position. Some of this coverage was permitted on an experimental test basis, some on a permanent basis. The trial most widely covered by television during this period occurred in Florida in September 1977. Fifteen-year-old Ron Zamora of Miami Beach was charged with murdering an elderly woman, whose money and car he used for a weekend spree. Defense argued that the boy's heavy viewing of violence on television had intoxicated him, "diseasing his mind."[14] This was the first trial televised in Florida's one-year experiment with electronic coverage. Noncommercial WPBT-TV covered it on a pool basis. One camera was allowed in the courtroom; lighting was kept to the minimum. The proceedings went smoothly. Zamora was found guilty, and Florida decided to make such coverage permanent.

The Floodgates Open

Here and there, gingerly, courts entered the Electronic Age. Then came a series of actions that opened the floodgates. In 1980, in *Richmond Newspapers v. Virginia,* the Supreme Court for the first time recognized that the press has a constitutional right of access to criminal trials.[15] On top of that, it ruled that Florida, in allowing cameras in the courtroom, had acted constitutionally.[16] The decision was a signal victory for broadcasters because it was unanimous and, as NBC's veteran law correspondent Carl Stern pointed out at the time, because it "dealt with the toughest situation —the presence of cameras in a criminal trial, before a jury, over the objection of the defendants."[17] By the next year 37 states were permitting some form of broadcast coverage.

In August of that year (1982) the American Bar Association, seeing so many states adopting their own rules, softened its stand. Its House of Delegates revised Canon 3A (7), which had replaced Canon 35, to say that under appropriate authority

> a judge may authorize broadcasting, televising, recording, and photographing of judicial proceedings in courtrooms and areas immediately adjacent thereto consistent with the rights of parties to a fair trial subject to express conditions which allow such coverage in a manner that will be unobtrusive, will not distract trial participants, and will not interfere with the administration of justice.

Obviously, neither the new canon nor the Supreme Court decision automatically, or completely, opened courtroom doors. No state court could admit radio or television unless standards for coverage first were laid down by that state's legislature or high court.[18] And federal courts still were off limits. They might, on occasion, admit cameras for a naturalization ceremony, but electronic coverage of a hearing or trial remained taboo.

As chief justice, Warren Burger was vehement in opposing the broadcast of proceedings in any federal court, including his own. To test just how strong his opposition was the Mutual Broadcasting System in 1986 offered to cover live and without commercial interruption oral arguments on the constitutionality of the Gramm-Rudman bill aimed at reducing the federal deficit. Burger had seemed to imply in a speech that, under certain conditions, he might relent.[19] But Burger's reply was unequivocal. "There is no basis whatever," he said, " 'to imply' that any circumstances would exist in which I would favor television coverage of Supreme Court proceedings."[20] Mutual seized on the word *television*. What about radio? Burger shot back, "It is not possible to arrange for any broadcasting of any Supreme Court proceedings."[21]

Burger has since retired, and the new chief justice, William Rehnquist, let it be known that he would not oppose electronic coverage of some federal courts on an experimental basis. On September 12, 1990, the Judicial Conference of the United States took a historic step. It authorized radio and television coverage of civil trials in various federal courts as a three-year experiment. The Supreme Court is not included in the test.

By the end of 1989 only five states and the District of Columbia forbade any kind of trial coverage by radio and television. Twenty-two states allowed the broadcast of criminal trials without the consent of the defendant. All states permitting radio and television in the courtroom reserved the right to bar coverage on a case-by-case basis.

44
The Longest Battle

No battle in broadcasting has been waged so fiercely and for so long as the battle over the Fairness Doctrine and Section 315 of the Communications Act of 1934. The doctrine's purpose has been enlightening of the electorate on controversial issues of public importance. To that end, broadcasters "must" afford reasonable opportunities for the presentation of contrasting views. The purpose of Section 315—the so-called equal time provision—is a fair shake for political candidates and a chance for the electorate to hear all sides. The section states that if a station allows a legally qualified candidate for public office to go on that station's air, it "shall" afford equal opportunity to all other qualified candidates for that office.

Broadcasters applaud these goals but demand the right that newspapers have to cover the news as they see fit. They argue that under the First Amendment government cannot, for whatever purpose, appropriate their editorial role. It is the mandatory nature of the Fairness Doctrine and the equal time provision—the *must* and the *shall*—that lies at the heart of the debate. The broadcast journalist's position was expressed forthrightly by Richard Salant when he was president of CBS News. He said:

> Let me make this point as crystal clear as I know how. While I am convinced that if the First Amendment is to mean anything to us in broadcast news it must mean that the government cannot investigate and regulate and tell us what to do and how to do it . . . I am equally convinced that this gives us no moral license to be wrong or careless or biased.
>
> The mark of a good journalist is that his eyes and ears and perceptions—the facts he selects and the facts he reports—are not colored by his personal predilections. . . . Morally and professionally, then, we have no right whatever to be wrong. Constitutionally, we must have the right to be wrong.[1]

As Salant spoke—it was 1968—the FCC was requiring the networks to justify their coverage of the recent tumultuous Democratic convention in Chicago. Twelve days after Salant spoke, Richard Cheverton of WOOD-TV, Grand Rapids, gave the keynote address at the annual convention of the Radio-Television News Directors Association. He spoke bluntly.

> Government is now demanding an accounting for an editorial decision. There is the inescapable conclusion that government would not demand an accounting unless they assumed a proprietary authority to either approve or disapprove of the network judgments. That, gentlemen, is not freedom of the press.[2]

The Man in the Uncle Sam Suit

Because of Section 315, broadcasters cannot do a program on one qualified candidate without doing programs on all qualified candidates. In a presidential campaign, there may be a score of minor party candidates, none with a chance of being elected. The result is that stations, and networks, have shied from doing programs they otherwise would have done. And the public is less well informed.

At first, Section 315 applied to the appearance of legally qualified candidates on any program, including newscasts. This requirement was eased in 1959 when Lar Daly, who liked to dress up in a red, white and blue Uncle Sam suit, ran for mayor of Chicago. Daly complained that he was not getting as much television coverage as Chicago's mayor, Richard Daley, who sought reelection. Although Daley, running the city, naturally was in the news more often, the FCC held that his opponent must have comparable air time. Shocked by the ruling, CBS President Frank Stanton said he feared what would happen "once crackpot candidates realized what a rich opportunity lay before them to be seen and heard."[3]

Recognizing the impracticality of the FCC decision, Congress acted to exclude newscasts, news interviews, and, ultimately, political debates from the equal time requirement. The same went for news documentaries so long as the appearance of the candidate was incidental to the subject of the documentary.

It was this suspension of equal time that made possible the Nixon–Kennedy debates. In 1975, the FCC went further. It ruled that all political debates carried in their entirety are news events and hence exempt from the equal time requirement. But there was a catch. The debates could not be conducted by either broadcasters or political managers. They had to be sponsored by an independent organization, which is how presidential debates came to be administered by the League of Women Voters. It was this outside control, the FCC reasoned, that made a debate a news event. Later, the commission went still further, broadening debate exemption by eliminating the requirement for third-party sponsorship.

To keep down campaign costs, Section 315 says that what a station charges a legally qualified candidate shall be the minimum rate. If a candidate buys time, the station is not obliged to provide his or her opponents with free time. But time has to be made available for opponents to buy. Another provision prohibits any broadcaster from censoring what a candidate wants to say on the air. Broadcasters, fearful of libel, were understandably apprehensive; what candidates say about each other can get pretty rough. The Supreme Court removed this worry in 1959 when, in just such a libel case, it held that stations are not liable.[4]

Another section of the Communications Act—Section 312—says that stations must allow legally qualified candidates for federal office reasonable access. "Reasonable access" includes political commercials, for which stations cannot charge any more than the least amount charged any other advertiser for the same kind of time. It is a law written by members of Congress for their own benefit since they hold federal office and often seek reelection.

The Fairness Doctrine Fight

While Section 315 appears full-blown in the Communications Act of 1934, the Fairness Doctrine evolved from a series of FCC decisions based on the Radio Act of 1927, which said stations must operate in the public interest. In one major decision, the commission said the fact that stations are not common carriers "in no way impinge[s] on the duty of each station licensee to be sensitive to the problems of public concern in the community and to make sufficient time available, on a nondiscriminatory basis, for full discussion thereof."[5] Quite a mouthful. In another case, the FCC referred to "a licensee's duty to make time available for the presentation of opposing views on current controversial issues of public importance."[6] This, too, became part of the Fairness Doctrine.

The birth date of the doctrine is given, arbitrarily, as June 1, 1949, when it became explicit in an FCC report lifting the ban on editorials. But it may be said to have come of age in 1964 when the FCC issued a primer summarizing its rulings and clarifying their intent. Clarification was needed.

The rulings had come out, one by one, as cases came up. There was no package of policy. Now there was. And because the underlying principle in both the doctrine and Section 315 was fairness, it was easy to be confused. (Section 315—equal time—applies only to political candidates. The Fairness Doctrine is more encompassing. To quote the primer, "It deals with the broader question of affording reasonable opportunity for the presentation of contrasting viewpoints on controversial issues of public importance.")

Nor was it just a matter of "affording" reasonable opportunity. The Fairness Doctrine, as presented in the primer, said that broadcasters had an "affirmative duty" to encourge the presentation of contrasting views over and beyond making their facilities available. The contrasting views did not have to be heard on the same program, it was the fairness of the station's overall performance that counted.[7]

The Red Lion Case

The Red Lion case is a landmark. The principals were the Reverend Billy James Hargis, a New York writer named Fred Cook, and the Red Lion Broadcasting Company, operator of radio station WGCB in Red Lion, Pennsylvania.

In 1964, in a broadcast over WGCB, Hargis accused Cook, among other things, of once working for a magazine that "has championed many Communist causes."[8] Cook took umbrage and demanded free time to reply. The station refused. Cook protested to the FCC, which ordered the station to give him time. It still refused, and the case went to the U.S. Court of Appeals for the District of Columbia, which found for the FCC.

At this point, the Radio-Television News Directors Association (RTNDA), supporting what it held to be broadcasters' First Amendment rights, asked the U.S. Court of Appeals for the Seventh Circuit to set aside the FCC's personal attack rule. The appellate court agreed that the FCC order constituted an abridgment of freedom of speech and press.

The victory was short-lived. The Red Lion and RTNDA cases, consolidated, wound up in the Supreme Court, which upheld the FCC in ruling that "if the honesty, character or integrity of a person is challenged on the air, the station must notify those attacked, supply a text or tape of the attack and offer airtime for reply." (Newscasts and, in general, remarks by political candidates were exempt.) The court stated:

> It is the right of the viewers and listeners, not the right of the broadcasters, which is paramount. . . . It does not violate the First Amendment to treat licensees given the privilege of using scarce radio frequencies as proxies for the entire community, obligated to give suitable time and attention to matters of great public concern.[9]

To the dismay of broadcasters, the nation's highest court had found that the Fairness Doctrine was valid and constitutional.

Miami Herald v. Tornillo

In 1913, the Florida legislature passed a law that amounted to a fairness doctrine for newspapers in that state. It said that if a newspaper attacked a political candidate, the paper had to give the candidate space for reply. There was no real test of the statute until 1972 when the *Miami Herald* ran two editorials attacking the candidacy of Pat Tornillo, Jr., director of a local teacher's union, in a primary election. When Tornillo gave the *Herald* his reply, the paper refused to print it. The Supreme Court sided with the *Herald*.

> The choice of material to go into a newspaper, and the decisions made as to limitations on the size and content of the paper, and treatment of public issues and public officials—whether fair or unfair—constitute the exercise of editorial control and judgment. It has yet to be demonstrated how governmental regulation of this crucial process can be exercised consistent with First Amendment guarantees of a free press.[10]

It was difficult for broadcasters to read the decision and not feel bitter. The court had repudiated the concept of right of access to the printed press, using the same argument that they—the broadcast press—had used in *Red Lion*. One had only to substitute the words *broadcasting station* for *newspaper*. Why the different treatment? A committee of the American Bar Association answered the question by saying that while the daily newspaper field "is technologically open to all," the field for broadcasters "is inherently not so open." The government, it said, "chooses one licensee for a frequency and forecloses all others, a crucial difference."[11]

Banzhaf v. FCC

In 1967, the FCC ruled that cigarette smoking constituted a controversial issue of public importance. Applying the Fairness Doctrine, it said broadcasters who accept cigarette advertising must "provide a significant amount of time for the other viewpoint,"[12] a ruling the Supreme Court let stand.

John F. Banzhaf III, a private citizen, had complained that WCBS-TV, New York, having aired numerous cigarette commercials, kept him, and others, from going on the station with contrasting views. In defense, the station cited its news stories dealing with the health hazards of smoking. The FCC said the station had not done enough. It suggested broadcasters correct the imbalance by airing public service announcements such as those prepared by the American Cancer Society, and this was general practice until Congress banned cigarette commercials, effective January 2, 1971.[13]

The WHAR Ruling

Up to now, FCC rulings had focused on balance, on insuring that audiences, in fairness, heard both sides. The commission had said little about the broadcaster's other duty under the doctrine, which was to cover controversial issues of public importance; the broadcaster could not skip over these issues, pretending they did not exist.

The FCC reminded broadcasters of this second duty in a 1976 ruling involving WHAR-AM, a top 40 station in Clarksburg, West Virginia. The issue was strip mining. Congress was considering legislation, favored by environmentalists, against that method of mining coal. The station refused to air a tape provided by Congresswoman Patsy Mink supporting the measure. The station argued that since it had not carried any programs on the strip mining controversy, there was no need to run the tape for balance.[14] The FCC said that that was not the point; the station had violated the Fairness Doctrine by failing to report on a controversial issue of obvious importance to the community and must remedy that failure. The station then covered the issue, pro and con, in compliance with the order. *Broadcasting* noted that "the United States government has, for the first time, given a news assignment to a broadcast station."[15]

The Pentagon Papers

The 1970s saw a whole series of major court decisions affecting the media.

In 1971, the nation witnessed a historic effort at prior restraint. This was the Pentagon Papers case in which the Justice Department, on national security grounds, tried to keep the *New York Times* from publishing a series of articles detailing hitherto unrevealed information on the origins of the Vietnam War. The Justice Department acted after three installments in the series, based on a Pentagon study marked "top secret," had appeared in the *Times* and several other papers, including the *Washington Post*.

In a 6–3 decision, the Supreme Court upheld the right of the papers to publish. It ruled narrowly. It decided only on the issue of prior restraint in this instance—it did not prohibit future restraint—and it left open the possibility of criminal prosecution once the material was published.[16]

Herbert v. Lando

"Herbert" was Anthony Herbert, a much-decorated retired Army officer who had served as battalion commander in Vietnam. "Lando" was Barry Lando, a "60 Minutes" producer. On the evening of February 4, 1973, Herbert said on "60 Minutes" that he had been dismissed from his command for reporting U.S. atrocities to his superiors. Mike Wallace, who interviewed Herbert on the program, cast doubt on his charges, and Herbert sued CBS for libel. Other defendants were Lando, producer of the "60 Minutes" segment, Wallace, and the *Atlantic Monthly*, which had carried a Lando article on the subject.

The case was in the courts for 12 years. In pretrial hearings, Lando's testimony on preparation of the segment ran 2,900 pages, but he refused on First Amendment grounds to divulge his thoughts while working on the story. His stand was argued in the lower courts until 1979, when the Supreme Court ruled that the First Amendment did not protect Lando from such examination. It said that as a public figure Herbert had to prove he was libeled maliciously—that is, with knowledge that the statements were false or with reckless disregard for whether they were false. This, the court reasoned, meant that the defendant's "state of mind," as well as the editorial process, had to be examined.[17]

There were more hearings arising from legal dispositions on other points until finally, in January 1986, a federal appeals court dismissed Herbert's suit, It held that if what a journalist reports about a public figure is substantially true, libel action may not be based on minor statements contributing to the thrust of the story. In a last-ditch effort, Herbert, assisted by the American Legal Foundation, petitioned the Supreme Court for review. Review was denied.

So the suit itself never came to trial. What did emerge from the marathon pretrial process was a Supreme Court decision many feared would discourage investigative reporting. Citing the cost in time and money involved in fighting such suits, *Broadcasting* said, "A chill on journalistic enterprise is inevitable."[18]

A Storm of Subpoenas

Journalists suffered a defeat in 1972 when the Supreme Court ruled that they had no right to withhold from grand juries information given them in confidence.[19] The ruling applied to three cases linked on appeal. Paul Branzburg, a reporter for the *Louisville Courier-Journal*, had refused to testify on illegal drug use he had witnessed. Paul Pappas of WTEV-TV, New Bedford, Massachusetts, and Earl Caldwell of the *New York Times* had withheld information about the Black Panthers movement. Media leaders saw the decision as freezing up news sources and preventing important stories from being reported.

The issuance of subpoenas in such cases was not a new thing. As early as 1857, a *New York Times* reporter was cited for contempt for refusing to reveal his source for a story about bribe taking in Congress. One of the earliest cases involving a broadcast organization came up in 1957, a hundred years later, when Marie Torre, a newspaper columnist who later anchored for KDKA-TV, Pittsburgh, quoted a CBS executive as questioning Judy Garland's fitness to perform on television. Torre was adamant in not giving the executive's name when the singer sued CBS. For that, she was jailed for ten days.

Few journalists were served with subpoenas until the Nixon administration launched its concerted campaign to discredit the press. Then workers in the media were deluged. Nor did the deluge end with Nixon and his "hit man," Spiro Agnew. In a highly publicized speech, ABC News' Howard K. Smith viewed what was happening with alarm:

> The courts' assault on the media has been spectacular and scary. By my count, in the 1960s there were 10 cases in which courts allowed subpoenas of reporters' confidential information—10 cases in 10 years. Suddenly in two years, 1970–1971, there were 150 such cases. And in the year 1978 there were 500 such cases.[20]

A short time before Smith spoke, the Supreme Court had let stand the conviction of both the *New York Times* and its reporter, Myron Farber, for contempt of court in refusing to give information obtained in confidence. The *Times* paid fines totaling $285,000, and Farber served 40 days in jail. In the same term, the court also let stand the contempt conviction of Joe Pennington, reporter for KAKE-TV, Wichita. Smith was addressing a "live" subject.

Two "reporter's privilege" cases involving broadcasters stand out, each a *cause célèbre*. Both subpoenas originated in the House of Representatives, and both were served on well-known figures at CBS. In 1971, Frank Stanton courageously defied a House subpoena for outtakes of "The Selling of the Pentagon," and that case is reported in chapter 41. In 1976, a veteran CBS correspondent, Daniel Schorr, refused to name his source in the leak of a House Intelligence Committee report, which he passed on to the *Village Voice*.

Schorr had broadcast highlights of the report before the House voted to bar publication. He believed the report dealing with unsavory CIA activity warranted broad public exposure, and through an intermediary, he turned the full text over to the newspaper without informing his bosses. Schorr, with a reputation for independent-mindedness as well as tireless pursuit of the facts, had had rows with his superiors before. But now, although CBS wanted his resignation, it assumed the cost of fighting the House subpoena because of the principle involved.

Schorr enunciated that principle when he was summoned before the House Ethics Committee. Addressing Chairman John Flynt, members of the committee, and spectators crowded into the hearing room, he said:

> "We all build our lives around certain principles, and without these principles our careers simply lose their meaning. For some of us— doctors, lawyers, clergymen and, yes, journalists—it is an article of faith that we must keep confidential those matters entrusted to us only because of the assurance that they would remain confidential.
> Now, for a journalist the most crucial kind of confidence is the

identity of a source of information. To betray a confidential source would mean to dry up many future sources. . . . The reporter and the news organization would be the immediate losers, but I would submit to you that the ultimate losers would be the American people and their free institutions.

And if you will permit one last personal word. . . . To betray a source would for me be to betray myself, my career and my life. And to say that I refuse to do it isn't quite saying it right. I cannot do it.

Solemnly, Chairman Flynt warned the veteran correspondent that persistence in refusing "will subject you to prosecution and punishment by a fine or imprisonment or both."[21] Schorr still refused. A week later, the Ethics Committee abandoned its effort to cite him. It settled for calling his action leading to publication of the report "reprehensible." Reporters, it said, are not infallible in judging what is good for the country.

Many reporters, including Seymour Hersh, Mary McGrory, Dan Rather, and I. F. Stone, had defended Schorr's stand. So had influential cartoonists like Bill Mauldin, Tony Auth, and Herblock. There were signs that CBS News might have liked to keep Schorr as a correspondent, but he resigned anyway.[22]

Shield Laws

The flood of subpoenas involving confidentiality spurred states into passing legislation to shield reporters from punishment for refusing to name sources. By 1990, shield laws, including old laws updated to include journalists in the new electronic media, had been passed in 28 states. Bills were introduced in Congress to provide a federal shield, but none was enacted. Nor is the protection afforded by state laws absolute. For example, in many states reporters are protected only as long as the information sought can be obtained by other means.

Zurcher v. Stanford Daily

The Supreme Court decision of 1978 in *Zurcher v. Stanford Daily* sent shock waves through newsrooms across the country. Police, armed with a search warrant, had ransacked the editorial office of the student paper at Stanford University, looking for photographs of participants in a demonstration. Lower courts found the search a violation of the Fourth Amendment, which prohibits unreasonable searches and seizures. The Supreme Court ruled otherwise.[23] Howard K. Smith, recalling how Hitler's Gestapo had once raided his office in Berlin, called the high court decision "a terrible blow."[24]

Two years later, after a raid on the newsroom of KCBI-TV in Boise,

Idaho, Congress passed corrective legislation. The Privacy Protection Act of 1980 requires law enforcement officers, in most instances, to obtain subpoenas instead of search warrants in cases in which journalists and others protected by the First Amendment are involved. The safeguard is that subpoenas, unlike search warrants, can be contested in court.

A Question for Solomon

A year after its decision in *Stanford Daily*, the Supreme Court ruled that reporters may be barred from pretrial hearings if the defendant, prosecutor, and judge agree.[25] Eight organizations, including the Radio-Television News Directors Association and the American Society of Newspaper Editors, joined in protest. They noted that in just seven weeks after the decision defense attorneys in 51 cases had sought orders clearing the court and that in 26 instances they were successful. "The impact of the decision," wrote columnist Anthony Lewis, "has almost certainly gone beyond what its authors expected."[26] The news media, print and broadcast, recognizing the threat to their freedom, increasingly were making common cause.

Important relief was afforded in 1980 when the Supreme Court held that "the right to attend criminal trials is implicit in the guarantees of the First Amendment."[27] It was, and ever would be, a question to tax the wisdom of Solomon: the conflicting right of fair trial prescribed by the Sixth Amendment and the First Amendment guarantee of free press.

Meanwhile, on the Fairness Front

Developments in the Fairness Doctrine battle had become like the action on a basketball court in the final minutes.

In 1984, the FCC found that WTVH-TV, a Syracuse, New York, station owned by Meredith Broadcasting, had violated the Fairness Doctrine. The complaint was that the station ran commercials endorsing construction of a nuclear power plant without airing opposing views. Curiously, at this same time, the commission itself had strong doubts about the doctrine and was looking into its effect on the dissemination of news, even its legality.

When the FCC released the results of its inquiry on August 7, 1985, it said the doctrine disserved the public and probably was unconstitutional. In view of this, Meredith quite logically asked for reconsideration. The commission refused, saying it would have to enforce the doctrine until the situation was remedied by Congress and the courts. The Radio-Television News Directors Association, and others, charged the FCC with grievous inconsistency in supporting a doctrine it did not believe in, and Meredith, heartened, took its case to the U.S. Court of Appeals in Washington.

But the court would have none of it. It remanded the case to the FCC, warning its members:

> Federal officials are not only bound by the Constitution, they must also take a specific oath to support and defend it. To enforce a commission-generated policy that the commission itself believes is unconstitutional may well constitute a violation of that oath.

More importantly, the court said the FCC had the power to hold the doctrine unconstitutional and throw it out.[28] Which is what the commission did.

That wasn't all. A year earlier, in 1986, the same appellate court had said that the Fairness Doctrine was not a statutory obligation imposed by Congress. The question whether Fairness had the status of a law passed by Congress or was merely an FCC edict had been long debated. It seemed to many that in 1959, when Congress exempted news from Equal Time, it had made Fairness law by saying broadcasters still had to afford reasonable opportunity for the presentation of conflicting viewpoints. After all, that was the doctrine's principal tenet. Now, for the first time, a court had ruled, saying Fairness was no law.

It was a ruling the doctrine's advocates in Congress lost no time acting upon. If it was not law, they would act to make it law. Section 315 and the Fairness Doctrine always have enjoyed support in Congress since they help members get time on the air. Nor have congressional advocates fought alone. Some broadcasters, notably Westinghouse, espoused the doctrine. Therefore the court's ruling caused a veritable eruption of bills in the House and Senate to codify the doctrine and make it law. Despite a vigorous lobbying effort by RTNDA and the National Association of Broadcasters, Congress in 1987 passed a codifying measure. President Reagan vetoed it, and the win was erased.

President Bush, like Reagan, opposes the Fairness Doctrine. Broadcast journalists also find encouragement in the Supreme Court decision of January 8, 1990, to let stand the ruling that the FCC does have authority to abolish the doctrine. "We hope," said RTNDA president David Bartlett, "that Congress will follow the court's example and put this unconstitutional interference with editorial judgment to rest."[29]

But few believed the fight was finished.

45
Cable:
A Major Competitor

Cable television was born, as most innovations, out of need. Where viewers could not get good reception with their rooftop antennae, entrepreneurs, for a fee, fed clear pictures directly into their homes by coaxial cable.

The industry had its start in the late 1940s in rural communities in Pennsylvania and Oregon, where mountains interfered with over-the-air reception. (In New York City, one of the first major cities to be wired, the interference came from skyscrapers.) Typical was Robert Tarlton's experiment in 1949. A television salesman in Lansford, Pennsylvania, Tarlton had trouble selling sets because of poor reception. To meet the problem, he erected an antenna on a neighboring mountain and strung cable down to homes in the valley. The master antenna pulled in television stations in Philadelphia, 65 miles away. He sold the service on a subscription basis and got rich.

Because cable television began as a community service, with subscribers sharing a single antenna, it became known as community antenna television (CATV). It caught on slowly. Others, here and there, did what Tarlton did, but for years there was hardly a hint that operators of such systems had what one day would become a bonanza. Twenty years after

Tarlton sent his clear signal down from the mountain only 5 percent of America's television households were receiving programs by cable. Not until about 1980 did cable's threat to over-the-air broadcasters—stations and networks—become serious. By that year the 5 percent penetration by cable had risen to 20 percent, with more than 4,000 cable systems operating in 10,200 communities. By 1983 the penetration figure had jumped to 35 percent and by late 1990 to 60 percent.

As cable proliferated, *Newsweek* predicted it would make "the tube as we know it . . . as obsolete as the Victrola."[1] That has not happened, but the traditional networks, losing viewers to cable and videocassettes by the millions, do have a formidable competitor. For their part, stations not only lost audience but saw distant cable systems appropriating their programs without payment, and, through the years, copyright has been the subject of hot debate.

Cable is regulated, but the regulation has been less stringent than for over-the-air broadcasting. At first, all regulation was local. To string their wires, cable systems had to meet city requirements. Then state and federal agencies became involved. A rule adopted by the FCC in 1972 was that cable companies in the largest markets had to set aside one channel each for educational, governmental, and public use, and that these channels, known as access channels, must be available at no charge. As this is written, Congress is wrestling with legislation to stifffen cable regulation.

Cable, with its wide band, provides an abundance of channels, so it is feasible to use a channel for just one kind of programming, be it motion pictures, weather, health, sports, business news, or news in general. The result is pay television, also known as subscription television. Cable viewers, by paying an extra fee, can watch a motion picture on Home Box Office (HBO) or bring in any other specialized service such as the Financial News Network (FNN) and the Cable News Network (CNN).

In the beginning, news played only a small part. Its presentation was primitive. The local cable company might simply roll a series of typed-up stories in front of a camera and send it down the line, or it might hire a part-time reporter who appeared on camera, perhaps with Polaroid pictures taken of a downtown fire. One of the first ambitious journalistic undertakings came in 1972 when TelePrompTer, which had a Manhattan franchise, provided live satellite coverage of President Nixon's historic trip to China.

Cable News Network (CNN)

"Every time he did something, he put all his chips on the table and rolled the dice."[2] The high-roller is Ted Turner, who, taking a historic gamble, staked his fortune on a 24-hour news service, the Cable News Network, with which cable news came of age.

It is deep in the character of Robert Edward Turner III to attempt. As a yachtsman, he tried for the America's Cup twice. He captured it on the second try. He established the first superstation, WTBS-TV, Atlanta, by distributing its programs by satellite to cable systems nationwide. Because of the larger audience he could charge advertisers more, and other stations like WGN-TV, Chicago, and WWOR-TV, New York, followed suit. In Moscow, he staged his own Olympics-style games and lost millions. He did it, he says, to help the American and Soviet peoples "get to know each other better and compete with athletics instead of missiles."[3] He bought the Atlanta Braves baseball team and the Hawks basketball team, and had the effrontery to try to buy CBS.

Turner founded CNN in 1980. With seed money from the sale of a station he owned in Charlotte, North Carolina[4] and profits from his superstation, he hired nonunion reporters and technicians cheaply and set up domestic and foreign bureaus. Central studios for what detractors called the "Chicken Noodle Network" were located, not in New York, but in Atlanta, headquarters of the Turner Broadcasting System (TBS). The debut was spectacular. Old Glory was raised, military bands played, and President Carter granted an exclusive interview. Occasionally a cue went awry, but it worked. News was going out around the clock to systems serving more than two million homes.

In its first years, CNN suffered such losses it seemed a sinkhole. Turner said later, "If I'd had a lot of experience in journalism [and knew the cost of such an operation], I wouldn't have done it."[5] Even in 1986, when CNN was reaching more than thirty million households and turning a profit, the parent company, TBS, was deep in red ink because Turner, ever the highroller, had spent a billion dollars to acquire MGM. (Ultimately, he sold off many MGM properties but kept the film library, which gives him hundreds of motion pictures to run on Turner Network Television, his new cable network with the dynamite initials TNT.)

CNN was, and still is, largely staffed by young, relatively low-paid people—many fresh from college—eager to get a foothold on the ladder. Among the cadre of seasoned professionals at the start were George Watson, former Washington bureau chief for ABC News, who would be vice president in charge of CNN in Washington, and Stuart Loory, managing editor of the *Chicago Sun-Times*, who would be bureau chief. Daniel Schorr, formerly of CBS, came on as senior Washington correspondent. Bernard Shaw, who had worked at both ABC and CBS, would be the principal Washington anchor. Peter Arnett, the Pulitzer Prize-winning AP correspondent, was another veteran casting his lot with CNN. CNN's first president was Reese Schonfeld, a law school graduate experienced in news syndication. Robert Wussler, former head of CBS Television and CBS Sports, joined TBS as executive vice president with responsibilities involving both the superstation and CNN. Another who cast his lot with the new network is its executive vice president, Ed Turner (no relation to the founder), who once worked at CBS and later headed Metromedia news. These people found an excitement in being involved in something so new and ambitious. "It was," said Jim Schultz of the Washington bureau, "like being in on the start of NBC or CBS."[6]

Changes were inevitable. Wussler left after nine years to become president of Comsat Video Enterprises. Watson and Schorr left because of policy differences. Mary Alice Williams joined NBC. In October 1989, Shaw and Catherine Crier, who replaced Williams, became co-anchors of a one-hour newscast called "The World Today." The new program goes head to head with the evening news anchored by Dan Rather, Tom Brokaw, and Peter Jennings, and is the centerpiece in CNN's 24-hour schedule. CNN's president is former *Los Angeles Times Mirror* executive Tom Johnson.

For subject matter, the schedule offers multiple choices ranging from the talk show "Larry King Live" to *National Geographic* Specials to sports. Business coverage is heavy with programs like "Moneyline" and "Business Day." Organizations from 91 countries contribute to the international news exchange program "CNN World Report," which premiered as a weekly broadcast in 1987 but has gone to a daily format. CNN programming is available in many hotels overseas. "CNN Newsroom," a 15-minute daily newscast designed for students, became available free to high schools in 1989.

With 1,600 employees—up from a starting staff of 250—CNN has proved itself journalistically. Because the service runs continuously with no entertainment programs to get in the way, it can report news more readily as it breaks. When Pan Am Flight 103 crashed in Scotland, killing 270 people, CNN was the first American network to report it. When the *Challenger* shuttle disintegrated in a fireball, it was the only full network to air the disaster live. Such is CNN's reputation for saturation coverage that governments monitor it in times of crisis, as when Iraq seized Kuwait.

And That's Not All

New Year's Day, 1982, saw the debut of CNN Headline News,[7] a 24-hour service that gives the news in brief in half-hour cycles. The news is repeated with updates as stories develop.

On the heels of Headline News came CNN Radio, a radio news network with around-the-clock reporting of hard news, business, life-style features, and sports, packaged in one-hour blocks. In a separate newsfeed service, raw news material is delivered to stations to use as they see fit. In its infancy, CNN Radio relied almost entirely on simulcasting the audio portion of Headline News. Today, much of the service is live. CNN Radio recalls NBC's News and Information Service (NIS) of the mid-1970s, which operated in much the same way and failed. As 1991 arrived, CNN Newsource was aggressively marketing its new video service to more than 170 stations.

Because CNN carried news through the night, ABC, NBC, and CBS have been challenged to compete. In 1982, NBC offered the one-hour program "Overnight," starting at 1:30 A.M., Eastern time. It lasted, honorably, for 17 months.[8] CBS came on with "Nightwatch," a four-hour block of news and information starting at 2 A.M., followed by "The Early Morning News" at 6, an hour before "The CBS Morning News." Similarly, ABC scheduled "World News This Morning" an hour ahead of "Good Morning America." NBC matched these shows with "Before Hours" and "Early Today," later renamed "NBC News at Sunrise." In 1983, ABC expanded "Nightline" to an hour but soon returned to the half-hour format.

Satellite News Channel (SNC)

In June 1982, two broadcasting giants, Group W and ABC, joined in launching the Satellite News Channel (SNC) to compete with Turner. "Two Goliaths take on Captain Outrageous," heralded *Newsweek*.[9] Throwing the switch for the new 24-hour service was none other than Leo Rosenberg, who 62 years earlier had reported the Harding–Cox election returns over Westinghouse station KDKA (see chapter 1).

Unlike CNN, whose reports are both live and taped, SNC boasted it was all live. It had more experienced personnel and the financial backing of the nation's largest station group and ABC. Nevertheless, it failed. After 16 months, CNN and Headline News were in 26 million households, while SNC was reaching fewer than 8 million. Turner bought his competition for 25 million dollars, then killed it.

The last anchor to appear on the SNC screen shortly after 6 P.M., October 27, 1983, was Ken Alvord. He said:

> In 11,825 hours, our first words and pictures have traveled nearly eight trillion miles, almost one-third the distance to Proxima and Centuri in the Milky Way. And they'll just keep on traveling out there even after we disappear and maybe, just maybe, somebody out there will see some of this and learn a little bit about all of us, what makes us tick, what makes us cry.

SNC will be remembered as television's first all-live 24-hour network.

C-SPAN

The acronym C-SPAN stands for the Cable Satellite Public Affairs Network, a 24-hour two-channel service offering unedited coverage of national events. It is best known for offering congressional proceedings in their entirety, but it also covers National Press Club speeches, public policy conferences, panel discussions, political caucuses, even demonstrations, as in 1983 when thousands of people massed in front of the Lincoln Memorial to petition the government for "jobs, peace, and freedom." C-SPAN covered the rally, without interruption, for six hours. In 1984, it was the only network to televise both national political conventions gavel to gavel. Most recently, it began televising action in the British House of Commons.

C-SPAN, which has been called "The Raw News Network,"[10] is the brainchild of Brian Lamb, who served in President Nixon's Office of Tele-communications Policy. It began as a nonprofit cooperative of the major cable companies in 1979 with a staff of four and a program schedule limited to coverage of debate in the House of Representatives. Today it has about 200 employees and, carried by 2,700 cable systems, reaches more than forty million homes. C-SPAN got a boost in 1986 when the Senate joined the House in allowing radio and television coverage of floor debate. When the Supreme Court finally is opened to electronic coverage, the public will be able to hear, unedited, the oral arguments on important constitutional issues.

46
The Fourth Revolution

Writing in 1970, the science writer Isaac Asimov listed what he believed to be the four revolutions in human communication. The first was speech. Second was the development of writing and the third the printing press. Fourth on his list was the electronic revolution, radio and television, culminating with the communications satellite, which flung open the door, making information more accessible and more widespread than at any other time in history.[1]

Arthur C. Clarke, author of *2001: A Space Odyssey*, foresaw the satellite as early as 1945 when he wrote of a transmitting station orbiting synchronously above the equator which could relay messages between various points on Earth.[2] The possibilities became apparent in 1961 when radio signals were bounced off an orbiting balloon called Echo, which the U.S Army launched from Cape Canaveral. The shiny balloon, 100 feet in diameter, became a sort of pet of the American people, who went out in the night to see it moving slowly across the sky like a wayward star. In the same year, the Army put up its Courier satellite. Unlike Echo, it could receive and transmit messages. More sophisticated was Bell Lab's Telstar, launched by the National Aeronautics and Space Administration (NASA), which in just the right orbital position could relay television pictures across the Atlantic.

A Vision of What Might Be

The first live transatlantic telecast by a space satellite was relayed by Telstar on July 10, 1962. The picture showed an American flag fluttering in front of the sending station in Andover, Maine. Eleven days later, Fred Friendly produced the first live television exchange between Europe and the United States. In this demonstration program, the networks collaborated in presenting a picture album of Americana, including the Statue of Liberty, the Golden Gate Bridge, and a herd of buffalo. It was this herd, grazing near Mount Rushmore, which produced the most bizarre cue in telecommunications history—the cry, "Cue the buffalo!" The cue came from David Buksbaum, who with Friendly was directing from the central control room in New York. The cue the buffalo heard was a volley of shotgun blasts.[3]

By comparison, the rest of the program was subdued, with the BBC and the European Broadcast Union showing American viewers places like the Roman Coliseum, the British Museum, and the Louvre.

On July 10, 1963, a year after the cueing of the buffalo, CBS showed in dramatic fashion how the new technology could be used to educate the public in international affairs. Participating in the live program, billed extravagantly as "Town Meeting of the World," were former President Dwight D. Eisenhower; Jean Monnet, father of the European Common Market; Heinrich von Brentano, majority leader in the West German Bundestag; and former British Prime Minister Anthony Eden. Walter Cronkite anchored the program. Again, Friendly was executive producer.

Due to a hitch—no fault of Telstar—the program was seen live only in the United States and Canada. Fearful that Monnet might say something offensive to President Charles de Gaulle, the French refused use of their ground station. As a result, viewers in Europe saw the program the next day, after CBS scurried and sent a tape recording back across the Atlantic by jet. Richard Salant, president of CBS News, announced that henceforth the network would air "Town Meeting of the World" on a regular quarterly basis. The broadcast the following October, in which church leaders in London, Princeton, and Rome participated, marked the first discussion ever seen live in the United States and Europe simultaneously.

Because the earliest satellites were placed in low orbit, communication was broken off as they passed over the horizon. The trick, ultimately mastered, was to place the satellites in synchronous orbit, that is, so positioned at an altitude of 22,300 miles that they were in synchronization with the rotation of the earth, just as Arthur C. Clarke had proposed. That way, they seemed to be standing still, and service was uninterrupted. The first communications satellite to operate successfully in synchronous orbit was Syncom II, launched by NASA on July 26, 1963.[4]

In that same year, the Communications Satellite Corporation (COM-SAT) was created. COMSAT was a private corporation, authorized by act of Congress, with half its stock owned by the general public and the rest by communications companies, including AT&T. In 1964, COMSAT joined a consortium, INTELSAT, for establishing a satellite system with ground stations in participating countries throughout the world.

Early Bird, owned by COMSAT, was synchronous, and it was the world's first commercial communications satellite. The television networks, as well as telephone companies, could buy time on it. Because Early Bird was stationed over the Atlantic, producers found it the quick, handy way to get correspondents' reports from Europe. In network newsrooms the instruction "Put it on the Bird" became commonplace.

Early Bird was launched by NASA on April 6, 1965. (Its real name was Intelsat I, but almost nobody called it that.) In the same way that they had celebrated the arrival of Telstar, the networks joined European broadcasters in producing a monumental program marking the new breakthrough. "This Is Early Bird," broadcast throughout America and Western Europe on May 2, was more news oriented then the Telstar program. It had its share of soft features, such as the Maibock Festival in Bavaria and exhibition of Aztec dancing in Mexico City, but viewers also saw French scientists trying to harness the tides, Dr. Martin Luther King, Jr., speaking at a church dedication in Philadelphia, Pope Paul VI blessing the crowds in Vatican Square, U.S. Marines patrolling in the Dominican Republic, and a medical conference in Geneva witnessing a heart valve operation in Houston. Jack Gould of the *New York Times* called the effect overwhelming. "If only," he said, "because it so clearly outlined the possibilities that lie ahead."[5]

The next day, starting with "Today" and ending with an ABC-TV special called "Melina Mercouri's Greece," network news producers were switching so enthusiastically from country to country via Early Bird that John Horn, the *New York Herald Tribune* critic, commented that they were "a bunch of kids with a new kite."[6]

It was natural for producers to be tempted to have fun with the new technology, and use it for overseas stories regardless of immediacy or merit. Recognizing the temptation, Friendly, as the new president of CBS News, instructed his people to resist it.

> Now that the Bird is working for us, CBS News must make sure it does not find itself working for the Bird. . . . There is a natural tendency to show what we can do physically with the satellite, but it is what we do with it as a news instrument that will distinguish CBS News. Let others turn it into a plaything for bland features. . . . Hard news content still counts most.[7]

It was instruction many producers, network and local, could have heeded with profit upon the arrival of Electronic News Gathering (ENG) a decade later.

In fact, economics enforced Friendly's judgment. Putting stories on the Bird was expensive, Besides what COMSAT charged, British postal authorities imposed a hefty fee for use of its ground station at Goonhilly Downs. CBS estimated that nightly use of the satellite for its evening news would run as high as $35,000 a week.[8] The networks began assigning fewer stories to Early Bird and sharing what time they did buy.

Although INTELSAT had three new satellites in 1967—one more over the Atlantic and two over the Pacific—the cost of transmission remained high. In the entire year 1967, CBS took satellite transmissions only 73 times, or about once every five days, and this at the height of the Vietnam War.[9] Gradually, advanced satellites were introduced. While Early Bird could handle only 240 telephone calls or provide a solitary television channel—it could not do both at the same time—eight years later Intelsat IV boasted 5,000 telephone circuits or 12 television channels, or a combination of these. With such increased efficiency—mass production, as it were—COMSAT cut its charges for satellite service almost in half. By this time—the mid-1970s—most overseas stories came to New York by satellite. It has been that way ever since.

47
Local
Ain't So Local
Any More

Technology always has shaped content in news broadcasts. It happened with the introduction of audiotape in the 1950s and videotape in the 1960s. More newsmakers were heard, not quoted, and because videotape proved more serviceable than film, more events were seen, not described. In these two decades, the "sound bite" and the "picture bite" were born.

Electronic News Gathering

Electronic news gathering (ENG) arrived in the mid-1970s. It sprang from development of a small, relatively light camera, the minicam, and a portable cassette pack that could record on tape both sound and what the camera "saw." After that came the camera with the built-in recorder, giving the photographer, who now had to carry only a camera, still more mobility.

At the same time came record-playback machines on which videotape could be edited electronically—no more splicing—and scenes slowed down, speeded up, stopped, or dissolved at the touch of a few buttons. All this, combined with digital switching, computer graphics, dish-mounted vans, and microwave linking, made ENG the way to get a story on the air more quickly than ever before. Stations publicized their ability to do live reports from anywhere in their market area. KPRC-TV, Houston, bought the cover of *Broadcasting* magazine to boast, "We bring the news back alive."[1]

Because ENG made it easy to do live remotes, there was a tendency, which has not altogether disappeared, to "go live" simply because the capability existed, as when a New York station, for no good journalistic reason, switched to a helicopter hovering over one of the city's parkways where a traffic snarl had occurred. The reporter in the helicopter told of long delays, but as he spoke the camera showed traffic moving normally. (The situation had cleared up an hour earlier when a pothole was repaired.) In this instance, the news director yielded to the temptation to go live not only because it was technologically possible, but also, one suspects, because he was justifying the cost of the helicopter to management.

In encouraging live reporting, ENG encouraged ad-libbing. This, in turn, placed added responsibility on the reporter, who had no editor to check the story beforehand. Also, because videotape production takes less time than film production, a reporter now had more opportunity to research the story, to think about what it meant and write the best possible script. Unfortunately, the assignment editor could have the reporter use that time to do another story.

Satellite News Gathering (SNG)

After ENG came SNG, newscasting's Big Bang. The explosion, triggered by a proliferation of domestic satellites, burst on the industry with such force that the old, never completely comfortable bond between network and affiliate was shattered. The fact was that the networks just were not that important to the affiliates any more. The affiliates no longer depended on networks for their programming as they had for more than half a century; they had become much more independent, and the old-line networks were in danger of becoming extinct.

This should have come as no surprise. The portents were there. One was that more and more syndicated programs were being produced and distributed, bypassing the networks. In the mid-1970s, stations had a tantalizing array of nonnetwork shows to choose from. From Louisville Productions a station could get author Cleveland Amory and economist Eliot Janeway, "Joe Carcione, the Green Grocer" from Mighty Minute Programs, Evans and Novak from RKO Productions, "Jane Goodall and the World of Animal Behavior" from Metromedia Producers Corporation, and from 20th Century Fox Television a 25-part blockbuster series featuring "the battles of the great dinosaurs, the power of the sun, killer earthquakes, the coming of bionic man, the deadly sharks, the fury of volcanoes, the dark world of caves."[2]

That's only a sampling. Other companies, including some associated with newspapers and magazines like Time-Life Television, the Newsweek Broadcasting Service, and NYT Syndication, a *New York Times* subsidiary, also were offering programs. Independent Network News and TVN, the news service of Television News, Inc., provided further competition.

Syndication provided an even larger role with the arrival of SNG, which, employing satellites, delivered programs more speedily and economically than over land lines or by Federal Express. Stations now had access to such an outpouring of all sorts of syndicated material, the choices seemed endless. Les Brown, writing in the *New York Times,* foresaw the impact. It is, he said, a development with revolutionary implications, "particularly in loosening the tight relationships between the major networks and their affiliated stations."[3]

The "loosening" was encouraged in other ways. For years, before either ENG or SNG, broadcast groups like Westinghouse and Cox Broadcasting maintained bureaus in Washington. So did a few individual stations. The explosion in Washington bureaus occurred in the early 1980s. In just five years, between 1980 and 1985, the number of local television news bureaus rose from 15 to more than 50.

Other stations signed up with Washington news agencies. An unusual agency is operated by the Medill News Service. Except for its director, Lou Prato, it is staffed by journalism students from the Medill School, Northwestern University, who work in Washington for three months, gaining experience and credit toward a master's degree. In 1989, it was feeding news to six television stations and eight radio stations. Most reports are fed to the stations by satellite. The fees charged are nominal and go to the university. The news from both bureaus and agencies is custom-tailored for their markets—the decision to close a local army base, for example, or an investigation into the conduct of a congressman from the station's district, perhaps an exclusive interview with the congressman—all news of local interest not necessarily covered by the networks. Says one agency vice president, "It's like it was a few years ago when everyone was buying a helicopter for the news department. Now if you're serious about Washington coverage, you make sure you have someone representing you in Washington."[4]

Sometimes stations in broadcast groups shared the Washington stories fed to them and thus formed ad hoc networks. This affected content in an unexpected way. Norman Wagy, who as bureau chief set up Storer Broadcasting's SNG operation, found that while news normally was covered with s single market in mind, "with all our stations able to see the same feed, we began broadening into more general interest stories."[5]

Bureaus often cover stories of general interest and at the same time tailor them for specific audiences. On April 3, 1989, families of the victims in the terrorist bombing of Pan Am Flight 103 held a memorial vigil in front of the White House. A general interest story. But in covering it, following the rule that local news is where local people are, Gillett Broadcasting's correspondent, Gary Nurenberg, interviewed relatives from cities where Gillett owns stations.

This is just what major stations have been doing more often at national political conventions since 1980, when scores of local reporters—no longer so local—covered delegations from their states with live satellite reports. By 1988, the figures for local representation at the Republican and Democratic conventions had soared dramatically to more than 4,000. There were anchors, reporters, producers, and technicians from 338 television and 275 radio stations at the Democratic convention and from 315 television and 245 radio stations at the Republican convention. Image enhancement was part of it, but the pursuit of news was real. For most stations covering the conventions the workhorse was the Ku-band[6] van, which as a mobile ground station for satellite transmission makes origination from almost everywhere possible.

Besides Washington bureaus maintained by local stations and broadcast groups, and such nonnetwork suppliers as Conus, Newsfeed, and N.I.W.S., the *Broadcasting-Cable Yearbook 1989* lists 15 firms in Washington that serve television stations around the country. All of these are invading what was traditionally network turf. At base is the fact that with increasing frequency affiliates can get from other sources what the founding networks once provided. And being less dependent has spelled independence.

Regional Networks

State radio networks grew in importance in the 1970s. Twenty-one of them were operating by the end of the decade. The Missouri network, called MissouriNet, was typical. It had almost 190 affiliates, 70 in Missouri and the rest scattered in nearby states. The news division fed its affiliates 13 programs a day and its farm division 19 programs. The network also distributed KMOX's St. Louis Cardinal and Kansas Chiefs broadcasts, as well as University of Missouri football and basketball. Today, MissouriNet comprises 314 stations, with 68 in Missouri and the rest in surrounding states. As from the start, coverage of state government is stressed.

Many states have more than one regional network. Kentucky, for example, has three, one devoted entirely to farm news. *Broadcasting-Cable Yearbook for 1989* lists 101 regional radio networks.[8]

Satellite technology spurred the founding of regional television networks. One of the first was the Florida News Network. In February 1984, Ken Middleton of WTSP-TV, St. Petersburg, called a meeting at which he and other news directors from Miami, Ft. Lauderdale, Jacksonville, and Orlando agreed to cooperate in a daily exchange of stories. Stations in Fort Myers, West Palm Beach, and Tallahassee soon joined. In Florida, as in more than a dozen other states, the station closest to breaking news covers the story and puts it on the satellite for other member stations. Cost of the coverage is shared.

Have Satellite, Will Travel

Until the 1970s, it was a rare station that sent a reporter abroad, even on short assignment. The practice grew with the growth in competion and satellite technology and became fairly common in the 1980s. Usually the report had a local angle, as when WBAL-TV, Baltimore, followed a Maryland congressman to El Salvador and KJRH-TV, Tulsa, covered a group of Oklahomans studying in China.

If one year can be taken as a breakthrough year for local reporting overseas, it is 1981. The big foreign story arousing local interest that year was the release in January of the 52 Americans held hostage by Iran. Scores of reporters and photographers from hometown stations flew to Wiesbaden, West Germany, to meet the hostages on their way out. Local reporting never would be so parochial after that.

Sometimes the "local" story obtained abroad was carried nationwide. This was the case when, later in 1981, Anne Odre of Buffalo, New York, was wounded in the attempted assassination of Pope John Paul II. WKBW-TV, Buffalo, rushed anchorman Don Postles to Rome, where he scooped the networks with a recording of the woman's bedside audience with papal representatives. Postles also got an exclusive interview with Odre, which was picked up by ABC's "World News Tonight." NBC benefited similarly when affiliate WCSH-TV in Portland, Maine, covered the 1983 visit to the Soviet Union of Samantha Smith, the Maine schoolgirl who wrote Soviet President Yuri Andropov of her yearning for world peace. Reports by correspondent John Dougherty and photographer Scott Wernig were used by both the "Nightly News" and "Today."[9]

And sometimes there was no local angle. It was simply a good story. Roger Grimsby of WABC-TV, New York, flew to South Africa and produced a one-hour documentary on the social crisis in that country. WOR Radio's Lou Adler reported from Ireland on "The Troubles." Jean Enersen of KING-TV, Seattle, made news in 1988 when Moscow aired four parts of her five-part series on life in the Soviet Union. In the unused segment, a Russian soldier recounted his experiences in Afghanistan. The program made Enersen the first journalist in the history of American commercial broadcasting to report to the Soviet people on events in their own country.

Observing how stations were going abroad for stories, *Broadcasting* concluded, "There's a new definition for the 'local' in local journalism. It is anywhere a satellite can reach."[10]

The Traveling All-Stars

The same Buck Rogers technology that redefined *local* has made foreign origination of the network evening news almost commonplace. Dan Rather, Tom Brokaw, and Peter Jennings no longer surprise anyone when they appear, in trenchcoat, in places as disparate as Red Square or St. Peter's square. NBC News is a pioneer in this respect. In 1984, Gordon Manning, NBC vice president for editorial projects, directed negotiations enabling his network to become the first to provide a full week of live coverage from Moscow. Four years later, NBC News originated all its programs for an entire week from the People's Republic of China.

Dan Rather has said that, in going abroad, his is "no traveling Chautauqua operation."[11] Although the star anchors, for purposes of image, occasionally may have gone abroad to cover stories their correspondents could have covered equally well, it was indeed "no Chautauqua operation" when Rather and Bernard Shaw of CNN were the lone network anchors in Beijing the night of June 4, 1989, when soldiers opened fire on students in Tiananmen Square. And Brokaw, Jennings, and Rather were covering one of the great stories of the century when, in 1989 they reported the collapse of Communism in Eastern Europe and the tearing down of the Berlin Wall. Brokaw achieved a coup by being in Berlin at the moment the wall came down. Rather and Ted Koppel scored with reports out of Baghdad on the heels of Iraq's seizure of Kuwait.

These were anchors aweigh. They reported competently and heightened viewer interest. Network correspondents normally covering China, Eastern Europe, and the Middle East, who presumably knew their bets intimately, were reduced to lesser roles.

48
Time of Trial

It was like the rise and the fall of empires. In the mid-1980s, the dynasties that had informed and entertained on the air for more than half a century, and had made so much money doing it, lost their monopoly. Competitors, led by cable, captured millions of their viewers. With the erosion of audience, profits fell. The situation was right for takeovers. In 1985, Capital Cities, a communications company with a reputation for cost-consciousness, acquired ABC. In 1986, General Electric took over NBC, and Laurence Tisch of the Loews Corporation took control of CBS, which had gone a billion dollars in debt fighting off takeover attempts by Ted Turner and an outfit called Fairness in Media, supported by Senator Jesse Helms. In one year, the old order created with so much enterprise and enthusiasm by Paley and Sarnoff had come to pieces.

The Ax Falls

The effect on the news divisions was immediate. Budgets that had doubled within a decade were slashed, and hundreds of news personnel were either dismissed or forced to take early retirement. Although some cost cutting was in order because of reduced income and swollen budgets, the new managements cut into muscle as well as fat.

In the first wave of firings at ABC, 350 people, including 32 in the news division, lost their jobs. Forty-three unfilled positions in news were eliminated. Several bureaus were closed, others streamlined with a reduction in staff. The bureau in South Africa was reinforced. The next year saw the layoff of almost one hundred news personnel, including more than one-third of the "Close-Up" documentary unit. Two veterans let go were Herb Kaplow, senior political correspondent, and Nicholas Archer, vice president, television news services. Thirty-eight were laid off at WABC-TV, ABC's flagship in New York. One who went was Roger Grinsby, an anchor at the station for 18 years. In 1987, about seventy more people at ABC News were dismissed.[1]

The cuts at ABC News were particularly painful. After years of striving, it had come from behind to equal and, in more than one instance, surpass the best effort of its rivals at CBS and NBC. "Sometimes," said Roone Arledge, president of ABC's news division, "the dreams get put on the shelf." He did not mean to lose sight of the dreams, he said.[2]

At NBC, General Electric, outdoing ABC, reduced the news staff by 400. Larry Grossman, as president of NBC News, resisted making so deep a cut and had to resign. Concerning GE's bottom-line approach, he said, "We were operating in different worlds."[3] His successor was Michael Gartner, a former president of the American Society of Newspaper Editors, who as an executive for the Gannett chain had a reputation for fearlessness and efficiency. In one of his first acts, Gartner whacked 15 million dollars out of the news division budget. Highly cost-conscious, he took the heat in 1989 for losing correspondent Connie Chung to CBS, which offered her more money.

CBS, which practically invented network news, suffered such adversity that a best-seller appeared with the title *Who Killed CBS?*[4] This was exaggeration: no dead company offers a prospective employee more than $1,500,000 a year, as CBS did Chung. Still, the network's experience between 1985 and 1988 proved the most traumatic in its history.

The changes came so fast it was difficult to keep track. In six years, CBS, Inc., had three presidents and CBS News four presidents. Gone was CBS' research laboratory, birthplace of the long-playing record. And gone, sold to SONY, was its lucrative records business. Then Tisch, who had said that he would not touch CBS News, chopped it down to what he regarded as proper size. Where would it end? Even the company's medical office for treating on-the-job injuries closed. It was CBS' own crisis story, a story of such interest that four books have been written about it and, before them, Fred Friendly's invaluable *Due to Circumstances Beyond Our Control*, which sets the scene.[5] It seemed to Tom Shales, even as the wrecking crews were getting started, that CBS had "lost something that was near and dear to the company during its golden years: a sense of decorum, an aura of dignity, a semblance of stability."[6]

High Noon at CBS News

It was not mere change but rather a transformation when late in 1981 Van Gordon Sauter succeeded Bill Leonard as president of CBS News. Leonard, past retirement age, had worked at CBS for almost forty years. Sauter had just marked his 46th birthday. Both had enviable track records, but Leonard was of the Murrow school and Sauter of the new "grab 'em" school. Working as a reporter for the *Detroit Free Press,* he also wrote for the *National Enquirer.* It was hard to picture Leonard doing that.

At CBS News, Sauter maintained an office that was as different from the typical executive's office as the chinos he wore were from typical executive dress. There sat his old rolltop desk, manual typewriter, wooden writing table, hat rack, and old-fashioned upright phone out of "The Front Page." The walls were covered with framed pictures, and among the oddly Victorian clutter was a large, stained-glass two-dollar bill inscribed "In Nielsen We Trust."

The inscription was prologue.

Few broadcast journalists had done as much as Sauter in so short a time. In just ten years, before ascending to the presidency of CBS News, he had been news director at WBBM-TV in Chicago, CBS bureau chief in Paris, vice president in charge of program practices (censor) for CBS Television, vice president and general manager of KNXT in Los Angeles, and president of CBS Sports. Now, as Laurence Tisch had come as a White Knight to rescue CBS, drained by the long-drawn-out Westmoreland case and attempted takeovers, Sauter came to CBS News. The evening news, apple of CBS' eye, was in trouble. It had been slow recovering from the predictable ratings slump suffered when Rather took over from Cronkite. Paley thought too slow. Sauter had a good ratings record at KNXT and seemed, with all his other experience, the man to turn the evening show's ratings around.

The formula lay in Sauter's character. From the beginning of his career, it was his ability to write movingly of human emotion that marked him. As a reporter for the *Free Press* and later for the *Chicago Daily News,* he seemed more drawn to feelings than to facts. Corresponding from Vietnam for the *Free Press,* he made what the fighting man felt the heart of his story. It was what he liked to do and what he believed newspaper subscribers liked to read. It was natural, then, that as head of CBS News, when Rather's ratings needed a boost, he enlivened the show with more stories evoking emotional response. "Goddammit," he said, "we've got to touch people. They've got to feel a relationship with us."[7]

There was in the formula more than a hint of sensationalism, which has precedent in print journalism. In 1976, Erik Barnouw gave a lecture in which he related how the introduction of advertising in newspapers affected their news content. Because of advertising, newspapers began vying for circulation—the more circulation, the more advertising revenue—and in this competition the papers went increasingly for stories that were sensational. Barnouw said the same thing had happened with television:

> We used to think of journalism, entertainment, education, politics, advertising, and religion as somewhat separate activities, each carried on in its proper domain, with its own procedures. But today the bright tube, in living color, has become the newspaper, theater, schoolroom, podium, billboard, and pulpit. In the process, all have gravitated toward the same dramaturgical techniques and appeals.[8]

Murrow had a kindred observation. He called broadcast journalism "an incompatible combination of show business, advertising, and news." He said, "Each of the three is a rather bizarre and demanding profession, and when you get all three under one roof, the dust never settles."[9]

The highly emotional stories, those that grab viewers, build ratings, and the higher the ratings, the more revenue. These were the stories Sauter enjoyed doing, and he knew revenue was what management wanted. In doing what he enjoyed and trying to give management what it wanted, he raised a great deal of dust. For all his intelligence, energy, and flair, he could not persist in doing the news he wanted without scandal. He had supporters, but Murrow, even after two decades, was still too strong a presence. It was not just the Old Guard within CBS and the split between it and the new generation of producers. A big part was the bad press. Critics had chosen Murrow, not Sauter, when it came to choosing. This was reflected in article titles like "Discord in the House of Murrow"[10] and "Is CBS Still the Tiffany of Network News?"[11] and headlines like "Darkening Skies at CBS News"[12] and

Ax Falls Hard at CBS News, Fatcats O.K.[13]

Not the kind of publicity any corporation likes to see spread about, let alone one operating in an increasingly competitive market and fighting for its good name.

"It Was Just Awful"

The layoffs hit CBS News in three waves. The first came in 1985. Seventy-four staffers were fired, receiving notice on a Thursday that they had until late Friday to clear out their desks. Fifty others were induced to take early retirement. In some cases, inducement approached threat: Retire with pension benefits or be assigned to a CBS outpost the equivalent of Siberia. Five correspondents including Dallas Townsend, the honored newsman hired by Paul White, were among those leaving. The famed "CBS Reports" unit virtually disappeared. The research staff for the morning news disappeared altogether. Correspondent Bob Schieffer, recalling that day, says, "It was awful. People running up and down halls crying. It was just awful."[14]

It was so awful Don Hewitt went to Gene Jankowski, president of the CBS Broadcast Group, about buying CBS News. If ever CBS News were for sale (CBS had just sold its St. Louis station and four musical instrument companies), he, Mike Wallace, Dan Rather, and others might buy it—a deal, it seemed to Hewitt, better than selling to an outsider unappreciative of what CBS News stood for. Jankowski, shocked by the suggestion, said CBS had no thought of selling the news division.

Hewitt wanted the right of first refusal. But he also had sent a signal, dramatically demonstrating to management how deeply he and others were worried about what was happening to CBS News. It was an audacious gesture.

It seemed to some, like Tom Shales of the *Washington Post,* that things could hardly get rougher,[15] but deeper cuts were coming. In 1986, CBS News let go another 70 people, including George Herman, one of the most hard-working, most respected journalists in television. He, too, had been hired by Paul White. In 42 years with the network he had served as war correspondent in Korea, chief White House correspondent, and moderator of "Face the Nation." Five other correspondents were dropped, along with producers in New York, London, and Paris.

The third round of dismissals in 18 months came on March 6, 1987, and was the most devastating. By now the president of CBS News was Howard Stringer, an ambitious, Oxford-educated producer of documentaries and the evening news who had started at CBS as a clerk logging commercials. Tisch had told Stringer that he would like to see a deeper cut in the news division budget, something like 50 million dollars. Recognizing an order, no matter how delicately phrased, Stringer cut the budget by 30 million dollars.

The cut translated into the loss of 215 people, including veteran correspondents like Jim McManus, Steve Young, and Ike Pappas, a firehorse of a reporter who in 20 years with CBS had covered stories all over the world, including Vietnam. It meant not having any correspondent stationed in West Germany, leaving only two in the Chicago bureau to cover all of the Midwest, and closing down the Seattle bureau, which had covered the Northwest. The widely praised "Sunday Morning" program lost five of its nine producers. Even "60 Minutes," the program making more money than any other program on television, lost five producers. In administering the blow, Stringer expressed regret that so many persons dedicated to CBS News "have been so ill-rewarded today."[16]

Morale at CBS News hit bottom. Dan Rather and Richard Cohen, a senior producer for the evening news, composed an "Op-Ed" piece for the *New York Times.* It was forthright:

> Our concern, beyond the shattered lives of valued friends and colleagues, is: How do we go on? How do we cover the world? Can we provide in-depth reporting and analysis with resources so se-

verely diminished? ... Tisch told us when he arrived that he wanted us to be the best. We want nothing more than to fulfill that mandate. Ironically, he has now made the task seem something between difficult and impossible.

The piece had 11 paragraphs. It carried only Rather's signature. Only he could have gotten away with it.[17]

Loyalty was involved. Loyalty to people and to tradition, although Rather himself, by expanding his role as anchor and making management-like decisions, and adopting much of Sauter's philosophy, was part of the new CBS. The organization to which Rather and others were devoted and in which they took pride was being wrecked. Some of them would say with Edwin Diamond, the media scholar, that it was total surrender, "the junk-yard rather than the repair shop."[18] The organization was torn, not only by the firings and closed bureaus, but by deep-rooted internal dissension regarding principle. While members of the Old Guard mourned the passing of news as Murrow saw it,[19] others cited the economic realities. Times had changed, they said, and if network news were to compete successfully in the new marketplace, it had to be what Sauter said it had to be: more interesting, which is to say more entertaining. It had to reach out and touch.

Morale at NBC News was not much better. It suffered when efficiency experts prowled the newsroom, checking on staffers' performance, as though they worked on an automobile assembly line. It suffered more during a four-month strike by editorial workers and technicians, and after Gartner came and took up the role of Mr. Efficiency himself. It was demoralizing to hear the network's president, Robert Wright, wonder out loud whether NBC really needed a nightly newscast and to see NBC Radio, where it had all started with David Sarnoff, sold to an upstart California company called Westwood One.

Roone Arledge had handled it better at ABC, where pains were taken to talk with people who were being laid off and explain the circumstances. And there was an excitement at ABC News. Arledge had snatched Chris Wallace from NBC and Diane Sawyer from CBS, and they were joining Sam Donaldson in a new prime-time series to complement, and perhaps match or exceed, the success of "20/20." Nor did it hurt that more often now ABC's "World News Tonight with Peter Jennings" was beating out the opposition in terms of ratings in the three-way evening news race.

But as 1991 began, and more events received pool coverage, staff reductions at all three networks continued.

Van Gordon Sauter served two tours as president of CBS News. The first was from February 1982 to September 1983, when, pursuing his ambition for corporate position, he became executive vice president of the CBS Broadcast Group, supervising both CBS News and the CBS-owned stations. In December 1985 he was back. Ed Joyce, who had been executive vice president of CBS News, served as president between tours, implementing so many of Sauter's unpopular decisions that he came to be regarded as his hatchet man. Until now, Joyce had had a distinguished career. By 1986, he and Sauter were both gone.

It was inevitable that Sauter would leave. He had come under fire in the press and created division in his own ranks through favoritism and what the Old Guard, led by Cronkite, saw as corruption of the evening news. With layoffs he had butchered "CBS Reports." He mishandled the morning news, choosing Phyllis George, a former Miss America with scant experience, to co-anchor the two-hour program. Honoring its contract, CBS had to pay her more than a million dollars after she was fired.[20] And it was Sauter, surrendering to bookkeepers, who finally gave up the morning news. Later, with Sauter gone, CBS News recovered the two hours.

Sauter's successor in October 1986 was Howard Stringer, who had made the deepest, widest slash of all in CBS News personnel. He was head of the news division only 20 months before rising to the presidency of the CBS Broadcast Group, overseeing all of the network's broadcast operations. The new CBS News president was David Burke, an astute fiscal manager who had been Roone Arledge's right-hand man at ABC and who once, with former Secretary of State George Shultz, coauthored a book on economics.

Burke lasted two years. Late in 1990 he was succeeded by Eric Ober, a veteran of 24 years with CBS News and now the seventh president of the division in ten yers. The appointment marks a return to the policy of promoting from within. "The Generation That Was" had not totally disappeared.

49
End of an Era

Looking back, one sees the landmarks. Some are mountainous: radio's coverage of World War II, television's coverage of Vietnam and the struggle for civil rights, broadcasting's impact on politics, and the technological breakthroughs, including cable. Each breakthrough—audiotape, videotape, the minicam, the computer, the satellite—changed what could be presented and how it was presented. In politics, radio and television, changing their ways, changed the news. Candidates going for the irresistible "sound bite" and "picture bite" created news by saying and doing things they otherwise would not have said and done.

Audiotape allowed radio audiences actually to hear the child cry, the artillery piece fire, the politician speak. Videotape speeded up the showing of what happened by eliminating the time required to process film and made possible the instant replay. The lightweight minicam, parlayed with electronic news-gathering equipment (ENG), allowed television to approach the flexibility and immediacy of radio. Domestic communications satellites revolutionized ENG. Satellite news gathering (SNG) provided an alternative to AT&T's land lines for long distance telecommunications. It enabled networks and stations using dish-equipped vans to pick up and transmit news anywhere from any uplink site by bouncing their signals off "birds" hovering 22,300 miles above the equator. SNG altered dramatically the close relationship between networks and their affiliates.

The computer became a major tool. Producers in computerized newsrooms could now store information on an almost infinite number of subjects and recall it in seconds. The computer holds previously used stories and retrieves them. No more searching through racks of audio or videotape. It also is used for editing. It conjures up graphics. It's the journalist's magic wand.

The Specialists

Today the air is full of reports by specialists: doctors, lawyers, agricultural experts, economists, meteorologists, gardeners, psychologists, cooks. Julia Child made preparing dinner look like an adventure. Many stations have consumer reporters; Betty Furness of NBC was one of the first. Business reporters have been hired and syndication services purchased to satisfy the appetite for financial news. Investigative reporters like Lea Thompson at WRC-TV, Washington, and Pam Zekman at WBBM-TV, Chicago, became stars. Outstanding at NBC are Ira Silverman and Brian Ross.

Increasingly, reporters of legal matters are lawyers. NBC's Carl Stern received his law degree, *magna cum laude,* from Cleveland State University. ABC tapped Tim O'Brien, graduate of Loyola Law School, to cover the Supreme Court. For years, CBS had Fred Graham, who boasted law degrees from both Vanderbilt University and Oxford. The networks have their space reporters. Most, like Walter Cronkite at CBS and Jules Bergman at ABC, who both pioneered in space reporting, came to the subject without science degrees but became expert through independent study. The networks also have reporters assigned specifically to covering developments in medicine.

This specialization is not new; it simply has grown. In 1921, Frank Mullen at KDKA was informing farmers on the life cycle of the corn borer. That same year, the University of Wisconsin's experimental station, 9XM, was airing weather forecasts. The first radio station to hire a full-time weather reporter was WLW, the powerful Crosley outlet in Cincinnati. The year was 1940, and the weatherman was James C. Fidler. Another pioneer in weather reporting was E. B. Rideout at WEEI, Boston. Developments on the New York Stock Exchange were reported by the University of Nebraska's experimental station as early as 1916. In 1924, WJZ, New York, had a Wall Street report each weekday. A medical program, "Your Health Today," began a long run on NBC Radio in 1932.

Specialization pervades all media, radio and television almost to the degree that it pervades magazines. Radio stations have their individual formats—country music, oldies, religion, news–talk, album-oriented rock. There are black and hispanic radio networks, just as there are black and hispanic television networks. Cable has channels devoted solely to one subject, such as business and sports.

Observers note a danger in this "narrowcasting." Audiences addicted to information pertaining only to their special interest may become audiences narrowly informed.

The News Boom

Television news in the early 1980s entered a period of unprecedented expansion. The networks began presenting news through the night, giving America, Fred Friendly said, "the best-informed insomniacs in the world."[1] Independent Network News (INN) offered a regularly scheduled half-hour newscast in prime time, something the founding networks never quite got around to doing, and local television stations, smelling money, made progressively more room in their schedules for news.

The boom was particularly noticeable in large markets. More, and longer, newscasts appeared in the morning. One-hour programs at noon became commonplace, and the early evening news was so spread out it could as well be called the late afternoon news. In an essay in the *Wall Street Journal*, Vermont Royster complained that the outpouring of local news followed by network evening news was "prolonging the drinking hour beyond good judgment and delaying dinner."[2] No matter. Stations in the larger markets went on giving more news. Sports got more attention than local government, weather more attention than city schools.

If It Bleeds, It Leads

Of profound consequence was a change in editorial standards. Generally speaking, news had been something broadcasters did because it was expected of them. Station owners provided it in part to keep their licenses, but many did news out of their own sense of duty. The reputation for public service was a medal worn with pride.

Then it was discovered that money—lots of money—could be made in news, and so in many instances it became, instead of competition for journalistic achievement, competition for audience. The "happy talk" school of newscasting was founded. One symptom is the inordinate amount of yukking it up between anchor, sports reporter, and whoever is doing the weather. The happy talk format, says critic John Leonard, "giggles its way to apocalypse."[3] As part of the format, Edwin Newman sees

> what now appears to be a competition in wishing the viewers well. They are urged to have a good day, have a good night, have a good weekend, have a good week. . . . A local New York anchorman signs off: "We care about what happens to you."

Newman asks, "What has this to do with news?"[4] Tom Shales, the *Washington Post* critic, once wrote a satire on the trivializing of news. After the

"Cronkite and Company" disco theme, the eminent anchor is forced to read:

> THIS is WAL-ter CRON-kite. Join me and the CBS News team tonight for exclusive coverage of the end of the world, live via satellite, at eleven-thirty Eastern, ten-thirty Central, right after all the latest sports scores on your local station.

The title of the broadcast envisioned by Shales was "Countdown to Bye-Bye."[5]

To a large extent, market researchers, not editors, determine the content of local newscasts. Since consultants have warned against the sin of boring anyone, pictures have become increasingly important, the more graphic the better—in traffic accidents, blood on the pavement; in homicide cases, bodies being removed in bags. No one argues that auto accidents and murders should not be covered; the question is what priority to assign them. To quote John Hart, "Too many producers select stories because they may seize an audience, instead of offering coverage designed to serve the audience."[6] Nor, in this, are network producers innocent.

A Question of Survival

It was this clash between public interest and corporate interest—between responsibility in news programming and profits—that concerned Murrow in 1958 when he spoke to the country's news directors and expressed his "abiding fear" of what it would do to society. Speaking boldly, realizing his own danger, he declared:

> Our history will be what we make it. And if there are any historians about fifty or a hundred years from now, and there should be preserved the kinescopes for one week of all three networks, they will there find recorded in black and white, or color, evidence of decadence, escapism and insulation from the realities of the world in which we live. . . . If this state of affairs continues, we may alter an advertising slogan to read: LOOK NOW, PAY LATER. For surely we shall pay for using this most powerful instrument of communication to insulate the citizenry from the hard and demanding realities which must be faced if we are to survive.

And he added, "I mean the word *survive* literally."[7] A quarter century later, John Chancellor, addressing the same group, spoke of how news had become a money center. "Our greatest challenge," he said, "is the corruption of success."[8]

Murrow was soon gone from CBS. The world in which he worked had changed, and he and that world had become incompatible. Broadcasting always had been a business, but never so big a business. Staffs had grown with growth in profits. The intimacy, the sense of comradeship, were gone.

Paley had built an empire, and in it Murrow's independent satrapy was out of place.

David Halberstam, writing of Murrow's reportorial role in World War II, observed:

> In normal times, there would have been no way for Murrow to have been Murrow. Excellent reporting might have pleased the intelligensia and his colleagues but angered vast portions of the public and the government and placed him in constant confrontation with management.[9]

Murrow, as we have already noted, saw that he no longer could be Murrow. He took a one-year sabbatical, returned for the 1960 elections, then accepted President Kennedy's offer of the directorship of the United States Information Agency. He was down but not out. He would not be out until 1965 when cancer brought on by his incessant cigarette smoking killed him.

It is fruitless, as well as mistaken, to look for villains in Murrow's departure from CBS. This was Greek tragedy, each player drawn, inextricably, to the final resolution. As it was inevitable that Murrow, possessing stature unparalleled in broadcast news, would exercise an independence annoying to Paley, so it was inevitable that Paley in his corporate position would place corporate interest first. And inevitable that Stanton, the other major player, would do Paley's will. It was hopeless. Anger, frustration, respect, loyalty, and rivalry had tangled in a knot that could not possibly be untied.

I worked closely with Murrow for nine years, and a question I often ponder is how he would have fared in these troubled times. Probably no better, if as well. He would have been bloodied and, possibly sooner than before, forced into exile. It is significant that neither CBS nor either of the other traditional networks could bring themselves to produce or broadcast the story of Edward R. Murrow, their most distinguished journalist. A cable company did it first and then not until two decades after his death.[10]

50

A New Age

Computers and satellites broke the boundaries. This last chapter is about the new chapter in telecommunications just beginning.

A spectacular development in the near future will be high definition television (HDTV). Wide-screen television has been around in theaters, bars, and other public places for a long time. Invariably, the 525-line image, greatly magnified, produced a picture that was fuzzy. Now, just as FM revolutionized radio, HDTV is about to stage its revolution, bringing pictures as sharp and almost as large as those in movie houses into viewers' homes.

Japanese scientists demonstrated the first feasible high definition television system in 1981. Its images consist of 1,125 lines, more than twice the American standard, allowing the picture to be enlarged and still exceed anything achieved before in terms of brilliance, fidelity of color, and detail. Just as years of research and corporate competition preceded adoption of a system of "colorcasting" in the 1950s (RCA with an all-electronic system beat out CBS), a battle over HDTV standards is raging today.

At issue is the design, and consequently the manufacture, not only of cameras and receivers for higher definition, but of videocassettes and VCRs. A major problem is that the system requires five times the spectrum space as a conventional television signal, which is to say that one HDTV channel monopolizes five conventional channels. Both Japanese and American companies are working on ways to compress the HDTV channel to manageable width. Besides this problem and the problem of commonality—the standardization of equipment—are questions relating to regulation and funding for development, questions which have involved the networks, the American National Standards Institute, the Society of Motion Picture and Television Engineers, the FCC, and the Congress, which, with an eye to the multibillion-dollar market in the next century, supports those policies that will help America in the high-tech race. Even the Defense Department is involved because of military applications.

HDTV will intensify television. Barnouw has noted how color film affected visual impact during the Vietnam War—"Mud and blood were indistinguishable in black and white; in color, blood was blood."[1] News footage, life-size, has to carry more force. Because of this, will televised politics—speeches and demonstrations—have different consequences than in the past, personalizing still further the political process? Will television as a whole become more powerful? Because as HDTV comes to over-the-air television, it comes also to cable.

"News Eye" in the Sky

Another entrant is space photography. Governments have used camera-equipped satellites as "spies in the sky" for years, but news organizations, print and broadcast, would like to have satellites of their own for taking pictures. The Defense Department has raised questions of national security. In response, the media, guarding their First Amendment rights, are asking who decides what images are to be withheld on security grounds and what procedures are to be followed.

Indeed, such pictures already have been used by the media. When the Chernobyl accident occurred in April of 1986, both ABC and CBS used videotape based on digital data from a satellite that happened to be over the site. The magazine *Aviation Week and Space Technology* has used satellite imagery for more than ten years. In such remote-sensing, expert interpretation is needed because of the low-resolution images now available for commercial use. Arrangements for allowing higher-resolution images to be used are being discussed. "Keep an eye on this act," says *Broadcasting*. "It will get bigger."[2]

"Much, Much More"

And there is, as they say in too many commercials, much, much more. On the horizon is more use of fiber optics. That is the relay of information on laser beams passing through glass filaments only slightly thicker than a strand of human hair, each filament capable of handling an almost limitless number of channels. Telephone companies, using fiber optics, want to get into cable television. There are legal obstacles. Will they make it? If they do, will they deliver news?

Undue emphasis on giving the public what it wants, rather than what it needs, has brought widespread tabloid journalism to television for the first time. Syndicated shows like "A Current Affair" attract large audiences with their sleaze. Has their popularity peaked?

Will network news, adapting, become an electronic version of the Associated Press?

To what extent will the traditional networks enter the realm of cable news? An ambitious, pioneering step in this direction was taken in January 1991 when NBC's News Channel began feeding up-to-the-minute reports to its television affiliates on a 24-hour basis.

Coming on strong is the remote tuner enabling viewers to "zap" commercials. What, in the marketplace and on news programming, which is paid for by advertisers, will be the effect?

No one knows how large a role direct broadcast satellites will play. With this technology, called DBS, no station is involved. Programs come down from satellites to dish-shaped antennae in the backyards of subscribers' homes. For the most part, the subscribers, with decoders for unscrambling the programs, live in rural areas not reached by cable, although, so far, most program suppliers have been the cable companies. Other companies have bet on DBS and lost millions. How will it fare?

The future of teletext, a means of delivering pages of textual information through television sets, also is shrouded. Expansion has been delayed by standardization problems and expense. Teletext's big advantage over newspapers is that it can be continually updated.

Over the horizon are spacey television sets with 3-D pictures, more AM stereo, more robotic studio cameras, more cameras with solid-state imaging instead of tubes, more solid-state transmitters, and more digital effects systems that can do more for less. Scientists are discovering superconductors that will make computers even faster. Satellites, besides serving television and other communications systems, are on their way to becoming giant jukeboxes in the sky, generating signals strong enough to be received on wristwatch radios.

The nation's population will pass the quarter-billion mark, and the radio audience, with the increase in population, will grow. Penetration by cable also will grow and proportionately the size of the over-the-air television audience will continue to shrink, bottoming out at best around a 50 percent share. New networks will appear, fragmenting the audience still further, although simple economics imposes a limit at some point because to support them there are only so many advertising dollars. The popularity of videocassettes will be undiminished. If shopping by television moves in any direction, it will be up. Pay-per-view television, in which cable viewers pay only for the program they want to see—the big sports event or stellar concert—seems to be taking hold.

Don Hewitt of "60 Minutes" envisions newspapers being delivered electronically, using techniques not too dissimilar from fax machines. They would reach the home via cable television or direct broadcast satellites, as would pay-per-view newscasts fed directly to a subscriber's VCR. Ted Turner's CNN could be the prototype for this new service. In any case, Hewitt considers today's network-affiliate setup for delivering news outmoded.[3]

Viewer Lib

The Department of Commerce, in a 672-page report, predicts such a dazzling array of advances by the twenty-first century that "viewers will have achieved full control over their television sets [and] be able to watch precisely what they want to watch when they want to watch it."[4] Attending the convenience is the danger of America's becoming a nation of electronic isolationists, each man and woman tuned to the channel of individual interest—news, business, health, entertainment, sports—learning more and more about less and less. Like cable, radio has adopted its formats for special tastes—golden oldies, country, adult contemporary, news, talk, religion, Top 40, rock. Television networks still broadcast a mix of entertainment and information, but so many viewers have strayed from them that not only audience but perceptions are fragmented. The public is losing its common, fundamental, shared base of information, a development, Richard Salant has warned, that threatens the democratic process.[5]

The day is coming when anyone, anywhere, can press a few buttons and call up on the screen whatever he or she wants to know, whether it be a mortgage rate or what is taking place in Yankee Stadium. The person learns the rate or the ball score and then, as journalist Emerson Stone has expressed it, "quits to play horseshoes or something and learns nothing else that day."[6]

Whither Network News

The traditional networks are "reinventing" their evening newscasts. NBC has abandoned the four-minute "Special Segment" format and replaced it with various series called "Focus," "On Site," and "Capitol Watch." ABC does the same with its "American Agenda" series. For its evening news, CBS has adopted a similar approach. With these series come more investigative reports, and more often now the anchors interview national and international leaders. They also interview correspondents who can contribute insights from their experience and special knowledge. Jonathan Alter, writing in *Newsweek,* notes the irony that "the technological revolution in local TV news means that network news programs will have to rely more on a non-technical advantage, their correspondents."[7]

The aim is to give viewers what local stations with their more limited resources cannot give. As Dan Rather says, the networks have to come up with "something special, the something special always being, 'Here's a piece that no way, no how, are you going to see a lot of other places because we put our worldwide resources together to do it'."[8] Because of these efforts at differentiation for the sake of competition, the network evening programs are becoming daily newsmagazines akin to the full-hour MacNeil-Lehrer broadcast. This is change, but network producers, limited to half an hour, are handicapped.

At the same time that the network news divisions strive for programming that sets them apart, they give the viewer more news of Hollywood celebrities, rock music, accidents, weather, and sports, precisely the same news that local stations provide. The two- or three-minute pro sports story, once a rarity on the evening news, has become commonplace. So have stories of murder and marital strife. Salant recalls that one night in the midst of the Iran–Contra hearings and other important happenings, the CBS evening news devoted three minutes to the Joan Collins divorce.[9]

The networks neglect commentary, an area in which they could excel. Since Bill Moyers left CBS in 1986, only John Chancellor of NBC comments regularly. The contribution to understanding made on CBS and ABC by Moyers and others like Howard K. Smith, Frank Reynolds, Eric Sevareid, and Edward R. Murrow has not been replaced. In commentary, National Public Radio and cable's "World Monitor" and CNN do better.

The network evening news programs are programs in search of a new identity. "At some point in this game," says Brian Lamb, founder of C-SPAN, "you're going to see one of the three networks go so far away from what they're doing now that it will overwhelm you when you see the difference."[10]

A Declaration of Independence

The competition has changed the network–affiliate relationship and nowhere more noticeably than in the news sharing that goes on between the networks and their affiliated stations. For a long time, the news feeds to affiliates consisted of leftovers. The best quotes and best visuals were saved for the evening news; affiliates were fed the scraps. Affiliates protested with little effect until competing news services appeared. No longer can the networks behave so high-handedly; they now give affiliates more of the stories they want. The cooperation at national political conventions is particularly close. At the 1988 conventions, the networks provided affiliates with anchor booths, Ku-band uplinks, and workspace for reporters— a far cry from the day when, at such political gatherings, the networks thought only of facilities for themselves.

The affiliates, now being wooed, often stray. They preempt network public affairs programs, especially documentaries, or run them in ghetto hours. (In early 1989, WUSA-TV, the CBS affiliate in Washington, was airing "Face the Nation" from 11:30 P.M. to midnight.) Radio stations cut away from 15-minute newscasts early, while more than a few television stations skip altogether the network newscasts scheduled for 10 and 11 o'clock on Sunday nights. It is in accommodation with this new independence, rudely declared, that the networks cater increasingly to station needs. With all their news sources and other programming available to them, the affiliates no longer live by the networks. The networks live by them. And both know it.

And Some Defect

In 1986, addressing the annual meeting of the Radio-Television News Directors Association, Fred Friendly said that if he were starting out today, he might well make local news his career.[11] That something is amiss with network news, once the shining goal of broadcast journalists, is demonstrated by its desertions. In 1973, when David Schoumacher left CBS to anchor the news on what is now WJLA-TV in Washington, it was an almost unheard-of move. In the 1980s, as obsession with ratings made work at the networks less appealing, distinguished correspondents like Fred Graham of CBS, John Hart of NBC, and Sylvia Chase of ABC forsook them for local television or cable though Chase has now returned.

Explaining her move from the bigtime to KRON-TV, San Francisco, Chase cited the cuts the networks made in their news budgets and the fact that "local news isn't just local anymore."[12] A crack investigative reporter herself, she was attracted by KRON's commitment in creating a ten-person investigative unit. Bernard Shaw, who has worked for both ABC and CBS, says of the early work at CNN, "It was exciting. We were working on something that nobody else had done or was doing. We felt we were pioneers."[13]

It was the same excitement that once existed in network newsrooms but which now, to an observable degree, is gone.

Fight for Survival

The traditional networks are not, to borrow from Dylan Thomas, going gently into that good night. As their share of the audience slips and they stand endangered, they are doing more than making allies of their affiliates. They have sold off valuable properties to raise capital and are joining—if you can't lick 'em, join 'em—competing systems.

CBS went into the business of selling videocassettes for home viewing as early as 1981. The first in its CBS News Collectors Series covered the Kennedy presidency and sold well enough to make the "Top 40" chart published by *Billboard*. At the same time, ABC was selling a videocassette of Pope John Paul's visit to the United States. Earlier, CBS had been doing the same thing with audiocassettes. After 1981, the network formed the CBS Video Club, from which members received videocassettes by mail. CBS/Fox Video had a hit with a set of four "I Love Lucy" cassettes after Lucille Ball died.

One by one, the networks went into producing programs for both domestic and foreign markets. They made in-flight video magazines for airlines. A book, *Dateline America,* written by Charles Kuralt and put out by CBS, sold 60,000 copies. Then there was NBC's bold step when it founded NBC Cable. From it sprang the Consumer News and Business Channel (CNBC). The network also began developing regional news services with cable operators. ABC bought into ESPN, the sports network.

Some of what the networks did for capital was painful, almost unthinkable. CBS sold its productive records division to SONY, and NBC, as we have noted, sold its radio network to the California-based Westwood One, which in 1985 had bought Mutual from the Amway Corporation. NBC Radio and Mutual shared headquarters in Arlington, Virginia. Inconceivably, WNBC-AM, which as WEAF had been the birthplace of NBC, no longer belonged to it. The station was acquired in 1988 by Emmis Broadcasting and is now all-sports WFAN-AM.

A sign of the seriousness of the competition networks face may be gleaned from a *New York Times* feature called "Television This Week." Each Sunday, in the Arts and Leisure section, the newspaper lists the top television programs of the coming week. A survey of listings for the month of June 1989 shows that out of 76 programs recommended, only 26 were aired by ABC, CBS, and NBC. Fifty, or almost twice as many, were carried on cable or by PBS. Cable carried 34 and PBS 16.[14]

In 1989, the crisis facing over-the-air television—"free TV," the industry calls it—led the National Association of Broadcasters to enlist Walter Cronkite as spokesman in a national promotional campaign. The message, carried across the country in prime time, was the need to preserve over-the-air television, which, the promoters said, had become an endangered species.[15]

Without question, the competition challenging the founding networks is formidable. Among those nibbling away at their audience are the Cable News Network (CNN), CNN Headline News, C-SPAN, the Financial News Network (FNN), the new Fox Network, the Christian Broadcasting Network (CBN), Turner Network Television (TNT), the Spanish International Network (SIN), AP Network News, the Discovery Channel, the Weather Channel, the Health Channel, the USA Network, Showtime, and Home Box Office.

Also taking nibbles are 9,300 cable systems serving 53 million subscribers, which translates into more than 100 million viewers. Well over half the nation's television households are now wired for cable. In 1989, 22 regional television networks also were taking their bites. The huge cooperatives—Conus, N.I.W.S., and Newsfeed—loosen further the bonds between founding networks and affiliates. More than four hundred television stations are independents, and these command the largest nonnetwork share of television viewing.

In radio, the Big Three and Mutual face National Public Radio, American Public Radio, the National Black Network, the United States Radio Network, the USA Radio Network, the Wall Street Journal Radio Network,

Reuters Radio, Associated Press Radio, the UPI Radio Network, the Sheridan Broadcasting Network, and 101 regional radio networks.[16] None of these lists is complete.

One hopes that the networks will not only survive but continue to report the news. For if in great contemporary moments the networks, including CNN, are not there to report them, who will? Not local stations. The task of sustained coverage of stories like Watergate and the civil rights movement is too overwhelming. The same holds true with events like the assassination of President Kennedy and what happened in Tiananmen Square, Eastern Europe, and the Persian Gulf.

Burton Benjamin, a great man in broadcast journalism, spoke on this subject not long before he died. It was in 1987, and the retired CBS News Executive, who was then a senior fellow at the Gannett Center for Media Studies, was speaking at the University of Nevada at Reno. He said:

> And so technology has closed the gap that once existed between local stations and the networks. And there are some observers who wring their hands and say network news is dead. I am not among them. I believe the networks will continue to grope for their proper niche. Some nights they are looking like MacNeil-Lehrer and other nights like "60 Minutes." I believe they should lead with and exploit their greatest strength—their journalism. That is how they can separate themselves from the pack. Not that local stations don't have good journalists. The networks simply have more of them and more appetite to use them.

Then he came down to the heart of it.

> The good journalist is a treasure, and they won't be able to develop or clone him in a laboratory. The problem that television faces, in my opinion, is for the creativity to keep up with the racing technology. I don't care whether or not a story is coming to you via satellite, has been written by computer and transmitted by a correspondent with an antenna implanted in his head. If he can't write, he can't write—by satellite or quill pen. If he can't report, he can't report. And all of the technology in the world can't save him. There is so much at stake today that if we simply go with the technology, we are going to be in trouble. There was never a time when . . . reporters who can write, report, analyze, ask the right questions were needed more.[17]

Telecommunications has expanded to the same degree that the six-foot HDTV screen dwarfs the four-inch screen exhibited at the New York World's Fair in 1939. The large, colorful, highly defined picture has replaced the small, grainy, black-and-white picture. Images flash instantaneously through glass fibers. The sky is crowded with moons bearing solar cells and transponders. But, for all that, what appears on the screen may be no more significant and the opportunity for abuse no less. As Murrow said, the instrument has no conscience.[18]

The same is true of radio. Radio and television are tools. They have been, still are, and will be no better or worse than those who use them. The history of the first century of broadcast journalism ends here. Broadcast journalists, riding the tiger of new technology, are making new history. But the issues arising—standards and freedom to broadcast—will be the old issues. They are everlasting.

As this book went to press, war broke out in the Persian Gulf, and the world was seeing a new, graphic demonstration of the role of radio and television in wartime, a revolution in journalism as well as high-tech weaponry. Up to this writing, much reporting of the Gulf war has resembled the reporting of other wars. Coverage of Saddam Hussein's seizure of Kuwait, the historic debate in Congress, and onslaught of Operation Desert Storm was typical in terms of bulletin interruptions, television specials, and Pentagon briefings. The anti-war demonstrations seemed a replay, and as in past wars the rush to report sometimes produced error and confusion. Correspondents still visited bomb shelters. They still fought for air time and performed valiantly. Fatigue dogged them and showed in their faces.

Viewers knew it was a different war when gas masks covered the faces. Air raid sirens had a familiar sound, but the grotesque image the masks projected was new. New too, was the swarm of satellites carrying the image and the pictures of Patroit missles and laser-guided bombs. New and nettlesome was the strict censorship imposed by the U.S. government, a product of the Vietnam experience. And just as more women were serving in the armed forces, more were reporting, though the number remained small. Never had the networks engaged so many retired generals to explain what was happening. Never on television screens had appeared so many maps.

It was a time when the broadcast media showed what their high-tech equipment could do. Producers seemed able at will to summon live reports from places like Dhahran, Riyadh, Amman, Tel Aviv, even Baghdad in the early days, not to mention military bases and ships at sea. And everywhere, in palaces, embassies, and parliaments, on farms and in Wall Street, people in record numbers were watching. Swarms of communications satellites and ground stations, linked with radio, television, and cable networks, notably CNN, made it what George Will called "the first war of the wired world."[19]

Chronology

1837   Samuel F. B. Morse invents telegraph.

1858   First transatlantic cable message.

1876   Alexander Graham Bell invents telephone.

1883   Paul Nipkow in Germany develops disk capable of scanning television images mechanically.

1886   Heinrich Hertz demonstrates nature of radio waves.

1895   Guglielmo Marconi transmits radio signals for short distances.

1898   *Dublin Daily Express* receives radio-telegraph coverage of Kingstown Regatta.
Lee De Forest begins study of high-frequency radio waves.

1901   Reginald Fessenden experiments with voice transmissions.

1904   Lionel James of London *Times* uses de Forest equipment to report Russo-Japanese War.

1906   Fessenden broadcasts Christmas program that includes music as well as voice.

1907   De Forest receives patent for first three-electrode vacuum tube for amplifying radio signals.

1909   Charles "Doc" Harrold uses "wireless telephone" to broadcast news reports.

1912   Radio Act of 1912 makes secretary of commerce responsible for licensing stations.

1915   David Sarnoff proposes manufacture of "radio music box."

1916   De Forest demonstrates first radio transmission from an airplane, broadcasts presidential election returns.
U.S. entry into World War I interrupts development of radio for general public.

1920   Frank Conrad broadcasts phonograph "concerts" from garage.

1921   WHA pioneers in voice reports on markets and weather.

1922   First commercials are aired on WEAF.

1923   Vladimir Zworykin develops the iconoscope for electronic scanning of pictures for television.

1924   Republican and Democratic conventions broadcast for first time.

1925   WGN covers Scopes trial.
Coolidge inauguration aired.

1926   National Broadcasting Company establishes radio network with 24 stations.

1927   Congress passes Radio Act of 1927. It creates Federal Radio Commission (FRC) and says stations shall operate in "the public interest, convenience, and necessity."

1928   William S. Paley creates the Columbia Broadcasting System (CBS).

1930   Philo T. Farnsworth develops orthicon tube.
Lowell Thomas begins network career on CBS.

1933   President Roosevelt broadcasts to the nation. In introducing Roosevelt, Robert Trout uses phrase "fireside chat."
Edwin Armstrong conducts successful demonstration of FM.
Popularity of broadcast news sparks press–radio war.

1934   Mutual Broadcasting System founded.
Congress passes Communications Act of 1934. Federal Communications Commission (FCC) replaces FRC.

1935   Verdict broadcast in Hauptman trial.

1936   H. V. Kaltenborn reports Spanish civil war battle live.
World hears King Edward VIII renounce throne for "woman I love."

1937   Herb Morrison reports *Hindenburg* disaster for WLS.

1938   First "World News Roundup" airs on CBS.
Orson Welles causes nationwide scare with "War of the Worlds" broadcast.
Kaltenborn reports Munich crisis around the clock.

1939   Hitler precipitates World War II with invasion of Poland.
CBS' William L. Shirer and NBC's Max Jordan report from Berlin.

1940   Eric Sevareid reports fall of Paris. Shirer scoops world press with live eyewitness report on French surrender.
Edward R. Murrow wins recognition with perceptive reports on Battle of Britain.

1941   Japanese bomb Pearl Harbor.
Cecil Brown of CBS is eyewitness to sinking of British battleship *Prince of Wales* and cruiser *Repulse*.
FCC, in Mayflower decision, bans editorializing.

1942   Elmer Davis leaves CBS to head Office of War Information.

1943   Murrow, after accompanying RAF bombers on Berlin raid, does "orchestrated hell" broadcast.
Edward Noble buys NBC's Blue Network, which becomes ABC.

1944   ABC's George Hicks uses wire recorder in reporting Normandy invasion.

1945   F.D.R. dies. All networks and most stations cancel commercial programs.
Murrow makes Buchenwald broadcast.
Japan surrender reported by radio from deck of battleship *Missouri*.

1946   Radar signals are bounced off moon.
FCC issues Blue Book.
Radio-Television News Directors Association is founded.

1947   Opening session of Congress televised for first time.
Murrow starts long-running series of 15-minute newscasts on CBS Radio.

1948   Television covers national political conventions.
Evening news, Monday through Friday, comes to network television: "Douglas Edwards With the News" on CBS and "Camel News Caravan" with John Cameron Swayze on NBC.

1949   Amending Mayflower decision, FCC lifts ban on editorials, establishes Fairness Doctrine.
ABC-TV enters evening news race with "John Daly With the World News."
Kentucky Derby telecast for first time.

1950   North Korean troops invade Republic of Korea, and networks cover a new war.
With arrival of audiotape, Murrow and Fred W. Friendly start "Hear It Now" radio series.

1951   Coaxial cable links East and West coasts. President Truman inaugurates transcontinental television with address from Japanese peace conference in San Francisco.
Television carries Senate hearings on organized crime.
Murrow and Friendly launch "See It Now" documentary series.
William R. McAndrew becomes head of NBC News.

1952   "Today" debuts on NBC-TV.
First nationwide gavel-to-gavel telecast of national conventions.

Nixon delivers "Checkers" speech.
Truman conducts first televised tour of White House.
NBC-TV airs "Victory at Sea."

1953   Eisenhower inauguration is first seen live on television.
Audiotape of presidential news conferences made available for broadcast.
Fighting ends in Korea.

1954   "See It Now" broadcast exposes Senator McCarthy's methods.
Army–McCarthy hearings carried live on ABC and DuMont.

1955   "Monitor" becomes hit on NBC Radio.

1956   Chet Huntley and David Brinkley replace Swayze on NBC's evening newscast.
Ampex demonstrates video recorder.

1957   Radio and television cover school integration crisis in Little Rock. Eisenhower sends troops.
"Twentieth Century" series bows on CBS-TV.

1958   CBS cancels "See It Now."
In RTNDA speech, Murrow challenges broadcast industry to live up to its responsibilities.

1959   Amendment to Communications Act requires broadcasters "to afford reasonable opportunity for the discussion of conflicting views of public importance." Section 315 is amended to exempt appearances by qualified political candidates on news programs from equal time requirement.
Fidel Castro appears on "Meet the Press."

1960   Campaign precedent set with Kennedy–Nixon debates.
"Harvest of Shame" airs on CBS-TV.
ABC launches "Close-up" documentary series.
"The U-2 Affair" becomes first of "NBC White Paper" specials.

1961   Murrow leaves CBS to head United States Information Agency.
Telstar satellite permits live transatlantic television.
Newton Minow delivers "vast wasteland" speech.
Kennedy allows live broadcast of presidential news conferences.
Jay McMullen produces "Biography of a Bookie Joint" for CBS-TV.
Richard Salant named president of CBS News, serves until 1964, then again from 1966 to 1978.

1962   Reuven Frank produces "The Tunnel" for NBC-TV.
Walter Cronkite succeeds Douglas Edwards as anchor for "The CBS Evening News."

1963   "The CBS Evening News" expands from 15 minutes to half an hour.
Huntley-Brinkley program follows suit.
President Kennedy assassination and Lyndon Johnson succession receive massive four-day coverage.

1964   FCC issues primer clarifying Fairness Doctrine.
        Evangelist on WGCB, Red Lion, Pennsylvania, makes personal attack on author Fred J. Cook. Cook demands free time to reply on basis of Fairness Doctrine. WGCB refuses on First Amendment grounds, and case goes to the courts.

1965   U.S. places Early Bird satellite in synchronous orbit.
        CBS Correspondent Morley Safer gives film report on burning of Vietnamese village.

1966   Friendly resigns as president of CBS News.

1967   FCC adopts rule that if an attack is made upon the character of an identified person or group during the presentation of news on a controversial issue of public importance, the person or group must have reasonable opportunity to reply.
        Frederick Wiseman produces "Titicut Follies."
        Public Broadcast Laboratory (PBL) is launched on educational television stations.
        President Johnson signs bill establishing Corporation for Public Broadcasting.
        ABC-TV expands evening news to half an hour.

1968   Tet offensive. Cronkite, in half-hour special, foresees Vietnam stalemate.
        Johnson stuns nation with broadcast announcement that he will not seek reelection.
        Martin Luther King, Jr., is assassinated. Robert Kennedy meets same fate two months later.
        Television cameras record clash between police and antiwar demonstrators outside Democratic convention in Chicago.
        Don Hewitt creates "60 Minutes."

1969   U.S. Supreme Court, acting in Red Lion case, upholds constitutionality of Fairness Doctrine.
        Moon landing is viewed in 94 percent of television homes.
        Vice President Agnew attacks "tiny and closed fraternity of privileged men" in television news who determine what America sees.

1970   "Civilisation" series airs on PBS.
        Congress bans cigarette advertising on television.
        National Public Radio (NPR) is created as nonprofit service.

1971   March on Washington; more than 13,000 antiwar demonstrators are arrested.
        House committee asks for outtakes of "Selling of the Pentagon," and CBS refuses. Full House votes down contempt citation.

1972   Broadcasters accompany Nixon on historic trip to China.
        "CBS Evening News" devotes unprecedented 14 minutes to recap of Watergate scandal.
        NBC airs "Pensions: The Broken Promise."

1973   Agnew, pleading no contest to tax evasion charges, resigns.

Nixon charges "outrageous, vicious, distorted reporting," particularly by television.

CBS temporarily abandons "instant analysis."

1974 Through radio and television, the nation attends House committee hearings on impeachment of Nixon.

Roper poll indicates majority of Americans rely more on television than on newspapers for their news.

The nation hears Nixon resign.

1975 Special reports aired on fall of Saigon.

ENG technology revolutionizes television news.

1976 Barbara Walters resigns from "Today," signs contract with ABC for five years at one million dollars a year.

"MacNeil/Lehrer Report" bows on PBS.

1977 Roone Arledge becomes president of ABC News.

1978 "20/20" starts on ABC-TV.

1979 Three Mile Island nuclear accident tests capability to report such highly technical stories.

Brian Lamb founds C-SPAN.

House of Representatives allows radio-television coverage of floor debate.

Iran takes U.S. embassy personnel hostage. ABC News starts late night series called "America Held Hostage," which after hostages' release becomes "Nightline."

"Sunday Morning" bows on CBS-TV.

1980 Ted Turner creates Cable News Network (CNN).

NBC scores with exit polls in presidential election.

Independent Network News (INN) is launched.

1981 Iran releases U.S. embassy personnel. Return of hostages and inauguration of Reagan on the same day strains network facilities.

Supreme Court rules that state courts may admit cameras.

Cronkite retires as "CBS Evening News" anchor; Dan Rather succeeds him.

Cameras record Reagan assassination attempt.

David Brinkley, NBC veteran, joins ABC.

Mark Fowler becomes FCC chairman, and period of deregulation begins.

Japanese demonstrate high definition television (HDTV).

1982 Turner starts CNN Headline service.

Sol Taishoff, publisher of *Broadcasting* and exponent of First Amendment rights for broadcasters, dies.

Public stations win right to editorialize.

1983 Stations expand coverage, foreign and domestic, with satellite facilities.

"Vietnam: A Television History" airs on PBS.

U.S. invades Grenada; coverage is highly restricted.

1984   Boom in videocassette recorders.

"MacNeil/Lehrer Report," expanding to an hour, becomes "MacNeil/Lehrer NewsHour."

ABC airs "To Save Our Schools, to Save Our Children."

1985   General William C. Westmoreland drops multimillion-dollar libel suit against CBS arising from documentary "The Uncounted Enemy: A Vietnam Deception"; CBS admits violation of standards.

ABC is bought by Capital Cities.

Turner fails in CBS takeover attempt.

Westwood One buys Mutual from Amway.

Rupert Murdoch starts up Fox Television Network.

General Electric buys RCA, corporate parent of NBC.

FCC concludes that Fairness Doctrine is not in the public interest but says it will enforce it because of 1969 Supreme Court decision upholding doctrine's constitutionality.

1986   Senate joins House in permitting radio-television coverage of floor debate.

Laurence Tisch gains control of CBS.

Declining audience share and revenue force ABC, CBS, and NBC to cut news staffs.

Space shuttle *Challenger* explodes as millions watch.

Bill Moyers reports "The Vanishing Family: Crisis in Black America."

Guidelines sought for covering news from space by means of reconnaissance satellites.

1987   NBC sells its radio networks to Westwood One.

ABC premiers "Capital to Capital" series, marking first time a broadcast is seen simultaneously in the United States and the Soviet Union.

1988   FCC, acting on appeals court decision, throws out Fairness Doctrine.

Turner launches new cable network, Turner Network Television (TNT).

Gannett's "USA TODAY on TV" and *Christian Science Monitor's* "World Monitor" start September 12. Gannet effort fails.

Reality programming spreads.

After a long battle, most state courts admit microphones and cameras.

1989   NBC introduces new television magazine, "Yesterday, Today, and Tomorrow." It is shortlived.

"Primetime Live" premieres on ABC-TV.

Telephone companies seek entry to cable television.

Time, Inc., and Warner Communications merge, creating world's largest media and entertainment conglomerate.

Audience share for "Big Three" networks continues to decline.

Fall of Berlin Wall, Eastern European revolutions seen live on U.S. television.

1990   Discovery Channel joins PBS in planning creation of a commercial-free educational cable network.

CNN, viewed in more than 90 countries, becomes a global news service.

ABC, CBS, and NBC expand affiliate news services.

Fox Network expands news operations.

NBC, Cablevision Systems, Murdoch News Corporation, and Hughes Communications plan, as partners, to launch a DBS system called Sky Cable.

1991   Radio-TV, with new technology, covers the Iraq war.

Notes

1. The Natal Circumstances

1. Richard H. Ranger, *The Radio Pathfinder* (Garden City, N.Y.: Doubleday, Page, 1922), p. 4.

2. The unit for measuring radio frequencies is the hertz, named for the German physicist. A hertz is one cycle per second.

3. *Fortnightly Review,* February 1, 1892.

4. John Allen, ed., *One Hundred Great Lives* (New York: Greystone Press, 1945).

5. Soon to become Marconi's Wireless Telegraph Company, Ltd. with a U.S. subsidiary called the Marconi Wireless Company of America. In 1913, it acquired the assets of Lee De Forest's rival company, United Wireless, and eventually became part of the Radio Corporation of America (RCA).

6. The American yacht *Columbia* defeated Sir Thomas Lipton's *Shamrock* in a clean sweep.

7. The term *radio* originated about 1912 when the U.S. Navy, finding *wireless* too inclusive, adopted the word *radiotelegraphy* for transmission of code. Transmission of voice became known as *radiotelephony.* In Britain, the term *wireless* is still used.

8. Eugene Lyons, *David Sarnoff,* pp. 59–60.

9. Erik Barnouw, *A Tower in Babel,* p. 19. In *Broadcasting in America,* p. 100, Sidney W. Head says, "From a technical viewpoint this event could be regarded as the birth of broadcasting."

10. Robert St. John, *Encyclopedia of Radio and Television Broadcasting,* p. 28. Some of the first radio news was distributed to passengers on ships at sea. The wireless operator

on the *Kroonland* was jotting down news bulletins for the ship's newspaper when by chance he picked up the Christmas music.

11. Lee De Forest, *Father of Radio*, p. 1.

12. In 1948, Kaltenborn declared the Republican presidential candidate, Thomas E. Dewey, victorious over Harry S. Truman, who had been expected to lose the election because of his poor showing in the polls. For years afterward, Truman enjoyed doing an imitation of Kaltenborn making his election night mistake.

13. De Forest, *Father of Radio*, p. 339.

14. Lyons, *David Sarnoff*, pp. 71–72.

15. *Ibid.*, p. 72.

16. *Radiola* was a word coined by Dr. Alfred Goldsmith, a former professor of electrical engineering at the College of the City of New York. He had come to RCA as chief broadcasting engineer.

17. The station became WWF on March 3, 1922, after using the call letters WBL for less than a year. It was 8MK until October 12, 1921.

18. Hoover's friend, Lowell Thomas, made his first broadcast on KDKA, talking about the around-the-world flight by U.S. Army fliers in 1924. "The date of my one-hour ad lib broadcast for KDKA was March 1925. At the time, one of the fliers, Lt. 'Smiling Jack' Harding, and I were doing a coast-to-coast tour, with films, telling the story of the flight. No copy of it exists." Correspondence, April 28, 1976.

19. Head et al., *Broadcasting in America*, p. 112.

20. The first program ended with a member of the paper's advertising staff playing "Taps." Such was the free-style approach to programming in those early radiophone days!

21. Mitchell V. Charnley, *News by Radio*, p. 1.

22. *Detroit News*, September 1, 1920.

23. Barnouw, *A Tower in Babel*, p. 64.

24. Charnley, *News by Radio*, p. 1.

25. Robert Lewis Shayon, *The Crowd-Catchers* (New York: Saturday Review Press, 1973), p. 44.

26. The Aeriola, Jr. was a small crystal set that sold for $25. It went on sale in June 1921. The Aeriola, Sr., boasting a vacuum tube, was marketed the next winter.

27. Rosenberg, correspondence, April 26, 1976.

28. Barnouw, *A Tower in Babel*, p. 70.

29. Before that, WBZ was located in Springfield, Massachusetts.

30. Rosenberg, correspondence, April 26, 1976, and May 20, 1976.

31. Baudino and Kittross, "Broadcasting's Oldest Stations: An Examination of Four Claimants," *Journal of Broadcasting*, Winter 1977.

32. Dr. Smith set forth his criteria in "Oldest Station in the Nation," *Journal of Broadcasting*, Winter 1959–60. Baudino and Kittross said they saw in the criteria an implied challenge to determine which station indeed is oldest, with the results reported here.

33. Baudino and Kittross, *Journal of Broadcasting*, Winter 1977.

34. *Ibid.*

35. De Forest tells in his autobiography, *Father of Radio*, how his friend, C. S. Thompson, and John F. Hubbard organized the company in an effort to sell transmitters to newspaper owners. The *Detroit News* was their first customer.

36. Baudino and Kittross, *Journal of Broadcasting*, Winter, 1977.

37. *Ibid.*

38. Ad appeared in *Radio in the Home*, August 1925. The reference is to Donald MacMillan, the American Arctic explorer.

39. It is no wonder that Barnouw chose *A Tower in Babel* as the title for the first volume of his three-volume history of broadcasting.

40. In his history of WLW, *Not Just a Sound*, Dick Perry says, "The power played strange ghostlike tricks on nearby communities, like never letting some of them turn off their houselights."

41. FCC figures.

2. Growing Pains . . . and Pleasures

1. Interview with Lowell Thomas, August 29, 1973.

2. *Broadcasting Yearbook, 1979.*

3. Barnouw, *Tower in Babel,* p. 99.

4. As the number of stations grew, the broadcast spectrum became crowded, and many colleges and universities, pressed for funds, sold their stations to commercial interests, which were hungry for available frequencies.

5. Werner Severin, *WHA, Madison: "Oldest Station in the Nation,"* paper, University of Texas at Austin, 1977, p. 13.

6. *Ibid.,* p. 18.

7. Ben Gross, *I Looked & I Listened,* pp. 57–58.

8. Charnley, *News by Radio,* p. 79.

9. Joe Weeks of CBS, who earlier announced the Long Ranger Series at WXYZ, Detroit.

10. William S. Paley writing in *Columbine,* April/May 1974. The first broadcast from an airplane may have been made in 1916, when Lee De Forest, on his first flight, took along a small transmitter with an antenna that trailed in the air. It was a test for the Army, and De Forest believed it was the first "radiotelephone set" ever installed in an airplane; *Father of Radio,* p. 339.

11. Robert Trout, correspondence, January 2, 1970.

12. Gross, *I Looked & I Listened,* rev. ed. p. 205.

13. Brokenshire, *This Is Brokenshire,* p. 49.

14. Gross, *I Looked & I Listened,* pp. 207–208. Writing in the *Washington Post,* November 4, 1979, George F. Will said that with its coverage of the Democratic National Convention in 1924 "radio become part of the nation's nervous system."

15. Brokenshire, *This Is Brokenshire,* p. 61.

16. *Ibid.,* p. 64.

17. John T. Scopes, and James Presley, *Center of the Storm: Memoirs of John T. Scopes* (New York: Holt, Rinehart and Winston, 1967), p. 53.

18. *Ibid.,* p. 101.

19. One of those present that morning was Charles Mack, a newsreel cameraman who one day would be a respected pioneer in television news.

20. Lowell Thomas denies published accounts that he was one of those who broke the news. "Alas," he says, "I wasn't on the air when Lindbergh made his flight." Correspondence, March 14, 1980.

21. Gross, *I Looked & I Listened,* rev. ed. p. 101.

22. Paley got his company (all 16 employes) out of the cramped Times Square quarters and briefly into the Steinway Building on West 57th Street; then, in 1929, into a new building at 485 Madison Avenue, where the network, in the beginning, leased six floors. The CBS headquarters since 1964 has been a monumental 40-story building at 51 West 52nd Street designed by Eero Saarinen and popularly known as Black Rock because of the dark Canadian granite used in its construction. That CBS at one time occupied the Steinway Building on West 57th Street is interesting on two counts: CBS one day would own the Steinway piano company, and the network's principal production studios in New York are now located on West 57th Street.

23. William S. Paley, *As It Happened,* pp. 37–38.

24. *Ibid.,* p. 40.

25. *Ibid.,* p. 39.

26. *Ibid.*

27. *Broadcasting,* January 5, 1976.

28. *Encyclopedia Brittanica Book of the Year, 1968,* p. 728.

29. Gross, *I Looked & I Listened,* rev. ed. p. 224.

3. The Founding Fathers

1. Paley had a good ear for potential singing stars, as he demonstrated again in 1942 when he signed up a skinny kid named Frank Sinatra.
2. Paley, *As It Happened,* pp. 119–120.
3. *San Diego Daily Journal,* August 16, 1948. All three were celebrated newspaper columnists.
4. *Broadcasting,* issue of March 15, 1932, refers to Glover as "director of news broadcasting." *Broadcasting,* issue of October 27, 1980, identifies him as "CBS director of news broadcasts."
5. J. G. Gude, correspondence, April 2, 1982.
6. Interview with Gude, February 23, 1982.
7. Interview with Thomas, August 29, 1973.
8. *Ibid.*
9. Gross, *I Looked & I Listened,* p. 159.
10. White, *News on the Air,* p. 32.
11. As this is written, WXYZ is owned and operated by ABC.
12. Schechter, *I Live on Air,* pp. 156–157.

4. "The World's Most Famous Baby Has Been Kidnapped"

1. *Broadcasting,* March 15, 1932.
2. J. G. Gude, correspondence, April 2, 1982. *Broadcasting* omitted mention of the poker game, reporting tactfully that "CBS press relations men by sheer coincidence happened to be in the studios."
3. *Broadcasting,* March 15, 1932.
4. White, *News on the Air,* p. 33.
5. *Broadcasting,* March 15, 1932.
6. Prosper Buranelli, interview, June 11, 1952.
7. NBC Radio, March 2, 1932.
8. CBS headquarters at 485 Madison Avenue.
9. Gude, correspondence, April 2, 1982.
10. *Broadcasting,* March 15, 1932.
11. Culbert, *News for Everyman,* p. 36. Through correspondence, Culbert checked Carter's claim with R. F. Harrison, registrar at Cambridge University.
12. *Ibid.,* p. 37.
13. *Ibid.,* p. 59.
14. Heatter, *There's Good News Tonight,* p. 71.
15. George Waller, *Kidnap: The Story of the Lindbergh Case* (New York: Dial Press, 1961), p. 344.
16. Heatter, *There's Good News Tonight,* p. 65.
17. No U.S. execution received comparable coverage until 1977 when Gary Gilmore went before a firing squad at Utah State Prison.
18. Fang, *Those Radio Commentators!,* p. 289.
19. Heatter, *There's Good News Tonight,* p. 80.
20. Schechter, *I Live on Air,* p. 259.
21. Bill Brannigan, correspondence, June 18, 1980.

5. The Press–Radio War

1. White, *News on the Air,* p. 30.
2. Charnley, *News by Radio,* p. 5.
3. Oliver Gramling, *AP: The Story of News* (New York: Farrar and Rinehart, 1940), p. 380.

4. One of the first stations to air a commercial was WEAF, New York, now WNBC. On August 28, 1922, it broadcast a ten-minute "message" for which it received $50. The sponsor was the Queensboro Corporation, a real estate company operating in Jackson Heights.

5. An estimated 2,000,000 sets in 1925, compared to 4,428,000 in 1929, according to *Broadcasting Yearbook, 1980*.

6. Charnley, *News by Radio*, p. 11.

7. Schechter, *I Live on Air*, p. 1.

8. White, *News on the Air*, p. 35.

9. *Ibid.*, p. 35.

10. CBS Radio, November 4, 1932.

11. Theodore F. Koop, in *Dateline: Washington*, Cabell Phillips (ed.), p. 83.

12. Lowell Thomas, speech, Hotel Plaza, New York, Oct. 21, 1970.

13. Henry Wefing, correspondence, February 17, 1977.

14. White, *News on the Air*, p. 41.

15. White, "Radio News, Past, Present, and Future," *Journalism Quarterly*, June 1946.

6. The First Fine Careless Rapture

1. Thomas, correspondence, October 8, 1979.

2. Later, the paper merged with the *Columbus Journal* to become the *Citizen-Journal*. It no longer exists.

3. Correspondence with Jack Shelley, October 24, 1979.

4. Article II, RTNDA Constitution and Bylaws, as amended in May 1988.

5. RTNDA Code of Broadcast News Ethics, 1987 revision.

6. "The Last Word," *RTNDA Communicator*, March 1979.

7. Vernon A. Stone, "News Directors Move for Professional Advancement," *RTNDA Communicator*, September 1988. Dr. Stone, who teaches at the University of Missouri, is RTNDA director of research services.

8. Walter Cronkite, speech, RTNDA convention, Miami Beach, December 13, 1976.

9. Eric Sevareid, speech, NAB convention, Los Angeles, March 28, 1977.

10. Heatter, *There's Good News Tonight*, pp. 84–85.

11. NBC Radio, December 17, 1939.

12. White, *News on the Air*, p. 305.

13. Schechter, *I Live on Air*, p. 133.

14. Schlesinger, *The Coming of the New Deal*, pp. 12–13.

15. Sherwood, *Roosevelt and Hopkins*, p. 43.

16. Schlesinger, *The Coming of the New Deal*, p. 13.

17. The CBS station in Washington.

18. Robert Trout, correspondence, January 2, 1970.

19. Excerpts from Roosevelt's recordings appeared in the February/March 1982 issue of *American Heritage*. The recordings were made during the 1940 campaign when Roosevelt's opponent was Wendell Willkie and were disclosed by R. J. C. Butow, a historian at the University of Washington.

7. The Oracles

1. *Will Rogers: His Life and Times* (New York: American Heritage, 1973), p. 341.

2. H. V. Kaltenborn, *Fifty Fabulous Years*, p. 109.

3. Theodore F. Koop, in Phillips, ed., *Dateline: Washington*, p. 79.

4. The salutation varied. Sometimes it was "Good evening, Mr. and Mrs. North America" or "Attention, Mr. and Mrs. United States."

5. Winchell, *Winchell Exclusive*, p. 256.

6. Conversation with Raymond Swing, circa March 1958.

7. Raymond Swing, *"Good Evening:"* (New York: Harcourt, Brace and World, 1964), p. 11.

8. *Ibid.*, p. 193.

9. MBS, September 23, 1940.

10. *New York Times,* August 26, 1966.

11. CBS Radio, May 19, 1958.

12. Not counting *Bare Living,* which he co-authored with Guy Holt.

13. Fang, *Those Radio Commentators:*, p. 182.

14. *Ibid.*, p. 183.

15. Interview with William J. Dunn, April 2, 1978.

16. CBS Radio, May 31, 1941.

17. Interview with Dunn April 2, 1978. It is remarkable that in his memoir, *Fifty Fabulous Years,* Kaltenborn makes no mention of Davis.

18. Interview with Robert Skedgell, February 9, 1979.

19. CBS Radio, June 23, 1935.

20. David Holbrook, *News for Everyman* (Westport, Conn.: Greenwood Press, 1976), p. 202.

8. "Time Marches On!"

1. Frederick Harris, "Time Marches On, But Not Easily," *Tune In,* October 1945.

2. Barnouw, *A Tower in Babel,* p. 277.

3. W. A. Swanberg, *Luce and His Empire* (New York: Scribners, 1972), p. 86.

4. Michael J. Arlen, "On the Trail of a Fine Careless Rapture," *The New Yorker,* March 10, 1980.

5. NBC, *The National Broadcasting Company in 1943,* p. 12.

6. A direct descendant of "America's Town Meeting of the Air" and "The American Forum of the Air" is the "National Town Meeting" program heard since 1974 on National Public Radio.

7. Forty-two years later, in 1980, WPFW-FM, the Pacifica station in Washington, D.C., aired a similar dramatization of a nuclear attack and drew criticism from the *Columbia Journalism Review* "for pulling an Orson Welles and scaring the daylights out of an already anxious audience." On October 31, 1975, ABC's Friday Night Movie was "The Night That Panicked America," based on the Mercury Theater production.

8. *Broadcasting,* August 1, 1937.

9. Saerchinger, *Hello, America!,* p. 264.

9. "Hello, America, London Calling . . ."

1. Paley, *As It Happened,* p. 121.

2. Cesar Saerchinger, *Hello, America!* (Boston: Houghton Mifflin, 1938), p. 4.

3. *Ibid.*, p. 5.

4. *Ibid.*, p. 9.

5. Saerchinger, *Hello, America!,* p. 260.

6. Barnouw, *Tower in Babel,* p. 249.

7. America's radio editors voted the nightingale feature the most interesting broadcast of 1932.

8. Saerchinger, *Hello, America!,* p. 282.

9. Quincy Howe, *The World Between the Wars* (New York: Simon & Schuster, 1953), p. 600.

10. Saerchinger, *Hello, America!,* pp. 237–238.

11. Saerchinger, *Hello, America!,* pp. 237–238.

12. *Ibid.*, pp. 243–244.

13. NBC Radio, December 11, 1936.
14. Robert MacNeil, *Wordstruck* (New York: Viking, 1982), p. 192.

10. Radio's First War Correspondents

1. De Forest, *Father of Radio*, p. 155.
2. Edward Gibbons, *Floyd Gibbons, Your Headline Hunter*, p. 277.
3. Gibbons definitely did another broadcast on Manchuria, but it was from Honolulu on his way back to the States.
4. Saerchinger, *Hello, America!*, p. 220.
5. *Ibid.*, p. 223.
6. Kaltenborn, *Kaltenborn Edits the News*, p. 12.
7. Kaltenborn, *Fifty Fabulous Years*, p. 201.
8. Kaltenborn, *Kaltenborn Edits the News*, p. 25.
9. Edward Gibbons, *Floyd Gibbons: Your Headline Hunter*, pp. 322–323.

11. Munich

1. William L. Shirer, *Berlin Diary*, p. 95.
2. Murrow had been in Salzburg to arrange a broadcast from the music festival.
3. Shirer, *Berlin Diary*, p. 80.
4. Shirer, *20th Century Journey: The Start, 1904–1930*, pp. 24–25.
5. *Ibid.*, p. 21.
6. Cowley was reviewing the first volume of Shirer's memoirs for the *New York Times Book Review*, October 10, 1976.
7. Half a century later, Shirer wrote, and Simon and Schuster published, *Gandhi: A Memoir*.
8. Shirer, *Berlin Diary*, p. 3.
9. CBS Radio, February 3, 1954.
10. Conversation with Bliss.
11. *Ida Lou Anderson: A Memorial*, published by the State College of Washington (undated), p. 18.
12. Alexander Kendrick, *Prime Time: The Life of Edward R. Murrow*, p. 121.
13. Paley, *As It Happened*, p. 130.
14. CBS Radio, March 12, 1938.
15. Shirer, *Berlin Diary*, p. 104.
16. CBS Radio, March 13, 1938.
17. Shirer, *Berlin Diary*, p. 105.
18. Sidney W. Head, *Broadcasting in America*, p. 146.
19. Shirer, *Berlin Diary*, p. 89.
20. Interview with William J. Dunn, April 2, 1978.
21. H. V. Kaltenborn, *I Broadcast the Crisis*, p. 9.
22. White, *News on the Air*, p. 46.
23. *Ibid.*, p. 9.
24. Culbert, *News for Everyman*, pp. 74–75.
25. Kaltenborn, *I Broadcast the Crisis*, p. 246.
26. *Ibid.*, p. 3.
27. Schechter, *I Live on Air*, p. 206.
28. The letter was in response to a request from Schechter for the details.
29. Schechter, *I Live on Air*, pp. 361–362.
30. Shirer, *Berlin Diary*, p. 145.
31. *Ibid.*, pp. 150–151.

12. "Steady, Reliable, and Restrained"

1. Eric Sevareid, *Not So Wild a Dream*, p. 4.

2. *Ibid.*, p. 29.

3. *Ibid.*, p. 41.

4. *Ibid.*, p. 47.

5. *Ibid.*, p. 67.

6. *Ibid.*, p. 107.

7. *Ibid.*

8. Just as Murrow fibbed about his own age when he applied at CBS, adding five years, he fibbed now, telling New York Sevareid was 29 when he was 26. Murrow would fib again on hiring Charles Collingwood, raising the young reporter's age by a year. He wanted these men—believed in them—and feared New York would hold their youth against them.

9. Sevareid, *Not So Wild a Dream*, p. 82.

10. Interview with Larry La Sueur, September 14, 1982.

11. Interview with Albert Maxwell, May 25, 1981.

12. Letter from Collingwood dated May 14, 1940. *Current Biography 1943* (New York: H. W. Wilson, 1944), p. 137.

13. A chain, 66 feet in length, used by surveyors. Ten square "chains" equal one acre.

14. Speech by Collingwood, New York, January 8, 1976.

15. *Current Biography 1943*, pp. 137–138.

16. Howard K. Smith, *Last Train from Berlin*, p. 4.

17. *Ibid.*, pp. 15–16.

18. Briefly, between Shirer's departure in December 1940 and Smith's employment, CBS was represented in Berlin by Harry W. Flannery, a St. Louis broadcaster selected by Paul White.

19. Correspondence with Hottelet, October 14, 1982.

20. CBS Radio, March 13, 1958.

21. Shirer, *Berlin Diary*, p. 42.

22. David H. Hosley, *As Good As Any of Us: American Female Radio Correspondents in Europe, 1938–1941* (Westport, Conn.: Greenwood Press, 1982), p. 6.

23. Marion Marzolf, *Up From the Footnote*, p. 140.

24. Interview, October 16, 1982. Breckinridge had visited England so often that English mannerisms had crept into her speech.

25. Interview, October 8, 1982.

26. Hosley interview with Wason, *As Good As Any of Us*, p. 38.

27. *Ibid.*

28. Hosley interview with Pupli, *As Good As Any of Us*, p. 19.

29. Hosley, *As Good As Any of Us*, p. 24.

30. Ruth Ashton, correspondence, August 9, 1978.

31. White, *News on the Air*, p. 364.

32. Bill Slocum soon left to write a column for the *New York Mirror*.

33. Lord also produced "Seth Parker" and played the part of Seth Parker in that long-running radio series on NBC.

34. Telephone conversation, March 22, 1978.

35. Helen Sioussat, *Mikes Don't Bite* (New York: L. B. Fischer, 1943), pp. 93–96.

36. *New York Times,* July 26, 1968.

37. *Ibid.*

38. Interview, Catharine Heinz, director of Broadcast Pioneers Library, Washington, D.C., November 4, 1982.

13. War: The People Listened

1. R. Franklin Smith, *Edward R. Murrow: The War Years*, p. 23.
2. NBC Radio, September 22, 1939.
3. *The Living Room War* was the title of Michael J. Arlen's book published by Viking Press in 1969.
4. Lowell Thomas, *Magic Dials*, p. 74.
5. *New York Daily News*, September 9, 1939.
6. John MacVane, *On the Air in World War II*, pp. 11–12.
7. Sevareid was delivering the fourth annual Elmer Davis Memorial Lecture at Columbia University, April 29, 1970.
8. Bill Dunn, taped statement to Bliss, August 10, 1978.
9. NBC Radio, March 1, 1940.
10. CBS Radio, April 12, 1940.
11. CBS Radio, February 21, 1940.
12. Burdett appeared before the Senate Internal Security Subcommittee on June 29, 1955. He had told the FBI and CBS of his former Communist connections four years before that.
13. Cecil Brown, *Suez to Singapore*, p. 8.
14. *Ibid.*, p. 9.
15. Schechter, *I Live on Air*, pp. 369–370.
16. *Ibid.*, p. 363.
17. For example, correspondents were prohibited from using the word *Nazi*. Censors said it had a bad connotation, as indeed it did.
18. Talk to journalism students at Boston University, December 1, 1976.
19. Mary Marvin Breckinridge had reported in a broadcast on CBS (April 28, 1940) that Dutch uniforms were being smuggled across the border into Germany.
20. Schechter, *I Live on Air*, pp. 136–142.
21. Swing, *Good Evening!*, p. 198.
22. Fourth annual Elmer Davis Memorial Lecture, Columbia University, April 29, 1970.
23. CBS Radio, May 28, 1940.
24. CBS Radio, June 10, 1939.
25. CBS Radio, "Farewell to Studio 9," July 26, 1964. It was from Studio 9, in the old CBS headquarters building at 485 Madison Avenue, that most CBS News programs originated from the time of the Munich crisis until 1963, when television studios were available at the new production center on West 57th Street.
26. Schechter, *I Live on Air*, pp. 215–216.
27. Sevareid, *Not So Wild a Dream*, pp. 152–153.
28. NBC Radio, June 19, 1940.

14. Ankara to Singapore

1. Cecil Brown, *Suez to Singapore*, p. 13.
2. *Ibid.*, pp. 37–38.
3. *Ibid.*, p. 151. "This is Singapore" recalls Ed Murrow's "This is London." In this chapter, all dates are Far East time, one day later than United States time because of the International Date Line.
4. *Ibid.*, p. 295.
5. *Ibid.*, pp. 314–317.
6. *Ibid.*, p. 325.
7. *Ibid.*, p. 333.
8. *Ibid.*, p. 348.
9. *Ibid.*, p. 361.
10. *Ibid.*, p. 368.
11. *Ibid.*, p. 409.

12. Now Djakarta, capital of Indonesia.

13. Brown, *Suez to Singapore,* p. 500.

14. *Suez to Singapore,* published by Random House, 1942.

15. Interview with Dunn, December 16, 1982.

16. *Ibid.*

17. Dunn, taped statement to Bliss, August 10, 1978.

18. The Allied headquarters in Batavia was called the American-British-Dutch-Australian Command (ABDACOM).

19. Dunn, taped statement to Bliss, August 10, 1978.

20. MacDougall was 36 hours in the water. While in the water he made a pact: If allowed to live, he would spend the rest of his life in God's service. After the war, he became a Roman Catholic priest. Quote is from a taped statement to Bliss, August 10, 1978.

15. The Battle of Britain

1. Kendrick, *Prime Time,* p. 189.

2. Sevareid has said that the most fearsome part of the Blitz was dashing about London in Murrow's little car. The author recalls driving with Murrow on the Maine Turnpike at better than 90 miles an hour. For several miles, the car was guided solely by an index finger resting lightly on the steering wheel.

3. Kendrick, *Prime Time,* p. 206.

4. Interview with LeSueur, April 1, 1980.

5. John MacVane, *On the Air in World War II,* p. 32.

6. CBS Radio, September 18, 1940.

7. Interview with LeSueur, April 1, 1980.

8. Larry LeSueur, *Twelve Months That Changed the World* (New York: Knopf, 1943), p. 58.

9. CBS Radio, June 2, 1940.

10. CBS Radio, August 18, 1940.

11. CBS Radio, September 8, 1940.

12. CBS Radio, September 13, 1940.

13. CBS Radio, September 18, 1940.

14. Paley spoke at a time when new controls on radio were being rumored. Senator Burton K. Wheeler, isolationist chairman of the Interstate Commerce Committee, wanted networks to submit copies of their commentators' scripts to him so he could see if they were propagandizing.

16. "We Interrupt This Program. . ."

1. Ironically, the one time Wilkins was heard live that historic day was when, through a switching error, he was carried on NBC.

2. *Washington Star,* February 2, 1976.

3. The quotes are from Paul Hollister and Robert Strunsky, eds., *From Pearl Harbor to Tokyo* (New York: Columbia Broadcasting System, 1945), pp. 39–40.

4. Kendrick, *Prime Time,* p. 240.

5. Bill Lawrence, *Six Presidents, Too Many Wars,* p. 56.

6. Koop, in Phillips, ed., *Dateline: Washington,* p. 87. Roosevelt had called December 7, 1941, "a *date* which will live in infamy."

7. During the Eisenhower, Kennedy, Johnson, and Nixon administrations, Koop was the country's standby censor should the need arise.

8. Barnouw, *The Golden Web,* p. 157.

9. The nine pages of instruction, dated December 1941, bear the title "Columbia's War Coverage: A Memorandum to the CBS News Organization."

10. Full-page advertisement in the *New York Times,* September 20, 1943.

11. Cuthbert, *News for Everyman,* pp. 88–89.

12. Barnouw, *The Golden Web,* pp. 136–137.

13. FCC, January 16, 1941.
14. Correspondence from Sevareid, March 25, 1980.
15. Letter from White to Brown, August 27, 1943.
16. White, *News on the Air*, pp. 205–206.
17. Kaltenborn was speaking at a joint meeting of the Association of Radio News Analysts and the news committee of the National Association of Broadcasters.
18. White, *On the Air*, p. 204.
19. Citation quoted in *Variety*, May 11, 1966.
20. The highly controversial program was shown on CBS Television March 9, 1954.
21. "Letters," *Newsweek*, April 12, 1954.
22. Kendrick, *Prime Time*, p. 195.
23. CBS Radio, December 3, 1940.
24. *Ibid.*, March 9, 1941.

17. Into North Africa and Italy

1. Harry C. Butcher, *My Three Years With Eisenhower* (New York: Simon & Schuster, 1946), p. 21.
2. Woodrow Wirsig, "Reporter to the Nation," *Esquire*, August 1943.
3. There is reason to believe that the opportunist admiral, realizing Vichy was finished—Hitler soon took over all of France—had planned to be in Algeria at the time of the invasion.
4. MacVane, *On the Air in World War II*, pp. 121, 133.
5. Sevareid, *Not So Wild a Dream*, p. 224.
6. Quincy Howe, *Ashes of Victory*, New York: Simon and Schuster, 1972, p. 205.
7. Letter from Collingwood, March 28, 1978. With no disparagement of Collingwood, MacVane believes his rival was helped by CBS' hustling publicity department.
8. CBS Radio, April 11, 1943.
9. CBS Radio, December 3, 1943.
10. Kendrick, *Prime Time*, p. 221.
11. Sevareid, *Not So Wild a Dream*, p. 399.
12. It operated in the early stage as the Blue Network Company, Inc. Mark Woods became president and Noble chairman of the board.
13. Correspondence with Donald Coe, April 10, 1978.
14. Interview with Thomas Velotta, February 21, 1983.
15. Correspondence, April 10, 1978. Later, the headquarters moved to Naples.
16. Fraser had done special events reporting for NBC under the name of Jack Fraser—his full name was John Gordon Fraser. But when Johnstone decided to make him a war correspondent, he regarded "Jack" as too casual or flip.

18. And Into Normandy

1. In a press release, the Blue Network told newspaper editors, "We will appreciate it, however, if you will identify Blue correspondents as such whenever it is possible." A "network" called American Broadcasting Stations in Europe (ABSIE) was set up for sharing the reports. ABSIE would have its own clear channel so no big story would be delayed.
2. The memorandum was dated February 29, 1944.
3. *Time*, March 20, 1944.
4. From the instruction sheet drawn up by Everett Holles, assistant news director, dated May 16, 1944.
5. Correspondence from Joel Tall, March 6, 1977.
6. Paul Hollister and Robert Strunsky, eds., *D-Day Through Victory in Europe* (New York: Columbia Broadcasting System, 1945), p. 5.
7. Correspondents reporting on sponsored programs received additional payments.

8. Interview with Cronkite, March 26, 1975.

9. Hollister and Strunsky, *D-Day Through Victory in Europe*, p. 12.

10. An NBC account of D-Day coverage written June 7 did not mention Murrow. It said the Order of the Day was read by "General Eisenhower's spokesman at Supreme Headquarters."

11. *Broadcasting*, June 12, 1944.

12. MacVane, *On the Air in World War II*, p. 210.

13. *Broadcasting*, June 12, 1944.

14. MacVane, *On the Air in World War II*, pp. 237–252.

15. For security reasons, Murrow could not give the location of the basement. It was in the Ministry of Information building.

16. CBS Radio, June 18, 1944.

17. Stringer was an American. His wife was Ann Stringer, war correspondent for UP.

18. John Gilbert Winant, *Letter from Grosvenor Square* (Boston: Houghton Mifflin, 1947), p. 165.

19. MacVane, *On the Air in World War II*, p. 294.

20. *Ibid.*, p. 295.

19. Victory in Europe

1. Interview with Cronkite, March 26, 1975.

2. Correspondence with Jack Shelley, March 12, 1978.

3. Collingwood wrote the broadcast for January 22, 1945, but it was not heard because of a breakdown in communications.

4. J. Fred MacDonald, *Don't Touch That Dial* (Chicago: Nelson-Hall, 1979), p. 304.

5. CBS Radio, December 13, 1942.

6. *Ibid.*

7. CBS Radio, April 15, 1945.

8. Smith, *Edward R. Murrow: The War Years*, p. 89.

9. CBS Radio, April 12, 1945.

10. White, *News on the Air*, p. 26.

11. Godfrey broke into broadcasting on WFBR, Baltimore. His first real success was on WJSV (now WTOP, Washington), the same station on which Robert Trout got his start.

12. CBS Radio, April 13, 1945.

13. NBC Radio, April 27, 1945.

14. The AP reporter who broke the embargo on Germany's surrender was Ed Kennedy, a correspondent who, earlier in the war, had protested what he believed to be unreasonable censorship. Now Allied commanders and fellow correspondents who had abided by the embargo were incensed, and, after loss of accreditation, Kennedy was sent home. Later, he covered the United Nations for the AP.

15. CBS Radio, May 7, 1945.

16. *Ibid.*, May 8, 1945.

20. The Other War

1. Full-page advertisement in *Broadcasting*, June 18, 1945.

2. Telephone interview with Dunn, February 8, 1978.

3. Clement-Attlee, upon becoming prime minister, soon replaced Churchill at the conference table.

4. The third crew member was Major Thomas Ferebee of Mocksville, N.C., the bombardier.

5. There was a rule that anything recorded had to be identified on the air as "electrically transcribed." Colonel Jack Harris, who was MacArthur's communications

chief, says, "I decided the hell with that—a historic event like this." *Broadcasting,* March 26, 1979.

6. *Broadcasting,* August 13, 1945.

21. A New Day

1. *The First 50 Years of Broadcasting,* p. 74. Letter from President Truman to Sol Taishoff dated July 3, 1945.

2. *Ibid.,* p. 79.

3. *Time,* October 20, 1941. For its war coverage, CBS in 1945 received the George Foster Peabody Award.

4. *Chicago Tribune,* June 21, 1978.

5. Sevareid, *Not So Wild a Dream,* p. 178.

6. *Pathfinder,* March 22, 1950.

7. White, *News on the Air,* p. 367. Presumably, "all our newsrooms" meant newsrooms at stations owned by NBC as well as the newsroom in New York.

8. Jack Shelley was writing in *The Newscaster,* issue of November 1945.

9. *Broadcasting,* December 2, 1946.

10. Charnley, *News by Radio,* p. 82.

11. Paley, *As It Happened,* footnote, p. 136.

12. Jap Gude had left CBS and was acting as Davis' agent. Among his other clients were James Thurber and William Lyon Phelps.

13. CBS Radio, May 19, 1958.

14. Culbert, *News for Everyman,* p. 147.

15. *Ibid.*

16. Sevareid spoke on April 29, 1970. The Davis quote is from *But We Were Born Free,* p. 113.

17. Robert Metz. *CBS: Reflections in a Bloodshot Eye,* p. 110.

18. Frank Thomas Roberts III, "Paul W. White: Broadcast Journalism Pioneer" (M. A. Thesis, University of Kansas, 1981), p. 79.

19. Margaret White, correspondence, January 23, 1978.

20. *Ibid.*

21. See chapter 16.

22. Telephone interview with Thomas Velotta, February 21, 1983.

23. Interview with John Daly, January 12, 1978.

24. *TV Guide,* April 19, 1980.

25. *Ibid.*

26. *Broadcasting,* November 26, 1979.

27. *Quill,* October 1980.

22. Radio's Revolution

1. From speech delivered April 11, 1979, before the Deadline Club in New York. Some radio stations scheduled news summaries on the half hour as well as on the hour, some only on the half hour.

2. *New York Times,* September 19, 1967.

3. In a letter to *Broadcasting* (August 19, 1983), Donald C. Keyes, president, WTAL, Tallahassee, said he had designed the all-news format at XETRA, sometimes confused with XTRA, the news service.

4. Joshua Mills, "Development and Refinement of All-News Programming at Radio Stations and Networks," paper presented at the annual meeting of the Association for Education in Journalism, Boston, August 1980, p. 3.

5. Richard Pack, correspondence, September 17, 1988.

6. Expense in terms of personnel is demonstrated by the fact that WINS in 1968 was employing 23 reporters (including anchors), 3 news editors, 6 writers, 26 technicians

and 72 other persons in supporting roles. One reporter was the late Jack Williams, respected teacher of broadcast journalism at the Medill School of Journalism, Northwestern University.

7. *Washington Star,* March 16, 1977.

8. Figures from the Radio Information Center, New York, were published in *Broadcasting,* September 24, 1990.

9. *Broadcasting,* February 24, 1975.

10. *Television/Radio Age,* January 15, 1979.

11. *Broadcasting,* November 22, 1976.

12. Ad in *Broadcasting,* May 2, 1983.

13. Emerson Stone, correspondence with Bliss, January 8, 1982.

14. The Senate Foreign Relations Committee was hearing testimony on U.S. involvement in Vietnam.

15. Marvin Barrett, ed., *Broadcast Journalism,* pp. 136–137.

16. Figures are from *Broadcasting,* October 30, 1989, and *Broadcasting Yearbook 1980,* p. A-7.

17. *RTNDA Communicator,* May 1983.

18. John Kittross letter to editor, *RTNDA Communicator,* July 1983.

19. *Broadcasting,* September 7, 1981.

23. Edward R. Murrow, V.P.

1. Ruth Ashton Taylor, correspondence with Bliss, August 17, 1978.

2. A William Bluem, *Documentary in American Television,* p. 68.

3. Taylor, correspondence, August 17, 1978.

4. Kendrick, *Prime Time,* p. 294.

5. Paley, *As It Happened,* p. 179.

6. *Berlin Diary* was published by Alfred A. Knopf in 1941.

7. Joseph E. Persico, *Edward R. Murrow: An American Original* (New York: McGraw-Hill, 1988), p. 252.

8. Kendrick, *Prime Time,* p. 295.

9. A. M. Sperber, *Murrow: His Life and Times* (New York: Freundlich Books, 1986), p. 283.

10. Harrison E. Salisbury, "Memoirs of an Iconoclast," *Washington Post,* February 9, 1990.

11. Sperber, *Murrow,* pp. 285–286.

12. Persico, *Edward R. Murrow,* p. 252.

13. Janet Murrow, correspondence with Bliss, May 12, 1990.

14. Kendrick, *Prime Time,* p. 324.

15. *The Rise and Fall of the Third Reich* was published by Simon and Schuster in 1960.

16. The novel was *Stranger Come Home,* published by Little, Brown in 1954.

17. William L. Shirer, *20th Century Journey: A Native's Return 1945–1988* (Boston: Little, Brown, 1990).

18. Shirer, *A Native's Return,* p. 102.

19. *Ibid.,* p. 107.

20. Dallas Townsend, correspondence with Bliss, April 12, 1990.

21. Shirer, *A Native's Return,* p. 104.

22. Interview with Bliss, February 14, 1990.

23. Shirer, *A Native's Return,* p. 104.

24. *Ibid.,* p. 93.

25. Sperber, *Murrow,* p. 286.

26. Shirer, *A Native's Return,* footnote, p. 108.

27. Sperber, *Murrow,* p. 281.

28. Interview with Bliss, April 10, 1990.

29. Persico, *Edward R. Murrow,* p. 253.

30. Eric Sevareid, conversation with Bliss, February 28, 1990.

31. Shirer, *A Native's Return,* p. 109.

32. C. E. Hooper, Inc. report for the twelve-month period ending August 31, 1946.

33. Letter to James M. Seward, executor of the Edward R. Murrow estate, June 22, 1966.

34. Shirer correspondence with Bliss, May 11, 1975.

35. *Ibid.*

36. Persico, *Edward R. Murrow,* p. 255.

37. "Edward R. Murrow with the News," CBS Radio, March 8, 1950.

38. *Ibid.,* September 29, 1947. As he would often say, no more infallibility than that of an individual whose voice is heard from one end of the bar to the other.

39. *Ibid.,* October 27, 1947.

40. *Ibid.,* June 9, 1949.

24. The Greatest Political Show on Earth

1. Audience Research, Inc., survey reported in *Broadcasting,* July 5, 1948.

2. Sig Mickelson, *From Whistle Stop to Sound Bite,* p. 29.

3. John Cameron Swayze, correspondence with Bliss, December 28, 1977.

4. Swayze, correspondence, December 28, 1977.

5. Interview with John Daly, January 12, 1978.

6. Interview with Joel Tall, July 16, 1980.

7. Heatter, *There's Good News Tonight,* p. 156.

8. *Broadcasting,* July 19, 1948.

9. *Ibid.*

10. *Ibid.*

11. *Ibid.*

12. Swayze, correspondence, December 28, 1977.

13. Robert J. Donovan, *Conflict and Crisis: The Presidency of Harry S. Truman, 1945–1948* (New York: Norton, 1977), p. 395.

14. Truman's forays were covered by the radio networks as news. His campaign swing through the West in June, for example, was covered by Bryson Rash of ABC, John Adams of CBS, Bill Hillman of Mutual, and Fred Bourgholtzer of NBC.

15. Donovan, *Conflict and Crisis,* p. 408.

16. *Broadcasting,* February 1, 1940.

17. Donovan, *Conflict and Crisis,* p. 432.

18. Interview with Daly, January 12, 1978.

19. *Ibid.* I attended the breakfast. Murrow's frustration permeated the room. He was an angry man. Cost, he believed, had taken precedence over responsibility.

20. CBS Radio, November 5, 1948.

21. Edward P. Morgan, ed., *This I Believe,* p. xi.

22. Howe, *Ashes of Victory,* p. 453.

23. CBS Radio, September 20, 1948.

24. CBS Radio, May 17, 1948.

25. Quoted in an article by Ted Berkman in the *St. Petersburg Times,* May 15, 1983. Berkman, a former ABC correspondent and author of several books, knew Polk when they were stationed together in Cairo.

25. The Roving Eye

1. An even more improved tube, the vidicon, was introduced by RCA in 1952.

2. Herbert Hoover participated in an experimental television program conducted by Bell Laboratories in 1927, but the program was transmitted between New York and Washington by cable, and Hoover was then secretary of commerce.

3. *Broadcasting,* September 19, 1977.

4. Gilbert Seldes, "Past and Present," in *Television USA: 13 Seasons* (New York: Museum of Modern Art, distributed by Doubleday, 1962), p. 8.

5. Robert Skedgell, correspondence, October 18, 1977.

6. WCBW's principal cameramen in the news studio were Edward Anhalt and Bob Bendick. Anhalt went on to become a Hollywood director, and Bendick, after becoming special events director at CBS, was associated in the production of "This Is Cinerama" and the "Today" show with Dave Garroway. Skedgell enlisted in the Army. He returned to CBS after the war and was a news executive there until his retirement.

7. The engineer-inventor, who would go on to found the Dumont Network, gave the station his own initials.

8. *Radio and Television Broadcast Primer* (Washington, D.C.: Federal Communications Commission, June, 1959), p. 10.

9. *Broadcasting Yearbook 1980,* p. A-7.

10. *Boston Globe,* June 8, 1978.

11. The word *anchor* is applied loosely. In this early period, television programs rarely switched to where news was being made.

12. Interview with John Daly, January 12, 1978.

13. Cronkite, correspondence with Bliss, December 12, 1979.

14. The concluding headlines served a practical as well as editorial purpose. In meeting time requirements, Swayze could cut the broadcast off neatly at any point.

15. Les Brown, *New York Times Encyclopedia of Television* (New York: Times Books, 1977), p. 421.

16. Cronkite, correspondence, December 12, 1979.

17. Douglas Edwards, correspondence, February 8, 1978.

18. *Ibid.*

19. *Ibid.*

20. *Ibid.*

21. *Ibid.*

22. *Washington Post,* June 22, 1979.

23. Interview with Don Hewitt, March 17, 1982.

24. Interview with Edwards, March 26, 1982.

25. Edwards, correspondence, February 8, 1978.

26. It was not the last that television audiences would see of Swayze. For more than twenty years he was the television pitchman for Timex watches. Invariably the commercial showed how a Timex watch could be abused—be stomped on by an elephant, for example—and still keep running.

27. *Variety,* December 18, 1957.

28. *Variety* had checked viewers of the Edwards program against circulation figures for the *London Daily Mirror, New York Daily News,* and *Life,* which were leaders in the newspaper and magazine fields.

26. Era of Fear

1. *Newsweek,* January 17, 1972.

2. Edward R. Murrow and Fred W. Friendly, eds., *See It Now,* p. xi.

3. *New York Times,* November 18, 1951.

4. Interview with Joseph Wershba, April 21, 1981.

5. Irwin Ross, "Thinking Man's Friend," *Television Age,* September 17, 1962.

6. Interview with Joseph Wershba.

7. Fred Friendly, *Due to Circumstances Beyond Our Control,* pp. xviii–xix. Friendly was particularly impressed by the awesomeness of the new atomic weapon, having seen Hiroshima and Nagasaki from a low-flying reconnaissance plane a few days after their devastation.

8. In the early 1980s, NBC Radio had a weekly magazine program hosted by Lloyd Dobins called "Hear and Now."

9. "Hear It Now," CBS Radio, May 18, 1951.

10. Kendrick, *Prime Time,* pp. 329–330.

11. Fred Friendly, speech at dedication of Edward R. Murrow Room, Fletcher School of Law and Diplomacy, Tufts University, April 16, 1971.

12. Friendly, *Due to Circumstances Beyond Our Control,* p. xix.

13. Palmer Williams, correspondence, July 6, 1983.

14. Friendly, *Due to Circumstances Beyond Our Control,* p. xix.

15. Visitors to CBS News in the 1950s, seeing "SIN" emblazoned in large letters outside the "See It Now" offices, often asked where *that* door led. It was something the staff rather enjoyed.

16. Williams, correspondence, July 6, 1983.

17. *Ibid.*

18. Kendrick, *Prime Time,* p. 42.

19. "A Conversation with Eric Sevareid," CBS-TV, December 13, 1977.

20. W. A. Swanberg, *Luce and His Empire* (New York: Scribner's, 1972), p. 286.

21. "Goodnight and Good Luck," BBC-TV, April 27, 1975.

22. Since September 1953 the series had been aired on Tuesdays in prime time.

23. Friendly, *Due to Circumstances Beyond Our Control,* p. 30.

24. Kendrick, *Prime Time,* p. 50.

25. *Ibid.,* p. 49.

26. Paley, *As It Happened,* p. 284.

27. Michael D. Murray, "Television's Desperate Moment: A Conversation with Fred W. Friendly," *Journalism History,* Autumn 1974.

28. Paley, *As It Happened,* p. 284.

29. *New York Times,* March 11, 1954.

30. *New York Herald Tribune,* March 11, 1954.

31. Kendrick, *Prime Time,* p. 61.

32. Roger Burlingame, *Don't Let Them Scare You* (Westport, Conn.: Greenwood Press, 1974), p. 299.

33. *Ibid.,* pp. 307–308.

34. Interview with Daly, January 12, 1978.

35. William Lawrence, *Six Presidents, Too Many Wars,* p. 200.

27. The Electronic Politician

1. *Time,* October 14, 1966.

2. Interview, "CBS Evening News With Dan Rather," CBS-TV, September 18, 1984.

3. John Corry, "What Is TV Doing to the Election Process?", *New York Times,* November 18, 1984.

4. Robert Pierpoint, *At the White House* (New York: Putnam, 1981), p. 174.

5. Eric Engberg, speech, Region 7 meeting, Society of Professional Journalists, Iowa City, March 8, 1986.

6. Peter Jennings, speech, national convention of Radio-Television News Directors Association, Nashville, September 12, 1985. For insight into how Nixon and his managers manipulated the broadcast media in the 1968 campaign, the author recommends Joe McGinniss' *The Selling of the President 1968* (New York: Trident Press, 1969).

7. Robert Lewis Shayon, "TV and Radio," *Saturday Review,* January 18, 1964.

8. William A. Henry III, "Campaign Books: Why Nobody Reads Them (Including Mine)," *Washington Journalism Review,* November 1987.

9. Thomas E. Patterson, "The Mistaken Image," *Television Quarterly* (1985), vol. 21, no. 4.

10. The name Precinct Profile Analysis (PPA) was used until someone pointed out that the first two initials, used repeatedly on Election Night, might cause embarrassment. By such concern for viewer reaction are network decisions made!

11. John Corry, "Has TV Helped Empty the Polls?" *New York Times,* January 22, 1984.

12. Cynthia Lowry, "Live and Ad Libbed," AP, January 26, 1961.

13. Max Lerner, "TV Revolution," *New York Post,* January 27, 1961.

14. Robert Pierpoint, *At the White House* (New York: Putnam, 1981), p. 70.

15. Dan Rather with Mickey Herskowitz, *The Camera Never Blinks,* pp. 12–20.

16. White House news conference, August 4, 1980.

17. Helen Thomas quoted in unsigned article, "Still Not in the Club," *The Quill,* June 1985.

18. At the Republican convention, speakers used a TelePrompTer for the first time. Herbert Hoover got ahead of the script unrolling on the new-fangled gadget and, ignoring the open mike, muttered, "Go on! Go on!"

19. *Broadcasting,* July 7, 1952.

20. Sig Mickelson, *The Electric Mirror,* p. 226. After all, newspaper reporters were being admitted into the room to witness the credentials battle.

21. *Broadcasting,* July 14, 1952.

22. These figures are from Gross, *I Looked & I Listened,* p. 220.

23. *Broadcasting,* July 14, 1952.

24. In *Six Crises* (New York: Doubleday, 1962), p. 103, Nixon says the "ploy" of using Checkers was inspired by Franklin D. Roosevelt, who spoke devastatingly in the 1944 campaign of Republicans attacking his dog Fala.

28. Korea

1. This was a radio program originating in Washington. The CBS network had no late evening television news.

2. Burlingame, *Don't Let Them Scare You,* p. 300.

3. CBS Radio, "Edward R. Murrow With the News," June 30, 1950.

4. *Ibid.,* June 27, 1950.

5. Cable dated July 13, 1950. It was addressed to Larry LeSueur, who anchored "Edward R. Murrow With the News" while Murrow was in Korea.

6. CBS Radio, "Edward R. Murrow With the News," July 7, 1950.

7. The initials M*A*S*H stand for Mobile Army Surgical Hospital. The final episode of the television series, aired on CBS-TV on January 28, 1983, attracted roughly fifty million viewers, a record for any single program up to that time. An actor in that final episode was Robert Pierpoint, the CBS correspondent, who played himself reporting from Seoul as he had 30 years before. Clete Roberts, another radio newsman in Korea, had appeared in an earlier episode.

8. Dunn says that when the Communists attacked, Folster cabled him in Manila, "Come work with me this time." In covering the Pacific campaigns of World War II, the two men had been keen rivals. Letter to Bliss, September 25, 1982.

9. Interview with Dunn, September 25, 1982.

10. William Lawrence, *Six Presidents, Too Many Wars,* p. 177.

11. CBS News biography, No. 06084, undated. Herman's narration was recorded separately on tape, not on film.

12. Correspondence with Bliss, October 22, 1989.

13. Kalischer would cover early stages of the Vietnam War for CBS.

14. Phillip Knightley, *The First Casualty,* p. 349.

15. Av Westin, *Newswatch: How TV Decides the News,* p. 87.

16. CBS-TV, "See It Now: Christmas in Korea," December 29, 1953.

17. *Ibid.*

18. Phillip Knightley, *The First Casualty,* p. 338.

19. CBS Radio, "Hear It Now," June 15, 1951.

20. Correspondence with Bliss, October 22, 1989. In his syndicated Scripps-How-

ard column, Ernie Pyle wrote almost exclusively of the life and miseries of the frontline G.I.

29. Time Out for Ratings

1. *Saturday Review,* January 8, 1972.
2. Full-page advertisement in *Broadcasting,* July 13, 1987.
3. Nielsen still uses diaries in measuring local TV audiences.
4. *New York Times,* July 16, 1965.

30. The Alarm Clock War

1. As Paar's popularity soared, the program title was changed to "The Jack Paar Show," just as with Carson it became "The Tonight Show Starring Johnny Carson."
2. NBC Nightly News, April 20, 1979.
3. *Washington Post,* August 28, 1975.
4. Robert Metz, *The Today Show,* p. 65.
5. *Ibid.,* p. 261.
6. Just as ABC for some perverse reason omits the commas demanded by good grammar in the date—day, month, year—at the start of "World News Tonight," it omits the requisite comma in its morning show title.
7. *Newsweek,* May 19, 1969.
8. AP, April 20, 1979.
9. *Broadcasting,* July 28, 1975.
10. Harry Waters, *Newsweek,* May 19, 1969.
11. Reacting to ABC's press agentry, National Public Radio took out a full-page ad in the *New York Times,* issue of October 4, 1976, to say: "We love you, too, Barbara, but you're not the first woman to cohost a national news program. Susan Stamberg has been co-anchoring [with Bob Edwards] a national news show ["All Things Considered"] since 1972."
12. *Newsweek,* May 3, 1976.
13. *Time,* May 3, 1976.
14. John Chancellor also refused to read commercial copy when he was host of "Today."
15. *Quest,* November 1980.
16. *Broadcasting,* April 4, 1983.
17. "A Case of Morning Sickness," *Newsweek,* March 13, 1989. In justice to Gumbel, he wrote the memo critiquing his colleagues at the behest of Marty Ryan, his boss.
18. "Calendar," CBS-TV, November 7, 1961.
19. *Before the Colors Fade* was published by Knopf in 1981.
20. *Variety,* April 9, 1969.
21. Although the book, *We're Going to Make You a Star,* published by Simon and Schuster in 1975, is highly critical of CBS News management, it is dedicated to Hughes Rudd, who Quinn says was sympathetic.
22. *TV Guide,* March 7, 1981.
23. *Minneapolis Star,* January 7, 1981.
24. *Boston Globe,* December 30, 1983.
25. *Newsweek,* January 20, 1975.
26. *Broadcasting,* October 20, 1975.
27. *Ibid.*
28. *Washington Post,* November 3, 1976.

29. *New York Times,* September 12, 1982.
30. *Time,* January 3, 1983.

31. Magazines of the Air

1. Cronkite, correspondence, June 29, 1978. Thousands of peacetime travelers knew the *Wakefield* as the S. S. *Manhattan.*
2. Opening words of the first program were "Hello, hello. What's the matter with this line?" Corwin thought the opening would catch listeners' attention, but CBS engineers in New York believed there were transmission difficulties and cut the program off the air.
3. A complete listing may be found in *The National Broadcasting Company in 1943* (New York: National Broadcasting Company, 1944), p. 34.
4. Ray Carroll, *Development of the Network Television Documentary,* paper presented to Radio-TV Division, Association for Education in Journalism, Boston, August 11, 1980, p. 10.
5. *New York Times,* June 27, 1975.
6. *Saturday Review,* November 4, 1967.
7. *Chicago Daily News,* November 6, 1967.
8. *New York Times,* November 6, 1967.
9. *Variety,* December 27, 1967.
10. *Time,* December 6, 1968.
11. *New York Times,* December 30, 1984.
12. *Variety,* October 30, 1968.
13. *Ibid.*
14. Bill Leonard, talk at American University, April 20, 1976.
15. *Variety,* October 30, 1968.
16. *Parade,* February 11, 1979.
17. Interview with Morley Safer, November 10, 1977.
18. *Washington Post,* November 18, 1970.
19. *New York* magazine, November 24, 1975.
20. Telephone interview with Don Hewitt, November 8, 1989.
21. *The New Yorker,* July 19, 1982.
22. Axel Madsen, *"60 Minutes": The Power and the Politics of America's Most Popular TV News Show.*
23. Westin, conversation with Bliss, April 19, 1974.
24. *Variety,* April 21, 1982.
25. Interview with Hewitt, January 16, 1985. The distinct, and distinctive, ticking of that stopwatch is no accident.
26. *The New Yorker,* July 19, 1982.
27. *Los Angeles Times,* February 6, 1964.
28. *New York Daily News,* February 4, 1964.
29. Hewitt, conversation with Bliss and others, September 26, 1984.
30. Mike Wallace and Gary Paul Gates, *Close Encounters,* p. 287.
31. Tom Shales, syndicated column, June 28, 1982.
32. *Television Quarterly,* Summer 1980.
33. Wallace and Gates, *Close Encounters,* p. 481.
34. Interview with Hewitt, January 16, 1985.
35. Author of the *WJR* article was Bill Carter, television critic for the *Baltimore Sun.*
36. "ABC Gears Up for 'Watershed' Year," *Broadcasting,* June 19, 1989.
37. "Chung's Glossy Magazine," *Washington Post,* September 25, 1989.
38. "TV View," *New York Times,* October 22, 1989.
39. *Time,* April 11, 1969.
40. John J. O'Connor, *New York Times,* December 18, 1984.
41. *Washington Post,* March 6, 1978.
42. *Saturday Review,* May 27, 1978.

43. *Broadcasting,* June 12, 1978.

44. *Newsweek,* June 19, 1978.

45. *Variety,* June 14, 1978.

46. *Ibid.*

47. *Washington Post,* March 31, 1983.

48. *Newsweek,* July 9, 1979.

49. *New York Times,* June 26, 1979.

50. "NBC Magazine With David Brinkley," September 26, 1980. The reference is to J. R. Ewing, the ruthless principal character on "Dallas."

51. *TV Guide,* September 19, 1981.

52. *Washington Post,* November 12, 1982.

53. Associated Press, September 15, 1983.

54. UPI, June 25, 1984.

55. *Time,* January 2, 1984.

56. *Variety,* April 4, 1984.

57. *Washington Post,* June 27, 1984.

58. *New York Times,* August 14, 1983. One recalls Ed Murrow writing his parents from wartime London that he was preaching.

59. Press release, December 22, 1980.

60. *Time,* October 26, 1981.

61. John Corry, *New York Times,* August 14, 1983.

62. Tom Shales, *Washington Post,* June 25, 1983.

63. Interview in *Broadcasting,* February 11, 1980.

64. *Washington Post,* December 24, 1978.

65. John O'Connor, *New York Times,* April 20, 1980.

66. *Ibid.,* May 4, 1980.

67. *Broadcasting,* August 1, 1983.

68. *Newsweek,* December 31, 1979.

69. Before "PM Magazine," Westinghouse syndicated two late-night talk shows called "PM East," originating in New York," and "PM West," originating in San Francisco. The western edition soon folded, but "PM East," with Mike Wallace as host, went on for another year.

70. *RTNDA Communicator,* October 1980.

71. *Washington Post,* December 2, 1971.

72. Quoted by Karl Vick, "Believe It or Not Television," *Washington Journalism Review,* March 1981.

32. "In Greater Depth and in Broader Scope"

1. "CBS Evening News with Walter Cronkite," September 2, 1963.

2. Memorandum by Frank Stanton to CBS employes, September 27, 1963.

3. Oliver Quayle and Company survey. In a Phillips-Sindlinger survey, 1974, Cronkite was rated "most trusted and objective television newscaster."

4. Dan Rather with Mickey Herskowitz, *The Camera Never Blinks,* p. 32.

5. *Ibid.,* p. 35. Twenty years later, delivering the Alfred M. Landon Lecture at Kansas State University, Rather quoted William S. Paley and Frank Stanton as saying, "What we are at CBS News is a public journal. A public journal is a public trust. Your job is never to forget it."

6. Barbara Matusow, *The Evening Stars,* pp. 27–28.

7. *Newsweek,* February 25, 1980.

8. It was widely reported that Rather had signed a contract calling for $8,000,000 spread over five years. On April 1, 1985, in an interview with *Broadcasting,* Rather credited Gene Jankowski, president of the CBS Broadcast Group, and Bill Leonard, retiring CBS News president, with persuading him that his future lay with CBS. It was not, Rather said, a question of money. He had received generous offers from all parties. CBS was the network with the most estimable news tradition.

9. *Washington Post,* March 3, 1982.

10. Brinkley, talk at the National Archives, Washington, D.C., January 15, 1976.

11. Joan Barthel, "When Will They Say Their Final Goodnights?", *TV Guide,* July 1, 1967.

12. Chet Huntley, *The Generous Years* (New York: Random House, 1968), p. 193.

13. Reuven Frank, correspondence, April 16, 1985.

14. NBC correspondents Frank McGee and Ray Scherer joined Huntley in defying the union. When Cronkite, like Brinkley, respected the picket line, his place as anchor on the CBS evening news was taken by a 28-year-old program administrator, Arnold Zenker. In 1952, when the Writer's Guild struck the networks, Murrow crossed the picket line to do his nightly broadcast. One of the pickets in the 1952 strike was Ernest Kinoy, who in 1985 wrote the docudrama "Murrow."

15. *New York Times,* March 22, 1974.

16. Murrow, speech before the annual meeting of the Radio-Television News Directors Association, Chicago, October 15, 1958.

17. *Broadcasting,* August 1, 1983.

18. *New York Times,* July 27, 1983.

19. Since the departure of John Cameron Swayze in 1956, the evening news at NBC has had four names: "The Huntley-Brinkley Report," "The NBC Evening News," "The NBC Nightly News," and "The NBC Nightly News with Tom Brokaw," giving him equal billing with "The CBS Evening News with Dan Rather."

20. *New York Times,* December 23, 1980.

21. The one-hour program, called "All-Star News," aired on Monday, Tuesday, Wednesday, and Friday nights. It was cut back to a half hour on Thursdays.

22. The soon to expire DuMont network carried the hearings to a much smaller audience.

23. *Congress and the Nation 1945–1964* (Washington, D.C.: Congressional Quarterly Service, 1965), p. 1721.

24. When Kintner died, he left a yet-to-be-published biography in manuscript form. In 1978, Kintner rejected my request for an interview, saying, "If you think I'm going to give away what's in my book, you're nuts." He spoke good-naturedly but meant it. The reaction was pure Kintner.

25. David G. Yellin, *Special: Fred Freed and the Television Documentary,* p. 218.

26. Julian Goodman, speech, March 22, 1976.

27. Both quotes are from a speech that Elmer Lower made at the annual meeting of the Radio-Television News Directors Association in Dallas in 1975.

28. *New York Times,* June 14, 1966.

29. CFJR-AM, Brockville, Ontario.

30. John J. O'Connor, *New York Times,* November 12, 1971.

31. "The Reasoner Report" (February 1973–June 1975).

32. *Variety,* April 5, 1967.

33. ABC News brochure, 1973.

34. *Newsweek,* May 3, 1976.

35. *Saturday Review,* June 12, 1976.

36. *Time,* May 3, 1976.

37. *New York Times,* May 2, 1976.

38. *Ibid.,* October 4, 1976.

39. *Washington Post,* October 5, 1976.

40. *USA Today,* December 4, 1984.

41. UPI, June 24, 1982.

42. Arledge, news conference, May 3, 1977.

43. *Time,* May 16, 1977.

44. *Newsweek,* August 20, 1979.

45. Such series, treating a single subject in more depth than customary on the evening news, have been appearing under different titles at all three networks ever since.

46. *Newsweek,* August 20, 1979.

47. *New York Times,* June 10, 1979.

48. Advertisement, *Washington Post,* April 16, 1979.

49. In 1989, Westin left ABC for King World Productions, where his title was senior vice president for reality programs.

50. "Good Morning America," ABC-TV, July 20, 1983.

51. *Washington Post,* July 21, 1983.

52. *New York Daily News,* February 26, 1986.

53. "ABC Earns News Parity & More," *Variety,* January 28, 1981.

54. *Time,* September 6, 1982.

55. Shortly after the premiere, the name was changed to "USA Today on TV."

56. Quoted in *New York Daily News* review, September 14, 1988.

57. Review, *New York Times,* September 20, 1988.

58. Robert Feder, "Newsman John Hart Leads 'Monitor' Team," *Chicago Sun-Times,* August 24, 1988.

33. "Let Freedom Ring . . ."

1. Telephone interview with Robert Schakne, August 21, 1986.

2. William A. Wood, *Electronic Journalism,* p. 105.

3. Bill Monroe, panel discussion, University of Missouri, November 16, 1965.

4. Harry Reasoner, *Before the Colors Fade,* p. 61.

5. Robert MacNeil, *The Right Place at the Right Time,* p. 180.

6. Byron Shafer and Richard Larson, "Did TV Create the 'Social Issue'?" *Columbia Journalism Review,* September/October 1972.

7. The victims were Andrew Goodman, Michael Schwerner, and James Chaney. In 1967, a federal jury convicted seven Ku Klux Klansmen of conspiracy to commit murder.

8. Dan Rather with Mickey Herskowitz, *The Camera Never Blinks,* p. 79.

9. MacNeil, *The Right Place at the Right Time,* p. 186.

10. *Television/Radio Age,* May 1979.

11. Telephone interview with Schakne, August 21, 1986.

12. "CBS Evening News with Walter Cronkite," CBS-TV April 5, 1968.

13. As far back as 1943, in the wake of the Detroit riots, CBS Radio had broadcast "An Open Letter on Race Hatred," a documentary produced by William N. Robson of the Columbia Workshop.

14. There is doubt today that Edmund Burke ever made the statement!

15. *Newsweek,* January 13, 1969.

16. *Newsweek,* June 15, 1964.

34. "If You're White and a Male, O.K."

1. When Worthy returned to the United States, his passport was revoked. With support from Edward R. Murrow and the American Civil Liberties Union, he filed suit in federal court on grounds that, barring actual wartime conditions, citizens have the right to free movement. The court decided for the State Department.

2. *Newsweek,* December 4, 1967.

3. *Washington Post,* April 25, 1968.

4. *New York Times Magazine,* September 15, 1968.

5. *Harper's,* June 1965.

6. *Report of the National Advisory Commission on Civil Disorders* (Kerner Commission) (New York: Bantam Books, 1968), pp. 366–385.

7. Lem Tucker, speech, RTNDA convention, New Orleans, September 10, 1981.

8. *Broadcasting,* April 24, 1989.

9. *Washington Journalism Review,* May 1981.

10. *Washington Star,* April 29, 1977.

11. Nancy Dickerson, *Among Those Present,* p. 82.
12. *New York Times,* July 4, 1976.
13. Statement released by ABC News, November 22, 1982.
14. Robert Pierpoint, *At the White House* (New York: Putnam, 1981), p. 31.
15. John Hart, RTNDA convention, Las Vegas, September 8, 1979.

35. A Season for Sorrow

1. Dan Rather with Mickey Herskowitz, *The Camera Never Blinks,* p. 119.
2. *Ibid.,* p. 120.
3. Interview with Robert Skedgell, December 6, 1989.
4. Eddie Barker, "President John F. Kennedy: DOA at Parkland Hospital," *RTNDA Communicator,* November 1988.
5. *Hearings Before the President's Commission on the Assassination of President Kennedy* (Washington: U.S. Government Printing Office, 1964), XX, p. 416.
6. Barnouw, *The Image Empire,* p. 231.
7. Rather says in *The Camera Never Blinks* (p. 127) that suggestions of how much *Life* paid for the Zapruder film range from $50,000 to $500,000. *Life* published still pictures and, within the week, sold them to newspapers. But the film itself was not shown on television until long afterward because broadcasters felt it was too gruesome for home viewing.
9. MacNeil was a correspondent for NBC from 1960 to 1967.
9. Robert MacNeil, *The Right Place at the Right Time,* pp. 215–216.
10. Melville Bell Grosvenor, "The Last Full Measure," *National Geographic,* March 1964.
11. *New York Times,* November 26, 1963.
12. *Broadcasting,* January 18, 1988.
13. *The First 50 Years of Broadcasting,* p. 166.
14. Brinkley, interview, *Broadcasting,* November 15, 1982.
15. Stanton, memorandum to all CBS employes, December 12, 1963.
16. Editorial, *New York Times,* November 25, 1963.
17. "The Long Watch," *Newsweek,* June 17, 1968.
18. *Ibid.*
19. Sirhan Sirhan, an unemployed clerk, was held in strict isolation from reporters until tried and convicted of murder. He was sentenced to life imprisonment.
20. Lawrence Laurent, "TV Responds to Tragedy," *Washington Post,* June 6, 1968.
21. UPI, June 29, 1967.
22. *Washington Post,* November 25, 1975.

36. War: The People Watched

1. Also represented at the Geneva conference were France, Great Britain, the Soviet Union, China, Laos, Cambodia, the revolutionary and predominantly Communist Viet Minh, and the Vietnamese government established by the French at Saigon.
2. "CBS Evening News With Walter Cronkite," CBS-TV, September 2, 1963.
3. "Huntley-Brinkley Report," NBC-TV, September 9, 1963.
4. The *New York Times* met its responsibility no better than CBS. In an article in *Nieman Reports* (September 1972), Tom Wicker says that following the supposed Battle of Tonkin Gulf and President Johnson's announcement of air attacks on North Vietnam in response, "we did no more [in the next day's editions] than parrot the President without any challenge or question." A large issue unexamined was the war-making powers of the president. The Tonkin Gulf resolution contributed to passage of the War Powers Act of 1973, curtailing the authority of the president to use military force.
5. Barnouw, *The Image Empire,* pp. 272–273.

6. William McGaffin, and Erwin Knoll, *Anything But the Truth* (New York: Putnam, 1968), p. 79.

7. I recall the screening of film shot inside a helicopter before and after it was shelled. One moment you saw an able-bodied airman; the next moment you saw his brain splattered on Plexiglas. No one in the CBS screening room argued for showing that.

8. Archibald MacLeish, speech, Waldorf-Astoria Hotel, December 2, 1940.

9. This is a list of network correspondents who reported from Vietnam. It includes those who came early and late. Some now work for different organizations or have died.

ABC: Charles Arnot, Steve Bell, Elliot Bernstein, Bill Brannigan, Hilary Brown, Malcolm Browne, Lou Cioffi, Kevin Delaney, Don Farmer, Ken Gale, Jim Giggans, Ken Kashiwahara, Ted Koppel, Mike McCourt, Roger Peterson, Marlene Sanders, Dave Snell, Craig Spence, George Watson. CBS: Ed Bradley, Charles Collingwood, Walter Cronkite, Morton Dean, Bruce Denning, Jed Duvall, Brian Ellis, Ed Fouhy, Murray Fromson, Jeff Gralnick, John Hart, Peter Herford, Phil Jones, Bernard Kalb, Peter Kalischer, Charles Kuralt, John Laurence, Bill McLaughlin, David Miller, Gerald Miller, Bruce Morton, Igor Oganesoff, Ike Pappas, Bill Plante, Bert Quint, Adam Raphael, Dan Rather, Hughes Rudd, Morley Safer, Bob Schakne, Eric Sevareid, Gary Shepard, Bob Simon, George Syvertsen, Richard Threlkeld, Mike Wallace, Don Webster. NBC: Lew Allison, Dean Breliss, David Burrington, Paul Cunningham, Neil Davis, Steve Delaney, Frank Donghi, Robert Goralski, Wilson Hall, Welles Hangen, Richard Hunt, Mike Jackson, Kenley Jones, Douglas Kiper, Jim Laurie, George Lewis, Ron Nessen, Jack Perkins, Jack Reynolds, John Rich, Jim Robinson, John Sharkey, Ron Steinman, Robert Toombs, Liz Trotta, Lem Tucker, Howard Tuckner, Garrick Utley, Bill Wordham.

10. After Hangen was declared dead, his widow, Patricia, and NBC gave the Museum of Broadcasting in New York a collection of his personal papers, as well as broadcast scripts and tapes.

11. Gordon Manning, correspondence, January 23, 1982.

12. *Quill,* September 1970.

13. Six years after the end of the Vietnam War, CBS News, together with *Newsweek,* arranged a reunion of surviving members of Charlie Company, which was broadcast in the "CBS Reports" series on December 12, 1981. *Newsweek,* issue of December 14, carried a detailed account. Never before had a network news organization and a national newsweekly engaged in such a cooperative effort.

14. One recalls Murrow, during the Korean War, speaking of "villages to which we have put the torch" and putting the question whether the people after their "pitiful possessions have been consumed in flames" will be more, or less, attracted to Communism (CBS Radio, August 14, 1950.)

15. David Halberstam, *The Powers That Be* (New York: Knopf, 1970), p. 491.

16. Friendly, letter to William S. Paley and Frank Stanton, February 15, 1966.

17. On May 23, 1966, three months after Friendly resigned, NBC took a full-page ad in the *New York Times* to boast that "when all three networks cover an event, it is NBC News which most often gets to the story first and stays with it longest." In particular, NBC cited its live coverage of the Senate committee hearings on the Vietnam War.

18. Gary Paul Gates, *Air Time,* p. 209.

19. News special, CBS-TV, February 27, 1968.

20. Barbara Tuchman, *The March of Folly* (New York: Knopf, 1984), p. 352.

21. *USA Today,* June 6, 1986.

22. Cronkite, letter to the *Wall Street Journal,* April 5, 1985.

23. "Goodnight, All!", *TV Guide,* August 1, 1970.

24. NBC-TV, 6:30–7:00 P.M., May 10, 1969.

25. *New York Times,* May 18, 1969.

26. "CBS Morning News With Joseph Benti" and "CBS Evening News With Walter Cronkite," CBS-TV, November 25, 1969.

27. Mike Wallace and Gary Paul Gates, *Close Encounters,* p. 234.

28. Alfred Balk and James Boylan (eds., *Our Troubled Press: Ten Years of the Columbia Journalism Review,* p. 123.

29. Kintner, memorandum dated August 1, 1963.

30. *CBS News Standards,* 1976, pp. 6–7.

31. *New York Times,* February 28, 1971.

32. "ABC Evening News With Howard K. Smith and Harry Reasoner," ABC-TV, April 1, 1971.

33. Kissinger, speech, October, 26, 1972.

34. "Vietnam: A War That Is Finished," CBS-TV, April 29, 1975.

35. *Ibid.*

36. CBS Radio, "Edward R. Murrow With the News." Typescript is undated except for year 1951.

37. CBS Radio, January 17, 1955.

38. Charles Mohr, "Once Again, Did the Press Lose Vietnam?", *Columbia Journalism Review,* November/December 1983. In a February 2 news conference, President Johnson called the Tet offensive a failure militarily.

39. Perry Deane Young, "Revision Reconsidered," *Quill,* May 1983. Young writes: "The reporters got it wrong because the MPs had it wrong. It was unfortunate, understandable, and human." The Viet Cong did penetrate the embassy compound.

40. Peter Braestrup, *Big Story,* pp. 718–719.

41. Peter Arnett, "Tet Coverage: A Debate Renewed," *Columbia Journalism Review,* January/February 1978.

42. Philip Caputo, "The War Returns to Your Living Room—With Some Answers," *TV Guide,* October 1, 1983.

43. *New York Times,* April 29,1975.

44. Alistair Cooke, *The Americans* (New York: Knopf, 1979), pp. 47–48.

37. Knights of the Camera

1. Erik Barnouw, *Documentary,* p. 154.

2. *Wall Street Journal,* October 20, 1983.

3. Bill Brannigan, correspondence, June 26, 1980.

4. Ed Bradley, correspondence, March 6, 1980, and April 3, 1980.

5. Wall Street Journal, April 1, 1971.

6. John Laurence, correspondence, June 30, 1980.

7. George A. Bailey and Lawrence W. Lichty, "Rough Justice on a Saigon Street: A Gatekeeper Study of NBC's Tet Execution Film," *Journalism Quarterly,* Summer 1972.

8. *Ibid.* Bailey and Lichty report that although an ABC cameraman was present, he did not film the actual shooting, only the scene leading up to it and the bloody aftermath.

9. Westmoreland, speech sponsored by Nova University, Fort Lauderdale, Florida, January 15, 1986.

10. John Laurence interview with Travis. Laurence correspondence with Bliss, June 28, 1980.

11. For their pictures, both Nick Ut and Eddie Adams received the Pulitzer Prize.

12. *Variety,* December 5, 1962.

13. *Quill,* June 1984.

14. CBS-TV, July 28, 1970.

15. Douglas Edwards, interview, November 10, 1982.

16. Friendly in his foreword to *See It Now,* p. xii.

17. Frank Bourgholtzer, correspondence, January 16, 1980.

18. Sevareid, *Not So Wild a Dream* (1969 ed.), p. 185.

38. Out of This World

1. The precise percentages reported by A. C. Nielsen were 92.1 and 93.9, respectively.

2. A Russian, Yuri Gagarin, made the first manned orbital flight on April 12, 1961.
3. CBS-TV, July 20, 1969.
4. CBS-TV, July 21, 1969.
5. *Times,* July 24, 1969.
6. *Ibid.*
7. Marvin Barrett and Zachary Sklar, *The Eye of the Storm,* p. 15.
8. *Variety,* July 23, 1969.
9. *New York Times,* July 18, 1969.
10. *Ibid.,* July 27, 1969.
11. CBS-TV, July 15, 1969.
12. The fact that lift-off came two hours late was a factor in the failure of the other television networks to catch the explosion live.
13. Bob Moon, "Something Went Wrong Here," *Network News,* newsletter published by Associated Press Broadcast Services, March/April 1986, pp. 1–2.
14. *New York Times,* January 30, 1986.
15. *The New Republic* in its issue of February 17, 1986, said in an editorial that "all day the network anchormen assumed the duty of telling us what to feel."
16. "Covering the Awful Unexpected," *Time,* February 10, 1986.
17. *Ibid.*
18. "60 Minutes," CBS-TV, February 2, 1986.

39. Those Panel Shows

1. George Harman in a guest lecture, School of Communication, American University, February 6, 1973.
2. Newsletter, AP Broadcasters, May 1976.
3. NBC News advertisement, *Broadcasting,* September 10, 1984.
4. Daniel Schorr, *Village Voice,* January 21, 1986.
5. *Washington Post,* August 18, 1979.
6. Robert MacKenzie, *TV Guide,* May 28, 1983.
7. "This Week With David Brinkley," ABC-TV, June 1, 1986.
8. *Village Voice,* February 8, 1983.

40. Conversations

1. "Justice Black and the Bill of Rights," CBS-TV, December 3, 1968.
2. *Saturday Review,* January 4, 1969.
3. "The Burger Years," CBS-TV, July 9, 1986. The interview was taped on June 17. By July 9, Warren Burger had retired.
4. UPI, May 27, 1977.
5. "See It Now," CBS-TV, January 4, 1955.
6. *Variety,* December 9, 1956. Because of a State Department ban on travel by American journalists to mainland China, the interview took place in Rangoon, Burma, where Zhou was visiting.
7. Bob Considine, *New York Journal-American,* September 24, 1956.
8. *Ibid.*
9. "Person to Person," CBS-TV, January 13, 1956.
10. *Time,* September 30, 1957.
11. Joseph Wershba, "Murrow vs. McCarthy: See It Now," *New York Times,* March 4, 1979.
12. "Small World," CBS-TV, October 12, 1958.
13. Harold Nicolson, *Diaries and Letters, 1930–1964,* Stanley Olson, ed. (New York: Atheneum, 1980), p. 393. The entry is for December 26, 1959.
14. In Jerusalem, Barbara Walters became the first journalist to interview Begin

and Sadat side by side. Cronkite and John Chancellor demanded and received the same privilege.

15. "TV diplomacy and Other Broadcast Quandries," supplementary report, the Alfred I. duPont-Columbia University Survey of Broadcast Journalism, Marvin Barrett, ed., *Columbia Journalism Review*, May/June 1979.

16. Mandela's statement of why he would not turn his back on Fidel Castro and Moammar Gadhafi—they had supported his movement—was picked up by the world press.

17. Tom Shales, "Kuralt's Ageless Americana," *Washington Post.*

41. Jewel in the Crown

1. A. William Bluem, *Documentary in American Television*, p. 18.
2. *Ibid.*, p. 145.
3. *Ibid.*, pp. 142–144.
4. Karl E. Meyer, "The Sunday Screen," *Saturday Review*, April 17, 1976.
5. John O'Connor, "NBC Gives a Personal View of America," *New York Times*, November 15, 1972.
6. Harry F. Waters, "Pulse of the Heartland," *Newsweek*, March 29, 1982.
7. Jack Gould, "What's a 12-Letter Word for 'Extraordinary'?," *New York Times*, October 18, 1970.
8. Bluem, *Documentary in American Television*, p. 214.
9. Interview with Bernard Birnbaum, February 4, 1986.
10. Barnouw, *The Image Empire*, p. 180.
11. *New York Times*, August 15, 1980.
12. Reuven Frank, "The Making of the Tunnel," *Television Quarterly*, Fall 1963.
13. *New York Times*, October 12, 14, 22, 1962.
14. Elmer W. Lower *et al.*, "The Making of 'Africa'," *Television Quarterly*, Fall 1967.
15. *Ibid.*
16. "Hunger in America," CBS-TV, May 21, 1968, and June 16, 1968.
17. CBS News brochure, undated.
18. Letter from Orville Freeman to Representative Carl Perkins, chairman of the House Education and Labor Committee, May 27, 1968.
19. "Hearts and Minds" won an Oscar as the best film documentary of 1975.
20. *New York Times*, February 24, 1971.
21. News conference, New Orleans, March 9, 1971.
22. On February 19, 1964, Salant had issued a memorandum, which said in part: "In no instance may a question or answer, or any part thereof, be edited to another answer or question, or any part thereof."
23. The program said the Pentagon has 30,000 offices. The number is more like 5,000.
24. Remarks at annual meetings of CBS stockholders, Los Angeles, April 21, 1971.
25. Telegram to Committee Chairman Staggers dated April 16, 1971.
26. Ben Bagdikian, "The FCC's Dangerous Decision Against NBC," *Columbia Journalism Review*, March/April 1974.
27. Letter to the FCC dated November 27, 1972.
28. Citation, George Foster Peabody Award for "Pensions: The Broken Promise," New York, May 2, 1793.
29. Speech at annual meeting of National Association of Broadcasters, Chicago, March 25, 1976. In 1974, while the legal battle over "Pensions" was still in progress, Congress passed a pension reform program.
30. Samuel A. Adams, "Vietnam Cover-up," *Harper's*, May 1975.
31. Don Kowet and Sally Bedell, "The Anatomy of a Smear," *TV Guide*, May 29, 1982.
32. In a CBS memorandum dated February 20, 1985, CBS News President Ed Joyce thanked Bud Benjamin for his report, saying: "Bud, you didn't volunteer for this

assignment, but I recall your telling me that you took on this burden because 'nothing was more important than CBS News'. How fortunate we all are that an individual of such unblemished integrity was willing to accept this kind of responsibility."

33. Joint statement, February 19, 1985.

34. *Washington Post,* February 27, 1985.

35. *Broadcasting,* June 6, 1983.

36. Talk at annual convention of Association for Education in Journalism and Mass Communication, University of Florida, August 7, 1984.

37. *New York Times,* October 4, 1983.

38. Review *Variety,* February 28, 1979.

39. Newton N. Minow, speech, National Association of Broadcasters, May 9, 1961.

40. John J. O'Connor, *New York Times,* October 18, 1973.

41. Roone Arledge, memorandum to ABC News personnel, January 2, 1979.

42. Friendly, *Due to Circumstances Beyond Our Control,* p. 92.

43. Stanton, speech, Ohio State University Institute of Radio and Television, May 6, 1959.

44. Robert MacNeil, *The People Machine,* p. 77.

45. Seventeen years after surviving the U-2 crash in the Soviet Union, Francis Gary Powers died in a helicopter accident in California. As pilot-reporter for KNBC-TV, Los Angeles, he was bringing footage of a brush fire back to the station when the helicopter crashed. The cameraman, George Spears, died with him.

46. John J. O'Connor, "Energy Crisis: Prime Subject in Prime Time," *New York Times,* September 5, 1973. ABC and CBS also broadcast prime-time specials on the energy crisis, which arose from a shortage of oil and lasted several years.

47. David G. Yellin, *Special: Fred Freed and the Television Documentary,* pp. 218–219.

48. Freed, "The Rise and Fall of the Television Documentary," *Television Quarterly,* Fall 1972.

49. "Eyes on the Prize," parts I and II, aired on PBS in 1987 and 1990.

50. Freed, "The Rise and Fall of the Television Documentary," *Television Quarterly,* Fall 1972.

42. Nixon vs. the Nets

1. A factor in the networks' decision may have been this sentence toward the end of Agnew's speech: "Whether what I have said to you tonight will be heard and seen at all by the nation is not my decision; it is not your decision; it is *their* decision." Also, for reasons having to do with integrity, it was practice to report what might be disadvantageous. When I was at CBS, the evening news leaned over backwards to report every finding made on the hazards of cigarette smoking; this at a time when the network was receiving millions of dollars in advertising revenue from cigarette manufacturers.

2. Marvin Barrett, ed., the Alfred I. duPont-Columbia University Survey of *(Broadcast Journalism) 1969–1970: Year of Challenge, Year of Crisis,* pp. 31–32.

3. *New York Times,* November 14, 1969.

4. *Ibid.*

5. *Ibid.*

6. One of the exceptions was the *Miami Herald,* which warned, "The suppressive power of federal authority is mighty and dangerous. Mr. Agnew is toying with this dynamite as no other federal official in modern times."

7. Spiro Agnew, speech, Montgomery, Alabama, Chamber of Commerce, November 20, 1969.

8. Small, *To Kill a Messenger,* p. 250.

9. Commentary, "The ABC Evening News With Frank Reynolds and Howard K. Smith," ABC-TV, November 18, 1969.

10. *Ibid.,* November 21, 1969.

11. Correspondence with Bliss, August 4, 1978. For his commentaries in 1969, Reynolds received the coveted George Foster Peabody Award.

12. "Good News Search," *Variety,* December 9, 1970.

13. Cronkite, speech, International Radio and Television Society, May 18, 1971.

14. Herbert Klein, speech, June 1, 1971.

15. William Safire, *Before the Fall* (Garden City, N.Y.: Doubleday, 1975), p. 341.

16. The antitrust suits were based on the fact that the networks produced many of their entertainment programs. NBC settled with a consent decree in 1977 and ABC and CBS in 1980. Under the settlements, the networks agreed not to acquire interest in independently produced programs and not to engage in domestic syndication.

17. Clay Whitehead, speech, Indianapolis chapter of the Society of Professional Journalists, Sigma Delta Chi, December 18, 1972.

18. *Washington Evening Star and Daily News,* December 20, 1972.

19. Julius Duscha, "Whitehead? Who's Whitehead?" *Progressive,* April 1973.

20. This was a segment of "The Great American Dream Machine" in which three youths said FBI agents engaged them to promote acts of violence as a means of entrapping campus militants.

21. There were more than 15,000 responses on behalf of the program, including donations.

22. "CBS Evening News With Walter Cronkite," CBS-TV, October 10, 1973.

23. Carl Bernstein and Bob Woodward, *All the King's Men* (New York: Warner Paperback Library edition, 1975), p. 21.

24. Lewis J. Paper, *Empire: William S. Paley and the Making of CBS,* p. 275.

25. The two reports were unusual in their length but not unprecedented. A few weeks earlier, the CBS evening news had carried a similar two-part series on a controversial multimillion-dollar wheat agreement with Moscow. Talking with Cronkite on the evening of October 31, I detected no sense of intimidation on his part. What disturbed him was the possibility that, coming so soon before the presidential election, the series might be construed as a plot to deny Nixon a second term. "It isn't that, of course," he said. "There are all these facts, confusing, scattered all around. To make sense out of them, they have to be brought together. We'd have tried to do it any time, as we did with the grain deal, another confusing story. It's just something we thought needed to be done."

26. Barbara Matusow, *The Evening Stars,* p. 130.

27. Theodore H. White, *Breach of Faith: The Fall of Richard Nixon* (New York: Atheneum, 1975), p. 229.

28. Rather was taken off the White House beat five days after Nixon resigned. Earlier reassignment would have had the appearance of yielding to pressure.

29. Dean's secretary gave Pierpoint the information over the telephone on April 19, 1973, and it was quickly confirmed.

30. Nixon news conference, October 26, 1973.

31. "ABC Evening News with Harry Reasoner and Howard K. Smith," ABC-TV, October 31, 1973. The *New York Times* called for Nixon's resignation on November 4, 1973.

43. Electronic Coverage: Congress and the Courts

1. "What TV Should Contribute to the U.S. As Seen by Eleven Distinguished Americans," *TV Guide,* June 28, 1975. What Minow said in 1961, addressing the National Association of Broadcasters' annual meeting, was that if you watch a television station uninterruptedly from sign-on to sign-off, "I can assure you that you will observe a vast wasteland." Of all broadcast criticism, this is probably the phrase best remembered.

2. Address before the Advertising Council, New York, December 15, 1969.

3. Sydney W. Head, *Broadcasting in America: A Survey of Television and Radio,* 3d ed. (Boston: Houghton Mifflin, 1976), p. 503.

4. Max Wylie, *Clear Channels,* p. 52.

5. *Congressional Record,* February 23, 1961, 107:2440.

6. The congressman was Representative Bud Shuster, Republican of Pennsylvania. The name he gave the duck in his performance of August 27, 1980, was Donald Democrat.

7. James Reston, editorial, *Broadcasting,* June 9, 1986.

3. "TV in the Senate: One Year After," *Broadcasting,* June 1, 1987.

9. Thomas P. O'Neill, interview, C-SPAN, March 19, 1984.

10. Hugh Terry, president and general manager of KLZ-AM-TV, Denver, led the fight against Canon 35 in Colorado and for his "significant contribution to radio and TV journalism" in 1956 received the first Paul White Award conferred by RTNDA.

11. Ben Silver, interview, April 10, 1983. Silver joined CBS News in 1966 and now teaches broadcast journalism at Arizona State University.

12. The proposal was made to the ABA's special committee on possible revision of Judicial Canon 35 on February 18, 1962.

13. *Estes v. Texas,* 381 U.S. 532 (1965).

14. "Florida Trial of 'TV Addict' Goes on the Air," *Broadcasting,* October 3, 1977.

15. *Richmond Newspapers v. Virginia,* 448 U.S. 555 (1980).

16. *Chandler v. Florida,* 449 U.S. 560 (1981).

17. NBC Newsletter, February 1981.

18. For example, when the Arizona Supreme Court authorized broadcast coverage its guidelines specified one pool camera and one still photographer with the work of both to be shared with all media. Members of juries were not to be photographed.

19. Warren Burger, National Press Club speech, December 19, 1985.

20. Burger, letter dated February 18, 1986.

21. Burger, letter dated March 6, 1986.

44. The Longest Battle

1. Richard B. Salant, speech, Oregon Association of Broadcasters, Portland, November 8, 1968.

2. Richard Cheverton, keynote address, RTNDA convention, Los Angeles, November 20, 1968. Today no speaker would address members of an RTNDA audience as "gentlemen." Scores of women have become news directors in recent years.

3. Quoted by Murrow on "Edward R. Murrow With the News," CBS Radio, June 16, 1959.

4. *Farmers' Educational and Cooperative Union of America, North Dakota Division v. WDAY, Inc.,* 360 U.S. 525, 79 S. Ct. 1302 (1959).

5. *United Broadcasting (WHKC),* 10 FCC 515, June 26, 1945.

6. *Petition of Robert Harold Scott for Revocation of Licenses of Radio Stations KQW, KPO and KFRC,* 11 FCC 372, July 19, 1946.

7. *Applicability of the Fairness Doctrine in the Handling of Controversial Issues of Public Importance,* 29 Fed. Reg. 10415, adopted July 1, 1964, printed July 25, 1964.

8. Program in "Christian Crusade" series WGCB-AM, November 27, 1964. The magazine to which Hargis referred was *The Nation.*

9. *Red Lion Broadcasting Company v. Federal Communications Commission, United States v. Radio-Television News Directors Association,* 395 U.S. 367 (1969). In *The Good Guys, the Bad Guys and the First Amendment,* Fred Friendly details how the Democratic National Committee used the Fairness Doctrine to discourage right-wing attacks on policies of the Kennedy and Johnson administrations. Example: "Virtually every time a Hargis . . . denounced the test ban treaty, a letter was sent out [to stations that aired the attack] demanding reply time under the Fairness Doctrine" (p. 34).

10. *Miami Herald Publishing Company v. Tornillo,* 418 U.S. 241 (1974).

11. "Electronic Journalism and First Amendment Problems," recommendations of Communications Law Committee, Section on Science and Technology, American Bar Association, *Federal Communications Bar Journal,* November 1, 1976.

12. *Letter from Federal Communications Commission to Television Station WCBS-TV,* 8 FCC 2d 381, June 2, 1967. In 1970, the FCC was asked, because of auto emissions, to

expand its ruling in *Banzhaf* to include commercials for gasoline and cars. It declined, saying it would not extend the ruling to include general advertising.

13. Congress' action cost broadcasters more than 200 million dollars a year in revenue.

14. Later, the station changed its statement to say that it had not aired any *locally produced* program on the strip mining issue.

15. Editorial, *Broadcasting,* June 21, 1976.

16. *New York Times v. United States,* 403 U.S. 713 (1971).

17. *Herbert v. Lando,* 441 U.S. 153 (1979). The court had held in *New York Times v. Sullivan,* 376 U.S. 254 (1964), that, in suing for libel, public figures must prove "actual malice" as well as falsehood. Herbert was a public figure because of his best-seller *Soldier,* written in collaboration with James Wooten and published—ironic twist—by Holt, Rinehart & Winston, owned by CBS. He also had appeared on talk shows and the lecture circuit.

18. Editorial, *Broadcasting,* April 23, 1979.

19. *Branzburg v. Hayes,* 408 U.S. 664 (1972).

20. Howard K. Smith, keynote address, RTNDA convention, Las Vegas, September 6, 1979.

21. Hearing, House Ethics Committee, September 15, 1976.

22. Dan Schorr, *Clearing the Air.* pp. 137–258.

23. *Zurcher v. Stanford Daily,* 436 U.S. 547 (1978).

24. Smith, address, RTNDA Convention, Las Vegas, September 6, 1979.

25. *Gannett Co. v. DePasquale,* 443, U.S. 368 (1979). The case involved a murder suspect whose attorney argued that the pretrial hearing be closed.

26. Anthony Lewis, "Stopping Secret Trials," *New York Times,* September 10, 1979.

27. *Richmond Newspapers, Inc. v. Commonwealth of Virginia,* 448 U.S. 555 (1980).

28. U.S. Court of Appeals, D.C., January 16, 1987.

29. "Supreme Court Rejects Appeal for Reinstatement of Fairness Doctrine," *RTNDA Intercom,* January 15, 1990.

45. Cable: A Major Competitor

1. *Newsweek,* July 3, 1978.

2. Irwin Mazo, Savannah investor and former business associate of Turner, quoted in the *Wall Street Journal,* June 5, 1987.

3. Edwin Diamond, "Ted Turner's Olympic Quest," *New York,* July 14, 1986.

4. WRET-TV.

5. Ted Turner was speaking at B'nai B'rith's Edward R. Murrow Awards ceremony, New York, May 28, 1987. Although Turner may not have realized how formidable a project he was undertaking, he did have the example of HBO, which in 1978 had plans for a 24-hour news service but abandoned them due to lack of support from advertisers.

6. Lincoln Furber, "Cable News Readies for June Debut," RTNDA Communicator, April 1980.

7. For awhile, at the start, CNN Headline News was called CNN2.

8. In 1984, a year after its passing, "Overnight" with Linda Ellerbee and Lloyd Dobyns received the prestigious duPont-Columbia Award.

9. "Has CNN Met Its Match?", *Newsweek,* June 28, 1982.

10. Laurence Zuckerman, "The Raw News Network Hits Its Stride," *Columbia Journalism Review,* March/April 1986.

46. The Fourth Revolution

1. Asaac Asimov, "Toward the Global Village: The Fourth Revolution," *Saturday Review,* October 24, 1970.

2. Arthur C. Clarke, "Extraterrestrial Relays," *Wireless World,* October 1945.

3. Details of how Friendly, Buksbaum, and others, overcoming what seemed impossible obstacles, produced the Telstar broadcast make one of the best stories in broadcasting. Nowhere is it told better than by Av Westin in his book, *Newswatch: How Television Gathers and Delivers the News.*

4. Syncom I blew up soon after launch.

5. Gould, "What Did the Early Bird Catch Today?," *New York Times,* May 9, 1965.

6. John Horn, "Early Bird Highlight: BBC's News of U.S.," *New York Herald Tribune,* May 4, 1965.

7. Memorandum to staff, May 4, 1965.

8. Richard K. Doan, "TV Worry: Early Bird Rates," *New York Herald Tribune,* May 13, 1965.

9. CBS memorandum, January 30, 1968. The Vietnam War was the first in which the networks employed satellites, though on a limited basis. When the Pacific satellite was used, film went by jet from Saigon to the network bureau in Tokyo. After processing in Tokyo the story was relayed by satellite to New York. At that time, Pacific satellite service cost $3,000 for a minimum of 10 minutes. The first war reported daily via satellite from a war zone was the Arab–Israeli conflict of 1973. This was possible because the film-processing facilities and an Israeli ground station were available.

47. Local Ain't So Local Anymore

1. Advertisement, *Broadcasting,* June 16, 1980.

2. Full-page advertisement, *Broadcasting,* January 10, 1977.

3. Les Brown, "TV Syndication by Satellite Is Set Up," *New York Times,* March 12, 1979.

4. Norman Wagy, "Piggyback Arrangement Speeds Same-Day Service from Washington to Storer Net," *RTNDA Communicator,* February 1980.

5. Bruce Finland of Potomac News, Inc., quoted in "End-Running the Networks" by Tom McNichol, *Columbia Journalism Review,* March/April 1985.

6. Ku-band is a range of broadcast frequencies higher than the frequency range known as C-band. Because Ku-band frequencies are more powerful than C-band frequencies, they make possible smaller, less expensive antennae and receiving dishes.

7. *Broadcasting-Cable Yearbook 1989* (Washington, D.C.: Broadcasting Publications, 1989), F69-F72.

8. *Broadcasting-Cable Yearbook, 1989,* pp. F67-F69.

9. The NBC Moscow bureau helped the WCSM-TV team with equipment and logistics.

10. Editorial, *Broadcasting,* November 16, 1987.

11. Monica Collins, "On the Road: Are Traveling Anchors Tracking Real News?," *USA Today,* April 1, 1985.

48. Time of Trial

1. After the round of cuts in 1986, the ABC News staff totaled about 1,070 and CBS News and NBC News about 1,300.

2. Peter J. Boyer, "The Spendthrift Turns Miser at ABC," *New York Times,* April 2, 1986.

3. Jennet Conant, "Michael Gartner: What's Behind the Bow Tie?" *Manhattan, Inc.,* March 1989.

4. Peter J. Boyer, *Who Killed CBS?* (New York: Random House, 1988).

5. *Due to Circumstances Beyond Our Control* is available in a paperback edition published in 1968 by Vintage Books. The others are *In the Storm of the Eye* by Bill Leonard, *Bad News at Black Rock* by Peter McCabe, *Who Killed CBS?* by Peter J. Boyer, and *Prime Times, Bad Times* by Ed Joyce.

6. Shales, "In the Storm of CBS' Eye," *Washington Post,* October 28, 1985.

7. Ron Rosenbaum, "The Man Who Married Dan Rather," *Esquire,* November 1982. Rosenbaum was quoting Rather, who said Sauter wanted "moments," defined as those times when "somebody watches something and *feels* it, *tastes* it, and *knows* it." Sauter, he said, wanted several such moments of intense feeling in every broadcast.

8. Eric Barnouw, Lecture, Library of Congress, May 7, 1976.

9. Murrow, speech, RTNDA convention, Chicago, October 15, 1958.

10. *Time,* November 4, 1985.

11. *TV Guide,* July 2, 1988.

12. *Washington Post,* March 10, 1987.

13. *Variety,* September 25, 1985.

14. Peter J. Boyer, *Who Killed CBS?,* p. 319.

15. Shales, "In the Storm of CBS' Eye," *Washington Post,* October 28, 1985.

16. Peter J. Boyer, "14 Reporters Among 215 Cut by CBS," *New York Times,* March 7, 1987.

17. Rather, "From Murrow to Mediocrity?", *New York Times,* March 10, 1987.

18. Diamond, "The Big Chill," *New York,* August 11, 1986.

19. Personal correspondence I have received expresses the mood of the traditionalists. An editor wrote, "The inmates have taken over the asylum." A correspondent said he was depressed by so many goodbye parties "and the journalistic schlock emanating from your own place of work." "I can't believe it," wrote a retiree who had worked with Murrow. "Everyone I meet says I should be glad I'm not there."

20. The blunder would have cost CBS another million dollars if Phyllis George had not let the network out of its contract for the second year.

49. End of an Era

1. Frank LePore, "No-Doz News," *The Quill,* October 1982.

2. Vermont Royster, "Thinking Things Over," *Wall Street Journal,* July 21, 1982.

3. *Life,* February 1971.

4. Newman. "Some Thoughts About the News Business," *Television Quarterly,* summer 1983.

5. Shales, *On the Air!,* pp. 194–195.

6. Hart, "Television News: What For?," *RTNDA Communicator,* September 1988.

7. Murrow, RTNDA convention, Chicago, October 15, 1958.

8. Chancellor, RTNDA convention, Las Vegas, September 24, 1983.

9. Halberstam, *The Powers That Be,* p. 40.

10. The docudrama "Murrow" was carried by Home Box Office during the week of January 19, 1986.

50. A New Age

1. Barnouw, *The Image Empire,* p. 301.

2. Editorial, *Broadcasting,* January 25, 1988.

3. Panel discussion, "The Future of TV News," sponsored by the Center for Communications, New York, March 1, 1988.

4. "NTIA Telecom 2000: Charting the Course for a New Century," National Telecommunications and Information Administration, U.S. Department of Commerce, October 1988.

5. Salant, speech, RTNDA national convention, Las Vegas, September 8, 1979.

6. Emerson Stone, "News Practices," *RTNDA Communicator,* June 1989.

7. Jonathan Alter, "Anchor Away: At Home Abroad," *Newsweek,* March 10, 1986.

8. Rather interview, *Broadcasting,* March 10, 1986.

9. Quoted by Arthur Unger, "The Future of TV News," part two, *Christian Science Monitor,* December 1, 1987.

10. Lamb interview, "Bringing Government to the People," *Broadcasting,* April 3, 1989.

11. Friendly, speech, RTNDA convention, Salt Lake City, August 29, 1986.

12. Sylvia Chase, "Why I Left a Network to Anchor Local News," *TV Guide,* October 11, 1986.

13. Bernard Shaw, "CNN's Anchoring Reporter," *Broadcasting,* April 24, 1989.

14. Survey conducted by Bliss. *New York Times* listings appeared June 4, June 11, June 18, and June 25, 1989.

15. "Manning the Barricades for Free TV," *Broadcasting,* April 25, 1989.

16. These figures from *Broadcasting-Cable Yearbook 1989* are for January 1989.

17. Scripps lecture, University of Nevada at Reno, April 2, 1987.

18. Murrow upon accepting the NAB's Distinguished Service Award, 1962.

19. George Will, "War's Long Echoes," *Washington Post,* January 18, 1991.

Bibliography

Abell, Tyler, ed. *Drew Pearson Diaries, 1949–1959*. New York: Holt, Rinehart and Winston, 1974.

Adams, William C., ed. *Television Coverage of the Middle East*. Norwood, N.J.: Ablex, 1981.

Adams, William C., ed., *Television Coverage of International Affairs*. Norwood, NJ: Ablex, 1982.

Adams, William C., ed., *Television Coverage of the 1980 Presidential Campaign*. Norwood, N.J.: Ablex, 1983.

Adams, William C. and Fay Schreibman, eds. *Television Network News*. Washington, D.C.: George Washington University Press, 1978.

Adler, Renata. *Reckless Disregard: Westmoreland v. CBS et al.; Sharon v Time*. New York: Knopf, 1986.

Agee, Warren K., ed. *Mass Media in a Free Society*. Lawrence: University Press of Kansas, 1969.

Agee, Warren K., Phillip H. Ault, and Edwin Emery. *Introduction to Mass Communications*. 9th ed. New York: Harper & Row, 1988.

Alcott, Carroll. *My War With Japan*. New York: Holt, 1943.

Alexander, Shana. *Talking Woman*. New York: Delacorte Press, 1976.

Altheide, David L. *Creating Reality: How TV News Distorts Events.* Beverly Hills: Sage, 1976.

Altheida, David L. *Media Power.* Beverly Hills: Sage, 1985.

Archer, Gleason L. *History of Radio to 1926.* New York: American Historical Society, 1938.

Arlen, Michael J. *The Living Room War.* New York: Viking Press, 1969.

Arlen, Michael J. *The View From Highway One.* New York: Farrar, Straus & Giroux, 1976.

Arlen, Michael J. *The Camera Age.* New York: Farrar, Straus & Giroux, 1981.

Aumente, Jerome. *New Electronic Pathways: Videotex, Teletext and Online Databases.* Newbury Park, Calif.: Sage, 1987.

Bagdikian, Ben. *The Information Machines.* New York: Harper & Row/Torch, 1971.

Baker, John C. *Farm Broadcasting: The First Sixty Years.* Ames: Iowa State University Press, 1981.

Balk, Alfred and James Boylan, eds. *Our Troubled Press: Ten Years of the Columbia Journalism Review.* Boston: Little, Brown, 1971.

Bannister, Harry. *The Education of a Broadcaster.* New York: Simon & Schuster, 1965.

Barber, Susanna. *News Camera in the Courtroom: A Free Press—Fair Trial Debate,* Norwood, N.J.: Ablex, 1986.

Barnouw, Erik. *Mass Communication.* New York: Holt, Rinehart & Winston, 1956.

Barnouw, Erik. *A Tower in Babel.* New York: Oxford University Press, 1966.

Barnouw, Eric. *The Golden Web.* New York: Oxford University Press, 1968.

Barnouw, Erik. *The Image Empire.* New York: Oxford University Press, 1970.

Barnouw, Erik. *Documentary: A History of Non-fiction Film.* New York: Oxford University Press, 1974.

Barnouw, Erik. *Tube of Plenty: The Evolution of American Television.* New York: Oxford University Press, 1975.

Barrett, Marvin. *Survey of Broadcast Journalism 1968–1969.* New York: Grosset & Dunlap, 1969.

Barrett, Marvin. *Survey of Broadcast Journalism 1969–1970: Year of Challenge, Year of Crisis.* New York: Grosset & Dunlap, 1970.

Barrett, Marvin. *Survey of Broadcast Journalism 1970–1971: A State of Siege.* New York: Grosset & Dunlap, 1971.

Barrett, Marvin. *Survey of Broadcast Journalism 1971–1972: The Politics of Broadcasting.* New York: Crowell, 1973.

Barrett, Marvin. *Survey of Broadcast Journalism: Rich News, Poor News.* New York: Crowell, 1978.

Barrett, Marvin, ed. *Broadcast Journalism 1979–1981.* New York: Everest House, 1982.

Barrett, Marvin and Zachary Sklar. *Survey of Broadcast Journalism: The Eye of the Storm.* New York: Lippincott & Crowell, 1980.

Barrett, Rona. *Miss Rona.* Los Angeles: Nash, 1974.

Bayley, Edwin R. *Joe McCarthy and the Press*. Madison: University of Wisconsin Press, 1981.

Beasley, Maurine and Sheila Gibbons. *Women in Media: A Documentary Source Book*. Washington, D.C.: Women's Institute for Freedom of the Press, 1977.

Benjamin, Burton. *The CBS Benjamin Report: CBS Reports "The Uncounted Enemy: A Vietnam Deception": An Examination*. Washington, D.C.: Media Institute, 1984.

Benjamin, Burton. *Fair Play: CBS, General Westmoreland, and How a Television Documentary Went Wrong*. New York: Harper & Row, 1988.

Bergreen, Laurence. *Look Now, Pay Later*. Garden City, N.Y.: Doubleday, 1980.

Bilby, Kenneth. *The General: David Sarnoff and the Rise of the Communication Industry*. New York: Harper & Row, 1986.

Bittner, John P. and Denise A. *Radio Journalism*. Englewood Cliffs, N.J.: Prentice-Hall, 1977.

Bittner, John R. *Broadcast Law and Regulation*. New York: Prentice-Hall, 1981.

Blair, Gwenda. *Almost Golden: Jessica Savitch and the Selling of Television News*. New York: Avon, 1988.

Blanchard, Robert O. *Congress and the News Media*. New York: Hastings House, 1974.

Bliss, Edward, Jr., ed. *In Search of Light: The Broadcasts of Edward R. Murrow, 1938–1961*. New York: Knopf, 1967.

Bluem, William A. *Documentary in American Television*. New York: Hastings House, 1965.

Blum, Daniel. *A Pictorial History of Television*. Philadelphia: Chilton Press, 1959.

Blyskal, Jeff and Marie. *PR: How the Public Relations Industry Writes the News*. New York: Morrow, 1985.

Bogart, Leo. *The Age of Television*. New York: Ungar, 1956, 1958, 1972.

Bortz, Paul and Harold Mendelsohn. *Radio Today—And Tomorrow*. Washington, D.C.: National Association of Broadcasters, 1983.

Bower, Robert T. *Television and the Public*. New York: Holt, Rinehart and Winston, 1973.

Boyer, Peter J. *Who Killed CBS? The Undoing of America's Number One News Network*. New York: Random House, 1988.

Braestrup, Peter. *Big Story: How the American Press and Television Reported and Interpreted the Crisis of Tet 1968 in Vietnam and Washington*. Boulder, Colo.: Westview, 1977.

Brewin, Bob and Sydney Shaw. *Vietnam on Trial: Westmoreland vs. CBS*. New York: Atheneum, 1987.

Broadcasting Magazine. *The First 50 Years of Broadcasting*. Washington, D.C.: Broadcasting Publications, 1982.

Broussard, E. Joseph and Jack Holgate. *Writing and Reporting Broadcast News*. New York: Macmillan, 1982.

Brown, Cecil. *Suez to Singapore*. New York: Random House, 1942.

Brown, Les. *Television: The Business Behind the Box.* New York: Harcourt Brace Jovanovich, 1971.

Brown, Les. *Encyclopedia of Television.* 2nd ed. New York: Times Books, 1986.

Bulman, David, ed. *Molders of Opinion.* Bruce: Milwaukee, 1945.

Campbell, Robert. *The Golden Years of Broadcasting.* New York: Scribner's, 1976.

Carnegie Commission of Educational Television. *Public Television: A Program for Action.* New York: Carnegie Corporation, 1967.

CBS *Election Guide.* New York: Columbia Broadcasting System, 1964.

Chancellor, John and Walter R. Means. *The News Business.* New York: Harper & Row, 1983.

Charnley, Mitchell V. *News by Radio.* New York: Macmillan, 1948.

Charnley, Mitchell V. and Blair Charnley. *Reporting.* 4th ed. New York: Holt, Rinehart and Winston, 1979.

Chester, Edward W. *Radio, Television and American Politics.* New York: Sheed and Ward, 1969.

Cole, Barry, ed. *Television Today: A Close-up View.* New York: Oxford University Press, 1981.

Collier, Barney. *Hope and Fear in Washington.* New York: Dial Press, 1975.

Columbia Broadcasting System. *Crisis.* New York: CBS, 1938.

Columbia Broadcasting System. *From D-Day Through Victory in Europe.* New York: CBS, 1945 (paper).

Columbia Broadcasting System. *From Pearl Harbor into Tokyo.* New York: CBS, 1945 (paper).

Columbia Broadcasting System. *10:56:20 P.M. EDT 7/20/69: The Historic Conquest of the Moon as Reported to the American People by CBS News Over the CBS Television Network.* New York: CBS, 1970.

Corcoran, Paul E. *Political Language and Rhetoric.* Austin: University of Texas Press, 1979.

Corry, John. *TV News and the Dominant Culture.* Washington, D.C.: Media Institute, 1986.

Corwin, Norman. *This is War!* New York: Dodd, Mead, 1942.

Craft, Christine. *An Anchorwoman's Story.* Santa Barbara: Capra Press, 1986.

Crosby, John. *Out of the Blue.* New York: Simon & Schuster, 1952.

Crouse, Timothy. *The Boys on the Bus.* New York: Random House, 1973.

Culbert, David Holbrook. *News for Everyman: Radio and Foreign Affairs in Thirties America.* Westport, Conn.: Greenwood Press, 1976.

Davis, Elmer. *But We Were Born Free.* Indianapolis: Bobbs-Merrill, 1952, 1953, and 1954.

De Forest, Lee. *Father of Radio: An Autobiography.* Chicago: Wilcox & Follett, 1950.

Diamond, Edwin. *Sign Off: The Last Days of Television.* Cambridge: M.I.T. Press, 1982.

Dickerson, Nancy. *Among Those Present.* New York: Random House, 1976.

Donahue, Hugh Carter. *The Battle to Control Broadcast News.* Cambridge, Mass.: M.I.T. Press, 1989.

Donaldson, Sam. *Hold On, Mr. President!* New York: Random, House, 1987.

Dorfman, Ron and Harry Fuller, Jr., eds. *Reporting, Writing, Editing: "The Quill" Guides to Journalism.* Dubuque, Iowa: Kendall/Hunt, 1983.

Dunlap, Orrin, E., Jr. *History of Broadcasting: Radio to Television.* New York: Arno Press and the *New York Times,* 1971. (Originally published in 1932 by Harper & Bros. as *The Outlook for Television.*)

Dunn, William J. *Pacific Microphone.* College Station, Texas: Texas A&M Press, 1988.

Dunning, John. *Tune in Yesterday: The Ultimate Encyclopedia of Old-Time Radio, 1925–1976.* Englewood Cliffs, N.J.: Prentice-Hall, 1976.

Efron, Edith. *The News Twisters.* Los Angeles: Nash, 1971.

Efron, Edith. *How CBS Tried to Kill a Book.* Los Angeles: Nash, 1972.

Ellerbee, Linda. *"And So It Goes".* New York: Putnam, 1986.

Emery, Edwin. *The Press and America: An Interpretive History of the Mass Media.* 3rd ed. Englewood Cliffs, N.J.: Prentice-Hall, 1972.

Epstein, Edward J. *News from Nowhere.* New York: Random House, 1973.

Epstein, Edward J. *Between Fact and Fiction.* New York: Random House, 1975.

Fang, Irving E. *Those Radio Commentators!* Ames: Iowa State University Press, 1977.

Fang, Irving E. *Television News/Radio News.* 4th ed. St. Paul, Minn.: Rada Press, 1985.

Faulk, John Henry. *Fear on Trial.* New York: Simon & Schuster, 1964.

Ferrell, Robert H., ed. *The Diary of James C. Hagerty: Eisenhower in Midcourse, 1954–1955.* Bloomington: Indiana University Press, 1983.

Fielding, Raymond. *The March of Time: 1935–1951.* New York: Oxford University Press, 1983.

Flannery, Harry W. *Assignment to Berlin.* New York: Knopf, 1942.

Fornatale, Peter and Joshua Mills. *Radio in the Television Age.* Woodstock, N.Y.: Overlook Press, 1980.

Friendly, Fred W. *Due to Circumstances Beyond Our Control.* New York: Random House, 1967.

Friendly, Fred W. *The Good Guys, the Bad Guys and the First Amendment.* New York: Random House, 1975.

Friendly, Fred W. *Minnesota Rag: The Dramatic Story of the Landmark Supreme Court Case That Gave New Meaning to Freedom of the Press.* New York: Random House, 1981.

Friendly, Fred W. and Edward R. Murrow (eds.), *See It Now.* New York: Simon & Schuster, 1955.

Fury, Kathleen. *Dear "60 Minutes."* New York: Simon & Schuster, 1984.

Gans, Herbert J. *Deciding What's News: A Study of CBS Evening News, NBC Nightly News, Newsweek and Time.* New York: Pantheon, 1979.

Garay, Ronald. *Congressional Television: A Legislative History.* Westport, Conn.: Greenwood Press, 1984.

Garst, Robert E. and Theodore M. Bernstein. *Headlines and Deadlines.* 4th ed. New York: Columbia University Press, 1982.

Gates, Gary Paul. *Air Time: The Inside Story of CBS News.* New York: Harper & Rowe, 1978.

Gelfman, Judith S. *Women in Television News.* New York: Columbia University Press, 1976.

Gibbons, Edward. *Floyd Gibbons, Your Headline Hunter.* New York: Exposition Press, 1953.

Gilbert, Douglas. *Floyd Gibbons, Knight of the Air.* New York: Robert McBride, 1930.

Gordon, Matthew. *News Is a Weapon.* Introduction by Elmer Davis. New York: Knopf, 1942.

Graham, Fred. *Happy Talk: Confessions of a TV Newsman.* New York: Norton, 1989.

Gramling, Oliver. *AP: The Story of News.* New York: Farrar and Rinehart, 1940.

Green, Maury. *Television News: Anatomy and Process.* Belmont, Calif.: Wadsworth, 1969.

Greenfield, Jeff. *Television: The First Fifty Years.* New York: Abrams, 1977.

Greenfield, Jeff. *The Real Campaign: The Media and the Battle for the White House.* New York: Summit Books, 1982.

Gross, Ben. *I Looked & I Listened.* New Rochelle, N.Y.: Arlington House, 1954, 1970.

Halberstam, David. *The Best and the Brightest.* New York: Random House, 1969.

Halberstam, David. *The Powers That Be.* New York: Dell, 1980.

Hallin, Daniel C. *The "Uncensored War": The Media and Vietnam.* New York: Oxford University Press, 1986.

Hammond, Charles M., Jr. *The Image Decade: Television Documentary, 1965– 1975.* New York: Hastings House, 1981.

Head, Sidney W., Christopher H. Sterling, and Rogert D. Wimmer. *Broadcasting in America: A Survey of Television, Radio, and New Technologies.* 6th ed. Boston: Houghton Mifflin, 1989.

Heatter, Gabriel. *There's Good News Tonight.* Garden City, N.Y.: Doubleday, 1960.

Hess, Stephen. *The Washington Reporters.* Washington, D.C.: Brookings Institute, 1981.

Hewitt, Don. *Minute by Minute.* New York: Random House, 1985.

Hiett, Helen. *No Matter Where.* New York: Dutton, 1944.

Hofstetter, Richard. *Bias in the News.* Columbus: Ohio State University Press, 1976.

Hohenberg, John. *Between Two Worlds.* New York: Praeger, 1967.

Hohenberg, John. *A Crisis for the American Press.* New York: Columbia University Press, 1978.

Hohenberg, John. *The Professional Journalist.* 4th ed. New York: Holt, Rinehart and Winston, 1979.

Hosley, David H. *As Good As Any: Foreign Correspondence on American Radio, 1930–1940.* Westport, Conn.: Greenwood Press, 1984.

Hosley, David H. and Gayle K. Yamada. *Hard News: Women in Broadcast Journalism.* Westport, Conn.: Greenwood Press, 1987.

Howe, Quincy. *The News and How to Understand It.* New York: Simon & Schuster, 1940.

Hulteng, John L. and Roy Paul Nelson. *The Fourth Estate.* New York: Harper & Row, 1983.

Husing, Ted. *Ten Years Before the Mike.* New York: Farrar & Rinehart, 1935.

Jakes, John. *Great Women Reporters.* New York: Putnam, 1969.

Jordan, Max. *Beyond All Fronts: A Bystander's Notes on This Thirty Years War.* Milwaukee: Bruce, 1944.

Joyce, Ed. *Prime Times, Bad Times: A Personal Drama of Network Television.* New York: Doubleday, 1988.

Juergens, George. *News from the White House.* University of Chicago Press, 1981.

Julian, Joseph. *This Was Radio.* New York: Viking Press, 1975.

Kahn, Frank J., ed. *Documents of American Broadcasting.* 2nd ed. New York: Appleton-Century-Crofts, 1973.

Kaltenborn, H. V. *Kaltenborn Edits the News.* New York: Modern Age Books, 1937.

Kaltenborn, H. V. *I Broadcast the Crisis.* New York: Random House, 1938.

Kaltenborn, H. V. *Fifty Fabulous Years.* New York: Putnam, 1950.

Kendrick, Alexander. *Prime Time: The Life of Edward R. Murrow.* Boston: Little, Brown, 1969.

Kierstead, Phillip O. *All-News Radio.* Blue Ridge Summit, Pa.: TAB Books, 1980.

Kintner, Robert E. *Broadcasting and the News.* New York: Harper & Row, 1965.

Kittross, John M. and Christopher H. Sterling. *Stay Tuned: A Concise History of American Broadcasting.* Belmont, Calif.: Wadsworth, 1978.

Klever, Anita. *Women in Television.* Philadelphia: Westminster Press, 1975.

Klurfield, Herman. *Winchell: His Life and Times.* New York: Praeger, 1976.

Knightley, Phillip. *The First Casualty.* New York: Harcourt Brace Jovanovich, 1975.

Kurtis, Bill. *Bill Kurtis: On Assignment.* Skokie, Illinois: Rand McNally, 1983.

Lambeth, Edmund B. *Committed Journalism: An Ethic for the Profession.* Bloomington: Indiana University Press, 1986.

Lang, Gladys Engel and Kurt Lang. *The Battle for Public Opinion.* New York: Columbia University Press, 1983.

Lang, Gladys Engel and Kurt Lang. *Politics and Television Reviewed.* Newbury Park, Calif.: Sage, 1984.

Lang, Kurt and Gladys Engel Lang. *Politics and Television.* Chicago: Quadrangle Books, 1968.

Larson, James F. *Television's Window on the World: International Affairs Coverage on the U.S. Networks.* Norwood, N.J.: Ablex, 1984.

Lawrence, William. *Six Presidents, Too Many Wars.* New York: Saturday Review Press, 1972.

Lazarsfeld, Paul F. and Harry Field. *Radio and the Printed Page.* New York: Duell, Sloan & Pearce, 1940.

Leapman, Michael. *Arrogant Aussie: The Rupert Murdoch Story.* Secaucus, N.J.: Lyle Stuart, 1985.

Leonard, Bill. *In the Storm of the Eye.* New York: Putnam, 1987.

Lesher, Stephen. *Media Unbound: The Impact of Television Journalism on the Public.* Boston: Houghton Mifflin, 1982.

Lewis, Carolyn Diana. *Reporting for Television.* New York: Columbia University Press, 1984.

Lichter, S. Robert, Stanley Rothman, and Linda S. Lichter. *The Media Elite.* New York: Adler & Adler, 1987.

Lichty, Lawrence W. and Malachi C. Topping, eds. *American Broadcasting: A Source Book on the History of Radio and Television.* New York: Hastings House, 1975.

Lippmann, Walter. *Public Opinion.* New York: Free Press, 1922.

Lunden, Joan with Ardy Friedberg. *Good Morning, I'm Joan Lunden.* New York: Putnam, 1987.

Lyons, Eugene. *David Sarnoff.* New York: Harper & Row, 1966.

MacDonald, J. Fred. *One Nation Under Television: The Rise and Decline of Network TV.* New York: Pantheon, 1990.

MacDonald, J. Fred. *Television and the Red Menace: The Video Road to Vietnam.* New York: Praeger, 1985.

MacDougall, Curtis D. *Interpretive Reporting.* 8th ed. New York: Macmillan, 1982.

MacNeil, Robert. *The People Machine.* New York: Harper & Row, 1968.

MacNeil, Robert. *The Right Place at the Right Time.* Boston: Little, Brown, 1982.

MacVane, John. *On the Air in World War II.* New York: Morrow, 1979.

Madsen, Axel. *"60 Minutes": The Power and the Politics of America's Most Popular TV News Show.* New York: Dodd, Mead, 1984.

Mankiewicz, Frank and Joel Swerdlow. *Remote Control: Television and the Manipulation of American Life.* New York: Times Books, 1978.

Marton, Kati. *The Polk Conspiracy.* New York: Farrar, Straux, & Giroux, 1990.

Marzolf, Marion. *Up From the Footnote: A History of Women Journalists.* New York: Hastings House, 1977.

Matusow, Barbara. *The Evening Stars.* Boston: Houghton Mifflin, 1983.

Mayer, Martin. *About Television.* New York: Harper & Row, 1972.

McCabe, Peter. *Bad News at Black Rock: The Sell-Out of CBS News.* New York: Arbor House, 1987.

McClendon, Sarah. *My Eight Presidents.* New York: Wyden Books, 1978.

McClure, Robert D. *The Unseeing Eye.* New York: Putnam, 1976.

McCormick-Pickett, Nancy, ed. *Women on the Job: Careers in the Electronic Media.* Washington, D.C.: American Women in Radio and Television, Women's Bureau, Department of Labor, 1984.

McLuhan, Marshall. *Understanding Media.* New York: McGraw-Hill, 1964.

McLuhan, Marshall and Quentin Fiore. *The Medium Is the Message*. New York: Bantam, 1967.

McNamee, Graham. *You're on the Air*. New York: Harper & Brothers, 1926.

McNeil, Alex. *Total Television: A Comprehensive Guide to Programming From 1948 to the Present*. New York: Penguin, 1984.

Metz, Robert. *CBS: Reflections in a Bloodshot Eye*. Chicago: Playboy Press, 1975.

Metz, Robert. *The Today Show*. Chicago: Playboy Press, 1977.

Mickelson, Sig. *The Electronic Mirror*. New York: Dodd, Mead, 1972.

Mickelson, Sig. *America's Other Voice: The Story of Radio Free Europe and Radio Liberty*. New York: Praeger, 1983.

Mickelson, Sig. *From Whistle Stop to Sound Bite*. New York: Praeger, 1989.

Mitchell, Curtis. *Cavalcade of Broadcasting*. Chicago: Follett, 1970.

Morgan, Edward P., ed. *This I Believe*. New York: Simon & Schuster, 1952.

Mosse, Baskett and Fred Whiting. *Television News Handbook*. Evanston, Ill.: Medill School of Journalism, 1986.

Mowrer, Paul Scott. *The House of Europe*. Boston: Houghton Mifflin, 1945.

Murrow, Edward R. *This is London*. New York: Simon & Schuster, 1941.

Murrow, Edward R. et al. *Ida Lou Anderson: A Memorial.* Pullman, Wash.: State College of Washington, undated.

Murrow, Edward R. and Fred W. Friendly, eds. *See It Now: A Selection of Text and Pictures*, New York: Simon & Schuster, 1955.

Myrowitz, Joshua. *No Sense of Place: The Impact of Electronic Media on Social Behavior*. New York: Oxford University Press, 1985.

National Broadcasting Company. *The Fourth Chime*. New York: NBC, 1944.

National Broadcasting Company. *Huntley-Brinkley Convention and Election Almanac*. New York: NBC, 1964 (paper).

Neustadt, Richard M. *The Birth of Electronic Publishing*. White Plains, N.Y.: Knowledge Industry, 1982.

Noble, Gil. *Black Is the Color of My TV Tube*. Secaucus, N.J.: Lyle Stuart, 1981.

O'Connor, John E., ed. *American History/American Television*. New York: Ungar, 1987.

Paley, William S. *As It Happened*. Garden City, N.Y.: Doubleday, 1979.

Paneth, Donald. *The Encyclopedia of American Journalism*. New York: Facts on File, 1983.

Paper, Lewis J. *Empire: William S. Paley and the Making of CBS*. New York: St. Martin's Press, 1987.

Patterson, Thomas E. *The Mass Media Election: How Americans Choose Their President*. New York: Praeger, 1980.

Patterson, Thomas E. and Robert D. McClure. *The Unseeing Eye*. New York: Putnam, 1976.

Pearson, Drew. *Diaries 1949–1959*. Edited by Tyler Abell. New York: Holt, Rinehart and Winston, 1974.

Persico, Joseph E. *Edward R. Murrow: An American Original*. New York: McGraw-Hill, 1988.

Phillips, Cabell et al., eds. *Dateline: Washington.* Garden City, N.Y.: Doubleday, 1949.

Pintak, Larry. *Beirut Outtakes: A TV Correspondent's Portrait of America's Encounter With Terror.* Lexington, Mass.: Lexington Books, 1988.

Powe, Lucas A., Jr. *American Broadcasting and the First Amendment.* Berkeley: University of California Press, 1988.

Powers, Ron. *The Newscasters: The News Business as Show Business.* New York: St. Martin's Press, 1977.

Powers, Ron. *Supertube: The Rise of Television Sports.* New York: Coward-McCann, 1983.

Quinlan, Sterling. *Inside ABC.* New York: Hastings House, 1979.

Quinn, Sally. *We're Going to Make You a Star.* New York: Simon & Schuster, 1975.

Ranney, Austin. *Channels of Power.* New York: Basic Books, 1984.

Rash, Bryson. *Washington Footnote.* McLean, Va.: EPM Publications, 1983.

Rather, Dan and Mickey Herkowitz. *The Camera Never Blinks.* New York: Morrow, 1977.

Reasoner, Harry. *Before the Colors Fade.* New York: Knopf, 1981.

Reck, Franklin M. *Radio From Start to Finish.* New York: Crowell, 1922.

Reinsch, J. Leonard. *Getting Elected: From Radio and Roosevelt to Television and Reagan.* New York: Hippocrene Books, 1988.

Robinson, John P. and Mark R. Levy. *The Main Source: Learning from Television News.* Newbury Park, Calif.: Sage, 1986.

Rooney, Andrew A. *A Few Minutes with Andy Rooney.* New York: Atheneum, 1982.

Routt, Edd. *Dimensions of Broadcast Editorializing.* Blue Ridge Summit, Pa.: TAB Books, 1974.

Rowan, Ford. *Broadcast Fairness: Doctrine, Practice, Prospects.* New York: Longman, 1984.

Ryan, Milo. *History in Sound.* Seattle: University of Washington Press, 1963.

Saerchinger, César. *Hello, America!* Boston: Houghton Mifflin, 1938.

Safer, Morley. *Flashbacks: On Returning to Vietnam.* New York: Random House, 1990.

St. John, Robert. *This Was My World.* Garden City, N.Y.: Doubleday, 1953.

St. John, Robert. *Encyclopedia of Radio and Television Broadcasting.* Milwaukee: Cathedral Square Publishing, 1967.

Sanders, Marlene and Marcia Rock. *Waiting for Prime Time: The Women of Television News.* Urbana: University of Illinois Press, 1988.

Savitch, Jessica. *Anchorwoman.* New York: Putnam, 1982.

Schechter, A. A. with Edward Anthony. *I Live on Air.* New York: Stokes, 1941.

Schmuhl, Robert, ed. *The Responsibilities of Journalism.* Notre Dame, Ind.: Notre Dame Press, 1984.

Schoenbrun, David. *America Inside Out: At Home and Abroad from Roosevelt to Reagan.* New York: McGraw-Hill, 1984.

Schoenbrun, David. *On and Off the Air.* New York: Dutton, 1989.

Schorr, Daniel. *Clearing the Air.* New York: Berkeley, 1978.

Schram, Martin. *The Great American Video Game: Presidential Politics in the Television Age.* New York: Morrow, 1987.

Schramm, Wilbur. *Communications in Modern Society.* Urbana: University of Illinois Press, 1948.

Schramm, Wilbur. *Responsibility in Mass Communication.* New York: Harper & Row, 1957.

Scott, Willard. *Joy of Living.* New York: Coward, McCann & Geoghegan, 1982.

Seldes, Gilbert. *The Great Audience.* New York: Viking Press, 1957.

Settel, Irving. *A Pictorial History of Radio.* New York: Citadel Press, 1960. Republished by Grosset & Dunlap, 1967.

Sevareid, Eric. *Not So Wild a Dream.* New York: Knopf, 1946. Republished by Atheneum, 1976.

Sevareid, Eric. *In One Ear.* New York: Knopf, 1952.

Sevareid, Eric. *This is Eric Sevareid.* New York: McGraw-Hill, 1964.

Shales, Tom. *On the Air!* New York: Summit, 1982.

Shaw, David. *Journalism Today.* New York: Harper & Row, 1977.

Shaw, David. *Press Watch.* New York: Macmillan, 1984.

Shirer, William L. *Berlin Diary.* New York: Knopf, 1941.

Shirer, William L. *20th Century Journey.* Vol. 1, *The Start: 1904–1930.* Boston: Little, Brown, 1976.

Shirer, William L. *20th Century Journey.* Vol. 2, *The Nightmare Years.* Boston: Little, Brown, 1984.

Shirer, William L. *20th Century Journey.* Vol. 3, *A Native's Return.* Boston: Little, Brown, 1990.

Shook, Frederick. *The Process of Electronic News Gathering.* Englewood, Col.: Morton, 1982.

Singh, Indu, ed. *Telecommunications in the Year 2000.* Norwood, N.J.: Ablex, 1983.

Sklar, Robert. *Prime Time America: Life On and Behind the Television Screen.* New York: Oxford University Press, 1981.

Shulman, Arthur and Roger Youman. *The Television Years.* New York: Popular Library, 1973.

Singleton, Loy. *Telecommunications in the Information Age: A Non-technical Primer on New Technologies.* Cambridge, Mass.: Ballinger, 1983.

Slate, Sam J. and Joe Cook. *It Sounds Impossible.* New York: Macmillan, 1963.

Slater, Robert. *This . . . Is CBS.* New York: Prentice-Hall, 1988.

Small, William. *To Kill a Messenger.* New York: Hastings House, 1970.

Small, William. *Political Power and the Press.* New York: W. W. Norton, 1972.

Smith, Howard K. *Last Train from Berlin.* New York: Knopf, 1943.

Smith, R. Franklin. *Edward R. Murrow: The War Years.* Kalamazoo, Mich.: New Issues Press, Western Michigan University, 1978.

Smith, Sally Bedell. *In All His Glory: William S. Paley the Legendary Tycoon and His Brilliant Circle.* New York: Simon & Schuster, 1990.

Spear, Joseph C. *Presidents and the Press: The Nixon Legacy.* Boston: M.I.T. Press, 1984.

Sperber, A. M. *Murrow: His Life and Times.* New York: Freundlich Books, 1986.

Steinberg, Charles S. *Mass Media and Communication.* New York: Hastings House, 1966.

Stephens, Mitchell. *A History of News: From the Drum to the Satellite.* New York: Viking, 1988.

Sterling, Christopher H. and John M. Kittross. *Stay Tuned: A Concise History of American Broadcasting.* Belmont, Calif.: Wadsworth, 1978.

Stone, Vernon A. *Careers in Broadcast News.* 4th ed. Washington, D.C.: RTNDA, 1985.

Swing, Raymond. *"Good Evening!"* New York: Harcourt, Brace & World, 1964.

Tall, Joel. *Techniques of Magnetic Recording.* Foreword by Edward R. Murrow. New York: Macmillan, 1950.

Tannenbaum, Percy H. and Leslie J. Kostrich. *Turned on TV/Turned Off Voters: Policy Options for Election Projections.* Newbury Park, Calif.: Sage, 1983.

Teague, Bob. *Live and Off-Color: News Biz.* New York: A&W, 1982.

Tebbell, John. *The Media in America.* New York: Crowell, 1975.

Tebbell, John and Sarah Miles Watts. *The Press and the Presidency.* New York: Oxford University Press, 1985.

Theberge, Leonard J., ed. *TV Coverage of the Oil Crisis: How Well Was the Public Served?* Washington, D.C.: Media Institute, 1982.

Thomas, Lowell. *Magic Dials.* New York: Lee Furman, 1939.

Thomas, Lowell. *History As You Heard It.* Garden City, N.Y.: Doubleday, 1957.

Thomas, Lowell. *Good Evening, Everybody.* New York: Morrow, 1976.

Thomas, Lowell. *So Long Until Tomorrow.* New York: Morrow, 1977.

Torre, Marie. *Don't Quote Me.* Garden City, N.Y.: Doubleday, 1965.

Tuchman, Gaye. *Making News.* New York: Free Press, 1978.

Tull, Charles J. *Father Coughlin and the New Deal.* Syracuse: Syracuse University Press, 1965.

Turner, Kathleen J. *Lyndon Johnson's Dual War: Vietnam and the Press.* Chicago: University of Chicago Press, 1985.

Wallace, Mike with Gary Paul Gates. *Close Encounters.* New York: Morrow, 1984.

Waller, Judith C. *Radio: The Fifth Estate.* Boston: Houghton Mifflin, 1950.

Westin, Av. *Newswatch: How Television Gathers and Delivers the News.* New York: Simon & Schuster, 1982.

Whedon, Peggy. *Always on Sunday.* New York: Norton, 1980.

White, Paul W. *News on the Air.* New York: Harcourt, Brace, 1947.

Wicklein, John. *Electronic Nightmare: The New Communications and Freedom.* 1981.

Winchell, Walter. *Winchell Exclusive.* Englewood Cliffs, N.J.: Prentice-Hall, 1975.

Winfield, Betty Houchin and Lois B. DeFleur, eds. *The Edward R. Murrow Heritage: Challenge for the Future.* Ames: Iowa State University Press, 1986.

Wittemore, Hank. *CNN: The Inside Story.* Boston: Little, Brown, 1990.

Wolf, Warner with William Taaffe. *Gimme a Break!* New York: McGraw-Hill, 1983.

Wolfson, Lewis. *The Untapped Power of the Press.* New York: Praeger, 1985.

Wolverton, Mike. *And Now the News.* Houston: Gulf Publishing, 1980.

Wood, William A. *Electronic Journalism.* New York: Columbia University Press, 1967.

Woodruff, Judy. *This Is Judy Woodruff at the White House.* Reading, Mass.: Addison-Wesley, 1982.

Wylie, Max. *Clear Channels: TV and the American People.* New York: Funk & Wagnalls, 1954.

Yellin, David G. *Special: Fred Freed and the Television Documentary.* New York: Macmillan, 1972.

Yoakam, Richard D. and Charles F. Cremer. *ENG: Television News and the New Technology.* 2nd ed. Hightstown, N.J.: McGraw-Hill, 1989.

Yorke, Ivor. *The Techniques of Television News.* 2nd ed. Stoneham, Mass.: Focal Press, 1987.

Zousmer, Steven. *TV News Off-Camera.* Ann Arbor: University of Michigan Press, 1987.

Index